CHARITY ACCOUNTS

A PRACTITIONER'S GUIDE TO THE CHARITIES SORP

Fourth Edition

CHARITY ACCOUNTS
A PRACTITIONER'S GUIDE TO THE CHARITIES SORP

Fourth Edition

Andrew Pianca, FCA
Partner and Chief Executive, Horwath Clark Whitehill LLP

Greyham Dawes, FCA
Director – Not-for-profit Unit, Horwath Clark Whitehill LLP

JORDANS

Published by
Jordan Publishing Limited
21 St Thomas Street
Bristol BS1 6JS

British Library Cataloguing-in-Publication Data

A catalogue record for this book is available from the British Library.

ISBN 978 1 84661 154 4

Typeset by Letterpart Ltd, Reigate, Surrey

Printed in Great Britain by CPI Antony Rowe, Chippenham, Wiltshire

ACKNOWLEDGMENTS

The authors acknowledge that any errors still to be found here are entirely their own and, if brought to notice by helpful readers or by other means, must be put right in the very next edition.

Whilst every care has been taken in connection with the preparation of this book, no liability whatsoever can be accepted in respect of any of the material contained herein by the authors or the publishers.

This publication is sold with the understanding, or on the basis, that the publishers are not engaged in providing accounting, legal, banking or other professional or financial services.

Andrew Pianca
Greyham Dawes
August 2009

PREFACE TO THE 4TH EDITION

The oldest forms of charitable institution, trusts established by Deed or by Will, and a number of bodies incorporated by Royal Charter or Act of Parliament, have been with us for centuries – some of them dating back well before the Charitable Uses Act of 1601. Though long since repealed, the preamble from that Act had been lingering on seemingly indefinitely, its archaic wording codified as the four heads of charity identified by Lord MacNaghten in the famous case of *Income Tax Special Commissioners v Pemsel*. Around this core there later grew the now flourishing 'Voluntary Sector', out of which were added the many unincorporated charitable associations and their increasingly popular limited-liability equivalent: the charitable company. But despite the setting up of the Charity Commissioners for England and Wales as a statutory body in 1853, there had been no serious attempt to standardise and regulate the public accountability of charities as such until the passing of the Charities Act of 1992 and its consolidation into the present Charities Act 1993 – itself soon to be superseded by further consolidation, this time with the Charities Act 2006. In the early '60s, then, even the setting up of a public register of charities under the Charities Act of 1960 was a daunting task for the time.

A hundred thousand charities had rushed to register, and with the meagre resources made available for the purpose it took 3 years before they could all be accommodated and numbered. As has since emerged from the Charity Commission's late 1990's initiative to overhaul and make it 'accurate' (an exercise still going strong and likely to last many years yet, what with the universal 'public-benefit testing' now required under the Charities Act 2006) the ongoing Review of the Register of Charities' also has to rationalise the basis of initial acceptance for registration at that time. That, it seems, had been granted after only the most cursory examination of what was submitted as the charity's 'governing document'.

Small wonder that the later Regulations made under the 1960 Act could not attempt to standardise the format, content and methodology of charity accounting for external reporting. Instead, charities were left to continue accounting according to their own traditions, or else to adapt, each in their own way (which in some cases could be breathtakingly idiosyncratic) the basic framework of 'true and fair' commercial accounting for limited companies and other enterprises as published by the old Accounting Standards Committee. The result was a glorious heterogeneity that defied description, and a dearth of data on the financial dimensions of the sector. Such data are only now coming online through recent innovations: the 'Guidestar' free public-access website database, the Charity Commission's graphic 'quick-view' Annual Return financial summary for those registered charities exceeding £500,000 gross income and the more comprehensive Summary Information Return ('SIR') for those above the Commission's 'public interest' threshold of £1m gross income, both being published on the charity's pages of the Commission's website.

Even the requirement to file accounts annually at the Charity Commission was only automatic in the old days if the charity had a permanent endowment. Other registered charities were only required to file every 5 years, with no other public right of access to charity accounts – except (for obvious reasons) via Companies House, for a charitable limited company. Such was the traditional confidentiality of charity trusteeship, such the level of trust and confidence normally enjoyed by those responsible for a charity's administration – until the advent of the Charities Act 1992, that is.

The earliest version of the Charities SORP, labelled 'SORP 2' by the ASC at the time to distinguish it from the one for the Pension Funds sector ('SORP 1'), appeared as early as 1988, but in the absence of any kind of statutory underpinning it was largely ignored by the sector. It used to come as no surprise to discover that a new charity client had been exceeding its powers by engaging in activities that were clearly not within the meaning of the charitable Objects declared in its governing document, or had failed to distinguish between its endowed funds, other restricted funds and unrestricted funds.

Many large charitable trusts had never before had to have their accounts audited, in the absence of any compulsion under trust law, unless here or there the Charity Commission, for its own purposes as the regulator, specifically required and paid for one. There was no automatic requirement for annual audit of a non-company charity unless stipulated in its governing document, so the Charity Commission's policy view, as communicated to many such charities prior to the Charities Acts of 1992/93, used to be that a professional audit was, in the absence of special circumstances, normally justifiable not more than once every 4 years.

Things are very different today. Charities in England and Wales now provide gainful employment for over half-a-million people, equivalent to some 4% of the UK labour force – except that most of them seem to work full-time for substantially less pay than those in the profit sector, thus providing a so far unacknowledged form of financial support for the sector. According to Charity Commission website figures, the *registered* charities now have a combined annual gross income of £50bn. The regulatory regime now guarantees the public availability of audited accounts in a more or less standardised charity-specific format to cover nearly 90% of this, plus a statutory annual report by the trustees in the case of all but the very smallest of the registered charities.

This regime is designed to strike the right balance between the conflicting needs for openness and public confidence on the one hand and simplicity and confidentiality on the other – something that the Charities Act 2006 seeks to refine even further, quite apart from its hotly debated focus on public benefit issues, as we have highlighted in the 4th edition of this book.

It is instructive to see how well charities are implementing the SORP's enhanced reporting requirements. This book therefore gives many examples from recently published charity accounts and annual reports. The statutory framework of charity regulation is a vast improvement on what went before. It is clear that the greater openness or 'transparency' of annual reporting now required has noticeably increased public confidence in the sector even further in recent years.

Many large charities generate a major part of their income from trading (nearly half of the sector's gross income seems to be raised through charitable trading) or from investment activities. A further significant proportion of the services charities provide for those in need is financed by voluntary contributions coming direct from the public – whether, for example, through donations in kind or in cash, including street collections and other appeals, in many cases under the Gift Aid Scheme or other tax-incentives, or through legacies.

However, SORP 2005 and the further changes it brought are a timely reminder that the setting up of a statutory framework for the regulation of charities was by no means the end of change in the area of financial reporting requirements. Inevitably, the revision of the SORP's related Regulations in line with the 2006 Charities Act has included yet more improvements, notably the long-promised harmonisation of the accounts scrutiny regime across the sector and the extension of the consolidated accounts rules from company law to charity law. This is not to say that the framework itself was faulty: simply that it was such a large step in such a diverse sector that there was bound to be much to learn in the process. For the future, the pressing need is for the Commission, as the relevant 'SORP-issuing body', now joined by OSCR as its equivalent in Scotland, to restart the present Charities SORP review that has been stalled by the ASB's convergence of its UK standards with those of the IASB, which seem to leave no standing at all for 'Industry SORPs' within the global commercial economy they are designed to serve. Whether the Charities SORP might find a more secure future within the EU's 'NPO Code of Conduct', now more than three years into its exploratory implementation to protect member-States' voluntary sectors from vulnerability to criminal exploitation, rather than as an adjunct of international commercial accounting, and whether this would then be seen as reflecting the SORP's natural affinity with the international public sector accounting standards whose closely reasoned modifications of the commercial standards have already gained global credibility, could be major issues to be covered in a 5th edition of this book.

In addition to all this, the charity sector itself has continued to change, and many outstanding issues still remain. These include, for example, the long-term effect of the Lottery on charitable service-provision; also whether, under the

Government's long-standing Care in the Community initiative, charities are adequately structured and equipped to cope with the commercial pressures of competitive contract tendering; whether the EC will have any significant effect on the UK charity sector (a sector that is not fully recognised elsewhere in the EC, where 'not for profit' tends to be the distinguishing feature rather than charity as such).

It is now a decade and a half since the issue of the original, 1995 Charities SORP together with the 1993 Charities Act's accounting and reporting regulations that first put teeth into the SORP – certainly as regards the larger non-exempt charities in England and Wales. That was the dawn of a new era of a world-leading regime of *public accountability* for the trustees of all charities in these countries, a regime set up to be regulated – if not quite standardised – by the Charity Commission and (in theory, if not always so in practice) enforced through statutory compliance-monitoring of the larger registered charities. To this has since been added Scotland's own regulatory regime under its enabling legislation of 2005, and more recently Charities Acts providing for similar regulatory regimes to be set up in Northern Ireland and in the Republic of Ireland.

Under the spotlight of the Charities SORP's necessary observance of our somewhat archaic and therefore little-understood common law of charitable trusts, the niceties of which can still catch us out if unwary, charity trustees, executives and advisers have in many cases had to struggle towards clarification of old ambiguities or obscurities affecting their charity's constitution, structure and administration in ways that had never seemed to matter much to anyone up to then. Others – especially where charitable trading or major grant-funding for service-provision are involved – have found it even more of a struggle to reconcile the conflicting needs of 'transparency' in charity accountability and commercial confidentiality in these increasingly competitive arenas.

For many of the 50,000 registered charities that are above the new threshold of £25,000 gross income threshold for routine annual filing, any anxieties they may have had about Charity Commission acceptance of their statutory Annual Report & Accounts as SORP-compliant have long since been overtaken by events. Most have found to their relief that they got away with just 'doing their best', since the Commission's transitional policy turned out to be broadly supportive where charities have clearly found it too difficult to get things right. That was only to be expected in any attempt to impose external regulation on the core of something as amorphous, idealistic and sensitive as the Voluntary Sector. What it has meant in practice, though, is that the Commission mainly contented itself with just pointing out the most significant deficiencies for corrective action in future annual accounts submitted for filing, so as to minimise the potential burdens of rectification and re-submission. Of course, such indulgence merely postpones the problem for the charity, as the same need for clarification of obscurities and correction of defective accounting treatments keeps coming up again year after year until properly dealt with – or until brought to light by some administrative crisis perhaps quite unrelated to public accountability in itself.

For the *auditors* of the 9,300 or so charities that are now above the statutory audit threshold, as well as for those of smaller charities *choosing* annual audit to support an appeal to the public or to a funding body, etc, such official indulgence of their client can be of little comfort. The professional regulatory standards imposed on charity auditors (including an increasingly strict audit quality inspection regime) do not permit them to turn a blind eye where significant defects in the annual accounts have to be reported on – no matter how sympathetic and understanding the regulator may be!

For better or worse, it continues to be the charity auditor's *professional opinion* that forms the keystone to the statutory regime of public accountability for charities. To update the professional guidance on best practice in this area, in December 2008 the Auditing Practices Board issued a revised version of its 2002 'Practice Note 11: The Audit of Charities' in the light of the accounting and reporting changes introduced by SORP 2005 and also the recent company law changes – but more importantly to reflect the APB's adoption of international auditing standards.

But while it may be unarguable that the actual *framework* of statutory regulation is largely unchanged apart from at last harmonising the regime for company and *non-company* charities, the *impact* of SORP 2005 on annual reporting – certainly by the larger charities – remains incisive, especially for the trustees' annual report. This is partly due to the close underpinning provided by the SORP's related Regulations governing the annual accounts of non-company charities not opting for a 'Receipts & Payments' accounting basis. That gives this particular SORP an enhanced status for the whole of the sector, making it so persuasive that compliance becomes, in principle, 'unavoidable' when it comes to the audit of charitable companies.

But the SORP 2005's impact is also mainly the result of work done by the Accounting Standards Board in recent years in areas relevant to charities even though not specific to them. Not the least of these areas is that of pensions provision, where the sector has had to come to terms with what we might call 'virtual' asset/liability recognition under FRS17 (pension scheme funding surplus/deficit accounting), as well as the accounting consequences of the Trustee Act 2000 and the increasingly popular use of the 'total return' basis of investing trust capital.

As regards the current FRSSE, all except the largest 500–750 charities could, if allowed to use the FRSSE's own (turnover-based) definition of size, claim to be 'small' enough to adopt it for their entity accounts and can then forget about the other standards, what with charities' commercial trading subsidiaries tending to be empty shells due to tax law constraints and thus immaterial for Balance Sheet purposes. Here one may note, in passing, that the main benefit of adopting the FRSSE is just an easier 'learning curve' for anyone new to 'true and fair' accounting, plus for some charities it can also lighten the burden of FRS15/11 compliance. This is only to be expected from the FRSSE's primary purpose of unburdening the *1,000,000+* 'smaller' reporting entities engulfed by the ever-increasing complexities of standards chiefly designed to curb antisocial 'creative accounting' by major public companies. The ASB's notable achievement with the FRSSE is a simple and compact alternative accounting standard that cuts out most of the esoteric stuff on profit-manipulation and concentrates on basics.

This edition, now called a *practitioner's* guide rather than just a practical one, to reflect the increasingly intricate nature of charity accountability for such a disparate sector, has been through a major overhaul in the process of updating from the 3rd edition, but the structure of the previous editions has again been largely retained, so that existing readers should easily be able to find their way around for updating purposes..

Andrew Pianca
Greyham Dawes
August 2009

CONTENTS

LIST OF APPENDICES IN 4TH EDITION OF CHARITY ACCOUNTS

Book only:

Appendix 1   The Charities SORP 2005 and its subsequent Information Sheets

CD ROM:

Appendix 1   The Charities SORP 2005 and its subsequent Information Sheets

Appendix 2   The Charities Act 1993, Part VI: Charity Accounts, Reports and Returns – as amended to date

Appendix 3   The SORP's related 2008 Regulations for England & Wales: The Charities (Accounts and Reports) Regulations 2008 – SI 2008/629

Appendix 4   The Charities and Trustee Investment (Scotland) Act 2005, Charities – Part 1: Charity Accounts

Appendix 5   The SORP's related 2006 Regulations for Scotland: the Charities Accounts (Scotland) Regulations 2006 – SSI 2006/218

Appendix 6   SORP compliance by charitable companies under Part 15 of the Companies Act 2006 and Regulations SI 2008/409 ('small' companies/groups) or SI 2008/410 (larger companies/groups)

Appendix 7   Charity Accounts & Reports under the Charities SORP 2005 – disclosures checklist

Appendix 8   Worked examples of SORP-compliant Charity Accounts & Reports

The National Disability Charity (a charitable company with subsidiary undertakings)

8.1a   Annual report and group consolidated accounts (audited) for the year to 30 April 2009

8.1b   Summary Information Return 2009

ABC Charity (a charitable trust with subsidiary undertakings)

8.2a   Draft annual report and group consolidated accounts for the year to 31 March 2009

8.2b   Draft Summary Information Return 2009

The Higher College Charity (an unincorporated charitable school with subsidiary undertakings)

8.3a   Annual report and group consolidated accounts (audited) for the year to 31 August 2009

8.3b   Summary Information Return 2009

Anytown Charitable Trust (a small charitable company)

8.4   Annual report and Companies Act accounts (independently examined) for the year to 5 April 2009

Handbell Ringers Association (an unincorporated membership charity, accounting on a receipts & payments basis)

8.5   Annual accounts (independently examined) for the year to 31 March 2009 with 2009 AGM Minutes as the annual report

TABLE OF STATUTES

References are to paragraph numbers.

TABLE OF STATUTORY INSTRUMENTS

References are to paragraph numbers.

TABLE OF OTHER MATERIALS

References are to paragraph numbers.

LIST OF ABBREVIATIONS

1960 Act	Charities Act 1960
1961 Act	Trustee Investment Act 1961
1985 Act	Companies Act 1985
1993 Act	Charities Act 1993
1995 Regulations	Charities (Accounts and Reports) Regulations 1995, SI 1995/2724
1995 SORP	Charities SORP 'Accounting by Charities'
APB	Auditing Practices Board
ASB	Accounting Standards Board
AUT	Authorised Unit Trust
CAF	Charities Aid Foundation
CIF	Common Investment Fund
CIO	Charitable Incorporated Organisation
Companies Regulations 1995	Companies (Summary Financial Statement) Regulations 1995, SI 1995/2092
DBERR	Department of Business, Enterprise and Regulatory Reform
DBIS	Department for Business, Innovation and Skills
DIUS	Department for Innovation, Universities and Skills
DTI	Department of Trade and Industry
EUV	existing use value
FASB	Financial Accounting Standards Board
FEI	Further Education Institution
FRC	Financial Reporting Council
FRS	Financial Reporting Standard
FRSSE	Financial Reporting Standard for Smaller Entities
FSA	Financial Services Authority
HEI	Higher Education Institution
HEFCE	Higher Education Funding Council for England
HMRC	Her Majesty's Revenue & Customs
IAS	International Accounting Standard
IFAC	International Federation of Accountants

IMA	Investment Management Association
IPSAS	International Public Sector Accounting Standard
IR	Inland Revenue
ISA	International Standards on Auditing
NED	Non-executive Director
NDPB	Non Departmental Public Body
OG	Operational Guidance
OIC	Open-ended Investment Company
OSCR	Office of the Scottish Charity Regulator
OTS	Office of the Third Sector
PPF	Pension Protection Fund
Regulations 2000	Charities (Accounts and Reports) Regulations 2000, SI 2000/2868
Regulations 2005	Charities (Accounts and Reports) Regulations 2005, SI 2005/572
Regulations 2008	Charities (Accounts and Reports) Regulations 2008, SI 2008/629
RSL	registered social landlord
SAS	Statement of Auditing Standards
SCIO	Scottish Charitable Incorporated Organisations
SFAS	Statement of Financial Accounting Standards (as subsumed in the FASB's 'Accounting Standards Codification' for financial years ending after 15 September 2009 in the USA)
SIR	Summary Information Return
SoFA	Statement of Financial Activities
SORP 2000	Charities SORP 'Accounting and Reporting by Charities'
SORP 2005	Charities SORP 'Accounting and Reporting by Charities'
SORP	Statement of Recommended Practice
SSAP	Statement of Standard Accounting Practice
STRGL	Statement of Total Recognised Gains and Losses
TA 2000	Trustee Act 2000
TFA	trust for application
TR	total return
UITF	Urgent Issues Task Force
UTR	unapplied total return

Chapter 1

THE CHARITIES SORP – SCOPE AND COMPLIANCE

SORP OVERVIEW

1.1 This chapter sets the scene for the rest of the book, and is therefore essential reading for anyone new to the charity sector. It gives an overview of the nature and purpose of the Statement of Recommended Practice, generally known as the Charities SORP, and its evolution to date, when and where it applies to any particular charity, how and where it is given statutory underpinning to facilitate the regulation of the UK sector and to what extent compliance with it is enforceable.

Origin and development of the SORP

1.1.1 The Charities SORP has its origin in the 1980s as No 2 in a series of industry-specific SORPs issued by the old Accounting Standards Committee as guidance for *voluntary* use in dealing with aspects not covered in the standards. With the passing of the Charities Acts of 1992 and 1993, it had to be completely overhauled and rewritten to make it rigorous enough to provide a sound basis for the detailed accounting and reporting regulations provided for in what is now Part VI of the Charities Act 1993 ('the 1993 Act'), as amended by the Charities Act 2006.

As soon as the Charity Commission, as the relevant SORP-issuing body, acting under the auspices of the Accounting Standards Board (ASB), was able to issue the 1995 SORP, the Home Office published the Charities (Accounts and Reports) Regulations 1995, SI 1995/2724 ('the 1995 Regulations') needed to give it statutory underpinning for the purposes of official regulation of the sector in England and Wales. (For the accounting and reporting regime applicable to charities elsewhere in the British Isles, see the end of this chapter.) The 1995 Regulations took effect for financial years commencing on or after 1 March 1996, ending a transitional period of voluntary compliance with the Charities SORP 'Accounting by Charities' ('the 1995 SORP') and making SORP compliance compulsory for all charities regulated by the Charity Commission and preparing annual accounts claiming to show a 'true and fair view'.

Much the same procedure was followed for the revised version of the Charities SORP issued in October 2000 after a detailed independent review by the Charities SORP Committee some 3 years after the 1995 SORP was issued. (The ASB normally requires SORP-issuing bodies to undertake regular reviews in the context of current practices in their sector, which is now being done annually for the Charities SORP, and to update their SORP at least every 3 years in line with further developments in accounting standards.)

Immediately following the publication of the revised Charities SORP 'Accounting and Reporting by Charities' ('SORP 2000'), the related new Regulations needed to renew its statutory underpinning were 'made' and published. As it was said at the time that these 'Regulations 2000' could be imposed only for financial years starting *subsequently*, which for practical reasons meant on or after 1 January 2001, they also provided for a transitional phase (see **1.1.8**) during which trustees could either continue complying with the 1995 SORP and Regulations or else (as a one-way street) opt for early *voluntary* adoption of SORP 2000 – when the related new Regulations automatically became binding on them. So, instead of the normal practice of just displacing the old SORP immediately upon publication, the new SORP carefully preserved the currency of its predecessor by declaring itself to be:

> '... applicable to all accounting periods beginning on or after 1 January 2001. Early adoption is encouraged.'

> *– SORP 2000, paragraph 1*

This procedure was again followed for the current version of the Charities SORP, issued in March 2005 after an extensive review exercise carried out by the Charities SORP Committee starting in 2003 and culminating in public consultation in the summer of 2004 on the Exposure Draft. Thus the ASB's normal requirement of 3-yearly revisions seems to have become a 5-yearly one in the case of the charity sector. With the publication of 'SORP 2005', its related new Regulations for statutory underpinning were 'made', published and laid before Parliament to await their passing into law, which due to the intervention of the General Election was not until late May 2005. Unlike the 'Regulations 2000', however, the SORP's Regulations 2005 were not 'forward-dated' but instead automatically came into effect for all financial years starting after 31 March 2005. Like their predecessor, though, they did provide for a transitional phase (see **1.1.8**) during which trustees could either continue complying with SORP 2000 and its Regulations or else (as a one-way street) opt for early *voluntary* adoption of SORP 2005 – whereupon its related Regulations 2005 automatically became binding on them. Thus SORP 2005 again carefully preserved the currency of its predecessor for charities' 2004/05 financial years by declaring itself to be:

> '... applicable to all accounting periods beginning on or after 1 April 2005. Early adoption is encouraged.'

> *– SORP 2005, paragraph 1*

In March 2008, new Regulations to replace those of 2005 were made by the Office for the Third Sector – the Cabinet Office branch which has inherited responsibility for the voluntary sector from the Home Office. The 2008 Regulations still point to SORP 2005 as the current SORP, but they implement for financial years from 1 April 2008 (or earlier voluntary adoption – as before) the 2006 Act's changes in the regime of public accountability for charities – principally the introduction of group-accounting by non-company parent charities, the extension of the 1993 Act's regime for audit or independent examination to cover 'small' charitable companies claiming company audit exemption and a new requirement for the trustees' annual report to focus on the public benefit that all charities must now demonstrate under the 2006 Act.

Role of the Accounting Standards Board

1.1.2 The policy of the ASB is to limit its own role to overseeing the development of SORPs, regarding them as 'further guidance [that] may be required to implement accounting standards effectively'. The ASB only carries out 'a review of limited scope' on new versions of any industry/sector SORP prior to publication, to guard against any fundamental contradiction of its own standards and other pronouncements – which it describes as 'primarily applicable to general purpose company financial statements'.

For this purpose, the Charity Commission and (latterly) the Office of the Scottish Charities Regulator (OSCR) are 'recognised' by the ASB as SORP-issuing bodies that jointly comply with the ASB's code of practice for the issue of SORPs. The code requires the Commission and OSCR to work through a representative independent committee of competent individuals approved by the ASB. It also requires the development process to include adequate public consultation. In return, the ASB publicly endorses each new version of the Charities SORP, and in a preface to the current (2005) version says:

> 'On the basis of its review, the Board has concluded that the SORP has been developed in accordance with the ASB's code of practice and does not appear to contain any fundamental points of principle that are unacceptable in the context of accounting practice or to conflict with an accounting standard or the ASB's plans for future standards.'
>
> *– SORP 2005, preface*

This is the normal 'statement of negative assurance' that the ASB now authorises for inclusion in each published SORP to signify official approval for its use.

Status of the SORP in relation to accounting standards

1.1.3 In the wake of the 1995 SORP came many media articles, workshops, seminars and conferences by members of the SORP Committee and the Commission itself, not to mention the independent publication of specialised SORP guidance to meet the needs of different parts of the sector. SORP 2000 did not produce quite so much buzz, and for SORP 2005 it was even less – perhaps because (unlike the ground-breaking 1995 version) the SORP is nowadays, to quote the Charity Commission, 'evolutionary, not revolutionary'. Yet, more than a decade after the implementation of the original legislation heralding charity regulation as we know it, there are still a number of fallacies about the Charities SORP that have not been finally laid to rest.

For example: *'the SORP is "only **recommended** practice", and therefore doesn't have to be followed'; 'charity X is not registered with the Commission, so it doesn't have to comply with the SORP';* and (infrequently, nowadays) *'charity Y is also a company and as such must produce an income and expenditure account, so it can't comply with the SORP's requirement for a Statement of Financial Activities'.*

All these comments misunderstand the status of the Charities SORP, which is backed up by Regulations and (certainly for all the larger charities) by strictly regulated professional audit, with trustees' compliance with their legal obligations capable of being enforced by the Charity Commission as the sector's default regulator. This also needs to be seen in the context of the continuing development of national (though not international) accounting standards, where the status of SORPs generally has been made very clear, if not greatly enhanced. The globalisation of accounting standards in the commercial sector has so far ignored the needs of the charity sector, and despite the ASB's current programme for converging its UK standards with those of the IASB (where there is no place for SORPs at all) by 2010 and the at present similarly biassed 'Conceptual Framework' now being developed by the IASB, there is now a real risk that the Charities SORP could be marginalised as a merely local accounting code for UK charities if the international community looks beyond it to prefer the already charity-friendly *International Public Sector Accounting Standards* developed since 2002 for governmental use and which we comment on further in this book.

The function of SORPs in relation to UK accounting standards is defined in Financial Reporting Standard 18 (FRS18), 'Accounting Policies', in these terms:

> 'SORPs recommend accounting practices for specialised industries or sectors. They supplement accounting standards and other legal and regulatory requirements in the light of the special factors prevailing or transactions undertaken in a particular industry or sector.'
>
> *– FRS18, paragraph 4*

Lest the reader should conclude that this confers *only* 'recommended' status, thus implying that SORPs can just be ignored where inconvenient, the Standard includes a *compliance* disclosure requirement, saying:

> 'Where an entity's financial statements fall within the scope of a SORP, the entity should state the title of the SORP and whether its financial statements have been prepared in accordance with those of the SORP's provisions currently in effect. In the event of a departure, the entity should give a brief description of how the financial statements depart from the recommended practice set out in the SORP, which should include:
>
> (a)   for any treatment that is not in accordance with the SORP, the reasons why the treatment adopted is judged more appropriate to the entity's particular circumstances, and
>
> (b)   details of any disclosures recommended by the SORP that have not been provided, and the reasons why they have not been provided.'
>
> *– FRS18, paragraph 58*

For all *non-company* charities (ie, not just those above the statutory audit threshold, as in previous Regulations), as well as all group consolidated accounts prepared under the 1993 Act, Sch 2 to the SORP's Regulations 2008 even makes this disclosure mandatory by requiring the accounts notes to include:

> 'a statement as to whether or not the accounts have been prepared in accordance with any applicable accounting standards and statements of recommended practice and particulars of any material departure from those standards and statements of practice and the reasons for such departure ...'.
>
> *– SI 2008/629, Sch 2, para 1(v)*

FRS18 goes on to make it clear that there is normally no 'requirement' to *quantify the effect* any such departure has had on the accounts:

> 'The effect of a departure from a SORP need not be quantified, except in those rare cases where such quantification is necessary for the entity's financial statements to give a true and fair view.'
>
> *– FRS18, paragraph 59*

This is reflected in the 'best practice' disclosure called for by paragraph 359 of SORP 2005 (see also chapter 12 (Notes to the Accounts)):

> '... the following details should be given for any material departure from this SORP:
>
> ...
>
> (c)   an estimate of the financial effect on the accounts where this is needed for the accounts to give a true and fair view.'
>
> *– SORP 2005, paragraph 359(c)*

On the other hand, if the SORP-departure amounts to a 'material *change*' of an accounting policy or assumption on whose basis the accounts are prepared from year to year, then – also regardless of the size of the (non-company) charity/group – it is *mandatory* to provide:

> '(b)   a description of (i) each of the accounting policies which (aa) have been adopted by the charity trustees, and (bb) are material in the context of the accounts of the charity, and (ii) the estimation techniques adopted which are material to the presentation of the accounts; [and] (c) a description of any material change to policies and techniques referred to in ... (b), the reason for such change and its effect (if material) on the accounts, in accordance with the methods and principles set out in the SORP ...'.
>
> *– SI 2008/629, Sch 2, para 1(b) and (c)*

Any *new* departure will thus be caught, making its quantification enforceable, whereas an old *continuing* departure would not have to be quantified. (For what is meant by 'material', see '"Immaterial" items', below.)

In response to popular request, SORP 2000 contained a new appendix on the relevance of the individual accounting standards, and this was updated as Appendix 2 in SORP 2005. Chapter 5 discusses the major practical problems that can arise from the divergent and sometimes incompatible aims of the profit sector and the charity sector, and how to resolve these problems to achieve full compliance with the SORP.

The need for compliance

1.1.4   SORP compliance is now a fundamental requirement for the annual accounts of almost the whole of the financial resources of the charity sector – even though tens of thousands of the smaller (non-company) charities can and do continue to opt for the alternative of an *unregulated* 'receipts and payments' basis as permitted by law.

This is because, for those who cannot opt out, the law requires charities' accounts to show 'a true and fair view'. Charitable companies have to do so under the Companies Act 2006. The 'exempt' charities (see **1.2**) are made to do so by their own sponsoring department, statutory regulator or other supervisory body. And the remaining charities – whether registered or excepted from registration – must (unless small enough to opt out) do so under Part VI of the 1993 Act and the Regulations made under it. For this purpose, full compliance with the Charities SORP, or with any other, more specialised SORP applicable instead, will normally be unavoidable.

The statutory regime of annual returns filing with the Charity Commission, to which all registered charities above the £10,000 ceiling for the 'light-touch' regime are subject in principle,[1] includes compliance checks of audited accounts against the SORP, with referral of serious non-compliance to the auditor's regulatory body, where this is considered appropriate in the public interest. For exempt and excepted charities, other bodies than the Commission will normally be responsible for monitoring compliance with official requirements.

For *non-exempt* charities this now means those exceeding £500,000 gross income, or £250,000 if the balance sheet value of their gross assets exceeds £3.26m (but see chapter 2 for a more precise description of the 1993 Charities Act's different size bands).

The Auditing Practices Board (APB) gives very clear guidance in its Practice Note PN 11, 'The Audit of Charities', saying that auditors are expected to ensure that accruals accounts comply with the SORP except where there are very good reasons for not doing so. Even then, if a material departure is not adequately explained and justified for a true and fair view it should result in a correspondingly qualified audit report for all to see, perhaps leading to other difficulties for the charity.

The possible consequence of any serious non-compliance was made very clear in the Charity Commission's introduction to SORP 2000 (but not in SORP 2005, where the Commission's foreword takes an altogether friendlier line instead):

> 'The Commission expects charities to comply fully with this or any other applicable SORP. In so far as a charity diverges from the SORP in material respects, the charity's accounts should identify any divergence clearly and provide a full explanation. If no explanation is given or the explanation is unsatisfactory, the Commission may raise the matter with the charity and, if circumstances warrant it, institute an inquiry.
>
> Where the Commission finds that difficulties have arisen as a result of any divergence from this or any other applicable SORP, the Commission will take such divergence and any explanation the Trustees have given into account. The failure of Trustees without good reason to apply the appropriate SORP principles may be relevant to their responsibility for the difficulties arising.'
>
> – *SORP 2000, preface*

Opting out of SORP compliance altogether, by adopting the 'receipts and payments' basis instead (as explained in chapter 16), however, is not a passport to total freedom in accounting matters. The *'proper accounting records'* required by statute must still be *'sufficient to show and explain all the charity's transactions'* – *and* enable any accounts that may be required to be prepared from them to comply with statutory requirements. This would include the possibility that for the next accounts the statutory option might *not* be exercised by whoever is then responsible (in an extreme case, a 'Receiver and Manager' (or 'Interim Manager', under the Charities Act 2006) appointed by the Charity Commission under its supervisory powers, for example).

---

[1]   In practice, however, for financial resource reasons, Charity Commission policy since November 2004 has been not to collect from charities below the statutory audit threshold any monitoring data at all. The Commission estimated at the time that this change would relieve some 54,000 charities from having to provide monitoring information.

Scope of the Charities SORP

1.1.5 The scope of the Charities SORP as 'best practice' extends throughout the UK (for previous versions it was the British Isles, but following Eire's withdrawal from the SORP Review Committee SORP 2005 applies only by individual voluntary adoption in the Republic) to cover all charities preparing accounts that are required to show – or otherwise claim to show – 'a true and fair view' *except where a more specialised SORP applies instead.* As SORP 2005 puts it:

> '... where a separate SORP exists for a particular class of charities ..., the charity trustees of charities in that class should adhere to that SORP ...'.
>
> *– SORP 2005, paragraph 5*

Although it affects only a few dozen charities, such is their financial significance that the Investment Management Association's (IMA) SORP is specially cited as an example here:

> 'The trustees of Common Investment Funds (CIFs) in England and Wales, other than pooling scheme funds[2] ... should prepare their accounts and Trustees' Annual Report in accordance with the relevant accounts and reports regulations for CIFs made under Part VI of the Charities Act 1993 (regulations planned for 2005 will ensure these requirements are consistent with the SORP for Authorised Funds issued by the Investment Management Association and any subsequent regulations which may be made ...)'.
>
> *– SORP 2005, paragraph 449*

Contrary to cherished opinion in some quarters, the scope of the Charities SORP does not stop short at the 'exempt' charities, either, but extends to them just the same as to any other charity. However, in each case it can apply only within the framework of the particular legislation governing the charity's accounting and reporting obligations. Here, unlike SORP 2000 where the position was stated quite clearly, the subservience of the Charities SORP to statute and common law is now acknowledged only obliquely, in the following terms:

> 'The SORP is compatible with the requirements of the law. The SORP clarifies how charity accounting is affected by legal requirements, including aspects of trust law ... Charity trustees should include any additional information which they are required by law to report and in order for the accounts to comply with current statutory requirements or the requirements of the charity's governing document to the extent that these exceed statutory requirements.'
>
> *– SORP 2005, paragraphs 22 and 23*

Whether this subservience extends to statutory *permissions* rather than '*requirements*' is another matter. Clearly, the Council of the National Trust and its auditors have agreed to differ on this point in relation to accounting standards – and therefore also to the SORP itself:

---

[2] These are *official* 'arrangements for the pooling of investments belonging to two or more charities administered by the same trustee body as the body managing the fund' (see the Glossary definition 46.1 in Appendix 1 to SORP 2005) – ie a 'pool charity' set up with or without a Charity Commission Scheme or one made by the courts. Being under common control, their accountability follows the normal rules, so it is the *Charities* SORP that applies to them – not the IMA one. This is reflected in the Regulations. For their accounting requirements, see chapter 9, dealing with Investment Assets.

As explained in Note 2 of the Financial Statements, no value is placed on the inalienable property or on other property held for preservation *[Authors' note: These are now called 'heritage' assets in SORP 2005]*. While this is permitted by the National Trust Act 1971, it is not in accordance with the requirements of Financial Reporting Standard 15 (FRS15). Except for this departure from FRS15, in our opinion the financial statements [for the year to 28 February 2008] give a true and fair view ... and have been properly prepared in accordance with The National Trust Act 1971 and the Charities Act 1993.

The National Trust – 2007/08 Auditors' Report

The interaction between the Charities SORP and the 1985 and now 2006 Companies Act is covered in detail in each chapter where either the occasional gap has had to be bridged over by the SORP or where a conflicting statutory requirement complicates the preparation of SORP-compliant accounts.

The slightly different requirements imposed by the Scottish legislation of 2005 and the 2006 accounting Regulations made under it are discussed at the end of this chapter.

Charities subject to a specialised SORP

Although the charities concerned are mostly exempted from Charity Commission supervision and so are no longer to be found on the Charities Register, an example of a specialised SORP often encountered in practice is that issued by the NHA to cover registered social landlords (RSLs) (previously known as housing associations). The focus of that SORP is the grant claw-back provisions of the statutory accounting requirements imposed by the Housing Corporation on all charities coming to it for funding. If the charity later attracts substantial special-purpose voluntary funding from other sources, a dilemma may await the charity trustees.

To account properly, in accordance with charity law and best practice, for these newly acquired special-purpose voluntary funds, which constitute endowed and other restricted trust funds, they would need to follow the relevant recommendations contained in the Charities SORP or their equivalent as a special departure, if necessary, from the overall requirement to follow the more specialised SORP issued for their sector. This need has become a *statutory requirement* under the Charities Act 2006: it imposes on the Government Department responsible for regulating such a charity a 'compliance obligation' (in conjunction with the Charity Commission if necessary) in respect of all its voluntary funds – thus solving a problem that the Accounting Standards Board had been unable to deal with.

Although FRS18's consultation draft, FRED21, did at the time seem to be opening the way for more than one SORP to be applied wherever *'a significant part of an entity's activities'* falls within the scope of this or that SORP, the negative response received by the ASB to this novel idea resulted in a return to the 'all or nothing' approach in the finalised version of that Standard. In practice, this means that such charities are caught up on FRS18's requirement that the accounting policies adopted must be those that are *most appropriate* to the reporting entity, so that they cannot just hide behind a SORP that, for them, is inappropriate in some material respect. If their accounts are really to be able to show a true and fair view they will therefore have no option but to depart from it in that respect, disclosing the fact, the reason and – because such substantial funds clearly have an impact on the mandatory true and fair view – the financial effect on their accounts.

One charity that seems to have come up with an unconventional solution to this problem is The Institute of Cancer Research: despite its dependency on government funding it prepares annual accounts not under the specialised SORP for higher and further education institutions that is normally applicable but the Charities SORP instead. However, its internal controls are internally audited under the 'Accountability and Audit: HEFCE Code of Practice' and periodically reviewed by the HEFCE Audit Service to satisfy the Higher Education Funding Council for England (HEFCE). The Institute is an exempt charity as a HEFCE-designated Higher Education Institution for funding purposes (as well as being a charitable company) through its connection with the University of London as one of its trustee-appointing bodies (see **1.2** below: Exempt Charities), and works closely with other cancer charities and one of the NHS Foundations Trusts (the Royal Marsden).

For other charities, the boundaries of the Charities SORP's scope may only become an issue for the preparation of group consolidated accounts (see **14.3** in chapter 14). For example, the 2007/08 accounts of the Charities Aid Foundation (CAF) made the following compliance disclosure in respect of its banking arm:

---

1. Basis of preparation of financial statements and accounting standards

The group financial statements have been prepared under the historical cost convention, as modified for the revaluation of fixed asset investments and property, and in accordance with United Kingdom Generally Accepted Accounting Practice (UK GAAP), 'Accounting and Reporting by Charities' Statement of Recommended Practice (SORP 2005), the Charities Act 1993 and the Charities (Accounts and Reports) Regulations 2005, except for the provision of SORP 2005 for all investments to be valued at market value, since certain debt securities which are normally held to maturity for balance sheet management purposes are valued at amortised cost. Included in these group financial statements are those of CAF Bank Limited, whose accounts are prepared in accordance with relevant Statements of Recommended Accounting Practice issued by the British Bankers Association.

...

2. Consolidation

The group financial statements include the accounts of CAF (the charity) and its subsidiary undertakings for the year ended 30 April 2008. ... The following entities are controlled by CAF and are consolidated in the group financial statements using the equity method:

Trading subsidiaries
CAF owns 100% of the equity share capital of the following:

- CAF Bank Limited, a bank for charities authorised and regulated by the Financial Services Authority ➡

- CAF Marketing Services Limited, a company authorised and regulated by the Financial Services Authority to market the CAF group's banking and investment products for charities.

UK registered charities
Southampton Row Trust Limited, which operates as CAF American Donor Fund, is a UK charitable company registered with the Charity Commission (No 1079020). Throughout the year it was wholly owned by CAF America (see below) and its ultimate controller is CAF. CAF American Donor Fund supports cross-order tax-efficient giving by enabling individuals liable for tax in both the UK and USA to obtain tax relief in each country on charitable gifts.

Overseas charitable entities
CAF controls the following overseas charitable entities:

- CAF America, a US public charity recognised by the US Internal Revenue Service. CAF America provides US citizens with the opportunity to make tax-effective gifts for the support of overseas charities. CAF's Chief Executive is the sole member of CAF America.

- CAF Australia group, which offers a range of charitable services to Australian donors and charities similar to those offered by CAF in the UK. CAF is the sole member and appoints the directors of the entities in the CAF Australia group.

- CAF Philanthropy Services LLC, which was founded in Russia by CAF and operates alongside our branch in Moscow. Together they work to raise awareness of NGOs and to advance giving and philanthropy in Russia.

Joint ventures
CAF Marketing Services Limited holds a 30% stake in CaSE Insurance (Charities and Social Enterprise Insurance LLP). CaSE provides insurance products designed specifically for the third sector. The partnership was formed in March 2007 and its results to 30 April 2008, which have been included in these accounts, do not materially affect the group results.

Branch
The results of CAF Russia, CAF's overseas branch, are included in the accounts of CAF.

...

Charities Aid Foundation – 2007/08 accounts

Smaller charities

SORP 2005 discarded the section on 'receipts and payments' accounting that had been included in SORP 2000, and which in any case went beyond the scope of the ASB. It summarised the principles and practices commended by the Charity Commission as regulator and already featured in its general guidance literature (see below). It also noted where the Scottish legislation required something different. However, there was no statutory underpinning for that part of the SORP – unlike most of its other parts. Here, in catering for a negligible proportion of the sector's financial resources, SORP 2000 could hardly have expected more than a negligible level of public interest. As it was put in paragraph 12:

> 'This SORP is intended to apply to all charities in the United Kingdom and the Republic of Ireland regardless of their size, constitution or complexity. It provides the basis for the preparation of accruals accounts to give a true and fair view and also provides recommendations in other cases e g on the preparation of receipts and payments accounts.'
>
> – *SORP 2000, paragraph 12*

Instead, paragraph 6 of SORP 2005 acknowledges that the Charities SORP's recommendations '*do not apply to charities preparing cash-based receipts and payments accounts*', as in any case it would not be in the public interest for the regulatory regime to be allowed to bear down too heavily on such smaller charities. This is supplemented in the SORP's Appendix 5 'Accounting for Smaller Charities':

> 'As this SORP is applicable to accruals accounts, no specific recommendations on cash-based receipts and payment accounts are provided within this SORP although as explained in paragraph 6 such charities are encouraged to analyse their receipts and payments based on the activities undertaken. The Charity Commission for England and Wales produces detailed guidance on the preparation of cash-based accounts.'
>
> – *SORP 2005, Appendix 5, paragraph 5.1.5*

This need for a *proportionate* approach to charity sector regulation becomes very clear from the table at **2.2**: Charity size-bands for statutory financial reporting.

The Commission's 'simplified guidance' for the smaller charity is now of two distinct kinds in the form of downloadable 'accounts packs' designed to be acceptable for filing purposes and with guidance notes showing how to 'fill in the boxes'. The guidance notes for the accruals-based accounts pack (CC17) makes use of those parts of the SORP most likely to be relevant to the thousands of small *non-company* charities that do not trade and have no charity branches, no subsidiaries/associates and no investment assets. It can be downloaded from the website or ordered from the Commission in print form, and aims to lighten the burden of compliance with the statutory 'true and fair view' requirement in such cases. The accruals accounts pack itself comprises a pro forma set of accounts for full compliance with the statutory requirements, together with a pro forma Annual Report. This enables you to prepare your charity's annual report and accounts by just following the guidance notes and filling in the appropriate boxes. You can then adjust the format to your liking and print out the finished result. The accruals accounts pack also includes a pro forma report for an independent examiner to complete.

For those *non-company* charities small enough to be able to opt out of the regulated form of 'true and fair' annual accounts, equivalent help and guidance is provided in the cash-based accounts pack coded CC16. This, too, is available as a booklet, explaining how to prepare statutory accounts on the alternative 'receipts and payments' basis as recommended by the Commission (with their own blank forms, if you want to use them), or else as a downloadable complete do-it-yourself 'accounts pack' including report-forms for optional use by an independent examiner and the trustees respectively.

Outline of the Charities SORP approach to annual reporting

1.1.6 For those charities that are within its scope, the Charities SORP is basically unavoidable nowadays if they are to be able to meet their reporting obligations under charity law. That, of course, is the purpose for which it was developed.

Naturally, this is subject to the relevant exemptions/options provided by statute, to any reliefs/dispensations granted by the regulator and also to those contained within the SORP itself. These can, depending on the charity's own circumstances and needs, eliminate or replace components from the list below to make up the full set of financial statements and reports that must be approved and issued by the trustees in each particular case.

The practicalities of SORP-compliance for each component or document that may be required or desired to complete the set in any particular case are discussed in the following chapters:

Document	Chapter
Annual Report of the charity trustees	4
Charity Statement of Financial Activities (SoFA) *to show a true and fair view*	6, 13
Similarly, a consolidated SoFA – if the charity's group exceeds the statutory audit threshold (currently £500,000 gross income for the year) – the SORP's ceiling for the 'small group' consolidation exemption	14, 13
Charity balance sheet *to show a true and fair view*	8–10
Similarly, a consolidated balance sheet for the group – unless it is 'small' (normally combined with the charity balance sheet in a columnar format)	14
Cashflow Statement – for 'large' charities/groups only	11
Summary Income and Expenditure account *showing a true and fair view* (companies only – if the required FRS3 compliance is not possible within the SoFA)	7
Notes to the accounts (*if* claiming to show a true and fair view)	12
As a statutory option in England and Wales for *non-company* charities up to £100,000* gross income for the year (outside the scope of the SORP):	16
Receipts and Payments Account summary – instead of the SoFA and Notes	
Statement of Assets and Liabilities – instead of the Balance Sheet and Notes	
Report on the Accounts by a professionally regulated charity auditor, or by an independent examiner if audit exemption applicable	17

*increased to £250,000 for financial years ending on or after 1 April 2009 by Ministerial Order (SI 2009/508) in line with Charity Commission recommendations for regulatory threshold changes following the Spring 2008 public consultation.

In addition, certain chapters of this book deal with the wider, more general aspects that may be essential reading for some – or just useful reminders for others more experienced in the field of charity accountability and wishing to keep up to date with developments.

Chapter 2, 'Charity Size-bands for Statutory Reporting', explains the graduated structure of the regulatory regime that governs charity accountability in England and Wales. You will need this information to be able to identify any statutory reliefs, exemptions or options that may be applicable to your charity to minimise or optimise the SORP-reporting package summarised above.

Chapter 3 discusses the principles of *fund-accounting* by means of which *charitable gifts* of all kinds and their proper use/investment can be reported to meet the strict requirements of charity law, thus discharging the trustees' duty of care under trust law. This goes to the very heart of the Charities SORP, as something peculiar to the voluntary sector but still largely ignored by the ASB – even though its counterpart in the USA issued the broadly similar FASB116/117 to standardise gift-accounting ('voluntary contributions') as long ago as 1993. This makes chapter 3 the natural starting-point for newcomers from the commercial sector.

For anyone preparing accounts that are to show 'a true and fair view', familiarity with accounting standards and their applicability is a prerequisite, as the SORP itself makes clear. However, some of them are irrelevant to charity accounting, while others can only usefully apply in a modified way because of the fundamentally different motivation of *public benefit*, to the virtual exclusion of any conflicting right to 'private' benefit – especially investor interests of an equity nature. Chapter 5 is therefore all about the practicalities of applying the relevant accounting standards to achieve the very particular objectives of the Charities SORP. Newcomers from the commercial sector will therefore find it useful as the next stage of their induction before moving on to the individual chapters listed above.

It should be noted here in passing that the Scottish legislation of 2005 covering *non-company* charities for the alternative (ie, cash-based) form of accounts provided for on that side of the border increased the income ceiling from £25,000 to £100,000, with no indication of any further increase to come. Also unlike the English legislation, the Scottish Regulations of 2006 prescribe the content of the Receipts and Payments Account for those opting out of the SORP. The statutory alternative to a balance sheet is also different in Scotland: it is a 'statement of balances', implying a more developed 'numerical' kind of record-keeping (ie 'double-entry' book-keeping) than the more rudimentary *descriptive* kind permissible under English law as 'proper' accounting records.

Finally, chapter 15 discusses the statutory requirements for *summarised* accounts if provided to its members instead of the full audited accounts by any charitable company, the Charity Commission's requirements for *Summary Information Returns* by the top ca. 5,500 registered charities that currently exceed £1m annual gross income and also what the SORP outlines as 'best practice' whenever summarised *non-statutory* accounts are published, and how useful the latter can be in all kinds of publicity material where full accruals accounts can be daunting – for example, as part of a non-statutory 'Annual Review'.

'Immaterial' items

1.1.7 The concept of 'materiality' is intrinsic to public accountability, and the SORP is no exception to the general rule that, for clarity's sake, annual reporting should concentrate on what is most likely to influence the reader and should not allow inconsequential information to obtrude. This rule therefore relegates as background information – even, in some cases, disregarding it – any 'immaterial item' that could otherwise lead to the annual report and accounts becoming so cluttered up with minutiae as to turn the reader off completely. In the words of the Charities SORP:

> 'Each accounting recommendation should be considered in the context of what is material ... to the particular charity.'
>
> – *SORP 2005, paragraph 4*

Guidance on deciding what is 'material' is extensive in the glossary to the current SORP, which owes much to the extremely rigorous treatment of the subject in accounting and auditing standards – as can be seen from the following quotation:

> 'An item of information is material to the accounts if its misstatement or omission might reasonably be expected to influence the economic decisions of users of those accounts, including their assessments of stewardship. Immaterial information will need to be excluded to avoid clutter which impairs the understandability of other information provided.
>
> Whether information is material will depend on the size and nature of the item in question judged in the particular circumstances of the case. Materiality is not capable of general mathematical definition as it has both qualitative and quantitative aspects. The principal factors to be taken into account are set out below. It will usually be a combination of these factors, rather than any one in particular, that will determine materiality.
>
> (a)   The item's size is judged in the context both of the accounts as a whole and of the other information available to users that would affect their evaluation of the financial statements. This includes, for example, considering how the item affects the evaluation of trends and similar considerations.
>
> (b)   Consideration is given to the item's nature in relation to:
>   (i)   the transactions or other events giving rise to it;
>   (ii)   the legality, sensitivity, normality and potential consequences of the event or transaction;
>   (iii)   the identity of the parties involved; and
>   (iv)   the particular headings and disclosures that are affected.
>
> If there are two or more similar items, the materiality of the items in aggregate as well as of the items individually needs to be considered.
>
> Trustees are responsible for deciding whether an item is or is not material. In cases of doubt an item should be treated as material.'
>
> – *SORP 2005, Appendix 1, Glossary GL 42*

This distinction in the SORP is also reflected in the current Charities (Accounts and Reports) Regulations, SI 2008/629 (Regulations 2008), as well as in the new s 44A (imposing the same 'whistle-blowing' duty on all charity auditors and independent examiners) inserted into the 1993 Act by the 2006 Charities Act, where the following clauses require only 'material' information to be disclosed:

Auditor's Report –

'[if in the auditor's opinion on accruals-based accounts] any information contained in the statement of accounts is inconsistent in any *material* respect with [the trustees' annual report] [the auditor's report must state that opinion and the grounds for forming it]' – *reg 24(1)(g)(iii) for a non-company charity*; or *reg 25(1)(h)(iii) for a small charitable company;* or *reg 30(1)(h)(i) for group consolidated accounts,*

'[whether in the auditor's opinion on accounts prepared on a receipts and payments basis] the account and statement adequately distinguish any *material* special trust or other restricted fund of the charity' – *reg 26(1)(f)(ii).*

– SI 2008/629

Whistle-blowing duty for all charity auditors and independent examiners –

'[The person acting as independent examiner or (if under Part VI of the 1993 Act) auditor must report in writing to the Charity Commission any matter of which the person becomes aware in his capacity as such] which relates to the activities or affairs of the charity or of any connected institution or body and which he has reasonable cause to believe is likely to be of *material* significance for the purpose of the exercise by the Commission of its [supervisory] functions under section 8 or 18 [of the 1993 Act].' – *section 44A,*

'[The same duty] shall apply in relation to a person acting as an auditor of a charitable company appointed under Chapter 2 of Part 16 of the Companies Act 2006 (appointment of auditors) ...' – *section 68A.*

– Charities Act 1993 (emphasis added)

Independent Examiner's Report –

'[The report must state] whether or not any matter has come to the examiner's attention in connection with the examination which gives him reasonable cause to believe that in any *material* respect—

(i)   accounting records have not been kept in respect of the charity in accordance with (aa) where that charity is a company, section 221 of the 1985 Act; or (bb) in any other case, section 41 of the 1993 Act; or
(ii)   the accounts do not accord with those records; or
(iii)   in the case of an examination of ... accounts ... prepared under s 42(1) of the 1993 Act (ie, accruals-based)], the statement of accounts does not comply with any of the requirements of regulation ... 8 as relevant other than any requirement to give a true and fair view – *reg 31(h)*;

[The report must give particulars wherever] there has been any *material* expenditure or action which appears not to be in accordance with the trusts of the charity – *reg 31(j)(i);* or

[for accruals-based accounts] any information contained in the statement of accounts is inconsistent in any *material* respect with [the annual report]' – *reg 31(j)(iii)/(iv). (emphasis added)*

– SI 2008/629

Accounts Notes disclosures –

'(a)   particulars of any *material* adjustment made [to comparative figures to show them on the same basis as this year's figures] under regulation 8(8);

(b)   a description of each of the accounting policies ... adopted ... and [which] are *material* in the context of the accounts ... [and of] the estimation techniques adopted ... which are *material* to the presentation of the accounts;

(c)   a description of any *material* change to the policies and techniques [in] (b) [above], the reason for such change and its effect *(if material)* on the accounts, in accordance with the methods and principles set out in the SORP;

(d)   a description of the nature and purpose of all *material* funds of the charity in accordance with the methods and principles set out in the SORP;
        ...

(i)   an itemised analysis of any *material* movement between any of the restricted funds of the charity, or between a restricted and an unrestricted fund of the charity, together with an explanation of the nature and purpose of each of those funds;

(j)   ... *where material*, [each subsidiary/associated undertaking's] turnover and net profit or loss for [that body's] corresponding financial year ... and any qualification expressed in an auditor's report on [its] accounts;
        ...

(t)   an analysis of all *material* changes ... in the values of fixed assets, in accordance with the methods and principles set out in the SORP;
        ...

(v)   [for a charity above the statutory audit threshold] ... particulars of any *material* departure from [applicable accounting] standards and statements of practice and the reasons for such departure; ...'.

– SI 2008/629, Sch 2, para 1(1) (emphasis added)

Elsewhere in the 2008 Regulations, too, the distinction between what is or is not 'material' is made only by *cross-referring* to the SORP itself – as has been done for trustee-disclosures. There, for instance, the Regulations require the accounts to disclose:

'such particulars of transactions of the charity, or of any subsidiary undertaking of the charity, entered into with a related party, as are required to be disclosed by the SORP.'

– SI 2008/629, Sch 2, para 1(1)(e)

However, it should be noted that the uncompromising stance taken by the Charities SORP at the insistence of the Charity Commission even in the 1995 SORP, to the effect that *all* trustee-transactions – however small and insignificant – must be considered 'material' in the public interest, is tempered by SORP 2005's specific disclosure exclusions. These very welcome reliefs, first introduced in SORP 2000, are discussed more fully in chapter 12 on the Notes to the Accounts.

Finally, it should be noted in passing that, where consolidated accounts are in question too, the same test of 'materiality' applies – as is acknowledged in paragraph 383(c) of SORP 2005 in relation to subsidiary undertakings, even if not also in its later paragraphs dealing with associated undertakings.

Transitional concurrency of old and new versions of the Charities SORP and/or its related Regulations

1.1.8   For a time after the issue of SORP 2005, ie, until all charities had commenced a new financial year *after* 31 March 2005, there was a transitional phase for which we needed to distinguish two concurrent versions of the Charities SORP and its related Regulations in their old and new versions.

By 'old versions' at that time, we mean SORP 2000 and its related 1995 and 2000 Regulations, which were both covered in depth by the second edition of this book. They had retained validity together as a transitional option to compliance with their newer versions for all financial years *commencing before* 1 April 2005. Thereafter, the old versions could no longer be used as the basis of the annual report and accounts and the new versions of each began to apply instead, being cross-linked and so inseparable.

March 2005 saw the publication of the new version of the Charities SORP, *'Accounting and Reporting by Charities'* (distinguished in the third edition of this book as the 'new' SORP), or SORP 2005, together with a new version of the related regulations, Regulations 2005, reg 13 of which, immediately upon taking effect for any charity, automatically revoked its precursors: SI 1995/2724 and SI 2000/2868.

Similarly, March 2008 saw the making of the 2005 SORP's new and greatly expanded 2008 Regulations revoking the 2005 Regulations for all financial years starting after 31 March 2008 and with a transitional provision allowing the 2008 Regulations to be adopted voluntarily in place of the 2005 Regulations for any earlier financial year.

The third edition of this book was written for use with the 2005 versions of the SORP and its Regulations, while this fourth edition is for use with SORP 2005 and its 2008 Regulations, but the book again retains much the same structure as the previous editions, and includes comment on older SORP/Regulations versions where appropriate. This will enable the reader familiar with the 'old regime' to see more readily how the compliance needs have changed in each area under the 'new regime'. It also maintains continuity for readers of the previous editions of this book.

Relationship with the SORP-based Regulations 2008

1.1.9   Any overview of the current Charities SORP would be incomplete without indicating how it interacts with the related SORP-based Regulations – in this book those of March 2008. These new Regulations were made by the Cabinet Office's 'Office of the Third Sector' (OTS) under Part VI of the 1993 Act to correspond with the Charities SORP in its current version in order to continue and extend (principally to group-accounting by non-company parent charities and to the Charities Act accounts-scrutiny regime for small charitable companies claiming company audit exemption) its essential statutory underpinning – without which the effectiveness of the whole regulatory regime would be patchy, to say the least.

The relationship between the current SORP and any new version of its related Regulations necessitates a transitional concurrence of the old and new versions, as explained above. Here, we need only concern ourselves with those Regulations that relate to the Charities SORP, as accounting for charities subject to specialised SORPs (CIFs, RSLs and HEIs) is outside the scope of this book.

Thus, after the end of the transitional 'voluntary' phase applicable for all financial years commencing prior to 1 April 2008, during which charities have been able to choose to remain with the old Regulations of 2005, or else as soon as they voluntarily 'migrate' (early) to the 2008 Regulations, charities can no longer make use of SI 2005/572, because it is revoked at that point by reg 4 of Regulations 2008.

The transition from the relevant provisions of the 2005 Regulations to those of 2008 in relation to SORP 2005 is shown in the following table:

2005			2008 Regulations			
Regs	Topic	General	Non-company	Company	Group	NHS
1, 2	Citation; Definitions	1, 2			9	
3	Form & Content of charity accounts	5	8		12; 15–18	
6	Financial year-ends and changes	3			10/11	
7	Audit (accruals or cash-based accounts)	20; 25/26	24; 26	25	29/30	27/28
8	Independent Examination (ditto)	22	31	31		32
9	Audit/Examination – supplementary	33				
10	Charity Commission dispensations	34				
11	Trustees' Annual Report	37	40	40	41	
13	Revocation/Transitional provisions	4				
Sch 1	Accounts Notes	Sch 2				

In the above table, it should be noted that the Charities Act provisions governing (i) the preparation of group consolidated accounts by 'auditable' charities apply not only to all *non-company* parent charities but also to parent *charitable companies* if group-accounting is not **required** under the 2006 Companies Act; and (ii) audit or independent examination apply to all *non-company* charities as well as also to *charitable companies* claiming company audit exemption as a 'small' company/group as defined by the Companies Act 2006.

Under the current legislative policy of simply *cross-referring* to the current SORP in making new Regulations, instead of extracting selected parts of the SORP and re-formulating them, as was done in the original (1995) Regulations, reg 8(5) of 2008 (like reg 3(6) of 2005) looks innocuous enough. Its effect, however, is to give to the Charities SORP a kind of rebuttable statutory presumption of applicability in the vital areas of the compilation and presentation of the financial information that *must* be provided in the entity SoFA and balance sheet of all *non-company* charities, as well as in every group SoFA and balance sheet not *required* by the Companies Act 2006. This is a precedent that makes the SORP virtually unavoidable for charitable companies. It thus seems that this change at the turn of the millennium did indeed herald the dawn of the 'statutory SORP'.

EXEMPT CHARITIES

1.2   Exempt charities are those listed in the 1993 Act, Sch 2 as amended by the 2006 Charities Act. Under s 3(5)(a) of the 1993 Act, these charities are not required to register with the Charity Commission, and although entitled to the Commission's help and guidance just like other charities, they are not subject to its supervisory powers except at the instigation of the exempt charity's principal regulator. Since the provisions of the 1993 Act make these two aspects, registration and supervision, practically inseparable, however, exempt charities are not allowed to register at all.

This follows Government policy generally to avoid dual regulation, since in most cases there will be a sponsoring Department of Central Government, or else some other authority, such as HEFCE, for example, responsible for supervising the body. The various classes listed in Sch 2, of which those in *italics* lose their exempt status under the regulatory regime changes in the Charities Act 2006 and must then register with the Charity Commission (unless small enough to be provisionally 'excepted' – see below), include:

–   most universities and university colleges# in England *(those in Wales are to lose their exemption and may be 'excepted' in future)*; also any institution* connected with one of them – see the illustration at **1.1.5**, for example (exemption here being granted by Privy Council order, if requested);

–   *#Oxford, Cambridge and Durham University colleges;*

–   **the students' unions of all the above universities and colleges as well as those below;*

–   most colleges of higher or further** education in England *(but not in Wales)*;

–   *Winchester and Eton Colleges;*

–   the old 'grant-maintained' schools that opted for exempt 'foundation' status under the reform of State-funded/provided education (those that did become part of the fully devolved State education system of nearly 30,000 schools – since a certain measure of independence from Government is considered intrinsic to charitable status under English law – no longer count as charities at all)**;

–   many of the major museums and galleries *(but not the Museum of London any longer)*;

(in the above cases the exemption extends to almost any charitable institution administered by or on behalf of them)

–   *the Church Commissioners and any institutions administered by them;*

–   registered social landlords (RSLs) with charitable status** and also charitable industrial and provident societies in England** (under the Charities Act 2006, to be exempt in future these must also be RSLs regulated by the Tenant Services Authority in succession to the Housing Corporation – see below).

– **exempt status for 'foundation' and 'voluntary aided' schools, for further education corporations in England and for RSLs and charitable IP Societies in England, will depend on whether agreement can be reached with suitable 'principal regulators';*

Strictly speaking, it is not any provision of the other legislation governing them that grants them exempt status. It just provides the justification for including the body in the list in Sch 2 to the 1993 Act as an 'exempt' body 'insofar as it is a charity'.

Charities Act accounting requirements

1.2.1 Section 46(1) of the 1993 Act preserves *without change* the rudimentary old accounting requirements of the Charities Act 1960 ('the 1960 Act') for these exempt charities, as a kind of safety net below their existing accounting obligations that are normally – but not always – under some other statutory enactment.

'(1) Nothing in sections 41 to 45 above applies to any exempt charity; but the charity trustees of an exempt charity shall keep proper books of account with respect to the affairs of the charity, and if not required by or under the authority of any other Act to prepare periodical statements of account shall prepare consecutive statements of account consisting on each occasion of an income and expenditure account relating to a period of not more than fifteen months and a balance sheet relating to the end of that period.

(2) The books of accounts and statements of account relating to an exempt charity shall be preserved for a period of six years at least unless the charity ceases to exist and the Commissioners consent in writing to their being destroyed or otherwise disposed of.'

– Charities Act 1993, s 46

It follows that s 46 had to exclude the exempt charities from ss 41–45's updated and more detailed provisions regulating all the other charities' accounting records, annual accounts preparation, audit or independent examination, retention and filing, and also annual (trustees') report preparation/filing. But they are subject – just like any other charity – to s 47's direct public access requirement, quoted below:

'...

(2) Where any person—

(a) requests the charity trustees of a charity in writing to provide him with a copy of the charity's most recent accounts or (if subsection (4) below applies) of its most recent annual report,[3] and

(b) pays them such reasonable fee (if any) as they may require in respect of the costs of complying with the request,

those trustees shall comply with the request within the period of two months beginning with the date on which it is made.

(3) In subsection (2) above the reference to a charity's most recent accounts is—

...

---

[3]   Under the Charities Act 2006, this has been extended to include the trustees' annual report (if any) prepared for that year – but allowing for the public to request either or both of these documents, even though they should be seen as inseparable under the SORP.

(d) in the case of an exempt charity, a reference to the accounts of the charity most recently audited in pursuance of any statutory or other requirement or, if its accounts are not required to be audited, the accounts most recently prepared in respect of the charity.'

– Charities Act 1993, s 47

SORP compliance

1.2.2 Where any accounts prepared by an exempt charity are required to show a true and fair view, or where they claim to do so, as will normally be the case, the Charities SORP will still apply, albeit only within the relevant requirements of that body's governing legislation and adapted to satisfy any non-conflicting requirements of its governing document – except where a more specific SORP applies to that particular charity, of course. But compliance will be an issue only for its auditors and its own sponsoring department or other supervisory body, with the Charity Commission being brought in only as the 'default regulator' under provisions contained in the Charities Act 2006 which are primarily aimed at securing due compliance with charity law in respect of any charitable trust funds administered.

The commonest examples where other SORPs apply are those for universities and colleges, known collectively as HEIs (together with the colleges known as Further Education Institutions – FEIs), and for the charitable and other housing associations (nowadays called RSLs) registered with the Tenant Services Authority (the sector's regulator from 1 December 2008 in succession to the Housing Corporation, whose capital funding activities were then transferred to the Housing and Communities Agency) – in both cases to satisfy the grant-control requirements of the public bodies responsible for funding them.

EXCEPTED CHARITIES

1.3 Apart from the financially very significant but relatively few exempt charities, there are also perhaps as many as 100,000 charities (most of them small local bodies with insignificant financial resources) that over the years – mainly soon after the 1960 Act – have been 'excepted' from the duty to register with the Charity Commission. This was to recognise what were then seen as adequate alternative arrangements through some sort of (usually non-statutory) supervisory body that ensured their public accountability. Unlike the exempt charities, excepted charities can register voluntarily – and therefore also de-register at any time – under the present 'excepting' orders and regulations. The reason for this difference becomes clear from the next section.

Following a decade-long moratorium from 1996 to allow time for a thorough review of the effectiveness or otherwise of what has always been, in effect, a *voluntary* supervisory system, the largest excepted charities (principally comprising the largest 2,000 or so of the 13,000 Parish Church Councils, those which currently exceed a £100,000 annual gross income level – though that threshold is expected to be revised downwards in due course) had to lose their excepted status under provisions contained in the Charities Act 2006 with effect from 31 January 2009 when the Charity Commission started registering them. The Commission expects to complete that process for all the hitherto excepted religious charities before October 2009.

By analogy with that precedent, the same provisional financial threshold has been set by the Charity Commission, with effect from January 2009 for a new class of excepted charity that includes the smaller Students' Unions connected with an exempt university or college, once the 2006 Charities Act's removal of all Students' Unions from the 1993 Act's list of exempt charities takes effect, which is now to be in November/December 2009 by agreement between the Commission and the National Union of Students. For the numerous service funds of the Armed Forces charities, registration of those exceeding the £100,000 ceiling for excepted status started in October 2008.

In addition to those charities that are *specially* excepted, by Charity Commission order or regulation, two *general* classes of excepted charity, one for churches, chapels, etc, that are registered elsewhere as being open to the public, and the other for very small charities as redefined in simpler terms by the Charities Act 2006, are preserved in s 3 of the 1993 Act:

'(5)   The following charities are not required to be registered—
        ...

(c)   any charity whose income from all sources does not in aggregate amount to more than £5,000[4] a year;

and no charity is required to be registered in respect of any registered place of worship.'

– Charities Act 1993, s 3(5)

Charities Act reliefs for the very smallest

1.3.1   Charities excepted because of extreme smallness are also excused from more or less all the regulatory requirements to which larger charities are now subject in the public interest:

'Nothing in sections 43 to 45 above applies to any charity which—

(a)   falls within section 3(5)(c) above, and
(b)   is not registered.'

– Charities Act 1993, s 46(3)

This means they are not required to have any kind of external scrutiny report on their statutory annual accounts, nor to prepare the statutory form of annual report. They do, however, have to keep 'proper' accounting records, to prepare annual accounts and to make those accounts available to members of the public upon request.

Charities Act annual reporting – other cases

1.3.2   Other excepted charities – those covered by an excepting order or regulation, or which are set up to operate a registered place of public worship – are excused from having to prepare and file a statutory annual report unless specially requested to do so:

---

4   Under the Charities Act 2006, the 1960 Act criteria for compulsory registration of any charity (however small) having either (i) permanent endowment or (ii) the (exclusive) use or occupation of land have been abolished, and the old £1,000 gross income registration threshold has been raised to £5,000, but with *voluntary* registration being allowed below that level.

'Except in accordance with subsection (7) below,[5] nothing in section 45 above applies to any charity (other than an exempt charity or a charity which falls within section 3(5)(c) above) which (a) is excepted by section 3(5) above, and (b) is not registered.'

– Charities Act 1993, s 46(4)

These excepted charities must not only keep proper accounting records, prepare statutory annual accounts and provide copies[6] to the public upon request, but also have the accounts audited or independently examined (unless their gross income remains below the respective thresholds of £500,000 and £10,000* a year, of course), (*or any higher threshold, eg, over and above the new £25,000 independent examination threshold under SI 2009/508 for financial years ending after March 2009.)

If they do opt to be on the Charities Register, then as long as they remain there they must prepare statutory annual reports just like any other registered charity and (if outside the 'light touch' regime – threshold £10,000) file them, with accounts, etc, attached, along with their statutory annual return to the Commission for regulatory purposes. Under SI 2009/508, those below the £25,000 gross income threshold for the new regime of 'Serious Incident Reporting' imposed on charity trustees by the Commission in its Annual Return regulations will not have to file annual reports and accounts routinely with the Commission for financial years ending on or after 1 April 2009, but instead, if above £10,000 gross income, they will be subject to random monitoring checks to ensure that they are still meeting their public accountability obligations nevertheless.

For *excepted* charities, under Part VI of the 1993 Act and its SORP-based Regulations 2008, the statutory annual report is normally not mandatory as long as they remain unregistered, but it is nevertheless *best practice* to prepare it, in accordance with the Charities SORP.

CHARITABLE COMPANIES

1.4   Charitable companies are defined by the 1993 Act, s 97(1). They include any charitable body corporate that is either on the Companies Register or otherwise subject to the (accounting) provisions of the 1985 Act.

They therefore do not include charitable corporations set up by Royal Charter or local Act of Parliament, for instance, unless their accounting obligations are specifically tied to the 1985 Act's provisions, as re-enacted in the Companies Act 2006 – see below.

Companies Act accounting requirements

1.4.1   The annual accounts of charitable companies are now (for financial years from 6 April 2008) governed by the Companies Act 2006, chapter 15. This rewrites all the main provisions of the 1985 Act, Part VII and other than the detailed form and content requirements as set out in Schs 4/4A for individual (ie, entity) and group accounts

---

5   This refers to the statutory power of the Charity Commissioners to require any such excepted charity to prepare and submit an annual report.

6   Under the Charities Act 2006, this obligation is extended to cover not only a copy of the latest available statutory accounts, as hitherto, but also of any statutory annual report they have (had to) prepare for that year.

respectively, and in Schs 8/8A for abbreviated accounts similarly, while s 468 of the Companies Act 2006 makes provision for new Regulations to be made on company accounting, including these detailed form and content requirements, as now set out in SI 2008/409 and 410 respectively for 'small' companies/groups and those defined as 'medium-sized' or large. Meanwhile, the above 1985 Act Schedules continue to apply. In accordance with EC Directives, the Act requires *all* companies to show 'a true and fair view' in accounts prepared under it. To achieve this, they will normally also find it necessary to comply with all applicable Financial Reporting Standards (FRSs) and Statements of Standard Accounting Practice (SSAPs), etc, *and any relevant SORP* – since these represent the generally accepted, 'tried and tested' ways and means developed for the purpose, as has been recognised by the courts.

Company accounts, which for a charity must be based on UK accounting standards as required by s 396 of the Companies Act 2006 (ie, they cannot be based on IAS like any other private company), must thus continue to comply with the same form and content requirements as were set out Sch 4 to the 1985 Act:

'1(1)   Subject to the following provisions of this Schedule—

(a)   every balance sheet of a company shall show the items listed in either of the balance sheet formats set out below in section B of this Part; and

(b)   every profit and loss account of a company shall show the items listed in any one of the profit and loss account formats so set out;

in either case in the order and under the headings and sub-headings given in the format adopted.

...

2(1)   Where in accordance with paragraph 1 a company's balance sheet or profit and loss account for any financial year has been prepared by reference to one of the formats set out in section B below, the directors of the company shall adopt the same format in preparing the accounts for subsequent financial years of the company unless in their opinion there are special reasons for the change.

(2)   Particulars of any change in the format adopted in preparing a company's balance sheet or profit and loss account in accordance with paragraph 1 shall be disclosed, and the reasons for the change shall be explained, in a note to the accounts in which the new format is first adopted.

3(1)   Any item required in accordance with paragraph 1 to be shown in a company's balance sheet or profit and loss account may be shown in greater detail than required by the format adopted. ...

...

(3)   In preparing a company's balance sheet or profit and loss account the directors of the company shall adapt the arrangement and headings and sub-headings otherwise required by paragraph 1 in respect of items to which an Arabic number is assigned in the format adopted, in any case where the special nature of the company's business requires such adaptation.'

– Companies Act 1985, Sch 4, Part I, Section A

What is vital for our understanding is in para 3(3): 'the directors of the company *shall* adapt the arrangement ... where the special nature of the company's business requires such adaptation' (the emphasis is ours). This is not optional. And in the absence of a more persuasive alternative in any particular circumstances it will be the Charities SORP – catering, as it does, for the special nature of charities generally and their particular reporting needs – that will normally inform the opinion of a company auditor in reporting whether or not the accounts as prepared by the directors do show 'a true and fair view' of the company's activities and financial position *as a charity*.

The SORP-compliant annual report and accounts of a charitable company can look so much like those of a non-company charity nowadays that often the only way you can tell them apart is by searching for the small, tell-tale signs such as:

–   the company number on the cover, as required by the Registrar of Companies;

–   references to the company's 'directors' – who are, by virtue of their office, also the 'charity trustees' for Charities Act purposes (and are perhaps referred to as 'trustees', particularly if so defined in the Memorandum and Articles. Some *non-company* charities refer to their *non-trustee* executives as (departmental) 'directors' – so that this word cannot be taken as an infallible sign of a company);

–   the disclosure of a 'company secretary' as an officer in the annual report (this being a *statutory* office, which under the Companies Act 2006 is now *optional*, and not to be confused with that of 'secretary' to the Council of Management of an unincorporated charitable association);

–   reference to 'members' and their limited personal liability in the event of a winding-up, normally limited not by any kind of share capital (rarely seen because such capital must be 'non-participating') but by nominal guarantees (usually of £1 each) – which is normally a pre-condition for omitting the otherwise compulsory 'limited' at the end of the company's name;

–   the company's 'registered office' address in the annual report (being a *statutory* disclosure for *companies* but not for *charities* – there being no such requirement under the Charities Acts);

–   the company directors' statutory declaration concerning 'relevant audit information' (unless company audit exemption is claimed on the face of the balance sheet);

–   the emphasis on the company's 'net income' or 'results' for the year – not only in the annual report but also especially in the audit report (where its 'income and expenditure' (*as a company*) will be mentioned in addition to its 'incoming resources and application of resources' *as a charity*) – and also the separation of its investment gains/losses between realised and unrealised, with the insertion of a sub-total for 'net income' (or expenditure) between them – in cases where there is no separate Summary Income and Expenditure Statement to make it obvious that this is a company;

–   reference to the Companies Act instead of the Charities Act in the audit report on the accounts of an auditable charitable company 'required to be audited' under

Part 16 of the Companies Act 2006 (ie, in the absence of a valid claim to the 'small company' audit exemption available under that Act – see above);

– the (inconsequential (in the view of the authors), yet statutory) disclosure in the balance sheet of any 'unrealised' element of company reserves resulting from revaluing corporate assets.

The format of the FRS3-compliant SoFA, described later in chapter 6, corresponds to Profit and Loss Account Formats 3 and 4, the same as were contained in Sch 4 to the 1985 Act, in that it adopts the total income and total expenditure approach rather than the vertical (or 'cascade') approach of Formats 1 and 2. The company formats are to be seen as adapted by the Charities SORP to meet the reporting needs of charities, the special nature of whose 'business' (the provision, independent of the State, of public benefit through charitable activities) is radically different from that of any company formed 'for profit'.

As will be seen in chapter 6, the first part of the SoFA accounts for 'income and expenditure' (plus any incoming capital/endowed funds), while the second part of the SoFA presents the required statement of 'other recognised gains and losses' and also the reconciliation of funds from last year's balance sheet to this one.

Where a charitable company does present a separate income and expenditure account, the SORP shows how best to summarise, and cross-link to, the relevant information as presented in the SoFA, which is entirely in accordance with the Companies Act's Profit and Loss Account format requirements.

The need for compliance with all of this follows inescapably from the view originally taken by the APB in the 2002 revised edition of its Practice Note PN 11: 'The Audit of Charities', for use by registered auditors (a view that – apart from the FRS18 reference (abbreviated as paragraph 18 in the revised PN11's April 2008 exposure draft – merits but a brief mention in Appendix 1 to that document). Paragraphs 192, 193 and 194 of the section on Reporting (referring to the requirements of 'Statement of Auditing Standards' No SAS 600), put the then current position under FRS18 (effective for accounting periods from 24 December 2001 onwards) quite succinctly:

'Requirements of the Companies Act 1985

192 Charities which are incorporated under the Companies Act 1985 are required to prepare annual financial statements which give a true and fair view of the charitable company's state of affairs at the end of the year and of its income and expenditure for that year.

193 The Companies Act 1985 requires companies to prepare financial statements which give a true and fair view. Paragraph 3(3) of Part 1, section A of Schedule 4 of this Act requires the directors (trustees) to adapt the headings and subheadings of the balance sheet and profit and loss account in any case where the special nature of the company's business requires such adaptation. The special nature of charities, particularly in relation to special trusts, will lead to adaptation of such accounts in order to reflect the legal position of such trusts and to show a true and fair view. In addition, the development and issue of the Charities SORP, which followed the ASB code of practice, provides authoritative guidance on the application of accounting standards in a manner that takes account of the particular circumstances of the charities sector.

194 FRS 18 – *Accounting Policies* requires trustees of charitable companies to state whether the financial statements have been prepared in accordance with the Charities SORP and, for any treatment that is not in accordance with the SORP, to give the reasons why the treatment adopted is judged more appropriate to the charity's particular circumstances. Details also need to be given of any disclosures recommended by the SORP that have not been provided and the reasons why they have not been provided. Auditors will be aware that non-compliance with the requirements of FRS 18 ordinarily results in a qualified opinion. In this context auditors of charitable companies need to give particular consideration to the impact of non-compliance with the Charities SORP on their audit opinion. If an adverse or qualified opinion is to be avoided, auditors need to be satisfied that any alternative treatment adopted is more appropriate in order to give the true and fair view required by company law.'

– PN 11: 'The Audit of Charities' (Revised 2002), paragraphs 192–194: Reporting

Role of Auditing Standards

1.4.2 To complement the original 1995 SORP by aligning charity auditing practice with it, the APB updated and published its previous guidance on charity audits in October 1996 as Practice Note PN 11: 'The Audit of Charities'. That guidance was again reviewed in 2001 and updated to take account of SORP 2000, but with only minor changes to paragraph 8 of the Introduction to the 1996 version, which as renumbered paragraph 15 in the 2002 version stated:

'The financial statements of a charity which are prepared to give a true and fair view under the requirements of either the 1993 Act or the Companies Act 1985 are required to be prepared in accordance with applicable law and regulations, Financial Reporting Standards, and Statements of Standard Accounting Practice, irrespective of whether they are subject to audit, independent examination or reporting under Section 249A of the Companies Act. The Statement of Recommended Practice "Accounting and Reporting by Charities" (the Charities SORP), issued by the Charity Commission ... and developed in accordance with the Accounting Standards Board's (ASB's) stated practice, supplements these general accounting principles and is intended to apply to all charities in the United Kingdom and the Republic of Ireland (unless a separate SORP exists for a particular class of charities) regardless of their size, constitution or complexity and indicates the current view of best practice in accounting for charities. In addition, FRS18 – Accounting Policies – requires a statement that financial statements have been prepared in accordance with the relevant SORP, and details of any departures from the recommended practice and disclosures. Consequently, it is normally necessary to follow the guidance set out in the Charities SORP in order to give a true and fair view, as required by both Acts.'

– PN 11: 'The Audit of Charities' (Revised 2002), Introduction, paragraph 15

The specific requirements for audit reports on the accounts of charitable companies were considered later in the Practice Note, where paragraph 195 of the 2002 revised edition retained the 1996 wording:

'The form of the auditors' opinion on financial statements of a charitable company reflects the different form of accounting appropriate to charities, as set out in the Charities SORP, and therefore includes the expression of opinion on the incoming resources and application of resources whilst retaining reference to income and expenditure.'

– PN 11: 'The Audit of Charities', 1996 edition, Reporting, paragraph 15

The 2008 version of PN11, issued in December by the APB in the light of responses to the public consultation up to 11 July 2008, has had to take account of extensive changes since 2002 not only in the regulatory regime for the charity sector but also of the replacement of the old UK auditing standards by a modified version of the international ones, which are noticeably stricter as regards reliance on, and documentation of, audit evidence. The new version also builds on the success of its precursor versions by only mentioning in passing many of the considerations that had had to be explained in some detail in those versions. We discuss PN11 in more depth in chapter 17.

SORP compliance under the Companies Act

1.4.3 Unlike other charities, for charitable companies prior to FRS18 there had been no direct statutory requirement to disclose the extent to which they followed the Charities SORP in preparing their accounts, although even before the introduction of the present regulatory regime for charities in 1996 many had done so voluntarily. However, FRS18 introduced such a requirement to make this disclosure for all financial years ending after 23 December 2001 (see **5.5.9**).

As already mentioned at **1.1.3**, that disclosure (under 'Accounting Policies'), is a specific requirement arising from further developments in accounting standards in recent years.

Furthermore, for any significant non-compliance with the Charities SORP, paragraph 359 of SORP 2005 – similar to the wording used in previous versions – says that:

'... the following details should be given for any material departure from this SORP:

(a)   a brief description of how the treatment adopted departs from this SORP;
(b)   the reasons why the trustees judge that the treatment adopted is more appropriate to the charity's particular circumstances; and
(c)   an estimate of the financial effect on the accounts where this is needed for the accounts to give a true and fair view.'

– SORP 2005, paragraph 359

The onus is then on the auditors to form and give their own independent opinion as to whether or not the accounts do show the required 'true and fair' view, which for a *Charities Act* audit (ie, of a 'small' auditable charitable company that has validly claimed company audit exemption) also requires the auditor to say whether the SORP's 'methods and principles' have in fact been followed (obviously, subject to 'immateriality') if that is claimed in the accounts – as is needed, of course, to satisfy FRS18.

If the audit opinion has to be that the accounts do not show such a view, the Auditing Standards require a statement of how and where the accounts do not comply, the reasons for that non-compliance and its financial effect on the accounts.

Enforcement

1.4.4 In the case of the very largest registered charities, the Charity Commission will pick up on such 'non-standard' or 'qualified' audit reports sooner or later. Where it is in the public interest (an exceptionally large charity or a 'high-profile' case), the Commission can make use of standing inter-departmental liaison arrangements and procedures to have the matter referred to the Financial Reporting Council's audit inspection unit, which may then result in closer scrutiny of the work of that audit firm as a 'quality control' issue for the highly sophisticated regime of professional audit regulation. Or if the Commission's major concern is not so much with the accounts themselves as with the administration of the company's charitable resources, it will obviously have to consider taking appropriate supervisory action itself to remedy the situation – which in the case of a charitable company would be in conjunction with the Department for Business, Innovation & Skills (DBIS, formed in June 2009 by combining the DIUS and DBERR (the renamed DTI)) as and when necessary. Either way, this is likely to be a painful experience for the directors.

OTHER REGISTERED CHARITIES

1.5 In earlier sections we discussed the special provision made in Part VI of the 1993 Act for exempt charities and the specific exclusion of charitable companies from its other provisions governing accounting records and the preparation of annual accounts and their audit, etc, except where the 'small' company/group exemptions apply under the Companies Act 2006, when Part VI will automatically apply for *accounts scrutiny* – as also for the preparation of any group *consolidated accounts*. In this section we discuss what those statutory requirements of Part VI are for *non-company* charities that are either on the Charities Register or else, being excepted charities, are above the registration threshold.

The great majority of non-company charities of any size to speak of will come into this category, and apart from those accounting on the receipts and payments basis (see **1.5.3**), with the Charities SORP applicable in nearly all cases. For the sake of completeness, however, **1.5.2** identifies those classes for which special provision is made in the Regulations of 2005 to allow for the fact that they have to follow other SORPs.

Charities Act accounting and reporting requirements

1.5.1 We have already observed that the accounting (as distinct from disclosure) requirements of the SORP's related Regulations have since moved far closer to those of the Charities SORP than was considered possible in 1995 – so much so that it is difficult to see daylight between what SORP 2005 says you *should* do 'for the very best' and what the Regulations of 2008 say you *shall* do 'at the very least'. Therefore throughout this book references to SORP 2005 in this area of SoFA and balance sheet methodology and information presentation can also be taken as covering the *statutory* requirements for charities above the statutory audit threshold.

For reasons that may be obvious to the reader, the *disclosure* requirements cannot always be the same, whether in the accounts notes or the annual report. There, we must distinguish carefully at all times between what the SORP *advocates* as 'best practice' (and the Charity Commission clearly presses for) and what the law *requires* as a basic minimum in the public interest.

Special requirements where another SORP applies

1.5.2 The Regulations of 2008 make special provision for the *accounts* of non-company, *non-exempt* charities to which a more specialised SORP applies.

CIFs

It is the IMA SORP, for example, that applies to the well-known CIFs (or 'Investment Funds' as they are now called in the Regulations) that any charity can generally invest in. Their subjection to what is now Sch 1 to the Regulations of 2008 continues effectively unchanged. These 'public' CIFs must not be confused with the 'private' CIFs or 'Investment Pool' charities that may, as an alternative to using the newer pooling power available in the Trustee Act 2000, be set up under a Charity Commission Scheme for a single body/board of trustees wishing to pool the investment funds of multiple charities under its/their *sole* control, as discussed at **9.6**, and which as such are outside the scope of the IMA SORP.

More particularly, Investment Pool charities serving only charities administered by the *same* trustees as those of the Pool are not subject to reg 6 (CIFs), together with its detailed provisions in Sch 1, Regulations 2008, but are covered by reg 8, Regulations 2008, and its related Sch 2, just like any other 'normal case' charity, and will thus follow the same accounting rules according to their status as either a main charity or a branch (see chapter 13).

RSLs and HEIs, etc

For these 'special case' charities, as they are referred to in the 2008 Regulations, a new reg 7 maintains the same very basic requirements, which have not changed: an income and expenditure account and a balance sheet – with both of them required to show a true and fair view. The methodology for this is to be found in the relevant SORP, with the skeletal provision made here dovetailing with the more particular accounting requirements imposed on these 'special case' charities by their respective statutory funding bodies. Another point to note is that Sch 2 to the Regulations of 2008 belongs to reg 8 and therefore applies only to 'normal' charities – not to these ones.

As to which ones they are, the term 'special case charity' is defined in reg 2 as meaning:

> '... a charity which either—
>
> (a)   is a registered social landlord within the meaning of the Housing Act 1996 and whose registration has been recorded under section 3(3) of that Act; or
>
> (b)   has during the financial year in question—
>
> (i)   conducted an institution in relation to which a designation made, or having effect as if made, under section 129 of the Education Reform Act 1988 has effect;
>
> (ii)   received financial support from funds administered by a higher education funding council within the meaning of the Further and Higher Education Act 1992 in respect of expenditure incurred or to be incurred by the charity in connection with that institution; and
>
> (iii) incurred no expenditure for charitable purposes other than the purposes of that institution or any other such institution.'

– SI 2008/629, reg 2

This is made rather clearer for our purpose by the helpful explanatory note to these Regulations, which simply says:

'Regulation 7 ... prescribes the form and content of statements of accounts prepared by charitable registered social landlords and certain charities conducting higher education institutions.'

– SI 2008/629, Explanatory Note

Apart from the CIFs discussed above, then, *these* are the charities that are excluded from the 'normal' provisions of reg 8 governing the form and content of accounts. They are covered instead by reg 7.

In all other respects (ie annual reports; changes to financial year-ends), the statutory requirements for 'special case' charities are the same as those for 'normal' charities.

SORP compliance

1.5.3 Only a *non-company* charity small enough for its trustees to be able to opt out of regulated annual accounts altogether (by choosing to prepare 'simple', cash-based unregulated accounts under s 42(3) of the 1993 Act) can legally ignore SORP compliance. The statutory requirement for the normal charity's accounts to show 'a true and fair view' is now contained in reg 8(4):

'The statement of accounts shall be prepared in accordance with the following principles—

(a) the statement of financial activities must give a true and fair view of the incoming resources and application of the resources of the charity in the financial year;

(b) the balance sheet must give a true and fair view of the state of affairs of the charity at the end of the relevant financial year;

(c) where compliance with paragraphs (5) to (10) would not be sufficient to give a true and fair view as required under sub-paragraph (1) or (b), the additional information necessary to give a true and fair view must be given in the statement of accounts or in notes to the accounts;

(d) if in special circumstances compliance with any of the requirements of paragraphs (5) to (10) would be inconsistent with giving a true and fair view, the charity trustees must depart from the relevant requirement to the extent necessary to give a true and fair view.'

– SI 2008/629, reg 8(4)

The requirement to comply specifically with the Charities SORP to achieve this is set out in just a single line at reg 8(5):

'The statement of accounts must be prepared in accordance with the methods and principles set out in the [Charities] SORP [2005].'

– SI 2008/629, reg 8(5)

Contrast this with para 3, Part III of Sch 1 to the 1995 Regulations, where the statutory requirement to comply with the SORP used to be much narrower:

'The values of assets and liabilities of the charity shall ... be determined in accordance with the methods and principles for inclusion of assets and liabilities in the balance sheet set out in the Statement of Recommended Practice for Accounting by Charities issued in October 1995.'

– SI 1995/2724, Sch 1, Part III, para 3

Enforcement

1.5.4 Paragraph 1(1)(v) of Sch 2 to the Regulations of 2008 makes non-compliance in any material respect by a *non-company* charity above the statutory audit threshold disclosable, requiring the accounts notes to include:

> 'a statement as to whether or not the accounts have been prepared in accordance with any applicable accounting standards and statements of recommended practice and particulars of any material departure from those standards and statements of practice and the reasons for such departure.'
>
> – *SI 2008/629, Sch 2, para 1(1)(v)*

In addition, regardless of the charity's size, para 1(1)(b) and (c) of the same Schedule also requires the SORP itself to be disclosed as part of the accounting policies on which the accounts are required to be prepared, saying that the accounts notes must include:

> '(b) a description of (i) each of the accounting policies which (aa) have been adopted by the charity trustees, and (bb) are material in the context of the accounts of the charity, (ii) the estimation techniques adopted by the charity trustees which are material to the presentation of the accounts; [and]
>
> '(c) a description of any material change to policies and techniques referred to in paragraph (b), the reason for such change and its effect (if material) on the accounts, in accordance with the methods and principles set out in the SORP.'
>
> – *SI 2008/629, Sch 2, para (1)(b) and (c)*

The SORP departure will also be highlighted in the audit report if the auditor of a *non-company* charity's entity (as distinct from group consolidated) accounts does not agree that the non-compliance was necessary in order to show a true and fair view, as reg 24 states:

> '(1) Where a statement of accounts has been prepared under section 42(1) of the 1993 Act for the relevant financial year, the auditor ... must make a report on that statement to the charity trustees which—
>
> ...
>
> (f) states whether in the auditor's opinion the statement of accounts complies with the requirements of regulation ... 8 ...; and ... in particular whether the balance sheet gives a true and fair view of the state of affairs of the charity at the end of the relevant financial year; and
>
> (2)(c) ... the statement of financial activities gives a true and fair view of the incoming resources and application of the resources of the charity in the relevant financial year'.
>
> – *SI 2008/629, reg 24*

Similar provision is made in reg 25(1)(g) for the case where the entity accounts of a 'small' *charitable company* are audited under Part VI, Charities Act 1993, when the requirement is for an audit report which:

> 'states whether in the auditor's opinion—
>
> (i) the company's individual accounts comply with the requirements of section 226A of the 1985 Act [now section 396, Companies Act 2006, for financial years starting after 5 April 2008] , and in particular whether (aa) the income and expenditure account gives a true and fair view of the income and expenditure of the charity for the relevant

financial year; and (bb) the balance sheet gives a true and fair view of the state of affairs of the charity as at the end of that year;

(ii) in any case where the charity has prepared a statement of financial activities ... that statement gives a true and fair view of the charity's incoming resources and application of resources in the relevant financial year;

(iii) in any case where the accounts state that they have been prepared in accordance with the methods and principles in the SORP, those methods and principles have been followed; '

– SI 2008/629, reg 25(1)(g)

And again, similar provision is made in reg 30(1)(g) for the case where the *group consolidated* accounts of any charity are audited under Part VI, Charities Act 1993, when the requirement is for an audit report which:

'states whether in the auditor's opinion the group accounts—

(iii) ... comply with the [true and fair view] requirements of regulation 15 and in particular whether (aa) the consolidated balance sheet gives a true and fair view of the state of affairs of the parent charity and its subsidiary undertakings as at the end of relevant financial year; [and] (bb) the consolidated statement of financial activities gives a true and fair view of the total incoming resources of the parent charity and its subsidiary undertakings and the movements in the total resources of the group in the relevant financial year; '

– SI 2008/629, reg 30(1)(g)

Note that instead of saying whether a true and fair view is shown of the application of the group's resources, as the Exposure Draft for the 2008 Regulations had put it, the requirement here is for the auditor to say only whether a true and fair view is shown of the movements in the total resources of the group. It remains to be tested whether the latter predicates a 'proper' application of all the parent charity's resources as required by charity law.

Where accruals accounts are independently examined instead of audited, the examiner can ignore the actual 'true and fair view' requirement, but must state within the statutory report on the accounts:

'whether or not any matter has come to the examiner's attention in connection with the examination which gives him reasonable cause to believe that in any material respect—
...
(iii) in the case of an examination of a statement of accounts which has been prepared under section 42(1) of the 1993 Act, the statement of accounts does not comply with any of the requirements of regulation ... 8 ... other than any requirement to give a true and fair view.'

– SI 2008/629, reg 31(e)

Wherever a charity has not complied with the Charities SORP and the matter is considered material, any non-compliance will become clear because of the requirement that:

'Trustees should include any additional information which they are required by law to report and in order for the accounts to comply with current statutory requirements or the requirements of the charity's governing document to the extent that these exceed statutory requirements.'

– SORP 2005, paragraph 23

This then needs to be read in conjunction with the disclosure requirement set out in para 1(v) of Sch 2 quoted above, and which in supporting reg 3(10) calls for:

'... particulars[7] of any material departure from [applicable accounting] standards and statements of practice and the reasons for such departure.'

– SI 2008/629, Sch 2(1), para (v)

GEOGRAPHICAL VARIATIONS

1.6   Apart from the SORP opt-out by Eire this time round, whose new Charities Act was enacted in February 2009 and is currently awaiting implementation for a broadly comparable regime of regulated public accountability, there was no geographical variation in the *applicability* of the Charities SORP 2005, despite its being issued by the Charity Commission for England and Wales alone, rather than jointly with other interested regulators. The Republic's regime of regulated charity accountability is likely to take at least two years to implement. In line with the UK regimes, it will entail the filing of annual reports and accounts (professionally audited – if the threshold for this, to be set at not more than €500,000 gross income or total expenditure, was exceeded in any of the last three years – or else independently examined) together with annual returns to the new 'Charities Regulatory Authority'. The new Act exempts companies, education bodies, designated 'centres for education' and any 'small' charity (one with gross income or total expenditure below a *de minimis* level to be set at between €10,000 and €50,000) from its accounting and auditing provisions and the detailed Regulations to be made for that purpose. It also allows any *non-company* charity to opt out of the 'statement of accounts' required by those Regulations in favour of an income and expenditure account and a statement of assets and liabilities under Regulations also yet to be made – provided its gross income or total expenditure did not exceed €100,000 for the year.

In producing the Charities SORP, the Commission was acting not as a regulatory authority but as the designated SORP-issuing body supported by the ASB, whose pronouncements are valid throughout the British Isles. Therefore the SORP can say:

'This SORP is intended to apply to all charities in the United Kingdom regardless of their size, constitution or complexity. ...

If a charity based in the Republic of Ireland chooses to adopt this SORP's recommendations they are encouraged to disclose that fact.'

– SORP 2005, paragraphs 3 and 8

---

[7]   These would include the SORP-departure's estimated financial effect (if quantifiable) on the accounts, as called for by paragraph 359(c) of the SORP itself – insofar as such disclosure 'is needed for the accounts to give a true and fair view'.

However, there are geographical variations in the *statutory underpinning* of the SORP. The way charities' accounts are presented in the different countries can therefore vary slightly due to variations in the law. Since these do not arise from the Charities SORP itself, however, they are not specifically covered within this book.

Although the legislation now differs only slightly in Scotland, it is still substantively different in Northern Ireland, pending the introduction of the new regulatory regime there, under the Charities Act (Northern Ireland) 2008, and which is based on the simpler model of the OSCR regime rather than that of the Charity Commission with its more comprehensive legal powers.

Scotland

1.6.1 Scottish charities are those managed and controlled in Scotland and previously recognised by the Inland Revenue (IR) in Edinburgh. The Scottish Charities Office did not maintain a register of charities, but the regulatory body for the sector, the Office of the Scottish Charity Regulator (OSCR), was set up in 2005 and immediately began compiling such a register from charities' own updates to the IR data as supplied to OSCR by Her Majesty's Revenue and Customs (HMRC).

English and Welsh charities operating in Scotland are subject to the charity reporting requirements of English charity law, but under Scottish charities legislation they have to register with OSCR (if occupying premises or holding meetings/events in Scotland) in order to comply with the Scottish regulatory regime – albeit subject to formal protocols between the two regulators in order to minimise the burden of any dual regulation.

For Scottish charities that are not companies, the primary accounting legislation prior to the Charities and Trustee Investment (Scotland) Act 2005 was the Law Reform (Miscellaneous Provisions) (Scotland) Act 1990. This was supported by detailed Regulations made under that Act in 1992: the Charities Accounts (Scotland) Regulations 1992, SI 1992/2165.

This old legislation required an income and expenditure account 'as a primary statement', but with the treatment of items within it being the same as for a SoFA. Thus the account was required to deal with unrestricted and restricted funds as required by the SORP, but obviously had to exclude endowed funds.

Chapter 6 (Accounts) of the 2005 Act was implemented for financial years from 1 April 2006 onwards, following the making of the necessary detailed accounting Regulations based on SORP 2005 – the Charities Accounts (Scotland) Regulations 2006, SSI 2006/218. The Scottish legislation defines gross income in order to decide whether the charity needs a statutory audit or needs to prepare group accounts or a cashflow statement, for which the thresholds were aligned with the English charity legislation (though how soon, if at all, they will be re-aligned with those English thresholds which, for financial years ending on or after 1 April 2009, are increased by SI 2009/508, made by the OTS with a view to a more 'proportionate' regulatory regime in the light of the 2008 public consultation, remains to be seen). It also defines the threshold of gross receipts (raised from the old level of £25,000 to £100,000, again for parity reasons) to decide whether a charity may alternatively prepare a receipts and payments account and a statement of balances (the Scottish description of what is essentially a listing of assets and liabilities with financial values disclosed) if it is small enough to be allowed to opt out of 'true and fair' accounts.

An odd difference from the public accountability regime for charities south of the Border was the inclusion of the trustees' annual report within the Scottish legislation's definition of the 'statement of account' that must be audited or independently examined in the case of a *non-company* charity – depending on whether its gross income is above or below the £500,000 statutory audit threshold. Unless the company audit regime were to be amended to require auditors to audit the directors' report, too, for the sake of the desired parity between the two regimes one must assume that the Scottish legislation has not done so either. That view has since been confirmed by OSCR, in that there was and is no intention to require an audit of the trustees' annual report, but only the intention to require auditors to consider and report on its consistency with the audited accounts – as is now required for audits under the Companies Act 2006.

It should also be noted here (see **14.3.8** of chapter 14) that the Scottish Regulations include an option enabling the annual accounts and trustees' reports of *connected* charities (administered together, akin to branches) to be collated (bound in together) and combined respectively – instead of being published separate from each other.

Northern Ireland

1.6.2 Pending the introduction of a new regulatory regime as provided for in the Charities Act (Northern Ireland) 2008, and which is expected to be based broadly on that operated by OSCR in Scotland, the accounting and reporting obligations of *non-company* charities in Northern Ireland are still governed by the Charities Act (Northern Ireland) 1964 and the Charities (Northern Ireland) Order 1987, SI 1987/2048.

There, the Department for Social Development has the power to scrutinise charities' accounts, for which the Charities SORP will be *informative* as representing generally accepted best practice. Furthermore, as is noted in SORP 2005:

> 'There is no register of charities for Northern Ireland, and no requirement for accounts to be filed with the Department, except where this is specifically directed by the High Court of Justice in Northern Ireland or the Department acting under specific statutory powers.'
>
> *– SORP 2005, paragraph 29*

The Charities Act (Northern Ireland) 1964 requires the trustees of a charity to 'keep proper accounts' and to preserve them for at least 7 years (s 27).

Companies in Northern Ireland have to comply with the Companies (Northern Ireland) Order 1986, SI 1986/1032 (as amended), and in preparing accounts to show the required 'true and fair view' those that are charities will, like their counterparts here, normally be unable to do so except by complying with the Charities SORP.

Republic of Ireland

1.6.3 Following the enactment in February 2009 (as the Charities Act 2008) of the long-awaited Charities Bill there, until the new Act is implemented Republic of Ireland charities are still governed by the Charities Acts 1961 and 1973. Neither of these Acts requires charities to register or to prepare and submit accounts, but again generally accepted best practice and the definition of true and fair view accounts would make following the UK Charities SORP informative at the very least – albeit now on an individual voluntary basis for the time being. The new Act preserves the presumption of public benefit for the advancement of religion but otherwise takes a similar line to that of recent Charities Acts in the UK, and provides for a Charities Regulatory Authority to take over the functions of the Commissioners of Charitable Donations and Bequests for Ireland.

Chapter 2

CHARITY REGULATION AND THE SORP

PROPORTIONATE REGULATION BASED ON CHARITY-SIZE

2.1 This chapter explains the *size-based* graduated structure of the regimes of regulated public accountability for England and Wales and for Scotland to maintain public confidence in the expanding charity sector in these countries. It provides an overview to enable you to see where your own charity fits in, depending on how 'large' it is (and also on whether or not it is a charitable company) and to what extent its *public accountability* is likely to be of interest to the regulator. (For Northern Ireland and the Irish Republic, see **1.6**.)

Aims of the SORP-based regulatory regimes

2.1.1 The *focus* of this book is on the practicalities of using the Charities SORP to report annually on a charity's financial resources in such a way as to give a 'true and fair view'. For the great majority of smaller *non-company* charities – over 85% of all registered charities (even more for excepted charities) – it is *not a statutory* obligation to do so. Charity accounting legislation lets these small and very small charitable trusts and societies/associations opt out by choosing to account on the traditional, basic and unregulated, 'receipts and payments' basis – subject to any constraints that may have been imposed by their founders/members or a funding body. This is a kind of deliberate legal loophole to avoid burdening them with what in their case would really have been just bureaucratic 'red tape', when you think how slight is the financial significance of their accounts (ie less than 10% of the aggregate gross income of all registered charities) for public interest purposes. Chapter 16 looks at their requirements in more detail.

In reality, the regulatory regime provided for in the Charities Acts largely relies on officially promoted 'best practice' annual reporting by all charities, as well as the development of 'operational standards' for their administration and, more particularly, the delivery of the required public benefit that has now become a focal point of the Charities Acts both north and south of the Border. *SORP compliance* is (in theory, at least) secured by compulsory annual filing with the regulator. This is on public record for England and Wales, but is required only for the top 50,000 registered charities (ie those above the 'light touch' regime's £10,000 gross income threshold **and**, for financial years ending on or after 1 April 2009, the new accounts filing threshold of £25,000). Only for the largest of them (mainly those with more than £500,000 gross income) is this reinforced by statutory audit and (in England and Wales) backed up by the collection and interrogation of the box-numbered data comprising key figures from the SoFA and Balance Sheet as called for in Part B of the Annual Return to the Charity Commission.

For the very few charities above the 'gross income' threshold of £10m a year or a gross assets value of £100m – some 700 charities which between them account for over 50% of the income of all charities on the Register – the Commission's accountants can monitor SORP compliance by scrutinising their annual reports and accounts each year.

The aim here is to minimise the cost to public funds of providing the required level of parliamentary assurance of the *proper administration* of the vast financial resources of *registered* charities in particular – now £50 bn a year and rising.

The *policing* of public accountability for the charity sector is now being more and more tempered by a strongly deregulatory approach towards the smaller registered charities, especially those below the statutory audit threshold – numbering more than 155,000 – in recognition of their relatively slight financial significance (just 10% of the Register's aggregate gross annual income) but also their sociological importance as the 'grass roots' of the voluntary sector. A dramatic example of the way the Government has moved here was the regulatory change mentioned in chapter 1, which for 2005 year-ends onwards relieved all registered charities below £250,000 gross income from having to continue providing the monitoring data previously collected from them in Part B of the Annual Return.

That this further deregulation is only common sense can be seen from the Table below.

PROFILE OF THE REGISTER OF CHARITIES

2.2   The Charity Commission's website publishes quarterly updates on changes to the Register, profiled in terms of the 'size' of charities by reference to their reported annual gross income from all sources (including any special trusts connected with them, as well as any other subsidiary charities for which they are made publicly accountable under the 1993 Act).

As they stood at January 2002, the figures summarised on *www.charity-commission. gov.uk* showed nearly 161,000 publicly accountable registered charities. These had reported gross income figures in their Annual Returns (mainly for December 2000 and March 2001 year-ends) amounting to nearly £27bn in aggregate.

By the time the December 2008 data appeared on the Commission's website, these two figures had grown to over 168,000 and £48bn. The aggregate income has since passed the £50bn level. The number of registered charities thus shows a compound growth rate of two-thirds of 1% a year, while their reported income shows a compound growth rate of nearly 10% a year – far exceeding the rate of inflation over this period. Whether such phenomenal income growth results from more comprehensive accounting rather than more successful income generation, however, is an unanswered research question for the time being – but one that may not have to wait too long before someone starts making use of the standardised summary data (Summary Information Return (SIR) – see chapter 15) available on the Charity Commission website and now being fed through to the free public access charity database launched by Guidestar UK late December 2005 – as well as being sold in CD-ROM format as part of the Register's public domain data for use by other customers for non-commercial research.

In our summary of the Charity Commission's website Register data as at the end of December 2008, as set out below, we have added two further columns to show how the incidence of charitable companies (based on estimates made originally from Companies Registry figures) varies with the size of charity.

Charity size-bands for statutory financial reporting

Income band:	Gross income £Bns	%	Total numbers '000s	%	Companies '000s	%No
Over £10m	25.3	52	0.7	0.5	0.5	70
£1m–£10m	14.5	30	4.1	2.5	2.5	70
£500,000–£1m	3.0	6	4.3	2.5	2	50
Charities over £500,000	*42.8*	*88*	*9.1*	*5.5*	*5*	
£250,001–£500,000	1.4	3	3.8	2.5	2	50
Charities over £250,000	*44.2*	*91*	*12.9*	*8*	*7*	
£25,001–£250,000	3.5	7.5	38.1	22	9	25
Charities over £25,000	*47.7*	*98.5*	*51.0*	*30*	*16*	
£10,001–£25,000	0.4	1	23.0	14	2	10
Charities over £10,000	*48.1*	*99.5*	*74.0*	*44*	*18*	
£0–£10,000	0.3	0.5	79.8	47	4	5
Unknown	-	-	14.5	9	-	
Totals	*£48.4*	*100*	*168.3*	*100*	*22*	*13*

(estimated)

(This is not the total number of all the registered charities, which is more like 200,000. For that figure, you must add back nearly 30,000 registered 'subsidiary' charities subsumed within the above 169,000 because they have no separate *public* accountability under the 1993 Act. On top of that, we must reckon with an uncounted number of non-registered special trusts administered by registered charities and whose income will largely be included in the above. Also, the Charities Act 2006 will precipitate a substantial influx of new registrations of previously excepted and exempted charities.)

The 9,000 charities above the £500,000 statutory audit threshold (of which around 1,000 are independent schools with up to 20% of the Register's total income) account for almost 90% of the financial resources of the Register but represent less than 6% by number – thus making for a highly cost-effective regulatory regime.

At the 'small' end of the Register, almost 50% of all the publicly accountable registered charities have between them only a half of 1% of the resources, a fact that led to their being given special relief (the 'light touch' regulatory regime) from the burdens of regulation, as explained below. Almost 10% of charities on the Register are of unknown size, not having responded to mailings for two years or more, but the Commission is gradually whittling these away as it identifies those that are moribund and in need of a legal scheme (eg, to appoint new trustees) or have ceased to exist and so must be removed.

DEREGULATION

2.3   The early 1990s saw a number of Government initiatives to get rid of 'red tape', with seven simultaneous 'task forces' reporting recommendations for deregulating various sectors of the national economy. An eighth, subsequently set up to do the same thing for the voluntary sector, delayed by nearly 2 years the implementation of the new regulatory regime provided for in the Charities Act 1992 and now forming Part VI of the 1993 Act.

After the publication of the Charities SORP's first exposure draft in March 1993, everything had to be put on hold while the Voluntary Sector Deregulation Task Force negotiated with the Home Office, the Charity Commission and other Government departments/agencies to achieve pre-agreement for its proposed recommendations. This involved considerable debate on the mutually exclusive aims of standardising annual reporting to achieve the desired 'transparency' and cutting red tape to avoid unduly burdening the sector.

Tessa Baring, who chaired that Task Force, and was later a part-time member of the Board of Charity Commissioners, emphasised these concerns in her introduction to the agreed Report:

> 'We suffer from many of the same problems as business, such as over-zealous enforcement of regulations, and assessment of the compliance cost of regulations particularly on small organisations which the Government has agreed to for business, is particularly relevant in the voluntary sector: it is estimated that 91 per cent of charities have an income of less than £100,000 per year, and 90 per cent of charities have no paid staff, relying entirely on voluntary effort. The effect of numerous regulations coming from different sources, and often not designed with the voluntary sector in mind at all, is particularly damaging, acting as a marked disincentive to thousands of small groups, such as village halls and community centres, which are often the mainspring of community life. The danger is that volunteers are beginning to say: "It's not worth the hassle" – a phrase that could be the death knell of voluntary activity in this country.'
>
> – *'Charities and Voluntary Organisations Task Force Proposals for Reform', July 1994*

The 'light-touch' regulatory regime

2.3.1   One result was the Deregulation and Contracting Out Act 1994 which, among other things, amended Part VI by providing for a 'light touch' regime that relieves 'small' charities up to a ceiling of £10,000 gross income and total expenditure from having to:

– complete and submit statutory annual returns (the basis of the monitoring system);

– submit their annual report and accounts for filing each year; and

– have a statutory independent examination if they opt out of audit under Part VI.

As already mentioned, recent initiatives for a more 'proportionate' regulatory regime include a Charity Commission recommendation (now implemented by the OTS in SI 2009/508) to relieve from April 2008 a further 23,000 charities up to £25,000 annual gross income from having to file annual reports and accounts with the Charity Commission with their annual return for the year, and also from the burden of independent examination.

Other deregulatory reliefs

2.3.2 Further agreed recommendations of the Voluntary Sector Task Force resulted in the Charities Act 1993 (Substitution of Sums) Order 1995, SI 1995/2696, raising the threshold for *non-company* charities' 'true and fair' annual accounts from £25,000 to £100,000 (ie allowing those below the specified level of gross income to be able to opt out and continue accounting on the traditional unregulated 'receipts and payments' basis) and the threshold for their statutory audit from £100,000 to £250,000.

Those recommendations also informed the then DTI's own deregulation measures at the time, resulting in the *charitable company* audit exemption threshold of £250,000 gross income. This remained unchanged until 27 February 2007, despite the issue of amending regulations that later raised the turnover threshold for the compulsory audit of non-charitable companies to £1m and then to £5.6m (since inflated to £6.5m) for alignment with EC company audit thresholds. The Charities Act 2006 has now doubled the £250,000 threshold for *all* charity audits for financial years starting on or after 27 February 2007, and applied the company audit 'gross assets' threshold (also doubled from the old £1.4m to £2.8m and since inflated to £3.26m) to the larger *non-company* charities (those exceeding £100,000 gross income) instead of the old 3-year test for compulsory audit.

Chapter 16 considers in detail the regulatory reliefs available for the accounts of *non-company* charities with gross income not exceeding the threshold of £100,000 per year (or for years ending on or after 1 April 2009 the £250,000 to which that figure is raised by SI 2009/508), while chapter 17 looks in detail at the audit exemption regimes for charitable companies and other charities.

Summary of reporting reliefs for smaller charities

2.3.3 The reliefs available for the smaller charity under the current regime of statutory annual reporting are considerably greater than those originally envisaged under the 1993 Act. Readers wishing to refer back to the legislation itself are advised to ensure that it is a fully updated version that they are using, since Part VI (accounts, reports and returns) has been extensively amended or supplemented by the following:

–   Companies Act 1985 (Audit Exemption) Regulations 1994, SI 1994/1935;

–   Deregulation and Contracting Out Act 1994;

–   Charities Act 1993 (Substitution of Sums) Order 1995, SI 1995/2696;

–   Charities (Amendment) Act 1995;

–   Charities (Accounts and Reports) Regulations 1995, 2000, 2005 and now 2008 (SI 2008/629); and finally by the

–   Charities Act 2006 together with its various Regulations harmonising the charity audit and independent examination regimes across the sector for financial years starting from 1 April 2008.

Appendix 4 on the CD ROM to this book includes an informal consolidation published by the Office for the Third Sector to show Part VI of the 1993 Act as the result of all these amendments, together with a summary of other relevant provisions of the Charities Act 2006. After determining where your charity fits into the size-based system of graduated regulatory requirements, as outlined in the rest of this section, you may find it useful to consult the checklist of annual accounts and trustees' report requirements for smaller charities, showing the options available to them, in Appendix 5 to SORP 2005 – as reproduced in Appendix 1 to this book.

SIZE-BANDS FOR CHARITABLE COMPANIES

2.4   Charitable companies are treated in exactly the same way as other charities for the purpose of annual *reporting* under Part VI of the 1993 Act. That is to say, charity size is measured for them, too, by reference to 'gross income' to determine what – if anything – they must file at the Charity Commission each year, whose requirements are independent of the filing requirements of the Registrar of Companies.

Regardless of what they may have filed at Companies House, which can be quite rudimentary if a charity takes full advantage of the filing exemptions for a 'small' company[1] to file only 'abbreviated' accounts there, with no activity statement or directors' report, it is their *full* accounts – as prepared for Companies Act compliance (not the reduced set of accounts excluding the parent company SoFA as normally distributed to members) – that they must provide to satisfy Charities Act requirements.

By the same token, while the 'annual report of the charity trustees' of a *non-exempt* charitable company that may have to be prepared under reg 40 or 41 of the Charities (Accounts and Reports) Regulations 2008, SI 2008/629 ('Regulations 2008') (and which may also have to be filed with the Commission) *can* – for administrative convenience – be combined with a statutory 'directors' report' as filed at Companies House, it does not have to be: each can just as easily stand alone, though that would, of course, involve a certain amount of duplication, and would in any case seem a little strange.

The interaction of the current Charities Act reporting requirements for *non-exempt* charitable companies with the relevant size-based accounting thresholds of the Companies Act 1985 ('the 1985 Act') as now collected together in Parts 15 and 16 of its successor the Companies Act 2006 for years from 6 April 2008 can be seen from the following chart:

Size of company £	Annual Report to be filed (with full accounts) at the Charity Commission	Minimum required report on the accounts
5,000** or less	None – unless registered, when a brief summary report could be asked for	None required#

---

[1]   The 'ceiling' for this category comprises any permutation of two out of three criteria: turnover – £5.6/£6.5m; gross assets – £2.8/£3.26m; employees – 50.

Size of company £	Annual Report to be filed (with full accounts) at the Charity Commission	Minimum required report on the accounts
25,000 (previously 10,000)* or less	Normally none, but a brief summary report could be asked for	None required#
500,000** or less ## and not liable audit	Brief summary report if registered; but only upon request, if excepted	Independent Examiner's report#
Over 500,000** ## or if liable to audit	Full report if registered; but only upon request, if excepted	Independent Auditor's report

*Gross income (the £10,000 was for years *ending* before April 2009 and, for financial years starting before 27 February 2007: total expenditure for year – as separate criteria)

**Gross income only

#Unless 10% or more of the members require an audit or other size criteria (see below) disallow company audit exemption. For financial years starting after 31 March 2008, partial exemption was abolished: company audit exemption now entails a Charities Act audit if gross income is above £500,000^ for the year or for smaller charitable companies an independent examination if income has exceeded £10,000 for a year ending up to 31 March 2009 or £25,000 for year-ends thereafter

(^ or £250,000 where the gross assets threshold is exceeded, subject to the recent increases in regulatory thresholds (ie, gross assets up from £2.8m to £3.26m for years from 6 April 2008 or ending on or after 1 April 2009; gross income up from £100,000 to £250,000 (and from £10,000 to £25,000) for years ending on or after 1 April 2009)

##Threshold doubled under the Charities Act 2006 for financial years starting on or after 27 February 2007

SIZE-BANDS FOR *NON-COMPANY* CHARITIES

2.5   For all *non-exempt* charities that are *not* charitable companies, the graduated minimum requirements of the law governing annual reporting are summarised in the Table below. Having covered in chapter 1 the SORP-compliance requirements for charities' accruals accounts, no more need be said about them here. The main thing to note is the absence of any Charities Act obligation on *excepted* charities (as long as they remain unregistered) to *prepare* an annual report unless the Charity Commission specially asks for one to be sent to it – when the full accounts must always be attached.

It should also be noted that in any particular case the Charities Act audit or independent examination requirements will be augmented *but not reduced* by a pre-existing, or even a subsequent, provision within the charity's governing document, but that in the public interest (and at the trustees' request) the Charity Commission readily assists wherever necessary with the removal of non-statutory audit provisions as long as this would not be unjustifiably inconsistent with the spirit of the intention at the time of that constitutional provision having been made.

Gross income £	Trustees' annual report to be filed for the year as a statutory requirement	Basis of accounts	Minimum required report on the accounts
5,000* or less	None – unless registered, when a brief summary report could be asked for	Optional Basis#	No report required

Gross income £	Trustees' annual report to be filed for the year as a statutory requirement	Basis of accounts	Minimum required report on the accounts
25,000 (previously 10,000)** or less	Normally none, but a brief summary report could be asked for	Optional Basis#	None as an option to statutory audit##
250,000 (previously 100,000)* or less	Brief summary report if registered; but only upon request, if excepted	Optional Basis#	Option: independent examination##
500,000* or less ### and not liable audit	Brief summary report if registered; but only upon request, if excepted	Accruals basis above 250,000* (was 100,000)	Option: independent examination##
Over 500,000 ### or if liable to audit	Full report if registered; but only upon request, if excepted	Accruals basis	Independent Auditor's report

*Gross income only

**Gross income (and, for financial years starting before 27 February 2007: total expenditure for year – as *separate* criteria)

#The statutory alternative to 'true and fair' accruals-based accounts is a receipts and payments account accompanied by a Statement of Assets and Liabilities (both documents unsigned)

##Except for financial years starting before 27 February 2007 where the charity had exceeded the £250,000 income/expenditure threshold in *either* of the two immediately preceding financial years, in which case an audit was still required. The Charities Act 2006 has abolished this exception thereafter, doubling the old threshold to £500,000, removing the prior years and total expenditure tests and (for charities exceeding £100,000 gross income) adding a 'gross assets' threshold of £2.8m – but imposing a new audit-exemption condition that only an eligible 'reporting accountant' (under the old rules for partial exemption from company audit) or CIPFA member or a Fellow of the Association of Independent Examiners can act as independent examiner within the charity size-band of £250,000 -£500,000 thus created. Note that under S.I.2009/508 for years ending on or after 1 April 2009 the £100,000 rose to £250,000 and the £2.8m rose to £3.26m

###Threshold doubled and rationalised under the Charities Act 2006, as noted above

REPORTING BY CHARITIES BELOW THE REGISTRATION THRESHOLD

2.6 Charities with no more than £5,000 annual gross income are not required to register with the Charity Commission but can register or remain registered if the trustees so wish. Prior to 23 April 2007, charities up to £1,000 annual gross income did not have to register so long as they had no permanent endowment or any 'use or occupation of land', the latter criterion implying a certain continuity and exclusivity of use that would normally involve liability for local rates or community tax assessments otherwise falling on the landlord. Under the Charities Act 2006, registration is compulsory above a provisional threshold of £100,000 for excepted charities from October 2009. This mainly affects the largest 2,000 or so Parish Church Councils of the Church of England, but also, with the loss of exempt charity status for all Students Unions affiliated to the universities and colleges of the higher education sector, to the great majority of them above that £100,000 threshold, below which they become excepted charities for the time being under a ruling by the Charity Commission.

These unregistered charities, too, are bound by the general requirements governing the keeping of 'proper' accounting records and the preparing of annual accounts, as well as copying their latest available accounts direct to any member of the public upon request.

If for *any* reason such a charity is registered, its reporting obligations will become the same as for any other registered charity below the next higher size-band. Whilst unregistered, though, they have no statutory obligation to prepare an annual report, or to file accounts with the Charity Commission, unless specially requested.

REPORTING BY CHARITIES IN THE 'LIGHT-TOUCH' REGULATORY REGIME

2.7   If registered, charities below the statutory £10,000 'light touch regime' ceiling of gross income for the year only need to complete Part A of the Annual Return form that the Charity Commission requires all registered 'main' charities to file every year, and which for larger charities is a statutory obligation under Annual Return regulations made by the Commission each year. These small registered charities are reminded of their basic duty to inform the Commission of any changes to their registration particulars, by checking and correcting the Register-updating section of the form, Part A, either online as preferred by the regulator or else by requesting a printed version for checking, amending, signing and returning for processing at the Commission's Liverpool Office.

Whether or not registered, there is *no* routine (automatic) requirement for them to submit annual reports or accounts to the Charity Commission. (Indeed, in anticipation of the accounts filing threshold increase under SI 2009/508, for 2008 year-ends even those up to £25,000 gross income were asked *not* to submit their annual report and accounts: only for larger charities is the Commission now making such documents available to the public on its website. If excepted and unregistered, they are not even required to prepare an annual report unless specially asked by the Commission.

Nor do registered charities in the 'light touch' regulatory regime normally have to have a statutory audit or independent examination report on their accounts unless ordered to do so by the Charity Commission.

REPORTING BY CHARITIES BELOW THE COMMISSION'S MONITORING THRESHOLD

2.8   SORP 2005 offers a number of annual accounting and reporting concessions to charities below the statutory audit threshold, with which the related Regulations 2008 accord, and which were provided with the 2006 Charities Act's doubling of the statutory audit threshold in mind. Regardless of whether those concessions are taken up, registered charities below the new audit exemption threshold of £500,000 gross income are no longer required to provide monitoring data from the annual accounts in their Annual Return to the Charity Commission.

Non-company charities can also invoke s 42(3) of the 1993 Act to opt out of SORP compliance for their accounts, as long as the year's gross income has not exceeded the old statutory threshold of £100,000 for compulsory accruals-based accounts (or now

£250,000 for years ending on or after 1 April 2009). The Charity Commission will normally allow the calculation for this purpose to accord with the accounts basis actually adopted – meaning that if, using the 'receipts and payments' basis, the charity's gross income is within the limit, then that basis is validated and the use of it will make the calculated figure the 'recorded' gross income.

The accounts must be audited (subject to Charity Commission dispensation in exceptional cases) unless the charity is below the £500,000 income threshold (£100,000/£250,000 if the book value of its gross assets exceeds £2.8m/£3.26m) and is not constrained by some constitutional obligation or by a funding body's requirement, and unless a valid independent examination has been carried out instead (again, see chapter 17).

Unless the charity is excepted and remains unregistered, the annual report and accounts, together with the appropriately completed annual return, must normally be submitted to the Charity Commission within 10 months after each financial year-end.

REPORTING BY CHARITIES ABOVE THE MONITORING THRESHOLD

2.9	For these charities, further size-based graduations provide a measure of relief from the full weight of the regulatory system until we come to the 700 or so above £10m gross income or £100m gross assets value – for which the Charity Commission is striving to establish the closest possible liaison based on a one-to-one communications relationship.

For those registered charities with more than £1m gross income, the *public domain* part of the Annual Return, the Summary Information Return (SIR) must be completed as Part C of the Return – see chapter 15.

For charities below the statutory audit threshold (which the Charities Act 2006 has doubled to £500,000 gross income for financial years starting on or after 27 February 2007, at the same time harmonising the criteria so that *non-company* charities are at last on a par with charitable companies), the SORP allows expense-type reporting of expenditure in the SoFA instead of the more sophisticated Objects-related activity basis now prescribed as best practice. It also provides a general relief from the FRS2 requirement to prepare consolidated accounts (as long as the group is also below the statutory audit threshold) – see chapter 14. The 'brief' form of trustees' annual report as specified in reg 40 of the SORP's related Regulations 2008 can also be used where the charity is below the statutory audit threshold – see chapter 4.

'GROSS INCOME'

2.10	In a marginal case it can become vital to clarify exactly what the Charity Commission will accept/require for a proper calculation of the charity's gross recorded income under the two alternative accounting bases. Since the Charities Act 2006 the Commission's guidance about this has become less and less specific, to the point where its Annual Return forms now say that 'gross income' means 'incoming resources' per the

SORP, excluding incoming endowments but including any endowment capital converted into income for spending, or else 'total receipts' excluding endowments if accounting on a Receipts & Payments basis.

'Gross income' is all too briefly defined by s 97(1) of the 1993 Act as the charity's *'gross recorded income from all sources including special trusts'*. But prior to the Charities Act 2006 (see below) this was qualified by a discretionary power given to the Charity Commission by s 96(4) of the 1993 Act to make a final determination of what on their own best estimate shall be taken as the figure for threshold purposes in any particular case, thus making further argument pointless:

> 'References in this Act to a charity whose income from all sources does not in aggregate amount to more than a specified amount shall be construed—
>
> (a) by reference to the gross revenues of the charity, or
> (b) if the Commissioners so determine, by reference to the amount which they estimate to be the likely amount of those revenues,
>
> but without (in either case) bringing into account anything for the yearly value of land occupied by the charity apart from the pecuniary income (if any) received from that land; and any question as to the application of any such reference to a charity shall be determined by the Commissioners, whose decisions shall be final.'
>
> – *Charities Act 1993, s 96(4)*

Paragraph 173(3)(b) of Sch 8 to the Charities Act 2006 removed that sub-section from the 1993 Act on 1 April 2008, the Commission having been empowered to determine the 'likely' amount of a charity's gross income for a financial year for registration purposes with effect from 23 April 2007 under s 3A(10) of the 1993 Act, as inserted by s 9, Charities Act 2006.

Faced with widespread anxiety at the time among smaller charities as to the possibility of a major 'capital expenditure' appeal or the sale of a property or investment transactions temporarily shunting them into a higher size-band and higher regulatory compliance costs when the regulatory regime commenced in March 1996, the Commission decided from the outset to interpret 'gross income' as excluding all realised/unrealised fixed asset disposals, whether of tangible assets or of investment securities.

While interpreting the 1993 Act's reference to 'revenues' as meaning 'earnings' such as trading turnover and also property rents and dividends/interest, the Commission also regarded it as including gifts of all kinds coming to the charity *other than those that endow it.* On the other hand, it was accepted that refunds of expenditure made in previous years must count as negative expenditure rather than as income, and also that insurance claim recoveries can properly be deducted from the expenditure being funded – whereas consequential loss claims in respect of (say) income depletion must count as income. All this was carefully explained in the guidance notes up to 2006 accompanying the Annual Return forms that the Commission provides for each charity to check, complete as appropriate and submit either online or (at the trustees' option) by post.

Nevertheless, much confusion has arisen from the fact that 'gross income' is not necessarily the same as the SoFA's 'total incoming resources' on a charity's income funds, so that in a marginal case the 'size' of the charity may not be clear from its accruals accounts. The required figure normally only has to be calculated for entry in the charity's annual return and nowhere else, so that its 'gross income' for the latest financial year for which accounts may have been filed can only be seen on the Charity Commission database once it has been added as part of the Register particulars that the Commission makes available to the public. The same applies where the accounts are prepared on the receipts and payments basis – even if the Commission's recommended formats are used.

To clarify the distinction where accruals accounts are prepared, SORP 2005 contrasts the meaning of these two terms in its glossary:

'Incoming Resources

Incoming resources means all resources which become available to a charity including contributions to endowment (capital) funds but excludes gains and losses on investment assets. Gross incoming resources includes all trading and investment income, legacies, donations, grants and gains from disposals of fixed assets for use by the charity ...

This term is to be distinguished from the statutory terms gross income and gross receipts (relating to Scottish charities) that are used for threshold purposes.'

– SORP 2005, Glossary GL 36

'Gross Income

Gross income is a term used within the Charities Act 1993 to determine the thresholds made by Regulations under that Act (and the Companies Act in relation to charitable companies). The thresholds govern the requirements (in England and Wales) for accounts scrutiny, the preparation of accruals accounts by non-company charities, submission of reports, accounts and an annual return to the Charity Commission. Gross income does not include the gains from disposals of fixed assets and investments, nor asset revaluation gains nor any resources[2] being received into the endowment funds. It will however include funds released from endowments.'

– SORP 2005, Glossary GL 31

By the same token, then, for *non-company* charities opting out of the SORP 'gross income' must be taken to mean only those 'total receipts' that are of an income nature, thus excluding not only endowments other than those converted into income for spending but also the proceeds of any disposals of fixed assets and any loans or loan repayments received, as well as the receipt of insurance claim monies other than for consequential loss.

LENGTH OF FINANCIAL YEAR

2.11   SORP 2005 does not enter into the question of the length of a charity's 'financial year', other than to remind you to disclose it for this year and last year:

---

[2]   This would apply to equipment given to a charity on condition that it is to be used for the work of the charity, thus as a fixed asset, or to a grant or donation of funds for that purpose.

'The corresponding figures for the previous accounting period should be provided in the accounts in accordance with generally accepted accounting practice. The duration of the current and previous accounting periods should also be shown.'

– SORP 2005, paragraph 31

This is because the determination of accounting year-ends is hardly a matter that can safely be left to 'best practice'. Moreover, it is already regulated by the relevant accounting legislation for charitable companies and for other charities, even though with changes constrained in a slightly different way to safeguard different aspects of accountability.

For most charities, the frequency and extent of permitted deviations from the normal duration of 12 months – or, alternatively, 52/53 weeks – are defined by legislation. The rules for charitable companies are exactly the same as for any other company under the 1985 Act, ss 223–225 – now ss 390–392 of the Companies Act 2006. The relevant legislation requires prior notice of any such change in statutory form, in the case of a company, or else 'exceptional reasons' that are disclosed and explained in the notes to the accounts, in other cases.

The rules for most other (non-exempt) charities are provided in reg 3 of the Regulations 2008 made under Part VI of the 1993 Act.

The two sets of rules are broadly similar in providing that accounting periods must be consecutive, can be varied in length by up to 7 days at will, and can generally be extended beyond the normal 12 months' duration (by up to 6 months) only once in 5 years for a company under s 225 of the 1985 Act or s 392 of the 2006 Act (other than to synchronise the financial year of a group member, or if the company is in insolvent administration); or once in 3 years for *non-company* charities.

While, under s 225/s 392, charitable companies may generally shorten their financial year as often as they like, other charities cannot do so more than once every 3 years. In any case, no *non-exempt* charity's accounting period can be shortened to less than 6 months.

Exempt charities (other than charitable companies) continue to be governed by the old rules, now preserved only in s 46(1) of the 1993 Act: accounting periods must be consecutive and no longer than 15 months each.

The freedom of charitable companies, and also of exempt charities (subject to any constitutional or other accounting obligations in the latter case), to shorten their financial year at will, may be contrasted with the constraint imposed on other (ie non-exempt) charities. This is quite understandable in view of what happens to the 'size' criteria under the Companies and Charities Acts when the financial year is lengthened or shortened. While the figures are flexed for companies, they remain unflexed for non-companies because the 1993 Act makes no provision for such flexing.

Frequent shortening of the financial year thus offers no administrative advantage under companies legislation but rather increases the costs of producing and filing accounts, while under charities legislation it could bring the smaller charity below some critical size threshold – for example, the 'light-touch' monitoring regime's £10,000 threshold; or the statutory audit or SIR thresholds; less obviously, perhaps, the 'small group' consolidation exemption for all *non-exempt* charities that for financial years starting after 31 March 2008 is currently set at £500,000 gross income by reg 18 of the SORP's related 2008 Regulations; or, for *non-companies* only, the accruals accounting threshold (raised from £100,000, to £250,000 for years ending on or after 1 April 2009). (For earlier financial years, in the absence of early voluntary adoption of the SORP's related 2008 Regulations by a *non-company* parent charity, its group consolidated accounts remain only a best-practice requirement under the SORP (ie, non-statutory), and the same for a parent *charitable company* claiming small group relief under the 1985 Act.)

THE REGULATORY REGIME FOR SCOTLAND

2.12   A regulatory regime of public accountability for Scottish charities that is broadly similar to the England and Wales one is effective for financial years from 1 April 2006 under provisions contained in the Charities and Trustee Investment (Scotland) Act 2005. This section discusses key differences between the two regimes.

The Act itself, in chapter 6 (Charity Accounts), provides for detailed accounting Regulations originally published for public consultation during 2005, and which as SSI 2006/218 broadly aligned the accounting thresholds with those of the English legislation at the time and give statutory force to the Charities SORP in Scotland. See Appendices 4 and 5 on the CD ROM respectively for the text of Scotland's primary and secondary legislation here.

Scottish charities other than companies, limited-liability Industrial and Provident Societies and Scottish Charitable Incorporated Organisations (SCIOs), up to the accruals accounting threshold of £100,000 gross income/receipts in line with English and Welsh non-company charities can opt out of SORP compliance by accounting on a receipts and payments basis instead. The content of such a rudimentary 'statement of account' is specified in Sch 3 to the Scottish regulations – unlike the English legislation, which imposes no detailed requirements. This fourfold increase from the old £25,000 accruals-accounting threshold was seen as a major deregulatory move – as was the raising of the statutory audit threshold for all Scottish charities to £500,000 gross income, again for parity reasons. Although company law is a reserved matter for the UK as a whole, the setting of the *audit thresholds* for charitable companies is a devolved matter, and after consultation it was decided that the same doubling of the audit threshold for English and Welsh charitable companies should apply to all Scottish charitable companies as well.

The 2006 Scottish Regulations continue to require specified accounts notes, as well as a 'Statement of Balances' in place of the English 'Statement of Assets and Liabilities'. The former – unlike the latter – must be signed by one of the charity trustees and must also show the date of approval of the accounts.

Whatever accounting basis is adopted, the Scottish audit exemption regime for even the smallest *non-company and company* charities (without any exemption even for those below £10,000 gross income – just as there is no size-based registration exemption for Scottish charities either) requires an independent examination of their accounts by a competent person (similar to that under the English legislation).

The Scottish Executive also decided that English charities having to register their Scottish operations under the new legislation will be able to choose between registering a separate charity operating in Scotland, for which Scotland-only report and accounts would be required, or registering the English-based charity with OSCR for its Scottish operations, for which OSCR would require a copy of the report and accounts of the UK charity. Any adjustment of the charity's report or accounts to meet the Scottish charity accounting regulations (eg, OSCR's requirement for the narrative reporting to disclose the charity's Scottish activities and achievements) will normally be minimal, as these regulations are intended to reflect existing UK recommended practice – ie the Charities SORP 2005.

The time allowed for filing a Scottish charity's annual report and accounts with OSCR has been reduced from 10 months to 9 months, failing which OSCR may make the default public, launch an inquiry into the charity and even appoint someone else to complete the accounts at the charity's expense.

The 2006 Regulations for the preparation of fully accrued accounts cross-refer to the *methods and principles* set out in the current Charities SORP as obligatory, but other than that are tailored to Scottish regulatory needs concerning the accounts format and the specific disclosures required. Cross-referring to the current SORP in this way is meant to provide increased flexibility, allowing the Regulations to adapt as accounting practices change.

Scottish charities are required to retain their accounting records for at least 6 complete years, and specifically to take all reasonable steps to protect them from risk of corruption by fire, flood, etc, and from loss of access due to IT failure or obsolescence, loss of passwords, etc.

Extending a Scottish charity's financial year beyond 18 months plus one week needs permission from OSCR (for which a justification of practicality and unusual circumstances will be required) under the Regulations, as will flexing the year-end by more than a week either side of the normal 12 months three times within a 5-year period. Other than that, all changes of year-end are at the charity's own discretion. This also differs from the English Regulations and UK company law in not setting a lower limit of 6 months. Pro rata adjustment in the statutory thresholds for accounting and audit purposes will follow automatically on any change of financial year – which is what happens under UK company law but not English charity law.

The Scottish Regulations (SSI 2006/218) require charities with subsidiary undertakings (whether charitable or not) to produce group accounts, subject to the specific exemptions available under FRS2 and a general exemption where the gross income of the group is below £500,000 (net of any consolidation adjustments). The group accounts, too, must comply with the methods and principles set out in the current Charities SORP.

By grouping together within a single annual report and accounts all the charities they manage and control in common, boards of trustees can avoid the additional effort and costs involved in separate public accountability – as long as all the information requirements of the new Regulations are met, based on those for the largest charity so grouped. Furthermore, no separate trustees' annual report is required for any charity included in the group accounts of another charity as long as they contain all the information required about it by the new Regulations, that it is wholly charity-controlled and that its own accounts indicate how a copy of the group report may be obtained.

New Scottish Regulations are currently under consideration with a view to tidying up certain ambiguities that have arisen in practice under the 2006 Regulations, but without substantively changing the present regime, other than perhaps to update the regulatory thresholds in relation to those under English law, and which are expected to come into force some time in 2010.

Chapter 3

FUND-ACCOUNTING

IMPACT OF TRUST LAW

3.1   To be able to record and report properly on the assets and activities of any charity, it is essential to be clear about any terms and conditions that may have been attached to its *voluntary* contributions – ie, those made by donors. Donor-requirements can become binding under English trust law – also in countries with similar legislative systems. The law then protects that gift's intended application, making the trustees personally liable at law for any subsequent loss to the charity to the extent of their responsibility for any 'misapplication'. Furthermore, the 'standard rules' of trust law protect the respective rights of *income* and *capital* (in a charity, the founder's intention to provide differently for present and future beneficiaries) where the trust is *endowed*, so that these rules can only be disregarded under special authority – either at the outset from the founder or subsequently from the High Court or the Charity Commission (e g investment on the 'total return' basis – see chapters 6 and 9, dealing with investment returns in the SoFA and investment assets in the balance sheet).

Resources given to further a charity's Object(s) without any narrower restrictions placed on them are part of its 'unrestricted' funds available for use as the trustees see fit. In the case of a charitable company, such resources form part of its 'corporate' funds – funds that are not held on trust at all but are its own absolute property and can obviously be used for any purpose within the Objects declared in the company's Memorandum of Association.

The trustees (or the company's directors) may designate or 'earmark' such funds for some particular present or future purpose, but they can also change their minds and use the funds for some other purpose – as long as this is still within the Objects of the charity. This means that fund-accounting distinctions are discretionary for all such funds, as the law does not require any discrimination within them (other than the irrelevant one imposed by the Companies Act 2006 (in succession to the 1985 Act for financial years from 6 April 2008) to distinguish between realised and unrealised corporate reserves on the face of a company's balance sheet – see chapter 10, on the subject of charity reserves).

It is different where assets are given with specific restrictions attached, either that they are to be used up on the activities of some particular project (restricted income funds) or that they are not to be spent (used up) but are to be retained as investment capital as a source of income, or else as capital resources for the charity's own long-term use (in both cases these are *trust* capital funds, i e 'endowments'). It then becomes essential that the different kinds of gift are recorded separately, and it is the principles of *fund-accounting* that then enable the annual accounts to demonstrate the proper application of such trust funds in accordance with their respective terms of trust as required by law.

Because the terms of any restriction of *purpose* must be within, but are narrower than, the Objects of the charity, it is acceptable for any restricted income fund in deficit to receive support from unrestricted funds. For restricted income fund money to be supporting either the general activities of the charity or another restricted fund for purposes outside its own permissible uses would be a 'breach of trust' unless the normal rules for commercial investment have been followed (a market rate of interest, a specified term for repayment and adequate security).

The trust law requirement is for the separate administration (other than for investment purposes, under the Trustee Act 2000 – see chapters 6 and 9), and therefore also a separate record, of each differently restricted fund. This can seem onerous where the restricted funds are numerous. It may be that, for practical reasons, the cash-book record includes both unrestricted and restricted monies, and even that these are kept in one bank account. In that case a separate record *must* be kept for each fund – either in columnar format within the cash-book itself or elsewhere in the accounting system (see also **3.11**, where we discuss the need for separate identification of the earnings of restricted funds). SORP 2005 summarises the impact of trust law here in much the same words as previous versions of the SORP:

> 'The main purpose of the accounts is to give an overall view of the total incoming resources during the year and how they have been expended, with a balance sheet to show the overall financial position at the year-end. There are additional requirements for charities that have to account for more than one fund ... under their control. The accounts should provide a summary of the main funds, differentiating in particular between the unrestricted income funds, restricted income funds and endowment funds. The columnar format of the Statement of Financial Activities is designed to achieve this ...
>
> Charities need to account for the proper administration of the individual funds in accordance with their respective terms of trust and accounting records must be kept in a way which will adequately separate transactions between different funds.'
>
> *– SORP 2005, paragraphs 65 and 66*

The main types of fund that may need to be distinguished in this way, and their characteristics and sub-types, can be summarised as follows.

UNRESTRICTED FUNDS

3.2   Unrestricted or 'general-purpose' funds comprise both the charity's free reserves (see chapter 10) and its designated funds, if any (see below), and represent assets which are available for the trustees to use at their discretion for any purpose within the Object(s) of the charity. Many charities will have *only* unrestricted funds, and therefore they will not need to maintain separate records for various funds or present the SoFA in columnar format.

For example, many charities set up to care for those in need in the local community, and relying on local health authority contracts gained under competitive contract tendering, will not have restricted income. They may, however, need to keep some sort of separate records, even if only for internal management purposes, to comply with the specific terms of each contract.

Designated funds

3.2.1 Designated funds, hitherto better known by many (including the authors) as 'earmarked' funds, arise when the trustees decide to set aside part of the unrestricted funds or 'charity reserves', ring-fencing them for a particular charitable project or administrative purpose they have in mind. This gives a clear indication to the reader that the trustees, for whatever reason, regard those funds as not available to spend on the general running of the charity. The vital distinction between restricted and designated funds is that the use of the latter is at the discretion of the trustees, who can change their minds and undesignate for use elsewhere those funds previously ring-fenced by the original designation. As the Charities SORP puts it:

> 'Unrestricted funds are expendable at the discretion of the trustees in furtherance of the charity's objects. If part of an unrestricted fund is earmarked for a particular project it may be designated as a separate fund, but the designation has an administrative purpose only, and does not legally restrict the trustees' discretion to apply the fund.'

– SORP 2005, Appendix 3.1(a)

Frequently, the actual designation merely formalises an existing reality rather than a future project. For example, some charities have been criticised in the media for not spending seemingly large reserves when in reality these mostly represent money already utilised to provide and equip the buildings within which the charity operates – or for some charities the outstanding soft loans to their beneficiaries or perhaps an investment in a charitable project being undertaken by a third party (both of the latter exemplifying the 'social' or 'programme-related' investment assets now given special treatment under SORP 2005). We discuss the remedy for this in **3.2.2**.

The example below gives two simple versions of a balance sheet, 'A' and 'B', to compare the general funds shown as unspent and therefore presumed to be available to spend on the general objects of the charity in the absence of any indication to the contrary:

BALANCE SHEETS	'A'	'B'
	£	£
Buildings and Equipment	680,000	680,000
Social Investment Assets	100,000	100,000
Net Current Assets	32,000	32,000
	812,000	812,000
Unrestricted Funds		
General Funds	812,000	32,000
Designated Fixed Assets Funds	–	780,000
	812,000	812,000

In this example, balance sheet 'B' shows that the charity has only £32,000 available to spend, whereas balance sheet 'A' appears at first glance to show that the charity has £812,000 available to spend, perhaps implying that the charity was too wealthy to need further donations.

Accounts presentation of designated funds

3.2.2 Since designated funds are a subset of the unrestricted funds of the charity, there is no specific requirement for a separate column to be shown for them on the face of the SoFA.

Funds for segregating designated activities

Where a designated ongoing 'activities' fund has its own incoming and outgoing resources that for one reason or another need to remain ring-fenced, and provided these are material enough to need highlighting, then as long as it does not result in too many columns some charities prefer to devote a column to that fund within the SoFA, with any further internal allocations to that fund being shown on the transfers line from an 'undesignated funds', or 'general purposes', column. Here is an illustration from the recent annual accounts of one of the 'household name' charities.

STATEMENT OF FINANCIAL ACTIVITIES FOR THE 52 WEEKS ENDED 30 MARCH 2008

		Unrestricted funds		Restricted funds		Total	2007 (52 wks)
		Operations	*Desig-nated*	*Project*	*Long term*		
	Note	*£000*	*£000*	*£000*	*£000*	*£000*	*£000*
Incoming resources							
Incoming resources from generated funds:							
– Voluntary income	2,3	21,774	116	1,479	3,613	**26,982**	25,175
Trading operations	26	6,543	0	0	0	**6,543**	6,130
Investment income		329	45	0	118	**492**	457
Incoming resources from charitable activities	4	18,850	0	0	0	**18,850**	16,673
Total incoming resources		**47,496**	**161**	**1,479**	**3,731**	**52,867**	48,435
Resources expended							
Costs of generating funds:							
– Costs of generating voluntary income		1,111	0	0	0	**1,111**	1,286
– Cost of trading operations	26	5,856	0	0	0	**5,856**	5,582
Charitable activities	5	39,003	1,766	1,400	2,466	**44,635**	42,087
Governance costs	5	169	0	0	0	**169**	190
Total resources expended		**46,139**	**1,766**	**1,400**	**2,466**	**51,771**	49,145

		Unrestricted funds		Restricted funds		Total	2007 (52 wks)
		Operations	Desig- nated	Project	Long term		
	Note	£000	£000	£000	£000	£000	£000
Net incoming/(outgoing) resources before transfers		**1,357**	**(1,605)**	**79**	**1,265**	**1,096**	(710)
Gross transfers between funds:							
– Capital and maintenance reserve		(1,350)	1,350	0	0	**0**	0
– Other		86	0	(86)	0	**0**	0
Net movement in funds		**93**	**(255)**	**(7)**	**1,265**	**1,096**	(710)
Reconciliation of funds							
Total funds brought forward	20	905	5,115	343	11,049	17,772	18,482
Total funds carried forward		**998**	**4,860**	**336**	**12,674**	**18,868**	17,772

STATEMENT OF FINANCIAL ACTIVITIES FOR THE 52 WEEKS ENDED 30 MARCH 2008

... The statement of financial activities incorporates an income and expenditure account. ...

The Royal National Theatre – 2007/08 accounts

Another example, specific to a particular sector but also of more general interest, is the 'school operating fund' recommended by the Independent Schools' Bursars Association in their guidance on applying the Charities SORP to independent schools, as illustrated by a worked example in that book. Paragraph 87 of SORP 2005 offers other suggestions on how a 'designated fund' column might be used in the SoFA in order to get a particular message across to readers.

Many charities, however, simply show the total movements on all their unrestricted funds within a single column of the SoFA, with sub-analysis in the notes to the accounts to highlight the movements on major designated funds and any further designations/undesignations, and explaining how each fund is being utilised.

Designation of 'fixed assets' funds for charitable/administrative use

An example of a quite different kind of designation is that of the 'fixed assets' fund – or some similar indicative name – used as a way of ring-fencing general-purpose funds that are no longer freely available, having been committed either (i) under a 'capital expenditure' budget to provide perhaps much-needed buildings and equipment for the functioning of the charity or (ii) to financing charitable projects intended to provide a financial return that can then be used for further project work. For example, many Benevolent Fund charities make 'soft loans' (repayable grants) to their beneficiaries, while charities in the newer charitable fields of urban regeneration, social development, heritage preservation, etc, may invest substantial funds as equity in, or securitised loans to, a non-charitable body set up to undertake a particular charitable project, as already mentioned.

Without the segregation of those committed funds in some way or other, it can be difficult for a charity to avoid giving potential donors the misleading impression that the large balance of 'unspent' general funds shown in the SoFA and balance sheet is contradicting its current appeals for further funding. For this kind of designation, a separate column in the SoFA is not really viable, since most of the column would be empty; it is more appropriate to use inset analysis of the brought-forward and carried-forward balances, referenced to the accounts notes to explain the movements. This can also be done in conjunction with the special note that used to be recommended in earlier versions of the SORP and which, for prominence, could be placed immediately following the SoFA as a way of highlighting for the reader the resource implications where the depletion of the charity's funds remaining available for core activities might otherwise go unnoticed:

'Note of Changes in Resources Applied for Fixed Assets for Charity Use

Where resources expended during the year on the acquisition of functional fixed assets is material, this fact should be explained in a note to the accounts to help the reader understand the impact on the more liquid funds of the charity. It may be useful for this note to follow on immediately after the reconciliation of funds at the bottom of the Statement of Financial Activities. The format should, where necessary, show:

(a)   net movement in funds for the year (from the Statement of Financial Activities);
(b)   resources used for net acquisitions (or obtained from net disposals) of fixed assets for charity use (ie the increase or decrease in the net book value of functional fixed assets);
(c)   net movement in funds available for future activities (ie those not held in functional fixed assets).'

– SORP 2000, paragraph 180

This, with illustrative figures inserted, including those for the 'social' investing now accorded an appropriate accounting treatment in SORP 2005, might then be the next accounts page after the SoFA – using the same columnar format for added emphasis:

Note of changes in resources applied for fixed assets used for charitable purposes

	Note	INCOME	FUNDS	ENDOWED FUNDS	TOTAL 2009	TOTAL 2008
		Unrestricted	*Restricted*			
		£000	*£000*	*£000*	*£000*	*£000*
Net movement in funds for the year	(SoFA)	3,750	1,000	500	5,250	1,500
Resources used for acquisitions (less disposals) of fixed assets for:						
– the charity's own use		(3,500)	–	(200)	(3,700)	(1,000)
– social investment		(500)	–	–	(500)	(100)

Note	INCOME		FUNDS	ENDOWED FUNDS	TOTAL 2009	TOTAL 2008
	Unrestricted		*Restricted*			
	£000		£000	£000	£000	£000
Net movement in funds *available for future activities*	(250)		1,000	300	1,050	400

SORP 2005, however, no longer recommends such special prominence for a note intended for this purpose, though it does acknowledge (paragraph 242) that '*charities also further their objectives by investing in tangible fixed assets to provide services*', and that '*such applications are charitable but do not decrease the funds of a charity*', before observing that this kind of information can be ascertained from a Cashflow Statement (see chapter 11). It then reformats the note to cover the reserves impact of investing in or divesting from fixed assets held either for use in the charity's own activities or else as loans, equity, etc, in a charitable project involving beneficiaries or some third party – for which see chapter 9. However the new recommendation unhelpfully links figures from the *Cashflow Statement* (if prepared) to the *SoFA* in making the following suggestion:

'A note summarising these effects, when material, can provide valuable information to readers of accounts in interpreting net movements in funds and help the reader understand the impact of such transactions on the liquid funds of the charity. Where relevant a charity may choose to provide in the notes to the accounts the following information:

(a)   total net movement in funds for the year;

(b)   net endowment receipts for the year (value of endowment receipts less any release of expendable endowment to income funds);

(c)   net expenditure on additions to functional fixed assets (cost of additions less proceeds of any disposals) for the year; and

(d)   net investment in programme related investments (cost of additions less proceeds of any disposals) for the year.'

– *SORP 2005, paragraph 243*

An unrelatable dataset like this (linking (a) from the SoFA's *total* column with (b)–(d) from the Cashflow Statement – which again gives only the charity-total figures and does not distinguish between fund-types) cannot tell the reader to what extent such activities of the year have locked up or unlocked the charity's unrestricted income reserves *over and above the net movement for the year as shown in the SoFA*. To achieve that, you will have to revert to the SORP 2000 format, updating it as shown above.

On the balance sheet, any *material* designated funds are in our* view best shown separately, as is recommended by paragraphs 245 and 247 of SORP 2005, perhaps listed along with the general fund under the 'unrestricted funds' subheading. That will also support the SoFA note highlighting the reserves implications of the year's movement on these two special kinds of designated fund, since the difference on each fund between the two year-ends will be the amount shown for it in that note. (*This refers to the assertion that fund-designations do not represent actual transactions and therefore cannot properly be shown on the face of the balance sheet. Against that view, we would cite the SORP's requirement to show inter-fund transfers on the face of the SoFA, but perhaps more fundamentally the need to record in the accounting records – and so also in the annual accounts – each and every exercise of the trustees' discretionary powers in administering their charity.)

A note to the accounts is required in any case, to analyse the net assets of the charity between restricted income funds, endowment funds and total unrestricted funds. There is no requirement for a further sub-analysis for designated funds (unless they are for non-accrued *spending* commitments – SORP 2005, paragraph 329) but, where such funds are material, the trustees may wish to provide such a note anyway, in order to make it clear that the assets are appropriate to the purpose of each major designated fund.

For example, an accounts note immediately below the SoFA of Marie Curie Cancer Care for 2004–05 sub-analysed the £12.5m increase in the balance sheet figure of designated funds (from £59.4m to £71.9m) to show that an extra £5m had been set aside out of the year's operating surplus to allow for further capital investment, while £0.1m represented reserves utilised to add to existing tangible fixed assets. The note went on to show that as well as those designations a further £4m had been set aside for a palliative care project, £3m for 'working capital' (a term borrowed from the commercial sector to indicate a need for free reserves) and £0.6m had been added to the revaluation reserve required under companies legislation, with the remaining £0.5m being added to the charity's uncommitted balance of unrestricted funds, which at the year-end stood at £4.5m. The annual report correctly grouped these last three categories together as free reserves, whose increase thus accounted for £4.1m out of the year's £13m increase in total funds.

Consolidated Statement of Financial Activities for the year ended 31 March 2005 (incorporating consolidated income and expenditure accounts)		Unrestricted funds	Restricted funds	TOTAL 2005	TOTAL 2004
	Notes	£000	£000	£000	£000
...		...	...	...	...
NET MOVEMENT IN FUNDS		**13,122**	**(100)**	**13,022**	**13,932**
Total funds at 1 April 2004	15	63,295	8,301	71,596	57,664
Total funds at 31 March 2005		**76,417**	**8,201**	**84,618**	**71,596**
APPLICATION OF NET MOVEMENT IN FUNDS					
Net movement in funds		13,122	(100)	13,022	13,932
Transfers (to)/from designated funds:	15				
Capital investment		(5,000)	–	(5,000)	(6,000)
Palliative care development		(4,000)	–	(4,000)	(4,000)
Working capital		(3,070)	–	(3,070)	(2,232)
Revaluation		(609)	–	(609)	(468)
Tangible fixed assets		100	–	100	(281)
Increase/(decrease) in General/Restricted funds		543	(100)	443	951

Marie Curie Cancer Care – 2004–05 accounts

Contrast that with the unhelpful equivalent 2007/08 SoFA footnote under SORP 2005:

Consolidated Statement of Financial Activities
for the year ended 31 March 2008 (incorporating consolidated income and expenditure accounts)

	Notes	Unrestricted funds £000	Restricted funds £000	TOTAL 2008 £000	TOTAL 2007 £000
...		...	...	...	...
NET INCOME FOR THE YEAR		2,004	834	2,838	5,499
(Loss)/Gain on investment assets	8	(4,061)	(8)	(4,069)	2,504
Pension Scheme actuarial gain/(loss)	18	130	-	130	(1,100)
NET MOVEMENT IN FUNDS		**(1,927)**	826	**(1,101)**	**6,903**
Inter-fund transfers		1,724	(1,724)	-	-
Total funds at 1 April 2007	15	87,267	6,874	94,141	87,238
Total funds at 31 March 2008		**87,064**	**5,976**	**93,040**	**94,141**
APPLICATION OF NET INCOME FOR THE YEAR					
Net income for the year		2,004	834	2,838	5,499
Add back: Depreciation Charge	7	1,502	894	2,396	2,398
Net income available for application		3,506	1,728	5,234	7,897
Application of net income:					
Contribution to DB Pension Scheme		(2,812)	–	(2,812)	(312)
Expenditure on ['own use'] fixed assets	7	(2,667)	(1,724)	(4,391)	(3,748)
Net income after application of funds		(1,973)	4	(1,969)	3,837

Marie Curie Cancer Care – 2007–08 accounts

Such an explanation does not show the reader how much of the year's increase/decrease in the charity's **total unrestricted funds** (ie, its net operating income **and** any 'holding gains' on its investments (losses, here) and other fixed assets) has affected readily available free reserves. (In this case, the investment losses were all 'realised' but excluded from 'net income' under FRS3 as if 'unrealised', by adopting a 'marking to market' accounting policy normally peculiar to the [taxable] trade of investment dealing but now allowed by SORP 2005 and sanctioned by the ASB in conflict with FRS3.) The Note has thus lost its point under SORP 2005 and could just as well be scrapped – unless you choose to stay with the really informative SORP 2000 form of it instead.

Designated funds v free reserves

3.2.3 There was much publicity about reserves levels in early years of regulated public accountability under SORP 1995, with charities being perceived as keeping them unreasonably high in some cases and far too low in others. Chapter 10 discusses the need to distinguish free reserves and how to calculate the actual figure, as well as the need to set and justify a reserves level and policy that will be seen as appropriate for the charity's circumstances, and to keep these under review.

The Charity Commission's concern to ensure that charities and their reserves are managed in accordance with clear and rational policies resulted in SORP 2000 containing a number of new disclosures being required in annual reports (chapter 4) and accounts (chapter 10). These were further expanded in SORP 2005, and are now underpinned by reg 40 (or for a group report, reg 41) of the Charities (Accounts and Reports) Regulations 2008, SI 2008/629 ('the 2008 Regulations'), requiring disclosure of the amount and purpose of all material designated funds as well as the timing of any future expenditure projects for which they are being held.

Even where some kind of discretionary power under the charity's governing document[1] permits general-purpose funds to be retained at will (other than by designating them for specific projects), it is still part of the general 'duty of care' to have regard to the needs of current, as well as future, beneficiaries and to make a rational and informed decision on how much should be designated for spending on projects that benefit the former and how much should be carried forward as free reserves.

To be able to formulate and maintain a reserves policy that can *convincingly* justify the retention of substantial funds without fear of public criticism, it will normally be necessary to have a clear strategic and business plan that can be used to distinguish in the accounts not just where funds have already been committed (as in **3.2.2**) but more particularly also where funds need to be earmarked to cover activity-commitments for which 'buffering' may be needed to protect vulnerable beneficiaries against the consequences of future income fluctuations (interruption of service, etc).

In some cases, it could be more persuasive to base such designations on actuarial valuations of the future needs of some particular class of beneficiaries or on the discounted present value of the anticipated future costs of a major charitable project that the trustees are saving to carry out. For the wealthier charity, we can expect to see rather more use being made of this kind of designated fund as a highlight of their accounts, as public awareness of, and interest in, charity reserves sharpens, increasing the need for explanation and justification.

In other cases, particularly where there are pressures of competition in charitable trading (eg the Independent Schools sector) or for the necessary grant-funding for many a worthy community-benefit project of the kind that somehow fails to excite popular sympathy, the opposite holds true.

Charities that have no prospect of ever building up free reserves worth speaking of may have little to gain and much to lose by creating designations that, in highlighting their lack of *uncommitted* reserves, merely expose a seeming financial vulnerability, inviting alarm and suspicion rather than trust and support. It is often only by dint of skilful cashflow management that such charities can maintain the 'tightrope' balance that has so far allowed them to remain financially viable from year to year.

The most they may then be able to say by way of a reserves policy is that the present level of their general funds is adequate for day-to-day immediate purposes, perhaps adding that ideally they would like to maintain a level of reserves that would facilitate longer-range strategic planning.

---

[1]   The corporate funds of a charitable company are perhaps the prime example of this: they are not held on trust at all but are *beneficially owned* by the company – even though they cannot lawfully be used for any other purpose than to further its charitable Objects.

Converting between unrestricted and restricted funds

3.2.4 Some charity trustees have a constitutional power in specified circumstances, or subject to certain conditions, to convert endowed funds into income for spending. Apart from the well-known example of gifts of money or investment assets coming to a charity on trust as 'expendable endowment', there is the less obvious example of a gift or grant of 'wasting' assets (or of the money to acquire them) where the donor requires the asset (or its equivalent) to be retained for the charity's own use on a continuing basis – thus as a 'functional' fixed asset, whose depreciation in use will then represent the annual conversion of capital into income in accordance with the terms of trust imposed by the donor.

In other cases, trustees may even be able to create irrevocable restrictions on their unrestricted funds. If a trustee-designation made under a specific power contained in the charity's governing document is going to be irreversible for lack of any counter-balancing power, special care will be needed, as the SORP obliquely warns in the latter part of paragraph 1(a) of Appendix 3, The Funds of a Charity:

> 'Some trustees have power to declare specific trusts over unrestricted funds. If such a power is available and is exercised, the assets affected will form a restricted fund, and the trustees' discretion to apply the fund will be legally restricted.'
>
> – *SORP 2005, Appendix 3.1(a)*

Such situations would include a discretionary power to capitalise income. Where the result is to add it to a permanent endowment, it makes a kind of one-way street that may be best avoided, as distinct from the dual carriageway afforded where it is a discretionary or 'expendable' endowment – the most flexible form of charitable fund you can have in this situation, as we will see in chapter 10.

Another example of the power to create a special trust, such as a school prize fund to be separately administered by the trustees themselves – or even by a separate body of trustees if the founder so wishes – would be the exercise of the (normally implicit) power of any body of charity trustees to make *charitable grants* for particular purposes within the donating charity's own Objects. The effect of using such a power is then the same as if the money had been given initially under that restriction. Since in doing this, by putting it into the hands of others, the trustees may be irrevocably limiting their future access to the money, it is not, in most cases, to be recommended except 'on advice'.

Up to 1999, the annual report and accounts published by the sole corporate trustee of The Wellcome Trust used to claim a two-way legal power: to capitalise unspent income and also to convert what was once upon a time (1936) a permanent endowment into income at will, the latter power having been sought and obtained by degrees, over the years, from the courts. The conversion of any unspent income of the year into capital therefore used to be shown on the inter-fund transfers line of the SoFA. Conversely, a deficit for the year could be eliminated by a transfer from capital in the same way.

This neat solution to the 'charity reserves' problem has been abandoned ever since the report and accounts for the year to September 2000, however, where it was explained that the distinction was considered 'no longer necessary' – no doubt the result of the Charity Commission Scheme for the Trust (the Scheme was published on the Commission's website at the time, in deference to public interest in such a giant charity), giving the trustee company full power to treat the charity's funds as capital or income at will (comparable to the *corporate* funds of a charitable company), thus unifying capital and income:

Trustee's Report for the year to 30 September 2000

Objects
The objects and powers of the Trust are currently set out in the Will of Sir Henry Wellcome as subsequently interpreted by the courts ... a new constitution has been agreed with the Charity Commission and went out for public consultation on 23 November 2000 for one month. This new document will update and modernise our constitution and make it more relevant to current times.

Notes to the Financial Statements for the year to 30 September 2000

1. Accounting policies

(h) Fund accounting
All the funds of the Trust are unrestricted funds with the exception of grants receivable in the financial statements of the Group which are not considered material.

In prior years, a distinction was made between income and capital gains and losses arising from the investment portfolio. These were taken to the Distribution and Capital Funds respectively, which were shown in separate columns in the Statement of Financial Activities. The Trustee no longer considers this distinction to be relevant, and accordingly the funds of the Trust are now in a single column format.

The Wellcome Trust – Annual Report and Accounts

RESTRICTED FUNDS

3.3   Restricted funds are subject to specific trusts which arise usually either because of an explicit instruction from the donor (or even a wish or intention that can be inferred from the circumstances) or because of the nature of an appeal. Normally, only gifts can give rise to restricted funds, not trading or investment income, unless specified by a fund donor. Therefore, funds, for example, received under a commercial contract, to carry out specific work, would not normally be restricted funds:

> 'Restricted funds are funds subject to specific trusts, which may be declared by the donor(s) or with their authority (e g in a public appeal) or created through legal process, but still within the wider objects of the charity. Restricted funds may be restricted income funds, which are expendable at the discretion of the trustees in furtherance of some particular aspect(s) of the objects of the charity. Or they may be capital (i e endowment) funds, where the assets are required to be invested, or retained for actual use, rather than expended.'
>
> *– SORP 2005, Appendix 3.2(a)*

The 'legal process' referred to above could be a Charity Commission Scheme to vary the purposes of an outmoded charity, for instance. As mentioned above, donor-authority does not always have to be expressly stated, but may be only implied. In certain situations, a binding trustee-declaration can be made long after a hastily mounted emergency relief appeal, and this then confirms or 'fixes' the Objects of that appeal, relying on the authority of a well-established legal precedent (*In re Mathieson*).

Where the restriction is solely on the purpose – rather than just on the timing – of the spending of the fund, it is a 'restricted income fund' that must be accounted for. That is to say, the trust law restriction is on the whole fund as income, and both in the Charities SORP and its related Regulations (and therefore also in this book) it is described simply as a 'restricted fund' – even though it is not the only kind of restricted fund a charity can have!

Alternatively, the restriction may be a requirement to retain the funds for the time being, or it may even operate to prevent the capital of the fund being spent at all. If it cannot be spent, or can be spent only if some specified event occurs, then this kind of restricted fund is thus capital in nature and is known as an endowed fund or *endowment capital* (see below).

The endowment will be for the *general* purposes of the charity unless a 'special' purpose has been indicated by the donor, or by the terms of appeal, in some way that has a binding effect under charity law.

Yet another way in which a charity may become accountable for restricted funds is where a separate charity is united with it for accounting purposes by means of a Direction issued by the Charity Commission under s 96(5) or (6) of the 1993 Act. The Direction makes the main charity publicly accountable for the charity that is deemed subsidiary to it, which is then treated as its 'charity branch' – but one that must be distinguished by showing it as part of the reporting charity's restricted funds.

Appeal funds

3.3.1   Restricted funds often arise where an appeal fund is started by the charity for a particular purpose – on the well-known basis that people are much more likely to give for a named project than for a charity's 'general purposes'. Unless stated otherwise, the voluntary contributions thus raised can be used only for that purpose. This obviously causes problems where insufficient money is raised for the purpose to be carried out, or where an excess of funds is raised and a surplus is achieved. In both cases, the charity either has to return the unspent money to the donors (frequently impractical or even impossible), or must apply to the Charity Commission for a scheme of arrangement in order to be able to use the money elsewhere (a time-consuming procedure).

It is, therefore, a common and recommended practice for appeal literature to contain a clause such as:

> 'In the event of there being insufficient funds to carry out the project or in the event of a surplus arising on the project any unspent funds will be used for the general purposes of the charity.'

Because the terms of any appeal literature can create a 'special trust', the wording used does need careful consideration to ensure that the proceeds achieve the desired result.

Accounts presentation

3.3.2 Trust funds can only be used for the particular purpose or purposes for which they have been given to the charity, and so each such fund needs to be separately administered and accounted for to ensure that there is always a record of how much of each fund remains to be spent on that purpose and to prove that the trustees have duly complied with the terms of trust in each case.

The strict view of the law is that separate administration is required, but this can often be achieved within a unified system, as has been recognised in practice by the Commission, so that guaranteed separation in accounting records is acceptable.

This separate accounting is so important for the maintenance of public confidence in the use of charity funds that, as emphasised at the beginning of this chapter, the split between unrestricted and restricted funds (and of the latter between income and capital, or 'endowed', funds) has to be shown on the face of the SoFA (see chapter 6).

Thus all the restricted income funds of a charity are normally grouped together under one column in the SoFA and then the movement on the material funds is analysed in the notes to the accounts. In addition, the assets and liabilities of the charity must be analysed in the notes between the unrestricted funds and each of the material restricted funds.

In some cases, where there are major individual restricted funds, these might be better presented in individual columns in the SoFA.

Gains and losses

3.3.3 It is essential to bear in mind that any gains or losses arising on assets held in a restricted fund of any kind, and regardless of whether such gains/losses are realised or unrealised, will normally form part of that same fund. Thus, if money in a restricted income fund was used to acquire shares whilst waiting to be spent on a project, gains or losses on those shares would be added to or deducted from the value of the fund.

By the same token, where unspent income from an *endowment* is invested *but cannot* be *accumulated as capital*, all investment gains and losses on the retained income will belong to income (restricted or unrestricted in line with the endowment's terms of trust) – not to capital.

A similar situation to capital accumulation arises where a 'total return' basis of investing a permanent financial endowment has been adopted on proper authority (ie from the founder, the High Court or the Charity Commission – see its website guidance OG83 on this), because that basis will then override the normal rules of trust law. Subject to the actual terms of that authority (eg perhaps requiring that the real value of the endowment *capital* must be preserved against inflation), all investment returns accrue as capital without distinction. These investment returns are then legally expendable by conversion into income at any time at the trustees' own discretion – but subject to a duty of care, imposed by the Trustee Act 2000, to be 'even-handed' in considering the needs of present and future beneficiaries.

Income arising

3.3.4 Where any fund (whether or not it is an endowment) held for a purpose that is *restricted* (ie to some particular part of the charity's declared Objects) is invested for the time being, the investment income arising will – unless the donor has indicated otherwise[2] – normally count as restricted income for that same purpose. This requires it to be accounted for in the *restricted* funds column of the SoFA – bearing in mind, of course, that the actual accounting presentation must always be subject to materiality. The converse holds good for the investment income arising from a general-purpose endowment: unless the donor has specified otherwise, that income belongs to the charity's general-purpose funds and is to be accounted for in the *unrestricted* funds column.

Expenditure

3.3.5 In order to comply with the terms of trust thus imposed, any express or implied instructions or intentions of donors when giving money or other assets required to be used only for a particular part of the activities of the charity must be adhered to – but this must not result in detriment to other trust funds administered in common with it. For this purpose, it is proper to charge the fund with not only the direct costs (including support costs) of carrying out the required activity but also a due proportion (ie, disregarding the donor's funding calculations: these cannot dictate the trustees' cost-allocation policies but only determine the amount of any deficit on that fund, to be funded out of the charity's own free reserves) of the charity's general overheads apportionable to that restricted fund.

As for calculating the amount of the *oncosts* to be apportioned to a restricted fund in any particular case, then, the basic trust law principle is that the individual *ongoing* special-purpose activities to which the charity has become committed for that particular fund should not be under-charged to the detriment of some other restricted fund of the charity through the resultant distortion of internal allocations and/or apportionments of central overheads between the charity's special-purpose activities and its general-purpose activities – even if a particular restricted fund is deliberately under-funded by the donor(s) for some reason, as has often happened with government funding.

On the other hand, a special-purpose activity that is only *transient* (rather than a continuing commitment) and *marginal*, in that it has no noticeable impact on the normal costs of running the charity (eg the use of a 'windfall' gift received to relieve some particular need that falls outside the charity's normal activities yet within its charitable purposes – such as the occasional overseas aid collection raised by many a church charity), can hardly be used to reduce the overhead costs of the latter.

However, any such administrative charges that exceed the limit (if any) specified by the donor will simply result in a deficit that must then be made good out of general funds. Indeed, with the increase in specific project-funding in the charity world and the consequent reduction in core-funding (ie funding for the general activities of the

---

[2]   As indicated in **3.3.3**, the adoption of a duly authorised 'total return' basis of investing a permanent endowment will also result in the investment income accruing to capital – but without affecting any existing restriction of the endowment's purpose. In such a situation the inter-fund transfer to be shown in the SoFA upon converting capital into income for spending will be from the endowment column to the restricted or unrestricted income column, according to whether or not there is such a purpose-restriction.

charity), it is advisable for charities to ensure that their funders do not unreasonably limit the proportion of their general fund expenditure that can be charged to the restricted funds. This problem has at last been dealt with by Government in its new commitment (albeit voluntary and – for good reason – not binding on any government department) to take full account of charities' core costs for fairer funding of special-purpose activities undertaken by these charities to deliver State services of one kind or another (the Commission for the Compact).

This is also particularly important in the case of EC funding, for example. Where apportionments out of a charity's central overheads are charged to a restricted fund, an accounting policy will need to be disclosed in the accounts to clarify the basis of calculation. That is a specific disclosure requirement under SORP 2005. The basis of charge to each fund could, for example, be a percentage of total staff hours spent on the particular project(s) for that fund, or perhaps just pro rata to each fund's total direct costs or some other acceptable and generally recognised costing basis that is easy to quantify. What is important is to have a 'fair' policy that is consistently applied across the charity's funds and from year to year.

If the restricted fund consists of a charitable project for which a particular tangible fixed asset is used either directly or indirectly (eg, in the latter case as part of central overheads), it is also correct to charge any attributable depreciation on the asset to that fund. This will be self-evident if the asset belongs to the reporting charity's *unrestricted income* funds (ie, to corporate reserves, in the case of a charitable company), as the reduction in the asset's carrying value is thus apportioned to the fund(s) using up the asset – but the same principle still applies even if the fund to which the asset belongs is an endowed fund. In the latter case, though, the preferred method (being more 'transparent' in the SoFA and Accounts Notes) may be to include the actual depreciation charge as part of the expenditure shown in either the unrestricted or restricted funds column of the SoFA (according to whether the use of the asset is for general or restricted charitable projects) and to offset this in total by means of a credit of the same amount to *unrestricted* funds (except to the extent of any *purpose-restriction imposed by the donor* of/for that asset, of course, as that is then a 'term of trust' and must be honoured in accounting for it) on the inter-fund transfers line against the depreciation charge to the endowed funds column on the same line. An alternative treatment, being more direct, and just as correct in the absence of any purpose-restriction imposed by the donor, is used by some charities to charge the depreciation straight to the endowed funds column as part of total expenditure.

Where a final surplus results on a restricted fund, in the absence of the necessary donor-agreement or the authority of the Charity Commission or the High Court the surplus cannot lawfully just be transferred to unrestricted funds as a contribution to general overheads, or for some other purpose, but must be accounted for to the donor.

Deficit balances

3.3.6 It is acceptable under charity law for a restricted fund to be in deficit, as long as it is effectively being financed for the time being by the charity's unrestricted funds – or at least without detriment to any other restricted funds of the charity. This is because the particular project being financed by the restricted fund must always be within the overall Objects of the charity, and therefore capable of being supported (funded) from wider – and/or general-purpose funds. The question that then arises where such a situation exists at the year-end is how best to reflect the true position in the annual accounts.

The deficit can properly be carried forward against the future income of that fund only where the trustees can reasonably take the view that it will not ultimately have to be made good out of general-purpose funds and that they can therefore continue financing it on a temporary basis. In such a case, they have really spent money out of the restricted fund in anticipation of receiving the relevant future funding. This may be done only where there are strong grounds for such an anticipation – for example, where future donations are promised under covenant from donors with a reliable track record, or where grant-funding depends on satisfactory completion and validation of each stage of the work being funded, and the trustees take the (reasonable) view that funding is secure enough not to hold up further work until the cash comes in.

Thus, the normal requirement will be that either the anticipated funding has since been received or its eventual receipt is reasonably certain on the basis of commitments made by the relevant funding bodies or other donors. But once any of the restricted fund expenditure has been subsidised by a charge to unrestricted funds in the annual accounts – perhaps due to the uncertainty of its being specially funded in full at the time – it is not permissible to reverse the charge the following year in order to offset that expenditure against a subsequent receipt in that restricted fund.

It is also not permissible for the *unrestricted* funds of a charity to be in deficit so that the deficit is financed by *restricted* funds. Were such a position to arise, the money given for particular purposes would then be financing the overall activities of the charity and this would amount to a *breach of trust* ('War on Want' Inquiry, 1991).

Nor is it permissible to use one restricted fund to finance a deficit on another restricted fund outside its own particular Objects or terms of trust.

Founders, but not subsequent donors to the same fund, can to some extent 'direct' the application of their gift, but they cannot set the charity trustees' policies without the risk of being held personally liable as if they had actually been appointed a trustee.

Donors can certainly restrict the use of the funds they provide within the Objects of the charity, and they can also restrict their contribution to the charity's overheads, so that the acceptance of their gift then entails a corresponding commitment for the reporting charity's general fund to contribute to that restricted fund – *but that must not be allowed to distort any apportionment of overheads to other restricted funds.*

ENDOWMENT FUNDS

3.4   Funds are often given to provide an asset-base to finance the future operation of the charity. These assets may, for example, be cash or shares invested to provide an income stream. As noted at **3.3.4**, where the gift is to fund *restricted* activities the income arising must always be accounted for within the *restricted* funds columns of the SoFA – but as *income*, thus not in the endowments column, as so many accountants have erroneously been doing for many years. (Even where the income is to be retained as capital under a power constituting part of the gift's terms of trust – as with the income-accumulation period of up to 21 years permitted by trust law – it cannot go directly to the endowments column but must first be recognised as income and only transferred to capital on the inter-fund transfers line of the SoFA.)

It is different where a financial endowment is invested on a duly authorised '*total return*' basis: as described above, the *special authority* needed for this replaces the 'normal rules' of trust law by taking *all* investment returns to a special capital 'supplement' from which the trustees can then make *discretionary* allocations to income from time to time. Clearly, on *that* basis, all 'income' returns *must* go to the *endowments* column, the same as for 'capital' returns (gains), because it is on the *inter-fund transfers* line that the allocations to income will be shown. Chapter 6 deals with this special aspect of investment accounting in more detail.

Alternatively, the asset could be freehold property or some other tangible asset *on trust for retention for the charity's own use*, meaning that it cannot just be sold off but must be regarded as a 'functional' fixed asset.

Whereas the former kind of gift will constitute a financial endowment, the latter kind will be a form of 'user-trust' endowment – usually wholly or partially expendable, in the absence (now more or less universal) of any 'sinking fund' requirement in its terms of trust to recoup the depreciation of the building or other 'wasting' asset and convert it over its depreciating life into invested endowed funds. The land on which the building stands, of course, will not normally be subject to such depreciation, but will be a permanent asset, to be retained for the charity's own use in perpetuity – unless the donor has specified otherwise.

Permanent endowment

3.4.1   A permanent endowment arises where money or some other asset received by the charity as a gift brings with it the restriction that the asset is to be treated as capital in perpetuity and thus may not be converted into income at all. This means that – unless wiped out in the course of time through inflation or (perhaps due to poor management) loss of market value in its underlying assets – the fund must be retained in perpetuity, thus permanently. Unless required to be retained *in specie*, though, the assets belonging to the endowment can normally be sold off – but then the proceeds can only be used for replacement assets of an 'equivalent' nature:

> 'Where assets held in a permanent endowment fund are exchanged, their place in the fund must be taken by the assets received in exchange. "Exchange" here may simply mean a change of investment, but it may also mean, for example, the application of the proceeds of sale of freehold land and buildings in the purchase or improvement of freehold property.'

> *– SORP 2005, Appendix 3.3(a)*

Any capital gain or loss arising on an endowment will accrue to that same fund, to be accounted for accordingly. The same holds true for the incidental costs of capital transactions and the *non-revenue* costs of managing (with all that this term entails nowadays) the endowment's constituent assets:

> 'Any expenses incurred in the administration or protection of endowment investments should be charged to capital. For example, the fees of someone who manages endowment investments, or the cost of improvements to land held as an endowment investment. Only

where the trusts of the charity provide to the contrary, or there are insufficient funds in the endowment to meet such costs, can they be charged against the other funds held by the charity.'

– *SORP 2005, Appendix 3.3(c)*

Furthermore, like the SORP, Sch 2 to the SORP's related 2008 Regulations requires the accounts to include:

'a description of any incoming resources which represent capital, according to whether or not that capital is permanent endowment.'

– *SI 2008/629, Sch 2, para 1(h)*

The investment income arising from a permanent endowment is to be used for the general purposes of the charity – unless the donor has imposed a further restriction that the income may only be used for a specific purpose. If so restricted, the income must obviously be accounted for not in the unrestricted funds column of the SoFA but in the *restricted* funds column – as explained above.

Expendable endowment

3.4.2 Sometimes the initial restrictions placed on funds given to the charity state that the funds are not to be expended unless or until some specified event occurs or the trustees, at their discretion, consider it expedient. The latter is often provided for in charitable settlements in order to give the trustees maximum flexibility to respond to changing social needs. Expendable endowment is, in fact, the most desirable form of capital for a charity to have.

> The Trustee may apply the Trust Fund without distinction between capital and income. It may, in its absolute discretion and without altering the expendable nature of the Trust Fund, treat such part or parts of the Trust Fund as capital as it thinks expedient for the prudent administration of the Trust. It may also make reserves out of income to recoup any expenditure funded out of capital, to smooth fluctuations in income or to provide for future income expenditure, or in any other manner permitted by the law of charity. The Trustee shall be free from any obligation strictly to distinguish assets or liabilities as between income and capital so long as it observes a proper balance between the need to allow for present demands on the Trust and the need to allow for future demands.

The Wellcome Trust – Clause 15(2), Charity Commission Scheme (2000)

To the extent specified by the donor, the trustees then have a corresponding power to convert capital into income whenever they wish, or whenever such an event arises, respectively, and this income will then be either restricted or unrestricted according to the original trusts. Such a power of conversion is normally only exercised at the point in time where the money is to be spent. The capital, however, must continue to be accounted for in the endowed funds column of the SoFA until so converted, and must be described in the accounts notes as expendable endowment.

Reserves used to build on endowed land

3.4.3 An unusual constraint can afflict trustees who have neglected to document and maintain the necessary accounting distinction between their unrestricted funds and a permanent endowment of land belonging to the charity and on which, over many years (perhaps decades), they have spent substantial sums out of non-endowed – usually unrestricted – funds to provide and equip buildings needed for the charity's own use.

Even where constructed of the finest stone on solid rock and subsequently maintained to the highest standards, such improvements will still – in theory, at least – be regarded as 'wasting' assets in the eyes of the law. What this means in practice is that you are not normally allowed to finance such improvements out of funds belonging to permanent endowment, which is probably why the trustees had to do it out of reserves in the first place.

If, to improve the charity's reserves by liquidating some of that 'capital expenditure', they later decide to sell part of the improved land, it may well happen that they are told after the event that – by analogy with landlord and tenant law – the whole of the proceeds now belongs to the permanent endowment, thus frustrating their plans.

Unless they can produce other evidence to support their contention that they always intended to maintain the distinction between the revenue-funded expenditure on buildings and the original endowment, their only option may now be to go cap-in-hand to the Charity Commission to request (and justify) an authority to *borrow back* the operational funds thus inadvertently converted into permanent endowment.

While the Commission's standard terms of business for such internal borrowings are known to be lenient to the point of indulgence in the best interests of the charity, this will nevertheless entail a *Recoupment Order* to repay on a pound-for-pound basis (ie, interest-free and ignoring inflation) the borrowed capital – albeit over many decades, if desired, and with the comforting prospect of cancellation of the order if ever the charity should fall on hard times and be unable to afford the repayments.

All of which goes to show that fund-accounting – or the lack of it – could have much more important practical implications than you might have thought possible at the beginning of this chapter!

Chapter 4

THE TRUSTEES' ANNUAL REPORT

INTRODUCTION

4.1   The Charities SORP recommends that the annual accounts, which of necessity report primarily in financial terms, should always be accompanied by *narrative* reporting. The recommendations for this are to be found in a separate section at paragraphs 35–59 of SORP 2005. Their purpose is to provide the wider *context* within which the trustees can demonstrate the *proper administration* of their charity, for which they alone are answerable under charity law. It is for this reason that the SORP says:

> 'The Trustees' Annual Report ... provides important accompanying information to the accounts and should therefore be attached to the accounts whenever a full set of accounts is distributed or otherwise made available.'

> – *SORP 2005, paragraph 37*

This narrative form of annual reporting is designed to acquaint the reader who may be new to the charity with essential background information as to its nature and purpose, its (financial) situation and circumstances and how it is structured, including its 'governance', as well as explaining its operating and financial management policies and summarising its aims, strategies and objectives, its activities and achievements or 'performance' and the external factors affecting these, and finally explaining its future plans.

That makes the trustees' report a most important document for the public, many of whom – not having the requisite accountancy training – must find 'true and fair' financial statements rather heavy going, if not indigestible. The report itself is therefore likely to have a much wider readership than the accounts. While its *format* is unregulated, its minimum contents are prescribed by regulations which apply to all charities other than those exempted from Charity Commission registration/supervision as listed in Sch 2 to the Charities Act 1993 ('the 1993 Act') or which are too small for registration.

Unlike the annual accounts, though, the public have so far (ie until the Charities Act 2006, in which clause 140(3)/(4) has amended s 47 of the 1993 Act here with effect from 1 April 2008) had no statutory right of direct access to the trustees' report, despite its clearly discernible purpose as a public document and the fact that – in contrast to the auditor's or independent examiner's report, for example – it is not required to be addressed to anybody in particular. The public can now also demand a copy of the trustees' report – if one has been prepared either as a routine statutory requirement or upon special request from the Charity Commission. The Charity Commission's right to receive the trustees' annual report, and also to retain it on public record, seems to have led to a feeling of proprietorship over it hitherto, but that will presumably now be dispelled. The explanatory notes to the SORP's related Regulations 2005 even referred to reg 11 as dealing with 'the annual reports which charity trustees are required to make *to the Charity Commissioners'*.

Being a statutory document, the trustees' report can also be a very convenient peg on which to hang other requirements. For example, for their own purposes in line with the Auditing Practices Board's Practice Note PN 11: *'The Audit of Charities'* (see chapter 17), charity auditors usually ask for the inclusion of a statement distinguishing the trustees' responsibilities from their own. As highlighted in this chapter, SORP 2005 has adds further disclosures on investment and reserves management, on governance and on operational and fundraising performance that may have more to do with charity monitoring than with assisting public understanding of, and confidence in, charities and their administration.

In an effort to get rid of the tempting 'checklist-ticking' approach to compliance with what some have described as the original SORP's overly prescriptive and perhaps burdensome expectations here, SORP 2000 had jettisoned most of the 1995 SORP's detailed recommendations on specific matters to be considered for narrative reporting. Instead, it simply required that this part of the trustees' report describe or explain *'what the charity is trying to do and how it is going about it'*.

SORP 2005 still retains those words at paragraph 36 as 'good reporting', but has also gone back to checklists with its prescribed disclosures under the six main headings set out in **4.3** below. As with the company directors' report (which can be combined with it, in the case of a charitable company), the trustees' report must naturally include commentary – however brief – on the accounts themselves, something that is not easy to specify in regulations.

SORP 2000 had seemed to call for compliance statements of a kind that would make it difficult to avoid *always* attaching the annual accounts to the trustees' report, as distinct from doing so just to meet statutory filing requirements at the Charity Commission or as a matter of best practice. Did this arise from a wish to bridge over the regulatory gaps that arise where the accounts of a smaller charity are unaudited – or even (if prepared on a receipts and payments basis in England and Wales) unsigned? It seems not, as the old SORP's ambiguously placed annual reporting requirement that *'Trustees should … confirm that the accounts comply with current statutory requirements, the requirements of the charity's governing document and the requirements of this SORP'* has now been moved to paragraph 358 of SORP 2005 as part of its *accounting policies note* requirements.

Satisfying the charity's 'stakeholders'

4.1.2 Although the trustees' report is clearly designed to serve as a public document, to satisfy the public need and to be on public record, public access to it prior to the changes brought by the Charities Act 2006 has not been as direct and reliable as it is for charities' *annual accounts* under s 47 of the 1993 Act:

'(1) Any annual report or other document kept by the Commissioners in pursuance of section 45(6) above shall be open to public inspection at all reasonable times—

(a) during the period for which it is so kept; or
(b) if the Commissioners so determine, during such lesser period as they may specify.

(2) Where any person—

(a) requests the charity trustees of a charity in writing to provide him with a copy of the charity's most recent accounts, and

(b) pays them such reasonable fee (if any) as they may require in respect of the costs of complying with the request,

those trustees shall comply with the request within the period of two months beginning with the date on which it is made.'

– Charities Act 1993, s 47

Many charities are *excepted* from the general statutory duty to *file* such a report unless specially requested to do so by the Charity Commission as regulator, while others are *exempted* from the duty to *prepare* one at all. For this reason it was seen as impractical to provide for *direct* public access to charities' annual reports. Not any more, however, as a Lords' amendment introduced into the Charities Bill 2005 in July 2005 resulted in adding the trustees' report (if required by law to be prepared) to s 47(2)(a), and adding the following extra sub-sections (the words in square brackets are ours).

'(4) This subsection applies if an annual report has been prepared in respect of any financial year of a charity in pursuance of section 45(1) [routine statutory requirement] or 46(5) [Charity Commission request] …

(5) In subsection (2) above the reference to a charity's most recent annual report is a reference to the annual report prepared in pursuance of section 45(1) or 46(5) in respect of the last financial year of the charity in respect of which an annual report has been so prepared.'

– Charities Act 2006, Sch 8, clause 140(4), amending s 47, Charities Act 1993

So, under the law as it stood prior to April 2008, but not now that the new law has come into force here, if the trustees are unwilling to co-operate in this matter the only way to be sure of getting a copy of their annual report for any year used to be to ask the Charity Commission for it – as explained in **4.1.5**, which deals with access to their public records.

A charity's *stakeholders*, however, are in a class of their own, as a subset of the public with whom the trustees will generally be only too willing to co-operate. If you happen to be in this class, you should have had no difficulty even under the old law. 'Stakeholders' is a collective name often used to describe all those who have any legitimate interest in a charity's activities for one reason or another (bearing in mind, of course, that this cannot normally include any kind of *equity* interest[1] in the residual funds of a charity).

The list of a charity's stakeholders is surprisingly long, and can include:

– its founders and patrons;

– the members, in the case of a charitable association – incorporated or unincorporated – as distinct from a charitable trust;

---

[1] This means a legal entitlement to a proportionate share of profits/gains: charitable and other 'not-for-profit' membership associations, whether incorporated or unincorporated, invariably prohibit any such distribution to the members, as this is a prerequisite for such a status.

- other donors (the public, in the case of appeals) and other potential supporters;

- grant-making bodies (official/corporate, and also other charities);

- the charity's beneficiaries – both current/future and potential;

- the charity trustees (of course);

- its employees and volunteers working for the charity;

- its creditors;

- any connected organisations (including those entitled to nominate trustees);

- the media, the rest of the voluntary sector, and academic and other researchers;

- the regulatory authorities – usually the Charity Commission (England and Wales) or OSCR (Scotland), but also HMRC in many cases.

The practical problem is that the requirements of these groups can differ considerably from each other, so that satisfying them all by means of the statutory annual report is almost as impossible as it is in the case of the statutory annual accounts. Many charities therefore supplement those statutory documents by distributing, for publicity purposes, simplified and sometimes highly colourful Summarised Accounts (see chapter 15) often contained within glossy *non-statutory* 'annual reviews' designed with their own immediate stakeholders' needs in mind.

Annual reviews tend to be longer, more detailed and more personalised than is possible for the more factual and objective statutory annual report, the contents of which are generally constrained by the auditor's concern for 'consistency' with the audited annual accounts. The Review often includes sections written from different perspectives, and in this way can be used to satisfy the different information requirements of their intended readership. Recognising the compliance problems that can and do arise from mixing the two kinds of annual reporting, SORP 2005 says:

> 'Legal requirements and this SORP do not limit the inclusion of other information within the Trustees' Annual Report or as additional information accompanying the accounts. Charity trustees may incorporate other material into their annual reporting, for example a chairman's report, environment report, impact assessment or an operating and financial review ...
>
> Charities may additionally use other means of providing information, outside of the accounting and reporting framework, about who they are and what they do. Such information is often tailored for the needs of particular audiences and presented through annual reviews, newsletters and websites. Whilst charity trustees might usefully refer to these other sources of information within their Trustees' Annual Report, such additional information should not be seen as a substitute for good statutory annual reporting.'
>
> – *SORP 2005, paragraphs 38, 39*

What seems certain is that annual reviews, as a complementary form of reporting to that afforded by the annual report, will continue to have an increasingly important part to play in 'marketing' the services of charities – as well as in public fundraising.

Drafting, approval and signing

4.1.3   Trustees often delegate the detailed drafting work. This is understandable, given their volunteer status in most cases. But the contents of this document are too important to the proper discharge of their duties for them to be able safely to leave it entirely to their staff, their auditors or their independent examiner. The tendency to delegate, however, was even acknowledged and accepted in SORP 2000, which referred at paragraph 28 to '*drafts being given to the trustees a reasonable time in advance*'. Those words no longer appear in SORP 2005.

On the other hand, to ensure that the public can receive a clear and consistent message about the charity, it is clearly important that the work of drafting it is undertaken by someone who understands the implications of the figures presented in the annual accounts and the picture they give of the charity, its work and its funding to those who know how to 'read' accounts.

If these two aspects, drafting the report and preparing the accounts, are dealt with independently without reference to each other, the resultant impression can be one of conflicting messages about the future development of the charity. This will tend to undermine its credibility in the eyes of those whose confidence in the charity may be crucial. But that is just where the auditor's duty to consider the *consistency* of the two documents can help the trustees.

Both the SORP and its related Regulations require the statutory annual report of the trustees to be signed and dated by a trustee *specifically authorised* for that purpose, to show that it has been formally considered by them and has been approved by a majority – it does not actually have to be all – of them. But SORP 2000 had also provided some useful – if perhaps slightly provocative – guidance for any dissenting trustee who might feel *too* uncomfortable about the majority decision, guidance that has also been dropped from SORP 2005:

> 'The usual procedure of charity trustees will not require the unanimous approval of the report and accounts. But any trustees who consider that the report and/or accounts should not be approved, or should not have been approved, should report to the Charity Commission (in the case of charities in England and Wales) or other regulator, any of their concerns which they are unable to resolve with their fellow trustees and/or with the auditors or examiners of the accounts.'

Prior to the coming into force of the SORP's 1995 Regulations, it was often the secretary or 'clerk' to the board of trustees (ie a non-trustee) who was instructed to sign the trustees' report – perhaps by analogy with company directors' reports, where the company secretary can legally sign instead of a director. Even after well over a decade of regulated public accountability, 'household name' charities like Help the Aged (see below), still maintain that tradition. However, reg 40 or (for a group) reg 41 of the current Regulations 2008, like reg 11 of the 2005 version, applies equally to charitable companies. This means that where – as is suggested by SORP 2005 at paragraph 40 – the directors' report and the trustees' report are combined into one document, *a company secretary who is not also a director cannot validly sign the amalgamated report for filing with the Charity Commission.*

Help the Aged

Registered Company Number 1263446
Registered Charity Number 272786 ...

Chairman's Report ...

Director General's Report ...

Help the Aged: aims, objectives, structure ...

– Combating poverty ...

– Reducing isolation ...

– Challenging neglect ...

– Defeating ageism ...

– Preventing future deprivation ...

- Helping developing countries ...

Our services
...

Financial review
Corporate Governance

– Governance and decision-making

– Statement of trustee's responsibilities ...

– Disclosure of information to auditors ...

– Risk and Internal Control ...

– Reserves ...

– Investments; Investment portfolio ...

– Grant-making policy ...
...
Approved by the Board and signed on its behalf on 17 July 2008 by:
(signed)
M Harvey
Company Secretary

Help the Aged – Annual Report 2007/08

Filing

4.1.4 It is only the trustees of registered charities *above* the 'light touch' regime's £10,000 ceiling of gross income who are routinely required by law to submit annual reports, though these must, under a new s 45(3A) inserted into the 1993 Act by the 2006 Act, still be prepared and therefore available to the public on request. However, with effect for financial years ending after March 2009 under SI 2009/508 only from charities above £25,000 are annual reports now routinely required for filing at the Charity Commission, to which report the trustees must then also 'attach' the annual accounts for that financial year, together with any audit, independent examination or (until abolished for financial years from 1 April 2008) 'company audit exemption' report applicable.

The Commission used to be entitled under s 45(3) of the 1993 Act to an original (ie signed) trustees' annual report – not just a copy of it. Trustees therefore needed to sign at least two identical originals – one for their own records and another to file with the Commission if so required. From 1 April 2008, however, only a *copy* of the signed annual report has to be filed with the Commission. The accounts to be attached can also, if prepared under s 42(1) and its related regulations, be a copy of the signed original. The signed set to be retained by the trustees is therefore the one to which the signed original of the audit or other external report on the accounts has to be attached, as only a *copy* of it has to be attached to the accounts sent to the Commission for filing. For financial years starting after 31 March 2008 the same applies to a *group* trustees' report – see below.

The statutory filing deadline is normally 10 months from the year-end, but the Commission's Liverpool Office (where the work of receiving, vetting and filing these documents is concentrated) will usually extend this without demur upon request – even if initially only by telephone, though it is always advisable for this to be confirmed in writing – if you explain to them what the problem is. The Commission does have statutory powers to enforce compliance in the event of 'persistent default' (eg after a third reminder has been ignored), which has been criminalised by s 49 of the 1993 Act to facilitate court proceedings and, ultimately, personal fines for obstructive trustees. In keeping with the 'voluntary principle' of charity trusteeship, however, and in the interests of the 'proportionate' regulatory stance to which it has had to become committed, the Commission now has a policy of first 'naming and shaming' significant default cases on the charity's pages on the Commission's website, in order to give defaulters every opportunity to make good without the need for such heavy-handed sanctions.

Public access

4.1.5 We discussed in **4.1.2** the reason why prior to the implementation of the Charities Act 2006 you, as a member of the public, could not just demand a copy of their latest annual report from the trustees *as of right*. That gap in the law has now been filled, as explained above. For a registered charity not so small as to fall within the 'light-touch' regulatory regime ('ceiling': currently £10,000 gross income for the year), nor below the £25,000 gross income where you would now be asked to go direct to the trustees with your request, you can normally inspect and copy (for a small copying fee) the trustees' filed annual reports and accounts within 5 working days of your request to any of the Charity Commission's three Public Registry offices – as long as these documents continue to be retained on public file, of course. The Commission used to have no time-limit for document retention but, with the rapidly expanding volume of records since the implementation of the Charities Acts of 1992 and 1993, a more pragmatic policy was developed to limit the retention of annual documents to 10 years.

That is the facility for *registered* charities within the Charity Commission's normal regulatory regime. For other charities, public access to their trustees' reports can be problematical.

Excepted charities as such are not required to prepare and file a trustees' report for any financial year unless specially requested by the Commission. The *very smallest* unregistered charities are not required by law to prepare trustees' reports at all. Although not relieved from the statutory duty to *prepare* trustees' reports, none of the smaller *registered* charities within the 'light-touch' regulatory regime have to *file* them with the Commission for any year unless specially requested to do so, and the same now goes for the next larger size-band: those up to £25,000 gross income.

This means that even under the new law the one way you can be sure to obtain a copy of the trustees' report for any charity if it is not on file at the Charity Commission (assuming the charity is not one of those below the registration threshold, of course) may still be to persuade the Commission to 'request' the report for itself, when it may also make it available to you as part of the public record.

Filing by charitable companies

4.1.6   Charitable companies used to be required to file with the Charity Commission an original (signed) trustees' report, just like any other charity, but can now just file a copy of it. In addition (though it can be combined in the same document – which must then comply with *both* Acts), the Companies Act 2006 (like the 1985 Act) allows the *directors'* report prepared under that Act to be filed at the Companies Registry with accounts appended that include the consolidated SoFA without the entity SoFA if the company so wishes – so long as this discloses how much of the net result for the year is dealt with in the accounts of the parent company.

The Charity Commission – unlike the Registrar of Companies – is also a *regulatory* authority, and for this purpose it has always been the *entity* accounts that were paramount. They are intrinsic to the need to demonstrate due compliance with *charity* law, which also covers the *corporate* funds of charitable companies through special statutory provisions contained in Part VIII of the 1993 Act. Although these entity accounts can be usefully *supplemented* by consolidated accounts, as is recommended by the Charities SORP, and now made mandatory for financial years starting after 31 March 2008 in respect of all charity groups above the £500,000 gross income threshold for a statutory audit, the information they provide cannot be entirely dispensed with if the Commission is to be able to police the sector effectively and be answerable to Parliament for its power to supervise the proper application of charitable resources.

Until the Charities Act 2006 inserted a new s 49A and Sch 5A into it, the 1993 Act contained no provision at all for consolidated accounts, but simply provided that the accounts to be attached to the trustees' annual report of a *charitable company* shall be:

'... a copy of the charity's annual accounts prepared for the financial year in question under Part VII of the Companies Act 1985 ...'.

– Charities Act 1993, s 45(5)

While that already allowed for the filing of trustees' reports where group consolidated accounts were prepared under *company* law, it is augmented for financial years starting after 31 March 2008 by specific provision in the Charities Act 2006 to require the filing of a *group* report by the parent charity's trustees wherever group consolidated accounts are prepared under the 1993 Act – see **4.1.7**, below.

Note the word 'prepared' here: not 'distributed to members', 'published' or 'filed with the Registrar of Companies'. It explains the Charity Commission interpretation that their entitlement is to a copy of the *full* accounts that the directors are required to prepare and the auditors to report on – which accounts as such do, of course, include the group parent's own (entity) financial activity statement even if for general publication that document is subsequently suppressed in favour of the consolidated one.

The Companies Act provides that the directors of a 'not-for-profit' company *shall* adapt the form and content of the statutory 'profit and loss account' to make it suit their reporting needs in annual accounts for the purpose of showing the required 'true and fair view' – but without telling them how to do it. Charitable companies therefore have to look elsewhere for this information. However, in contrast to its status for other charities, the Charities SORP is not actually *mandatory* for charitable companies preparing accounts under the Companies Act – in the absence of any special provision for them there (eg a special Schedule to that Act, as has been done for other companies in regulated sectors of the economy). For charitable companies, therefore, except for 'small group' consolidated accounts that have to be prepared under the 1993 Act and so are governed by the SORP's related Regulations 2008, the Charities SORP remains quite simply 'best practice' in normal circumstances for a true and fair view in the annual accounts – with which the trustees' report also needs to be consistent for audit purposes, of course.

A special regulation, reg 40 of Regulations 2008 (or for group reports reg 41 – see below), like previous versions of the SORP's Regulations, governs the contents of the trustees' annual report – *including that for a charitable company* – except that certain additional information will be required in it if the trustees' report is also to be filed at Companies House as the 'directors' report' under companies legislation. Details of the additional requirements for companies are specified in the disclosure checklist in Appendix 7.

Charity trustees are defined in the 1993 Act as:

'... the persons having the general control and management of the administration of a charity.'

– Charities Act 1993, s 97(1)

This means that, by virtue of their office, the 'company directors' and the 'charity trustees' will always be the same persons, and it is good practice to make this clear in the wording of the charitable company's combined annual report – for example:

> The directors, who are also the trustees of the charity, at the date of this report, and those who served during the financial year, together with the dates of any changes, are as set out [on page x].

To avoid any problems when filing the report and accounts at Companies House, it is also important to make clear in the title or in an opening sentence that the combined report is both the 'trustees' report' and the 'directors' report'.

Statutory requirements

4.1.7 Both the *preparation* of the trustees' report (for non-exempt charities above the registration threshold) and its *filing* with the Charity Commission by registered and non-registered (ie excepted) charities, are statutory requirements under s 45 of the 1993 Act as amended by the 2006 Act:

'(1) The charity trustees of a charity shall prepare in respect of each financial year of the charity an annual report containing—

(a)   such a report by the trustees on the activities of the charity during that year, and
(b)   such other information relating to the charity or to its trustees or officers,

as may be prescribed by regulations made by the Minister.

...

(3) Where in any financial year of a charity its gross income exceeds £25,000*, a copy of the annual report required to be prepared under this section in respect of that year shall be transmitted to the Commission by the charity trustees—

(a)   within ten months from the end of that year, or
(b)   within such longer period as the Commission may for any special reason allow in the case of that report.

(3A)   Where in any financial year of a charity its gross income does not exceed £25,000, a copy of the annual report required to be prepared under this section in respect of that year shall, if the Commission so requests, be transmitted to it by the charity trustees—

(a)   in the case of a request made before the end of seven months from the end of the financial year to which the report relates, within ten months from the end of that year, and
(b)   in the case of a request not so made, within three months from the date of the request,

or in either case, within such a longer period as the Commission may for any special reason allow in the case of that report.

(4) Subject to subsection (5) below[2], any copy of an annual report transmitted to the Commission under this section shall have attached to it a copy of the statement of accounts

---

[2]   This refers to charitable companies. It replaces the reference to accounts produced under the regulations by a reference to any accounts produced under Part VII of the 1985 Act (now Part 15, Companies Act 2006) to allow also for the possibility of accounts audited or else independently examined under the 1993 Act being appended to the copy of the trustees' annual report for filing with the Commission by a smaller charitable company.

prepared for the financial year in question under section 42(1) above or (as the case may be) the account and statement so prepared under section 42(3) above, together with—

(a) where the accounts of the charity for that year have been audited under section 43 ..., a copy of the report made by the auditor on that statement of accounts or (as the case may be) on that account and statement;

(b) where the accounts of the charity for that year have been examined under section 43 ..., a copy of the report made by the person carrying out the examination.

...

(7) The charity trustees of a charity shall preserve, for at least six years from the end of the financial year to which it relates, any annual report prepared under subsection (1) above which they have not been required to transmit to the Commission.'

– Charities Act 1993, s 45 (as amended)

(*Threshold amended by SI 2009/508 for financial years *ending* after 31 March 2009)

Group reports for consolidated accounts

For financial years starting after 31 March 2008 there is now an *additional* filing requirement for both *company* and *non-company* parent charities under the 1993 Act. This applies wherever a group annual report and group consolidated accounts have to be prepared under the new Sch 5A and the SORP's related 2008 Regulations (for charitable companies this will be where the group is 'small' under the Companies Act 2006, making consolidated accounts *non-mandatory* under that Act):

'10.—

(1) This paragraph applies where group accounts are prepared for a financial year of a parent charity ...

(2) The annual report prepared by the charity trustees of the parent charity in respect of that year under section 45 of this Act shall include—

(a) such a report by the trustees on the activities of the charity's subsidiary undertakings during that year, and

(b) such other information relating to any of those undertakings, as may be prescribed by regulations made by the Minister.

(3) [those] regulations ... may make provision—

(a) for ... (2)(a) to be ... in accordance with such principles as are specified or referred to in the regulations;

(b) enabling the Commission to dispense with any requirement [of] (2)(b) in the case of a particular subsidiary undertaking or a particular class of subsidiary undertaking.

(4) ... any reference to the charity's gross income in the financial year in question [in s 45(3) means] the aggregate gross income for the group in that year.

(5) When transmitted to the Commission ... the copy of the annual report shall have attached to it both a copy of the group accounts prepared for that year ... and—

(a) a copy of the report made by the auditor on those accounts; or

(b)   where those accounts have been examined under section 43 ... a copy of the report made by the person carrying out the examination.

(6)   The requirements in this paragraph are in addition to those in section 45 of this Act.'

– Charities Act 1993, Sch 5A, paragraph 10

In practice, however, it seems hardly likely that the Charity Commission would or could insist on two sets of filing by a parent charity that prepares group consolidated accounts. Not only does the SORP itself make clear the Commission's requirement for the key figures from the parent charity's *entity* SoFA to be disclosed in the notes to the consolidated accounts, but in its related 2008 Regulations reg 41 (governing the contents of the group report) and reg 40 (governing the contents of the trustees' report where no group consolidated accounts are prepared) are in most respects clearly alternative to each other – not supplementary. Elsewhere in this chapter we comment on those few disclosure requirements where reg 41 differs from reg 40.

FORMAT AND CONTENTS

4.2   There are no *format* requirements for the narrative and administrative sections of the report, so it is up to each charity to decide how best to present the information. It has, however, become almost standard practice for the section giving the required legal/administrative data (which can usually be kept to a single page) to be presented at the beginning (or sometimes the end) of the published annual report and accounts. In such cases (unless it is clearly a preface) it may need to be *cross-referenced* from within the signed report's narrative in order to make that report technically complete.

A detailed comparison of the requirements under the Charities SORP, its related 2008 Regulations and the amended 1993 Act is to be found in the checklist in Appendix 7. This chapter therefore mainly concentrates on the newer disclosure requirements individually, as well as discussing those older ones that are likely to continue to present practical problems.

SORP 2005, with its strong emphasis on *governance* and *performance-reporting*, seeks a more standardised information content by setting out its requirements for the Trustees' Report under half a dozen principal subject-headings, the everyday meaning of which (similar to the wording used on many a charity's website) we have indicated alongside each one as a reminder that you don't have to use the SORP's terminology, just as you can also vary the order of all these disclosures at will:

1.	Reference and Administrative Details	Who we are
2.	Structure, Governance and Management	How we do things
3.	Objectives and Activities	What we set out to do
4.	Achievements and Performance	What we have done so far
5.	Financial Review	About our finances
6.	Plans for Future Periods	What we plan to do next

There is also a potential seventh disclosure for those comparatively rare cases where a charity (or its trustee-body) holds assets as 'custodian' for a *separately accountable charity*, in which case brief details are required in accordance with the SORP and also with reg 41(3)(s) for a group report, or – no matter how small the charity – by reg 40(3)(r) of the 2008 Regulations in other cases.

ADMINISTRATIVE INFORMATION

4.3 For *all* charities, the SORP's related Regulations 2008 underpin most of its legal/administrative information requirements, which are designed to acquaint the reader with the charity – but with some interesting variations. These are discussed below, grouped by category, in each case quoting the relevant regulation, followed by how this relates to what the SORP recommends, and also the practicalities involved.

Identifying the charity

4.3.1 The 2008 Regulations, like those preceding them, call for the following particulars:

'(a)   the name of the charity as it appears in the register of charities and any other name by which it makes itself known;

(b)   the number assigned to it in the register and, in the case of a charitable company, the number with which it is registered as a company ...'.

– *SI 2008/629, reg 40(3) and reg 41(3)*

This means, in the first place, the 'official' name as set out in whatever 'governing document' (original/amended – see below) defines the constitution of the charity, but, in the second place, also those sometimes very different 'working' names, such as abbreviations, acronyms, branch names, etc that many charities find it convenient to use either to describe their activities or else in fundraising from the public.

For example, The Royal Commonwealth Society for the Blind works under the name 'Sight Savers'. Harrow School is run by a charity whose official name is 'The Keepers and Governors of the Free Grammar School of John Lyon', which also runs a day school called 'John Lyon School'. Dulwich College was originally named 'Alleyn's College of God's Gift'. There are many other examples on the Register of Charities.

Although charities typically strive to establish a unique and recognisable personality for themselves and their work, some can have confusingly similar names – perhaps comprised entirely of commonly used words (e g The Home Help Charity) – making it difficult to find them on statutory registers from the name alone. Hence the requirement for identifying registration numbers to be given as well.

If an *excepted* charity that has not registered voluntarily is requested by the Charity Commission to prepare and file an annual report for a particular year, there is, of course, no need for it to state the obvious: that it has no charity registration number.

Purpose and constitution

4.3.2   Here, the 2008 Regulations require two items of administrative information that, as we shall see, SORP 2005 puts in the narrative sections of the Report:

> '(h)   particulars, including the date if known, of any deed or other document containing provisions which regulate the purposes and administration of the [reporting] charity; ... [and]
>
> (l)   a summary description of the purposes of the [reporting] charity.'
>
> – *SI 2008/629, reg 40(3) and reg 41(3)*

In respect of the second of these disclosures, the original 1995 specification was 'a description of the trusts of the charity'. Technically speaking, it seems that did not perhaps quite cover charitable companies – even though the primary legislation under which these Regulations are made says:

> '"trusts" in relation to a charity, means the provisions establishing it as a charity and regulating its purposes and administration, whether those provisions take effect by way of trust or not, and in relation to other institutions has a corresponding meaning.'
>
> – *Charities Act 1993, s 97(1)*

The newer wording used in the Regulations since 2000 fills the gap by covering both:

(i)   the declared purposes (aims/objects) for which any *trust* property is owned and administered by or for the charity (even if that charity is a company) or else by the same body of trustees reporting under a Charity Commission 'Uniting Direction' for a number of perhaps disparate charities being accounted for collectively in the public interest (see chapter 14); and

(ii)   the declared *Objects* of a charitable company for the use of its *corporate* property – which, of course, it owns beneficially and not on trust at all.

This corresponds to the more loosely worded requirement in the SORP at paragraph 47(a), under 'Objectives and Activities', for:

> '(a)   an explanation of the objects of the charity as set out in its governing document.'
>
> – *SORP 2005, paragraph 47(a)*

As discussed in more detail below, the SORP (like the Regulations) thus glosses over the fact that 'multi-cellular' charities (ie those comprising multiple trust funds) must have multiple governing documents.

There could also be some confusion in trustees' reports between these enduring charitable purposes which under the 2006 Act must now be shown to be for the public benefit and the key annual *objectives* that SORP 2005 expects to be set and declared by trustees within the operating policies they adopt to further or pursue those purposes, as well as within the *statement of Public Benefit aims* it expects to be declared for the charity along with *'an explanation of ... the changes or differences it seeks to make through its activities'* – see **4.4.6**.

The Board of Trustees of the British Heart Foundation submits its statutory Report and Accounts for the year ended 31 March 2008.

...

Principal Aim and Activities

The aim of the British Heart Foundation is to play a leading role in the fight against disease of the heart and circulation so that it is no longer a major cause of disability and premature death. We are striving to achieve a world in which people do not die prematurely of heart disease. To this end, the Foundation continues to pursue five strategic objectives:

- to pioneer research into the causes of heart disease and improved methods of prevention, diagnosis and treatment

- to provide vital information to help people reduce their own heart health risk

- to press for government policies which minimise the risk of heart and circulatory disease

- to help attain the highest possible standards of care and support for heart patients

- to reduce the inequalities in levels of heart disease across the UK.

...

The total amount committed to the Foundation's principal objective of supporting research represented 68% of the [£106.9m] charitable expenditure in the year, and we continue to be the largest single contributor to UK cardiovascular research. Education of the public and the medical profession, together with expenditure on the care and rehabilitation of heart patients accounted for the remaining 32% of the total.

...

Governance

Organisational structure

The Foundation operates as a company limited by guarantee, under the terms of its memorandum and articles dated 28 July 1961 and last amended on 29 January 2008 ...

British Heart Foundation – 2007/08 Annual Report

It is also important to note that the statutory disclosure requirement under reg 40(3)(h) or 41(3)(h) is more demanding than the 'best practice' requirement of the SORP, which merely asks for:

'The *nature* of the governing document (eg trust deed; memorandum and articles of association; Charity Commission Scheme; Royal Charter; etc) and how the charity is (or its trustees are) constituted (eg limited company; unincorporated association; trustees incorporated as a body; etc).'

– SORP 2005, paragraph 44(a)

The practical problem for many trustee-bodies is again the 'multi-cellular' nature of the *entity* for which they are publicly accountable under charity legislation – see chapter 14, where we consider the ramifications of branch-accounting versus consolidation. For example, independent schools established as charities tend to attract multiple trust funds to found scholarships and prize funds, etc. Each of these will have its own governing document, in many cases with quite distinctive Objects not necessarily to be inferred from those of the main charity alone (eg providing for pupils to progress to further/higher educational institutions on leaving school).

In such cases the reporting charity is actually a *collection* of separate charitable institutions united by a common purpose under that trustee-body's *ultimate* – if not immediate – control. The nature of such a collection can be difficult to encapsulate in a brief description of the main charity's overarching declared charitable purpose – in legal parlance the 'Objects' of the main charity.

Under English trust law, the trustees of a charity of any kind can become legally responsible for the proper application of the funds of an unlimited number of separately constituted *charity branches* that have been added on through donors wishing to distinguish some special aspect of the charity's work as requiring separate administration. Where empowered to do so by their charity's governing document, the trustees themselves can achieve the same result by *splitting* funds. Alternatively, they might choose to set up branch or group subsidiary charities to which they then make grants for particular purposes. Furthermore, as explained in chapter 14, s 96(6) of the 1993 Act empowers the Charity Commission, in the public interest, to issue a 'Uniting Direction' requiring what may even be a disparate collection of charities administered by the same trustee-body to be accounted for collectively under Part VI of the 1993 Act. The Objects of the constituent members of such a reporting 'entity' will then not be directly related to each other, but only to the external purpose that justifies their being accounted for as a *notional* reporting charity, which must therefore feature in any summary of their Objects – for example, 'purposes to do with the improvement of the *local community's* health, recreational, employment and other facilities'.

Thus we should note here that the SORP's apparently simple and obvious requirement for 'an explanation' of the nature and constitutional type of the 'governing document' is actually a *generic* one that must be amplified by compliance with the closer specification contained in the Regulations. Reg 40(3)(h) or 41(3)(h) can really only be fully complied with by identifying *each* currently valid 'document' governing (regulating) the proper activities (purposes and administration) of any *legally distinguishable* parts (unless immaterial financially, of course) of the accountable entity or of the group parent (respectively) as defined by the 1993 Act for external reporting purposes under Part VI.

These are, of course, the defining documents that anyone is entitled to inspect (and take copies of) at the Charities Registry – if the charity is registered with the Charity Commission, that is. A currently valid 'governing document' is now a routine requirement for registration of any charity with the Commission – either as a 'main' charity with a unique registration number of its own or as a 'subsidiary' charity with perhaps just a suffix to the registration number of an existing main charity.

In the simplest possible case of a reporting charity that has no 'charity branches' – ie endowed or other 'restricted' funds – to be accounted for, you only need to state the *type* of governing document by which it is constituted (the SORP gives the most common examples) and also under the Regulations the *date* of that document in its latest amended or updated version. However, it would seem to be implicit in the SORP that the same information should also be given for any (significant) *charity branch* covered by the annual report and accounts if that branch does have its own legal constitution. This is a counterpart to the SORP's requirement at paragraph 44(d) for a description of the charity's *organisational structure,* discussed at **4.4.8** in some detail.

In addition, because annual reporting under Part VI of the 1993 Act requires a 'subsidiary' charity (ie a separately constituted charity branch – see chapter 14) to be publicly accounted for only within the statutory accounts of the relevant 'main' charity as defined by s 97(1) for 'special trusts', or as directed by the Charity Commission under s 96(5) or (6) in any other case, to meet the requirements of the legislation you will need to disclose *how* each of those subsidiary charities, if accounted for as charity branches, (as well as the main charity itself) is constituted – and *when*.

Trustees, officers, agents and professional advisers, etc

4.3.3   The Regulations require not only the charity trustees themselves to be named but also any *other* person (external to the charity) empowered to nominate or appoint them, as well as anyone else holding property (funds) belonging to the charity. But while the Regulations continue to provide for 'officers' to be included in this (see below) they also continue to ignore the SORP's further requirements at paragraph 41(f) for the Chief Executive and so on (ie the person(s), if any, to whom the trustees have delegated the day-to-day running of the charity) to be named, and at paragraph 41(g) for the names and addresses of 'relevant organisations or persons' including bankers, solicitors, auditors (or equivalent), investment or other principal advisers to be given.

This is generally taken to mean *retained* advisers – ie only those acting on a continuing basis – and it can include all sorts of other specialists, according to the kind of charity, its assets and activities. Logically, although not mentioned as such in the SORP, any third party acting as the charity's retained *agent* should also be named here. Where a charity has extensive property interests, for instance, the list could obviously also include managing agents, property surveyors and insurance advisers. Even without the compulsion of the Regulations, most charities do seem to comply with the SORP here by including such details in the administrative section of the trustees' report.

Perhaps taking their cue from the influence of companies legislation on the reporting style adopted for charitable companies (these now number nearly 75% of all registered charities above the £1m gross income level), many charities go beyond the strict requirements of the SORP here by also naming all their senior paid executives, such as chief executive, finance director/manager, etc. This can be seen as information needed by the reader to understand 'how decisions are made' – paragraph 44(d) of SORP 2005. In going on to ask in particular what kind of decisions are delegated to staff or reserved to the trustees themselves, the SORP's requirement here also reflects the reliance of the largely *non-executive* boards of trustees of larger charities on the delegated management structure they need to put in place for the sake of administrative efficiency. This again is a counterpart to paragraph 44(d)'s further requirement for charities above the statutory audit threshold to provide 'a description of the organisational structure of the charity' – see **4.4.7**, dealing with *management* structure.

The Regulations were cleverly expanded in 2000 (see the sections that were new at that time, as *highlighted* below) and are merely renumbered now in reg 40(3) and 41(3) of the 2008 Regulations to require:

'...

(i)   the name of any person or body of persons entitled *by the trusts of the [reporting] charity* to appoint one or more new charity trustees, *and a description of the method provided by those trusts for such appointment*;

(d)   the name of any person who is a charity trustee of the [reporting] charity on the [date of approval of the report], *and, where any charity trustee on that date is a body corporate, the name of any person who is a director of the body corporate on that date*;

(e)   the name of any other person who has, at any time during the financial year in question, been a charity trustee of the [reporting] charity;

(f)   *the name of any person who is a trustee for the [reporting] charity on the date [of approval of the report]e*;

(g)   *the name of any other person who has, at any time during the financial year in question, been a trustee for the [reporting] charity ...*'.

– SI 2008/629, reg 40(3) and reg 41(3)

Where the trustees number more than the SORP limit of 50 *as at the date of signing the report*, reg 40(5)(a) and 41(5)(a) limit the requirement of (d) above to the names of any 50 of them, so long as this includes every *current* 'officer of the charity'. This means what the SORP calls 'office-holders': Chair, Secretary (unless a *non-trustee*), Treasurer, etc.

Note also the separate requirements for disclosure of the names of all:

(i)   *charity trustees of* the charity; and

(ii)   trustees *for* the charity, as well as the careful distinction (not new) between the date of signing the report and the financial year being reported on – which can normally have ended up to 10 months before that, longer if the filing deadline has been extended on request.

The words we have emphasised distinguish:

(i)   the *charity trustees*, as the persons who have the legal responsibility for managing and controlling the charity, from

(ii)   other persons holding charity assets – which comprises a number of categories that had not been specified by the original 1995 Regulations.

The nearest they came was in the requirements of reg 10(2)(g) of the 1995 Regulations concerning *'any assets held by the charity, or on behalf of the charity by any trustee of the charity, for another charity'* – so as to distinguish any custodian trusteeship holdings from the charity's own holdings of assets.

The Regulations would therefore now seem to require the following kinds of person (individual or body corporate) – if different from (i) – to be considered and perhaps disclosed as trustees *for* the reporting charity in some way or other:

– 'holding' or custodian trustees (normally applies only to land holdings, the most obvious example being the Official Custodian for Charities – the Commission's own land-holding service for the sector – as a 'safe haven' in any case where both the charity and its trustee-body are unincorporated and conveyancing costs would otherwise have to be incurred to satisfy any incoming trustee);

– nominees (normally only for convenience in dealing with investment securities);

– the charity trustees of a 'special trust' or of any other subsidiary charity included within the reporting charity's *entity* accounts as required by the 1993 Act; and

– anyone else in possession of property (funds) belonging to the charity – whether or not this is with the charity's agreement (eg funds raised for the charity by a 'friends group') or, perhaps having arisen from some legal claim against them of which the charity is or should be aware, whether it is only because they are accountable to it as a 'trustee for the charity' *in that respect* (eg unauthorised private benefits obtained by somebody legally entitled to appoint and remove a majority of the charity trustees – apart from the Charity Commission itself, of course, which as a public body exercising judicial functions would not have to be named here).

Prior to 2005, the SORP mentioned only 'custodian trustees' in this connection, which the glossary definition then amplified by saying that the term *'includes ... any other non-executive trustee in whose name property belonging to the charity is held'*. This is now, in the interests of clarity, turned the other way round in SORP 2005. It refers specifically to 'trustees of the charity' and 'trustees for the charity' – with Glossary definition GL 59 explaining that the latter term includes a custodian trustee.

The SORP thus now makes it clearer that the disclosure requirement (as before) is for accounting information to be provided to the reporting charity's trustees by (effectively) *any* other person holding property (ie funds) on its behalf.

It is interesting to note that reg 40(3)(i) and 41(3)(i), as quoted above, seem to narrow down the intended meaning of the SORP's paragraph 44(b) by making the disclosure mandatory only in respect of appointors/nominators of trustees of *trust funds*. This would mean *all* the trusts, of course, where the reporting charity includes 'restricted' funds. But the use of the word 'trusts' does mean that this *obligation* cannot strictly apply to a charitable company *itself* – even where, as an exception, it has directors appointed by some external body or individual rather than by the company's members.

On the other hand, disclosure of the name of the trustee-appointor *is* mandatory where a *trust fund* for which the company is accountable within its entity accounts empowers somebody other than the company to administer that fund as a charity trustee of it. This must catch any special trusts that are not administered solely by the company itself. Less commonly, it would also catch other subsidiary charities (as determined by the Charity Commission) where the company has only majority – as distinct from total – board control.

It is also noteworthy that reg 40(3)(i) and 41(3)(i) provide statutory underpinning for the SORP's recommendation to disclose the *method of appointment* prescribed – but only where this is provided for as a *term of trust* on which that fund is administered.

A further point to note is the requirement of reg 40(3)(d) and 41(3)(d) above, mirroring what the SORP now wants to know about *all* corporate trustees (in contrast to the original 1995 SORP's interest, which was only in companies acting as *sole* trustee):

> '... where any charity trustee disclosed is a body corporate, the names of the directors of the body corporate on that date.'
>
> – *SORP 2005, paragraph 41(d)*

The intention is clearly to force out into the open the identity of the *individuals* currently (ie as at the date of signing the annual report) in ultimate control of the charity, which can all too easily be hidden through the use of a series of corporate trustees. The inquiring reader would otherwise have needed to search other databases such as the Companies Registry for the required information – hopefully without a dead end at the point where the director is some overseas company. In other cases, too (eg that of an NHS trust), such information may not be easy to access by other means. This information does not seem to be required in relation to the financial year itself, however.

The Trustee and the Board of Governors

The sole trustee (the 'Trustee') of the Wellcome Trust is The Wellcome Trust Limited, a company limited by guarantee (registration number 2711000), whose registered office is 215 Euston Road, London NW1 2BE ... The directors of the Trustee (known as Governors) ... are shown on pages 72 to 74.

... The incumbent Governors make appointments to the Board of Governors, after advertisement and wide consultation.

The Wellcome Trust – 2007/08 Annual Report

The pioneering use of a non-charitable company in this way, established many decades ago, to administer an unincorporated charity as sole corporate trustee, is noteworthy and now beneficially adopted by many charities. Unless they exceed their company's powers, these 'Governors' are protected by company law from the unlimited personal financial liability involved in running such a gigantic charitable trust, since the company itself is the only 'person' regarded by charity law as the 'charity trustee' – not its officers (unlike a *charitable* company).

Charity Commission dispensation from all these 'personal identification' disclosures is provided for by reg 40(4) and 41(4) as a necessary protection where it is considered that such disclosure could lead to trustees or their (external) nominators/appointors being placed in 'personal danger'. The SORP makes similar specific provision (at paragraph 42) for non-disclosure in order to guard against any such danger to the charity's *executive staff* whose names would otherwise be given as a matter of best practice under paragraph 41(f).

For a *charitable company*, this protection given by the SORP's Regulations cannot stop the statutory particulars of its directors and company secretary being accessed from the

Companies Registry database – even in cases where advantage is taken of the abbreviated filing options available for small companies in order to avoid filing a directors' report.

The SORP no longer asks specifically for the (non-mandatory) disclosure of any *sub-committees* of which a trustee is a member. Instead, paragraph 44(d) of SORP 2005 (dealing with the charity's *organisational structure* (which the Regulations *do* require to be disclosed if the charity exceeds the statutory audit threshold)) also wants to know 'how decisions are made' – but this, too, is a non-mandatory requirement. However, as the principles and practices of corporate governance spread to charity reporting, as a matter of best practice in the interests of transparency the largest charities tend to list any significant committees on which the reporting trustees rely, together with their terms of reference and their membership. We take a closer look at the disclosure of such committees at **4.4.7**, this being an aspect of the *internal* organisational, or management, structure of the reporting charity, as well as at trustee-recruitment and training, these being further aspects of governance for larger charities where the disclosure requirements in SORP 2005 are also underpinned by the Regulations of 2008.

'Place of business'

4.3.4 Many charities are located in the *virtual* rather than the physical world, having no actual address of their own, thus operating on a 'shoestring' for economy's sake. Their administration is through periodical meetings of the trustees in some convenient location (perhaps even on the Internet – as long as they can all see and communicate with each other directly, as with video-conferencing facilities), with the accounting and other records kept at the home of one of them and all charitable activities delegated to volunteers working wherever the need is to be found. For larger charities, it is normally more efficient to centralise these functions in some *physical* location as a 'business' address or HQ.

It is this address – or the main one, if they have several of them (plus, of course, any *other* address registered at Companies House) – that the 2008 Regulations, in line with paragraph 41(c) of SORP 2005, continue to require:

> '(c) the principal address of the [reporting] charity and, in the case of a charitable company, the address of its registered office.'

– SI 2008/629, reg 40(3) and reg 41(3)

This is subject to the same dispensation provision as discussed above for the names of the charity trustees, etc, and with the same proviso for a charitable company's *registered office* – which, however, can always be made the address of a confidential professional adviser or other 'correspondent' in order to minimise any risks arising from easy public accessibility.

On the Register of Charities, including the Internet version, it is – for the reason given above – the charity's designated 'correspondent' that is the common feature, whose address then determines which of the Charity Commission's three operational offices normally deals with the charity. The Commission imposes no rules as to who may be so designated, but does make it clear that all correspondence will normally be addressed to that person in the first instance. And that address can obviously be given as the charity's 'principal' address if it has no other.

Custodian holdings for other charities

4.3.5   Having covered at **4.3.3** the requirement to disclose the names of those acting as custodian trustee(s) for the reporting charity, we also need to look at the relatively unusual situation where the charity (or any of its trustees – but, interestingly enough, not any of its *subsidiaries* in the case of a *group* report) is looking after the assets of another *publicly accountable* charity. SORP 2005 covers this only at the end of its section on trustees' reports as an afterthought, but its close affinity with the administrative disclosures discussed above may be inferred from the regulatory requirement.

The Regulations have been greatly extended here from those of 2000 (which had remained unchanged from 1995, and which had applied only to charities above the statutory audit threshold) to require the following disclosure:

> '... a description of any assets held by the [reporting] charity or by any charity trustee of, or trustee for, the charity, on behalf of another charity, and particulars of any special arrangements made with respect to the safe custody of such assets and their segregation from assets of the charity not so held and a description of the objects of the charity on whose behalf the assets are held.'
>
> – *SI 2008/629, reg 40(3)(r) and reg 41(3)(r)*

For all charities, however small, it is thus mandatory to disclose these details, which SORP 2005 at paragraph 59 in much the same words deems to be 'best practice', where *any* custodian activities are undertaken for another charity.

NARRATIVE INFORMATION

4.4   In the preamble to SORP 2000, the Charity Commission, as the SORP-issuing body, had summarised how the narrative reporting recommendations had been changed since the 1995 SORP:

> 'The detailed requirements for narrative information (as distinct from legal and administrative information) have been reduced in order to encourage charities to expand on their activities and the achievement of their objectives, rather than answer a series of questions.'

In the light of experience since then, SORP 2005 seems to have turned the clock back by reverting to the 1995 SORP's more prescriptive approach – only now with a special emphasis on the topical areas of 'governance' and performance-reporting. We look at the practicalities of each of these major innovations in turn, along with older policy-disclosures where problems can arise from the SORP's enhancements: charity reserves and investment- and beneficiary-selection.

Whereas the 1993 Act merely outlines the statutory requirement for an annual report by the charity trustees, its specification is to be found in the detailed 'Charities (Accounts and Reports) Regulations' now made by the Office for the Third Sector under that Act to underpin each new version of the SORP. These Regulations comprise (in theory, at least) those SORP recommendations that are officially considered to be *minimum* requirements for the effective regulation of the sector in the public interest.

But since the SORP and its related Regulations have moved so much closer together than was thought possible in 1995, for compliance purposes it is nowadays easier to focus on what the Regulations require and then to consider what *else* the SORP requires, rather than the other way round.

Requirements for *all* charities

Reserves (level / justification / policy)

4.4.1   The Regulations require even the smallest[3] charity's trustees' report to include:

'a description of the policies (if any) which have been adopted by the charity trustees for the purpose of determining the level of reserves which it is appropriate for the charity to maintain in order to meet effectively the needs designated by its trusts, *together with details of the amount and purpose of any material commitments and planned expenditure not provided for in the balance sheet which have been deducted from the assets in the unrestricted fund of the charity in calculating the amount of reserves, and where no such policies have been adopted, a statement to this effect...*'.

– SI 2008/629, reg 40(3)(p)

The equivalent regulation governing a *group* report to be prepared by a parent charity's trustees also highlights the extent to which any reserves held by the rest of the group impact on the *parent* charity's reserves policy:

'(p)   where the charity trustees have adopted policies for the purpose of determining the level of reserves which it is appropriate to maintain in order to meet effectively the needs designated by its trusts, (i) a description of those policies *including in particular whether account has been taken of any reserves held by its subsidiary undertakings in determining the appropriate level of reserves*; (ii) details of the amount and purpose of any material commitments and planned expenditure not provided for in the balance sheet which have been deducted from the assets in the unrestricted fund of the charity in calculating the amount of reserves;

(q)   [or if they haven't,] a statement that no such policies have been adopted'

– SI 2008/629, reg 41(3)(p)/(q)

To this minimum requirement, in which we have italicised what differs for a *group* report and in other cases what is *new* this time round, we must add, for best practice, the SORP's *further* recommendation (which is not new) that the report should more particularly state:

'... the level of reserves held and why they are held ...'.

– SORP 2005, paragraph 55(a)

The 'why', of course, can only really be informative where actual reserves greatly exceed the level set by the declared policy – which will have to be a reasonable one in all the circumstances if it is to satisfy the law. This is because a valid policy is itself

---

3   In practice, only in exceptional circumstances could this impact on a *very* small charity within the 'light touch' regulatory regime – e g one whose activities out of income from a substantial endowed investment portfolio may have been artificially depressed by one-sidedly investing for capital gains to the detriment of current beneficiaries. By specially requesting the filing of the charity's annual accounts and trustees' report, the Charity Commission would then be able to enforce this particular disclosure as a means of highlighting the administrative problem with a view to its correction.

the explanation in all other cases. As a special case, many a well-endowed charity has no need of reserves where the trustees have a constitutional power to convert capital into income at will. If their policy is to do so year by year to fund income-deficits on their charitable activities, it will be useful (even though not mandatory) to say so as the *reason* why the charity has no reserves policy, the bald fact of which will be disclosable under the above regulation in each case.

Only if reserves cannot be contained within reasonable limits, but continue to climb despite reworking the trustees' strategic plan for the charity's future activities and setting up the necessary *designated funds* to ensure that those activities will not be under-funded, is it then 'best practice' to go further than the regulatory requirement and comment on why the excess is being carried forward and (by implication) what steps the trustees are taking to remedy the situation.

This was exemplified by the classic case of *Bridge House Estates* at one time, until the trustees were able to obtain a Charity Commission Scheme to widen the charity's Objects beyond the archaic aim of keeping the City of London's bridges in good order (instead of this being undertaken by the State, as is normal elsewhere), thus unbottling millions of pounds in excess reserves built up over decades to be put to good use at last for the wider benefit of the local community.

Thus we should note that the *statutory* disclosure is of the *policy* only (or that there is none) – not of the facts and figures themselves, the *materiality* of which will be critical for the extent of any required *best practice* disclosure in the annual accounts for a true and fair view. On the other hand, as a matter of best practice to comply with the SORP, both the actual and desired level of reserves, as well as the reasoning behind the policy and what is being done by way of reserves-management, would need to be disclosed.

Similarly, the statutory disclosure of the amounts and purposes of any *designated funds* for unaccrued expenditure commitments and intentions, which is an interesting way of drawing public attention to them as 'committed reserves' (in view of their obvious susceptibility to manipulation if trustees are hard-pressed to minimise their 'free reserves'), neither calls for the timescale envisaged for spending those designated funds nor does it include funds already tied up in fixed assets held for the charity's own use. The latter two disclosures, being 'best practice' items under SORP 2005, are thus likely to feature as a regulatory matter only in exceptional circumstances.

It will often be possible to meet the minimum requirement here in a few brief words – or just to declare 'none' if the trustees have not yet formulated a policy, perhaps because in their own charity's situation the very idea of 'reserves' is a mere pipe dream: not an uncommon situation for 'trading' charities and those that have to depend on statutory funding to finance ongoing 'community benefit' provision. Common sense suggests that an actual 'policy' needs to be thought out, and therefore reported, *only* where the charity has (or can reasonably expect to achieve within the near future) reserves that are *financially significant* in relation to its year-on-year activities.

The need to say *why* charity funds are being held in reserve, and to *justify* the amount so retained, has long been highlighted by the Charity Commission. May 1997 saw the publication of its comprehensive guidance leaflet on the subject: CC19 *Charities' Reserves*, following a thorough public airing in a Consultation Draft. Chapter 10 goes into the practical details of *how* to establish a reserves policy. Here, we are concerned only with how that policy should be presented. The following extract is taken from one of the six SORP 2005 worked examples commissioned from the sector at that time for website publication and downloading along with the SORP itself:

Reserves policy

The trustees have established the level of reserves (that is those funds that are freely available) that the charity ought to have. Reserves are needed to bridge the funding gaps between spending on productions and events and receiving resources through admission charges and grants that provide funding. Reserves are also held to cover possible emergency repairs to the theatre and other expenditure. In addition, short term reserves will also be needed to sustain operations over the period when it is anticipated that some of the income generating activities may be curtailed temporarily whilst the anticipated redevelopment project at ACT Park is carried out. The trustees therefore consider that the ideal level of reserves as at 31st March 2006 would be £500,000, reducing to £400,000 at March 2007.

The actual reserves at 31st March 2006 were £380,000, which is £120,000 short of our target figure of £500,000. In calculating reserves, the trustees have excluded from total funds the restricted income funds (£12,000), tangible fixed assets (£830,000), and the designated development fund (£167,000) which is required either as funding should the redevelopment of ATC Park go ahead or for essential smaller scale changes should the grant application be unsuccessful. We anticipate that this designation will be expended within a 2 year period in line with development plans ...

Annual Report – 'Arts Theatre Trust Limited'

This illustration from ActionAid's 2007 Annual Report is of strict compliance with the SORP's requirements in speaking about the reserves of the company's unspent trust funds (ie its restricted funds – see the illustration at 4.4.12) as well as (here) those of its corporate (ie 'unrestricted' funds):

RESERVES POLICY

Our supporters give us money with the expectation that we deliver on our vision – so we take care not to hold excessive funds.

Our policy is to hold unrestricted funds sufficient to cover three months' UK expenditure. This provides us with both the cash to run our day-to-day business, and a certain amount of insulation from unanticipated shocks. On this basis we were slightly over at £4.3 million (target £4.2 million) at the end of 2007.

ActionAid's trustees judge that this is the correct level in the context of reserves held elsewhere in ActionAid International (please see financial review for ActionAid International for more details).

Most restricted funds are passed directly to ActionAid International Secretariat. Some funds, mostly from the EU, are managed by ActionAid. To the extent that such income has been received but not spent at the year end, this will show as restricted reserves and will be spent in the following year.

At the year end, four EU-funded projects showed a deficit balance exceeding £10,000 – the total of all deficit balances totalled £346,000. Fund balances can be➡

> in deficit when expenditure is made on a project that is expected to be reimbursed by the European Union, but at the end of the financial year not all the conditions have been met that would justify this income being recognised within the accounts. The trustees are satisfied that the likelihood of reimbursement is sufficient to justify carrying the deficit fund balances at the end of the year for all projects.

ActionAid – 2007 Annual Report and Accounts

Oxfam's Annual Report illustrates how the disclosure of reserves policy, level and justification can more usefully be set in the context of the charity's *non-reserve* funds:

Reserves Policy

The Council of Trustees has established a general Reserves Policy to protect the organisation and its charitable programme by providing time to adjust to changing financial circumstances. This limits the risk of disruption to the programme in the event of a downturn in some of Oxfam's various sources of income, or an unexpected need for additional expenditure. The Policy also provides parameters for future strategic plans and contributes towards decision-making. Oxfam's Reserves Policy establishes an appropriate target range for the level of general reserves; the target range for 2007/08 was established as between £33 million and £37 million. The range is based on a risk assessment of the probability and likely impact on Oxfam's charitable programme that might be caused by a decline in income, an inability to meet financial obligations, or an inability to reduce expenditure in the immediate short term. The Policy ensures a balance between spending the maximum amount of income raised as soon as possible after receipt, while maintaining the minimum level of reserves to ensure uninterrupted operation. The Policy and the target range are reviewed annually to reassess the risks and reflect changes in Oxfam's income, financial obligations and expenditure. The risks surrounding the pension liability have been taken into consideration when calculating the target range. Since Oxfam is confident that it can meet the required pension contributions from projected future income without significantly impacting on its planned level of charitable activity, it continues to calculate its 'free' or general reserves without setting aside designated reserves to cover the pension liability. We comment on this year's reserves performance below.

General Reserves (unrestricted)

General reserves are not restricted or designated for use on a particular programme – or for some other defined or designated purpose. General reserves decreased by £4.0 million during 2007/08, with the balance of general reserves being £44.6 million by the end of April 2008. This decrease reflects the planned increase in unrestricted programme activity during 2007/08, which was planned given the high level of general reserves brought forward into the year (caused by several one-off income streams in 2005/06). Our intention is still to bring general reserves back into the target range of £33 million to £37 million by the end of April 2009 by once again allowing unrestricted programme expenditure to exceed unrestricted income during 2008/09. General reserves are represented by net current assets and are equivalent to just over three months' unrestricted expenditure at 2007/08 levels.   ➡

Pension Reserves (unrestricted)
The valuation of Oxfam's pension scheme at 30 April 2008, for the purposes of FRS17, showed a funding deficit of £13.0 million (2006/07: £20.1m), (see Note 20d). This deficit represents the difference between the liabilities of the pension fund and the value of its underlying assets; it does not represent an immediate cash commitment, as the cash flow required to meet the £13.0 million deficit relates to future pension contributions. The valuation of the pension scheme's assets under FRS17 is different from the triennial actuarial valuation, which determines the pension contributions required to reduce the deficit. Current financial projections indicate that Oxfam will be able to make these contributions as they fall due. FRS17 requires a pension reserve to be established to meet the pension deficit. The defined benefit pension scheme was closed to new members during 2002/03.

Designated Funds (unrestricted)
Designated funds are those unrestricted funds that have been allocated by the Trustees for particular purposes. The Designated Fund for Fixed Assets of £14.1 million (2006/07: £14.9m) represents resources invested in the charity's fixed assets (excluding investments), that are, therefore, not available for other purposes. The retained profits of the microcredit scheme in Azerbaijan, which totalled £0.9 million at the end of April 2008 and whose accounts have been consolidated for the first time, have been set aside in a designated fund, as they are only available for use in Azerbaijan. Further details of the Designated funds and their movements during the year are shown in Note 19 of the accounts.

Restricted funds
These funds are tied to particular purposes, as specified by the donor or as identified at the time of a public appeal. They are not available for use in other Oxfam work. At the year-end, unspent restricted funds were £27.4 million (2006/07: £24.5m). The largest restricted fund balance of £4.7 million (2006/07: £7.5m) relates to Oxfam Unwrapped, which primarily represents income from the Christmas catalogue, which, in line with our policy, we intend to spend by April 2009, the end of the following accounting year. The restricted fund balance includes total deficit balances of £10.4 million. These deficit balances have arisen on projects where total expenditure has exceeded income; it is expected that the expenditure will be reimbursed by a government or other agency in the following accounting year (see Note 18 for further details).

Endowment Funds
Endowment funds of £2.7 million (2006/07: £2.6m) represent monies received from donors where there is some restriction on the use of the capital (see Note 17).

Financial Position
The Council of Trustees considers that there are sufficient reserves held at the year-end to allow the organisation to manage any disruption in the event of a downturn in future income, and that there is a reasonable expectation that Oxfam has adequate resources to continue in operational existence for the foreseeable future. For this reason, the Council of Trustees continues to adopt the 'going concern' basis in preparing the accounts.

Fund-deficits; subsidiaries with negative reserves

4.4.2   One of the consequences of the separate reporting of a charity's reserves is that the SORP no longer asks (as it did in 1995) for a fund-by-fund commentary on the ready availability and adequacy of the charity's assets in relation to its obligations, but instead only requires the annual report to disclose:

> 'where any fund is materially in deficit, the circumstances giving rise to the deficit and details of the steps being taken to eliminate the deficit.'
>
> – *SORP 2005, paragraph 55(b)*

We quoted from the annual report and accounts of ActionAid at **4.4.1** to illustrate the disclosure of reserves, which also provides an illustration of the disclosure of Restricted Fund deficits.

The important point to note here out of that illustration is, of course, how these deficits are covered by the charity's corporate reserves. It should be noted in general that this disclosure requirement does not refer only to a charity's *restricted* funds: it refers even more urgently to its unrestricted funds – where, for obvious reasons, the explanation of how the deficit arose would have to cover any implied *breach of trust*.

The related Regulations, however, do not ask for the 'why'. They also effectively defer to the *following* financial year the duty to disclose how the trustees have dealt with any new deficit, in that it only says that the trustees' report must:

> 'where any fund of the charity was in deficit at the beginning of the relevant financial year and the charity is one in respect of which a *statement of accounts has been prepared under section 42(1) of the 1993 Act* for the financial year, contain particulars of the steps taken by the charity trustees to eliminate that deficit.' [*Authors' emphasis*]
>
> – *SI 2008/629, reg 40(2)(c)(i)*

The exemption thus provided for:

(i)   *non-company* charities whose trustees (validly) opt for a receipts and payments accounting basis; and

(ii)   charitable companies (which in any case have no such option),

is an interesting one. The implication of (i) is that the Charity Commission will either require the filing of a separate receipts and payments account for each distinct charitable trust fund administered by those trustees or else will ignore any breach of trust arising in such a small charity, since it must (by definition) be immaterial for regulatory purposes. The implication of (ii) is even more interesting: the Commission can hardly be seen to ignore a material breach of trust by a charitable company as trustee of its trust funds, so could it be that separate accounts will be required in future for a charitable company's (a) corporate funds and (b) trust funds (if any)? That needs only a minor amendment to s 97(1) of the 1993 Act to exclude charitable companies from its references to 'charity' in defining a 'special trust' – or, more alarmingly, the major charity law reform hinted at by the Cabinet Office Strategy Unit in its 2002 Report, which at the time promised in connection with the proposed introduction of a completely new corporate form of charity (the Charitable Incorporated Organisation, 'CIO') that charitable company status 'would remain available for at least the next 5 years'.

Regardless of such regulatory indulgences, however, the earliest possible reporting of fund inadequacies of this kind is vitally important to the Commission as regulator. Surprising as it may seem, though, this is not out of concern for the solvency of the *charity*, since that is considered basically a private matter for the trustees to work out with their creditors.

Where a *group* report has to be prepared by the trustees under reg 41 of the SORP's related 2008 Regulations, ie, to accompany mandatory *group consolidated* accounts, in addition to the above fund-deficit disclosure requirements the trustees also have to highlight any subsidiary with *materially negative reserves*. Reg 41 says the report must:

'(d)   where any fund of the parent charity was in deficit at the beginning of the financial year in question, contain particulars of the steps taken by the charity trustees to eliminate that deficit;

(e)   where the total of capital and reserves in any of the parent charity's subsidiary undertakings was materially in deficit at the beginning of the financial year, contain particulars of the steps taken by the relevant undertaking or undertakings to eliminate that deficit.'

– SI 2008/629, reg 41(2)(d)/(e)

Charity solvency is not, of itself, a matter of public interest – but rather of prime concern to (apart from existing creditors, of course) an intending donor. Once a charity's funds are fully spent, it can have no further activity (other than out of the trustees' own resources, ultimately speaking). It has then 'ceased to exist', and in the case of a *registered* charity, its trustees are duty-bound to notify the Charity Commission to enable it to be 'removed' from the public Register of Charities. That is all there is to it – assuming its funds to have been 'properly applied' to further its declared Objects, of course.

The Commission's real concern must be the risk of loss resulting from any *breach of trust* caused by the unauthorised use of a 'restricted' fund for purposes falling outside its own Objects – for example, by means of 'internal borrowing' from the fund's liquid assets (cash and investments) to cover a deficit on another – perhaps even the reporting charity's general-purposes – fund.

A famous case in point here was that of *War on Want* (1991), where an unrecognised solvency situation had subsequently deteriorated almost to the point of collapse before the charity found rescue through a Charity Commission investigation which led to a £400,000 out-of-court payment to the charity by its ex-auditors to settle a negligence claim.

A less obvious scenario is where, within a key fund of the charity, short-term liabilities are inappropriately 'matched' with long-term (ie 'fixed') assets held for the charity's own use – thus leading to the potential insolvency of that fund unless remedial action can be taken in good time.

A deficit can also arise where responses to an appeal launched for some special project lag behind the urgency of the work to be done. As long as there is reasonable certainty that subsequent appeal income will cover the year-end deficit and that in the meantime it is fully covered by available reserves, it can quite properly be left unfunded in the accounts, with the situation briefly explained in the trustees' report and (preferably) also in the accounts notes.

One of the Commission's main concerns has always been to see that the required *separate administration* of distinct charitable funds under trust law is properly reflected in the way the trustees account for all the funds under their control, and more particularly that the liquidity of each such fund can be seen to be adequate to enable its obligations to be met as they fall due (one of the two primary tests of solvency).

Smaller charities only – 'activities and achievements'

4.4.3 With some 95% of all registered charities being below the current £500,000 statutory audit threshold, a strongly de-regulatory line continues to be taken here by the SORP's related Regulations, which require that the trustees' report shall:

> 'in the case of a charity which is not an auditable charity, be a brief summary setting out the main activities undertaken by the charity to further its charitable purposes for the public benefit; and the main achievements of the charity during the year;'
>
> – *SI 2008/629, reg 40(2)(b)(i)*

For the vast majority of charities, then, the trustees' report *can* be kept as 'short and sweet' as you like here – as long as it indicates *how* the year's activities are considered to have furthered the charity's declared Objects – noting that for financial years starting after 31 March 2008 the narrative reporting here will have to show *what public benefit is intended by these Objects* and the *appropriateness* of these activities and achievements to that end – and also *what* progress has been achieved in this direction.

The SORP itself helpfully distinguishes between smaller and larger charities for all its Annual Report requirements, though it still calls for *best practice* in *everything* – even from the smallest. However, it would be more realistic to focus on matters of interest to such a charity's closest stakeholders rather than the general public: you will then be able to skip over the remaining sections of this chapter dealing with the requirements for charities above the statutory audit threshold.

For example, among the many tens of thousands of smaller unincorporated *membership association* charities all over the country are a great number for whom the preparation of a statutory annual report by their management committee just to satisfy the strict requirements of the Regulations was felt to impose an unacceptable burden even in 1995. In response to popular request at the time, the Charity Commission agreed to accept AGM minutes as a form of annual report for filing with the annual accounts of such charities – so long as the necessary legal and administrative information is included. An illustration of this format of the annual report is included in Appendix 8.

In this respect, what needs to be explained is primarily the *expenditure* of the smaller charity's resources, and *why* these resources have been expended (ie, how the intended public benefit provision is being aimed for, thus meeting the new requirement of the Charities Act 2006 for *all* charities to demonstrate that they are set up *for public benefit*, even if the hoped-for delivery of such benefit is still only a reasonable expectation of ultimate success) – or else why they are still being retained as reserves.

Activities undertaken to provide public benefit in furtherance of the charity's Objects are therefore the primary consideration here. Other activities (or part-activities) undertaken 'merely' *to generate resources* (ie in appealing for gifts; in raising revenues by levying fees/charges for the charitable services provided; the same for 'ancillary' trading activities; in holding charity lotteries and conducting 'fundraising' trading as permitted by law) may be vital for the charity's *future viability*. But insofar as these are merely *ways and means of funding* (refinancing) the charity such revenue-raising activities can only really be of secondary interest in charity reporting.

For a charity below the audit threshold, then, their reporting is not a statutory requirement, since such *fund-generating* will be of interest for meeting the public benefit test only if done *in relation to the charity's Objects* – which will only be the case for dual-purpose activities, as where a public appeal, for example, aims to increase public awareness of beneficiary needs as well as soliciting donations to meet those needs. That is conceptually difficult, because of the legal view that 'fundraising' as such is *not* a *charitable* activity.

It therefore misses the point entirely if trustees merely comment here on the year's gross and net 'results', with the mistaken idea that they can safely follow what has become standard practice for directors' reports to a company's shareholders.

Larger charities – other narrative reporting requirements

Organisational structure

4.4.4 Reg 40(3)(k) (as qualified by reg 40(7) exempting charities below the statutory audit threshold), or – in the case of a group report – reg 41(3)(k) for both the parent charity and its subsidiaries, requires *larger* charities to describe their '*organisational structure*' as another of those disclosures that in SORP 2005 are 'encouraged as a matter of good practice' for *all* charities – but which are likely to excite little public interest below the audit threshold.

There are actually two complementary aspects of 'organisational structure' envisaged by the SORP. The *management* structure will *always* need to be described by the larger charity, as it is *mandatory*. The other aspect is the *constitutional* structure of the reporting charity, which (in general) may have:

(a)   charity 'branches' (or 'subsidiary charities') making up either the 'entity' or else the 'group' for the purposes of the reporting trustees' statutory public accountability; and/ or

(b)   *non-charitable* subsidiary 'undertakings' (limited companies, normally) within a group structure headed by itself as 'parent' undertaking.

In **4.4.4.2** we look at (a) under the heading of *organisational (branch) structure*, and in **4.4.4.3** we look at (b) under *connected (group) non-charitable bodies*. In **4.4.4.4** we then contrast the SORP's (again, non-statutory) requirements for the disclosure of information on other (ie non-group) connected organisations.

Management structure and 'governance'

4.4.4.1   In *management* terms, the required description of the 'organisational structure' should, above all, include:

(a)   how the reporting charity is organised for its ongoing operational work (in effect, an outline of the 'chain of command'), naming any major departmental divisions and their (top) managers responsible to the trustee-body;

(b)   to what extent the reporting trustees have *delegated* any of their powers, identifying the persons/bodies concerned and indicating how the necessary management control is then exercised; and

(c)   trustee-recruitment and training requirements, indicating the policies and procedures in place for ensuring 'good governance'.

The relatively new disclosure in (c), the only specifically mandatory one out of the three, will surely enhance the quality of governance-*reporting* by charities – even if not their actual governance. The requirement is clearly justified in respect of remunerated trustees and also those appointed as having relevant professional skills, but it may also need to be tempered by consideration of the implications of the 'voluntary principle' for charity trusteeship which the Government still seeks to maintain through the 2006 Charities Act's carefully worded provision for statutory authority to allow a minority of a charity's trustees to be remunerated for 'non-trustee' services.

If no distinction is to be made between the standard of care that can reasonably be expected of remunerated/professional trustees and genuinely volunteer trustees, the many charities for good causes without popular appeal must find it harder to attract new trustees. This is exacerbated by the requirement of reg 40/41(3)(j) for:

> 'a description of the policies and procedures (if any) which have been adopted by the charity trustees for the induction and training of charity trustees, and where no such policies have been adopted a statement to this effect.'
>
> – *SI 2008/629, reg 40(3)(j) and reg 41(3)(j)*

Requiring a 'nil' disclosure here could possibly be seen as implying that without such formalities charity trustees are incompetent, thus incapable of equipping themselves with the information needed to fulfil their duties. The argument that governance 'problems' detract from a charity's 'enterprise' and 'quality commitment' for lack of appropriate trustee skills, knowledge and expertise does presuppose a certain type of charity: a service-provider funded by Government either through procurement contracts or performance-related grant control agreements.

Most auditable charities do not seem to fall into that category. For them, the argument does not stand up to scrutiny – especially where the charity uses investment returns to finance grant-making for a variety of good causes, but also where it competes in the market place to provide public benefit.

In any case, the largest of them (certainly the top 700 or so above £10m gross income or £100m gross assets) will already have well-developed governance 'policies and procedures' to meet their own particular needs – albeit often subject to membership representation constraints that impede board recruitment on a skills-only basis. For this reason, the extension of the disclosure requirements here from trustee-selection powers to trustee-recruitment and -training ought perhaps to have discriminated between those charities that do need to make such disclosures in order to satisfy their 'stakeholders' (ie any principal funding bodies) and those that don't.

The inverse of commercial corporate governance

Charity 'governance', as an import from the corporate sector, has slowly but surely taken root here since the initial enthusiasm with which it was greeted a decade or so ago. The reason for the slowness may have been that, for charities, the governance issue is the *inverse* of the problem identified in the Cadbury Report. Charity law generally prohibits all 'trustee benefits' not provided for by the charity's founder in keeping with the public-benefit purpose intrinsic to charity. Charity Commission registration procedures routinely query trustee-benefit arrangements of any kind. While the Commission does nowadays accept the argument for charities to be able to remunerate some of their trustees in certain cases, these have so far mostly been confined to situations where professionals/specialists are needed for *decision-making*, as distinct from just advising the Board. Even then, the general rule, as now incorporated into the provisions of the Charities Act 2006 in this area, is that the governing document must restrict trustee remuneration to a *minority* of the trustees at all times, with adequate 'conflict-of-interests' protocols in place to protect the charity and its work from detriment. This severely cautious official attitude is to guard against the risk of the charity's 'public interest' aims being somehow outweighed by the trustees' *private* interests. The 'golden rule' in the charity sector is that any unavoidable private benefit must be seen to be only 'incidental' to the public benefit requirement on which charitable status is judged.

Solving the governance problem

Charity trustees are normally all *non-executive* volunteers, for whom *special authority* is then needed for their charity to be able to pay them at all. For this reason s 66 of the 1993 Act modifies company law to make any subsequent authorisation of the provision of such benefits by a charitable company conditional on prior written consent from the Charity Commission. The 'rule of thumb' here, under charity law prior to the Charities Act 2006, has been that trustee remuneration not already authorised in the governing document must be specially justified to the Charity Commission so that the regulator's consent can be obtained before the remuneration can safely be paid. As it is normal for the trustees of larger charities, being largely unpaid, to be 'non-executive' in any case, the governance issue for charities has been not perhaps whether non-executive trustees are prevented from being active but rather whether they themselves may have adopted too passive a role by relying on delegation to their paid staff/agents without maintaining adequate controls over the exercise of such delegated powers.

As an alternative to bringing paid executives onto the Board of Trustees, charities with a large workforce and management structure have traditionally appointed some of the trustees to sit on special-purpose sub-committees alongside non-trustee executives – or they have delegated tasks completely to non-trustee executives/agents. The Independent Schools sector is a prime example here, with all the day-to-day management normally delegated to the Head – or perhaps Head and Bursar.

The 'voluntary' principle of charity trusteeship

The general principle followed in Charity Commission Leaflet CC11: *'Remuneration of Charity Trustees'* is that donated charity funds (including funds derived from them) should not be arbitrarily diverted from the public benefit for which they were given. However, 'remuneration' as defined by the Charity Commission on the basis of existing charity law is much wider than the 'reward' proscribed by charity law. This suggests that for an effective and useful clarification of the issue in the context of modern society and its needs, our ideas of 'trustee-benefit' also need rethinking to exclude all trustee-remuneration that merely removes personal *dis*advantage to the trustee – as distinct from remuneration that confers personal *advantage* on the trustee. The first step in that direction, by the Cabinet Office Strategy Unit's 2002 recommendation that all charities should have a statutory power to remunerate their trustees for any 'non-trustee' services they may provide to meet the needs of the charity, led to specific provision for this being included in the Charities Act 2006, as we have already noted.

As new legislation affecting charities' activities – particularly those of a business nature – continues to increase in both weight and complexity (much of this seemingly in response to EC Directives) it increases the burden of legal responsibility resting on charity trustees beyond what to the ordinary person seems tolerable for volunteer activity. This must tend to shrink the pool of available volunteers having the personal skills needed to fulfil such an over-demanding role at their own expense and risk.

It is also only natural – given that the great majority of the 5,500 registered charities over £1m gross income are limited companies – that corporate governance concepts and the like will influence the sector's management structures more and more, which will tend to sharpen the distinctions (and thus the tensions) between paid *non-trustee* executives and unpaid *non-executive* trustees. The reliance – if not dependence – of the latter on the former is, in many cases, almost total. As the Charity Commission guidance on the subject ('Trustee Responsibilities'), has put it:

> 'Charity trustees should be selected for what they can contribute to the charity. They should not be appointed for their status or position in the community alone; this is the function of patrons. Charity trustees need to be prepared to take an active part in the running of the charity and therefore need to be able – and willing – to give time to the efficient administration of the charity and the fulfilment of its trusts. We recommend that they be selected on the basis of their relevant experience and skills.
>
> The growing awareness of the need for "stakeholder-representation" on the boards of decision-making bodies has frequently given rise to calls for the appointment of "staff-trustees", "user-trustees", and so on, as representatives of their class of "stakeholder". This has bolstered the argument for recompensing trustees for any personal disadvantage (loss of earnings, etc.) that may be entailed, especially where remuneration for non-trustee services provided to the charity, and which was entirely proper up to then, suddenly becomes an unauthorised personal benefit upon being appointed a trustee.'

As 'Trustee Responsibilities' went on to explain:

> 'Prospective trustees should consider whether there would be any possible conflicts of interest if they were to be appointed as a trustee. This is particularly important where personal interests may be significant enough to make it difficult for the individual concerned to make a full contribution to the trustees' discussions and decisions. We recommend that charities have arrangements in place for identifying and managing conflicts of interest and that all trustees are aware of these arrangements. Trustees should also be aware that some

transactions affected by a conflict of interest will be at risk of being invalid, unless they are authorised, either by the governing document of the charity or by an Order from us or the court.'

But there are also less personal kinds of conflict-of-interests situations to trip up the unwary. As an old version of 'Trustee Responsibilities' explained:

'Sometimes an individual is nominated by an outside organisation to be a trustee of a charity. The usual reason for this is to give a voice in running the charity to a member of a group which has an interest in its work, such as a user or a funder. For instance, some of the members of the committee of management of a village hall charity may be nominated by regular users of the hall such as a playgroup. The trustees of a recreation ground charity may include nominated trustees from sports clubs who use its playing fields. A local authority may want to nominate one or a number of trustees onto the governing body of a charity which operates in its area and for which it has provided funding.

... nominated trustees will need to be aware that having two roles may bring conflicting demands, especially where the nominated trustee is also a member of the outside organisation that nominates him or her. For instance a trustee nominated by the local authority will need to recognise that the interests of the charity and its beneficiaries may not be the same as those of the local authority and its tax- and rate-payers. It is not the role of the nominated trustee to represent the interests of the organisation which nominated him or her. All trustees must act solely in the best interests of the charity.

Where a potential conflict of interest for a trustee arises on a particular issue, he or she should not take part in the discussions or vote on that issue. For example if you are a local councillor and also a trustee of a charity which is negotiating the sale of land to the local authority for development, you should not vote on the issue and should withdraw from any meeting at which the proposed sale is considered. You may also need to consider, with the charity's legal advisers, whether on such a major issue we should be asked to authorise such a transaction. Without that authority, the presence on the trustee body of trustees with conflicts of interest may lead, in some circumstances, to the transaction being invalidated.'

What this superseded guidance didn't make clear enough at the time was that only where the conflict arises from a *personal* interest must you:

(i)   ensure equality of information on both sides of the transaction by declaring the other interest (as is also necessary even if that interest is only an *im*personal one), but also

(ii) absent yourself from all discussion and deciding of the matter, and either

(iii) account to the charity for any unauthorised personal benefit arising from the transaction, or (as the case may be)

(iv) make proper disclosure of any authorised benefit (citing its authority) in the charity's annual accounts.

Trustee-appointment/removal powers

An external person/body may have appointment and/or removal powers over a majority of the board of trustees to the extent that this amounts to a right to determine the composition of the board. This is then seen as bestowing a degree of 'control' that automatically entails a charity law obligation to account (ie to make restitution) to the charity for any unauthorised private profit or benefit derived from transactions with the charity – another trap for the unwary!

For completeness here, we should perhaps also note, in passing, the other ways a trustee may be removed from office. Quoting 'Trustee Responsibilities' again:

'The law disqualifies from continuing to be, or from becoming, a trustee those who:

- have been convicted at any time of any offence involving deception or dishonesty, unless the conviction is legally regarded as spent; or
- are bankrupt or, having made compositions or arrangements with their creditors, have not yet been discharged as such; or
- have at any time been removed by the Commissioners or by the court in England, Wales (or by the Court of Sessions in Scotland) from being a trustee because of misconduct; or
- are disqualified from being company directors; or
- are subject to an order made under s 429(2) (b) of the Insolvency Act 1986.'

Delegation of trustee-powers: the charity law 'duty of care'

As we have noted already, you can use sub-committees and audit committees to bridge over internal control gaps between non-executive trustees, executive staff and the membership of a charitable association, thus resolving perhaps otherwise intractable governance problems in the voluntary sector. Such delegation does not, however, release the trustees from their charity law duty of care in the absence of special authorisation (eg delegation of investment-selection powers under the Trustee Act 2000). It is merely a way of fulfilling that duty by 'remote control', due care being required over the selection of reliable and trustworthy persons to whom to delegate, with adequate controls and report-back procedures in place to monitor how well the delegated task is being performed. The Trustee Act 2000 ('TA 2000'), the example cited above, only protects trustees personally from any defaults by their investment managers where the delegation of investment decision-making is under a written control agreement and a written investment policy issued by the trustees and against which actual investment performance is regularly reported to them and reviewed by them.

'Internal Controls' as an aspect of governance

Internal controls are seen as an important aspect of corporate governance, with listed companies nowadays having to report annually on their compliance with Stock Exchange requirements in this area. This seems to have prompted the Charity Commission to follow suit in the Exposure Draft of SORP 2000 at the time, which had proposed to require the trustees' annual report to include 'a statement regarding the adequacy of internal controls'. On finalisation, however, that idea was dropped in favour of a broader 'corporate governance' statement on the mitigation (or 'management' in SORP 2005) of 'major risks'.

It remains to be seen to what extent the further development of Stock Exchange thinking and that of the authorities more generally on this subject – as exemplified by the 2003 *Smith Report* as well as the *'Combined Code'*, supplemented by the more voluminous *Higgs Report* (*'Review of the Role and Effectiveness of Non-Executive Directors'*) and then in June 2006 the Financial Reporting Council's issue of a revised version of the 2003 Combined Code in the light of its 2005 review and consultation: the

'*Combined Code on Corporate Governance*', compliance with which (following due process in the form of the usual public consultation) has since been made compulsory by the Financial Services Authority (as UK Listing Authority) under its statutory powers to make Listing Rules – will be able to continue to influence governance concepts in the *charity* sector.

The Smith Report recommended that Audit Committees should have:

- at least three independent non-executive directors;

- at least one member with significant, recent and relevant financial experience;

- its main role and responsibilities set out in writing.

It also recommended that these responsibilities should include:

- monitoring the integrity of the financial statements;

- reviewing significant financial reporting issues and significant judgments made;

- reviewing the company's internal control system and risk management systems;

- monitoring/reviewing the effectiveness of the company's internal audit function;

- making recommendations to the Board on external auditor appointments;

- agreeing the external auditors' remuneration and terms of engagement;

- monitoring the external auditors' independence, effectiveness and objectivity;

- implementing a policy on the external auditors supplying non-audit services.

The key points of the Higgs Report were:

- a wider pool of available non-executive directors (NEDs) is needed;

- the role of NEDs should be clearer;

- a Chief Executive should not be made Chairman of a company;

- major shareholders should have a right to meet with NEDs;

- better training should be provided for NEDs.

The first of the Higgs recommendations is considered extremely relevant to the charity sector, where the feeling – certainly on the part of the Charity Commission – is to get away from the old tendency for trustee boards either to be recruited from among the board members' close personal connections or else to be elected on a popularity vote of the charity's membership – in both cases often with little regard to the spread of skills that may be needed for the most effective administration of the charity. Therefore 'skills audits' and 'trustee-competencies' are among the current buzz-words in the sector.

The third recommendation is relevant here only because it was implemented in July 2004 at the Charity Commission itself, where the post of Chief Charity Commissioner was then split into two: a part-time Chair of the Board of Commissioners, recruited from the sector (currently Dame Susie Leather), and a full-time Civil Service career post of Chief Executive (Andrew Hind).

These recommendations provided detailed support for the revised *Combined Code on Corporate Governance*, which in its comprehensive requirements for best practice by public-interest companies in the *profit* sector is likely to become the *de facto* standard for major charities as well – subject to the 'voluntary principle' of charity trusteeship, as now updated and formalised in the Charities Act 2006.

This will mean that public-interest charities as defined by the FRC (ie those with a gross income of more than £100m) will in future be expected, like listed companies, to disclose (i) how their governance policies relate to the Code's *principles* and (ii) depending on charity size and complexity, the extent to which they comply with the Code's detailed *provisions* where relevant to them, and explaining any departures from those provisions.

To summarise: the fact that almost all the trustees of large charities with devolved management structures are *non-executive volunteers* does make it necessary to tread carefully in importing these increasingly sophisticated governance concepts from the commercial sector.

Perhaps the more searching question to be asked here is whether the increasing focus on the formalities of charity governance is necessarily in the public interest for *all* the larger charities – or only for those with a significant dependency on public support.

For many *privately endowed* charities the extra cost burden imposed by these undifferentiated reporting requirements under SORP 2005 and its related Regulations is not easily justified by any perceptible public benefit to 'stakeholders and supporters' where the charity is self-sufficient and makes no appeal to the public but simply gets on with the job of providing public benefit in accordance with the wishes of its founder. Often, the latter will have made specific provision concerning trustee-appointments, perhaps in order to perpetuate a family ethos of philanthropy, and in such cases it is arguable that in the absence of any clear signs of maladministration the quality of the charity's governance is more a matter of internal good management than of external or even public concern.

For the smaller auditable charity below the £1m gross income threshold for standardised public domain 'SIR' reporting (see chapter 15), and where 'hands-on' management by the trustees themselves is normally needed in order to run things within such a small budget, assisted mainly by volunteer helpers to supplement the very small team of paid staff that is all the charity can afford for coping with certain routine day-to-day tasks, it may be enough to say here that the charity is managed by the trustees personally, with professional advice as and when needed, including the processes of trustee-recruitment and maintaining personal competence as trustees, or else to say which of them undertake this, and how (perhaps in committee), on behalf of the whole Board.

If, to take the other extreme, the trustees leave everything to an agent/correspondent to deal with, restricting their own involvement to periodic reviews of activity-reports and the approval of recommendations for action, then they should say how and to what extent they have delegated the different aspects of the charity's day-to-day management, identifying the person(s) responsible for them in each case.

In fact, many of the larger charities adopt a similar approach, delegating to their most senior executive staff rather than to an external agent. The governing bodies of independent schools, for example, often delegate all the day-to-day management to the school's head teacher, also perhaps to the deputy head and bursar, naming these as key staff in the administrative information section of their report.

Where the management structure is one based on committees empowered by the trustee-body to undertake particular aspects of the charity's management (eg grant-awards, finance and general purposes, etc) it may be sufficient to describe their functions, indicating the committee(s) on which each trustee sits – or the principal ones, if there are too many – and perhaps also identifying the non-trustee members. As mentioned earlier, this is one of those 'corporate governance' disclosures increasingly regarded as *best practice* – especially among the largest charities.

Organisational (branch) structure

4.4.4.2 Here, we need to consider the other aspect of the broad requirement of SORP/Regulations for *'a description of the organisational structure of the charity'*. This aspect should be seen in the context of the SORP's unsupported further requirement at paragraph 44(f) to explain *'the relationships between the charity and related parties, including its subsidiaries, and with any other charities and organisations with which it co-operates in the pursuit of its charitable objectives'*.

The scope of the latter was considerably widened by SORP 2000's inclusion of *related parties* where the 1995 SORP had limited itself to 'connected charities' – a step too far, perhaps, seeing the ramifications of the accounting standard (FRS8) from which it is drawn. The widening brought in not only the *non-charitable* bodies discussed in **4.4.4.3** but also any other body (or individual) 'related' to the reporting charity or its trustees by one side or the other being in a dominant position giving (in theory) the potential to distort transaction-values unilaterally for ulterior purposes. Thankfully, this one is not a regulatory requirement at all. Also, we can note in passing that SORP compliance *here* does *not* have to entail lists of related parties, still less of any transactions with them.

The explanation it calls for can be met by disclosing what each *kind* of relationship is, indicating its relevance and significance, for example:

–   special trusts and other linked charities where a control relationship is recognised under charity law are accounted for as *charity branches*;

–   controlled charitable companies not accounted for as branches are accounted for as subsidiary undertakings in the consolidated accounts (or else more fully described in the charity's (entity) accounts);

–   non-charitable subsidiary/associated undertakings that are used for generating funds (and/or for a charitable project) are accounted for in the consolidated accounts (or else more fully described in the charity's (entity) accounts);

–   certain (named) charities are co-operating in this or that charitable project (charity 'partnerships');

–   it is the policy of the Board to conduct all business with any other related party at arm's length.

Of course, this statement can be slimmed down almost to vanishing point for the very simplest of 'stand-alone' charities. The advantage of the basic format suggested here is that it can cater for the most complex of situations without having to be greatly expanded. The *comprehensiveness* of the SORP requirement, however, is not new. It is only differently expressed and widened in deference to FRS8.

As regards *charity branches*, we can observe that the structure of some charities is akin to that of the hub and spokes of a bicycle wheel, their activities from place to place in this country and/or overseas being managed locally but with legal control concentrated in a central unit or hub. Local operational units may have similar or quite different activities. This may require them to be organised and controlled either geographically or departmentally – it does not matter here. Even if such an operational unit is set up as a separate charity with its own 'governing document', it will count as a 'branch' for *charity* reporting purposes if the central trustee-body has 'control' rights enabling it legally to compel the proper application of the local funds *to serve its own (charitable) aims* – naturally within any constraints imposed by trust law in each case.

A special kind of 'charity branch' is identified and provided for in s 97(1) of the 1993 Act. Trust law allows a charitable trust (A) to be established *and independently administered* by its own trustee-body for the exclusive purpose of furthering the work of another charity (B) in some particular way, with A's Objects then 'pointing' to B and recognisable as a sub-set of B's Objects. The 1993 Act says that A is then a 'special trust', and (unless the Charity Commission, acting in the public interest, specifically determines otherwise by issuing a 'Disuniting Direction' under s 96(5) of the 1993 Act) *automatically* makes B publicly accountable for A by means of branch-accounting – although A is in other respects autonomous!

In between these two kinds is the *deemed* charity branch to cover 'common control' situations where, in the public interest, public accountability for the two connected charities (C and D) is *combined* by 'linking' them on the Charities Register. The reporting trustees of, say, C as the designated 'main' charity must then account for D as its designated 'charity branch' having no separate public accountability of its own, so that any annual accounts prepared for D itself will be 'branch accounts' as described in chapter 15 – thus *non-statutory*. This requires a Charity Commission 'Uniting Direction' issued under s 96 of the 1993 Act for the purpose.

All these variations and their accounting consequences are considered in more detail in chapter 14, where we discuss the various kinds of charity branch that you can have, and how to identify their legal status and accountability in each case.

For now, we need to note that where the charity *does* have a 'branch' structure in any of the ways outlined above, the reporting trustees should, if only for the sake of transparency, identify the different *legal entities* that – for the purposes of their trustees' report if under reg 40 of the SORP's related 2008 Regulations (thus also for their statutory *entity accounts* – see chapter 14) – are treated as one, and especially to distinguish these from any other subsidiary charities and any non-charitable bodies included in *group consolidated accounts*, making reg 41 applicable instead of reg 40. However, such disclosures are still not generally to be found in the published annual reports and accounts of charities. There is only the ready availability of a listing of all the *registered* subsidiary charities linked with them for charity accounting purposes on the Commission's website – but not of the many thousands of special trusts that are still *unregistered charities*, often simply because the trustees have never realised that the 1993 Act automatically exempts them only from separate public accountability – not from registration:

> '... "special trust" means property which is held and administered by or on behalf of a charity for any special purposes of the charity, and is so held and administered on separate trusts relating only to that property but a special trust shall not, by itself, constitute a charity for the purposes of Part VI of this Act.'
>
> – *Charities Act 1993, s 97(1)*

In any case, the 'related parties' referred to at paragraph 44(f) of SORP 2005 would certainly include all such 'controlled' connected charities (as well as any others where there are enough trustees in common to fall within the commercially driven FRS8 definition, were it not that the constraints of charity law counterbalance such relationships, arguing for exemption – see chapter 12).

While the smaller charity can choose whether or not to describe them, for full compliance with the Regulations and the SORP their description does, for the reasons outlined above, need to be seen as *mandatory* by larger reporting charities.

Connected (group) non-charitable bodies

4.4.4.3 Having dealt with connected *charities* accounted for as 'charity branches' (normally in the reporting charity's *entity* accounts – except where (as explained in chapter 14) for a 'non-small' parent *charitable company* the Companies Act takes priority over the Charities Act, when consolidation is recommended instead), we now need to discuss what is meant by the reporting charity's (beneficial) interests in connected *non-charitable bodies* – bearing in mind that their disclosure *here* (as distinct from the accounts notes) is not at present a regulatory requirement for *any* charity but simply 'best practice'.

Where the charity's interest is a 'controlling' one, it makes that non-charitable body its 'subsidiary undertaking' for group-accounting purposes: a member of the 'group' of which the reporting charity is the 'parent undertaking'.

Where it is only a *significant* minority interest entitling the charity to take an active part in the management and control of the body's activities and affairs, that body will be regarded for group-accounting purposes as its 'associated undertaking' – or even as a 'joint venture' undertaking, if control is *shared* with other interested parties without any party being able to exercise sole control.

If the charity's interest is less than this, being no more than that of a passive investor, thus without active participation in the management and control of the body, there is said to be no 'participating' interest and the body can be disregarded here. There is more in this than meets the eye: an investing charity may be invited to provide or nominate a charity trustee with particular skills or expertise to join the board of the investee – especially where this is to advise and assist with some charitable project carried out by the latter, funded by the former (ie 'social' or programme-related investment). SORP 2005 offers the following guidance:

'An associate will be created if the nomination or appointment is used in conjunction with a formal or informal agreement to exercise significant influence through direct involvement in setting the [investee's] operating and financial polices. Where the charity trustee appointment is simply used to provide advice or expertise to the [investee] ... whilst allowing the [investee] to adopt its own policies and strategies then an associate relationship is unlikely to be created.'

– SORP 2005, paragraph 410

For the avoidance of doubt, the SORP continues to offer a very practical 'rule of thumb' here, drawn from the accounting standard itself:

'Where a charity beneficially holds 20% or more of the voting rights in any undertaking, it will be presumed to have a participating interest and significant influence over its operating and financial policy, unless the contrary is shown.'

– SORP 2005, paragraph 409

For the purpose of 'related party' and other accounting disclosures, the Regulations 2005 defined 'connected' as meaning a *controlling* interest (as explained below) or a *participating* one (as explained above):

'"*institution or body corporate connected with the charity*" ... means ... an institution ... controlled by, [or] a body corporate in which a substantial interest is held by, the charity ...'.

– SI 2005/572, reg 2

The 2008 Regulations under Part VI of the 1993 Act, with its new group-accounting rules, take a different approach, so the above definition has been dropped. Instead, reg 2 (Interpretation) speaks only of a 'parent charity' and of a 'subsidiary undertaking', defining these terms by referring you to the 1993 Act as amended by the Charities Act 2006, where the new Sch 5A (Group Accounts) defines a 'parent charity' and a 'subsidiary undertaking' in para 1(2) by reference to the company law definitions of 'parent' and subsidiary' 'undertakings'.

There, 'control' (meaning sole control, even if subject to a minority interest held by a third party) plus 'benefit' (which need not be financial but can be just the furtherance of the reporting charity's own Objects) are the deciding factors.

This is then qualified by excluding any charity branches included in the reporting charity's entity accounts and extending the meaning of 'undertaking' to include any *other* controlled charities that, as *trusts*, are excluded for Companies Act purposes:

'(3)   Each undertaking in relation to which a parent charity is (or is to be treated as) a parent undertaking in accordance with those provisions is a "subsidiary undertaking" in relation to the parent charity.

(4)   But sub-paragraph (3) does not have the result that any of the following is a "subsidiary undertaking"—

(a)   any special trusts of a charity,
(b)   any institution which, by virtue of a direction under section 96(5) of this Act, is to be treated as forming part of a charity for the purposes of this Part of this Act, or
(c)   any charity to which a direction under section 96(6) of this Act applies for those purposes.

(5) "The group", in relation to a parent charity, means that charity and its subsidiary undertaking or undertakings, and any reference to the members of the group is to be construed accordingly.

(6) For the purposes of—

(a)   this paragraph, and
(b)   the operation of the provisions ... of this paragraph,

"undertaking" has the meaning given by sub-paragraph (7) below.

(7) For those purposes "undertaking" means–

(a)   an undertaking as defined by section 259(1) of the Companies Act 1985, or
(b)   a charity which is not an undertaking as so defined.'

– *Charities Act 1993, Sch 5A, para 1*

As for what is meant by 'controlled', the SORP says:

'*"Controlled"* means that the charity is able to secure that the affairs of the institution are conducted in accordance with its wishes.'

– *SORP 2005, Glossary GL 50: 'Related Parties'*

While information about a charity's *group* interests must be more reliable if contained within audited accounts, it has been impractical up to now to enforce disclosure for the greater number of (non-exempt) charities other than by calling for it in the trustees' report – where, as already mentioned, it is still 'only' a matter of best practice for *all* charities. That has changed, however, with the Charities Act 2006 group-accounting provisions having been implemented for financial years starting after 31 March 2008.

For completeness, what is really needed is a statutory requirement to disclose (in the trustees' report, if the information is not given in the annual accounts) a list of all 'connected' charitable and non-charitable institutions/bodies. This should disclose which ones are included in the reporting charity's entity accounts and which ones in its group consolidated accounts. For any others, the disclosure should include the kind of brief particulars prescribed by the Companies Act for group members, or else an indication of where the reader can obtain such information.

The difficulty of enforcement in this area up to now has partly been due to inadequate statutory underpinning for the SORP's disclosure requirements in respect of charitable companies of any size. It has also been an inevitable result of the 1993 Act's understandable preoccupation up to now with the 'proper application' of charities' resources and its consequent (deliberate) non-provision hitherto for the group-accounting that is such an important feature of the 1985 Act and now the 2006 Companies and Charities Acts.

In the case of *non-company* charities, though, it also seems to have reflected official policy towards the smaller ones that validly opt out of 'true and fair' accounts by choosing the receipts and payments basis instead.

Other connected charities/organisations

4.4.4.4   Although the SORP is non-mandatory in calling for the trustees to describe the reporting charity's relationships with '*related parties ... and ... charities and organisations with which it co-operates*' other than the above, as well as with any '*wider network ... where this [relationship] impacts on the operating policies adopted by the charity*', to quote paragraph 44(e), the need for transparency in such matters can still – if significant transactions are involved – be vital to the public interest if the other body is neither a charity branch nor a subsidiary/associate.

For the statutory accounts, of course, this sort of disclosure may be seen as falling into the category of:

> 'any additional information ... (ii) may reasonably assist the user to understand the statement of accounts.'
>
> – *SI 2008/629, Sch 2, para 1(y)*

It may even be arguable that (apart from charity networks and their 'umbrella body' charities, where to comply with the SORP you will normally only need to identify the network and the number of its members – the *relationship* being obvious), the particulars to be disclosed should be on similar lines to those required by FRS9 for 'associates', etc.

At the very least, for compliance with best practice the *significance* of the relationship for the charity's own governance needs to be made clear.

The British Red Cross Society ('the British Red Cross') has pleasure in presenting the Trustees' report and the audited consolidated financial statements of the organisation for the year ended 31 December 2007.

...

Organisation

...

The British Red Cross is a prominent member of the International Red Cross and Red Crescent Movement, with volunteers and staff contributing to a number of initiatives within both the International Federation of Red Cross and Red Crescent Societies (Federation) and the International Committee of the Red Cross (ICRC).

The British Red Cross Society – 2007 Annual Report

Report of the Board of Trustees

About ActionAid

For the purpose of these accounts it may be useful to clarify what we mean by the various uses of 'ActionAid'.   ➡

When we say ...	We mean ...
ActionAid International	the global ActionAid 'family', of which ActionAid is a member. This family includes six fundraising members and more than 40 country programmes
ActionAid International Secretariat	the management body of ActionAid International globally

Whenever we want to refer to a particular member of the ActionAid family we will add the relevant country name, eg, ActionAid Cambodia or ActionAid Italy. ...

Our total income is almost £68 million and this represents 53% of ActionAid International's total income. ...

The accounts of ActionAid International show the full financial performance and position of the ActionAid family worldwide. These are available at www.actionaid.org.

ActionAid – 2007 Annual Report

Operational performance

4.4.5 For charities *above* the statutory audit threshold, as well as for parent charities and their subsidiaries in the case of a group report [as we have indicated in square brackets, below], the 2008 Regulations underpin most of SORP 2005's extensive 'best practice' recommendations on *operational performance* by *requiring* that this part of the trustees' narrative report shall:

'be a review of the significant activities undertaken by the charity during the relevant financial year to further its charitable purposes for the public benefit , or to generate resources to be used to further its purposes, including details of—

\#   details of the aims *and objectives* which the charity trustees have set for the [reporting] charity [for a **group** report: and its subsidiary undertakings] in that year,

\#   the *strategies adopted* and significant activities undertaken in order to achieve those aims and objectives;

\#   the achievements of the [reporting] charity [for a **group** report: and its subsidiary undertakings] during the year, measured by reference to the aims *and objectives* which have been set;'

– SI 2008/629, reg 40(2)(b)(ii) and reg 41(2)(b)

'Objectives and activities'

The words *highlighted* above underpin what were *new* requirements in SORP 2005, thus beyond those contained in the 2000 Regulations. The required publication of annual objectives or targets, together with the trustees' (short-term) *strategies* for achieving them (information that for many charities is commercially sensitive and therefore traditionally confidential to top management) puts key internal management information – or the lack of it – into the public domain. That also brings a need to guard against public expectations being used to limit the trustees' freedom of decision to adapt the charity's operating and financial management policies, and thus its future activities, in the light of experience – especially if too many of these management objectives or 'key performance indicators' are published. Charities will need to weigh the pros and cons very carefully before deciding which data are safe to publish and which to keep confidential.

In general, only *high-level* annual objectives and their strategies can safely be published, if only in order to avoid frequent changes of comparative figures in the required SoFA analysis of activity-costs, which needs to be aligned with (i) these published annual objectives in order to describe, as required by paragraphs 47(e) and 48 of SORP 2005, activities considered 'significant' for the year's achievements in support of the charity's claim to be meeting the *public benefit* test now extended to all charities by the Charities Act 2006, and (ii) (for charities above £1m gross income) the SIR's analysis of the costs of the most significant activities in that context – see chapter 15.

Problems can arise here for charities set up for 'general charitable purposes' – which many of them fulfil by simply making grants to institutions in support of charitable work with which the trustees of the donating charity may feel there is a particular affinity. Prior to the Charities Act 2006, with its radical provision to make charitable status subject to continual public-benefit testing against specified criteria, the trust law duty to ensure that a charity's resources have been 'properly applied' has been discharged at the point of payment in the case where a grant is made to another charity. That has always made grant-making trusts set up for *general charitable purposes* an attractive proposition for many a wealthy philanthropist.

Whether that will now change may depend to some extent on how easily such charities can collect the relevant *performance* information to be able to show that there is a 'reasonable' expectation of public benefit in their grantmaking. This information must surely come from the institutions whose work they choose to support, and they can only be sure to obtain it under a grant-control agreement. Second-hand data of that sort may not be reliable enough for putting on public record – quite apart from the duplication entailed. In any case, it would be hard to justify the extra cost burden imposed on them in having to summarise what is essentially internal control data to inform the trustees' beneficiary-selection policy, and then having to publish it as the donating charity's own objectives for what it aims to achieve through its grant-making.

To comply fully with best practice in line with the SORP's paragraphs 47 and 48, the trustees' report should add to the Regulation's disclosure requirements as set out above *'the changes or differences [the charity] seeks to make through its activities'*.

'Achievements and performance'

Similarly, it should not only show to what extent the achievements of the year have met the immediate aims and objectives the trustees had previously set themselves (these normally being as declared 'for future periods' in the previous year's annual report – see below), but should also identify, in line with the SORP's paragraph 53, any *'benchmarks against which the achievement of objectives is assessed by the charity'* and furthermore explain any *'measures or indicators'* that are *'used to assess **the outcome of activities'***.

That this more demanding requirement of *performance-reporting* is no mere paper exercise, to be completed perhaps in the light of the next year's third-quarter management accounts, is clear from the SORP's further requirement also to disclose the objectives the trustees have set *for the future.*

'Future plans'

These are to be seen as steps along the way to implementing the trustees' long-term strategy for furthering the charity's Objects, and should therefore outline what they have *now* planned for the future, corresponding to their *aims* derived from prioritising those Objects. But where SORP paragraph 57 speaks of *'key objectives ... set for future periods'*, clearly meaning annual, the Regulations are strangely imprecise:

> 'a description of the aims and objectives which the charity trustees have set for the [reporting] charity in the future, and of the activities contemplated in furtherance of those aims and objectives.'
>
> *– SI 2008/629, reg 40(3)(q) and reg 41(3)(r)*

Subsidiaries' activities and achievements

As a further ramification now underpinned by the 2008 Regulations, but only for financial years starting after 31 March 2008, SORP 2005 adds at paragraphs 47 and 53 that the reporting of activities and achievements should, where significant, include those of any subsidiary undertakings. This allows for the reporting of charitable activities that are furthered less directly, by the *group* rather than by the charity itself.

Where a *group* trustees' report has to be prepared under the 2008 Regulations, reg 41 now governs its contents, as the alternative to reg 40, which applies in all other cases, in order to extend the required disclosures to cover both the reporting charity itself, ie, the group parent, and also its subsidiary undertakings – whether these be charities or non-charities. In keeping with the spirit of the SORP, this should distinguish their activities that aim to deliver public benefit from those undertaken to generate funds for the group.

The need for *identification* of these and other group members is discussed at **4.4.4**.

The annual cycle of performance-reporting

To sum up, then, a *model* operational performance review will be one that relates the charity's declared Objects for the public benefit to the trustees' aims to further those Objects as best they can and to their current long-term strategic plan for doing so, and more particularly to the year's actual activities and those planned for the coming year – both within the context of current and future objectives and any limitations imposed by the charity's circumstances. There are widely differing views on what gives *insight* into the ongoing management of the work of the charity – as can be seen from the following two illustrations.

Aims and objectives

The National's continuing objective is to present a balanced artistic programme. The repertory system is a key to this, not as a good in itself, but as the means of taking artistic risks and responding to audience demand. The NT endeavours to produce to the highest standards by attracting the best artists to work in an environment that enables and stimulates them to realise the fullest extent of their talents. ➡

These are the NT's constant objectives. Alongside are two long-term and interlinked strategies. The NT seeks to broaden the work on its stages, by nurturing new plays and new forms at the Studio, by commissioning, and by active project development of all kinds, in which Associate Directors, associates and other consultants are involved. It seeks to broaden its audiences through the programming choices it makes, by keeping ticket prices down, and by making manifest its ambition to be bold, contemporary and accessible.

Specific objectives for 2007–08:

- to develop new work for the two large stages

- to develop the NT's international links

- to continue digital developments

- to conclude arrangements for a season of Sunday performances

- to re-define NT Education

- to re-establish the Studio, with the NT Archive and Education studio under the same roof

- to continue the development of the exterior spaces

- to develop a designs trategy for the NT building as a whole

- to reduce further the NT's use of energy and water

... Paid attendances ... as % of capacity: 2003/4 91%; 2004/5 94%; 2005/6 84%; 2006/7 85%; 2007/8 87% ...

Unrestricted reserves have now reached their target level of £1m. This sum has been determined by the Trustees as the target level of unrestricted reserves required to maintain financial stability on an ongoing basis. It is recognised that there is particular uncertainty around box office receipts and £0.5m is held to recognise the volatility in box office revenue as between budget and actual out-turn and £0.5m reflects the impact that the unexpected and therefore unplanned replacement of a major piece of capital equipment would have on the charity.

The Royal National Theatre – 2007/08 Trustees' Report

OUR MISSION
WWF's mission is to stop the degradation of the planet's natural environment, and to build a future in which humans live in harmony with nature by:

- conserving the world's biological diversity;

- ensuring that the use of renewable natural resources is sustainable;   ➡

- reducing pollution and wasteful consumption.

REVIEW OF ACTIVITIES TO MEET OBJECTIVES
In last year's Trustees' Report, nine objectives were indentified for 2007/08. We report back on them as follows:

- Objective 1. Continue our substantial investment in developing Network Initiatives with partners across the Network. ...

- Objective 2. Engage in the negotiations for agreeing a post-Kyoto climate settlement programme. This will include lobbying and working with governments and stakeholders to ensure that the new settlement contains robust measures to address climate change. ...

- Objective 3. Influence government, including the devolved administrations, and seek cross-party commitment to a Climate Change Bill and a Marine Act. ...

- Objective 4. Continue the first year of our new partnership with HSBC Holdings pc by examining the effect of climate change on freshwater ecosystems in Brazil, China, India and the UK. ...

- Objective 5. Develop new business partnerships embracing our business and industry engagement policy that ensures we are proactive in pursuit of partnerships, aspiring to achieve transformational change while generating income. ...

- Objective 6. Renew our Partnership Programme Agreement with DFID. ...

- Objective 7. Invest in developing brand understanding among potential supporter audiences. ...

- Objective 8. Develop our vision of a One Planet Future and communicate to our supporters so they are better informed, involving some of them as active campaigners. ...

- Objective 9. Make the best of available digital technologies to improve communications with stakeholders and streamline our systems for better effectiveness. ...

OUR FOCUS FOR NEXT YEAR

Our objectives for 2008/09 are:

Strategy launch and communicate our new five-year Strategic Plan

Safeguarding the natural world ... Network Initiatives [to] protect the world's most special wildlife and places ... Marine Acts [for the] UK ... ➡

> *Tackling Climate Change*   ... Copenhagen in December 2009 ... and ... Earth
> Hour in March ... Climate Change Acts [UK] which commit to substantial
> reductions in greenhouse gas emissions
>
> *Changing the way we live*   ...
>
> *Communicating and influencing*   ...
>
> *Funding our work*   ...

WWF-UK – Annual Report, year to 30 June 2008

Investment policy/performance

4.4.6   For a charity above the statutory audit threshold, and also for a group (where a group trustees' report is required, as indicated in square brackets below) with *material* investment assets, the Regulations now require:

> '... a description of the policies (if any) which have been adopted by the charity trustees [or
> as the case may be the subsidiary undertaking,] for the selection, *retention and realisation* of
> investments for the charity, *including the extent (if any) to which social, environmental or
> ethical considerations are taken into account* ...'.
>
> *– SI 2008/629, reg 40(3)(o) and reg 41(3)(o)*

This extension of the policy disclosure to cover not only the selection of investments but also their retention and realisation seems at first sight to be simply a clarification in the light of the statutory duty of care imposed on all trustees by the TA 2000 – as does the reference to any 'social, environmental or ethical' considerations affecting that policy. Indeed, the very wording of the Act in imposing a duty to consider the 'suitability' of trust investments seems to imply that charity trustees *must* give due consideration to social and environmental as well as ethical issues in order to avoid conflicting with their charity's Objects for the public benefit by investing in incompatible industries or sectors of the economy that could detract from that public benefit. That is a far cry from when Charity Commission guidance used to insist that charity investment must pursue the best possible commercial return, and that special authority was needed for trustees to be able to override this and adopt an ethical investment policy, in view of the *performance-sacrifice* involved for the charity. However, the advent of 'socially responsible' investment expectations as more and more environmental issues begin to attract public attention, coupled with stricter environmental safeguards imposed on industry by the authorities, has long since shown that ethical investment does not necessarily correlate with under-performance.

Furthermore, when the 2005 SORP's draft Regulations were made available for public consultation early in 2005, concerns were expressed by some respondents at the possible implications of what the consultation document called a 'proposed requirement to disclose the trustees' policy on *the exercise of voting rights attached to their investments*'. In the event, no such requirement was included in the Regulations actually made, nor more recently in the SORP's 2008 Regulations, but even the fact that the idea was part of official thinking at that time may be seen as a pointer to possible future developments in this area. If that were to happen, charities with significant holdings in particular industries or sectors of the national (or global) economy would need special guidance on the extent to which they could properly use their voting power to influence the operating and management policies of the investee company, presumably to secure the furtherance of the investing charity's own charitable Objects where relevant – but also as to the possible group accounting consequences of doing so. Any such guidance would also need to cover what might be seen elsewhere in the EC as an unacceptable 'conflict of loyalties' necessitating divestment as the only way to avoid subordination of the investee's interests to those of the investing charity in a case where the business of the two parties is 'unrelated'.

In addition to *policy* disclosures, these 'auditable' charities (see **4.4.5**) must disclose the actual *performance* of their investments, in accordance with reg 40(3)(n) or its *group* alternative, reg 41(3)(n), in the latter case noting that *separate reporting* is required for (a) the parent charity and (b) the rest of the group – which at the very least will mean highlighting the income yield of, and the rate of growth achieved by, their portfolio for the year as figures that can easily be derived from the accounts disclosures. For the purpose of inter-charity comparisons, these two figures can be combined to disclose the portfolio's *total return* for the year in line with normal practice in the financial sector.

To compensate for the well-known volatility of capital markets the world over, the charity's investment performance may also be worth reporting both *cumulatively* (to show the longer-term trend on which serious investors – as distinct from speculators – normally put more weight) and also *subsequently* (in the context of short-term market fluctuations that may have spanned the year-end, perhaps momentarily depressing the balance sheet valuation to the detriment of annual performance).

To the *minimum requirement* again, we must add from SORP 2005 the further best-practice recommendation to include a performance *comparison*:

> 'Where material investments are held, details of the investment performance achieved against the investment objectives set; …'.

– SORP 2005, paragraph 53(c)

This cannot be done, of course, if no policy objectives or targets for the year have been set – without which it would then also be difficult to comply with the TA 2000 by reviewing against the required written policy the performance of any investment manager exercising *delegated* powers of investment decision-making.

For *small* investment funds (some say anything up to £0.5m), meaning those below the normal threshold for economical professional investment management on an individual client basis, the expedient thing to do prior to the TA 2000 was always to invest in the CIFs that were a specially authorised investment, ie 'special range' investments under the Trustee Investments Act 1961, for all charities (a course traditionally recommended by the Commission at the time).

For many, this had become custom and practice – not a reasoned policy decision at all. If now it is felt that something must be said about a policy, and properly documented, then it may have sufficed for the trustees to minute the fact and to report that their policy was *to invest exclusively in CIFs in accordance with the Charity Commission's general guidance*. For that to be able to continue under the TA 2000, however, 'proper advice' as to their suitability, etc, is necessary.

In practice, you are likely to be pressed for a *comparative performance* statement only if your investment portfolio is considered financially significant in relation to your charity's (or charity group's) activities and funds, and viable as a separate unit in the market for professionally managed funds – in which case you would be expected to have looked at other options besides CIFs.

Investment *policy* disclosures under SORP 2005 no longer need to include a summary of specific investment powers and their authority – something that was recommended in SORP 2000 from before the TA 2000 came into force (February 2001), bestowing such wide-ranging investment powers on all trustees, subject to specific 'duty of care' safeguards, that any constitutional empowerment in this area became irrelevant.

On the other hand, many charities receive gifts of investment assets on restricted terms of trust requiring retention *in specie*, and thus constraining diversification to such an extent that any policy on *re*investment would be wishful thinking. Even before the advent of tax incentives for charitable giving popularised gifts of quoted securities (often with disposal embargoed within a specified period, eg during a price-sensitive flotation), founders of charitable settlements have often used this kind of inalienable gift to lock in charity control of a successful family business.

In such a case, there would now be a legal obligation to disclose the donor-required policy of non-diversification of specifically inalienable investment gifts like this, unless of course their current value happens to be immaterial, since the existence of such a 'retention' policy can hardly be denied.

Where investment management powers have been *delegated*, the extent of such delegation needs to be part of the description of the investment policy that ought then to be set by the trustees, as would any performance criteria they may (or should?) have set. The TA 2000 does make the issue of such a policy obligatory in such cases. (See chapter 9 for a review of the TA 2000's impact on investing charitable *trust* funds – in particular, **9.5**.)

The following illustration is of special interest because investment is mostly in income units issued by a separately accountable investment pooling charity, a Common Investment Fund (CIF) for Army charities, but primarily because of a crisp and clear statement of the performance of a virtually unendowed charity's *long-term* portfolio, worth some £32m at March 2008:

INVESTMENT MANAGEMENT

The Fund's investments are largely held in distribution units of the Armed Forces Common Investment Fund (AFCIF), formerly the Army Common Investment Fund (ACIF) . . . At the year-end the market value of the Fund's AFCIF holding was £32,281,356 (2007: £33,738,943).

The ACIF was launched in September 2002 to provide Army charities with a professionally managed investment management and administration service at relatively low cost. As a Common Investment Fund it is a charity in its own right, with a Corporate Trustee and an independent Advisory Board, comprising elected representatives of the participating charities and senior City individuals appointed by the Army Board. In the previous year the ACIF was renamed the AFCIF, recognising that it is open to all charities of the armed forces. ➡

The sole performance objective of the AFCIF is to seek to outperform its customised, composite benchmark by 1% per annum. The total return for the year to 31 March 2008 was (0.8)% compared to the benchmark return of (5.8)%; since the launch the total returns have been 79.1% and 67.3% respectively. The income distribution in the year to 31 March 2008 was 4.50p per unit, and at the current rate the distribution for the year to 31 March 2009 will be 5.00p per unit.

Although, the AFCIF has its own independent Advisory Board the Army Benevolent Fund's own Finance and Investment Committee and its Trustee Board monitor the AFCIF performance against its benchmark.

The Trustees of the Fund are quite clear that the Fund is a long-term investor in AFCIF, and accordingly look beyond the day-to-day fluctuations in the market. This means that the portfolio will sometimes under-perform the market as a whole in-year; the Trustees accept this limitation and are aware that the value of the investment portfolio can fall as well as rise.

The Army Benevolent Fund – 2007/08 Annual Report

The crucial question, then, for many charities is: What sort of investment policy is *reasonable* for the trustees to adopt in our own situation?

It is here that trustees will mostly have been looking to their professional fund managers to offer guidance on what kind of policy they would find it reasonable to work to – and to be judged against on performance. That, however, can only produce appropriate wording for *policy disclosures* in the annual report as a by-product of the intensive reviews, research and discussions needed between the larger charities and their investment and financial advisers (e g auditors).

What is immediately obvious is that the continuing retention of donated investments – unless this *must* be done to comply with donor-restrictions (see above) – needs to be seen as their *selection by default*, in view of the trustees' general duty to diversify investments for a safer balance between risk and reward. In any case, the TA 2000 *requires* a policy to be set by the trustees where investment management is *delegated*.

If investing *only* in CIFs, for example, it might suffice to report (usually in percentage terms) the year's income and net gain/loss on the total holding(s), or just the aggregate of these as the 'total return', and comparing this with the previous year if no different objective was set for this year, and also to confirm the policy of retaining the investment unchanged if that is considered on the basis of 'proper advice' to be in the charity's best interests for the time being – but if making an informed choice between CIFs or perhaps alternative investment vehicles, the basis or 'policy' used will have to be indicated as well, even if only briefly.

While a portfolio of immaterial value will hardly warrant much 'in depth' review, so that its performance can just be reported factually, for the larger portfolio any poor investment performance will tend to be spotlighted by the SORP's requirement here for a comparison with the trustees' objective(s) – which will therefore need to be realistic. At the very least, market comparisons may need to be given so that an apparently under-performing portfolio can be seen in the proper context before going on to outline the basis of the objective(s) against which that performance is to be evaluated.

Charitable companies already have absolute investment powers for their *corporate* funds in any case. For their *trust* funds, as with those of other charities, any specific investment clauses in *pre-August 1961* governing documents – and even those in subsequent ones if, despite the use of any different wording, the clause was obviously intended merely to provide for the old statutory powers – were *superseded* by the TA 2000 as from 1 February 2001, as we have already noted. The trustees of these 'liberated' funds do not even need to state that the TA 2000 applies to them – only to mention any constitutional restrictions that still apply.

The following suggestions for the wording of an appropriate disclosure of investment performance against the objective(s) set for the year in line with the trustees' policy are adapted from Appendix J of the Independent Schools' Bursars Association/ Incorporated Association of Preparatory Schools booklet: *SORP 2005 Guidance for Independent Schools.*

However, it should be noted that the actual wording to be used in the trustees' report can only be finalised by reference to the reporting charity's particular circumstances. The text therefore cannot just be copied over, as from a template.

To meet both the statutory requirement and the further (non-statutory) requirement of SORP 2005 to compare the performance with the year's objective(s), charities with investment funds will need to include the following elements:

–   commentary on the reporting charity's total investment income and gains for the year (these have to be shown in the SoFA, with comparatives, in any case) compared with the previous year's total return as this year's implied objective (if no other objective was set) – this can be in terms of the annualised percentage return achieved this year on the opening value of total invested funds, adjusted for any new investment or divestment (the movement on Fixed Asset Investments forms part of the analysis note required to support the balance sheet figure); and

–   an indication of the investment criteria used during the year to review/change the charity's existing investments and for new investment/divestment (this may need to include not only 'ways and means', such as delegated investment management or the use of a sub-committee, but also any 'benchmark' performance-indicators (eg WM Charity Universe; FTSE All-Share Index; MSCI World Index) or longer-term performance objectives/targets (eg 'to preserve the real value of the retained fund(s)', or 'of the charity's permanent endowment'), etc – which clearly must be conditioned by the capital/income needs of each particular fund); and

–   the extent of any under-/over-performance against those criteria.

While circumstances may dictate a more detailed review than the very basic wording used in the texts below, it is suggested that these would at least meet the minimum requirements.

Charity A (those with more than, say, £4m to invest)

> The annualised total return [of x%] achieved for the year on the charity's investment assets exceeded the [y% for the] previous year by [(x-y)%]. The Board's policy is to maintain a balanced budget to cover annual expenditure requirements➡

for each invested fund within the prevailing constraints of the investment markets while endeavouring to preserve the real value of funds invested to provide for long-term needs, using WM Charity Universe as the benchmark. *The Board's policy is not to invest in industries and sectors of the economy that are generally considered detrimental to [the furtherance of our Objects or the welfare of our beneficiaries].* The Board are advised that this constraint will not invalidate the use of that benchmark, as the under-performance that may result is not likely to be material in that context. While this year's income return was in line with that policy, the capital return was z% below/above benchmark. What with the general decline of the markets in recent years, the endowed funds are still below their long-term target level, although the Board are advised that their existing investment policy is appropriate in the circumstances and can therefore continue unchanged.

Depending on the significance of any long-term investment funds, this sort of performance review could be slanted as follows:

Charity with a financial endowment to fund its activities

A predominantly long-term (endowments) policy could make the capital growth target more of a priority, with a correspondingly relaxed target for income returns if either:

(i)   the charity's activities are mainly self-financing; or

(ii)   it has substantial income fund retentions that can be used for deficit-funding.

If investing on a properly authorised 'total return' basis (see **6.4.3** and **9.5** respectively), you can forget about 'income returns' as such: the duty of even-handedness then shifts to the informed use of the discretionary power to convert part of the unapplied total return into income each year.

Charity using annual fundraising, grant-aid or charitable trading income to finance its activities

A medium-term (unendowed funds) policy may need to take the opposite view by relaxing the requirement to maintain 'real value' so that priority can be given to the charity's need to maintain predefined levels of annual cashflow to cover spending requirements incorporated in the latest business plan.

Charity B (those with investment funds of £1m–£4m)

There may not be much latitude for varying the relative priorities from the above formulation – especially if operating margins are constrained or capital expenditure needs must be given priority. In either case, it may be best just to shorten the text to avoid appearing to set unrealistic targets for either capital or income returns – subject to the same proviso about investing on a 'total return' basis, of course.

Charity C (those with investment funds approaching £1m)

Investment funds of such a small size seem to be of little interest to most professional investment managers. Prior to 1 February 2001, when the TA 2000 came into force, the easy option was to invest in a CIF specialising in income or capital funds as appropriate. These were classed as 'special range' investments authorised by the Charity Commission *without the need for investment advice*. However, under the 2000 Act, trustees of even the smallest investment funds must have regard to the standard investment criteria of suitability and diversification – as well as of even-handedness, of course, when investing endowment capital. While this does not invalidate CIF investment, it must entail informed comparison with alternative investment vehicles such as authorised unit trusts or other forms of investment pooling under professional management – or even of direct investment, if the portfolio is large enough to be an economical proposition. For this level of investment, therefore, something along the following lines might suffice.

> The existing policy of CIF investment is considered appropriate to the size of funds available, with the investment return for the year as shown in the accounts amounting to x% in total against the year's target/expectation of y%, but the trustees continue to keep alternative investment vehicles under review as regards the balance of risk and reward compared with CIF holdings.

Whatever its circumstances, however, any charity in category A or B (or C, if changes are in mind) will need access to expert investment advice that takes account of the capital/income nature of its investing funds, as well as of their Objects – and, within that context, also of their longer- and shorter-term spending needs, if annual performance comparisons of any kind are to be made against realistic objectives/targets/expectations under what is now expected to be an 'informed' policy.

Grant-making and 'social' investing *beneficiary-selection* policy

4.4.7 Wherever a charity above the statutory audit threshold, or having to prepare a *group* trustees' report under the 2008 Regulations, makes grants or what SORP 2005 calls 'social' (or 'programme-related') investments, the Regulations now require:

> 'a description of the policies (if any) which have been adopted by the charity trustees [of the reporting charity] **for** the selection of individuals and institutions who are to receive grants or other forms of financial support out of the assets of the charity; ...'.

> – *SI 2008/629, reg 40(3)(m) and reg 41(3)(m)*

Although reg 41 does not specify any policy disclosure where the grant-making is only by a subsidiary, rather than by the parent charity of the group, the effective requirement of the regulations that the consolidated accounts must be prepared as if the group comprised a single charitable institution and the need for consistency of narrative reporting in the trustees' report would in practice make the disclosure unavoidable.

The 'other forms of financial support' typically mean 'soft loans' (repayable grants) to needy beneficiaries, for example, of a benevolent fund charity, but the term also covers equity and/or loan investments made in *non-charitable* bodies set up to carry out charitable projects through which the investing charity can further its own Objects while (as a secondary consideration) looking for an investment return as a way of wholly or partly recycling such resources for further activities. SORP 2005's Glossary also calls this 'programme-related' – or you could say 'project-related' – investing:

> 'Programme related investments (also known as social investments) are made directly in pursuit of the organisation's charitable purposes. Although they can generate some financial

return (funding may or may not be provided on commercial terms), the primary motivation for making them is not financial but to further the objects of the funding charity. Such investments could include loans to individual beneficiaries (e g for housing deposits) or to other charities (for example, in relation to regeneration projects).'

– *SORP 2005, Glossary GL 47*

Resources used in this way show up as assets in the balance sheet to the extent that they are still considered recoverable, or as charges in the SoFA if irrecoverable. SORP 2005, paragraph 309 specifies a historical cost basis for the asset's carrying value and classifies the write-offs as *charitable grants* – hence the requirement here to disclose the *selection policy* adopted for deciding who is to benefit from this kind of 'social investing'.

Extending the beneficiary-selection policy disclosure to cover this kind of financial support for a charitable project, however, ought not to include situations where the reporting charity takes a participating interest in a non-charitable institution (or finances it on 'soft loan' terms), because the primary purpose in doing so must be to benefit the project and the investor – not the investee. After all, the Regulations do not require this kind of policy disclosure where the project is undertaken in-house by the charity alone, nor for beneficiary-selection by service-providing charities generally.

Yet again, the point to note is that the *statutory* information requirement here is a *policy* disclosure only, not a lengthy explanation of what may have become custom and practice in your charity – though of course there is nothing to stop you using this opportunity to include a summary of your standard requirements as well, if that helps to cut down the administration work involved in screening out unwanted applications. For example, many grant-making charities make it clear in their annual report that as a matter of policy they do not consider unsolicited grant applications but only award grants to beneficiaries they themselves select in accordance with their own criteria. The same will often hold good for 'social investment' decisions.

Risk-mitigation

4.4.8 The SORP's related 2008 Regulations require the trustees of *larger* charities and of groups (where a group trustees' report has to be prepared) to include in their annual report:

> 'a statement as to whether the charity trustees have given consideration to the major risks to which the charity is [or (**group** reports only): and its subsidiary undertakings are] exposed and satisfied themselves that systems or procedures are established in order to manage those risks.'

> – *SI 2008/629, reg 40(2)(b)(ii)(ee) and reg 41(2)(c)*

This differs from the SORP itself only by allowing for the possibility that risk may not actually be a major factor (e g in the case of an endowed general-purpose charity whose 'business' consists entirely of making grants for particular purposes to other charities) – whereas SORP 2005 assumes it always is. Having duly considered the question itself, the further requirement of the Regulations can be satisfied by undertaking from time to time a *cost/benefit review* of the options available for minimising any loss to the charity resulting from the risks that must be inherent in the day-to-day running of the business of any economic enterprise – however charitable – and then implementing any management action needed. The SORP is more demanding here in a sense, because it assumes there will always be some major risk (while allowing for the possibility that –

despite having done your best to fulfil your 'duty of care' under charity law – you might still be unaware of it) and that if you are aware of it you must *always* have to take action:

> 'A statement should be provided confirming that the major risks to which the charity is exposed, as identified by the trustees, have been reviewed and systems or procedures have been established to manage those risks.'
>
> – *SORP 2005, paragraph 45*

The Exposure Draft for SORP 2000 had proposed to require the trustees to confirm that their control systems were 'adequate'. During the public consultation, some had suggested that this was too 'strong' to be a reasonable statement for any trustee to have to make, and that 'adequate' should be watered down to 'appropriate for the charity' – acknowledging that charities cannot all be expected to put in place the kind of control systems that are now considered appropriate for multi-national listed companies. The problem here was that 'adequate' might be taken to mean 'in all circumstances' (ie regardless of cost/efficiency/practical considerations), whereas 'appropriate' would clearly take account of such issues. Instead, the risk statement that was substituted (without any further consultation) and is still retained in SORP 2005 seems every bit as onerous as what was rejected by the sector. One therefore cannot help feeling that there must have been an ulterior motive: to economise on the monitoring of the larger registered charities by adding this item – once considered confidential to the top management of any organisation – to *all* trustees' public reporting responsibilities.

The question that must have arisen for many readers was: How did we get here, with the regulator *expecting* us to employ such sophisticated business-optimisation practices? The answer is to be found in the repeated efforts during the 1990s, and which have continued ever since, to put in place strict codes of practice in the area of 'corporate governance' for the better regulation of public companies in the interests of their shareholders.

As long ago as 1992, the report of the Cadbury Committee on the Financial Aspects of Corporate Governance had highlighted the need for 'audit committees', and for reporting on the effectiveness of internal controls. In 1998, the Hampel Committee's 'Combined Code' essentially upheld and updated the Cadbury recommendations, reaffirming in particular the benefit to be expected from 'positive' reporting on internal controls.

With few public companies having already begun to comply, the Turnbull Committee published its 'Internal Control – Guidance for Directors of Listed Companies' in September 1999 to show the way. Their published accounts are now required to include a Board statement on the system(s) of internal controls and their effectiveness. This presupposes annual reviews, supported by internal audit where necessary; for the purpose of which a *risk-based* approach is to be preferred, recognising that internal control systems are not the only way of reducing risk, and that risk-management itself should be an 'embedded' process within corporate governance.

It is not just in the corporate sector that a 'corporate governance' framework has been developing; the principles are spreading through the not-for-profit sector. Examples include the 1995 Code of Practice for Housing Associations, introducing formal corporate governance reporting, and updated in 2000. This closely mirrored the listed companies model, but tailored the Cadbury requirements to the specific issues facing

RSLs. Friendly societies, under the Friendly Societies Act 1992, were required to demonstrate compliance with the 'criterion of prudent management', thus a system of Control and Inspection and Report – effectively an internal audit. The management committees of Friendly Societies have to make an annual report to the Financial Services Authority (FSA) (previously to the Friendly Societies Commission until the transfer of its regulatory functions to the FSA under the provisions of the Financial Services and Markets Act 2000) confirming that *adequate* internal control systems have been in place throughout the year. That report also has to include a statement by the society's auditors.

Risk-assessment is not confined to *financial* loss, however. Audited charities will generally have financial controls already, controls that are tried and tested and therefore do mitigate the risk of immediate loss. But there are also wider questions to be asked in a review of *all* major risks – for example, what of the risks inherent in strategic business/development planning, where far-reaching assumptions often have to be made, leading to the choices that may turn out to be far from optimal?

For many charities, major risk can arise from the increasingly onerous compliance requirements of laws governing the operational activities they are set up to undertake – for example, in areas such as health and safety, food hygiene, employment and human rights, etc.

Other operational risks may be to the charity's name or reputation, to the physical security of its property, or even to its beneficiaries and/or staff. There are also newer risks of major loss from our increasing reliance on information technology, such as data protection (including the need for 'fail-safe' data-storage/data-recovery systems and for anti-virus programs), systems development/maintenance, etc. Environmental risks (eg pollution and its consequences) and now terrorist activity may also need special consideration in some cases.

To be able to say that they have duly considered (reviewed) their charity's major risks and how best to 'manage' them, trustees will have to undertake a 'risk-mapping' exercise to prioritise each of these perceived risks in terms of how it impacts on the charity's effectiveness, efficiency and economy. This will provide a rational basis for deciding whether to eliminate the risk by 'avoiding action' or else to keep it within tolerable limits by means of some sort of control system, or simply to insure against it – or even ignore it altogether.

Risk-identification, the 'themed' approach and 'risk-mapping'

Through 'facilitated discussion' internally, you can involve all the charity's decision-makers in the necessary clarification process. A 'themed' approach can then be used to enable you all to delve deeper in identifying the major risks in need of mitigation, as illustrated by the following list of possible risks of a general financial nature (not to speak of more specialised aspects like fundraising, investing, purchasing, staffing and the use of volunteers):

– Weak or ineffective financial controls

– Systems and controls not operating as intended

– Written financial procedures poor or non-existent

- Inappropriate authorisation and approval processes

- Inadequate financial planning

- Trading revenue-levels inadequate

- Capital expenditure plans lacking

- Charity assets not adequately safeguarded

- Inadequate insurance cover

- Ineffective/inefficient treasury management

- Inability to meet financial obligations as they fall due (as a 'going concern')

- Poor or untimely management information systems

- Unprotected exposure to foreign exchange movements

- Insufficient long-term committed funding

- Lack of financial supervision by the charity trustees

- Defective statutory accounts

- Heavily qualified statutory audit report

- Failure to implement auditors' management report recommendations

- Inadequate scope of internal audit function

- No direct communication lines between internal audit and the charity trustees

- Lack of control over outsourced services

- Formal reserves policy not established or not recently revisited

- Inadequate fund-accounting

- Unauthorised non-charitable trading

- Unplanned Tax/PAYE/VAT liabilities

The table below sums up how to minimise risk by this 'common-sense' approach:

Probability	High	Low
Major loss	*Avoid*	*Insure*

Probability	High	Low
Minor loss	*Control*	*Accept*

Whatever the approach, it needs to be *formalised* for compliance purposes, perhaps using a Risk Register to record who is tasked with monitoring each major risk identified, with reports on the periodic review of the system's effectiveness, and any recommendations/decisions arising, being minuted by the Board, together with any management action resulting, as the basis for the disclosure to be made in the trustees' report. In some areas, specialist advice may be needed. In others, the risks may already have been adequately addressed, and the Board need only minute the existing precautionary measures as representing what *at that time* they consider to be *appropriate* 'systems' designed to manage the charity's major risks.

Risk-management is clearly a developing area, with plenty of room for further discussion and more precise guidance. David Taylor, during his time as the Charity Commissioner responsible for charity accounting matters, went on record as saying that the Commission would be looking to the sector itself to develop best practice in this area, and specifically to professional advisers to give a lead. Against that, the Charity Commission website includes a very comprehensive guidance leaflet on the subject, which (although aimed at helping trustees of larger charities fulfil their reporting obligations) is also recommended reading for others as well – as long as you do not feel too daunted by its lengthy checklist of potential risks to be considered!

It is interesting to note that the following officially approved risk management statement from SORP 2000's companion booklet of worked examples seems to have anticipated SORP 2005 here:

The Trustees have assessed the major risks to which the charity is exposed, in particular those related to the operations and finances of the Trust, and are satisfied that systems are in place to mitigate our exposure to the major risks

---

Example Annual Report: 'The Edinburgh Educational Trust'

Some may have felt that this was unwisely 'bullish' then. Five years on, none of the worked examples under SORP 2005 had exceeded its requirements, while one did not seem to have moved on from SORP 2000, saying only that a *strategy* has been adopted to establish and implement the required systems and procedures – with no explicit confirmation that they now exist:

The trustees have a risk management strategy which comprises:

- an annual review of the risks the charity may face;

- the establishment of systems and procedures to mitigate those risks identified in the plan; and ➡

> •   the implementation of procedures designed to minimise any potential impact on the charity should those risks materialise.

Example Annual Report: Arts Theatre Trust Limited

Here is one of our own seminar examples, which is quite specific enough, but with qualifying statements such as 'risks *identified*' and '*appropriate*' systems and procedures. Perhaps not so very different, but enough to stop trustees (unlike Governments) being held responsible for the results of fuel shortages, flooding, etc:

> The task of monitoring the Charity's financial control systems and procedures is delegated to the Audit Committee. In conjunction with the Charity's internal auditor, the Audit Committee has reviewed and reported to us on the working of these systems and procedures in relation to the wider issue of managing major risks identified as arising from or in connection with the Charity's activities. We continue to keep under review the adequacy for this purpose of the systems and procedures now in place and those in operation during the year. These appear to us to be appropriate to the Charity's size and the nature of its operations.

Example Annual Report: 'The ABC Charity'

The following alternative suggestion is regarded by the authors as reasonable, in line with best practice – subject to adapting it to the particular circumstances of the charity:

> The Board is responsible for the management of the risks faced by the charity.
>
> Detailed considerations of risk are delegated to the Audit Committee, who are assisted by senior charity staff. Risks are identified, assessed and controls established throughout the year.
>
> A formal review of the charity's risk management processes is undertaken on an annual basis.
>
> The key controls used by the charity include:
>
> –   Formal agenda for Board activity
>
> –   Detailed terms of reference for all sub-committees – Audit, Investment, Fund-Raising
>
> –   Comprehensive strategic planning budgeting and management accounting
>
> –   Established organisational and governance structure and lines of reporting
>
> –   Formal written policies
>
> –   Hierarchical authorisation and approval levels
>
> –   Comprehensive internal audit function   ➡

Through the risk management processes established for the charity, the trustees are satisfied that the major risks identified have been adequately mitigated where necessary.

It is recognised that systems can only provide reasonable but not absolute assurance that major risks have been adequately managed.

The wording used in the 2007/08 annual report of Save the Children illustrates how even major charities may wish to tread cautiously in formulating public statements about their approach to risk-management in order to comply with best practice:

Risk management and internal control

Save the Children exists to help the most vulnerable children in the world. To keep our promises to those children, we have to operate in some of the most fragile and high-risk countries. To fulfil those promises effectively, to safeguard our staff, and to meet our obligations to those who provide funding, we must be fully aware of – and effectively manage – the risks faced in those countries. We achieve this through:

- recording major risks, significant threats to the implementation of our strategy, and changes to our risk profile in the strategic risk register, which then indicates current measures in place to mitigate the risks and any planned actions to further reduce exposure; and

- support from the Global Risk Assurance Manager, appointed in 2007/08, who ensures that we have robust mechanisms in place to identify both strategic and operational emerging risks, and that we have appropriate steps in place to mitigate those risks. The Global Risk Assurance Manager also works to effectively embed risk management throughout all levels of the organisation.

Major risks are those that have a high likelihood of occurrence, and that would – if they occurred – have a severe impact on our work, our reputation, or our ability to achieve our ambitions. These risks are reported to Trustees through the risk management process, so that the Audit Committee, and all Trustees, can challenge any assumptions and concentrate their efforts on ensuring that the most serious risks are being managed effectively. The Trustees recognise that in order to achieve the objectives of the charity, it is necessary to accept some risks that are outside Save the Children's control, and which cannot be fully mitigated. Where this happens, executive directors are charged with actively monitoring those risks. However, it is recognised by the Trustees that any system of risk management cannot completely eliminate risks, and therefore provides reasonable, but not absolute, assurance that the organisation is protected.

This year the most significant risks we discussed were: the sustainability and potential for growth of various income streams in order to deliver our strategic objectives; attracting the right people to lead our pioneering work throughout the world; and effectively managing our relationships with institutional donors.

Save the Children's internal audit department carries out regular audits. The reviews are prioritised using a risk-based approach and each audit expresses a➡

> view on the controls in place and their operation in practice. Recommendations are systematically followed up and reports on implementation are received. The Head of Internal Audit submits regular reports to the Audit Committee, ensuring that the controls are continually reviewed.

Save the Children – Annual Report 2007/08

Fundraising performance

4.4.9   The effectiveness of fundraising activities is an area where the SORP has not yet had any statutory underpinning at all, despite the fact that fundraising performance remains one of the Charity Commission's major concerns – as can be seen from the continuing inclusion of this aspect in the detailed fundraising data gathered from charities above the £1m 'SIR' threshold (see chapter 15) for the maintenance of public confidence in the sector as a whole.

The inclusion of *fundraising effectiveness* as a specific new reporting requirement in SORP 2000 therefore came as no surprise at the time. The only regret must be that the detailed guidance needed for compliance had been dropped. This was what the 1995 SORP had provided in its requirement for the narrative review to be sufficiently informative to enable the reader to appreciate:

> 'where the charity was set up to undertake a specific project, the progress of that project. This part of the review should give cumulative figures of funding and expenditure on the project to date, with estimates of the additional costs and period of time required to complete it ...'.

> *– 1995 SORP, paragraph 28(c)(ix)*

For medium- to long-term fundraising campaigns, start-up costs can be dauntingly high, and even where the eventual achievement of the funding target seems to be reasonably certain the campaign's financial efficiency from the donor's viewpoint can look very poor in the early stages. An indication, by means of *cumulative* reporting as outlined above, of how the fundraising efficiency has improved over time could therefore be very helpful and reassuring to the reader.

For major fundraising campaigns extending over several years, this could usefully include a statement of aims for the campaign, together with its timescale and the updated forecast to completion compared with cumulative actual costs and proceeds.

For different kinds of fundraising activity, the ratio of costs to gross proceeds as a measure of efficiency can vary widely. For the many 'charity shops' run by 'household name' charities selling cast-offs donated by the public to help their favourite charity finance its activities, the costs can be as high as 85% of turnover, whereas for a major capital appeal the cost ratio ultimately achieved over the appeal's life-cycle could be less than 5% of proceeds. For direct marketing campaigns of all kinds seeking voluntary contributions, the annual ratio can be as high as 30–40% or even higher – especially in the early years of building up a donor-base.

Legacy 'marketing' is another example where start-up costs can dramatically distort the long-term ratio: the success achieved annually in terms of wills written or amended to benefit the charity can take many years to 'mature' into actual bequests.

The SORP offers no methodology for all this, instead calling in paragraph 53(b) for disclosure of the charity's fundraising performance against the objectives set, and also for additional commentary to explain how any *'material expenditure for future income generation'* has affected (i) the fundraising return for the year and (ii) *'anticipated income generation in future periods'* – whatever that may mean.

This focus on 'investment in the future', which should also be read in the context of the charity's *future plans* (see **4.4.5**), together with the disclosures nowadays required for *designated funds* (see **4.4.1**) seems to have been intended to meet Accounting Standards Board expectations at that time in respect of a good *Operating and Financial Review* in the corporate sector – including also the current level of capital expenditure. The charity sector equivalent of that form of 'investment in the future' is, of course, the Fixed Assets Fund set up by many charities to show the extent to which their *general-purpose* funds (reserves), having been committed to future activities, are no longer freely available for current activities.

Financial *management* policies

4.4.10 As part of the *financial review* called for by SORP 2005, paragraph 55 explains that the trustees' financial management policies include not only managing the charity's reserves and any fund-deficits, each being a mandatory disclosure for the larger charity, but also as a further mandatory disclosure its *'principal funding sources'*. The SORP then extends the sentence by calling for an explanation of *'how expenditure in the year under review has supported the key objectives of the charity'* – a disclosure that is not supported by its related Regulations. Nevertheless, this is now being seen by the Charity Commission as a peg on which to hang its information-gathering for Public Benefit assessments under the Charities Act 2006, on the basis that what the SORP really means here is that the Trustees' Annual Report should show how the year's expenditure on charitable activities supports their *Public Benefit* aims.

However, that lack of statutory underpinning makes no real difference for charities above £1m gross income, as they have to give much the same information to the Charity Commission in the SIR (see chapter 15) as part of their statutory annual return.

Volunteer-help

4.4.11 At paragraph 51, SORP 2005 calls for an explanation if the reporting charity *'makes significant use of volunteers in the course of undertaking its charitable or income generating activities'*. This is a *mandatory* requirement for the larger charity, in that reg 40(2)(b)(ii)(cc) or, for a **group** report, reg 41(2)(b)(iv), calls for *'details of the contribution'* made to the charity's activities by volunteers.

During the public consultation on the *SORP* 2005 Exposure Draft at the time, the Charity Finance Directors' Group, having studied the feasibility of recognising volunteer-help at a financial value in charity accounts, put up proposals for this to become a SORP requirement. That idea was firmly rejected as impractical due to 'measurement issues' – an allusion to the difficulty of trying to audit such an estimate.

Instead, paragraph 51 of the SORP goes on to point to the importance of information on the use of volunteers, saying that it *'may ... quantify the contribution in terms of hours or staff equivalents, and may present an indicative value of this contribution'*; but that does reflect the practical impossibility of putting a *reliable* financial value on this sector-wide charitable resource that can sometimes be indispensable to certain kinds of charity, and which popular opinion in some quarters says therefore ought to be highlighted in the annual report.

Volunteer-help is essentially one of those unquantified 'dependencies' which the original 1995 SORP required to be acknowledged in a statement about those on whose goodwill the charity is dependent. That was not so much to do with public recognition for the benefactors, though the opportunity for that should not be overlooked, but it was – and is – much more to do with recognising constraints on the trustees' freedom of action. That aspect is no less important for the public and the Charity Commission to know about now, under SORP 2005, than it was then.

What has changed since 1995 is that these public-interest disclosures are largely covered by the 'related parties' disclosure requirements of SORP 2000 as preserved in SORP 2005, and which feature both here (see **4.4.4.2–4.4.4.3**) and in the accounts notes.

Chapter 5

THE SORP AND ACCOUNTING STANDARDS

INTRODUCTION

5.1   In 1995 the Charities SORP had said little about its relationship with individual accounting standards – except where a modified treatment was needed to comply with charity law. This need for a *charity-specific* application of the commercially oriented general Standards was mainly

(i)   to account properly for **endowment capital** (ie, fund-accounting for all *non-revenue* gifts/grants accruing to a charity) and

(ii)   in accordance with their respective terms of trust, to account separately for all *special-purpose* **restricted funds** of an income, or revenue, nature (these will be either gifts/grants intended for spending on the specified *activities* or income derived from endowment capital given to the charity for such activities),

(iii)   to exempt legally or operationally 'inalienable' assets from capitalisation, and

(iv)   to require investment assets to be accounted for at their 'current value' where feasible.

Apart from that, the SORP explained the impact of what were then the four 'fundamental accounting concepts', and laid down a general requirement now reiterated in SORP 2005 as:

'In meeting the obligation to prepare accounts showing a true and fair view ... accruals accounts should follow the standards and principles issued or adopted by the Accounting Standards Board, or its predecessors or successors and set out in:

(a)   Statements of Standard Accounting Practice (SSAPs);
(b)   Financial Reporting Standards (FRSs);
(c)   Urgent Issues Task Force abstracts (UITFs);

and in addition take note of:

(d)   The Interpretation for Public Benefit Entities of the Statement of Principles for Financial Reporting (a discussion paper issued by the Accounting Standards Board in May 2003).

This SORP provides guidance and recommendations that supplement accounting standards in the light of the special factors prevailing or transactions undertaken with the charity sector, and, as with the law, does not seek to repeat all of their requirements. Appendix 2 provides a summary of these accounting standards and of their general applicability to charities.'

– SORP 2005, paragraph 61

SORP 2005 was not only updated to keep pace with the further development of the Accounting Standards Board's (ASB's) standards and principles – especially the ASB's International Accounting Standards (IAS) convergence programme for all UK standards – but, like SORP 2000 before it, includes a special appendix to list them all, indicating (unfortunately only very briefly) in what way each one is or is not relevant to charity accounts for a true and fair view. Helpful though that is, such a cursory reminder can hardly suffice for those not already familiar with commercial and charity accounting practice, and we have therefore retained and updated the more informative summary from the previous edition of this book (see the Table at **5.4**).

SCOPE OF ACCOUNTING STANDARDS

5.2   Before considering their applicability to charity accounts, it is important to understand why we need to consider accounting standards at all, since these are really just a set of rules that have been developed over the last century to curb malpractice in the world of *commercial* accountability with its 'bottom line' of distributable profits. Latterly, the traditionally backward-looking emphasis on stewardship accounting has given way to the ASB's forward-looking concept of 'fair value' accounting, with the intention of making the annual report and accounts more reliable as a tool for *investor-decisions*. None of this seems to have much in common with the altruistic world of charity, where annual reporting has, for centuries, been purely historical, factual and objective – that is, until the overlapping of these two worlds in the charitable company (primarily for its use as a trading vehicle) and the eventual formulation of the Charities SORP. Thus for all charities preparing accounts intended to show a true and fair view, compliance with relevant accounting standards is normally a necessity, *insofar as these are not inconsistent with, or inadequate for, the need to demonstrate that the charity law duty of 'proper application' of all charitable resources has been satisfied by the trustees.*

However, the sharp distinctions needed to show strict compliance with donor requirements concerning gifts made *on trust* are not always so clear in SORP 2005. This can be traced to the SORP's careful alignment with the ASB's proposed general principles for joined-up financial reporting throughout the public and private sectors – itself part of a global striving for consensus on best practice in this field. For better or worse, the approach of the UK standard-setters seems to have been to build onto the commercially oriented standards new terminology for 'public benefit interpretations' and (for pure gifts and other 'non-exchange' transactions – e g taxes – that are peculiar to the governmental public benefit sector) special treatments. The result is a focus on perceived common principles rather than established common law, ie, on equity rather than trust law, with 'fair value' reliability for future economic decisions competing with the historical stewardship reporting that has always been needed for charity trustees to be able to show due compliance with the duty of care imposed on them by the common law of charitable trusts.

Charitable companies are, of course, specifically required by the Companies Act to prepare their accounts in accordance with relevant accounting standards, albeit with due consideration for their *not-for-profit* nature and therefore for any necessary adaptation required in order to meet the overriding objective of showing a true and fair view *as charities*, for which specific purpose the standards themselves were not developed in the first place and therefore must be approached with caution (much like a pedestrian when crossing a busy road).

But there is a further issue to consider here: the status of SORPs in relation to accounting standards.

The ASB's 'Foreword to Accounting Standards' and 'Explanatory Foreword to Statements of Recommended Practice' explain the general relationship between the two types of pronouncement. This is that SORPs are formulated by and for particular industries or sectors of the UK national economy, taking into account the principles of accounting standards and having regard to the 'spirit and reasoning' underlying the relevant standard.

Where a SORP modifies the application of an accounting standard, it does so in order to assist in the preparation of accounts that will give a true and fair view in the *special* circumstances of that particular industry or sector, in this case the charity sector. This means that even where there is no legal underpinning for them the accounting treatments proposed in a SORP, being of narrower application and therefore more particular, will necessarily have to take precedence over those of accounting standards, which are more general, *unless this would impair the truth and fairness of the accounts in the circumstances*. A parallel can be seen here with the relationship between a special trust and the main charity it points to.

FINANCIAL REPORTING STANDARD FOR SMALLER ENTITIES (FRSSE)

5.3   Issued originally in November 1997 for immediate adoption at their own option by 'small' companies and other reporting entities meeting the same size criteria, the Financial Reporting Standard for Smaller Entities (FRSSE) represented a radical departure from the general tendency towards more and more complex accounting standards in response to what has now come to be described as 'aggressive accounting' or 'financial engineering' in the world of the multinational conglomerates. The current version is FRSSE 2008, effective only for financial years starting from 6 April 2008 onwards, being basically the 2007 version updated to refer to the 2006 Companies Act instead of the 1985 Act, and in which specific provision continues to be made for SORPs to be able to limit the application of the FRSSE for their own purposes.

Any charity, whether incorporated or not, can adopt the current FRSSE for the preparation of its own (ie, entity) accruals accounts – provided the charity (together with its consolidated group interests) counts as 'small' as defined by the 2006 Act and before it that of 1985. This means that two out of the following three criteria must be satisfied year-on-year, with the proviso that the first year for which this fails to happen will not prevent adoption of the FRSSE. Once having failed to qualify as 'small', though, it will need two consecutive financial years of satisfying the condition to qualify again.

Because of the wording used in the FRSSE, *non-company* charities and their groups also have to satisfy similar conditions:

-     turnover (replaced by 'gross income' in Appendix 4 of SORP 2005 and in its Appendix 5: 'Accounting for Smaller Charities' – but not in the text itself[1]) not exceeding £6.5m (groups: or that figure plus 20% before the consolidation adjustments required by the Act);

-     balance sheet total (ie total assets before deducting liabilities) not exceeding £3.26m (groups: or that figure plus 20% before the consolidation adjustments required by the Act);

-     employees not exceeding an average of 50 in number.

To overcome this perceived problem (see footnote), which does not in any way prejudice *charity* accounting as prescribed by the SORP, the FRSSE's use of 'turnover' to measure size is modified by SORP 2005's Appendix 4, where 'gross income' is given as the *charity equivalent* to be used instead. While this may have become binding for *non-company* charities under the SORP's related 2008 Regulations, it seems to be the only way the SORP can bring a charitable company's *trust* income (ie its 'restricted income') within the size-definition. However, for the typical charity dependent on substantial gift-funding – as distinct from the *trading* that is the primary focus of accounting standards – the unfortunate result is that the SORP seems intent on denying access to the FRSSE for thousands of charities below the £6.5m turnover ceiling. See also the decision tree for FRSSE adoption at **12.2.8**.

Charities adopting the FRSSE must disclose the fact in their accounting policies note, and will then be exempt from the normal requirement to comply with the other accounting and financial reporting standards and ASB pronouncements – except for consolidated accounts. For the latter, the FRSSE refers the accounts-preparer to FRS2 and 9, also FRS6/7 and FRS10 – whereas the SORP is more enigmatic:

> 'If a charity applying the FRSSE prepares consolidated accounts, it should apply the relevant accounting practices and disclosures required by accounting standards and the SORP in relation to consolidated accounts.'
>
> *– SORP 2005, Appendix 5.2.2(f)*

As a kind of safety net when accounting for any transaction/event not specifically covered there, the FRSSE refers you to the full range of Standards – 'not as mandatory documents, but as a means of establishing current practice'.

RELEVANCE OF THE UK STANDARDS TO CHARITY ACCOUNTABILITY

5.4   As an unforeseen result of the current globalisation of accounting standards following a string of major corporate accounting scandals in the profit sector, the Charities SORP, as something of an endangered species, being based on the UK

---

[1]   Although, in the *company audit exemption regulations* before the 1985 Act's special regime for charitable companies was abolished for financial years from 1 April 2008, 'turnover' was replaced by 'gross income' in the case of a charitable company (but not for any group to which it belonged for that Act's purposes) there is no legal authority for the FRSSE – or for the Charities SORP itself, for that matter – to have done likewise. The problem seen here by the Charity Commission is that both voluntary and investment income (the major sources of revenue for most charities) fall outside the 1985 Act definition of 'turnover'.

standards, has now had to be given statutory protection under both company law as well as charity law, for as Mary Keegan, reporting as Financial Reporting Council (FRC) Chairman at the time, commented:

> '... the IASB has not yet had time to consider standards or guidance for particular sectors, and IASB standards are not designed to apply to some reporting entities such as those in the public benefit sector. The implications for SORPs will therefore need careful consideration if we are to avoid creating a gap ... The ASB . . . proposes an all-embracing new definition for the [public benefit] sector: public benefit entities which have a primary objective to provide goods or services for the general or social benefit, rather than a financial objective relating to returns to equity shareholders ... Public Benefit Entities [thus include] both government entities and charities ... We have noted in particular that the IASB has made clear that its standards are not designed to apply to not-for-profit activities. As its standards increasingly become the model for international financial reporting, however, we consider it important to provide a "bridge" from profit-orientated reporting to the public benefit sector.'

– Financial Reporting Council: 2003 Report

Which suggests that the true convergence for *charity* accounting standards may well be ultimately with something entirely different: the specially developed collection of *International Public Sector Accounting Standards* (IPSASs) and their successors (IPSFRSs), the extant set of which was published as long ago as 2002 by an offshoot (see below) of the New York-based *Committee of the International Federation of Accountants* (IFAC) – whose membership includes standard-setting bodies around the world. The entire set of these 'not-for-profit' international accounting standards can be freely downloaded from the IFAC website.

For ease of reference, the following tables indicate to what extent the charity sector will normally find the current UK Standards to be relevant, and where else in this book that relevance is explored further:

Financial Reporting Standards (FRS) and earlier Statements of Standard Accounting Practice (SSAP)

Standard	Subject	Relevance	Comments on special aspects
FRSSE	Financial Reporting Standard for Smaller Entities (2008)	Most (only for entity accounts)	The 'small charity' option: a cut-down version of all the (commercial) Standards – see above
FRS1	Cashflow Statements (revised 1996)	Most – albeit as a useless exercise	See chapter 11
FRS2	Accounting for subsidiary undertakings	Most	See **5.5.3**, and also **13.12** and **14.18–14.23**
FRS3	Reporting financial performance	Charitable companies: most	See **5.5.2**, also chapters 6 and 7
FRS4	Capital instruments	Not for any debt-financing convertible into equity	*Non-convertible* securitised debt (or its equivalent) could apply to charities – eg, Schools
FRS5	Reporting the substance of transactions	All	Some tensions with trust law compliance-needs

Standard	Subject	Relevance	Comments on special aspects
FRS6	Acquisitions and mergers	Little, other than for non-charitable group-members	**Charities** can be merged, not commercially *acquired*. See chapter 14
FRS7	Fair values in acquisition-accounting	Little	Both FRS6 and 7 do concern *non-charitable* undertakings (but not transfers of **trusteeship** of charities) – see chapter 14
FRS8	Related party transactions	Most	See chapter 12
FRS9	Associates and Joint Ventures	Most – but it is not yet 'charity-friendly'	See **5.5.3** and also **14.24**
FRS10	Goodwill and Intangible Assets	Little	See **5.5.4** and **5.5.7**
FRS11	Impairment of Fixed Assets and Goodwill	Some	See **5.5.5–5.5.6** and chapter 8
FRS12	Provisions, Contingent Liabilities and Contingent Assets	Some	Applies especially to (external) charitable commitments. See **5.5.7**
FRS13	Derivatives and other Financial Instruments – Disclosures	Little, other than their use in risk-mitigation	Special disclosures now required by SORP 2005
FRS15	Tangible Fixed Assets	All	See **5.5.5–5.5.6** and chapter 8
FRS17	Accounting for Staff Retirement Benefits	All	See chapter 12; also **5.5.8** and **6.18**
FRS18	Accounting policies	All	See **5.5.9** and chapter 12
FRS21	Post Balance Sheet events	All	For accounts starting from 1 January 2005 replaces SSAP17
FRS23	Effects of changes in foreign currency exchange rates (re. FRS26)	Charitable companies using 'fair value' accounting rules	Accounts starting from 1 January 2006
FRS24	Hyper-inflation (re. FRS26)	Charitable companies using 'fair value' accounting rules	Accounts starting from 1 January 2006
FRS25/26 and 29	Financial Instruments (Derivatives, Hedging, etc.)	Charitable companies using 'fair value' accounting rules	Accounts starting from 1 January 2006 (2007 for FRS29)
FRS27	Life Assurance business	None	Inapplicable to most charities
FRS30	Heritage Assets	All	See chapter 8
Pre-ASB Standards not yet superseded:			
SSAP4	Accounting for government grants	Some	See **5.5.1** below

Standard	Subject	Relevance	Comments on special aspects
SSAP5	Accounting for VAT	All	
SSAP9	Stocks and long-term contracts	Most	Principally concerns trading and contracting by charities/groups
SSAP13	Accounting for research and development	Little	Concerns the commercial value of 'private' research – e g by medical research charities/groups
SSAP19	Investment properties	Some	Fully covered by the SORP
SSAP20	Foreign currency translations	All	See also FRS23/4
SSAP21	Accounting for leases and hire purchase contracts	All	See also UITF28
SSAP25	Segmental reporting	Little	See chapter 15 on Summarised and Segmental Accounts

'Urgent Issues Task Force' Consensus Pronouncements[2] (UITF Abstracts) extant as neither subsequently withdrawn nor subsumed in a Standard or its revision:

Abstract	Subject	Relevance	Comment on special aspects
UITF4	Long-term debtors in Current Assets – presentation	All	Now modified by the SORP's 'social investment' rules
UITF5	Transfers from Current Assets to Fixed Assets	Some	Must be at existing carrying value, removing any revaluation gains/losses from 'net income'
UITF9	Accounting for operations in hyper-inflation economies	All	Relates to SSAP20 (Foreign Currency translation)
UITF21 & Appendix	Accounting issues arising from the proposed introduction of the Euro	Some	
UITF23	Application of FRS15's transitional rules on splitting out asset-components having a different useful economic life	Was: All	
UITF24	Asset-accounting for start-up costs	Little	Not: websites – see UITF29
UITF26	Accounting for the real cash value of barter transactions for advertising	All	(Implications for barter-deal valuation more generally)

---

[2]   Other than those dealing with equity interests – for obvious reasons.

Abstract	Subject	Relevance	Comment on special aspects
UITF27	Revisions to estimates* of the useful economic life of goodwill and intangible assets (*no retrospective adjustment)	Little	
UITF28	Operating lease incentives (Incorporates UITF12 on lessee-accounting for e g reverse premiums, rent-free periods, etc)	All	Relates to SSAP21 (Accounting for Leases and HP Contracts)
UITF29	Website development costs can be capitalised only for an 'enduring' asset whose costs are considered recoverable from future cashflows (or from other economic benefits)	All	Build-costs for an educational website could also be added to (tangible) fixed assets – but only to the extent of demonstrable (non-cash) future benefits
UITF31	Exchange of a business or other non-monetary assets for an interest in a subsidiary, joint venture or associate	Some	Constrains the carrying value of retained interests in underlying assets for control/participating interests valued under FRS2/9 in consolidated accounts, etc
UITF32	Employee Benefit Trusts and other Intermediate Payment Arrangements (Under FRS5, any funds passed to an intermediary are presumed to create an asset until vesting unconditionally in identified beneficiaries)	Little	
UITF33	Obligations in capital instruments where a liability might not normally accrue	None	Charities cannot issue equity of any kind, so no doubts arise
UITF34	Pre-contract costs incurred before the deal is secured cannot be carried forward	All	Applies to trading by charities and their group-members
UITF35	Death-in-service and Incapacity benefits	All	Re FRS17 Defined Benefit Scheme uninsured benefits
UITF36	Contracts for sales of capacity	Little	(Revenue recognition rules for swaps, barter-deals, etc)
UITF 40	Revenue recognition from contracts for services	Little	Refers to FRS5 and Application Note G

ASPECTS REQUIRING SPECIAL ATTENTION

5.5   For a UK charity with substantial locally-run international operations to overcome the problem of being locked in to UK/AS, restructuring as a group of national charities under a *non-charitable* **not-for-profit** UK (or overseas) parent company would be necessary. The group consolidated accounts would not then be tied to UK/AS. Under the Companies Act they could follow appropriate international standards instead

– which (in line with the group's public benefit purpose) would of course need to be those derived for use in *public benefit* financial reporting and first published in 2002 by the then Public Sector Committee of the New York based IFAC (the global umbrella body for financial reporting standard-setters) as IPSAS/IPSFRS.

That Committee, now renamed the International Public Sector Accounting Standards Board (IPSASB) is committed to the further development of IPSAS/IPSFRS. These are IAS *adaptations* clearly more suitable for adoption by all 'public sector' bodies – which includes not only governmental non-profit bodies but also the 'private' not-for-profit sector in general if only the body is established for the public benefit, thus charities in particular.

However, due to funding uncertainties even for its core activities supported by national governments, the IPSASB (or PSC, as it was known at the time) was unable to focus on issues specific to charities and other private sector bodies as *independent* public benefit providers. The gap this left (and still leaves) was highlighted in the 2004 report of a strategic review panel (independently chaired by the then head of the UK Government Accounting Service):

> 'The Panel notes that the private not-for-profit sector is currently outside the scope of both the International Accounting Standards Board (IASB) and the PSC. Whilst the Panel considers that this leaves a significant gap in terms of the coverage of global financial reporting standards it would be premature to extend the scope of the PSC to include the private not-for-profit sector until the forward funding of the Standards Program is assured. However, the PSC should have a medium term objective to include the private not-for-profit sector within its scope and should communicate such an aim to its constituents.'

'Capital expenditure' grants (SSAP4)

5.5.1 Under SSAP4, 'Accounting for Government Grants', one way to account for 'capital expenditure' grants from statutory authorities used to be to deduct the grant from the cost of the fixed asset – unless the charity was a company, as the Companies Act does not allow such a treatment. But this option was later withdrawn by the ASB, so that now the only way to achieve the required matching of 'related' income and expenditure in reporting the activities of the year is to spread the recognition of the grant as income in line with the depreciation charges in respect of the asset concerned.

Because the 1995 SORP did not particularly dwell on the charity law principle here, many accountants assumed that a 'deferred income' treatment was in order, but failed to notice that this could only fully satisfy the SORP's *gift-accounting* requirements (based on the common law of trusts) where the grant is accounted for as an *expendable endowment*. While the Charities SORP continues to specify *restricted fund* accounting initially for such grants, saying that it is the nature of the restriction that will decide the accounting treatment, the necessary special explanations were also included in SORP 2000 and are still to be found in SORP 2005. The problem is that they are not very easy to locate.

Trust law constrains *all* gifts/grants of money/assets intended to equip the charity with fixed assets *with the legally binding intention of their continuing use*. Such a 'term of trust' then makes the gift one of endowment capital, as a *special* case where the donor-restriction is not discharged until the charity has had the *use* intended by the donor.

Although the SORP does continue to clarify this distinction in an appendix (see below), the text of the SORP specifies only the more general treatment of 'restricted fund' accounting for such gifts, saying that funds given just to 'provide' the fixed asset will become unrestricted upon its acquisition and should then (according to paragraph 111 of SORP 2005) be 'designated' and amortised over the life of the asset to satisfy the spirit of SSAP4. That is also the line taken by the ASB in its proposed advisory 'Interpretation for Public Benefit Entities of the Statement of Principles for Financial Reporting' as part of its convergence agenda to align UK/AS with IAS, based on commercial rather than trust law, and with which the SORP itself is now aligned, as noted above.

For strict compliance with the enduring principles of *English trust law*, however, it is left to the accounts preparer/auditor to check whether there is *also* a 'continuing use' requirement imposed on the gift as a further 'term of trust' – in which case it must, to satisfy charity law, be shown in the *endowments* column of the SoFA. That is, in our view, unless the asset is only short-lived (say, not more than 2 years), or its value is below the threshold for capitalisation under the charity's accounting policies.

In the case of a *wasting* asset the endowment is automatically *expendable* over the asset's life and should be amortised accordingly on the 'transfers' line of the SoFA in line with the annual depreciation expenditure charges, thus satisfying SSAP4. (In the rare situation where the donor has clearly imposed an obligation to preserve the original value of the gift, a 'sinking fund' would have to be designated out of the charity's own reserves in order to honour such a wish.) As an alternative treatment that – although not mentioned in the SORP – may commend itself to the reader as being simpler and more transparent, the annual depreciation charge itself can instead be taken direct to capital in the endowments column of the SoFA, obviating the need for an entry on the inter-fund transfers line. This parallels the need to credit to that same column any investment income on endowed funds invested on the (properly authorised) 'total return' basis, as explained at **6.4.3**.

Any *material* contingent liability to make repayment (e g on early disposal) during the first few years of use will normally only need disclosure in the notes. It cannot justify deferring recognition of the gift in the first place:

> '… the possibility of having to repay the incoming resources does not affect their recognition in the first instance.'

> *– SORP 2005, paragraph 111*

Unfortunately, SORP 2005, like that of 2000, takes rather a circuitous path if you want 'chapter and verse' as to the proper treatment of such gifts/grants: it sends you from paragraph to paragraph to land up eventually in Appendix 3, which only obliquely covers 'actual use':

> 'Restricted funds may be restricted income funds, which are expendable at the discretion of the trustees in furtherance of some particular aspect(s) of the objects of the charity. Or they may be capital (ie endowment) funds, where the assets are required to be invested, or retained for actual use, rather than expended.'

> *– SORP 2005, Appendix 3.2(a)*

What you really want in order to be able to quote 'chapter and verse' is now buried in the *Glossary* at GL 34, where despite the misleading heading of 'Inalienable Asset' the proper accounting treatment is precisely stated:

> 'Normally the asset will belong to the charity's "permanent endowment" where it is held on trusts which contemplate its retention and continuing use but not its disposal. However, in the case of a gift-in-kind of a "wasting asset", such as a building, a long lease or a non-durable artefact, the terms of trust may not have provided for its maintenance in perpetuity or its replacement. In that case the endowment will be treated as expendable to the extent of the aggregate amount of its depreciation or amortisation properly provided for in the annual accounts (ie based on its currently anticipated useful life).'
>
> – *SORP 2005, Glossary GL 34*

These explanations – however tortuous it may be to track them down in SORP 2005 – do at least make it clear that the restricted fund will be capital in nature (ie an endowment) if the grantor of the asset (or the money for it) imposed a binding condition of *retention for the charity's own use on a continuing basis*. Where – as is normally the case – the grant is of/for a 'wasting' (ie depreciating) asset, this will make the fund an *expendable* endowment – to be amortised either:

(i)   by annual transfers from capital to income in the SoFA in order to offset in the latter column the annual depreciation charges reflecting the consumption of the asset's net cost over its useful economic life (which also means taking into account any special terms of trust that may have been imposed concerning the disposal of the residual asset); or

(ii)   by charging that annual depreciation direct to the endowment column in the SoFA, as explained above.

Net income/expenditure statement (FRS3)

5.5.2   Because of the need to retain comparability of the accounts of all companies for DBERR purposes, SORP 2005, like 2000, makes it clear that, for charitable companies only, a separate Summary Income and Expenditure Statement will be required in order to satisfy FRS3 only in the rare situation where the SoFA cannot be adapted to achieve the necessary compliance through the SoFA alone. We deal with those requirements in chapter 7.

Non-charitable subsidiary/associated undertakings (FRS2/9)

5.5.3   While the consolidated SoFA under SORP 2005 automatically segregates the revenues and costs of all *subsidiary* (FRS2) undertakings within the two basic headings of charitable activities and activities to generate funds, no such segregation is possible in complying with the charity-unfriendly treatment the SORP continues to specify for FRS9 undertakings. We deal with the latter problem in chapter 14.

In the balance sheet, the FRS9 requirement is for associated undertakings and corporate joint ventures (including consortium undertakings) to be equity-consolidated to show the group interest in their net assets. The SORP, of course, continues to require all *investment* assets to be shown in the balance sheet at their current market value – except where:

(i)   valuation difficulties make this impracticable, when historical cost figures can (continue to) be used instead; or

(ii)   the asset is a 'social' or 'programme-related' investment, when historical cost and annual impairment reviews are specified.

This requires a distinction to be drawn between the use of such a non-charitable undertaking primarily to serve the charitable/administrative (ie functional) purposes of the group parent (when (ii) above will apply) and its use for other (ie commercial investment) purposes (when (i) above may apply). The carrying value of the reporting charity's interest in it should, however, be the same in both the entity and consolidated balance sheets.

The strict view taken in FRS9 that such interests are under *shared* control – not the sole control required for full consolidation in group accounts – and must therefore be segregated to make the fact clear, is at the root of their awkward treatment by the SORP, which under such a constraint can't distinguish fully in the SoFA between their charitable uses and their fundraising uses – unlike FRS2 interests. In the balance sheet, while a segregated presentation under the 'social investment' classification in SORP 2005 is now feasible, their carrying value remains constrained by FRS9's equity-accounting rules. These prevent the adoption of the SORP's historical cost basis for them, because the commercial purpose of the FRS9 treatment is to show the fair value of resources held outside the group and under shared control. However, where that is done to further a charitable project, not just to make money, it is arguable that the economic aspect should take second place to the charitable one.

On the other hand, the balance sheet treatment required by the SORP at paragraph 406 under FRS2 continues to be that the group's *charitable* funds should always be distinguished from any *non-charitable* funds retained by group members (ie subsidiaries) operating outside the Objects of the group parent. See chapter 13, where we highlight at **13.5** this often overlooked fund-accounting requirement.

SORP 2005 makes it clear at paragraph 383(d) that, for *charitable* subsidiary undertakings, the 'branch' accounting provisions of Part VI of the Charities Act 1993 ('the 1993 Act') pre-empt the consolidation provisions of the Standards – except that in the special case where both the parent and its subsidiary/associate are charitable *companies*, their statutory *entity* accounts, being outside Part VI altogether, can only be grouped together by *consolidation*, as discussed more fully in chapter 14.

Capitalisation of goodwill and intangible assets (FRS10)

5.5.4 FRS10, the Standard regulating how goodwill and intangible assets should be accounted for, can be of little relevance to most charities, insofar as the distinction drawn between purchase and creation (of goodwill and intangible assets) is mainly of concern as to their commercial value. Professional bodies, and certain other kinds of membership association, established as charities, might find that the use of commercially valuable publication titles forms a part of their activities.

For obvious reasons, however, charities would otherwise find it difficult to justify retaining such assets as 'qualifying investments'.

Capitalisation and depreciation of 'own use' fixed assets (FRS15/11)

(a) The carrying value of the asset

5.5.5 One of the most important developments in accounting standardisation, and one that has a considerable impact on charities with valuable old buildings, is FRS15. This specifically deleted SSAP19's permissive disapplication to charities as a now redundant exception. FRS15 has not otherwise addressed the subject of investment properties and their revaluation – it only excluded them because their review was still going on as a separate exercise at that time.

The main impact of the FRS on charities (other than those adopting the FRSSE, where a certain latitude is allowed) has been in relation to 'own use' fixed assets, in particular the basis of their:

(i)   valuation (other than of gifts in kind) or revaluation; and

(ii)   depreciation (or non-depreciation) especially of buildings, but also of other long-lived assets.

The FRS did in part endorse the SORP's special rules on fixed-asset accounting for gifts in kind, but it then relegated to an explanatory paragraph its rather limited acceptance of the validity of the 1995 SORP's non-capitalisation of certain inalienable/historic, etc, *functional* fixed assets – ie those that charities are effectively unable to dispose of without detriment to the furtherance of their Objects. In SORP 2005, however, the rules here were tightened up by narrowing that definition to *heritage* assets (see chapter 8) and disregarding inalienability completely.

It can be seen from FRS15's Appendix IV, 'The Development of the FRS', paragraphs 6–9, that the ASB accepted the practicality of not capitalising *donated* inalienable/historic tangible fixed assets that are difficult to value reliably (e g based on a recent market transaction or inheritance tax valuation – as noted in paragraph 287 of SORP 2005) – but not those purchased out of 'special trust' funds donated for the purpose where the acquisition is after first implementing FRS15.

This effectively ring-fenced the accounting treatment adopted by charities for *pre-FRS15 acquisitions* where justified on cost-benefit grounds (ie the valuation costs entailed in capitalising the asset exceeded the value of the information to the reader, any actual realisation being so improbable as to be only a remote contingency).

The valuation basis to be used when capitalising tangible fixed assets donated in kind to a charity, as noted at paragraph 255(c) of the SORP, is:

> 'The initial carrying amount of tangible fixed assets received as gifts and donations by charities should be the current value of the assets at the date they are received.'

– FRS15, paragraph 17

'Current value' is less subjective than the SORP's 'value to the charity', as is apparent from the way the Standard defines the term:

'The current value of a tangible fixed asset to the business is the lower of replacement cost and recoverable amount. [Recoverable amount is] the higher of net realisable value and value in use.'

– FRS15, paragraph 2: Definitions

'Value in use' is then cross-referenced to FRS11 for its definition and calculation as given there. For charities adopting the FRSSE, however, this is simplified to 'the lower of market value and value in use' at the date of gift.

The option to capitalise at either historical cost or a valuation is constrained by the FRS's requirement that *revalued* assets must then be carried in the balance sheet at their *current* 'value in use' – ie the revaluation must not be allowed to become out of date. This is, of course, subject to FRS11, and – as with (b) below – does not affect the SORP's requirement to recognise gifts of fixed assets at a deemed historical cost equal to their estimated market value at the time of gift, however, since that does not amount to 'revaluation' – even if later revised by way of correction.

The view taken at the time in FRS15's Exposure Draft (at paragraph 28 of Appendix IV) was that the residual values of tangible fixed assets in the longer term will invariably be less than initial capitalisation values – but this merely reflects the effect of requiring the measurement of those residual values to be by reference to prices ruling at the time of acquisition or revaluation (ie thus eliminating currency inflation).

This was confirmed by the way FRS15 softened the uncompromising language of its Exposure Draft, in that it does not, after all, exclude the *appreciation* that can arise from changes in supply and demand (eg 'heritage' value; 'alternative use' potential) – but instead imposes an FRS11-type annual impairment review to substantiate cases where little or no depreciation is being charged (eg on grounds of immateriality).

The FRSSE relaxes the regime yet further by not imposing any such annual review on the smaller charity.

Impairment reviews are required not only in the absence of any material depreciation charges but also where the depreciation period is extended beyond 50 years for what may, for example, be a substantial and well-maintained institutional property used for carrying out charitable purposes. The frequently used argument that depreciation charges at such low rates as 1% or 2% are 'immaterial' in any particular case must also deal with the materiality of the accumulated charge needed to reflect the ratio between the currently anticipated remaining life and the total life of such a property.

By thus tightening the rules in this way, FRS11 and FRS15 made it a difficult and demanding exercise for many non-FRSSE charities to measure gross and net carrying values in the balance sheet in respect of tangible fixed assets capitalised for their own use.

This aspect of balance sheet accounting is dealt with more fully in chapter 8, where a flowchart is provided at **8.5** to assist readers with the decisions needed to ascertain the correct accounting treatment in any particular case.

(b) 'Impairment' of a capitalised asset's carrying value

5.5.6 Where a reporting charity carries any of its functional (ie 'own use') fixed assets at a *revaluation* it is required under FRS11 to carry out a special review if any 'impairment' of the asset's value is suspected. The FRS was not intended to catch assets carried in the balance sheet at historical cost less accumulated depreciation unless there are *indications* of impairment.

However, its catchment area was later clarified by FRS15 – see (a) above – to say that an impairment review is required *annually* for all tangible 'own use' fixed assets on which little or no depreciation is being charged – regardless of whether carried in the balance sheet at historical cost or current value – unless the FRSSE is adopted, which instead requires all functional fixed assets to be written down to their 'recoverable amount if necessary'.

This means that, for non-FRSSE charities, the only situation where FRS15 will not *automatically* impose an annual impairment review is where a fixed asset continues to be depreciated over an unexpired life of less than 50 years and:

(a)   is a revalued asset whose residual value is not suspected of impairment; or

(b)   is capitalised at either:
  (i)   historical cost, in the case of purchased/constructed assets; or
  (ii) 'deemed' historical cost equal to its estimated market value at time of gift, in accordance with the SORP, even where that value is subsequently adjusted in the light of further information – provided no attempt is made to revalue the asset as at a later date.

The appropriate value at which to carry an 'impaired' asset is always the lower of its present balance sheet value (net) and its 'recoverable amount'. The recoverable amount is either its net realisable value if sold off now or, if higher, its 'value in use'. The difficulty in applying the Standard to charities is that 'value in use' is normally determined for commercial accounting purposes by a calculation of net present value based on the future cashflows that the use of the asset is expected to generate.

This being so, FRS11 makes the following provision:

> 'If a fixed asset is not held for the purpose of generating cash flows either by itself or in conjunction with other assets, for example certain fixed assets held for charitable purposes, it is not appropriate to measure the asset at an amount based on its expected future cash flows. In such cases it may not be appropriate to write down the fixed asset to its recoverable amount – an alternative measure of its service potential may be more relevant.'
>
> – *FRS11*

Such service potential is normally likely to produce a relatively high figure (it being much easier to continue using fixed assets for charity work long after they have ceased to be economically viable if used primarily for generating profits). It is therefore felt that the calculation will rarely (eg if declining demand for the free public benefit it provides left surplus capacity for which no other charitable/economic use could be found) yield an impairment requiring a charity's asset values to be written down. This is therefore an important relief for charities.

In any case, 'impairment' reviews as such are almost vestigial in the FRSSE, in that they are not unconditionally *annual* but only 'where necessary'.

Commitments arising from charitable grant awards (FRS12)

5.5.7 Just as with FRS8, where the Charities SORP and the needs of the Charity Commission as regulator had already worked out what disclosures in respect of 'trustee-transactions' are required in the public interest to satisfy the strict accountability of charity trustees under the existing law, making the real impact of that standard effectively a kind of reinforcement of the Charities SORP in the case of *charitable company accounts*, so FRS12 effectively reinforced the Charities SORP requirements in 2000 concerning the recognition of liabilities and the disclosure of contingencies. Things have moved on since then, however, and SORP 2005 seeks to impose liability-accrual for *any* charitable commitment where, as noted below, a third party can be shown to have had a 'valid expectation' of its fulfilment and the charity has no control over whether any outstanding entitlement conditions will be met. That (apart from the morality of letting such a mindset become binding in honour – with all the implications such a non-existent 'beneficiary-entitlement' must have for the would-be donor) seems to beg a more fundamental question: the uncertainty that distinguishes non-accruable *contingent* liabilities. See **6.7.1** for a detailed consideration of the impact of the SORP's interpretation of this Standard.

Grant-commitments to be accrued as liabilities

The catch for some charities, however, is that the SORP now makes no exception for awards expressed as being payable only out of future income – an exception carefully made in the 1995 version. The overriding principle expressed in the FRS, and also in the SORP since 2000, is that an 'operational liability' should be provided for where the award of a charitable grant has been notified to the intended beneficiary in terms that have 'created a valid expectation' (ie in the mind of the prospective recipient, or of some other party) of its fulfilment, leaving the charity with a 'present obligation (legal or constructive) as a result of a past event'.

Grant-commitments to be noted (or designated) but not accrued

This cannot so easily happen where the grant award is manifestly in excess of available funds (eg as evidenced by the charity's latest accounts on public record), but that cannot suffice to negate the expectation. Something more will be needed to put the question beyond doubt. Where such an award is clearly subject to pre-conditions of any kind (including eligibility criteria set by the grant-making charity – particularly where annual reviews are stipulated), then unless there is reasonable certainty of those conditions being met it cannot properly be provided for as a liability but should instead be disclosed as a charitable commitment unless (in appropriate cases) covered by designated funds set aside for that purpose.

'Performance-related' grants with income-entitlement pre-conditions

SORP 2005 clarifies the proper accounting treatment required where charities make or receive this unique kind of 'zero-tolerance' grant for charitable activities: income must be recognised in the SoFA each year *in line with the related expenditure* for revenue grants (typically awarded by a Local Authority or Central Government Department, but grant-making charities could also impose such terms) where the grant-control agreement denies the recipient charity any legal entitlement to the grant-monies until certain specified output requirements (as regards the level/quantity and/or quality of service to be provided) have been met to the donor's satisfaction. This is a special case because the denial effectively defers the gift's 'perfection' (completion) for trust law purposes until the expenditure it is to fund has been incurred, so that the charity never does possess any unspent trust funds as such, for which this kind of grant-control agreement has 'zero-tolerance'. Until then, any grant monies advanced under the control agreement remain legally the property of the donor, necessitating at best a 'deferred income' treatment for such cash advances (if not liability-accrual) until they qualify for recognition as income of the year.

Notional asset/liability for staff pension scheme under-funding/over-funding (FRS17)

5.5.8 The 5-year phased implementation of this contentious Standard called for progressively more detailed accounts notes disclosures additional to SSAP24, which was only superseded upon full implementation of FRS17 with its recognition of the notional asset/liability for pension-funding in accounts for financial years starting on/after 1 January 2005 in respect of single-employer 'defined benefit' ('final salary') schemes or multi-employer schemes of the same kind that identify each employer's share of the underlying assets and liabilities in the scheme on a consistent and reasonable basis. For further information about the disclosures required in the accounts notes, see under 'Staff costs' at **12.3.5**.

Those (larger) charities whose accounts are materially affected by this need to ring-fence the notional asset in a designated fund of its own so that it does not result in *inflated reserves*, or else they may have to consider abating lower-priority designated funds correspondingly in order to avoid the notional liability resulting in apparently *negative reserves*. We deal with the impact on the balance sheet at **10.5.1** and the impact on the SoFA at **6.7.6**.

Accounting policies and assumptions (FRS18)

5.5.9 The strict and detailed requirements of this Standard mean that the trustees of a charity are expected to exercise *informed judgment* in order to 'select those accounting policies judged to be *most appropriate* to its particular circumstances for the purpose of giving a true and fair view'.

All policies and assumptions must comply with two 'principles' (unless stated otherwise in the accounts notes) and a further four 'objectives'.

These are discussed in more detail in chapter 12.

Chapter 6

THE STATEMENT OF FINANCIAL ACTIVITIES

INTRODUCTION AND BACKGROUND

6.1   The SoFA was originally introduced by the 1995 SORP as a totally new 'primary accounting statement' for charities. It was designed to overcome the limitations of the Income and Expenditure Account, with its inappropriate exclusion of endowment capital funding and commercially 'unrealised' resources. The key phrase is 'Financial Activities', because the Statement combines a comprehensive account of the income and costs of all operating *activities* as well as reporting *all* movements in *financial* resources, both capital and income.

The Income and Expenditure Account is essentially the voluntary sector's equivalent of the commercial Profit and Loss Account, but as such it cannot cope with the more complex needs of *charities* for full compliance with *charity law*. Not only is it confined to the year's 'realised' gains and operating surplus/deficit, but it cannot handle movements on endowed funds (*trust capital* movements).

Worse than that, until the 1995 Charities SORP put a stop to the practice, many charities did not include *restricted* funds in their Income and Expenditure Account at all, and the commercially inspired practice of treating them as 'liabilities' in the balance sheet was widespread. Charities had even been known to contact a major donor to suggest the imposition of some sort of restriction on the use of the donation so that it need not be shown in the Income and Expenditure Account but could be 'played down' as a movement on restricted funds as disclosed in the accounts notes. Such 'window dressing' was able to make many a fundraising charity look misleadingly 'poor', when in reality it may have had huge special-purpose or even endowed funds.

The SoFA solves this and other charity accountability problems by presenting in single-page format a *complete* picture of all movements in the charity's funds. Far from hindering fundraising, this actually facilitates it through the greater credibility afforded by its comprehensiveness and 'openness'.

In his treatise, *A Study of Charity Accounts after the Publication of Statement of Recommended Practice 2: Accounting by Charities* (Charity Finance Directors Group, 1991), Dr Ken Ashford, as an academic long before becoming head of the operational accountancy unit at the Charity Commission's Liverpool Office, outlined many of the problems inherent in the use of the Income and Expenditure Account for charities, due to the fact that it was originally designed for trading operations.

Combination Statement

6.1.1   The Income and Expenditure Account's *supplementary* financial statements under FRS3, the Statement of Total Recognised Gains and Losses (STRGL) and the Funds Reconciliation Statement, are neatly combined in the SoFA as a composite primary accounting statement adapted to charities' distinctive reporting needs. For the authors, this represented a major victory in freeing charity accounting from the straitjacket of DTI standardisation in company reporting of distributable profits.

Although the SoFA looks radically different from an Income and Expenditure Account, this is mainly due to its lack of focus on a 'bottom-line' surplus/deficit figure, its more comprehensive inclusion of capital (endowed funds) movements and especially the way it distinguishes between the different types of trust fund that the charity has ('fund accounting').

In chapter 7, we discuss the need for a separate Statement of Income and Expenditure for any charitable company unable to format the upper section of its SoFA to comply fully with FRS3. For *non-company* charities this is no longer an issue as the ASB accepts that it is inappropriate for them to be required to show a 'realised' net result (the not-for-profit sector's equivalent of 'net profit' – or 'net loss') for the year in accordance with that Standard. However, for the *charitable company's* SoFA to satisfy FRS3 and the DBERR it must in all cases include a clear reference to the company law requirement (see chapter 7) by adding, for example, the words '(incorporating an income and expenditure statement)', or simply '(Income and Expenditure)' after or immediately below the title.

Columnar format

6.1.2   Since the SoFA has to report all the charity's incoming resources in the year and all expenditure of its resources in that year, essentially distinguishing between each of the principal types of fund, it has a columnar style of presentation for the sake of clarity, a format that in principle has since become *mandatory* for *non-company* charities under the related Regulations, and now also for the consolidation of small charity groups, and (for audit purposes) unavoidable for charitable companies in other cases. As the Charities SORP puts it:

> 'The statement should consist of a single set of accounting statements and be presented in columnar form if the charity operates more than one class of fund; ...'.

> *– SORP 2005, paragraph 30(a)*

> 'If it has more than one type of fund, the statement should show, in columns, the movements in the different types of funds as well as the total movements of all the funds.'

> *– SORP 2005, paragraph 84*

In particular, separate columns are required for endowed funds, other restricted (ie income) funds and unrestricted funds, adding up to the total funds column. Where necessary to enable the reader to come to a proper understanding of the charity and its activities, this is to be supplemented by supporting analysis of major individual funds in the notes to the accounts.

Obviously, a column can and should be omitted where there are no movements for the year, or where the figures are immaterial. In the latter case, you must of course include the relevant information in another fund column, appropriately re-titled – such as: 'Unendowed Funds – general and special-purpose', as distinct from *endowed* funds, or 'Restricted Funds – capital and income', which for a charitable company could be: 'Trust Funds – capital and income' to distinguish them from its *corporate* funds), but with any *material* figures (eg year-end fund balances) segregated by showing them on a separate line in the appropriate section of the SoFA, and with an explanatory note at the foot of the statement to avoid distorting the true and fair view. A fairly common example is where relatively small gifts have been added to a substantial endowed fund in the year.

It also goes without saying that where necessary these columns can always be *sub-divided* to show more than the statutory minimum – for example, by splitting the unrestricted income column into designated and free funds, or the restricted income column between categories of restriction, or even the endowments column into permanent and expendable endowments, or between general-purpose and special-purpose endowments.

In chapter 3, the illustration we used from the annual accounts of *The Royal National Theatre* (see **3.2.2**) also shows the use of a 'Designated Activities' fund, while the following illustration, *The Army Benevolent Fund*, shows how the SoFA can be used to highlight *grant-aid commitments* ring-fenced as a fund of 'intended' awards already notified to the prospective beneficiaries.

	General Fund	Designated Funds (Note 2)	Restricted Funds	Total	2007
INCOMING RESOURCES	£	£	£	£	£
Voluntary income					
from the public:					
– Donations and appeals	2,298,365	535,454	25,000	2,858,819	1,677,666
– Legacies	1,071,554	–	–	1,071,554	1,766,125
	3,369,919	535,454	25,000	3,930,373	3,443,791
from the Army:					
– Army Units	306,634	–	–	306,634	271,087
- Army Central Fund	-	250,000	-	250,000	-
- Army Dependants Trust	19,004	-	-	19,004	181,706
– Regimental & Corps Benevolent Funds	672,098	–	–	672,098	607,296
– Edinburgh Military Tattoo	150,000	–	–	150,000	140,000
	1,147,736	250,000	–	1,397,736	1,200,089
Investment income	874,032	13,379	180,177	1,067,588	901,941
Activities for generating funds:					
Music on Fire!	-	-	-	-	1,081,943

	General Fund	Designated Funds (Note 2)	Restricted Funds	Total	2007
Other donations and events	1,089,178	–	–	1,089,178	937,349
Total income	**6,480,865**	**798,833**	**205,177**	**7,484,875**	**7,565,113**
RESOURCES EXPENDED					
Costs of generating funds					
– Fundraising trading costs	1,095,517	–	–	1,095,517	2,027,798
– Costs of generating voluntary income	1,150,478	47,416	–	1,197,894	1,077,210
		2,245,995	47,416	–	2,293,411
Net incoming resources available for charitable activities	4,234,870	751,417	205,177	5,191,464	4,460,105
Charitable activities					
– Grants to other charities	1,951,153	100,000	328,990	2,380,143	2,497,171
– Grants to Regiments/Corps for individuals	1,735,197	124,305	376,556	2,236,058	2,039,213
	3,686,350	224,305	705,546	4,616,201	4,536,384
– Support costs	232,721	2,510	41,208	276,439	304,678
	3,919,071	226,815	746,754	4,892,640	4,841,062
Governance costs	69,548	–	–	69,548	46,607
Total expenditure	**6,234,614**	**274,231**	**746,754**	**7,255,599**	**7,992,677**
Net income (before investment gains, etc.)	**246,251**	**524,602**	**(541,577)**	**229,276**	**(427,564)**
Exchange losses	(733)	-	-	(733)	(175)
Investment gains / (losses)	(734,792)	(14,498)	(201,354)	(950,644)	2,082,093
Net movement in funds	**(489,274)**	**510,104**	**(742,931)**	**(722,101)**	**1,654,354**
Income fund balances at 1 April	33,812,910	482,933	6,638,307	40,934,150	39,279,796
Transfer between funds	(50,000)	50,000	-	-	-
Income fund balances at 31 March	**33,273,636**	**1,043,037**	**5,895,376**	**40,212,049**	**40,934,150**
Permanent Endowment Funds				45,996	45,996
Total Funds at 31 March				40,258,045	40,980,146

	General Fund	Designated Funds (Note 2)	Restricted Funds	Total	2007

[Accounts Note] 2 Designated funds
The Designated Funds consist of the Northern Ireland Special Relief Fund (NISRF) and the Current Operations Fund (COF). The NISRF has been set up to meet the special requirements for aid occasioned by events in Northern Ireland, with the COF being established in 2007 to provide a continuing fund for soldiers, ex-soldiers and their dependants in times of need who are suffering distress as a result of military operations being undertaken at that time and all subsequent military operations.

The Army Benevolent Fund – 2007/08 accounts

As another example in common use, some independent schools show a designated fund column in the SoFA to segregate the 'trading' income and expenditure of the school itself as an operating unit from all the other unrestricted income and expenditure of the charity. This enables them to show the school's operating surplus/deficit on the face of the SoFA instead of only in the accounts notes. Another, if less useful, example is that given in SORP 2005 itself, where paragraph 87 suggests that the school '*may have two unrestricted fund columns, one containing the resource movement connected with teaching, another welfare and other costs*'.

Sectional structure

6.1.3 The sectional structure of the SoFA is carefully specified and illustrated both diagrammatically and by means of a table, the essential elements of which are set out below:

Description	Unrestricted Funds	Restricted Income Funds	Endowment Funds	Total Funds
Incoming Resources from				
generated funds:				
– Voluntary (solicited/unsolicited gifts, etc)	A1a	A1a	A1a	A1a
– Activities (inc events, charity shops, etc)	A1b	A1b		A1b
– Investment income	A1c*	A1c*		A1c
charitable activities	A2	A2		A2
other sources	A3	A3	A3	A3
Total incoming	**A**	**A**	**A**	**A**
Resources expended				
Costs of Generating Funds:				
– Gift-fundraising (appeals, etc) costs	B1a	B1a	B1a	B1a
– Fundraising trading costs	B1b	B1b		B1b

Description	Unrestricted Funds	Restricted Income Funds	Endowment Funds	Total Funds
– Investment management costs	B1c	B1c	B1c	B1c
Sub-total	B1	B1	B1	B1
[Incoming resources available for charitable activities = A-B1](optional)	*[A–B1]*	*[A–B1]*	*[A–B1]*	*[A–B1]*
Charitable Activities**	B2	B2	B2	B2
Governance costs	B3	B3		B3
Other resources expended	B4	B4		B4
Total Expenditure (= B1+B2+B3+B4)	**B**	**B**	**B**	**B**
Net Incoming Resources before Inter-fund Transfers (= A–B)	**C**	**C**	**C**	**C**
Inter-fund Transfers (gross)	D	D	D	Nil
Net Incoming Resources before Other Gains/Losses (= C+D)	**E**	**E**	**E**	**E**
Net Gain/Loss on revaluing Fixed Assets held for Own Use	F	F	F	F
Net Gains/Losses on Investment Asset Disposals/Revaluations	G	G	G	G
Net movement for year (= E+F+G)	**H**	**H**	**H**	**H**
Total Funds brought forward	I	I	I	I
Total Funds carried forward (= H+I)	J	J	J	J

* As a notable exception to the normal rule here, these items accrue not to income but to capital wherever a duly authorised 'total return' investing basis has been adopted for a permanent financial endowment. They must then be shown in the Endowment Funds column instead – see chapter 3.

**For activities having different charitable objectives (purposes) the total costs (including support costs) of each activity are to be shown on a separate line here, together with a sub-total line, instead of this single line – except that where grant-making is the sole or main charitable activity it is considered more informative to put all its support costs (if material) on a separate line. Also, *no* distinction is made here between service-provision and grant-making.

Section headings

6.1.4 The SoFA is designed to include all *endowed* (ie capital fund) movements, so the section for 'incomings' is normally worded as Incoming Resources rather than Income. Similarly, the separate sub-sections for Expenditure (or 'Resources Expended') introduced by SORP 2000 are described by very distinctive headings. The 2005 SORP still allows a certain latitude as regards *minor* variations in form and content. It 'ring-fences' only:

(i)   the basic structure; and

(ii)   actual disclosure of all required information.

The freedom this offers to adapt the layout and style of the SoFA, not only to show how particular incoming and outgoing resources are related (eg trading turnover and costs, 'performance-related' grants and the costs they have funded, fundraising proceeds and their costs, etc) but also to suit a charity's own particular reporting needs, allows for special solutions to practical problems of presentation – such as how best to show an occasional endowment movement, or the (material) turnover and operating costs of a 'shell' subsidiary that trades outside the charity's Objects and remits all its profits by donation under the GiftAid Scheme. (Of course, the corresponding group consolidated figures in the latter case might also need showing in some way on the face of the charity SoFA.) By utilising a suitable set of 'designated activities' funds (if a single SoFA column is used for this, it can be sub-analysed in a supporting accounts note), it is even possible to accommodate the need of many church and other membership association charities to distinguish (i) committed ongoing 'core' activity costs and their voluntary funding from (ii) all other, perhaps only occasional and/or less predictable, general-purpose income and its expenditure.

The SORP can safely accommodate all this because whatever it decrees for the preparation of the SoFA is made *obligatory* by its related Regulations – certainly for *non-company* charities and the consolidated accounts of all 'small' charity groups, while for charitable companies in other cases any significant departure will need concurrence by the charity's auditors to avoid the risk of a qualified audit opinion:

> 'The Statement of Financial Activities may be adapted to give a true and fair view, but disclosure requirements should always be met and the underlying structure should not be changed. Trustees should balance the provision of information with clarity.
>
> Category headings should be omitted where there is nothing to report in both the current and preceding periods.'
>
> – *SORP 2005, paragraphs 86 and 91*

This is to signal that it is acceptable to use more specific SoFA headings to fit the charity's circumstances. It is only that the generic terms used by the SORP are designed to cover *all* requirements for compliance with standards *and* charity law. For example, if a charity has no (material) incoming endowments it is quite in order to describe the top section of the SoFA as 'income' rather than using the wider description of 'incoming resources' as offered in the SORP.

It must also be borne in mind that the SoFA is in effect a summary statement that *aggregates* (*not* consolidates) all the individual charitable funds being accounted for as a 'collection' of differently constituted *and therefore separately administrable* charitable institutions. The *integrity* of their transactions must therefore be respected within the combination statement in which their *proper administration* is to be reported.

As a *summary* statement, the SoFA must nevertheless show the individual movements *gross* on each of the main fund categories, since these are distinct from each other under charity law and therefore cannot properly be netted off in annual reporting if the accounts are to serve their ultimate purpose of discharging the trustees' duty to account for their *stewardship* of the resources of *each* of these charitable institutions for which they are answerable at law.

This applies to *any* transaction between funds of the reporting charity that are legally distinct from each other and which trust law therefore doesn't allow to be merged together. Although transactions between, say, the unrestricted funds and a restricted fund (e g a pupil's school fees being defrayed out of a scholarship award from a 'special trust' fund administered by the school) will not have affected the overall resources available to the charity, they will certainly have affected the position of the individual trust fund concerned. So they must be shown *gross* in the respective columns and sections of the SoFA, as well as in any sub-analysis of major funds in the accounts notes, just as inter-fund transfers must be shown gross of any transfers in the opposite direction. We discuss the inter-fund transfers section of the SoFA at **6.10**.

Having arrived at the net incoming/(outgoing) resources for the year, the SoFA then continues with what in the commercial sector would be a separate primary statement reporting any *other* funds-movements in what FRS3 entitles the 'Statement of Total Recognised Gains and Losses'.

This section reports the results of any FRS15-compliant annual revaluation of tangible fixed assets held for the charity's own use and carried at 'current value' and (more rarely) any FRS10-compliant revaluations of *intangible* assets, as well as any realised/unrealised gains/losses on investment assets (see chapters 8 and 9 for further details).

The final section adds to the net movement in funds for the year the opening balances from the previous balance sheet on all the charity's funds, the result of which must then agree with the balance sheet figures of funds carried forward for future activities or for the benefit of the charity, as appropriate.

No 'bottom line'

6.1.5   Although in many cases it can (e g for FRS3 compliance) be modified to do so, the SoFA is not designed to focus on a single figure as the charity's surplus/deficit for the year. Although many charities do in fact trade (e g independent schools), and charitable trading turnover now represents almost half the aggregate gross income of all registered charities, it would be missing the point of charitable status to lock onto a particular line and column of the SoFA in order to spotlight an 'operating result' – especially where the charity undertakes significant grant-making activities or voluntarily funded charitable services.

This follows from the fact that the primary aim of a charity must be the provision of public benefit in accordance with its declared objects – not 'profit or gain' for its own sake, even in cases where trading is priced to result in a surplus that can be used to fund *other* charitable activities.

For a charity, therefore, any annual surplus/deficit is entirely a matter for internal management and budgetary control; it is not in itself a valid measure of 'success' or 'failure'. Even the Charity Commission's cherished ideal of a 'balanced budget' is something that must be left to the discretion of the trustees, having due regard to all the circumstances.

In any case, it may well be that a charity has been given a large amount of funding (not as a 'performance-related' grant – see below), or perhaps even a large legacy, to be spent on either 'core' or 'special' projects which have only just started. In that case, there will initially be a large positive 'result' on unrestricted or restricted funds as the case may be, whereas in future years there may well be a negative 'result' as the bulk of the project expenditure is incurred.

This again highlights the importance of the annual report, where the SORP requires the trustees to explain what the charity is trying to do and how it is going about it, thus putting all the SoFA figures into the proper perspective.

Impact of the Regulations

6.1.6   Regulation 8 (Form and Content) of the SORP's 2008 Regulations (SI 2008/629 – see Appendix 5) puts the flesh on the bones of s 42(1) and (2) of the Charities Act 1993 ('the 1993 Act') in the case of unincorporated charities by the simple device of making *all* the SoFA (and balance sheet) requirements of SORP 2005 *mandatory*:

> 'The statement of accounts must be prepared in accordance with the methods and principles set out in the SORP; ...'.
>
> *– SI 2008/629, reg 8(5)*

Regulations 15 and 16 of the same SI effectively impose that obligation also for any *consolidated* accounts (see chapter 14) prepared under the 1993 Act, with special provision for parent charitable companies of 'small' groups not **required** to prepare group accounts under the Companies Act, (which Act nevertheless still regulates the parent's *entity* accounts to the exclusion of the Charities Act):

> 'The group accounts prepared under this regulation must ... (b) in any case where the parent charity is a company, be prepared as if its charity trustees had been required to prepare a statement of accounts under section 42(1) of the 1993 Act.'
>
> *– SI 2008/629, reg 15(5)*

Comparative figures

6.1.7   The Charities SORP *requires* comparative figures only for the SoFA's *total* column but not for the analysis columns:

> 'Comparative figures for the previous financial year, given on the face of the statement will normally only be given for the row totals (e g voluntary income,[1] investment income etc) rather than for the analysis of each row across the various categories of funds.'
>
> *– SORP 2005, paragraph 84*

This is then made mandatory by the related 2008 Regulations as follows:

> '(6)   Subject to paragraphs (7) to (9), the statement of accounts must, in relation to any amount required to be shown in the statement of financial activities ... show the corresponding amount for the financial year immediately preceding the relevant financial year.

---

[1]   SORP 2000 referred to 'donations' here, though clearly meaning bequests as well. As SORP 2005 provides no separate line in the SoFA for gifts that *endow* the charity, clearly such voluntary incoming *capital* resources are not meant to be excluded here either.

(7)   Where a charity has more than one fund, only amounts corresponding to the entries in the statement of financial activities relating to the totals of both or all of the funds of the charity need be shown.

(8)   Where the corresponding amount referred to in paragraph 6 is not comparable with the amount to be shown for the item in question in respect of the financial year, the corresponding amount is to be adjusted.

(9)   Where ... an amount was required to be shown in respect of that item in the statement of accounts for the financial year immediately preceding the relevant financial year, [it must still be shown as the corresponding amount even] if [the] amount ... in the statement of accounts for the relevant financial year [is] nil.'

– SI 2008/629, reg 8

This means it is only where a column of the SoFA is sub-analysed in the accounts notes in order to show the movements on any *major* individual funds that it may be necessary, *for the sake of best practice*, to show each fund's comparative figures (ie for each column in the sub-analysis). This is *not* a regulatory requirement. As can be seen from the quotation below, Sch 2 to the SORP's 2008 Regulations carefully exempts three categories of accounts note – inter-fund transfers (i), grant-making expenditure (o) and gains/losses and other movements on fixed assets (t) – from its 'comparative figures' requirements for all the accounts notes it specifies in para 1(a)–(t), among which any sub-analysis of movements on individual funds is not to be found. Thus, para 1(u) requires to be shown:

'in the case of any amount required by any of the preceding sub-paragraphs (other than sub-paragraph (i), (o) or (t)) to be disclosed, the corresponding amount for the financial year immediately preceding the relevant financial year.'

– SI 2008/629, Sch 2, para 1(u)

'Netting off'

6.1.8   It is because charity law prohibits any expenditure that is not a 'proper application' of the charity's resources, either in furtherance of its declared Objects or else for the charity's own benefit, that the Charities SORP requires compliance here to be demonstrated by showing all incoming resources *gross* in the SoFA – ie without netting off any related expenditure (unless the effect is immaterial). The original, 1995 SORP did make certain exceptions to this rule, allowing the following items to be shown net of the related expenditure:

–   the results of *non-charitable* trading (but with an *inset* note of the turnover); and

–   the proceeds of small-scale fundraising events for (rather than by) the charity, in cases where the costs were difficult to ascertain.

It is only the latter exception that is now preserved in SORP 2005 – and even then only with a strict proviso:

'All incoming resources should be reported gross whether raised by the charity (or by volunteers working at the charity's direction) or its agents. However where funds are raised or collected for the charity by individuals not employed or contracted by the charity, the gross incoming resources of the charity are the proceeds remitted to the charity by the organisers of the event, after deducting their expenses.'

– SORP 2005, paragraph 95

This is because the SoFA groups together all the costs of any activities undertaken primarily 'to generate funds', showing them in a special sub-section immediately after the 'incoming resources' section of the SoFA.

'INCOMING RESOURCES' SECTION

6.2 All *new and additional* financial resources accruing to the charity in the year (ie not inter-fund transfers, nor 'incremental' gains in asset-values – other than from disposing of assets held for the charity's own use, dealt with below) must be reported within this section. In this, the Charities SORP requires immediate recognition in full of all incoming resources accruing to endowed funds and also normally to other restricted funds – whatever the nature of the restriction – but has special rules for *time-restricted* income gifts, including those to unrestricted funds, as below.

'Deferred income'

6.2.1 The accounting rules for the recognition of *trading income* are the same for charities as for commercial entities: costs and related revenues must be 'matched' by recognising them in the same accounting period. This requires a 'deferred income' treatment for 'unearned' trading receipts by *postponing* their recognition in the SoFA:

'Some charities earn income by providing goods and/or services in return for a fee as part of their charitable activities. Such contractual income is recognised as incoming resources in the Statement of Financial Activities to the extent that the charity has provided the goods and/or services. Where such incoming resources are received in advance then a charity may not have entitlement to these resources until the goods or services have been provided. In this situation incoming resources received in advance should be deferred ... until the charity becomes entitled to the resources.'

– SORP 2005, paragraph 98

The SORP similarly requires a 'deferred *voluntary* income' treatment only until the donor's pre-conditions (if any) for the charity's use of the gift are met (eg 'this gift is only for use in a [specified] future accounting period'):

'Charities are normally entitled to incoming resources when they are receivable. Recognition of a grant or donation without pre-conditions should not be deferred ... even if the resources are received in advance of the expenditure on the activity funded by the grant or donation. In such cases the charity has entitlement to the resource, with the timing of the expenditure being within the discretion of the charity. Incoming resources cannot be deferred simply because the related expenditure has not been incurred. Similarly, a condition that allows for the recovery by the donor of any unexpended part of a grant does not prevent recognition. A liability for any repayment is recognised when repayment becomes probable.'

– SORP 2005, paragraph 110

... or until some specified *performance* requirement has been met (eg cash advanced under a 'performance-related' grant-funding agreement – ie one that denies legal entitlement to the cash *as income* until the performance requirement has been met):

> 'Certain grant arrangements may not be contractual in law but nevertheless have the characteristics of a contract, in that the conditions attaching to the grant only give entitlement to the recipient of the funding (and a liability to the grant provider) as the goods or services specified in the grant terms are provided. Such arrangements are termed performance related grants ...'.

– SORP 2005, Glossary GL 30.3

There is a very fine line being drawn here. Under trust law the recipient charity's trustees are accountable to the donor for the proper use of such a grant for its intended purpose. If they account for it as a restricted trust fund they will not need to accrue for the residual trust law liability to repay whatever is ultimately not so used unless and until that liability crystallises.

Once upon a time it was custom and practice for charities to account for *all* unutilised restricted trust funds as 'liabilities' by analogy with commercial accounting concepts. That treatment, which made many charities' ongoing activities look grossly under-funded, was outlawed by the 1995 SORP. However, by saying here (in GL 30.3) that the monies advanced under the agreement shall not become a grant until the activities they are to fund have been carried out as specified, and that the grant-maker only then becomes liable as such, the latter has effectively provided a 'soft loan' initially – not an outright grant at all. The accounting then needs to reflect that position.

The 1995 SORP's 'deferred income' treatment for donor-imposed timing restrictions applied only where the donor-condition was *without restriction of purpose* – a clarity that seems to have become blurred in SORP 2000 and 2005. Yet the SORP's basic fund-accounting approach then and now fully provides for the necessary segregation of *special-purpose* income funds as well as of all *trust capital* funds:

(a)   gifts *on trust for spending* on activities restricted by the donor (restricted funds);

(b)   gifts *on trust for retention* for the general benefit of the charity or else to facilitate activities restricted by the donor (endowed funds).

In this context, it might be thought contradictory and misleading to postpone the recognition in the SoFA of *Restricted Income* merely because the donor has stipulated a *delay* of use (spending) to an extent that does not amount to a long-term retention requirement turning the gift into capital (expendable endowment), or even to a lack of entitlement. Until SORP 2000, as long as voluntary income of any kind for *general purposes* (ie unrestricted funds) was subject to a (temporary) donor-imposed *timing* restriction – for example, a grant for the charity's activities in each of the following three financial years – it could not be recognised at all in the SoFA.

Under SORP 2000 and now 2005, this includes all *special-purpose* voluntary funding as well – ie restricted income funds. Instead of accounting for a time-restricted special-purpose gift (grant) for activities by immediately recognising it as restricted income, with a supporting note to disclose the timing delay, the gift has to be carried forward in the balance sheet as 'deferred income' just like any general-purpose gift, until the donor-imposed pre-condition for 'use and enjoyment' of the gift (as distinct from entitlement to it as income of the charity) has been satisfied.

This unfortunately subordinates trust law compliance to the commercial concept of 'disposable income'. While only a small step towards the desired convergence of profit-accounting with public-benefit accounting, likewise of UK with international standards, it nevertheless reduces the SORP's usefulness as a means of evidencing the charity's proper administration in compliance with the strict demands of trust law.

The 1995 SORP's treatment for deferred voluntary income was also slightly different, spotlighting such time-restricted general-purpose resources by requiring them to be taken into the SoFA as incoming resources in the normal way – only to be taken out again on the next line as 'deferred income' (adjusted for any previous deferments now qualifying as income) – as well as being analysed in the accounts notes. It is only the latter requirement that is now retained:

> 'Where any incoming resources have been deferred the notes to the accounts should analyse the movement on the deferred account between incoming resources deferred in the current year and amounts released from previous years. Incoming resources of a similar nature can be grouped together in the notes as appropriate.'

> *– SORP 2005, paragraph 114*

Performance-related grants

SORP 2005 thus prohibits income recognition in the SoFA wherever *pre-conditions* for *entitlement* (and therefore also for 'use and enjoyment') cannot be met: such a resource is not yet 'incoming' for SoFA purposes, not yet 'owned' (irrespective of whether on trust or absolutely) in the sense of *unconditional* entitlement, but merely 'received in advance'. As such, it cannot be recognised in the SoFA at all, but must be accounted for as *a liability to the owner who has advanced it*, with the reason for the transaction being explained in the accounts notes.

Simple as this rule may be in concept, its practical interpretation has been a stumbling block for some, leading to the following clarification in SORP 2005:

> 'Conditions such as the submission of accounts or certification of expenditure can be seen simply as an administrative requirement as opposed to a condition that might prevent the recognition of incoming resources.'

> *– SORP 2005, paragraph 107*

Prior to the Finance Act 2000's tax incentives for charitable giving (eg the GiftAid Scheme), a common example of deferred income was the prepaid element of a 4-year charitable deed of covenant for the charity's general purposes where the donor 'deposited' a lump sum to be applied as income of the charity as and when due, or (commonly) in the event of the premature death of the donor (ie no refund required).

Life-membership subscriptions

Another example still to be found, and one that is special to charitable associations, is 'life membership' charitable (ie *non-benefit*) subscriptions. In calculating the 'future years' element to be carried forward as 'deferred income' in the balance sheet, the amount may be ascertained by comparing the current 'life' and annual subscription rates – actuarially, if need be (ie if the figures are material enough to influence the membership). This implies a donor-imposed timing restriction intended to eke out the life subscription evenly throughout the commutation period (eg 10 years) on which the rate is based. It also equates to the commercial matching principle whereby *membership-benefit* life-subscriptions are reported as income only as and when the benefits are provided – which for a 10-year commutation period would normally be 10% per annum.

That is also the accounting treatment used for life membership subscriptions giving free access as a visitor to National Trust's portfolio of heritage properties:

[Accounts Note] 25. **Life Membership Equalisation Account** Life membership subscriptions are credited to an equalisation account and released over ten years.		
The movements during the year were:	**2008**	2007
	£'000	*£'000*
Balance at 1 March	**11,228**	11,104
Amounts received in the year	**3,555**	2,456
Transfer to income (Note 5)	**(2,506)**	(2,332)
Balance at 28 February/29 February	**12,277**	11,228

National Trust – 2007/08 Accounts

School fees-in-advance schemes

A more interesting example is the use of commutation schemes to encourage the prepayment of school fees – often to cover the entirety of the child's attendance at a charity-run school. The attraction of such schemes is the financial discount given by the charity.

The advance payment can, where the terms of contract allow, be used and accounted for as a debt due under a capital instrument (the contract) in accordance with FRS4 (as amended by FRS25) – thus as a form of debt-financing for the charity. This accounting treatment, though not mentioned in the Charities SORP itself, is highlighted in 'Guidance for Independent Schools on Reporting under the Charities SORP 2005', published by the Independent Schools Bursars' Association for the circa 1,250 fee-paying charity schools represented by the Independent Schools Council.

For other kinds of Advance Fee schemes, the accounting treatment must accord with Application Note G to FRS5, as indicated in the SORP. This is where the scheme takes the form of a long-term contract which provides for each advance payment to be received simply as a discounted prepayment of future fees – in which case it would be taken to be income at its 'entry value' (ie the actual cash payment) as and when utilised in settlement of termly school fees.

Classification of incoming resources

6.2.2 In line with the ASB's convergence programme for the UK and international commercial standards, SORP 2005 has continued its predecessor's drift away from the strict UK tax law and charity law definitions followed by the 1995 SORP, which had classified charities' funding sources as:

(a)   voluntary contributions (income and capital);

(b)   charitable/non-charitable trading; and

(c)   income returns on invested funds,

plus the usual 'other' as a fourth category.

SORP 2005 extracts from (a) and (b) all income closely related to charitable activities and classifies it as 'incoming resources from charitable activities'. What remains of (a) and (b), together with (c), is then grouped under the heading of 'incoming resources from generated funds' as:

(i)   voluntary income;

(ii)   activities for generating funds; and

(iii) income returns on invested funds (the same as (c) above).

In the case of (c) and (iii) above, the need to supplement the Trustee Act 2000 ('TA 2000') with a solid legal basis for charities to be able to benefit from the investment professionals' adoption of a 'total return' approach to optimising performance in the capital markets resulted in the Charity Commission introducing a new kind of Order to authorise this for permanent endowments. The adoption of a total return investing basis then requires the income returns on endowed investments to be shown in the *capital* column of the SoFA instead of in one of the income columns. The detailed rules for this are now reflected in the Charities SORP as well as being set out in operational guidance (OG83) on the Commission's website. See **6.4.3** and also chapter 9 for the authors' summary of what is now the officially preferred solution to the problem of how best to account for investment returns in the SoFA where a 'total return' investment policy has been adopted.

In keeping with the spirit of FRS5, SORP 2005 follows its predecessor's 'substance over form' approach by glossing over some of the more difficult legal distinctions in order to focus on the *economic* realities instead. Chapter 13, covering special aspects of 'operating activities' in the SoFA, therefore explores those voluntary incoming resources that, although legally 'gifts', are so closely tied in with *business activities* that they behave like their *derived revenues* and must therefore be reported as such. These are mainly:

–   goods donated to the charity for resale (e g charity shops income);

–   'performance-related' grant-funding for the provision of goods/services whereby the service-level is closely regulated by the funding agreement in order to serve some specific purpose of the funding body (eg community services to local authority standards);

–   corporate sponsorship in cash/kind involving the charity's *active* participation in a commercial relationship (ie advertising/favouring the sponsor); and

–   membership subscriptions bringing membership benefits at a cost to the charity.

The SORP's current portrayal of charity income in terms of business activities and their equivalent tends to obscure the old charitable/non-charitable trading distinction inherent in the 1995 SORP, as well as the more fundamental distinction of voluntary contributions (ie pure gifts), so that the accounting classification of income derived *from* charitable activities is now more compatible with the commercial accounting concept of operational activities. The corollary of this is the grouping together of nearly everything else under the other main heading of 'incoming resources from generated funds' – including all spontaneous giving. Thus the primary categories of 'incoming resources' under SORP 2005 are now effectively:

(1)   *Voluntary contributions*, comprising all sorts of 'pure gift' donations (except the retail proceeds of the 'charity shop' type of gifts in kind to fund activities), legacies/bequests, the gross proceeds of Appeals, and all kinds of grants (except under local authority service agreements and the like – ie 'performance-related' grants), which despite the inaccurate terminology of the SoFA format at Table 3 (paragraph 85 of the SORP) must be split by means of the SoFA's columnar format into their three basic kinds as follows:
(i)   endowment funds (gifts on trust to retain as capital);
and as *income funds* other gifts that either:
(ii)   by law can only be spent for *restricted* purposes; or
(iii)   are *unrestricted* as to the purpose for which they can be used within the reporting charity's declared Objects.

(2)   *Activities to generate funds* – thus grouping together the gross proceeds of fundraising by such means as lotteries, car boot sales, concerts and other promotional events/activities (except for the 'pure gift' proceeds of appeals included in (1) above) with any corporate sponsorship income excluded from (1), the turnover of charity shops and the like (goods donated for sale as well as those bought in for resale), and also any 'ancillary' trading excluded from (4) because its primary aim is to raise funds, plus any licensing income and also any letting/hiring out of *non*-investment properties/equipment temporarily surplus to operational requirements.

(3)   *Investment returns* of an *income* nature (including the gross rents from investment properties), bearing in mind that all 'realised' capital returns (disposal gains) are confined to the gains/losses section lower down the SoFA – unless and until some future revision of the SORP brings them up into the incoming resources section (by analogy with disposals of non-investment fixed assets), thus allowing the realised element of the total return on investment assets to be reported here.

(4)   *Activities to further the [reporting charity's] Objects* – thus grouping together – even though in different columns – the turnover of any activities undertaken under

contract law *primarily to achieve/facilitate that end* and as gross revenues any 'restricted' grant-funding, for example, from a local authority, of *closely regulated* charitable activities undertaken under trust law (these two variants being sometimes virtually indistinguishable from the wording of the legal agreements – even to the lawyers involved!).

(5) *Other incoming resources* (e g realised gains on disposing of 'own use' fixed assets – according to whether they belong to endowed or unendowed funds).

Within these five basic categories, the actual sub-headings used – as well as the order of presentation, depending on materiality – must, of necessity, vary according to the nature of the charity and its activities, circumstances and relationships:

> 'The Statement of Financial Activities may be adapted to give a true and fair view, but disclosure requirements should always be met and the underlying structure should not be changed. Trustees should balance the provision of information with clarity.'
>
> – *SORP 2005, paragraph 86*

For *material* items, the SORP also requires 'a description of the sources', as well as supplementary analysis not only for the voluntary contributions but also for operating revenues:

> 'An analysis of incoming resources from charitable activities should be given in the notes to the accounts to supplement the analysis on the face of the Statement of Financial Activities. It should be sufficiently detailed so that the reader of the accounts understands the main activities carried out by the charity and the main components of the gross incoming resources receivable from each material charitable activity.'
>
> – *SORP 2005, paragraph 146*

In the next section we consider the SoFA treatment of the various kinds of 'voluntary contribution' a charity may have to account for, before going on to the treatment of investment returns and, to conclude this section of the SoFA, the disposal of fixed assets held for the charity's own use.

Because the practicalities of accounting for them are more involved, there is a separate chapter devoted to investment assets (chapter 9) and another to the SoFA treatment of trading and other 'operating activities' (chapter 13).

After incoming resources, this chapter looks at the remaining sections of the SoFA:

– expenditure;

– inter-fund transfers;

– gains/losses; and, to link last year's and this year's balance sheets, the

– reconciliation of funds.

VOLUNTARY CONTRIBUTIONS

6.3   Under this sub-heading (which now excludes the gross income of what are in substance, if not also in legal form, 'economic' activities as categorised at **6.4.1**) we need to consider everything that SORP 2005 brings together, whether solicited (fundraised) or unsolicited, by way of donations, legacies, pure grants and similar incoming resources – the generic description for which is surely 'voluntary contributions' as used in the USA for the Financial Accounting Standards Board's (FASB's) Accounting Standards No 116/117 on gifts and donor-compliance as long ago as 1993 to describe all forms of charitable giving. This includes gifts that endow the charity with capital, which under trust law must then be distinguished from the charity's income funds.

Legacies

6.3.1 The treatment of legacies has remained somewhat contentious ever since the original 1988 precursor ('SORP2') to the Charities SORP banished the old legacy equalisation account, with its overly pragmatic 3-year rule to even out the inherent 'lumpiness' of this source. In the hope of achieving greater standardisation in the recognition of legacies and other incoming resources in the SoFA, in 2000 the SORP introduced three criteria that must be considered in each case. The first (entitlement) is refined in SORP 2005 by superimposing a distinctly commercial view of that term, based on control over use and enjoyment, onto the strict rules of trust law governing the trustees' immediate accountability for *all* gifts made to their charity.

To these, we might add a fourth where legacies are in question: *awareness* of the legal entitlement, the importance of this aspect being heightened by the duty of care imposed by law on charity trustees. This requires them to take reasonable steps to be aware of, to gather in, to protect and to apply 'properly' all the resources that belong to their charity – not just those that have fallen into their hands.

Once the charity's legal entitlement[2] arises (ie at the death of the testator), thus 'when the will matures' (as they prefer to describe it in the USA), the process of recognition in the annual accounts cannot even begin until the trustees become aware that they do have an entitlement – hence the need to be on the alert for such news as it breaks.

Where the SORP's SoFA-recognition rules can be critical is in the area of 'residual' legacies of *non-monetary* assets. That seems to be where the widest variation in current accounting practice is to be found. Such gifts can only be *properly* accounted for at their value at the *date of gift* (ie of the death itself), that value being estimated, if necessary, from the best information available at the time of preparing the accounts, even if this figure has to be corrected in a subsequent year's accounts.

Once the trustees *are* aware of it, recognition in the SoFA as an incoming resource – capital or income as appropriate – is governed by paragraph 94 of the SORP, which says:

'This will be dependent on the following three factors being met:

---

[2]   This is, of course, subject to the 'proving' (probate) of the will, also to any successful contesting of its provisions by third parties affecting the charity's own claim.

(a) *entitlement* – normally arises when there is control over the rights or other access to the resource, enabling the charity to determine its future application;

(b) *certainty* – when it is virtually certain that the incoming resource will be received;

(c) *measurement* – when the monetary value of the incoming resource can be measured with sufficient reliability.' (emphasis added)

– *SORP 2005, paragraph 94*

Since the would-be executors cannot obtain the court's grant of probate without filing an estimate on public record of the value of the testator's estate for HMRC purposes, even though that estimate remains subject to correction until completion of the administration of the estate and discharge of the executors (a process that can easily take 2 years, sometimes more), it would be difficult to sustain an argument that the probate value of a legacy entitlement under the will is not reliable enough for it to be brought into account once its ultimate receipt is reasonably certain.

What this means in practice is that:

– the death must have occurred before the end of the financial year;

– the charity's entitlement under the will must have been confirmed by the executors (even if only after the year-end, since the confirmation merely reduces uncertainty, based, if need be, on 'adjusting[3] events' such as probate); and

– the amount to be recognised must be free of any *likely* substantial claims.

However, such is the contention surrounding legacy accrual that SORP 2005 still has to leave a grey area – albeit less than under previous versions of the SORP – within which the rules are open to subjective interpretation – leaving the charity's auditor to decide whether the result can be said to give 'a true and fair view' in the circumstances. Thus paragraphs 125 to 127 make it clear that an interim distribution received after-date from – or promised by – the executors can be accrued as receivable, but only:

'… where … it is clear that it had been agreed by the personal representatives *prior to the year end* (hence providing evidence of a condition that existed at the balance sheet date) …'. (emphasis added)

– *SORP 2005, paragraph 127*

The grey area here is indicated by the emphasised words, which disregard an *after-date* admission by the executors as audit evidence of the charity's entitlement as at the balance sheet date – an entitlement that arose at the death of the testator and was merely made legally enforceable by the proving of the will and the grant of probate.

---

[3]   This refers to FRS21: 'Post Balance Sheet Events' – in particular, those taking place prior to finalisation of the accounts and affecting the financial reporting of transactions or events of the year or of situations existing at the year-end. As SORP 2005 succinctly puts it,
'*adjusting events* are 'those that provide evidence of conditions that existed at the balance sheet date for which the entity shall adjust the amounts recognised in its financial statements or recognise items that were not previously recognised' … as distinct from those [events] that are indicative of conditions that arose after the balance sheet date for which the entity does not adjust the amounts recognised in its financial statements (non-adjusting events).'
– *SORP 2005, Appendix 2*

Again, the SORP *exemplifies* (but shies away from defining) 'certainty', doubts (without denying) that reliable measurement is possible before that point, and for good measure reminds us of the well-known fact that *reversionary* interests in expectancy cannot be accrued as receivable:

> 'There will normally be reasonable certainty of receipt for example, as soon as a charity receives a letter from the personal representatives of the estate advising that payment of the legacy will be made or that the property bequeathed will be transferred. It is likely that the value of the resource will also be measurable from this time. However, legacies which are not immediately payable should not be treated as receivable until the conditions associated with payment have been fulfilled (e g the death of a life tenant).'
>
> *– SORP 2005, paragraph 124*

The next paragraph's reliance on the executors' letter of intent delineates another grey area by doubting (but not quite denying) the possibility of any accruable entitlement in its absence – ignoring the situation where entitlement to a specific bequest has been confirmed as certain but for reasons of their own the executors have not yet indicated when they will be ready to hand over the asset(s):

> 'It is unlikely in practice that the entitlement, certainty of receipt and measurability conditions will be satisfied before the receipt of a letter from the personal representatives advising of an intended payment or transfer.'
>
> *– SORP 2005, paragraph 125*

At the other extreme, a *residuary* entitlement, if still not confirmed by the executors, could be problematical. Any part of the entitlement that on the above basis cannot be accrued, also its anticipated value to the charity, may then need to be disclosed by way of note – unless it can properly be considered immaterial, of course.

Life tenancy and remainder interests, life policies, etc

As charities become more resourceful in their efforts to meet an ever-widening range of public benefit needs, their fundraising becomes more competitive and ingenious. This in turn is bringing new problems in accounting for some gifts or bequests that fundraising managers now need to value as part of the results (proceeds) of a successful appeal or other initiative to generate voluntary funding.

The problem here may be what value to place on a life, where a charity's legal interest in gifted property (e g a life tenancy or the freehold reversion on the death of a life tenant), or in financial assets such as a life assurance policy, is in some way dependent on that person's life.

The SORP still doesn't have much to offer here by way of guidance, even though a reliable actuarial valuation can be accepted in probate cases. Instead, it merely calls for explanatory information if, despite the obvious legal entitlement and ultimate certainty of possession and enjoyment of the asset, it cannot yet be recognised in the SoFA as an incoming resource for lack of 'measurability' – for example:

> '... an indication should be provided of the nature of any material assets bequeathed to the charity but subject to a life tenancy interest held by a third party.'
>
> *– SORP 2005, paragraph 128*

Wherever the SORP's SoFA recognition conditions are not fully satisfied in respect of a material legacy expectation, so that it cannot be accrued as receivable, the accounts notes should include a best estimate of the amount(s) expected but not yet brought into account.

In practice, legacies that include some assets that cannot be valued 'with sufficient reliability', cannot just be *wholly* excluded from the SoFA, which would surely make it misleading. It is only the part that is subject to uncertainty that should be noted instead of being accrued. In any case where the amounts involved are material, the actual accounting policy followed, which should be consistent as well as reasonable, and in particular how the three criteria have been interpreted, will need to be explained as well.

Gifts 'in kind'

6.3.2 This means gifts of physical assets other than money – for example, quoted securities, popularised by the Finance Act 2000's US-style innovation of total tax deductibility for the wealthy philanthropist. It does *not* mean the free use of premises/equipment and other facilities on loan, or of money on 'soft loan', nor free or subsidised services, nor 'seconded' staff – all of which are dealt with in **6.3.3** as 'donated services and facilities' (what earlier versions of the SORP called 'intangible income').

Excluded from here, as well as from the next section, are also the services of the millions of volunteers on which the charity sector depends for so much of its service-provision. This exclusion simply reflects the extreme unreliability of the possible ways of measuring the financial value that must be attributed in order to account for this kind of voluntary contribution. Various suggestions (even one from the Charity Finance Directors' Group, as part of the SORP review process) have been made over the years, including the rather arbitrary use of national minimum wage rates – but none of these suggestions copes satisfactorily with the differences between skilled/unskilled help from those in or out of work or the sacrifice of working versus leisure hours, holidays, etc. Instead, the SORP recommends that any significant contribution made by volunteers to the charity's work be disclosed in the trustees' annual report, quantified if need be. The National Trust, like some other major charities largely reliant on volunteers, even goes a step further, by disclosing an estimated financial value for the donated hours, though without saying how this is calculated.

As a movement inspired from its birth by the volunteer spirit, we are proud to have 52,000 volunteers helping us across the full range of our work. This year, our volunteers contributed a total of 3,093,771 hours, equating to a notional value of £22.3 million.

National Trust – 2007/08 Annual Report

British Red Cross had been able to cap that (even before SORP 2005) in highlighting an estimated annual value for its army of volunteers – as a footnote on the face of the SoFA:

Voluntary support

The financial statements do not incorporate any value attributed to the number of voluntary hours devoted to the service of the British Red Cross by its➡

---

membership. In earlier years it was estimated that these hours amounted to at least 5 million, and this figure is not considered to have changed significantly. Based on national average hourly earnings rates, duly weighted to reflect the membership of the British Red Cross, of £8.16 per hour, (2006 £7.94 per hour) the value to the British Red Cross, and therefore to the community, of the work undertaken was about £41m for the year ended 31 December 2007 (2006 £40m).

British Red Cross – 2007 Accounts

On the other hand, the award-winning volunteer-charity *par excellence* contents itself under SORP 2005 with simply acknowledging in the Trustees' Annual Report the total number of its volunteers (44,147 – over 50% ranging from age 5 to 25) and the total number of hours of service they provided in 2004 (5,567,781), supplemented by the following Accounting Policies note:

Trustees' Report

Overall, during 2007 the total number of our volunteers decreased slightly to 43,000, while the number of hours of voluntary service given was 5.6 million, reduced from 5.7 million in 2006.

Accounting policies

d. Incoming Resources

The accounts reflect no amounts in respect of time provided by volunteer members of St John.

The Priory of England and the Islands of the Order of St John (St John Ambulance) – 2007

Goods donated to the charity for *distribution in kind* are to be recognised as *income* in the SoFA *only when distributed* (paragraph 129(a) of the SORP). Under paragraph 130, this must be at 'a reasonable estimate of their gross value to the charity', normally by reference to open market prices for 'an equivalent item', as the SORP puts it, but obviously with due regard to the availability of any cheaper alternative items that could suit the charity's purpose, also to any charity discounts on offer. For fund-accounting purposes, though, it will be inconsequential whether this is in the restricted or unrestricted funds column, since it is at the same value that they must also be shown as expenditure of the year in which they are distributed. In the meantime, and if they are of material value, an indication of the kind of goods undistributed at the year-end, and an estimate of their value, is to be given in the accounts notes (paragraph 132 of the SORP).

Where, instead, the goods are donated for the charity's *own use*, paragraph 129(b) requires their *immediate* recognition in the SoFA – but then ignores 'consumables' (implying the same accounting treatment as assets for distribution) to focus on fixed assets only: it adds a further paragraph reference directing the reader on a magical mystery tour in search of the fund-accounting rules that will determine in which *column* that is to be if the gift is of or for fixed assets. Suffice it to say that the treatment of *endowed* gifts for a charity's own use is fully explained at **5.5.1**.

In short, if the donor's intention creates what lawyers call a 'user trust', meaning one for retention for 'own use' by the charity, then the endowed funds column is indicated. If not, it will be an income funds column – restricted, if the goods are provided for some purpose narrower than the charity's general purposes, otherwise unrestricted. Whatever the column, paragraph 130 also requires these donated goods be brought in at 'a reasonable estimate of their gross value to the charity', while paragraph 131 requires the valuation basis to be disclosed (in the accounts notes – see chapter 12).

The treatment of goods donated 'on trust for sale' is also conditional: it will depend on whether the donor intended the proceeds to be:

(i)   spent on activities (ie as income); or else

(ii)   retained for the benefit of the charity (ie as an investment or else to finance the provision of fixed assets for the charity's own use).

If (ii), they are to be recognised immediately in the SoFA at their 'gross value to the charity' as stated above, except that this will normally be their *open market value* (these normally being readily marketable assets, often quoted securities) – and with paragraph 130 of the SORP also requiring that value to be adjusted by reference to the subsequent sale proceeds (if the disposal is in a later year).

In the case of (i), paragraph 129(c) acknowledges that immediate recognition is 'not practicable' and instead requires them to be brought into the SoFA only when sold off. That is because such goods (which can also include quoted securities intended to be sold off and spent on activities rather than reinvested) have to be accounted for as current assets until sold, with SSAP9 then requiring them to be valued at the lower of cost (ie nil) and market value. In passing, we should note that although this applies equally to goods donated for 'charity shops', car boot sale events and the like, paragraph 137(c) of the SORP now requires these to be accounted for not as 'voluntary contributions' but as 'income of activities for generating funds'.

This is in keeping with their distinctly *economic* bias, which can involve a lot more than simple cash realisation, having significant operating costs like any other 'business', perhaps including repairs and improvements of the donated goods, and often mixed in with a significant content of bought-in goods. Chapter 13 deals with trading and similar operating activities in detail.

Also excluded here more often than not are the kinds of hard-to-value gift in kind or split-interest gift highlighted earlier as tied in to someone's life expectation – see **6.3.1** – unless the charity's auditors can be persuaded that the actuarial valuation basis that will have had to be used to recognise the gift as an incoming resource in the SoFA is reliable enough for a true and fair view.

We should note that a gift of this kind may be (a) a financial asset that can only be held as an investment (eg a life assurance policy or an annuity on someone's life), or a functional one such as (b) the tenancy of a property for the charity's own use for the remainder of someone's life, with reversion to the donor's estate, perhaps – or it may even be the other way around: (c) where the charity is given only the reversionary interest. In the case of (b), the asset would have to be accounted for as income unless received on trust for retention and use by the charity on a continuing basis, when it will be endowment capital.

In some cases these can be very valuable assets, so much so that it is to be hoped that in due course a future version of the SORP can include the valuation guidance needed to assist trustees in accounting properly for them instead of just noting their existence.

Donated services and facilities ('intangible income')

6.3.3 Here, SORP 2005 changed the rules from SORP 2000 by using as a reference point not actual donor-*costs* as such but *market values* for whatever would be appropriate to the charity's needs as determined by the trustees – especially where the gift is of services or facilities 'usually provided by an individual or entity as part of their trade or profession for a fee' (paragraph 134). The benefit/use of all donated facilities (other than volunteer-help, of course) and soft loans should as before, be valued and included in the SoFA only if material and where it is 'reasonably quantifiable and measurable' – and in so far as needed by the charity.

> 'Donated services and facilities recognised in financial statements would include those usually provided by an individual or entity as part of their trade or profession for a fee. In contrast, the contribution of volunteers should be excluded from the Statement of Financial Activities as the value of their contribution to the charity cannot be reasonably quantified in financial terms.'
>
> – *SORP 2005, paragraph 134*

In particular, paragraphs 133–136 of SORP (supported by GL 20) require the SoFA to include as matching income and expenditure any valuable and financially quantifiable free or heavily subsidised benefits such as:

–   employed staff seconded to the charity (thus *not volunteer-help* – see above);

–   rent-free/reduced-rent accommodation;

–   equipment made available on free/subsidised loan;

–   'soft loans'; and

–   other facilities made available free-of-charge or at heavily subsidised rates,

where the arrangement is clearly intended to provide a *charitable* donation. This means that any subsidy must be seen to be more substantial than can be expected from an economic incentive such as a trade discount, an advertising incentive or a value-for-value commercial transaction dressed up as a 'sponsorship' arrangement.

The valuation rule for this purpose is that the amount to be recognised in the SoFA is to be the estimated *value of the benefit to the charity*.

> 'The value placed on these resources should be the estimated value to the charity of the service or facility received: this will be the price the charity estimates it would pay in the open market for a service or facility of equivalent utility to the charity.'
>
> – *SORP 2005, paragraph 133*

This looks simple enough at first sight, but could be problematical when it comes to benefits such as the occupation of a long-lasting freehold building in a prestige location.

If, on the other hand, the market value of (say) a leasehold property is immaterial (perhaps because the space donated has restrictions on its commercial use, or, at the time, represents unsaleable surplus capacity on the property market), the rule could even yield a nil value for recognition in the SoFA.

Other kinds may present the opposite problem. Clearly, the value to be attributed to the benefit of using *seconded* staff will be somewhere between the normal sales value (or its equivalent) to the employer of the staffing facility thus provided during the secondment, while the lower limit must be the minimum rate of pay and benefits at which the same job could be done by the charity's own staff (or by volunteers?) to a standard that is acceptable to the trustees.

Another difficult problem is that illustrated below:

SoFA extract (Restricted Funds were immaterial)		30 Sept 2008	30 Sept 2007
		£m	£m
Income			
Appeals: Donations/Legacies, etc		37.2	33.0
Activities to generate funds:			
– Investment/Other income		5.0	4.5
	Total income	**42.2**	37.5
Resources expended			
Costs of generating funds		1.7	1.6
Charitable Activities:			
– Grants (including support costs)		38.4	33.3
Management and administration (Governance)		0.3	0.3
	Total expenditure	**40.4**	35.3
Net income before investment gains/losses		1.8	2.2

BBC Children in Need – 2007/08 Accounts

You might expect a TV-based appeals charity for a popular cause to be a classic example of the required transparency in annual reporting by charities. Certainly the phenomenal fundraising efficiency (95%) shown by the accounts of the BBC Children in Need Appeal is unmatchable for *revenue*-funding (as distinct from US-style capital fundraising appeals) by charities unable to get the airtime needed to reach the donating public on such a scale. Yet the significant value of the BBC's major gift of a whole day's free air-time for its annual charity appeal has never been reflected in the accounts of the grant-making charity it set up for the purpose. The problem under SORP 2000 used to be that the donor (being funded out of TV licence-monies on a statutory basis) is prohibited from selling advertising time and the donor-costs for a day's air-time could not readily be established – as is always explained in the accounts. However, under SORP 2005 it is *the value the charity would be willing to pay* on the open market to obtain the needed facility that should be included as income and expenditure in the SoFA, and a reliable *market value* for such a generous gift could obviously be based on the commercial air-time charges of the rival TV channels. That this 'household name' charity's accounts still omit such valuable user-information is regrettable from a 'transparency' perspective, to say the least.

Grants and donations

6.3.4 Having considered the complexities of most of the *special* forms in which gifts may come to a charity (ie legacies/bequests and tangible/intangible gifts in kind), we cannot avoid saying something about the simplest form of voluntary contribution: gifts of money – even though you might have thought the accounting treatment must be self-evident. It certainly wasn't under SORP 2000, while under SORP 2005 it is now precisely stated but technically exacting to follow and apply.

When gifts of money from the authorities, other public bodies or other charities come to a charity *as principal* (as distinct from a mere agent, whose accountability is solely to the *owner* as principal) on terms that leave sufficient discretion over the use of the money for the recipient charity to be responsible under charity law for its proper application, such gifts are called 'grants' – but when it comes to their presentation in the SoFA under SORP 2005, the category of *voluntary income*:

> 'will include grants which provide core funding or are of a general nature provided by government and charitable foundations but will not include those grants which are specifically for the performance of a service or production of charitable goods, for instance a service agreement with a local authority.'
>
> – *SORP 2005, paragraph 121*

Unfortunately SORP 2000 (saying essentially the same thing as the above) had failed to resolve the fundamental question of whether the grant-control agreement was made under contract law or trust law (see chapter 13), thus leaving an ambiguity here, so SORP 2005 makes it clear, in full compliance with trust law, that the income/expenditure matching principle of contract-accounting applies wherever the grantor has imposed terms and conditions *denying legal entitlement* to grant monies **as income** until the stipulated output requirements are met by the grantee:

> 'Certain grant funding arrangements may contain conditions that closely specify the service to be performed by the charity. The terms of such funding may be set out in a service level agreement where the conditions for payment are linked to the performance of a particular level of service or units of output delivered, for example, number of meals provided or the opening hours of a facility used by beneficiaries. Entitlement to the incoming resources derived from such performance-related grants ... may be conditional upon the delivery of the specified level of service and in such circumstances should be recognised as incoming resources to the extent that the charity has provided the services or goods.
>
> ... Entitlement to the grant in such cases only arises as the performance conditions are met. This can be contrasted with a restriction that whilst limiting how a charity may expend funds to particular purposes does not require a specific and measurable output to be delivered by the recipient charity as a condition of a charity's entitlement to the funds.'
>
> – *SORP 2005, paragraphs 99–100*

This is reinforced by the SORP's earlier warning:

'In order to understand how accounting standards apply to different funding arrangements, charity trustees need to determine for each source of funds:

- what legal arrangements (eg contract or trust law) govern the terms of the arrangement and how any disputes arising are to be settled;
- whether entitlement to the funding requires a specific performance to be achieved (a contract or performance related grant) ...'.

– SORP 2005, paragraph 97

Thus for strict compliance with SORP 2005 you will need to check all grant-control agreements which specify a measurable output and look for any clause linking the grantee's performance to its *entitlement* to the grant monies provided for. This is not at all the same as the customary 'clawback' clause written into government grant agreements, making grant monies repayable if not utilised for their intended purpose. The SORP says that such a clause does not give rise to an accruable liability as long as the latter is *contingent* rather than probable.

Where the reporting charity is acting as an *intermediary* to channel or distribute (at least to some degree at its own discretion) money provided for the purpose by another funding body (eg the regional arts charities funded by the Arts Council for England), the SORP explains that it will also be necessary to explain the relationship and the nature of the transactions between the three parties. (Even where acting only as an agent, thus without any charity law responsibility, such explanations will be required by paragraph 319 – but in that case a note of the agency assets and liabilities is also required, as they cannot be included in the accounts.)

When money is given to/for a charity by individuals, for example under the GiftAid Scheme or the Payroll Giving Scheme, or else in response to a public collection or to any other special-/general-purpose appeal, it is commonly called 'donations'. SORP 2005 counts these as *voluntary contributions* in the relevant column of the SoFA – unless they are actually the proceeds of certain kinds of fundraising event:

'Activities for generating funds ... will include (a) fundraising events such as jumble sales, firework displays and concerts (which are legally considered to be trading activities); (b) those sponsorships and social lotteries which cannot be considered as pure donations; (c) shop income from selling donated goods ...'.

– SORP 2005, paragraph 137

What the SORP cannot provide for, since even the charity often can only guess, is which 'pure donations' (and other voluntary contributions, such as legacies) came from active (and perhaps initially quite costly) fundraising projects to build up and exploit a 'donor-base', and which ones are 'unsolicited'.

Nevertheless, the statutory annual returns by which the Charity Commission used to monitor registered charities above what was then the £250,000 statutory audit threshold required an estimate of the total proceeds of all the charity's fundraising activities. A detailed analysis of costs against the related proceeds for each of the main kinds of fundraising effort undertaken is now required instead as 'public domain' information (in that respect transferring charity-monitoring from the regulator to the general public) in the Summary Information Return (SIR) as Part C of the Annual Return by charities above £1m gross income. This is for assessing their efficiency in relation to the related costs which are highlighted in the SoFA as 'costs of generating funds'.

That at last overcomes the SoFA's problem, enabling the reader of the SIR to assess the true efficiency of the charity's fundraising expenditure. This can vary enormously from the best, capital fundraising, with insignificant costs (ie below the threshold of 'materiality', which in normal circumstances is generally set at 5% of the whole[4] – here: gross proceeds), to the worst, where *annual* costs can even exceed proceeds during the early stages of a donor-base creation programme.

When they are from the *corporate* sector, charitable donations – unless made under the GiftAid Scheme, with its minuscule allowance for any private benefit to the donor – very often come wrapped up as some kind of 'corporate sponsorship' package. This may be due to the not insignificant commercial self-interest that, understandably, will often be intrinsic to the relationship. As indicated above, the SORP requires that it is only the 'pure donation' element of corporate sponsorship income that is shown as 'voluntary contributions' in the SoFA, with the rest being shown as 'income from activities' – of a charitable trading or a fund-raising nature as may be appropriate in accordance with the primary reason for undertaking them.

Finally, we should note here that the special topic of grants receivable in respect of fixed assets for the charity's own use is covered at **5.5.1**, in the context of SSAP4.

Appeals, collections and other 'fundraised' voluntary contributions

6.3.5 Where the 1995 SORP solved an intractable audit problem by showing how to account for the exercise of proper control over 'cash collections' as a particularly vulnerable class of charitable resource, based on the trustees' charity law duty to exercise proper control over *all* resources as soon as the charity becomes legally entitled to them, this aspect of charity administration, the need to demonstrate *proper control*, is no longer featured in the SORP. This may in part be due to the requirement for the annual report to include disclosure of the trustees' policy on managing 'major risks' and of their systems of controls for this purpose – but it may also reflect the different approach that had to be taken by the SORP in 2000 in the light of FRS18 (Accounting Policies), as discussed at **12.2.4**.

Rather than dwelling on the mechanics of measurement and control in what has always been a difficult area, *incoming donations*, the SORP contents itself with a prescriptive set of rules for *recognising* incoming resources as such in the SoFA. We quoted the three rules at **6.3.1** in connection with legacy-recognition, but they are also especially applicable here – where the requirement to be 'prudent' when in doubt about accounting for a donation must not be taken as a licence to ignore it until *received in cash*. Rather, it presupposes effective control over its use as a resource to enable *reliable* reporting of the receivable donation in the accounts. In the words of FRS18's exposure draft at the time, FRED 21, which can be applied just as much to incoming resources as to changes in the value of existing resources:

> '... the approach to prudence in SSAP 2 used the concept of realisation as a way of dealing with gains under conditions of uncertainty ... The FRED focuses on reliability, rather than realisation, in its approach to prudence.'

---

[4]   This was at one time recognised in the SORP, where the 'ceiling' on immaterial grants had been set at 5%: 'If in any accounting year a charity makes grants totalling at least 5% of its total resources expended in that year the charity should regard its grant-making as material.'
    – SORP 2000, paragraph 139

Bearing this in mind, the accounting rules for the recognition of *donations* as part of voluntary incoming resources (just like legacies – see **6.3.1**), as declared by the SORP (except that we should note, in passing, that 'conditions' really means 'outstanding pre-conditions' – for obvious reasons), are as follows:

> 'A pre-requisite of recognition of a promised grant or donation is evidence of entitlement. ... Where entitlement is demonstrable, and no conditions are attached, such promises should be recognised as incoming resources once the criteria of certainty and measurability are met.'
>
> – *SORP 2005, paragraph 104*

What this means in practice is that appropriate financial controls and procedures remain indispensable for reliable estimation of the results of significant fundraising activities – especially where cash predominates and the scale is such that the trustees cannot keep in touch directly and thus satisfy themselves that everything is in order. These procedures need to be designed to afford a reasonable level of security for the charity from the moment the donor makes the gift, thus minimising the risk of its non-arrival. That this is not only a charity law duty but also a prerequisite for proper accounting makes it all the more regrettable that the necessary recommendations are no longer to be found in the SORP.

Bearing in mind the provisions of the Charities Act 2006 here (controls over professional fundraising and public collections), this will normally require different procedures to protect the proceeds of fundraising in the charity's name by:

– agents properly appointed to seek/collect gifts for the charity;

– 'friends' groups' seeking to raise funds under what are often very informal arrangements made with the trustees; and even

– other individuals/bodies holding out to the public that they are collecting on behalf of the charity and thus making themselves 'trustees *for* the charity' in respect of the gross proceeds so raised – but only to the extent that the charity trustees themselves can reasonably be expected to be aware of such activities.

Similarly, controls are also needed over, for example, the issue and return of unsold raffle (lottery) tickets sent out by the charity itself. These can have a face value of tens of thousands of pounds and offer tempting opportunities to the unscrupulous to turn charitable gifts into private wealth. Unless their take-up is closely monitored, with adequate control checks maintained at critical points where the risk of loss is considered greatest, with secure feedback and expert evaluation of the results, the necessary assurance required by an auditor as to the completeness of the charity's records of voluntary income/capital funds raised may be impossible to obtain after the event.

If, taking the same example, gross proceeds of only £35,000 are raised from the issue of 100,000 £1 lottery tickets for a particular event:

– How many unsold tickets are due to be, and have been, returned, with what serial numbers, by whom and with what time-lag?

– Were the time-limits imposed on collectors as strict as they could and should be?

–   Were the public within the charity's area of activity sufficiently informed about the project, and especially how to recognise authorised collectors, in order to minimise the danger of donors being tricked by fraudulent misrepresentation?

–   How reliable are the records of issues and returns, and how secure against subsequent falsification or loss?

–   Are the precautions taken against the risk of counterfeiting such tickets for the purpose of 'fraudulent fundraising' considered adequate?

Fundraising by 'friends' groups'

6.3.6   For some large charities the root problem has always been their uncertainty as to the actual legal status of their 'friends' groups', whose activities often seem to be beyond the control of the charity trustees for one reason or another. If the friends' group members of Charity 'A' have bound themselves to a written constitution with declared Objects that are exclusively charitable under English law, or even if they have merely made it known to donors that their appeals are for the purpose of making *discretionary charitable grants*, they will have become accountable as a charitable institution in their own right.

Where these Objects point only to Charity A, being entirely within its Objects (e g for some special project for which funds are being sought), the friends' group – despite their administrative independence – will be accountable to Charity A itself, rather than to the public at large. If in doubt about what to do for the best in their relationship, both sides will need to seek clarification and advice from their legal advisers and, ultimately, from the Charity Commission.

In order to avoid such accountability, friends' groups often refrain from committing themselves to *exclusively* charitable purposes. Because they then remain free to do their good works outside the boundaries of charity law (which confines itself to the protection of voluntary funds set up to provide *only* some 'recognised' public benefit), they find themselves in a kind of 'default' position within the voluntary sector, as a not-for-profit organisation rather than a charity.

Fundraising as such is not regarded as a charitable purpose in its own right, so such a friends' group can happily trade on the sympathies aroused by the charity's name (where they have been able to include it as part of their own name) and then use the funds so raised to make discretionary grants to their charity – or perhaps to provide benefits that the charity itself cannot lawfully provide.

Of course, the lack of charitable status means that they are not subject to the Charities SORP, nor can they hold and invest funds on a tax-free basis, although under charity law they are, of course, accountable as trustees *for* Charity A in respect of any funds raised specifically on its behalf. And, under the SORP and its related Regulations, the annual report of Charity A will have to name them as such – see **4.3.5**. This will not matter unduly, so long as funds raised for Charity A are not stockpiled but are promptly handed over to the charity, which is partly why many charities make a special point of asking their friends' groups to remit as much as possible to them before each financial year-end.

We should also note an exception here to the SORP's 'golden rule':

'All incoming resources should be reported gross when raised by the charity (or by volunteers working at the charity's direction) or its agents. However where funds are raised or collected for the charity by individuals not employed or contracted by the charity, the gross incoming resources of the charity are the proceeds remitted to the charity by the organisers of the event, after deducting their expenses.'

– SORP 2005, paragraph 95

The other reason for care here is the need to *monitor and control* the use of the charity name by others, in order to guard against undue risk of detriment to the charity. If friends' groups using that name to arouse sympathy for fundraising purposes other than by agreement with the charity trustees resist attempts to regulate their activities, viewing it as 'interference', there may be no other way to resolve the problem but by seeking advice from the Commission, preferably as a joint application by both parties.

Perhaps as a direct result of the statutory regime of public accountability, the charity name (including 'working names', 'brand' names, trade marks and logos, etc) is now increasingly seen as a valuable intangible asset capable of generating significant economic benefits. Thus, wherever fundraising by others clearly relies on a charity's particular name, the trustees of that charity can find themselves obliged to pursue the matter of accountability for the funds so raised, on the basis that by making use of the name in this way the fundraiser has become trustee *for* their charity in respect of those funds. This can be a delicate matter requiring careful handling in order to avoid the danger of alienating enthusiastic supporters.

TRADING, INVESTMENT AND OTHER INCOMING RESOURCES

6.4 While for most charities *gift-accounting* will be the primary consideration, in many cases with little or nothing to report from year to year under these other sub-headings, for many others it is increasingly the other way round. A charity may have been founded and funded in the traditional way by some wealthy philanthropist so that it has always been able to live off the investment returns from the initial funding to finance its activities. Or it may be that essentially modern phenomenon: a *'trading charity'* with perhaps little or no popular appeal for its cause and no wealthy founders to buffer it against economic uncertainty. Or, again, it may be something of a hybrid, deriving its funding from sources that cannot quite be characterised as voluntary or as trading, but only as something in between. All these cases, where significant income-streams have to be reported other than under the sub-heading of voluntary contributions, can involve special aspects that you then need to consider.

Income from charitable and other economic activities

6.4.1 As already mentioned above, the complexities of this source of charity funding by undertaking 'economic activities', encompassing both charitable/ancillary trading and the non-charitable kind (especially through a *non-charitable* trading subsidiary, but often to some extent even within the charity itself since the introduction of a 'de minimis' statutory authority for the latter, as contained in the Finance Act 2000), as well as 'performance-related' grant-funded service-provision and also the sale of donated goods as a continuing business activity, need to be covered in a chapter of their own: chapter 13 is where we look in detail at the treatment of all these 'operating revenues' in the SoFA.

Here, we should just take note that *which column* the income is to be shown in will depend on whether it is subject to contract or trust law, for as the SORP says in its Glossary definition GL 30 (Grants/Contract Income):

> '(a) a contractual payment will normally be unrestricted income of the charity, but a grant for the supply of specific services will normally be restricted income;
> (b) the nature of the payment may be relevant to its VAT treatment.'

> *– SORP 2005, Glossary GL 30.1*

Investment returns

6.4.2 Once upon a time, it seemed self-evident that dividends, interest and rental income can only accrue to an *income* fund – unless, of course, they belong to an endowment on trust terms *requiring* (*not:* allowing) all income to be rolled up as capital each year. It would be impossible to provide public benefit at all out of the invested fund if neither income nor capital could ever be spent, so it could only have been set up like that as a way of saving up for a permanent fund large enough to achieve the founder's aims. In any case, the *law against perpetuities* limits the validity of trust income 'accumulation' provisions (whether obligatory or discretionary) to 21 years from the date of the trust or the death of a named person living at the time, thus making this unusual treatment in the SoFA a transitory phenomenon, to be seen only in the early years of the trust's life.

However, while trustees who are *obliged* (by the terms of their trust) to accumulate income as capital could justifiably claim to account for all income returns on their investment assets by showing them in the endowments column of the SoFA, those who make use of a *discretionary power* to achieve the same end do not have any such justification. Instead, they must account for the endowment's investment income in the normal way, showing it in the restricted/unrestricted income funds column of the SoFA as appropriate, and showing as a *transfer to capital* the amount of income they choose to convert into endowment capital each year, using the inter-fund transfers line further down the SoFA.

It is different for trust funds invested on the (duly authorised) 'total return' basis – as explained at **6.4.3**.

Accounting implications of trust law

Thus, before income returns can be shown in the endowments column at all, it needs special authority for their accounting to override the normal rules of trust law, which decree that *income returns accrue as income and capital returns accrue as capital*. (Moreover, the latter cannot be shown as *incoming resources* at all under the Charities SORP in its present form, but instead must be shown in the gains/losses section, in the lower half of the SoFA.) This donor-authority can be bestowed by the governing document of the trust – either explicitly by the founder or else under a suitable power of amendment. If made or amended since the Trustee Investments Act 1961 (August 1961), it will then condition the application of the TA 2000 in this respect. However, many trustees will probably prefer to rely on *official* authorisation for the purpose.

The same considerations apply equally to the endowed and other restricted funds of a charitable company, since these are all held *on trust* – but not to its *un*restricted or *corporate* funds, since these are governed not by trust law but by company law (albeit subject also to certain regulatory constraints imposed by Part VIII of the 1993 Act – unless the charity is exempted under Sch 2 to that Act).

The legal procedures and sector guidance needed to achieve this special authority for *permanently endowed* investment funds were put in place by the Charity Commission only after the issue of SORP 2000 and are set out in its 'Operational Guidance' on the subject, together with the necessary guidance on the accounting requirements – now also summarised in SORP 2005 (see **6.4.3** below).

'Special-purpose' trust income

The SORP highlights the trust law rule under which income from investing a restricted fund must, if that is an *income* fund, be added back to it unless the donor has specified otherwise, while an *endowment's* investment income will normally belong to *restricted* income if the endowment is held for a restricted purpose but to *unrestricted* income if the endowment is for the charity's general purposes:

> 'Many charities hold funds that can only be applied for particular purposes within their objects. These are restricted funds and have to be separately accounted for. The restriction may apply to the use of income or capital or both. Income generated from assets held in a restricted fund (eg, interest) will be legally subject to the same restriction as the original fund unless either
>
> (a)   the terms of the original restriction specifically say otherwise (for example the expressed wishes of a donor or the terms of an appeal), or
> (b)   the restricted fund is an endowment fund, the income of which is expendable at the discretion of the trustees.'
>
> – *SORP 2005, paragraph 69*

This is then amplified in Appendix 3, 'The Funds of a Charity':

> '… Income derived from the investment of capital (endowment) funds may be applied for the general purposes of the charity (unrestricted income), unless a specific purpose has been declared by the donor for the application of the income from the capital fund in question. Such income will be applicable for that purpose and will be restricted income.'
>
> – *SORP 2005, Appendix 3.6*

This follows from the fact that the endowed funds column, as defined by the SORP, splits out all *capital* from the restricted funds column, so that the latter is only a 'restricted *income* funds' column.

Income rolled up as gains

Of course, an endowed fund will receive no income returns at all if invested in a 'capital accumulation' investment vehicle whose fund-manager – as distinct from the investing charity – chooses to roll up all its income as capital (together with all the manager's fees/costs[5] which are deductible as *internal* charges and – except in the special case of an 'internal' *investment pooling charity* (see chapter 9) – cannot show up in the reporting charity's SoFA). All investment returns on that fund for the reporting charity then come to it as *capital* growth (net of all investment management costs) which the SORP says must be shown as part of revaluation/disposal gains in the endowments column, below the transfers line of the SoFA. The same thing happens where *unendowed* funds are invested in such a 'one-sided' way (ie with nothing to show in the incoming resources section of the SoFA), with this difference: since there is no actual trust capital involved there is no need to seek the special authority that would be required to satisfy the trust law requirement (now enshrined in the provisions of the TA 2000 – see **6.4.3**) to be 'even-handed' as between income and capital beneficiaries of the trust. Regardless of whether they accrue as incoming resources or as gains, *all* investment returns on unrestricted and restricted income funds have to go into those same columns in the SoFA, ie it really does not matter how they accrue – as long as they do accrue!

'Total return' investment accounting in the SoFA

6.4.3   In the old days, it was 'custom and practice' for charities to set separate objectives or targets for:

(a)   the level of *investment income* required to balance their budget, thus to help fund their activities; and

(b)   *capital growth* – often expressed as a requirement to maintain or increase the 'real' value of the portfolio (ie over and above the prevailing level of inflation).

With the phasing out of charity tax relief in respect of the underlying corporation tax on 'franked' investment income (equity dividends), income as such lost its long-held tax advantage over capital gains, making it advisable to review investment policy and align performance targets with market pricing – based as it is on the *total* return expected from each investment.

The 'total return' basis of investing cuts across income/capital distinctions, so that the SoFA treatment of 'realised' returns can distinguish only between:

(i)   *non-disposal* receipts, to be shown as incoming resources of the fund; and

(ii)   *disposal* gains/losses by reference to the asset's carrying value at the time – to be shown in the lower section of the SoFA as part of investment gains/losses (see **6.11**).

(It is also blind to the traditional capital/income distinctions in its treatment of *investment management costs*, simply deducting them from the total return and leaving the reporting charity's trustees with an accounting problem of no concern to the investment manager at all – see **6.6.4**, where we consider this aspect separately.)

Because this treatment conflicts with the normal rules of trust law, it will thus need special authorisation if applied to the investment of *endowed* funds – though this may only become critical for the efficient administration of a *permanent* endowment with

---

5   For further consideration of this aspect, see **6.6.4**, on the practicalities of accounting for investment management costs.

insufficient income, possibly also one that is *expendable* (usually at the discretion of the trustees) but that is generating surplus income that cannot be added to capital.

In the Charity Commission's website 'Operational Guidance' on the subject of investing permanently endowed funds on a 'total return' basis, OG83, the necessary accounting guidance is at OG83–B5. OG83 also sets out the *administrative* requirements for a permanent endowment to be invested under *proper authority* on a 'total return' basis and to comply with the TA 2000.

In short:

–   The trustees can choose *any base-date* (present or past – as far back as they like, as long as they have complete supporting data for the analysis) and 'freeze' the then value of the permanent endowment as its *deemed* 'gift value' as at that date.

–   All investment returns (realised/unrealised) from that base date less all amounts taken out as income are accumulated to form the 'unapplied total return' (UTR).

–   The UTR represents a *capital supplement* to the permanent endowment's frozen 'gift value' (ie it is *not* to be regarded as 'income-accumulation').

–   Allocations out of the UTR balance can be made at any time at the trustees' own discretion into a 'trust for application' (ie income) on the authority of a Charity Commission order under s 26 of the 1993 Act or else some provision within the governing document of the permanent endowment, if the trustees prefer.

–   Such allocations are subject to a statutory duty under the TA 2000 to be 'even-handed' as between present and future beneficiaries (capital v income).

–   The annual accounts must explain how the UTR is being administered and under what authority, and in particular the accounts note must:
     (i)   analyse the year's movements in the UTR;
     (ii)   distinguish the amount of the actual or deemed historical gift value of the related permanent endowment and the base date used; and
     (iii) disclose the name of the investment adviser currently being relied on.

For a comprehensive solution, the accounting guidance has to show how the various kinds of charitable fund in different situations should administer and account for the three components of the year's total return:

–   non-disposal distributions of money receivable on the investment assets;

–   the proceeds investment asset disposals (including part-disposals); and

–   the annual revaluation gains/losses on the remaining investment assets,

as well as:

–   any discretionary allocations to income for the year out of the total return to date since starting to invest on this basis (ie the UTR), under whatever legal authority the trustees are relying on for the purpose.

OG83 goes on to explain what to do in the most urgent situation where investment values have declined so far that the UTR balance has fallen to zero: nothing (ie no further allocations to income can be made out of it). It also explains what to do if the UTR falls *below* zero, the result of further disposal/revaluation losses: again, nothing – this time because you must wait until the markets rise again to the point where the UTR has a positive balance once more before you can extract any spending money from it.

Yet another, if less common, special situation explained in the guidance is the treatment of Charity Commission *recoupment orders* providing for the replacement of previous or new borrowings from the invested permanent endowment for some authorised purpose or other (this is most usually for the provision/improvement of buildings, usually on the charity's own land, that the charity needs for its own use).

The recommended *accounting* treatment, as summarised in Appendix 3(g)–(k) and paragraphs 75(e) and 214 of SORP 2005 and explained more fully below, for a *permanent endowment* (the only kind of fund for which the Commission is prepared to make an order under OG83) offers the most practical SoFA presentation consistent with the relevant accounting standards:

(1)   Adopting the total return basis of investing effectively prevents *any* investment returns being accounted for as *income*, but instead requires all receipts *other than those representing a disposal or part-disposal* to be accounted for as *incoming capital resources* (of the UTR).

(2)   The inter-fund transfers line of the SoFA is the obvious place to show all amounts taken out of UTR into income under the terms of the trustees' authorisation to exercise their new discretionary power to make such allocations.
        As an alternative SoFA treatment, it might be possible to cut out this inter-fund transfer by showing as *income* the total amount for the year that has been taken out of the UTR, counterbalanced by the same amount being either deducted or shown as a charge on the same line *in the endowments column*. The only real objection to that seems to be that it is less 'transparent' than using the transfers line to show what is, after all, the exercise of a significant discretionary power akin to the conversion of expendable endowment into income.

(3)   Under the SORP/Standards at present, it simply is not possible to put either realised or unrealised investment gains/losses into the 'incoming resources' section of the SoFA. But since the only place where you will need to distinguish between the two component parts of the invested permanent endowment (the part that is frozen at gift-value and the UTR as its 'supplement') is in the accounts note, this line of the SoFA will not be affected at all.

The four illustrations below summarise the SoFA presentation on the above basis in years 1 to 4 from the start of 'total return' investing. For a clearer presentation of the essential principles, we have split what would normally be a composite column for all endowment funds into the two components of the permanent endowment under consideration. We have also set the base date as the beginning of year 1 of the new investing basis, rather than going back into previous years, as OG83 says you can do, to set an earlier base-date from which to calculate a UTR figure to bring forward into year 1. (The only advantage of going back into the past like that is if you can claw back substantial gains to enlarge the UTR pot and thus buffer your new policy against future market falls.) We are therefore starting year 1 with a *nil* balance on UTR.)

Total Return investment-accounting: Year 1	Income	Endowed Funds		Total
	Funds	UTR	Gift-value	Funds
Incoming resources:				
– Gift of shares as PE	–	–	100	100
– Non-disposal investment returns	–	10	–	10
Total incoming resources for the year	–	**10**	**100**	**110**
Expenditure for the year	(4)	–	–	(4)
Net incoming resources before transfers	**(4)**	**10**	**100**	**106**
Transfer to Income from UTR	5	(5)	–	–
Net incoming resources before Gains/Losses	**1**	**5**	**100**	**106**
Net disposal/revaluation gains for the year	–	20	–	20
Funds balances brought forward	10	–	50	60
Funds balances carried forward	**11**	**25**	**150**	**186**

Total Return investment-accounting: Year 2	Income	Endowed Funds		Total
	Funds	UTR	Gift-value	Funds
Incoming resources:				
– Gift of shares as PE	–	–	–	–
– Non-disposal investment returns	–	10	–	10
Total incoming resources for the year	–	**10**	–	**10**
Expenditure for the year	(6)	–	–	(6)
Net incoming resources before transfers	**(6)**	**10**	–	**4**
Transfer out of UTR	5	(5)	–	–
Net incoming resources before Gains/Losses	**(1)**	**5**	–	**4**
Net disposal/revaluation losses for the year	–	(30)	–	(30)
Funds balances brought forward	11	25	150	186
Funds balances carried forward	**10**	–	**150**	**160**

Total Return investment-accounting: Year 3	Income	Endowed Funds		Total
	Funds	UTR	Gift-value	Funds
Incoming resources:				
– Gift of shares as PE	–	–	50	50
– Non-disposal investment returns	–	5	–	5
Total incoming resources for the year	–	**5**	**50**	**55**
Expenditure for the year	(7)	–	–	(7)
Net incoming resources before transfers	**(7)**	**5**	**50**	**48**
Transfer out of UTR	–	–	–	–
Net incoming resources before Gains/Losses	**(7)**	**5**	–	**48**
Net disposal/revaluation losses for the year	–	(10)	–	(10)
Funds balances brought forward	10	–	150	160

Total Return investment-accounting: Year 3	Income	Endowed Funds		Total
	Funds	UTR	Gift-value	Funds
Funds balances carried forward	3	(5)	200	198

Total Return investment-accounting: Year 4	Income	Endowed Funds		Total
	Funds	UTR	Gift-value	Funds
Incoming resources:				
– Gift of shares as PE	–	–	25	25
– Non-disposal investment returns	–	–	–	–
Total incoming resources for the year	–	–	25	25
Expenditure for the year	(8)	–	–	(8)
Net incoming resources before transfers	(8)	–	25	17
Transfer out of UTR	10	(10)	–	–
Net incoming resources before Gains/Losses	2	(10)	–	17
Net disposal/revaluation gains for the year	–	25	–	25
Funds balances brought forward	3	(5)	200	198
Funds balances carried forward	5	10	225	240

It can be seen that in year 3 it is not possible to allocate any spending money out of the UTR, as last year's allocation used it all up, while this year's revaluation/disposal losses of £10m less the £5m non-disposal investment returns result in a negative balance of £5m to carry forward. This can be left to recover on its own in accordance with the trustees' (no doubt well-informed) policy of investing for growth in the longer term, and with no particular remedial action needed – other than perhaps a change of investment managers if they no longer have the trustees' confidence!

In year 4 it has been possible to resume allocations to income from the UTR, despite the absence of any non-disposal returns for the year, as a new and more aggressive investment policy (or perhaps just a general recovery in the markets) has resulted in revaluation and disposal gains that have more than wiped out the negative UTR balance brought forward – so much so that here the trustees decided to double up on the allocation to income this year in order to make up for last year.

OG83 sets out exactly how the Commission provides the legal authority in individual cases where the trustees can show that they need the Commission's help and that it is for the benefit of the charity to be officially allowed to adopt the 'total return' basis of applying *permanently endowed* funds held for investment. This constraint affects investment funds only if *permanently* endowed, since the trustees have full legal power to spend capital returns on investments that are *un*endowed or that belong to a *discretionary* endowment.

In the latter case, of course, it should also be possible to get the Commission to accept as reasonable the temporary retention of 'excess' income returns as a reserve to even out market fluctuations where the trustees' policy is to avoid depleting the capital – even by erosion due to inflation.

Summing up, then, we note that the 'standard' rules of trust law remain untouched by the TA 2000 – a fact made clear by the Commission's July 2000 public consultation document: *Endowed Charities – A Fresh Approach to Investment Returns?* In the guidance that followed, OG83, the Commission's explanation of the mechanics of the 'total return' basis of investment includes, among other things:

'The trustees of charities that have assets held on trust for investment (capital) must be even-handed in the way they treat current and future beneficiaries. Trust law underpins this duty with a series of rules for the allocation of investment returns. These have been developed to ensure the interests of all beneficiaries (present and future) are protected. In this guidance these rules are referred to as the "standard" rules.

Without a specific power in its governing document setting out how it should allocate investment returns, a charity must comply with the standard rules for this. The standard rules dictate that particular types of investment return should be added to the trust for application (income) and that particular types of investment return should be added to the trust for investment (capital). Legislation will be needed to change the standard rules to affect all trusts (including charitable assets held on trust). The Law Commission is examining the present general law in this area.

The general thrust of responses to the consultation was overwhelmingly in favour of the Commission's proposals to offer trustees flexibility in the allocation of investment returns. Taking the responses into account, we are willing to offer the trustees of endowed charities a power to allocate the investment return derived from assets held on trust for investment (capital) at their discretion, rather than in the way dictated by the standard rules. We are able to do this on an individual charity basis.

The power we will give will only be exercisable within the trustees' underlying duty to be even-handed in their treatment of present and future beneficiaries.

The policy set out in this guidance only applies to the assets of charities which are held on trust for investment (capital) and to the returns from such investment. It does not apply to other assets of charities. The policy:

– enables trustees to invest charitable funds in a way they judge will produce the best returns for the charity, regardless of the form in which the returns are received.
– recognises the need for trustees to take a long-term view on the generation and the allocation of investment returns. The policy draws trustees' attention to the fact that investment returns and inflation fluctuate from year to year – markets can go down as well as rise. It also explains their duty to make fair decisions about the resources to be spent on current and future beneficiaries.
– *does not* undermine the principle of permanent endowment nor the right of founders to establish a charity with a trust for investment (capital). Instead, it highlights the core principle of taking full account of the needs of present (not past) and future beneficiaries in an even-handed way that is consistent with the objects of the charity – and which recognises that the charity is intended to be permanent.'

– from OG83/A1

'What the power does and does not do

By introducing an adjustment to the administrative framework of charities with permanent endowment we aim to help them to more effectively balance the needs of present and future beneficiaries. The power we will give trustees will create flexibility in the process of allocating an appropriate part of the investment return to the trust for application (income).

The power does not extend beyond the allocation of part of the investment return to the trust for application (income). Once a part of the investment return has been allocated to the trust for application (income) (in accordance with the directions in the model order), that part must be applied for the purposes of the charity within a reasonable period of allocation in just the same way that a charity's income must be applied under the standard rules.

The power does not authorise trustees to add any part of the total return allocated to the trust for application (income) to the resources representing the actual gifts to the charity. A separate power of accumulation will be required for this purpose, as is the case under the standard rules.

Trustees will not normally need to retain funds for any length of time in the trust for application (income). This is because any part of a charity's unapplied total return may be allocated to the trust for application (income) at any time. However, on each occasion the allocation must be compatible with the discharge of the trustees' duty to be even-handed in their treatment of present and future beneficiaries. There is therefore no need for trustees to build up reserves in the trust for application (income) to cover a year when the investment returns for that year are minimal or negative (see OG 83 C4). But if funds are retained in the trust for application (income) this should be done in accordance with a proper policy on the maintenance of reserves. Our publication CC19 provides guidance in this area.

In making each allocation from the unapplied total return to the trust for application (income), the trustees must have regard to their duty to be even-handed and to the other duties attached to the use of the power – see section 2 of OG 83 B2. Under-allocation to the trust for application (income) would prejudice the interests of current beneficiaries. Over-allocation to the trust for application (income) would prejudice the interests of future beneficiaries.

The power does not authorise the expenditure of the charity's investment fund. A separate power will be required to authorise the expenditure of any part of this fund. Our policy on authorising the expenditure of part of the investment fund of a charity that is operating a total return approach to investment is set out in OG 83 B4. The model order to be used to provide such authority is given in OG 83 C6. It is therefore clear that the concept of permanent endowment (i e assets held on trust for investment (capital)) is not affected by the power we propose to give trustees. We recognise a donor's right to create a charity that will have future as well as present beneficiaries.

Changing back to the standard rules

Once trustees have started to use the power given by clause 1 of the model order they cannot use any other method of allocating the investment return of the charity without the prior approval of the Commissioners.

It may be impractical for trustees to go back to analysing the investment return on the basis of the standard rules. During the period when the total return approach was used, investment returns would have been received and allocated to the trust for application (income) without drawing any distinction between income and capital. It would therefore be difficult to say, at the date the trustees chose to return to the standard rules, which part of the unapplied total return held at that time was retained income and which part was capital.

However, we do acknowledge that there may be special circumstances in which it would be appropriate for trustees who have begun to use the total return power to then revert to an approach to investment based on the standard rules. The model order states that the prior approval of the Commission is required to do this …

New charities

New charities may be established with a power to operate a total return approach to investment, rather than the standard rules approach. In such circumstances we would recommend that the charity's governing document includes trustee duties similar to those set out in the model order. The promoters of such a charity will need to recognise that where a total return approach to investment is adopted and there is no unapplied total return, then there will be no resources that can actually be applied for the purposes of the charity.'

– *from OG83/A2*

Gains/losses on disposing of fixed assets for the charity's own use

6.4.4 The treatment of both realised and unrealised gains and losses on tangible (and other) fixed assets held for a charity's *own use* – ie those arising from their *disposal* and their year-end revaluation, respectively – is unchanged from the original SORP (other than to clarify the impact of 'impairment' – see **6.11**). Thus a net gain on the year's disposals of such assets is to be shown here, under 'other incoming resources', while a net loss on the year's disposals is to be included on the appropriate line(s) of the 'resources expended' section, in each case in the column proper to the fund to which the asset belongs.

'RESOURCES EXPENDED' SECTION

6.5 For larger charities, meaning those *exceeding* the statutory audit threshold (the Charities Act 2006 doubled the old £250,000 gross income figure for this, at the same time simplifying and harmonising the rules for all charities for financial years starting after 26 February 2007), SORP 2005 requires a strictly *purpose-based* presentation of all expenditure in the SoFA. That means classifying all costs and expenses according to the *operational objectives* for which they have been incurred (ie for public benefit or else to benefit the charity itself) – usually (but not necessarily) characterised by the nature of the activity in each case – rather than the nature of the cost/expense itself. Any 'support' costs (see **6.5.1**) included in the SoFA figures (together with the basis and result of 'cost-spreading' onto the direct costs of the charity's activities), as well as the total of any grants included within those direct costs, must then be sub-analysed in the accounts notes.

Further analysis of the SoFA figures by type of expense is required across the board only for staff costs (see below), with sub-analysis of non-staff costs being required only for support costs, costs of generating funds and governance costs – ie not for the costs of charitable activities as such.

It was here that SORP 2000 had introduced perhaps its most distinctive mark on the SoFA, in reformatting this expenditure section by means of a fundamental split of the larger charity's total expenditure between:

(i)   costs of generating funds; and

(ii) charitable expenditure – which SORP 2005 splits into (a) 'charitable activities' and (b) charity 'governance' (previously called 'management and administration of the charity').

These main expenditure headings are dealt with at **6.6** and **6.7** respectively.

The 'natural' or expense-type classification was then to be summarised in the notes, for example, staff costs, consumable supplies, utilities, communications, premises (but with depreciation often, by convention, being shown separately, if material), professional services, etc – whereas apart from staff costs this is no longer required for *charitable* activities under SORP 2005, which instead wants sub-analysis by project/objective, as noted above.

The original, 1995 SORP said that this expense-type classification, traditionally used in charities' income and expenditure accounts until then, 'may be shown in the notes'. But SORP 2000 said: 'The major items of expenditure within each type of charitable activity should be appropriately analysed in the notes to the accounts.' That requirement was dropped by SORP 2005.

It has become common practice to meet the SORP's requirement here by supplementing the SoFA's expenditure presentation with a table in the accounts notes using the very broadest of expense-type headings over which the SoFA figures were spread. The following illustration typically breaks out just the support costs from the grant-awards and other direct costs where under SORP 2000 the same charity took the costs shown in the total column of the SoFA and analysed each functional heading into its components of staff costs, depreciation and 'other costs' – as well as (in this case) the grant-awards comprising the charity's main purpose-related direct charitable activity cost.

[Note] 6 **Gross Expenditure**	Awards	Other direct Costs	Support costs allocated	**Total 2008**	*Total 2007*
	£000	£000	£000	£000	**£000**
Costs of generating funds					
Fundraising	-	16,053	1,679	17,732	17,435
Publicity	-	596	221	817	893
Retail costs	-	67,934	263	68,197	62,096
Investment management costs	-	756	-	756	711
	-	85,339	2,163	87,502	81,135
Charitable Expenditure					
Research	71,640	462	221	**72,323**	*50,414*
Cardiovascular Initiative – research	(97)	–	–	**(97)**	*(384)*
Prevention and care	10,679	22,561	1,458	**34,698**	*35,275*
	82,222	23,023	1,679	106,924	85,305
Governance	–	255	574	**829**	*733*
	82,222	108,617	4,416	**195,255**	*167,173*

British Heart Foundation – 2007/08 Accounts

To avoid clutter, detailed analysis of all the SoFA's main categories of expenditure on activities can be relegated to the accounts notes:

> 'The Statement of Financial Activities or the notes to the accounts should include an analysis of the sub-activities, services, programmes, projects or other initiatives that contribute to a particular activity category.'

– SORP 2005, paragraph 177

Smaller charities (companies *and* non-companies), however, ie those below the statutory audit threshold, can do more or less what they like here:

> '(a)   ... smaller charities do not need to analyse either resources expended or incoming resources by activity categories within the Statement of Financial Activities. They may instead choose resource classifications to suit their circumstances.
>
> (b)   Where a small charity adopts an alternative approach to analysis within the Statement of Financial Activities certain note disclosures may no longer be necessary, for example, where these disclosures relate to the constituent costs of an activity category or where relevant information is provided on the face of the Statement of Financial Activities. ...'.

– SORP 2005, Appendix 5.3.1

Allocation/apportionment of 'support costs'

6.5.1   Such is the great diversity of charities' objectives and activities that the SORP cannot give detailed guidance on how to achieve the required purpose-related and fully activity-based analysis to be shown in the SoFA by allocating/apportioning those support costs that are incurred for multiple purposes – usually 'central overheads'. In terms of the functions involved:

> 'Support costs include the central or regional office functions such as general management, payroll administration, budgeting and accounting, information technology, human resources, and financing.'

– SORP 2005, paragraph 164

One achievement of SORP 2000 in reformatting the SoFA's expenditure section, however, was that it did marginalise charities' competing efforts at narrowing down the definition of 'other expenditure' under the 1995 SORP: it simply transferred 'fundraising and publicity' costs to a larger sub-section ('activities to generate funds'), together with the management of investment assets, and highlighted 'charity management and administration' (which SORP 2005 calls 'governance') as a separate category of expenditure.

That made the spreading of 'support costs' all the more interesting, because that is where charities' 'indirect costs' had mostly migrated anyway – and because the logical next step as charity accounting/reporting developed further was clearly to require the full absorption of all support costs (even if not yet charity governance costs) in the presentation of expenditure by *Objects-related* functional activity.

To that end, the revised guidance in SORP 2005 went beyond what was possible in 2000, though still essentially repeating what paragraph 150 of the 1995 SORP originally had in mind, in setting out much more concise rules:

'In attributing costs between activity categories, the following principles should be applied:

(a)   Where appropriate, expenditure should be allocated directly to an activity cost category.

(b)   Items of expenditure which contribute directly to the output of more than one activity cost category, for example the cost of a staff member whose time is divided between a fundraising activity and working on a charitable project, should be apportioned on a reasonable, justifiable and consistent basis.

(c)   Depreciation, amortisation, impairment or losses on disposal of fixed assets should be attributed in accordance with the same principles.

(d)   Support costs ... provide the organisational infrastructure that enables output producing activities to take place. Such costs should therefore also be apportioned on a reasonable, justifiable and consistent basis to the activity cost categories being supported.'

– SORP 2005, paragraph 169

Therefore, the process of support costs allocation/apportionment under SORP 2005 starts out as one of elimination from *total expenditure* of all the costs that can be directly attributed, or else apportioned, to one or other of the activities to be reported within the expenditure section of the SoFA (and sub-analysed, if need be, in the accounts notes).

That leaves as a 'grey area' any costs that can only be attributed or apportioned to *intermediary* (ie supporting) *function-based* categories that are now invisible in the SoFA. Each functional component of the 'grey' area, ultimately what in total many charities have always called 'central overheads', is simply the result of a similar (and normally simultaneous) process of attribution and apportionment of each kind of expense incurred, and can then be reviewed for apportionment to the various reportable activities it serves. To comply with FRS18, the apportionment basis adopted must be not only rational and consistently applied, but also 'the *most* suitable' in the charity's circumstances. Under SORP 2005 it must, together with the results (percentages or amounts), unless the figures are immaterial, be disclosed in the accounts notes (to illustrate which the SORP provides a pro forma table showing the relationship between the activity costs shown in the SoFA and the support costs included within them – see chapter 12).

To optimise effectiveness and efficiency – if not also economy – any charity's activities entail a certain amount of expenditure on control and supervision (as an indispensable support cost) over and above the costs of running the charity as such. But now that both categories of component cost (direct and indirect) for 'charitable activities', and likewise for 'fund-generating activities', have been merged in the SoFA to achieve *objective-based* reporting, the distinction between them becomes less critical. This can make it harder to justify the use of sophisticated accounting bases for apportioning central overhead costs.

There are some half a dozen generally accepted alternative accounting bases for this, each with a different result – but none intrinsically better than the others. SORP 2005 exemplifies only staff time, headcount, floor area and 'usage' (of direct costs – ie pro rata to them), but some charities may find units of output (or even of input) better, or perhaps (direct) staff costs, rather than their time.

Therefore for consistency from year to year you would be advised to stick to the same methodology once it has been worked out and adopted, as a change of basis must in any case be disclosed under accounting policies (see chapter 12). Having said that, it is equally true that the basis/bases currently in use must be regularly reviewed and adjusted where necessary. Changes or adjustments, however, must be justifiable, and a consistent approach is clearly a necessity to facilitate a proper understanding of how a charity's activities as reported in the SoFA may have changed from year to year.

By way of example, if (using a 'time' basis) the finance director spends 10% of his time on project management, this cost is a support cost of the project services, and so 10% of his salary and (depending on the sophistication of the charity's costing system) related costs such as secretarial support, etc, should be allocated to it.

Central office costs, for instance, may be best apportioned on a 'space' basis, by estimating the floor area occupied for the purposes of each of the functional activities – departmentally in the largest charities. It is vital to work through the allocations and costs on a systematic basis. Whatever the system of cost allocation/apportionment adopted, however, care is needed to ensure that this is not unduly complex or costly in relation to the reporting needs of the charity.

The detailed disclosure requirements in relation to the SoFA are discussed in chapter 12 (Notes to the Accounts).

'COSTS OF GENERATING FUNDS'

6.6   Examples of SORP 2000's function-based expenditure-reporting under this heading included the costs of undertaking all kinds of:

–   charity appeals of any kind; as distinct from

–   'charity fundraising' events (including dinners, concerts, sponsored walks, etc);

–   'non-charitable' trading (but also 'ancillary' trading to *finance* service-provision);

–   commercial sponsorship activities (ie in which the charity is not 'passive');

–   charity lotteries; and

–   investment securities/estate management costs.

SORP 2005 still requires those that are significant for the charity to be differentiated. This need no longer be within the SoFA, but it does need to be presented in such a way as to show their relationship to the funds generated/raised – if necessary by means of the supporting accounts note. Where the activity is one of fundraising for *voluntary* income, however, SORP 2005 is more explicit:

> 'Where the costs of generating voluntary income are material, details of the types of activity on which the costs were expended should be shown in the notes to the accounts. Types of activity could include collections (eg street and house-to-house collections), sponsorship, legacy development and direct mail. As far as possible the analysis provided here should match the detailed analysis of voluntary incoming resources ...'.

– SORP 2005, paragraph 183

For *non-company* charities and also for 'parent' *charitable companies* of 'small' groups (as defined by the Companies Act 2006) in respect of any group accounts they must prepare under the Charities Act 1993, the requirement for this separate reporting of the different categories of expenditure in the SoFA is made mandatory by the SORP's related 2008 Regulations – whereas in the accounts notes this is so only for charitable activities and all support costs, not for activities to generate funds.

For some charities, the way the SORP spotlights charity fundraising (in its broadest meaning) by showing the relevant costs in a prominent position in the SoFA, usually *above* the section devoted to 'charitable activities' (see **6.7**), could be unhelpful. Perhaps this is because the charity is fortunate enough not to have to devote significant resources to *asking for help*, as distinct from just getting on with it and providing the public benefit (free or at a fee, as appropriate) for which it was set up in the first place. In such a case the SORP's emphasis here is just a minor nuisance to be tolerated for the sake of the sector.

In other cases, however, it could attract unwelcome attention to what may be relatively high costs of, eg, running charity shops or perhaps organising a celebrity concert, compared with the gross proceeds or 'turnover' of these and any other activities whose primary purpose is clearly to generate either voluntary funds or trading revenues – or both. As a not untypical example of the poor returns achievable even with the benefit of volunteer help and shop rental concessions in many cases, we can see (from the SoFA extract, below) that of the British Red Cross Society's total incoming resources of £241m for 2007, nearly £22m came from its charity shops. But £21m of this went on overheads (the goods themselves having been largely donated), leaving very little available for its real work – unless indeed the main benefit was the High Street presence needed to maintain donor-awareness. As the SORP's optional line for 'net incoming resources available for charitable activities' has not been included in the published SoFA, we can infer that it is unhelpful to the charity's cause.

Consolidated Statement of Financial Activities

Year ended 31 December 2007	Notes	Unrestricted £000	Restricted £000	2007 Total £000	2006 Total £000
Incoming resources					
Incoming resources from generated funds					
Voluntary income	2	51,668	49,795	**101,463**	79,031
Trading activities	3	22,270	16	**22,286**	22,076
Investment income		2,135	990	**3,125**	3,253
[sub-total]		76,073	50,801	**126,874**	104,410
Incoming resources relating to charitable activities					
Emergency response		15,654	30,431	**46,085**	46,619
Short term crisis care &c		27,735	920	**28,655**	28,326
Supporting & strengthening the Red Cross Movement		-	35,736	**35,736**	15,675
[sub-total]	4	43,389	67,087	110,476	90,620

Consolidated Statement of Financial Activities				
Year ended 31 December 2007	Unrestricted	Restricted	**2007** **Total**	2006 Total
Other incoming resources ...	4,435	(160)	3,446	6,232
Total incoming resources	**123,897**	**117,728**	**241,625**	**201,936**
Resources Expended				
Costs of generating funds				
Voluntary income	21,096	1,735	**22,831**	17,268
Trading activities	20,837	5	**20,842**	18,922
Investment management costs	96	–	**96**	54
[sub-total]	42,029	1,740	**43,769**	36,244
...				

British Red Cross – 2007 Accounts

Unless the special reasons for apparent under-performance are carefully explained, such activities could begin to suffer from lack of credibility with donors as they become aware of it in accounts presented in the format required by the SORP. Of course, the SORP does recommend commenting on the performance of any significant fundraising activities in the annual report, but without offering further advice – for example, to compare a campaign's target-figure with cumulative figures of gross funds raised and costs incurred, etc, in order to put into proper perspective the start-up costs often involved. Furthermore, the largest charities nowadays have to provide public domain data in this area, as part of their Summary Information Return to the Charity Commission, thus necessitating special explanations if donor confidence is to be maintained wherever such activities seem to be under-performing.

Charities vulnerable to the kind of misunderstanding that could well lead to 'donor-fatigue', if the relationship between 'funds raised' and 'costs of generating funds' is not properly explained under SORP 2005 (in descending order of risk), can be seen as those with:

–   costly fundraising, including failed 'high-risk' appeal events, exemplified by:
    –   public appeals using street collectors employed by professional fundraisers;
    –   'donor-base' development in its early years (eg for legacy-fundraising); or
    –   a major 'pop concert' appeal that is a 'wash-out' or loses its 'star turn';

–   low-margin business-type activities for revenue-raising purposes, such as:
    –   'charity shops' using *paid* staff (other than beneficiaries, of course) to sell off goods donated in response to appeals; or
    –   non-charitable trading (because of having to gross up the costs);

–   charitable trading that is dependent on:
    –   unusually high borrowing costs (in the absence of the necessary reserves); or
    –   heavy marketing and/or sales-administration costs.

Let us therefore take a look at the treatment of the costs of each of the main types of activity involved.

Fundraising and publicity

6.6.1 Publicity incurred to attract funds needs to be distinguished from *educational* publicity – or indeed any kind of activity to inform the public (and especially potential beneficiaries) of the availability and nature/extent of charitable benefits on offer, including any eligibility criteria and procedural requirements. It can be a difficult distinction to make if the educational or awareness-raising information is provided 'in the context of a fundraising activity', and the SORP says that for the costs to be properly apportioned between charitable activities and this heading:

> 'a distinction should be drawn between:
>
> (a)   publicity or information costs involved in raising the profile of a charity which is associated with fundraising (costs of generating funds) and
> (b)   publicity or information that is provided in an educational manner in furtherance of the charity's objectives (charitable expenditure).'

– SORP 2005, paragraph 172

The Charity Commission's *SORP 2000 Information Sheet 1* published in 2002 had clarified this point in order to deal with the situation where the trustees combine '*information about the aims, objectives and projects of a charity*' with '*fundraising activities such as mailshots, collections and telephone fundraising*', resulting in '*uncertainty ... as to whether the provision of such information creates a joint cost that may be allocated to other activities in accordance with the guidance provided in paragraph 153 of SORP 2000*'. The Commission's clarification, now part of SORP 2005, offered three criteria for expenditure to qualify as charitable:

> 'In the context of a fundraising activity, for publicity or information to be regarded as charitable expenditure, it must be supplied in an educational manner. To achieve an educational purpose, information supplied would be:
>
> (a)   targeted at beneficiaries or others who can use the information to further the charity's objectives;
> (b)   information or advice on which the recipient can act upon in an informed manner to further the charity's objectives; and
> (c)   related to other educational activities or objectives undertaken by the charity
>
> Where information provided in conjunction with a fundraising activity does not meet these criteria, it should be regarded as targeted at potential donors and therefore relating wholly to the fundraising activity.'

– SORP 2005, paragraph 173

Adverse media coverage in 2000 of NSPCC's 'Full Stop' campaign had showed how easily this area of a charity's activities can be misunderstood if not carefully explained. The following extracts from their 1999/2000 Accounts did provide the necessary explanations – but obviously this was not enough to avoid subsequent speculation in the national press suggesting that this amounted to wasteful fundraising expenditure, until that was countered by statements from both the charity and the Commission:

SoFA extract (Summarised)	Unrestricted	Restricted	Total
	£'000	£'000	£'000
INCOMING RESOURCES			
Donations and gifts	26,836	1,251	28,087
Donations and gifts – FULL STOP appeal	22,485	2,475	24,960
Legacies	12,371	–	12,371
Income from statutory sources	–	8,144	8,144
[Investment and Other Income]	...	...	...
Total incoming resources	66,851	11,580	78,431
RESOURCES EXPENDED			
Costs of Generating Funds			
Fundraising & publicity – regular income	6,019	–	6,019
Fundraising & publicity – FULL STOP Appeal	7,976	–	7,976
	13,995	–	13,995
Available for charitable application	*52,856*	*11,580*	*64,436*
Charitable Expenditure			
Local/National services	...	...	...
Policy development and influencing	11,068	353	11,421
Public education	9,161	–	9,161
Support costs & Administration	8,290	8	8,298
	50,906	10,042	60,948
Total expenditure	64,901	10,042	74,943
Net incoming resources before transfers	1,950	1,538	3,488

*Note 4: Allocation of expenditure on communications to the public
Communication with the public serves the dual purpose of educating and fundraising. Documents defining our public policy encourage readers to fund its implementation. Conversely, documents requesting funds need to explain the policy to gain financial support. Part of the expenditure incurred each year ... is specific to either [one or the other]. The remainder is allocated between [them]:

	Attributed	Allocated	Total
Total fundraising & publicity	4,190	9,805	13,995
Policy development and influencing	11,421	–	11,421
Public education	–	9,161	9,161
Total	15,611	18,966	34,577

NSPCC – 1999/2000 Accounts

Comment

In fact, fuller reading of the charity's report and accounts and relevant publicity material at the time would have made it abundantly clear that this was in fact a highly successful campaign with the dual aim of prevention through increased public awareness and also a target of a quarter of a billion pounds to fund future activities in the charity's efforts to put a stop to child abuse. Although its achievements were lauded in the 2000/01 Annual Report, the Full Stop campaign's financial dimensions were not discernible in the 2000/01 Accounts. What this 'media experience' had made painfully clear to the sector is that publicity can be a high-risk activity – even for a 'household name' charity.

Third-party fundraising

The SORP also points out (at paragraph 180) that fundraising *agents'* costs are to be included here, while (as noted at **6.1.8**) paragraph 95 carefully explains that only costs incurred by *other* external fundraisers can be netted off (ie ignored) in accounting for what comes to the charity as the proceeds of fundraising events or other activities undertaken by them. This is because the charity, having neither commissioned nor undertaken such fundraising, has no legal responsibility (and therefore no public accountability) for its costs. Fundraising for the benefit of a charity by its independently constituted and run 'Friends' Group' is a typical example.

Fundraising by a subsidiary or associated undertaking of the charity is a special case, however, in that the charity's proportionate share of the fundraising costs must of course be grossed up under FRS2 or FRS9 respectively – see chapter 14. As the SORP 2005 now puts it:

> 'In the case of consolidated accounts any such costs incurred by any subsidiary companies or other entities should be consolidated on a line-by-line basis.'

– SORP 2005, paragraph 180

Apart from that, you could reasonably group together here the costs of *all* events and activities whose proceeds primarily represent purely *voluntary* funding of any kind – other than goods specifically for resale, of course, which come under the next heading. This could therefore include such events as charity dinners/concerts, sponsored walks/runs (eg the London Marathon) and other fun activities designed to excite donor-participation for the purpose of attracting voluntary contributions from them or others – insofar as the costs do not count as 'valuable consideration' for any part of the proceeds, of course – otherwise they fall into the next category, at **6.6.2**.

Funding application/re-negotiation costs

In addition, the 'costs of ... applying for a grant for a charitable activity' belong here, having been seen as part of 'costs of generating funds' in accordance with paragraph 132 of SORP 2000. This is clearly to be taken as self-evident in SORP 2005, where instead the focus is now on accounting for the 'post-contract' situation, previously ignored:

> 'Costs of generating funds should not include:
>
> ...
>
> (b)   the costs of any subsequent negotiation, monitoring or reporting relating to the provision of goods or services under the terms of a grant, contract or performance-related grant.'

– SORP 2005, paragraph 179

Fundraising for the future

While expenditure on 'fundraising for the future' still cannot generally be capitalised or even just carried forward as a prepayment, SORP 2005 opens a door that might one day lead to a solution to the difficult question of using the SoFA to demonstrate fundraising performance:

> 'Some fundraising costs may be incurred in starting up a new source of future income such as legacies, or in developing a supporter database.
>
> (a)   Start-up costs of a new fundraising activity should be treated in the same manner as similar cost incurred as part of a charity's ongoing activities. In most cases, it will be inappropriate to carry forward start-up costs as prepayments or deferred expenditure as the future economic benefits that may be derived are usually not sufficiently certain (see Appendix 2: UITF Abstract 24 – Accounting for Start-up Costs).
>
> (b)   Data capture costs of internally developed databases may only be capitalised where future benefit can be demonstrated and the resulting database has a readily ascertainable value.'
>
> – *SORP 2005, paragraph 181*

The key point here must be the reliability of the charity's (reasonable) expectations of the future voluntary funding stream whose periodic reassessment by the fundraising managers involved is unavoidable to justify the charity's ongoing efforts at identifying, cultivating and appealing to donors for this purpose, even once those efforts begin to bear fruit as firm commitments or promises made by donors. That reliability will to some extent be dependent on the ready availability of comparable statistical data on the results achieved from such longer-term initiatives as 'legacy marketing', capital appeals, relationship fundraising for major gifts, etc – either by charities themselves or by the professional fundraisers serving their needs.

'Business' activities for revenue-raising purposes

6.6.2   This means trading and similar *economic* activities not undertaken primarily in order to provide public benefit. Although it is the costs of *non-charitable trading* that will most commonly be found here, the SORP regards the costs of dealing in donated goods (eg charity shops, 'second-hand goods' stalls in bazaars, fairs/markets and village/church halls, car-boot sales, etc) as falling into the same category. To this, it then adds in the costs of other 'operating activities' that, while also undertaken primarily to raise funds, have more of a business nature than the category at **6.6.1**, in that the funds raised are not really 'voluntary contributions' as such but the revenues of 'commercial' or 'value-for-value' transactions, of which some obvious examples might be:

–   lotteries, concerts/dinners, fun events and similar promotional events/activities;

–   corporate sponsorship activities in which the charity is not 'passive';

–   'ancillary' trading excluded from **6.6.3** as primarily to raise funds;

–   licensing of the use of charity assets (eg intellectual property rights);

–   letting/hiring out of non-investment properties/equipment while surplus to operational requirements for charitable activities.

Until the Finance Act 2000, any significant non-charitable trading on a continuing basis was traditionally hived down into a subsidiary trading company to avoid trouble with the Inland Revenue and the Charity Commission. Charities have a *statutory* concession under the Finance Act 2000 allowing them to trade *tax-free* outside their Objects up to a maximum annual turnover of £50,000 – depending on the size of the charity by reference to its annual gross income.

We discuss trading and similar activities of a business (ie economic) nature in chapter 13. Here, it is only necessary to note that the SORP requires the presentation of their costs to be clearly related to the presentation of the related income in the SoFA, as already mentioned.

Finance/marketing/sales-administration of charitable trading businesses

6.6.3 The golden rule for the SORP to be able to conform to the principles of trust law is that the costs of any kind of activity undertaken *other than* primarily to provide public benefit or to manage/administer the charity ('governance') can only properly be shown as part of the costs of 'activities to generate funds'. Thus *financing* even a primary-purpose trading activity can no more be said to be incurred directly in furtherance of the charity's Objects than can any other kind of fundraising. Surprising though it may be to those coming from the profit sector, this leads to the further conclusion that interest payable on all external borrowings – including trade-financing costs of any kind – belongs under the heading of 'Cost of Generating Funds'. More recently, however, the SORP Review Committee seems to have been veering away from such charity-specific thinking and now offers the commercially inspired (non-binding) interpretation in its Information Sheet No 1 that the costs of financing a particular activity should 'generally be allocated to that activity', with other financing costs being apportioned along with 'other support costs'. It remains to be seen whether this view of 'activity', which fails to distinguish whether its purpose is a public benefit one or a self-benefit one (ie, like all 'activities to generate funds'), will prevail or be corrected by deeper thinking in the next version of the Charities SORP.

Again, sales-administration and marketing, insofar as these activities cannot be shown to be *primarily* incurred for the purpose of finding/informing beneficiaries and extending or improving the charitable service actually provided to them, can only properly be accounted for as part of 'Cost of Generating Funds'.

On the other hand, the collecting in of sales debts arising from a *charitable* trading activity (as distinct from one to generate funds), like other costs of the realisation or conversion of *non-investment* assets that are not dedicated to fundraising activities, will – by the same reasoning – come within the Charitable Activities section, with those that cannot be included in 'support costs' there being part of 'governance' (previously 'charity management and administration'). The same thing goes for the costs of safeguarding such assets and controlling their proper application – as part of 'internal control'.

Management of investment assets (including properties)

6.6.4 The traditional method of remunerating agents in connection with the management of investment assets used to be by means of 'transaction' charges, which the agent added to the purchase price or deducted from the sales proceeds or income collected/remitted, respectively. The same method works in the same way for securities as for land. In accounting for these investment assets and their management, any 'incidental' costs of acquiring the asset are treated as part of its initial cost (the costs of any subsequent additions and improvements being added in as well), while the incidental costs of disposal are treated as reducing the sale proceeds in calculating the gain/loss, with the annual income from the retained asset being accounted for in the SoFA net of agents' costs if immaterial – otherwise gross.

However, the economies of scale achievable through computerisation, as well as those inherent in the management of larger investment portfolios/estates, have inevitably led in many cases to the streamlining of all the agents' charges. These are then replaced by a negotiated composite annual fee for all the services provided, which cannot easily be broken down into its component parts for accounting purposes, resulting in confusion about how much to write off through the SoFA (and where) and how much to take straight to the balance sheet as additional costs of the retained asset. The problem has been exacerbated by the far-reaching developments that have taken place in the world of investment management in the second half of the twentieth century, culminating in the TA 2000's liberalisation and regulation of *trust fund* investment from 1 February 2001.

The investment vehicles, instruments and methods now available to charities can cut right across the normal trust law rules of capital and income distinction – on which also the (commercial) accounting standards are based. At **6.4.2** we noted what happens to the investment management costs where a fund is invested in some external investment vehicle that accumulates all the returns as capital, but it also applies where the vehicle is designed to produce only an income return. And again at **6.4.3** we touched on the impact of the 'total return' basis when it comes to accounting for the costs of managing endowment investments.

On top of all that, the SORP requires incoming resources to be shown without netting off their related costs unless these are immaterial (though netting off continues to be the norm for investment gains/losses).

Are agents' fees a charge on income – or on capital – or both?

This then makes it necessary to say something about where to charge these costs – especially where subsumed in composite fees covering both transactional services and more general portfolio/estate management services such as reviews/advice and valuations. But in clarifying that question for *endowed fund* investment assets, the SORP seems to gloss over the critical question of the split between capital and revenue of this composite annual fee where the endowed fund is a *permanent* one:

> 'Any expenses incurred in the administration or protection of endowment investments should be charged to capital. For example, the fees of someone who manages the endowment investments, or the cost of improvements to land held as an endowment investment. Only where the trusts of the charity provide to the contrary, or there are insufficient funds in the endowment to meet such costs, can they be charged against the other funds held by the charity.'

– SORP 2005, Appendix 3.3(c)

Apart from anything else, the terminology is confusing. While the guidance is clearly right in saying you must (subject to any specific terms of trust) *pay* out of capital the costs of administering/protecting/improving the *capital* assets of an endowed fund, or if the cash cannot be found within the capital of that fund – even by (duly authorised) borrowing from it – then out of (related/general) income, that guidance fails to address the *accounting* question.

In the example cited above, the cost of improving permanently endowed investment land *cannot be written off in the SoFA*, since (by definition) it does not represent any consumption of resources, but must be accounted for by increasing the balance sheet's *carrying value* of the land – *not* instead by reducing the capital value of the fund, as 'charged to capital' seems to be implying. The transaction, if funded out of capital (and not, as is more often the case, out of reserves), is simply a conversion of endowed assets from cash to land in the balance sheet. If that would leave the endowed fund with a *negative* cash balance, it will entail a compensating transaction to convert some other capital asset of that fund into cash to clear/avoid the inter-fund 'overdraft'.

The professional costs of managing/administering investment assets need to receive the same accounting treatment where those costs are incidental to a specific asset's acquisition, improvement or enlargement. On the other hand, they must – as has long been general practice – be deducted from the sales proceeds in computing the gain/loss to be shown in the SoFA if they are incidental to this or that asset's disposal. But this is not so easy where composite annual fees are charged by the investment manager. As an alternative to their presentation as charges in the endowments column of the SoFA under the heading of 'costs of generating funds', the older accounting treatment of grouping together the capital component of investment management fees and the year's gains/losses was not invalidated by SORP 2000 nor by SORP 2005. It therefore still applies to professional fees:

(i)   for reviewing/advising on the asset-mix of an endowment's investment portfolio/estate with a view to capital gain, thus enhancing its value; but *not*

(ii)   for managing its income yield, nor for providing annual accounting valuations, since these are revenue-related costs and must therefore be accounted for as expenditure out of the income of that fund, or else out of general income.

But when it comes to the costs of *accounting valuations* (and presumably also other expenses of annual reporting by a permanently endowed charity) the SORP may have inadvertently moved the goal posts. Thus the very next paragraph of Appendix 3 incorporates the Charity Commission's 2002 *SORP Information Sheet* clarification of SORP 2000 on the point by saying:

> 'However, where charities have land held as endowment investments, then rent collection, property repairs and maintenance charges would normally be charged against the relevant income fund as would the cost of rent reviews. Valuation fees and other expenses incurred in connection with the sale of such land would normally be charged to capital, ie, against the gain (or added to the loss) realised on the disposal. Valuation fees incurred for accounting purposes would normally, in the case of endowment investments, be charged to capital and recorded in the governance category of resources expended.'
>
> – *SORP 2005, Appendix 3.3(d) and (e)*

The questions this must raise for the *founders* of *permanent* endowments, and thus also for those who later have to interpret their intentions (ie the High Court and Charity Commission, and last but not least the charity trustees themselves) must be:

– Where does that leave the boundary line between 'capital' and 'income' for the different kinds of recurring expense incurred by charity trustees within the above 'governance category' of the SoFA in complying with the founder's wish to provide perpetual public benefit? Isn't the line the same for investment use as for the charity's own (functional) use? How, then, should we treat fire insurance premiums/claims on a permanently endowed property for the charity's own use? Or the costs of maintaining security guards/equipment to keep such a property safe? And if an accounting valuation happens to be downwards, is the argument for charging revaluation costs to capital still the same in both cases – ie for functional and investment assets?

– As *Information Sheet 1* specifically disclaimed any binding status for itself, while the SORP's Appendices (other than the Glossary's definitions of terminology, of course) are clearly not meant to be taken as part of the text of the SORP itself – is this clarification to be taken as an invitation for trustees to seek a Charity Commission Order here, too, to enable them to override the standard rules of trust law by paying all sorts of administrative costs out of permanent endowment, not out of income as hitherto?

– If the case *Carver v Duncan (Inspector of Taxes)*; *Bosanquet v Allen (Inspector of Taxes)* [1985] 1 AC 1082 (the basis for the SORP's Appendix 3.3 as above) is a valid precedent for a permanent (charitable) endowment, where the 'tenant-right' to day-to-day use of the capital assets or to spend any revenues derived from them is interminable (thus making it hard to equate the perpetually unspendable charitable trust capital with the non-charitable interest in remainder that must one day become absolute), does this mean that charity founders must now explicitly prohibit recourse to capital if they wish to protect gifts of permanent capital from being gradually 'expensed' through the SoFA in defraying what seem to be costs of providing current charitable benefits? Clearly, they are not incidental costs of providing or disposing of capital assets, which we all agree are a charge on capital.

Apart from that, charging an entire composite annual fee for investment management services to *capital* would (except on the 'total return' basis of investing – see below) normally be contrary to the terms of trust of the endowment (if a permanent one) if the result is that the *revenue-related* component of the fee is not charged to the relevant *income* fund. That the SORP does not mean this to happen seems clear from paragraph 178(c), which says that 'Costs of Generating Funds' includes *'managing investments for both income generation and capital maintenance'*.

This is also supported by the SORP's Appendix 3, where paragraph 3.3(a) explains the meaning of 'permanent endowment', saying:

> 'An endowment fund where there is no power to convert the capital into income is known as a permanent endowment fund, which must generally be held indefinitely. This concept of "permanence" does not however necessarily mean that the assets held in the endowment fund cannot be exchanged ... nor does it mean that they are incapable of depreciation or loss. What it does mean is that the permanent endowment fund cannot be used as if it were income (ie to make payments or grants to others), however certain payments must be made out of the endowment, such as the payment of investment management fees *where these relate to investments held within the endowment* ...'.

– *SORP 2005, Appendix 3.3(a)*

The use of italics is ours, and is just for emphasis here. We can see this sentence as a warning that only fees relating to the investments themselves – *not to their revenues* – are payable out of the endowment fund to which these investments belong. It reminds us that revenue costs cannot be charged to capital in the absence of *special authority* under trust law. In contrast to such fleeting allusion to the need for due compliance with charity law in this respect, we find clarity in the Charity Commission's published Operational Guidance (OG83: 'Endowed Charities: A Total Return Approach to Investment'), which can be freely downloaded from the Commission's website.

Overriding the normal capital/income trust distinctions

That guidance makes it clear that the liberalisation brought by the TA 2000 does *not* confer any statutory power to override the existing 'standard' rules of trust law distinguishing between the respective entitlements of income and capital beneficiaries of a 'trust for investment' – in other words, a permanent *financial* endowment. Furthermore, the exercise of the discretionary powers bestowed by the TA 2000 is subject to a statutory 'duty of care' – except to the extent (if any) that this may have been excluded by the governing document of the trust.

Thus only where authorised by the trust's Founder (ie in the governing document) or by the courts (thus also by an order of the Charity Commission) can the trustees lawfully adopt *special* rules to replace the standard ones – for example, to pay revenue costs out of capital or vice versa. And the legal power to pay investment management fees out of the UTR on a permanent financial endowment on the 'total return' basis follows automatically from the authorisation to invest on that basis – see **6.4.3**. The fees then become chargeable in the *capital* column of the SoFA, within the 'Costs of Generating Funds' section, the UTR itself being capital in nature since its legal status is that of a 'supplement' to the (frozen) endowment. This nicely fits in with the trustees' statutory duty to be even-handed as between present and future beneficiaries in exercising their duly authorised discretionary power to make allocations to income out of the UTR from time to time.

'Playing fair' in handling endowment capital

It is worth reminding ourselves that an actual accounting problem can arise here *only* in the case of a *permanent* endowment (and occasionally where it is an expendable one), because that is where the standard rules of trust law oblige charity trustees to pay revenue-related costs only out of income and capital costs only out of (available) capital resources – rules that cannot be ignored without putting the trustees at risk of personal liability for breach of trust.

Clearly, this constraint must apply equally to the costs of raising voluntary funds for *activities* or for *endowment*, as also to the costs of maintaining or enhancing investment assets (including estate management costs) – except that in the latter case trustees are free to *choose* to invest general reserves in, say, improving permanently endowed land without unwittingly converting those reserves into capital as long as they make their intentions clear by maintaining through their accounting records and annual accounts the existing capital/income distinctions in the fund-ownership of the assets concerned.

Special authority

What is also clear in OG83 is that the trustees of a permanent endowment are tightly constrained by the standard rules of trust law both for their administration (spending) and for their annual accounting and reporting – except to the extent that these standard rules have been replaced by *special rules* on the authority of the founder (as provided for within the endowment fund's governing document) or of the courts (the Charity Commission). Clearly, trustees will need to have obtained such authority before they can safely pay out of capital any *revenue-related* professional fees charged by their investment manager – or vice versa. The accounting rules must logically follow suit, as exemplified above for the 'total return' basis of investing.

Where these fees are a composite to cover all aspects of managing the investments of a charity's trust funds, including the purchase and sale of securities, perhaps also the provision of nominee services, portfolio valuation/performance reports and the collection/distribution of income returns, trust law will normally require a proper split between income and capital in order to protect the respective rights of present and future beneficiaries – certainly of *permanent* endowment funds – unless the capital is invested on the (duly authorised) 'total return' basis, as already explained.

Incidental costs of acquiring/improving capital assets?

Unfortunately, it seems many are now pointing to the Charities SORP as authorising *all* investment management fees to be charged to capital (presumably only in the case of an endowed fund) whether or not invested on the 'total return' basis. They then conclude that they must show these fees under 'Costs of Generating Funds' in the *endowments* column of the SoFA, in order not to treat them as the 'incidental costs' of acquisition/retention of the investment assets themselves (with the consequent need to apportion them to individual assets when calculating realised gains and losses!).

Not only would it be illogical to treat the whole of these annually recurring fees as 'incidental costs' (especially where investments are, for good reason, retained unchanged), but it would also stop them being shown in the SoFA under 'Costs of Generating Funds'. Instead, they would become part of the investment gains and losses figure below the FRS3 line of net income/expenditure.

That such a simplistic interpretation cannot be right must be self-evident from the fact that the SORP itself has no power to override trust law. On the contrary, the SORP can and must harmonise charity accounting with charity law governing the proper administration of charity resources, even where this requires a modified application of this or that accounting standard.

Finally, it is also worth noting the reference to 'trust funds' (ie in the plural) where s 32 of the Trustee Act 2000 empowers trustees to remunerate an investment manager 'out of the trust funds'. In particular, the wording used at s 32(2)(b) gives the trustees recourse to the capital fund as well as the income fund of an endowed trust, but only for such fees as are 'reasonable' for the services provided, which accords with the standard rules of trust law:

'Remuneration and expenses of agents [etc]

(1)   This section applies if, under a power conferred by Part IV or any other enactment or any provision of subordinate legislation, or by the trust instrument, a person other than a trustee has been—

(a)   authorised to exercise functions as an agent of the trustees, or
(b)   appointed to act as a nominee or custodian.

(2)   The trustees may remunerate the agent, nominee or custodian out of the trust funds for services if—

(a)   he is engaged on terms entitling him to be remunerated for those services, and
(b)   the amount does not exceed such remuneration as is reasonable in the circumstances for the provision of those services by him to or on behalf of that trust.

(3)   The trustees may reimburse the agent, nominee or custodian out of the trust funds for any expenses properly incurred by him in exercising functions as an agent, nominee or custodian.'

– *Trustee Act 2000, s 32*

A few simple rules

In conclusion of this sub-section, it may be helpful to draw out a few simple rules.

The SoFA costs of managing/administering investment assets should:

(a)   have a line of their own (unless immaterial) under 'Costs of Generating Funds';

(b)   exclude any identifiable 'incidental costs' of asset-improvement/acquisition (this would include *portfolio review* costs (including valuations for that purpose – as distinct from the purpose of public accountability, which is an annual cost of governance) apportionable pro rata to asset-values as an incremental cost of the entire portfolio regardless of any individual asset disposals resulting from the review – noting that this accords with the traditional accounting treatment of adding those costs to the asset's carrying value in the balance sheet (before revaluing it at the year-end, meaning that they will decrease the revaluation gain, or increase the loss, in the *lower* section of the SoFA, below the 'net income' line);

(c)   always be charged in the relevant income column if the asset itself is *un*endowed;

(d)   be charged in the endowment column only if the asset itself is endowed and the charge[6] cannot be treated as an incidental cost of improving its market value *and*:
    –   *either* it is not for the work of income-management/-generation (e g estate lettings, property maintenance, income collection) under the normal or 'standard' rules of trust law – that would put it in the relevant income column;
    –   *or* the 'total return' investment basis applies, under which even the revenue-related costs are to be taken out of the 'unapplied total return', and so they must all be shown in the endowment column.

---

[6]   As an example, agents' services for safekeeping, safeguarding, etc, of such assets.

Relating operating activities' costs to their revenues

6.6.5 We have already noted the requirement for the SoFA presentation of operating costs and their related revenues to make the relationship clear by means of similar terminology, supported by additional information in the accounts notes (eg to show the net results of different major activities). As a way of highlighting in relation to incoming resources any *further* implications of the 'costs of generating funds', the SORP provides for an optional sub-total line immediately after this sub-section:

> 'Some charities may also find it informative to their readers to insert additional subtotals. For example, after [Costs of Generating Funds] an additional subtotal [line] "net incoming resources available for charitable application" may be added.'
>
> – *SORP 2005, paragraph 88*

This does, of course, interrupt the flow of information down the page, in that the optional line then separates the two sub-sections that go to make up the figure for total expenditure as required by the SORP. To avoid confusion, it may then be advisable for the optional sub-total line to be distinguished from other information on the page (eg shaded, boxed or in square brackets).

'CHARITABLE ACTIVITIES' COSTS

6.7 This sub-section of the SoFA was reshaped by SORP 2000 to include the costs of managing and administering the charity as well as all expenditure *primarily* incurred for the purpose of furthering the objects of the charity, both direct costs and 'support costs'. It was further reshaped by SORP 2005 not only to group together under *objectives-related* sub-headings *all* the costs (grant-making and/or service-provision) incurred to provide public benefit as such, but also to *exclude* those charity management and administration costs (which are to be reported in a sub-section of their own as 'governance' costs).

It thus includes all 'ancillary' trading costs incurred *primarily* to support or to facilitate charitable grant-making or service-provision (rather than primarily to *finance* such activities). This corresponds to the SORP's classification of the related income under *income from charitable activities* (as distinct from *activities to generate funds*):

> 'ancillary trades connected to a primary purpose ...'.
>
> – *SORP 2005, paragraph 145(f)*

As SORP 2000 went on to clarify, to be 'connected' to a primary purpose the 'principal aim' must be the provision of public benefit – a clarification regrettably omitted in SORP 2005. Depreciation, impairment and losses on disposal of fixed assets *used* for charitable activities are also included in this category, of course.

However, the SORP's main contribution to the development of charity accountability here does seem to be this requirement for *all* 'charitable activity' expenditure to be presented in the SoFA by reference to what the trustees are trying to achieve (above all, the public benefit objective(s) they are pursuing in undertaking these activities) rather than *how* they are going about it:

'Resources expended on charitable activities should be analysed on the face of the Statement of Financial Activities or in a prominent note to the accounts. This analysis should provide an understanding of the nature of the activities undertaken and the resources expended on their provision. This analysis may, for example, set out the activity cost of the main services provided by the charity, or set out the resources expended on material programmes or projects undertaken by the charity.'

– *SORP 2005, paragraph 191*

But before we can consider the SoFA presentation of 'charitable activities' expenditure in more depth we need to take a look at a more fundamental question: the recognition of liabilities and provisions under SORP 2005.

When does *charitable activity* expenditure become accruable?

6.7.1   For certain kinds of expenditure it has always been more difficult for charities than for commercial organisations to decide when to recognise the expenditure as 'incurred'. For the latter, all trading and other activities undertaken are primarily 'for profit', so that there is generally a clear value-for-value exchange: some valuable 'consideration' is given in return for goods/services or the commitment to provide them. Although a contract-performance liability can arise at the date of a contract, for accounting purposes what is fundamental is the concept of 'matching' related income and expenditure within the same accounting period by means of 'accruals', in which it is necessary to look at the date when 'consideration' passes or 'legal entitlement' arises. However, apart from the special case of charitable *trading* (e g the independent schools sector), *charitable* expenditure does not usually involve the receipt of any kind of material consideration (i e it is an altruistic giving of 'something for nothing').

For this reason, the question of when to account for charitable grant commitments as 'expenditure' remained debatable even under SORP 2000, until SORP 2005 clarified the complementary question of 'deferred income' (see **6.2.1**) in respect of grants receivable for activities. *Performance-related* grants (which the SORP defines as those where the grant-control agreement denies legal entitlement to grant monies *as income* until the reporting charity has met certain specified performance criteria) can only be recognised as income in line with the incurring of the related *qualifying* expenditure, so that any grant monies received in advance of this pre-condition being met must be carried forward within the creditors figure in the year-end balance sheet as 'deferred income' – just like a commercial contract.

Where instead the reporting charity is the grantor, the same principle makes the grant commitment fully accruable as expenditure as soon as the beneficiary has met or is likely to meet all imposed pre-conditions for entitlement (i e ownership) of the grant monies as income, which then leaves no reasonable basis for the reporting charity to be able to withdraw from the commitment without detriment to its reputation.

For this reason, charities making substantial grants for longer-term projects (2 years or more), and which since SORP 2000 have been making *payment* of future years' grant instalments conditional upon the beneficiary meeting specified performance criteria, may now need to go one step further by denying the recipient any *legal entitlement to grant monies as income* until those pre-conditions are met – thus turning each *payment* into a mere advance or loan, not a grant instalment at all.

SORP 2005 also clarified the accounting rules here by emphasising that any such criteria must be real (which means they must leave enough uncertainty to prevent accrual at the year-end – a more fundamental issue than the 'control' emphasised by SORP 2000) and not just a 'paper exercise' or perhaps a rarely-invoked clause included in the grant-control agreement 'just in case'.

SORP 2000, for strict compliance with FRS12, had said that where either a legal or a 'constructive' obligation (liability) arises – even if only in the longer term – it must be recognised immediately in full within the SoFA.

A merely *internal* decision committing the charity to make a grant or to provide some charitable service, however, will not of itself create a liability in the absence of a legal obligation unless there is a valid expectation in the mind of the other (or a third) party, and so under FRS12 nothing can be accrued for it and charged as expenditure in the SoFA – even if the trustees feel under a moral obligation to honour their commitment.

In the words of SORP 2005:

> 'Evidence that such a "valid expectation" has been created might be provided by the charity's current and past practice in discharging such obligations and the specific communication of a commitment to the recipient ... before the balance sheet date ...'.

– SORP 2005, paragraph 155

Where there is no 'liability', the trustees may wish to earmark funds by designating them to carry out such a decision or to honour such a moral obligation, and this can be done by means of a transfer from the undesignated funds of a charity. Care is needed here, however, to ensure that this earmarking is recorded as having taken place before the year-end – even if only as a Board decision made 'in principle' and subject to executive review of the exact amount to be shown in the accounts for that year. Otherwise by analogy with the ASB rule that proposed dividends to shareholders cannot be shown in the accounts unless the dividend was proposed before the year-end it could be argued that the earmarking is a post balance sheet non-adjusting event, not an accounting transaction of the year, meaning that the designated fund cannot be shown as such in the accounts.

The way the SORP's Glossary defines a 'liability' has not really changed since 1995 – other than to stop describing it as 'a claim against an accounting entity'. Instead, it is now described as 'an obligation of an entity to transfer economic benefits' which:

'(a) is expected to be settled by the entity parting with assets or in some way losing an economic benefit; and
(b) results from past transactions or events; and
(c) embodies a present duty or responsibility to one or more other entities that entails settlement at a specified or determinable future date, on the occurrence of a specified event, or on demand; and
(d) results from a duty or responsibility which obligates the entity either legally, or practically (a constructive obligation), because it would be financially or otherwise operationally damaging to the entity not to discharge the duty or responsibility.'

– SORP 2005, Glossary GL 40

Where the charity has entered into a *charitable* (ie not contractual) commitment for some years into the future, the practical questions arising for accounting purposes are:

–   Is the commitment for *future years* now unavoidable (i e now accruable)?

and for fund-accounting purposes *only* (e g in case of any resultant deficit):

–   What funds (present or future) can be relied on as 'available' to meet a liability for future years' instalments?

The tightening of the rules here by SORP 2000 to comply with FRS12 had abolished the 1995 SORP's special treatment of future commitments that are intended only to be met from *future* income – a change that alarmed many charities when it appeared in the Exposure Draft of SORP 2000, which had proposed at paragraph 125 to say: '... *where it is reasonably certain that payment will be made, a liability should be accrued'*. That was intended to replace what paragraph 145 of the 1995 SORP had said: '*In some cases charitable commitments are made only to be funded from future income, and in these cases it is not appropriate to account for the liability which will be met from such future income.'*

At the time, this had reflected the common practice of making the commitment for the future years conditional on *future* funds being available, to avoid depleting existing (or even non-existent) reserves by having to accrue a liability – this 'term' or 'condition' of grant was intended to put recipients on notice that the award was not to be regarded as creating an immediate liability on the part of the charity.

But FRS12 does not allow for niceties like disregarding what for grant-makers is nearly always a fairly reliable future income stream, so unless the charity can point to uncertainties on other grounds it will not be able to avoid accruing *that* kind of forward commitment as an immediate liability. Actually, with a little forethought it is usually not at all difficult to make these multi-year grant-awards subject to performance conditions and annual reviews to the point where future payments can no longer be taken for granted – as already discussed.

In the event, the wording used in SORP 2000 was carefully amended to allow for the *uncertainty* needed to prevent future years' grant commitments becoming immediate liabilities under FRS12. In SORP 2005, however, rather than uncertainty (an *objective* condition perhaps so self-evident it needs no mention?) the emphasis is on 'controllability':

> 'A charity may enter into commitments which are dependent upon explicit conditions being met by itself or the recipient before payment is made or upon future reviews. A liability, and hence expenditure, should be recognised once such conditions fall outside the control of the giving charity. If the conditions set remain within the control of [the] giving charity, then the charity retains the discretion to avoid the expenditure and therefore a liability should not be recognised.'
>
> – *SORP 2005, paragraph 158*

A case in point is the situation of many ex-services charities serving the needs of an ageing class of beneficiaries dating from World War II – now over half-a-century ago.

Where a beneficiary seems to be dependent on the charity's continuing help (e g in a residential home, or a life-annuity to help pay for domiciliary care), accounting under FRS12 could require some kind of *actuarial* calculation of the present value of the costs likely to be borne by the reporting charity in honouring an implied 'operational commitment' to continue providing future benefits at the current level (or as otherwise expected by such beneficiaries and persons closely connected with them). This would then impact on the level of reserves, raising implications for fundraising and the future viability of the charity.

However, even such a charity's *non*-accruable commitments to the rest of its diminishing beneficiary-class could justify setting aside reserves designated to help meet their remaining lifelong needs (thus neatly spotlighting the *charity's* future funding needs), since the relevant historical trends can be fairly reliably projected into the future on an actuarial basis.

Commitments to provide *staff* retirement benefits on a *charitable* (as distinct from a contractual) basis make an interesting example of a different kind. Where the benefit-provision remains purely discretionary, with the charity bearing the full cost, and not related to any 'operational liability' arising out of the contractual terms of their employment, the most that can be said in favour of FRS12-compliant accrual of the full commitment (actuarially assessed, of course) is that the nearer the staff come to retirement age the greater will be any 'valid expectation' of its fulfilment. Until then, annual staff-performance reviews alone would seem to mitigate against any certainty of future employment. (Considerations of the reasonableness or otherwise of any assumption of continuing employment in future years may also have a bearing on how *future* editions of the Charities SORP should interpret the requirements of FRS17 – see **6.8.**) In such cases, the appropriate treatment would seem to be to *designate* the funds needed for the purpose, or else to disclose in the accounts notes the extent of this voluntary commitment.

This is not altogether dissimilar to the problem faced by the Religious Order charities, many of them with an ageing membership of full-time volunteer workers who – bound by vows of poverty involving the renunciation of all their worldly goods and a lifelong personal commitment to voluntary service – are in no position to provide for their own retirement needs and must therefore be provided for as beneficiaries of the charity.

That is to be contrasted with the *liability* arising where staff employment contracts include some kind of contractual contributory/non-contributory pension scheme. The recognition of liabilities and the disclosures required in the notes to the accounts are then regulated by accounting standards. FRS17 on accounting for any material under-funding/over-funding of 'defined benefit' staff pension schemes (and any related 'constructive liabilities' for extra benefits outside the scheme rules – see paragraphs 4 and 5 of the FRS) is fully covered in SORP 2005 – see **6.8**. In addition, readers may wish to note the references to this subject in chapter 5, where we summarise the impact of accounting standards on charities under SORP 2005, and also in chapter 12 on the disclosure of staff costs, and also especially the website guidance issued by the Charity Commission in respect of the implications of FRS17 deficits for the reporting of charity reserves – see chapter 10.

Provision of grants to individuals/institutions

6.7.2   Where a charity's grant-making covers different purposes (objectives), it is clearly helpful and informative for the costs of pursuing these objectives to be analysed in the accounts notes in support of what is summarised on the face of the SoFA as specified by SORP 2005. Under **6.5**, the total costs of making British Heart Foundation's research grants, for example, are shown in the SoFA within their respective categories of charitable objective – thus including their support costs. Such a SoFA presentation then needs to be supplemented, as we have shown there, by detailed analysis of the actual grants and (separately) their support costs as a *requirement*, since the Charities SORP calls for certain extra information if any of the figures are 'material' in their proper context (ie for each grant-aided institution, also for all grant-making and for all charitable activities), specifying the kind of information and why it should be provided:

> 'Grantmaking charities may undertake their entire programme of work through grantmaking activities, whilst other charities may undertake their activities through a combination of direct service provision and grant funding of third parties. In either case, further analysis of grantmaking, where material, should be provided.'

– SORP 2005, paragraph 197

> 'Where activities are carried out through ... grant funding of third parties, the notes to the accounts should identify the amount of grantmaking expenditure, using the note to explain the activity funded.'

– SORP 2005, paragraph 193

> 'The further information provided in relation to grantmaking should provide the reader with a reasonable understanding of the nature of the activities or projects that are being funded and whether the financial support is provided directly to individuals or to assist an institution undertake its activities or projects. In the case of institutional grants, information as to the recipient(s) of the funding should be provided so that the reader can appreciate the type and range of institutions supported.'

– SORP 2005, paragraph 198

> 'The trustees may give further analysis and explanation of the purposes for which grants were made as part of the Trustees' Annual Report or by means of a separate publication. Such further analysis does not excuse the trustees from providing sufficient detail in the notes to the accounts as is needed to provide a true and fair view.'

– SORP 2005, paragraph 205

The SORP thus continues to require the direct cost of grant-making activities, if material, to be sub-analysed in the accounts notes (see chapter 12) between individuals and institutions, saying in each case for what purpose(s). For 'material' grants to institutions, it specifically requires the name and the total amount for the year to be disclosed for as many as you consider necessary for the reader's understanding, but now with no ceiling on numbers (only the top 50 were disclosable under SORP 2000) and no absolute threshold of significance (it was £1,000 under SORP 2000) – and subject to special provisions (paragraphs 208 and 209) for non-disclosure on grounds of possible 'serious prejudice' to either party's furtherance of its own purposes.

As a special case, it should be mentioned here that the Charities Act 2006 has amended Part VI of the 1993 Act with effect from 1 April 2008 to provide total exemption from these disclosures by any charitable trust during the lifetime of its settlor or the latter's spouse or civil law partner. The June 2008 reprint of SORP 2005, as an exception to the general legal rule prohibiting any substantive changes to the edition (March 2005) cited in its related Regulations (now 2008), makes special reference at paragraph 200(e) to this new statutory exemption – no doubt for completeness in summarising all the disclosure-reliefs currently available here.

As for the *kinds* of charitable purpose being funded in this way, paragraph 204 says:

'The analysis of grants should provide the reader with an understanding of the nature of the activities or projects being funded by the grantmaker. This analysis of grants should relate to the charity's objectives, for example, categories covering social welfare, medical research, the performing arts, the welfare of people in financial need or help to people seeking to further their education, depending on the nature of the charity. Some charities may decide that it is appropriate to provide further levels of analysis, for example, showing a geographical analysis of the value of grants made.'

– SORP 2005, paragraph 204

This is supported by the SORP's further requirement for grant-making *policy* to be disclosed in the annual report if the grant-making is *material* (the 'rule of thumb' here has usually been taken as 5% plus) in relation to all the charity's public benefit activities (not to total expenditure, as under SORP 2000). But regs 40(3)(m) and 41(3)(m), respectively, of the SORP's related 2008 Regulations make that disclosure in the annual report (for charities/groups liable to statutory audit) mandatory only in respect of the '*selection* policy' adopted by the reporting charity – if any.

The *support costs* of grant-making are still considered to be of public interest, so if material they must be disclosed in the accounts notes, and in this context SORP 2005 explains that this includes preliminary as well as subsequent costs.

'Support costs related to grantmaking will include:

(a)   costs incurred before grants are made (pre-grant costs) as part of the decision making process;
(b)   post-grant costs e g monitoring of grants; and
(c)   costs of any central or regional office functions such as general management, payroll administration, budgeting and accounting, information technology, human resources, and financing.'

– SORP 2005, paragraph 196

Provision of goods/services to/for beneficiaries

6.7.3   There is less difference under SORP 2005 in the regulator's attitude towards charities' provision of public benefit in cash or in kind, which is just as well in view of the difficulty you may have at times in trying to distinguish between the two – bearing in mind that 'cash' refers to actual money, as distinct from the many kinds of goods and services that can readily be turned into cash in today's world, bartered or otherwise dealt with as commodities, such is the sophistication of the marketplace.

A charity in the field of community care, for example, with a focus on the needs of long-term, full-time volunteer carers rather than the cared-for, can deliver the same benefit by making relief-holiday grants direct to the carer, or en bloc to a package holiday provider (charitable or commercial) under a grant-control agreement covering, say, a specified catchment area or category of need, so that carers can tailor each package to suit themselves. Or, instead, a block of popular holiday packages can be bought in for free distribution to eligible carers. In the first case the SORP requires disclosure of only the total amount paid out in grants to individuals for each of the charity's main objectives, projects, etc. In the second it requires the institutional grants total, sub-analysed to show the main types (again by objective/project) of grant being made and naming the recipients of a sufficient number of the material grants to give the reader a reasonable understanding. In the third case it only requires analysis of the costs of providing all charitable benefits for each of the main objectives/projects comprising these activities.

In fact, nothing like the SORP's extensive institutional grant-disclosure requirements is to be found when it comes to reporting charitable service-provision or goods-supply – or grants to individuals for that matter. And yet the trustees' charity law duty to ensure the proper application of *all* resources is the same regardless of the form in which those resources are held/applied.

But where SORP 2000 seemed brief to the point of indulgence in this central area of charity accountability, requiring only that the SoFA presentation of the costs of charitable service-provision be 'function-based' and 'appropriate', SORP 2005 with its blanket requirement for an *objectives-based* SoFA analysis of *all* expenditure – whether on charitable activities, fundraising or governance – has, as we saw in the first part of this section, effectively levelled the playing field for every charity that is subject to statutory audit.

This must, of course, be seen in context, as the SORP does also have certain annual report disclosure requirements that clearly have a bearing on the subject and must therefore influence the interpretation here for the sake of the charity's credibility with its stakeholders:

> 'The report should help the reader understand the aims and objectives set by the charity, and the strategies and activities undertaken to achieve them ... In particular the report should provide:
>
> ...
>
> (e)   details of significant activities (including its main programmes, projects, or services provided) that contribute to the achievement of the stated objectives.
>
> ...
>
> The details of significant activities provided should focus on those activities that the charity trustees consider to be significant in the circumstances of the charity as a whole. The details of activities should, as a minimum, explain the objectives, activities, projects or services identified within the analysis note accompanying charitable activities in the Statement of Financial Activities ...'.
>
> – *SORP 2005, paragraphs 47 and 48*

In view of this stricter requirement for meaningful reporting of all consumption of charitable resources, it may be useful to offer a few common examples of informative and useful 'objectives-based' expenditure descriptions under this heading, pointing to the need to ensure that these are clearly related to the charity's declared Objects (or those of the particular trust fund) so that presentation will be specific to the type of public benefit the charity provides:

'teaching', 'welfare', 'seminars/conferences/shows', 'lectures', 'exhibitions', 'educational publicity', 'awareness campaigns', 'day centres', 'advice services', 'counselling', 'rehabilitation', 'residential care', 'respite care', 'inspection services', 'disaster relief', 'concert/drama performances', 'heritage preservation', etc.

'GOVERNANCE' COSTS

6.8   Contrary to the restricted interpretation traditionally favoured by some charities competing in public appeals, SORP 2005 makes it clear that this heading covers rather more than just the obvious costs of trustees' and (if applicable) membership meetings, of preparing and publishing the statutory report and accounts and of the annual audit. Under the same heading must also come any 'back office' costs (if these really are 'material' and therefore in need of separate consideration) whose relationship with the charitable activities' *direct* costs is too distant/general to allow their inclusion in 'support costs', but which also have no causal connection with the other main expenditure sections, where the primary purpose is 'to generate funds'. This means also items such as legal and other costs in connection with the charity's constitutional structure, as well as the costs of strategic planning for long-term financial viability (as distinct from project-planning, day-to-day operational management, etc.), internal audit, risk assessment and everything else to do with charity law compliance generally.

Thus where the SORP was previously content merely to indicate that 'central management and administration costs', including their share of any 'indirect costs', were to be included under this heading, SORP 2005 is quite explicit:

> 'Expenditure on the governance of the charity will normally include both direct and related support costs. Direct costs will include such items as internal and external audit, legal advice for trustees and costs associated with constitutional and statutory requirements e g the cost of trustee meetings and preparing statutory accounts. Where material, there should also be an apportionment of shared and indirect costs involved in supporting the governance activities (as distinct from supporting its charitable or income generation activities).'
>
> *– SORP 2005, paragraph 211*

Our own view is that even the separation of these institutional/constitutional costs of ensuring the proper and effective running of the charity as such (ie its 'governance') from the costs of planning, controlling, supporting and facilitating its charitable and other activities will ultimately come to be seen as 'hair-splitting', in view of the more pressing need for simplicity and clarity in financial reporting as it becomes more and more comprehensive and standardised, and as the special disclosure of any significant matters becomes the norm for a proper understanding of the charity and what it is trying to achieve by way of public benefit.

STAFF PENSION SCHEME COSTS UNDER FRS17

6.9   The accounts must include recognition (within the appropriate section of the SoFA) of FRS17's specified components of the year-on-year movements in what is required to be carried in the balance sheet as a kind of asset or liability representing the net present value of the charity's (or group's) *notional* interest or liability in the actuarially assessed over-/under-funding of any 'defined benefit' ('final salary') staff pension scheme or equivalent <u>and</u> of any other operationally binding retirement-benefit arrangements it has made (even if these are only voluntary and unilateral) for its staff.

That then decreases or increases the apparent value of the charity's remaining funds by the difference between the calculated values of the FRS17 deficit/surplus from last year-end to this year-end – apart from employer contributions made for the year, of course, since they will already have been recognised in the SoFA.

For some major charities, it may even be worthwhile devoting a special column to FRS17 in the SoFA, thus avoiding the distortion that can result from combining a substantial FRS17 *notional* deficit (or surplus, for that matter) with their general (ie unrestricted) funds *real* balance in the SoFA. See Appendix 8 for the worked example illustrating this solution: 'The National Disability Charity'. It was also used to good effect by SCOPE in its accounts for the years to March 2005 and March 2006. The impact this could seem to have on some charities' reserves, and on the disclosure of reserves policy, is discussed in chapter 10. Here (and in chapter 12) there are more immediate questions – such as the validity of the FRS17 view that there will be no great volatility in the figure of the expected total return on the underlying investments, since this is calculated by taking (as at each year-end) the *long-term* total return expected on the market value of those investments.

> 'The expected return on assets is based on long-term expectations at the beginning of the period and is expected to be reasonably stable.'
>
> – *FRS17, paragraph 54*

Be that as it may, and subject to any residual problem of how to deal with post-service liabilities, it now looks as if the entire Standard could one day become redundant – judging by the continuing trend in the wake of the 2000/01 stock market decline and, following the usual cyclical upswing, the even deeper decline compounded by the near-collapse of the world's banking system and the resultant 'credit-crunch' of 2008/09, with more and more employers closing down or limiting their now embarrassingly volatile and expensive 'defined benefit' schemes, and opting instead for the cheaper and less troublesome 'defined contribution' and 'stakeholder' schemes.

A further consideration may one day be the advisability of charities with a significant dependency on voluntary funding being allowed to restrict their annual assessment of any under-funding 'liability' by reference to an *adjusted* actuarial calculation of scheme liabilities as if *closed by termination of all employments one year hence* – thus avoiding the apparent depletion of what are in many cases meagre reserves through the 'notional' accrual of liabilities that can only arise from the charity's continuation as a 'going concern' beyond the minimum period required under FRS18. Where the charity does not have sufficient free reserves out of which to provide for such further continuation, nor a sufficiently secure future income stream in the economic sense (ie disregarding any voluntary contributions), such longer-term continuation clearly cannot just be taken for granted, so common sense would seem to suggest that the liability calculation be restricted accordingly. Such a view may be seen as the converse of that taken by the ASB in rejecting any reduction of liability due to *prospective* redundancies – ie those not yet 'made':

> 'Expected future redundancies are not reflected in the actuarial assumptions because the employer is not committed (either legally or constructively) to making such redundancies in advance. When the employer does become committed to making the redundancies, any impact on the defined benefit scheme is treated as a settlement and/or curtailment …'
>
> It is not appropriate to assume a reduction in benefits below those currently promised on the grounds that the employer will curtail the scheme at some time in the future.'
>
> – *FRS17, paragraphs 29 and 31*

Each year's net movement in the balance sheet value of the Defined Benefit Scheme asset/liability (other than that arising from employer contributions to the Scheme) must be recognised in the appropriate section of the SoFA, with this annual movement itself comprising up to six separate items. As to exactly which section in each case, the SORP seems to take quite a relaxed stance:

> 'Pension costs may be allocated between the resources expended categories of the Statement of Financial Activities on the basis of the charity's own computations. The basis of the allocation should be reasonable and consistent. Allocations of pension costs based on the staff costs of employees within the scheme is one approach, although other approaches (e g allocation based on pension contributions payable) may also produce an equitable allocation.'
>
> – *SORP 2005, paragraph 437*

Keeping to the numbering used in paragraph 50 of FRS17 (in case you want to refer back to the source (rather than only to the 'overview' guidance given in SORP 2005) in what is admittedly still a very new area of charity accounting), items (a)–(c) and (e)–(f), as explained below, belong in one or other of the Income/Expenditure sections of the SoFA, while item (d) belongs in the Gains/Losses section.

Staff costs

These include:

(a)   the *current service* cost ('periodic costs'); and also, as 'non-periodic' costs,

(e)   any *past service* costs; and

(f)   any gains/losses on 'settlements and curtailments' (e g on redundancies, closure of the Scheme, etc).

The Standard is quite specific about how to calculate 'service cost':

> 'The current service cost should be based on the most recent actuarial valuation at the beginning of the period, with the financial assumptions updated to reflect conditions at that date … Any contributions from employees should be set off against the current service cost.
>
> The current service cost will be based on the discount rate at the beginning of the period and will therefore reflect current long-term market interest rates at that time.'
>
> – *FRS17, paragraphs 51 and 52*

The attribution, allocation or apportionment (as appropriate, depending on the accounting policy adopted) of these three components to each expenditure category obviously need to follow the methodology used for reporting the respective staff salary and pension contribution costs in the SoFA.

'Financing' activities

It seems only logical for the SORP's expenditure heading of 'Costs of Generating Funds' to include the net (if a cost) of the following two components identified by FRS17 as other 'periodic costs', which it regards as 'finance costs', being the excess (if any) of:

(b)   the *interest cost*; over

(c)   the expected return on assets.

On the other hand, if (c) exceeds (b) the FRS requires the net figure to be reported as *income* and shown *'adjacent to interest'*. This would seem to preclude treating it as part of the revenues of 'Activities to Generate Funds' (which is where you might have expected to put it, by analogy with the cost treatment), as *Investment Income* is the category that comes closest according to the FRS concept.

SORP 2005, however, is not very helpful here. Instead of pointing to 'Costs of Generating Funds' as the appropriate expenditure section, it implies an apportionment based on staff costs (the emphasis is ours here), while on the income side it leaves an unanswered question:

> 'Pension finance costs arising from changes in the net of the interest costs and expected return on assets should be allocated to *the appropriate resources expended categories* ... Income arising from these changes should be recognised as an incoming resource and separately disclosed where material.'
>
> – *SORP 2005, paragraph 437(b)*

Again, the Standard is quite specific about how to calculate these two components:

> 'The interest cost should be based on the discount rate and the present value of the scheme liabilities at the beginning of the period. The interest cost should, in addition, reflect changes in the scheme liabilities during the period.
>
> ... For quoted corporate or government bonds, the expected return [on assets] should be calculated by applying the current redemption yield at the beginning of the period to the market value of the bonds held by the scheme at the beginning of the period. For other assets (for example, equities), the expected return should be calculated by applying the rate of return expected over the long term at the beginning of the period (given the value of the assets at that date) to the fair value of the assets held by the scheme at the beginning of the period. The expected return on assets should, in addition, reflect changes in the assets in the scheme during the period as a result of contributions paid into and benefits paid out of the scheme. The expected rate of return should be set by the directors (or equivalent) having taken advice from an actuary.
>
> For quoted fixed and index-linked securities, the expected return can be observed from the market. For other assets, the expected return has to be based on assumptions about the expected long-term rate of return. The rate of return expected over the long term will vary according to market conditions, but it is expected that the amount of the return will be reasonably stable.'
>
> – *FRS17, paragraphs 53–55*

Gains/losses section

Here is where you have to show – on a separate line – item (d): 'Actuarial Gains and Losses'. This figure is also defined by FRS17 as 'periodic costs' – even though it will sometimes turn out to be a net gain. As can be seen from the quotation below, it contains three possible elements:

– *any increase/decrease in the long-term value of the Scheme's investments,* ie the annual gain/loss arising from updating the assumed long-term return on the underlying investments from last year's valuation to this one;

– any increase/decrease in long-term liabilities, ie changes on actuarial reassessment of:
  (i) the Scheme's liability for pensions and other retirement benefits; and (if applicable)
  (ii) any 'constructive obligation' incurred by the charity as employer (eg by promising extra benefits to its staff); and

– *any increase/decrease in 'disregarded' Scheme surpluses,* ie those from which the employer cannot benefit in terms of refunds and payment holidays, etc, under the Scheme rules.

The FRS puts it this way:

'Actuarial gains and losses arising from any new valuation and from updating the latest actuarial valuation to reflect conditions at the balance sheet date should be recognised in the statement of total recognised gains and losses for the period.

Actuarial gains and losses may arise on both the defined benefit scheme liabilities and any scheme assets. They comprise:

(a) on the scheme assets, differences between the expected return and the actual return (for example, a sudden change in the value of the scheme assets);
(b) on the scheme liabilities,
  (i) differences between the actuarial assumptions underlying the scheme liabilities and actual experience during the period and
  (ii) the effect of changes in actuarial assumptions; and
(c) any adjustment ... resulting from the limit on the amount that can be recognised as an asset in the balance sheet.'

– FRS17, paragraphs 57–58

The following illustrative figures, adapted from FRS17 itself in less stressful times, show how FRS17's requirements impact on the SoFA.

	This year	Last year
Pension Scheme [internal] operating costs:	£m	£m
Current service cost	3.4	2.5
Past service cost	1.2	–
– SoFA: Staff Costs within Expenditure headings	**4.6**	**2.5**
Pension Scheme [internal] finance return/cost:		
Expected return on scheme assets	7.3	6.8
Interest on pension scheme liabilities	(5.3)	(5.7)
– SoFA: Incoming Resources (/Expenditure) – see above	**2.0**	**1.1**
Pension Scheme [internal] gains/losses:		
Actual less expected return on assets	48.0	13.8
Experience gains/losses on liabilities	(5.8)	(0.6)
Changes in assumptions underlying the present value of the scheme liabilities	(14.6)	(4.1)
– SoFA: Gains/Losses (net actuarial gains)	**27.6**	**9.1**

Source: FRS17

FRS17 Allocations to Restricted Funds

6.9.1 When it comes to the question of allocating any of these FRS17 notional costs/credits to restricted funds, however, the SORP does have some really helpful guidance to offer:

> 'A pension asset should be recognised as accruing to a restricted fund only where it can be demonstrated that the economic benefit of the asset will accrue to a particular fund through reduced contributions or refunds. Similarly, a pension liability should be allocated to a particular fund only where it is demonstrable that a constructive liability arises to fund the deficit and could properly be met from the particular fund. Such a situation may arise where staff are specifically engaged on a long-term project funded from restricted income. This allocation may be undertaken on the basis of the charity's own computations ...
>
> Any allocation of a pension asset or liability to a restricted fund should be reviewed on an annual basis. Where staff changes or cessation of a particular project indicate that the economic benefits or obligations will no longer accrue to that particular fund then the asset or liability should be allocated to the unrestricted funds by means of a transfer of funds through the Statement of Financial Activities.'
>
> *– SORP 2005, paragraphs 438 and 439*

The Pension Protection Fund (PPF) levy

6.9.2 It is another question when it comes to how best to account for the impact on charities of this subsequent innovation of pensions legislation: the PPF levy, which is post SORP 2005. For 2006/07 onwards the PPF has imposed on all employers with a Defined Benefit Scheme (DB Scheme) an actuarially computed *risk-based* annual levy that could be anything from zero up to a maximum of 0.5% of Scheme liabilities (it was amusingly likened by the PPF to investment fund managers' charges), starting from a baseline date of 31 March 2006 to which all Scheme valuations had to be updated, and relying heavily on a Dun & Bradstreet country-based rating of each employer's short-term 'failure risk' (ie insolvency within the next 12 months) – as distinct from the more familiar 'credit ratings' available from such institutions.

PPF levy is payable on a sliding scale wherever the DB Scheme is not Government-backed to guarantee the employees' retirement benefits and the asset-cover available to the Scheme trustees (including 'contingent assets' such as employers' pledges of property or securities/cash or their bankers' guarantee or letter of credit) does not amount to at least 125% of Scheme liabilities calculated in accordance with the strictly actuarial basis specified by s 179 of the PPF legislation.

The levy aims to build up a national contingency fund for recourse wherever the employer goes out of business leaving the DB Scheme short of funds to meet its remaining liabilities. For charity accounting, the levy thus looks like an optional kind of *staff employment cost* to be weighed against the feasibility of designating any available reserves comprising investment assets that will then need to be *pledged* in favour of the Scheme trustees via the PPF in order to avoid or at least minimise the annual levy. The pledge itself, once made, will be disclosable as a *contingent liability* in the accounts notes – but will clearly sharpen charity auditors' focus for a critical evaluation of the credibility of the 'going concern' assumption (quite apart from 'credit-crunch' considerations – see above) on which the accounts are normally based.

Any levy actually payable each year, being irrecoverable, would seem to represent an annual cost of minimising the charity's funding of its DB Scheme for staff covered by that Scheme, making it simply an additional employer-contribution for SoFA and accounts note purposes.

INTER-FUND TRANSFERS

6.10   The Charities SORP calls for all transfers between different funds of the charity to be shown gross (where material) – because netting them off can all too easily make them incomprehensible:

> 'All transfers between the different categories of funds should be shown on the transfer row of the Statement of Financial Activities ...
>
> Material transfers should not be netted off but should be shown gross on the face of the Statement of Financial Activities.'
>
> *– SORP 2005, paragraphs 214 and 215*

This does not, however, require all these transfers to be *itemised* on the face of the SoFA – especially for transfers between reserves and designated funds, as the latter distinction is usually neither possible nor even desirable within the SoFA. This itemisation can quite properly be done entirely within the accounts notes:

> 'Material transfers between different funds and allocations to designated funds should be separately disclosed, without netting off, and should be accompanied by an explanation of the nature of the transfers or allocations and the reasons for them.'
>
> *– SORP 2005, paragraph 75(d)*

Furthermore, the SORP's related 2008 Regulations make it mandatory for a charity preparing accruals accounts under the 1993 Act generally to explain in the accounts notes each and every transfer into or out of a *restricted* fund (bearing in mind that in legal terminology this means funds that are restricted either as to income or capital – or both). The requirement is for:

> 'an itemised analysis of any material movement between any of the restricted funds of the charity, or between a restricted and an unrestricted fund of the charity, together with an explanation of the nature and purpose of each of those funds.'
>
> – *SI 2008/629, Sch 2, para 1(i)*

While this statutory requirement is not applicable for charitable companies that are required to prepare consolidated accounts for a group that does not qualify as 'small' under company law (in the oddly continuing absence of any special Schedule in, or Regulation under, the Companies Acts providing for the proper presentation of *trust* funds under their control, among other matters) the specific Companies Act requirement for not-for-profit companies to adapt the statutory profit and loss account to suit their own circumstances effectively makes SORP compliance unavoidable for them, too.

Without such information to explain and confirm the authority for any material transfers affecting their *trust funds* (ie endowed and other restricted funds), their accounts would have to be regarded as grossly misleading in view of the strict charity law requirements governing the administration of these trust funds by the company.

'GAINS AND LOSSES' SECTION

6.11   This section of the SoFA covers all *investment asset* gains/losses and also, on a separate line, any revaluation gains/losses arising on *non-investment* fixed assets – ie those held for the charity's own use. Under SORP 2005, like SORP 2000 before it, while their methodology remained unchanged, it is clear that the realised and unrealised investment gains/losses lines can be merged – except where the charity is a company and the SoFA is formatted to comply with FRS3.

In that case the line for *realised* (ie disposal) gains/losses on investment assets must be shown separately, immediately followed by a sub-total line to show the required 'net income/expenditure for the year', before going on to show all *unrealised* (ie revaluation) gains/losses, using separate lines for:

(a)   investment assets; and

(b)   non-investment fixed assets.

Again, the SORP continues to require *revaluation* gains/losses on (b) to be shown in this section of the SoFA (in the appropriate column, of course) – except to the extent that either:

–   a gain reverses 'impairment' charged as expenditure in previous years; or

– a loss represents an impairment charge this year over and above any previously recognised revaluation gains!

In these two cases, the SORP requires the impairment reversal or charge, respectively, to be included (in the appropriate column, again) within the appropriate line of the expenditure section of the SoFA.

Prior to the introduction of FRS11/15 and the requirement for impairment reviews, it was unusual to restate (b)'s carrying value at all, thus creating an 'unrealised' gain (or, more rarely, a loss) here. Certainly, apart from the 'impairment' question there is no requirement in the Charities SORP to do this other than:

– to correct an initial estimate of the value of donated assets; or

– to comply with the requirement of FRS15 to *maintain* 'current value' for the entire class if any asset of that class:
  – was *re*valued prior to FRS15's implementation and not subsequently 'frozen' at that value in the year of implementing FRS15 under transitional rules; or
  – is *re*valued thereafter.

Within the Gains and Losses section these items will always need to be shown on a separate line from *investment* asset gains/losses.

In addition, as discussed at **6.8**, this section must also include (on a separate line) the recalculated/updated actuarial gains/losses component of the annual movement in the balance sheet value of the charity's *notional* asset/liability in respect of any defined benefit staff pension, etc, scheme/arrangements it operates.

'FUNDS RECONCILIATION' SECTION

6.12 One of the great advantages of the SoFA is the standardisation it has achieved in the presentation of the net movement from year to year on the various funds of the charity and the relationship between this movement and the opening and closing balances as shown in the previous and current balance sheets.

The SoFA's standardised presentation of the charity's total (income) funds from year to year and their gross and net movements for the year satisfies the FRS3 requirement for (company) accounts to include a 'reconciliation of funds' statement, but it has also effectively outlawed the presentation of restricted funds (other than timing restrictions imposed by general-purpose donors, of course) as 'liabilities' in the charity balance sheet. As a 'commercial' view of the charity's financial position, and one presented by some surprisingly large charities at the time, such a treatment is now seen to have been inappropriate – flawed by non-compliance with charity law. For, in the SORP's own words:

'The Statement of Financial Activities should reflect the principal movements between the opening and closing balances on all the funds of the charity. ...'.

– SORP 2005, paragraph 74

The Charities SORP also makes it clear that this information needs to be supplemented by sub-analysis explaining the nature and purpose of any major funds included within any of the three main types of fund shown in the individual analysis columns of the SoFA, as well as reconciling the movement of these individual funds between the two balance sheets:

> 'The notes to the accounts should provide information on the structure of the charity's funds so as to disclose the fund balances and the reasons for them differentiating between unrestricted income funds (both general and designated), restricted income funds, permanent endowment and expendable endowment as well as identifying any material individual funds among them. In particular:
>
> ...
>
> (b)   Disclosure of how each of the funds has arisen (including designated funds), the restrictions imposed and the purpose of each fund should be provided. An indication should be given as to whether or not sufficient resources are held in an appropriate form to enable each fund to be applied in accordance with any restrictions. For example, if a charity has a fund which is to be spent in the near future, it should be made clear in the notes whether or not the assets held (or expected to be received) in the fund are liquid assets.
>
> (c)   Any funds in deficit should always be separately disclosed. An explanation should be given in the Trustees' Annual Report ... Designated funds should never be in deficit ...'.

– SORP 2005, paragraph 75

> 'Separate sets of statements may be produced for each major fund and linked to a total summary. The trustees should decide on the most suitable form of presentation, bearing in mind:
>
> (a)   the complexity of the fund structure,
>
> (b)   the need for the total provided in the summary to agree to the primary statements (Statement of Financial Activities and Balance Sheet), and
>
> (c)   the need to avoid confusion between the movements on the various funds. ...'.

– SORP 2005, paragraph 76

Chapter 7

THE SUMMARY INCOME AND EXPENDITURE ACCOUNT

INTRODUCTION

7.1 This chapter is primarily about FRS3 compliance by *charitable companies* unable to achieve this in the SoFA, ultimately due to material movements on endowed funds – to exclude which would undermine the very purpose of the SoFA. As a special case, the consolidated SoFA for a 'small' group above the charity audit threshold, where the consolidated accounts must be prepared under s 49A and Schedule 5A, Charities Act 1993 instead of the Companies Act 2006 (being 'not required' by the latter), serves the special purpose of *charity* accountability and is of no public interest *commercially*, so that FRS3 compliance in this respect is not relevant. Charitable companies are required by the Companies Act 1985 in any other case to report the not-for-profit equivalent of the 'surplus' or 'deficit' for the year, thus their (realised) net income or expenditure, because the Department for Business, Innovation & Skills (DBIS, the recently renamed DBERR alias the old DTI) continues to see this as essential to achieve inter-company comparability of annual 'net results' across the Register of Companies. Consequently, the SORP is unable to allow the 'Companies Act accounts' of charitable companies the same latitude as *non-company* charities, which can ignore FRS3 as irrelevant to the charity SoFA (unless, of course, their governing document requires them to report on the same (commercial) basis – ie to prepare an 'Income and Expenditure Account').

For charitable companies, then, if (under the Companies Act) the SoFA's essentially fund-by-fund view of the totality of all incoming and outgoing financial resources and valuation changes cannot accommodate the narrower focus of FRS3 on turnover and net result and the impact on them of any new/ceased activities, the Charities SORP continues to say that a separate primary statement should be prepared in order to satisfy FRS3.

To avoid duplicating information, it can be seen from paragraph 425 of the SORP that this additional statement should *summarise* just the *charity totals* of the operating and other income, and of expenditure, *without regard to individual funds of the charity.* The SORP says the Summary Income and Expenditure Account should be cross-referenced to the detailed figures shown in the SoFA, from whose accounting policies it must not deviate. This FRS3-compliant format is dealt with more fully at **7.3**.

Although the point is not brought out in the Charities SORP at all, the fact is that summary operating statements of this kind can be made to serve as useful sidelights to the SoFA even under SORP 2005. This is because they can ignore fund restrictions and concentrate instead on showing the gross and net results of mainstream activities that are wholly/partly self-funded (ie charitable trading) and any contribution made by gifts, investment earnings and fundraising trading or other events/activities. For some charities this may perhaps be clearer than using a separate column of the SoFA for the purpose.

Thus the summary income and expenditure account could be made to serve a useful function, even for *non-company* charities with different kinds of funded activity, by means of a little reformatting to show the surplus or deficit on each of those activities *from the trustees' perspective rather than that of donors*, as well as the extent to which the charity's various kinds of other activity have consumed or contributed income.

One way of doing this – and thus providing *really* helpful information to complement the fund-by-fund movements analysis needed to satisfy the requirements of charity law concerning the proper administration of each distinct trust included in the published accounts (an analysis missing from many charities' accounts even now, more than a decade after the 1995 SORP) – is as set out below:

	Residential Care services	Other Charitable Services	Non-charitable trading	Investment and other activities	2009 Total	*2008 Total*
	£'000	£'000	£'000	£'000	£'000	*£'000*
Income						
– Voluntary funding	700	9,480	–	–	10,180	*7,730*
– Turnover	1,200	–	1,140	–	2,340	*1,900*
– Investment income	–	–	–	400	400	*475*
Total	**1,900**	**9,480**	**1,140**	**400**	**12,920**	*10,105*
Operating costs						
– Charitable services	(2,430)	(7,060)	–	–	(9,490)	*(9,405)*
– Other expenditure	–	(690)	(870)	(90)	(1,650)	*(1,370)*
Total	**(2,430)**	**(7,750)**	**(870)**	**(90)**	**(11,140)**	*(10,775)*
Net operating income for year	(530)	1,730	270	310	1,780	*(670)*
Disposal Gains						
– Fixed Assets for own use	–	–	–	20	20	*30*
– Investment assets	–	–	–	100	100	*250*
Net income for year	**(530)**	**1,730**	**270**	**430**	**1,900**	*(390)*

Where a charitable company's SoFA fully satisfies FRS3's information requirements for an income and expenditure account, it can of course replace the latter in the accounts presented for filing at Companies House as well as at the Charity Commission. However, the following extract from Barnardo's 2007/08 accounts provides an interesting illustration of an opportunity missed:

SoFA & Note 22 extract	Unrestricted [Income]	Restricted Income	Endowment [Capital]	Total Funds
	£'000	£'000	£'000	£'000
Incoming Resources (in total)	**204,041**	**10,140**	**1,104**	**215,285**
Resources expended				
Costs of generating funds (in total)	40,012	-	83	40,095
Incoming Resources available for charitable activities	*164,029*	*10,140*	*1,021*	*175,190*
Charitable activities costs (in total)	153,263	10,743	-	164,006
Governance costs	1,292	–	-	1,292
Total expenditure	**154,555**	**10,743**	**-**	**165,298**
Net incoming/(outgoing) resources	9,474	(603)	1,021	9,892
Endowment Investments' total return converted from capital into income	550	-	(550)	-
Net incoming/(outgoing) resources after inter-fund transfers	10,024	(603)	471	9,892
Investment Gains/(Losses)*	(1,887)	-	(1,361)	(3,248)
Pension Scheme actuarial gain/(loss)	(4,500)	-	-	(4,500)
Net Movement in funds	**3,637**	**(603)**	**(890)**	**2,144**
*Notes 10/22a: Investment gains/losses				
– Disposal gains/(losses)	189	-	(3)	186
– Revaluation gains/(losses)	(2,076)	-	(1,358)	(3,434)

Barnardo's – from the 2007/08 Accounts

Comment

Barnardo's is one charitable company unable to square the requirements of FRS3 with those of the Charities SORP. Here, the insuperable problem is the legal device known as a "Total Return" Order, issued by the Charity Commission (at the trustees' request) to authorise the company, as the charity trustee of its permanent financial endowment (valued at ca.£21m), to invest that capital without regard to the normal trust law distinctions between capital and income, administering *all* investment returns as *expendable capital* – out of which ca. £0.5m was converted into income this year for spending (and so must be shown as an 'inter-fund transfer' in the SoFA). Under the Order, the income distributions (ca. £1m) receivable on those investments must be accounted for as accruing to *capital* in the SoFA, which then cannot present FRS3-compliant figures for total income of the year. So the SoFA has to be accompanied by a separate Statement of Income and Expenditure – the SORP's 'default' treatment for FRS3-compliance by a charitable company.

THE NEED FOR AN 'INCOME AND EXPENDITURE' STATEMENT

7.2   Since the advent of SORP 2000, this need has been confined to charities subject to the Companies Act 1985 ('the 1985 Act') or its replacement of 2006 – and even then only in a small minority of cases. SORP 2005 now says (paraphrasing the 2000 version):

'Charity accruals accounts should comprise:

...

   (b)   an income and expenditure account where this is a legal requirement. This applies to ... certain charitable companies ... Paragraphs 423 to 426 fully describe the circumstances in which a summary income and expenditure account is necessary for companies in addition to the Statement of Financial Activities ...'.

– SORP 2005, paragraph 30

The cross-referral to paragraphs 423–426 is to where the SORP goes on to say that:

'Circumstances where it will probably be required may arise where the income and expenditure account cannot be separately identified within the Statement of Financial Activities and there are items which may be open to challenge if they are included in an Income and Expenditure Account, such as:

   (a)   movement on endowment (capital) funds during the year; and
   (b)   unrealised gains and losses arising during the year.'

– SORP 2005, paragraph 423

Exclusion of capital transactions

7.2.1 The problem at (a) arises from the structured way in which the SoFA has to report not only all the unrestricted and restricted income fund movements but also all *endowed fund* movements (if any). Where in such a case the SoFA has both unrestricted and restricted income columns, they could easily be sub-totalled in a special column alongside the endowed funds column.

For this to satisfy FRS3's requirement to report total income and expenditure, however, the *comparative* gross and net income totals will also have to be shown, and this is not so easy to achieve without adding two extra columns for the comparative figures.

Realised and unrealised gains/losses on investment assets

7.2.2 The problem at (b) is a more subtle one, with implications that can easily be missed:

'Particular attention may need to be given to impairment losses and reversals which, in accordance with the guidance in FRS 11, are realised in some circumstances and unrealised in others.'

– SORP 2005, paragraph 424

For a charitable company's accounts prepared under the Companies Act 2006, it is necessary to comply with that Act's specific requirement that 'not-for-profit' companies *shall* adapt the statutory profit and loss account to suit their nature (but with the general requirement for 'a true and fair view' still applying only to their *net* income/expenditure and turnover – not to all the *gross* figures as is required for non-company charities and also for any consolidated accounts prepared under the 1993 Act in respect of a 'small' group headed by a charitable company).

What this means for company 'income and expenditure' statements prepared under company law is that, as an overriding requirement:

'only profits realised at the balance sheet date must be included in the profit and loss account ...'.

– para 13(a) of Sch 1 to Small Companies and Groups (Accounts and Directors' Report) Regulations 2008, SI 2008/409, and to Large and Medium-sized Companies and Groups (Accounts and Reports) Regulations 2008, SI 2008/410

To avoid losing sight of the unrealised variety, FRS3 therefore requires an additional primary accounting statement to report 'total recognised gains and losses'. However, the boundary line between these two separate statements, so conveniently joined together in the SoFA, must still be carefully observed and respected for FRS3 compliance in a charitable company's accounts *if prepared under company law*. This will mean splitting the SoFA's merged line for investment gains/losses and inserting a sub-total line, suitably worded, after the 'realised' line and before the 'unrealised' line – unless the directors choose to draw their 'net income/expenditure' line *before* realised gains/losses as having been 'taken directly to reserves', as is actually *required* by (charity) law.

For this purpose, the directors would have to rely on the argument that FRS3 '*Reporting Financial Performance*' is not sufficiently 'relevant' to charity law, which in this respect also governs the activities of charitable companies, and that this entitles them to parity with investment companies as regards the exclusion of realised investment gains/losses from 'net income for the year':

'Gains and losses may be excluded from the profit and loss account only if they are specifically permitted or required to be taken directly to reserves by this or other accounting standards or, in the absence of a relevant accounting standard, by law.'

– FRS3, paragraph 13

'Gains and losses may be excluded from the profit and loss account only if they are specifically permitted or required to be taken direct to reserves by this standard or by companies legislation or equivalent legislation.'

– FRSSE 2008, paragraph 3.2

The reasoning here is that, in so far as charity law prohibits any kind of profit distribution by a charity, **all** its funds are *undistributable reserves*.

The authority for claiming such a specialised accounting treatment must be the supervisory power of the Charity Commission in its role as a branch of the Chancery Division of the High Court. The Charity Commission is empowered by statute to intervene where necessary to enforce the proper application even of the *corporate* funds of a charitable company in furtherance of its declared charitable purposes. This power effectively constrains the use of these funds, certainly to prevent their distribution by way of profit or gain, and is thus the basis of the standard 'profit-distribution' prohibition in the Memorandum and Articles of every charitable company, thus giving its corporate funds the character of 'reserve' funds within the meaning of companies legislation.

The same legal power further authorises their continued retention as 'charity reserves' so long as this is operationally justified by the needs of beneficiaries – as, for example, with the provision of lifelong charitable support for the disabled, longer-term charitable research into causes and cures, etc.

Typically, charities seeking to build up reserves for such longer-term purposes tend to re-invest their investment disposal proceeds as a matter of policy, rather than spending them on current activities. This fact makes a nonsense of having to disclose disposal gains/losses as part of 'net income for the year'. Where the provision of redundant information also entails a cost-burden, so that the charity has chosen to omit it, the policy of the Commission in charity monitoring has been to turn a blind eye to the omission.

In other cases, instead of full re-investment there may be material *divestment* to make funds available for spending on activities – or even, perhaps, for 'capital expenditure' on assets for the charity's own use. It may not then be quite so easy to sustain the above argument, and the normal requirement of FRS3 to show realised investment gains/losses as part of 'net income' will then have to be met somehow or other.

Instead, SORP 2005 appears to have modified the application of FRS3 to charitable companies by allowing them to adopt the kind of 'marking to market' accounting policy (see below) normally used only for *trading* in investment securities, and which for an investment held as a fixed asset cannot really accord with the FRS3 concept that its existing carrying value must be either its historical cost or a revaluation included in the previous year's balance sheet. Furthermore any such trading, being a non-primary-purpose activity for a charity, would surely count as a taxable income source above the statutory concession ceiling of up to a £50,000 turnover.

However, the SORP's Appendix on compliance with accounting standards makes it clear that FRS3 – like all other UK standards – can apply only within the framework of the reporting entity's relevant accounting legislation, which for *non-company* charities, and for the consolidated accounts of 'small' groups headed by a *charitable company*, is Part VI of the Charities Act 1993 and the SORP's related Regulations made under Part VI (or in Scotland the 2005 Act and its 2006 Regulations that underpin SORP 2005 there). The implication is that the accounts of such charities do not need to disclose a 'result' for the year at all in the sense of FRS3's 'distributable profits'.

That aside, 'marking to market' is a policy which must be hard for any charity to justify under FRS18 as one that is considered *'the most suitable'* in the charity's particular circumstances, in that it purports to revalue all fixed asset investments by reference to current market prices *immediately prior to disposal*, thus making all disposal gains and losses nil – neatly disposing of the FRS3 requirement to include all realised gains/losses in the net result (income) reported for the year. Nevertheless that is what SORP 2005 sanctions at paragraphs 219 and 423:

> 'Any gains and losses on investment assets (including property investments) should be included under the gains and losses on the revaluation and disposal of investment assets. Realised and unrealised gains and losses may be included in a single row on the Statement of Financial Activities. In particular this approach will be necessary where a charity adopts a "marking to market" or continuous revaluation approach in relation to its investment portfolio.'

– SORP 2005, paragraph 219

'... where charities adopt a policy of continuous revaluation of investments (as explained in paragraph 219) there may be no realised gains to report and all the revaluation movements will be classified as unrealised gains.'

– SORP 2005, paragraph 423

The following example shows (in bold type) how the insertion of a sub-total after the line for realised investment gains/losses would affect the appearance of the SoFA:

	Note	Unrestricted Funds	Restricted Income Funds	2009 Total	2008 Total
		£	£	£	£
Total Incoming Resources	2	500,000	90,000	590,000	517,000
Total Resources Expended	5	440,000	100,000	540,000	496,000
Net Incoming/Outgoing) Resources before Fund Transfers		60,000	(10,000)	50,000	21,000
Transfer: Restricted Fund deficit	6	(5,000)	5,000	–	–
Net Incoming/(Outgoing) Resources after Transfers		55,000	(5,000)	50,000	21,000
Realised Investment Gains/(Losses)	7	(2,000)	(1,000)	(3,000)	10,000
Net Income/(Expenditure) for year		**53,000**	**(6,000)**	**47,000**	**31,000**
Unrealised Investment Gains/(Losses)	7	5,000	2,000	7,000	(1,000)
Net Movement in Funds for year		58,000	(4,000)	54,000	30,000
Fund Balances at start of year		150,000	40,000	190,000	160,000
Fund Balances at end of year	10	208,000	36,000	244,000	190,000

Income/capital conversions

7.2.3 Where a summary income and expenditure account is needed for *company law* compliance, it will also have to show the income arising from any (duly authorised) conversion of capital (ie endowed funds) for spending on the charity's activities. The most likely situations where this will apply are:

–   to amortise an *expendable endowment* grant/gift in line with the recognised annual depreciation of the related assets because they are required by the donor to be retained for the charity's own (ie functional) use on a continuing basis;

–   on conversion of *expendable endowment* into income for spending (most commonly as the exercise of a discretionary power given by the Founder);

–   allocations to income out of the unapplied total return where a *permanent endowment* is invested on that basis on special authority (see chapters 5 and 9);

–   in the year of borrowing from a *permanent endowment* as authorised by law, which in England and Wales means by an order of the Charity Commission (normally under a recoupment order to repay the borrowed capital out of the income of subsequent years).

By the same reasoning, it could be argued that it should also show any reduction of income as a result of the exercise of a legal power to 'accumulate' income by adding it to capital, which is a specialised meaning of 'capitalisation' in which the charity converts the unspent income into capital. Strictly speaking, this cannot be called 'expenditure' – but it certainly impacts on FRS3's 'bottom line' of net income as distinct from capital.

Dual regulation of charitable companies

7.2.4 Constitutionally, charitable companies are seen by the DBIS (alias DBERR, the old DTI) as just a special class of 'not-for-profit' company, being subject to charity law regulation as well. Among other things, this prevents the members from diverting to non-charitable uses any *corporate* funds acquired as a charity either as trading/ investment income or as a gift.

The proper application of *their* trust funds is subject to the same regulation as those of non-company charities. Not so their corporate funds, which (as their own absolute property) are held outside trust law. A charitable company's corporate funds can thus be disposed of at will – so long as this stays within the boundaries of the company's declared Objects and constitutional rules. These, however, can be changed – for example, to provide for non-charitable transactions – by means of a members' special resolution under company law.

But this is where Part VIII of the Charities Act 1993 ('the 1993 Act') intervenes to constrain changes made to the Memorandum and Articles (or other written constitution) of any incorporated charity. Section 64 of the 1993 Act invalidates any such change without the prior written consent of the Charity Commission; but it also protects the charitable application of existing funds, by providing that:

> 'Where a charity is a company or other body corporate having power to alter the instruments establishing or regulating it as a body corporate, no exercise of that power which has the effect of the body ceasing to be a charity shall be valid so as to effect the application of—
>
> (a)   any property acquired under any disposition or agreement previously made otherwise than for full consideration in money or money's worth, or any property representing property so acquired,
> (b)   any property representing income which has accrued before the alteration is made, or
> (c)   the income from any such property as aforesaid.'
>
> – *Charities Act 1993, s 64(1)*

This legislation effectively ring-fences corporate funds arising from 'absolute' gifts to incorporated charities (including all income and gains from their investment or reinvestment or from operational use for trading/fundraising) to much the same extent as gifts made on charitable trusts.

While it may be a moot point whether (b) would also catch a retained surplus on charitable *trading* (ie 'value-for-value' transactions, thus with no 'gift' element) carried out by a charitable company out of corporate capital subscribed for that purpose, it is quite clear from the Charities SORP that the 'profit and loss account' adaptation needed for charitable companies to recognise their nature as charities is far more extensive than that necessary for other not-for-profit companies.

Despite these narrower supervisory limits, however, the DBIS (and therefore the ASB) continue to require charitable companies to present as part of their annual accounts a primary statement showing a 'net result' for the year *comparable with the profit and loss statement of companies as a class.*

FORMAT

7.3   The summary income and expenditure account will need to show essentially the same entity/group information as the SoFA but only in summary form and excluding all movements on capital account (ie those within endowed funds). SORP 2005 adds that the summary 'should be derived from and cross-referenced to the corresponding figures in the [SoFA]', and further that:

> 'It need not distinguish between unrestricted and restricted income funds but the accounting basis on which items are included must be the same as in the Statement of Financial Activities. It should show separately in respect of continuing[1] operations, acquisitions and discontinued operations:
>
> (a)   gross income from all sources;
> (b)   net gains/losses from disposals of all fixed assets belonging to the charity's income funds;
> (c)   transfers from endowment funds of amounts previously received as capital resources and now converted into income funds for expending;
> (d)   total income (this will be the total of all incoming resources – other than revaluation gains – of all the income funds but not for any endowment funds);
> (e)   total expenditure out of the charity's income funds;
> (f)   net income or expenditure for the year.
>
> In practice, the format may need to be modified to comply with specific statutory requirements or those of the charity's own governing document.'
>
> *– SORP 2005, paragraph 425*

What does need emphasising is the requirement to cross-reference the figures in the summary income and expenditure account to those in the SoFA wherever the relationship is not self-evident – for example, where two or more figures in one statement have been added together in the other statement.

---

[1]   It should be noted here that FRS3 does not require any statement to the effect that there are only continuing operations, if in fact the SoFA/summary does not actually distinguish any discontinued or new ones. Overlooking this, many charities still continue to make such a redundant statement of the obvious.

Chapter 8

THE TREATMENT OF TANGIBLE AND OTHER FIXED ASSETS HELD FOR A CHARITY'S OWN USE

INTRODUCTION

8.1   This chapter is about how to account, under SORP 2005, for all *non-investment* fixed assets whose retention normally cannot be viewed in purely economic terms but rather in terms of their *public benefit* utility. This means those assets which are held primarily for the charity's *own use* on a continuing basis – including (at **8.3**) the SORP's *special* treatment of 'heritage' assets. That is a narrower class than the 'inalienable' or 'historic' assets or 'treasures' that had to be distinguished under SORP 2000, being a class subsequently redefined by the ASB in its new Standard, FRS30, effective from April 2010 (or earlier voluntary adoption from June 2009 when it was issued), to focus more closely on educational and cultural attributes. This chapter deals with the SORP's requirements for all 'own use' fixed assets for:

–   their 'capitalisation' and presentation in the balance sheet (and the exemptions);

–   writing them off as expenditure in the SoFA as having been 'consumed' in the course of the charity's activities;

–   their 'impairment' in use (however seldom this may occur in the charity world);

–   gains/losses arising from their eventual disposal; and in the meantime for any revaluation of such assets.

It also shows how all this is affected by the type of fund to which the asset belongs.

A separate chapter (chapter 9) deals with the treatment of investment assets – both fixed and current – as well as the *hybrid* class of 'social investments' by means of which more and more charities now seek to provide public benefit by recycling rather than expending their over-stretched resources.

These 'functional' assets include the usual 'tangible' (ie physical) assets like buildings occupied on freehold or leasehold land, together with all sorts of fixed and movable/mobile equipment besides furniture, fixtures and fittings, including communications network installations, computer and other equipment (some of it highly specialised), motor vehicles, etc. Some of these may be the heritage assets already mentioned, if used for a 'qualifying' purpose – see **8.3**.

But they also include *intangible* assets that, although still something of a rarity among charities, are now commonplace in the commercial world – ie 'intellectual property' rights/licences (eg covering the use/exploitation of trademarks and logos, patented designs, author's copyright, etc), goodwill in a (profitable) business, and even in some cases 'brand names' where perhaps a franchising operation has been able to quantify their marketable value on a reliable basis.

THE REQUIREMENT TO CAPITALISE

8.2   In principle, as required by FRS15, and subject to practicality (see **8.3.4**) and materiality (see **8.5**), all assets held by a charity for its own use on a continuing basis are required to be capitalised (ie carried forward in the balance sheet) under SORP 2005. This applies whether or not the asset is owned by outright purchase, self-constructed, a gift/grant, or held under a finance lease or a hire-purchase agreement. In theory it also applies whether or not the asset was included in the balance sheet prior to FRS15. However, where the asset used is held under an operating lease (eg a leased vehicle, computer or photocopier) not bestowing substantially all the rights and obligations of ownership, it should not be capitalised – at least, not for the time being, though current thinking among the standard-setting bodies is that perhaps it should be, after all. In the case of a leased property, then with that exception, unless it is only of short duration any alterations/improvements should be capitalised and amortised over the term of the lease.

The SORP devotes considerable space to explaining the very strict rules that must be followed for compliance with FRS15 and FRS11 here. But the complexity of these two Standards is such that even such lengthy guidance may not be in enough depth to save charities having to read up the full requirements for themselves in some cases. The main impact of these rules depends on the accounting policy adopted for:

–   valuation/revaluation (if used instead of original gift-value or purchase cost); and

–   depreciation (or non-depreciation);

of *land and buildings* in the main (but perhaps also of other major fixed assets), held for the charity's own use or 'functioning' – ie operational use, as distinct from investment use.

'Frozen valuations' under FRS15

8.2.1   Under the 1995 SORP, capitalised assets held for the charity's own use could be carried in the balance sheet either at their historical cost (with original gift-value counting as the 'deemed' cost) or at some subsequent valuation if preferred. All that changed in 2000. SORP 2000 had to follow FRS15 very closely by requiring any *re*valuations post-FRS15 to be *kept up to date* in future. This then entails the adoption of a 'current value' accounting policy (except where a previous valuation has been 'frozen' under FRS15's transitional provisions) in order to be able to revalue any asset *and the same for the whole class of assets of that kind.*

These transitional provisions gave a once-and-for-all 'window of opportunity' in the year of implementing FRS15 (see below): you could 'freeze' the carrying value of any already revalued asset as brought forward from *the previous balance sheet* without becoming committed to a 'current value' basis. If you did this for any asset at that time, you have to disclose the fact every year, as it must form part of your Accounting Policies, and FRS15 requires you also to say that the asset's carrying value 'has not been updated' – see **12.2.7**.

The only other way was to abandon the old revaluation by reverting to historical cost – ie the original purchase price (or its gift-value at the time, if applicable) – if the figures were still available!

Although charities were *required* to implement FRS15 anyway for 23 March 2000 and later balance sheets to be able to show a true and fair view, the new rules were included in the first edition of this book more than a year before SORP 2000 was finalised and issued in October 2000. Nevertheless, in the light of the feedback from experience and extensive writing and lecturing on the subject since then we have since found it useful to continue to reiterate them here.

Valuing *gifts* of fixed assets

8.2.2   The general rule under the Charities SORP is that *gifts* of fixed assets received 'on trust for retention' by a charity for its own use on a continuing basis (ie on 'user trusts') must be recognised in the SoFA at their *fair value for use by the charity* at the time of gift, that initial valuation being deemed to be their historical cost, capitalised at that same value in the balance sheet and depreciated in the normal way, in the case of 'wasting' assets.

What this now means in practice for the 1995 SORP's two special exemptions – for legally or operationally *inalienable/historic* assets and for the arguably rarer class of assets that can have *no reliable carrying value* – is that the first has been abolished to achieve FRS15 compliance and the second widened as if by way of compensation. Instead, inalienable/historic assets were just specially highlighted under SORP 2000, whereas under SORP 2005 the asset class itself has been further narrowed down to highlight only 'heritage' assets without regard to the question of any inalienability imposed by charity law or dictated by operational needs. For a closer look at this aspect, see **8.3**.

The way paragraph 17 of FRS15 specifies the valuation basis to be used when capitalising tangible fixed assets donated as 'gifts in kind' to a charity for its own use is:

> 'The initial carrying amount of tangible fixed assets received as gifts and donations by charities should be the current value of the assets at the date they are received.'

– FRS15, paragraph 17

'Current value' for this purpose is then modified by the SORP to become *'a reasonable estimate of their gross value to the charity'*. In 2000, this was taken to mean 'value in use' – a concept that could offer considerable latitude to charities by reference to their charitable aims (as distinct from profit-motivated ones). To minimise that latitude, in line with ASB aspirations, SORP 2005 goes on to clarify that:

> 'Where gifts in kind are included in the Statement of Financial Activities at their estimated gross value, the current value will usually be the price that [the charity] estimates it would have to pay in the open market for an equivalent item.'

– SORP 2005, paragraph 130

The initial value at which to capitalise a major gift (eg a substantial freehold property) intended for the charity's own use as a fixed asset is thus pinned to the open market price for that kind of property without regard to (i) any disposal restrictions imposed under trust law by the donor or (ii) the gift's actual suitability for the charity's own use (bearing in mind that the gifts we are offered are not always what we would choose to buy for ourselves – a thought seemingly outside the remit of commercially oriented Standards, but well within the remit of the SORP itself when accounting for donated services/facilities in the SoFA!).

However, by reference to the 'impairment' rules of FRS11 it is clear from paragraph 256 of the SORP that for non-commercial fixed assets (ie those held and used primarily for public benefit provision on a non-economic basis, thus free or at uneconomic charge-rates) such a commercial carrying value can then be immediately reduced to what the Standard calls the asset's 'recoverable amount' (ie the higher of its 'net realisable value' and its 'value in use') – see **8.2.4**, and also **8.7** where we discuss the impairment rules in more depth.

> 'Where the net book value of a fixed asset is higher than its recoverable amount, it will be impaired and should be written down to its recoverable amount …'.

– SORP 2005, paragraph 256

In chapter 10 (at **10.3.8**) we discuss the case of the National Trust, whose huge collection of non-capitalised heritage properties was – at least until 2007 – insured for buildings-reinstatement at a figure of nearly £5.7bn,* excluding the land values (which could be enormous, depending on planning permission for any redevelopment), but which are subject to perpetual maintenance obligations in the national interest – obligations whose present value is so high as to justify the Trust calling these 'negative assets'. In support of that view, it is understood that the Trust refuses to accept such gifts unless they come with a sufficient financial endowment to neutralise the obligation. All of which makes one wonder why for strict compliance with FRS15/11 these assets couldn't have been capitalised in the first place and then immediately written down to zero to recognise their 'impairment' subject to the legislation under which the Trust is permitted to avoid putting 'negative assets' on the balance sheet. (*This figure is taken from the Trust's 2006–7 Annual Report and Accounts – an illuminating if incomplete disclosure that seems, regrettably, to have been dropped for the year 2007–8.)

While legal (and, to a lesser extent perhaps, even operational) inalienability must depress an asset's ultimate disposal value and while its non-economic use mitigates against 'income stream' assessment of 'net realisable value', the concept of 'service potential' for assessing an asset's 'value in use' in order to arrive at a reliable 'value to the charity' is subject to the SORP's careful warning against 'window-dressing'. The implications here for gift-accounting as well should not be ignored:

'Value in use calculations should not be used to manipulate the write down of fixed assets. For instance when a new specialised asset is purchased, although it may have a low net realisable value, it is unlikely that it will suffer an impairment in service delivery within the first years after acquisition.'

– SORP 2005, paragraph 271

The Charities SORP has a strangely labyrinthine way of saying so, but the requirements of charity law do make such a gift (ie one given *on trust* to be retained for the charity's own continuing use) an incoming *endowment* – which will be of a permanent nature except where there is an express or implied power to expend capital. Wherever the gift is of (or money for) a 'wasting' asset, such as a building on freehold land, or a leasehold property, or equipment, vehicles, etc, such a power of expending the capital will normally be implied by the asset's very nature.

The SORP's rather general specification of 'restricted funds' treatment should then be interpreted more specifically as meaning '*endowed* funds' – to be amortised in line with the annual depreciation charges within the appropriate income fund column of the SoFA. As also explained in the SORP, the asset's ultimate disposal proceeds will become unrestricted, spendable income unless there are indications that the donor intended otherwise.

Grants/gifts of money *for* fixed assets

8.2.3 Funds given on trust for the purchase or construction of such assets must follow the same treatment, of course, corresponding to their terms of trust.

Where, instead, this donor-intention of 'continuing use' is absent or is only a 'non-binding' wish (perhaps because the donor says so) the trustees' decision, made at their own discretion, to retain and use the asset – rather than perhaps to sell it and use the proceeds for something else – makes the gift (or the money provided to acquire the asset) unrestricted, as indicated by the SORP itself.

Revaluations: the requirement for a 'current value' basis

8.2.4 'Current value' as an *accounting policy* under FRS15 has been made less subjective in its possible interpretation for gift-accounting purposes (see above) than the SORP's 'value to the charity' – as is apparent from the way the Standard defines the term at paragraph 2:

'The current value of a tangible fixed asset to the business is the lower of replacement cost and recoverable amount. [The latter is] the higher of net realisable value and value in use.'

– FRS15, paragraph 2

'Value in use' is then cross-referenced to FRS11 for its definition and calculation as given there. The special problems this raises for charities are discussed below.

This requirement does not in any way conflict with the requirement of the SORP to recognise incoming gifts of fixed assets at a deemed historical cost equal to their estimated fair value – or, more specifically, 'gross value to the charity' – at the time of gift, however, since that does not amount to '*revaluation*'.

The 1995 SORP's introduction of a fundamental requirement to carry all *investment assets* at market value in the balance sheet led many charities to think they also had to revalue fixed assets held for the charity's own use. Although this was certainly not so at the time, it *is* now so if you do not adopt the historical cost basis – as modified by the already described rules for the 'deemed' cost of gifts and for 'freezing' pre-FRS15 revaluations, of course.

On first capitalising assets previously not included in the accounts (see **8.3**), their recognition is not *re*valuation. It *will* be a change of accounting policy involving a 'prior years' adjustment, as they have to be brought onto the balance sheet at *depreciated cost* (or the best estimate thereof).

A charity may, for any one of a number of reasons, nevertheless wish to restate assets held for its own use at their current value for that particular use – notably land and buildings. Where it does so, it should normally base the value on at least an informal valuation from an experienced person, such as a member of the Royal Institution of Chartered Surveyors, who publish clear guidelines as to the manner and principles of such valuations.

For other assets, there is usually a ready market, with prices publicly available, such as for second-hand cars (eg *Glass's Guide* and others).

Generally speaking, however, it will not normally be in a charity's best interests to adopt current value instead of historical cost in the balance sheet as if these assets were akin to investment assets. In the authors' view, it would be a gross distortion for charities to have to account in such a way as to facilitate commercial calculations of a 'notional income return' on their total net worth – the ultimate aim behind 'fair value' balance sheet accounting – as if public benefit assessments could be reduced to a common denominator of money or a financial value put on a human life.

While a commercial entity might properly measure its 'return on capital employed' by this means, such an idea amounts to a denial of the essentially different motivation of charities. Not only does it fail to recognise that the real value of a charity's activities is *non-commercial*, being about putting something into society rather than taking it out, but also – at considerable administrative expense to charity funds – it would produce asset values which in many cases would be misleading. Some charities could only operate from the specific buildings they occupy, some of which came as a gift, perhaps as a permanent endowment, and some will have specially adapted their buildings to suit their own purposes, and a revaluation to depreciated replacement cost in such a case could seriously affect their SoFA figures.

Once having adopted a 'current value' policy for any class of their 'own-use' tangible fixed assets, the trustees must ensure that their valuations are kept reasonably up to date and also provide additional information in the accounts notes:

> 'The trustees may use any reasonable approach to valuation at least every five years, subject only to obtaining advice as to the possibility of any material movements between individual valuations. Where a charity has a number of such assets, it will be acceptable for valuations to be carried out on a rolling basis over a five year period. Independent formal professional valuations are not mandatory in the case of a charity, which instead may obtain a valuation from a suitably qualified person who could be a trustee or employee …'.

– SORP 2005, paragraph 265

'Where any class of tangible fixed assets of a charity has been revalued, the notes to the accounts should give:

(a)   the name and qualification (if any) of the valuer and whether they are a member of staff or a trustee or external to the charity;
(b)   the basis or bases of valuation;
(c)   where records are available, the historical cost less depreciation;
(d)   date of the previous full valuation;
(e)   if the value has not been updated in the reporting period, a statement by the trustees that they are not aware of any material changes since the last valuation.'

– SORP 2005, paragraph 277

HERITAGE ASSETS

8.3   The fundamental point to bear in mind here is that the Charities SORP's special rules for the separately disclosable class of 'heritage' fixed assets apply *only* to those held for the charity's own use for qualifying purposes. Thus they cannot extend to 'investment assets'. The term is defined in SORP 2005 to mean assets retained for *preservation or conservation purposes*:

'To fall within the definition of heritage assets, the charity must hold the relevant assets in pursuit of preservation or conservation objectives. The objective of the charity may be specifically of a preservation or conservation nature, or the heritage assets may be integral to a broader objective such as educating the public in history, the arts or science as in the case of museums and galleries.'

– SORP 2005, paragraph 281

However, this definition is no longer conclusive, as ASB thinking has since moved on. Its latest ideas on accounting for heritage assets were contained in FRED42, as finalised and issued in June 2009 in the form of FRS30, under which the rules for capitalisation follow FRS15 instead of the compulsory *current value* accounting that had been advocated by its ill-fated predecessor, FRED40. Furthermore, under FRS30 fixed assets will count as 'heritage' only if they have:

'historic, artistic, scientific, technological, geophysical or environmental qualities [and are] held and maintained principally for [their] contribution to knowledge and culture'.

– paragraph 2, FRS30

This is subtly different from the SORP's concept of 'preservation/conservation purposes', in that using an asset (say) to teach with/in is not at all the same as using it to teach people about it. Thus a Grade 1 Listed Building would not count as heritage if used as classrooms for general educational purposes unless that use can be shown to be secondary to a primary use of educating the public about the history or architectural style, etc. of that particular building, or preserving/conserving it as a cultural treasure in its own right. Similar considerations would seem to apply to the artefacts that many long-established charities retain as 'treasures' collected over the centuries as part of their history.

Apart from that, the only change to the SORP's present treatment of heritage assets is that as well as being segregated in the balance sheet (distinguishing between those at cost and those at current value, if adopted) and supported by the kind of descriptive accounts note recommended in SORP 2005 (which under FRS30 should also provide some understanding of the asset-*values* involved – even where heritage assets are not capitalised), a five-year movements summary will have to be built up from the date of implementation of the new Standard.

It is clear from the text elsewhere that SORP 2005 uses the word 'objective' here to mean the charity's legally defined 'Object', the lawful aim or purpose for which it was set up in the first place, not just some management objective which at best could only be *ancillary* rather than *integral* to the furtherance of that legal purpose. Thus even a listed building acquired and used as, say, a school or residential care home, would not be a heritage asset if the charity could equally well further its purpose(s) by using a non-listed building instead. What the SORP doesn't bother to tell you, though, is that the owning charity does not have to be the reporting charity itself, but can be just a *special trust* of it, thus a restricted fund (capital or income) within its entity accounts – a fine distinction, perhaps, but one whose only parallel in the commercial world is with a subsidiary undertaking in group consolidated accounts.

The 1995 Charities SORP originally allowed inalienable/historic assets acquired by gift – or even, in certain cases, by purchase – for the charity's own (charitable) use on a continuing basis (ie as a fixed asset) to be expensed immediately. This option had to be *withdrawn* by SORP 2000, which in order to comply with FRS15 had to require capitalisation regardless of categorisation wherever an identifiable and reliable cost can be attributed to the asset – see **8.3.4**. Instead, since 'special' considerations govern their retention (if not also their actual use), SORP 2000 merely required (i) segregation in the balance sheet of any inalienable/historic assets that are capitalised, and (ii) adequate description of all such assets, both capitalised and non-capitalised, in the accounts notes – subject to (iii) safeguards against detrimental/prejudicial disclosures. The change under SORP 2005 was that only *heritage assets* are to be segregated and described in this way, while inalienability is no longer a factor to be considered for this purpose, and the non-disclosure exception has also gone.

'Heritage' versus 'inalienable' and 'historic' assets

8.3.1   The Glossary to SORP 2005 defines 'heritage' assets as:

> '... assets of historical, artistic or scientific importance that are held to advance preservation, conservation and educational objectives of charities and through public access contribute to the nation's culture and education either at a national or local level. Such assets are central to the achievement of the purposes of such charities and include the land, buildings, structures, collections, exhibits or artefacts that are preserved or conserved and are central to the educational objectives of such charities.
>
> Examples of these assets are:
>
> (a)   Charities with preservation objectives may hold specified or historic buildings or a complex of historic or architectural importance or a site where a building has been or where its remains can be seen.
> (b)   Conservation charities may hold land relating to the habitat needs of species, or the environment generally, including areas of natural beauty or scientific interest.
> (c)   Museums and art galleries hold collections and artefacts to educate the public and to promote the arts and sciences.'

– SORP 2005, Glossary GL 32

The SORP thus specifically disregards inalienability for this purpose – perhaps because of the success some charities have had in persuading the authorities that their prevailing circumstances now justify either borrowing on the security of the inalienable asset or even annulment of the long-standing disposal restriction, thus freeing up a perhaps substantial source of funding for the charity's public benefit activities. 'Inalienability' in the legal sense means a binding obligation, usually imposed by a founding donor or the terms of an appeal, as a *charity law* impediment to disposal of an asset representing a charitable gift. This may require unconditional retention, perhaps in perpetuity, or it may only stipulate replacement with something equivalent. It normally amounts to 'permanent' endowment – except that if the asset is obviously a 'wasting asset' the annual wastage will (by implication, if not expressly provided for) be a proper charge to capital as amortisation or depreciation.

In the case of some ancient religious and secular charities, and also the 43 Diocesan Boards of Finance of the Church of England, the statutory alienation of user-rights over certain school premises they own, premises now occupied and used on a rent-free but full-repairing basis by publicly funded statutory governing bodies running Voluntary Aided (VA) Schools quite independent of the school's founding body, had – prior to the advent of FRS15 and SORP 2000 – been cited as the justification for merely disclosing their ownership of such *uncapitalised* assets, as in the illustration below. Under FRS15 and SORP 2000, the argument may have been different but the result was the same, since the freehold land reversion that is all they have left can hardly have a material historical cost. The VA School body seems to have all the rights and obligations as sole user of the premises, rather than the freeholder, and so under FRS5 it must therefore be up to the former, not the latter, to capitalise all material expenditure on the buildings additions/extensions/improvements – however financed.

Principal accounting policies

Tangible fixed assets

Voluntary-aided schools
The freehold of the land and buildings legally owned by the charity and occupied rent free on behalf of the trustees of the governing bodies of Catholic voluntary-aided schools, which are separate charities and publicly funded, are valued at £nil. The trustees consider that no meaningful value can be attributed to these assets, since they are not used directly by the charity, do not generate income and cannot be disposed of in the open market or put to alternative use while such occupation, which may be indefinite, continues.

Sisters of Charity of St Vincent de Paul – 2007 Accounts

With its disregard of inalienability, the narrowed-down category of *heritage* assets in SORP 2005 still includes some of the 'historic' assets identified under SORP 2000, so that the current terminology must be taken as extending to both *endowed* and *un*endowed 'historic' assets of cultural (artistic or scientific) importance nationally or locally where held for the charity's own use, provided they are held *as part of the owning charity's asset-preservation/-conservation Objects* – ie not just to support/facilitate the furtherance of perhaps unrelated Objects. Thus their continuing use – even if severely restricted or only in replica form, where the original is considered too vulnerable, perhaps even irreplaceable – must not only directly provide a charitable benefit but that benefit must be of a heritage-education/cultural nature and also, under FRS30, the *primary* reason for retaining the asset.

Thus the few examples given in the SORP also include the scientific and artistic 'collections' of museums and galleries where the aim is public education/appreciation of 'heritage'.

The same criteria apply equally to such environmental heritage assets as nature reserves and wildlife sanctuaries acquired by conservation and preservation charities, where these assets are generically intrinsic to the furtherance of the charity's Objects – if, under FRS30, these focus on 'knowledge and culture'. Similarly with *non-investment* 'treasures' – again, see below.

Assets that, on the above basis, need to be segregated in the balance sheet and/or referred to in the notes would therefore seem to include such examples as:

(a)   the church buildings needed for the continued functioning of the religious community – but only where the building itself has special historic interest in relation to that religion so that the building's own "contribution to knowledge and culture" can be seen *as the primary reason for its continuing retention* – regardless of whether or not some external permission (ie external to the charity itself) is a precondition for disposal;

(b)   a nature reserve acquired by a conservation charity and retained on a long-term basis for the charity's own use in furtherance of its Objects *of an educational and/or cultural nature*, thus not as an investment;

(c)   a collection of artefacts or 'treasures' retained for preservation on a long-term basis for the sake of their cultural importance for, and in inseparable connection with, the effective furtherance of the owning charity's Objects – even if they themselves are only ancillary to that purpose (as with the perhaps quite valuable paintings, sculptures, memorabilia, etc of past presidents or other particularly significant features of the history of an old-established charity if it seems its effectiveness would decrease without them *and their preservation is primarily for what they can contribute to 'knowledge/culture'*).

Interestingly enough, SORP 2005 looks at this from the very opposite direction, only exemplifying as *non-heritage* assets (the emphasis here being ours):

'... where a charity:

(a)   holds and occupies an historic building as its administrative offices or as part of a property investment portfolio *unrelated to any preservation or educational purpose*;

(b)   has in its possession works of art, or a collection of historic importance, or antique furnishings within its boardroom, as a store of wealth, the retention of which is *unrelated to any objectives of preservation or education*;

(c)   occupies a functional property that is used to house or display a collection of heritage assets *(unless the property itself is held for preservation or conservation purposes)*.'

– SORP 2005, paragraph 289

The 'economic benefits' rule

8.3.2   As already mentioned above, the impact of FRS15 on the Charities SORP was to abolish the charity-specific capitalisation exemption under the 1995 SORP, and at the same time to modify the old SORP exemption for assets incapable of financial measurement by restricting it to *non-business* assets whose *reliable valuation* for capitalisation purposes is impossible or impracticable. This kind of asset is characterised as one that:

– provides little or no 'economic benefits' and so is not retained primarily for such purposes; *and* either

– even before FRS15 was exempted under SORP 1995 – otherwise it would surely have been capitalised before now; or

– has been donated since then as a *long-held* asset of the donor (ie no recent purchase data available); and

– cannot be valued by reference to any similar asset; and

– would be too expensive to value on any other basis (eg 'depreciated replacement cost' valuation of a gifted specialised institutional property?).

By superimposing its own commercial rules in place of the original 1995 SORP's *charity-specific* exemptions from capitalisation, FRS15 effectively subordinated this aspect of charities' *stewardship* accountability to the ASB's ultimate goal of 'fair value' balance sheets as a *reliable decision-making tool for 'investors'* – even though these are non-existent as a class when we speak of charity's 'stakeholders'. This must surely be counted as an 'own goal' by the Charity Commission, whose standard-setting authority as the regulator of a unique sector of the national economy of England and Wales (one that is dedicated to public benefit) goes far beyond that of a SORP-issuing body but still seems to have been dominated by the DBIS's (previously DBERR's) highly professional yet nonetheless *commercially driven* standard-setting body.

Thus, although the FRS itself recognises that charities do have special needs, the SORP is still unable to modify its application enough to meet those needs: apart from the principle of segregation (see below) it simply takes the commercial line of the FRS, declaring that in principle *all* tangible fixed assets – including the charity sector's heritage assets and regardless of whether or not an asset is inalienable – are to be capitalised in recognition of the:

– *future economic benefits* expected from them (not necessarily cash inflows);

– *stewardship* responsibilities of the trustees in respect of them; and

– *investment* of charity funds in them (acquisition, restoration, maintenance, etc).[1]

---

[1]   There must be serious reservations about the logic of the ASB's assumption here and in its published draft *'Statement of Principles for Financial Reporting: Proposed Interpretation for Public Benefit Entities'* in treating *charitable giving* (either *by* the charity in the course of its delivery of public benefit or *to* the charity in the form of donors' gifts of substantial fixed assets for its own use) as 'economic activities' in the same league as the *commercially* motivated transactions that are the proper focus of its standards.

Finally, we should note here that in its press briefings in connection with FRS30's precursor, FRED42, the ASB indicated that it would be monitoring what happens to the International Public Sector Accounting Standards Board's proposals on accounting for heritage assets in the wake of the IPSASB's 2008 consultation paper for a new Standard, the contents of which were based largely on those of the ASB. The point here is that the charity sector is clearly the alternative provider of public benefit where that is not provided by government to meet society's needs – hence the great relevance for the future development of charity accountability of these specialised international Standards that have been (and are continually being) derived by the IPSASB from the commercially oriented ones developed by the IASB and with a view to their voluntary adoption by governments around the world. As mentioned in an earlier chapter, these 'Public Benefit Accounting Standards', as we might best describe them, have been published and promoted as IPSAS/IPSFRS since 2002 by the New York based International Federation of Accountants Committee (IFAC) through the independent Board (IPSASB) it has set up for this purpose, and are rapidly gaining ground as the generally accepted basis internationally for reporting on public benefit provision.

Segregation in the balance sheet

8.3.3 Paragraphs 246–250 and 288 of the SORP specify a separate line in the fixed assets section of the balance sheet, below other functional fixed assets (intangible and tangible) and above investment fixed assets, in order to distinguish this special class of asset whose continuing retention and use is in some way bound up with, if not central to, the charity's stated purpose(s), thus making its continued retention operationally indispensable.

> 'Heritage assets should be included in a separate row in the balance sheet and can be further analysed, in the notes to the accounts, into classes appropriate to each charity, e g collections, artefacts and historic houses.'
>
> – *SORP 2005, paragraph 288*

As mentioned above, FRS30 requires the balance sheet presentation to distinguish between cost and current value (if adopted). This is to be supported by a suitable explanatory note, as discussed below.

Non-capitalisation

8.3.4 Many charities would have had accounting problems from 2000 onwards if they had been forced by the loss of all exemption to capitalise and depreciate these *special purpose* fixed assets at their 'fair value' in the absence of reliable information on historical cost or original gift value. Often, such an asset has been withdrawn from the 'marketplace' a long time ago, and its use is so bound up with the owning charity's primary purpose as to be effectively non-disposable, with any revenues from that use being subordinate to its main purpose of *facilitating the provision of public benefit*. Not having been acquired for economic reasons in the first place, heritage assets thus cannot reasonably be grouped together with normal 'business assets' whose retention and use is determined solely on economic grounds. In the event, the ASB took the line in FRS15 that it was the absence of an 'income stream' that was decisive – which is quite understandable, as it is one of the principal methods of measuring 'fair value'. Therefore *'unreliability'* forms one of the only two grounds for continuing non-capitalisation under the SORP:

'(a)   reliable cost information is not available and conventional valuation approaches lack sufficient reliability ...'.

– SORP 2005, paragraph 283

This is then heavily qualified by paragraph 287, which seeks to limit the scope of paragraph 283 by requiring that:

'Where assets are purchased by the charity or by another party who then shortly afterwards donates the asset to the charity, the purchase price should be considered as reliable cost information and could be used as a reference point for the fair value of donations of similar assets. Where an asset is partly purchased by the charity and partly donated, a reasonable estimate of the cost or value to the charity should be able to be made. Gifts on death or lifetime transfers of significant value may also carry valuations for inheritance tax purposes that may provide sufficient reliability.'

– SORP 2005, paragraph 287

What this caveat means in practice is that (apart from the special case of heritage 'collections' – see below) you can get away with non-capitalisation here only if your view that the initial carrying value would be too unreliable is not contradicted by *similar* assets having been donated by someone to another charity at a known capitalisation value.

There is a further 'grey' area in which a reliable value could possibly be arrived at, but only at a significant cost in professional advice/valuation fees which, in the charity sector (where economic value takes second place to the provision of *public benefit*), could all too easily outweigh the relatively slight benefit of capitalisation – perhaps burdening the charity unnecessarily. Fortunately, the ASB was persuaded that this does give ground for exemption for the sake of the public interest in charities, so that the SORP has been able to *extend* its exemption from capitalisation to where:

'(b)   significant costs are involved in the reconstruction or analysis of past accounting records or in valuation which are onerous compared with the additional benefit derived by users of the accounts in assessing the trustees' stewardship of the assets.'

– SORP 2005, paragraph 283

Many substantial properties gifted to charities for their own use are so specialised that a market-based valuation is impracticable, in which case a 'depreciated replacement cost' calculation by a property valuation expert may be the only way to obtain a reliable enough figure for capitalisation. But in the case of a *heritage* property its uniqueness in relation to the owning charity's legal purpose(s) can make even this problematical, perhaps leading to the conclusion that no reliable valuation is possible in the circumstances:

'... particular issues can arise in attempting to estimate the replacement cost of achieving the same service potential of certain historic buildings. The uniqueness of certain structures that are associated with particular locations, events, individuals or periods in history may be irreplaceable in terms of recreating the same service potential. The same service potential in terms of its heritage value or educational benefit to the public may only be achieved through the original structure or site.'

– SORP 2005, paragraph 285

Trustees would normally be expected to ensure that assets of this kind are not only properly protected but also insured for their replacement value – except where some lower level of insurance cover would be in the charity's best interests (eg the assets are irreplaceable or economically uninsurable, the insurance claim proceeds (monies) could be put to better use, or the charity is unable to pay the insurance premiums).

A word of caution is needed here concerning the disclosure, or especially the use for capitalisation purposes, of such an asset's insured value. Not only can the information incite the criminal mind, but it can also be misleading without knowing the basis, type and extent of cover in relation to the assets concerned. 'New for old' values can be very different from those based on 'fair wear and tear'. While 'replacement as new' may best satisfy charity management, 'current value for existing use' is clearly more meaningful to the reader of the accounts. Nor should it be overlooked that in the case of heritage properties, too, the *land* value will not normally be reflected in the property's fully insured 'replacement' value – which is assessed by reference to the expected 'rebuild' cost of making good the total loss (eg by fire) of only the buildings/contents, not the land.

Although for most charities not perhaps of much interest in themselves, being of quite limited scope, the SORP does offer the following as examples of hard-to-value heritage assets:

> '(a)   museum and gallery collections and other collections including the national archives;
> (b)   mediaeval castles, archaeological sites, burial mounds, ruins, monuments and statues.'
>
> – *SORP 2005, paragraph 286*

The 'collections' at (a) above are an interesting example for another reason: as can be inferred from item (c) of the examples cited in the SORP's Glossary definition at **8.3.1**, they can be regarded as a single asset whose components, the individual items making up the collection (or perhaps belonging to a class of item within it), can be replaced or exchanged at will without invalidating the basis on which the collection is excluded from, or segregated in, the balance sheet and identified in the accounts notes as a heritage asset. What this means in practice is that, as long as you can still claim that your 'off-balance-sheet' collection (or a class of item within it) remains 'unpriceable' as described above, you can keep on expensing the costs of improving/enlarging it (eg restoration, adding items of the same kind, etc), the corollary being that you must also bring any sales proceeds into the SoFA as well – certainly if these are to be spent on activities, or invested to produce a return for that purpose, or else used to acquire more utilitarian assets, rather than just being used to purchase replacement items.

> 'The assessment of the costs involved in establishing a cost or valuation for heritage assets and the benefits derived by users of accounts from this information will involve the separate consideration of any material sub-classes of assets held within the heritage asset category. Whilst the cost/benefit test may not be practical to apply on an individual asset by asset basis, it should considered in the context of particular parts or sub-classes of an overall collection. For example, in the context of a general museum valuing a fossil collection may be onerous but valuing its collection of vintage cars may not.'
>
> – *SORP 2005, paragraph 284*

In all these cases, however, the heritage assets, whether or not capitalised, must be described by way of note as explained at **8.3.6**.

'Treasures'

8.3.5 As with any fixed asset, the criteria for classification as *heritage* would seem to apply equally to 'treasures' permanently retained not primarily for their investment value but primarily for their contribution to 'knowledge and culture' under FR S30 (see above) and because for this purpose they are considered indispensable in the pursuit or furthering of the charity's wider-ranging Objects, being so much an intrinsic part of the charitable benefit being provided or aimed for that it would be detrimental for the charity not to continue using them in this way. Many long-established independent schools, professional associations, learned societies and the like have over the years – centuries, in some cases – acquired treasures of this kind, whose age, historic relevance and scarcity (if not uniqueness) tend to make up-to-date valuations unreliable or prohibitively expensive and whose cost or original gift-value gradually becomes immaterial due to inflation.

Although constituting a potentially valuable source of convertible wealth in situations of last resort, such as part-closure, 'down-sizing', etc, such assets may be no less misleading in a charity balance sheet prepared on a 'going concern' basis than would the capitalisation of the value of a 'friends' group' or supporter-network in recognition of their pledges of financial support to be called upon in time of need.

Such treasures will come within the SORP's as well as FRS30's definition of 'heritage' – provided they fulfil the SORP's essential 'public benefit' criteria by being held not just *for preservation or conservation purposes* within the owning charity's Objects but primarily to contribute **in themselves** to *knowledge and culture*. In short: the public must benefit directly in an educational/cultural sense from the retention and use (even if only in replica form) of 'treasures' by charities before they can properly be regarded as 'heritage' assets, and this would normally entail their *necessary* preservation/ conservation. This latter criterion (though not that of 'knowledge/culture') has been to some extent (ie, subject to the constraints of FRS30) recognised and obliquely provided for in the SORP in the context of the valuation and capitalisation of heritage treasures:

> 'Abbeys, Monasteries, Cathedrals, historic Churches and ancient centres of learning may not meet the heritage asset definition as the preservation of the buildings they occupy is unlikely to be the *primary* objective of the charity ... Similar issues may arise in the context of artefacts contained within and associated with such structures e g religious artefacts contained within a cathedral or historic church.' (emphasis added)
>
> *– SORP 2005, paragraph 293*

The meaning of the highlighted word 'primary' here seems analogous to that in 'primary purpose' trading, as defined in tax legislation, since elsewhere the SORP only requires such an objective to be specific to the Objects (ie declared legal purpose) of the owning charity – which itself could be a small part (e g a special trust) of the reporting charity as an entity:

> 'To fall within the definition of heritage assets, the charity must hold the relevant assets in pursuit of preservation or conservation objectives. The objective of the charity may be specifically of a preservation or conservation nature, or the heritage assets may be integral to a broader objective such as educating the public in history, the arts or science ...'.
>
> *– SORP 2005, paragraph 281*

Note 1(a) Tangible fixed assets
Heritage assets acquired prior to October 2006, comprising substantial collections of books, artefacts of scientific and historical interest and other museum pieces, are not capitalised as, in the view of the Trustee, the cost of valuing the entire collection would be onerous compared with the benefit derived by users of the Financial Statements in assessing the Trustee's stewardship of the assets. Significant purchases of heritage assets are capitalised.

The Wellcome Trust – Accounts for the year to 30 September 2008

Prior to FRS15, the 1995 SORP had been invoked as the authority for not capitalising these 'heritage' assets of the charity, which were described as 'inalienable', then in later years as 'historic'. Clearly, they are held as having special relevance for the trust's own continuing *charitable* use in furtherance of its Objects and not primarily for investment or other revenue-earning purposes. Now the authority relied on – subtly reworded in anticipation of the ASB's proposed new off-balance-sheet option where the collection as a whole is mostly (by value) unquantifiable or unreliable (as distinct from individual assets being in that category) – has to be one of the only two grounds left under FRS15: the significant administrative costs of bringing such assets onto the balance sheet would outweigh the benefit of the additional information to the user of the accounts.

Heritage asset disclosures

8.3.6   For all heritage assets – regardless of whether capitalised or not – paragraph 294 of the SORP requires the accounts notes to describe these assets in sufficient detail to enable the reader to appreciate their age/scale and nature and also the use being made of them by the charity. To this we must add FRS30's requirement for the disclosure to give the accounts-user an understanding of the asset-values involved. Even where the provision of such information is thought to constitute an unacceptable security risk, it cannot be entirely suppressed, as no such ground for non-disclosure is currently available under SORP 2005. However, the accounts note can be minimised to avoid duplicating detailed information already publicly available elsewhere, and descriptions can be made generic rather than specific to individual assets – a solution favoured by some charities. In many cases the public have viewing access (as in an art gallery) or assets have to be on show at public functions. Often, the most interesting and valuable of these (usually non-capitalised) assets are depicted in published catalogues, in many cases also on a free public access website, to which the accounts note could then easily be cross-referenced.

But the SORP also requires the following financial as well as the above narrative information:

> '… either:

> (i)   details of the cost (or value) of additions and disposals of heritage assets during the year; or
>
> (ii)   where details of cost or value are not available (non-capitalisation in previous periods), a brief description of the nature of the assets acquired or disposed of, together with the sales proceeds of any disposals …'.

– SORP 2005, paragraph 294(b)

Under FRS30 the above disclosure will have to be built up into a five-year summary of movements on heritage assets.

For *capitalised* heritage assets, the current-year information required under (i) can most easily be summarised within the usual fixed assets movements analysis note (see **8.4**) by showing them in a separate column (after a sub-total column for all other tangible fixed assets for the charity's own use), whereas (ii) clearly requires equivalent information in respect of any *non-capitalised* heritage assets. Since the difficulty of obtaining a reliable enough cost or gift value is currently the only acceptable reason for omitting any material fixed asset (heritage or otherwise) from the balance sheet, the alternative requirement here is logically for a description of all significant acquisitions and disposals in the year, the disclosure of sales proceeds for the latter presumably being meant to provide sub-analysis of the SoFA's 'Other Incoming Resources' category.

ASSET CLASSES/MOVEMENTS ANALYSIS

8.4   Not only must the balance sheet value of tangible fixed assets held for the charity's own use be split to distinguish any 'heritage' assets figure on a line of its own, as mentioned at **8.3.3**, but the total value for each of these two lines must then be analysed in the accounts notes in the usual way to show the year's movements in value for each of the following asset classes under specified headings:

'Tangible fixed assets for use by the charity should be analysed in the notes to the accounts within the following categories:

(a)   freehold interest in land and buildings;
(b)   leasehold and other interests in land and buildings;
(c)   plant and machinery including motor vehicles;
(d)   fixtures, fittings and equipment; and
(e)   payments on account and assets in the course of construction.

These are broad categories and any charity may, within reason, split the headings or adopt other narrower classes that meet the definition of a class of tangible fixed assets and are appropriate to its operations.'

– SORP 2005, paragraph 273

These classes (a) to (e) mirror those of the Companies Act 2006 and its Accounting Regulations – the difference being that the SORP excludes 'investment properties' here, requiring them to be accounted for as investment assets (see chapter 9). It is also noteworthy that non-company charities and charitable companies preparing consolidated accounts for a small group under the 1993 Act are not required by the SORP to distinguish between long and short leases, though charitable companies preparing accounts under company law must do so. In practice, heritage assets will rarely fall into any other category than (a) and (d), so that it will usually be possible to combine the current year's movements analysis for both heritage and non-heritage assets within the one accounts note by the insertion of additional columns as described at **8.3.6**.

Furthermore, each of the year's movements on each class of asset and in total must be disclosed in an accounts note, to illustrate which the SORP offers at paragraph 274 the following basic pro forma table (to save you having to twist your neck or the text around to read vertical print as in the SORP, we have used the above alphabetical referencing from the SORP for the column headings in respect of each required asset-class):

Analysis of Movements – Fixed Assets held for the Charity's own use

	(a)	(b)	(c)	(d)	(e)	Total
	£	£	£	£	£	£
Assets at cost/valuation or current value:						
Balance brought forward						
Additions						
Less: Disposals						
Revaluation adjustments						
Transfers between classes						
Balance carried forward						
Depreciation and impairment provisions:						
Balance brought forward						
Less: Disposals						
Revaluation adjustments						
Impairment charges						
Transfers between classes						
Charge for year						
Balance carried forward						
Net Book Value carried forward						
Net Book Value brought forward						

'Mixed use' for both functional and investment purposes

8.4.1 Many charities now find it expedient to exploit the commercial potential of spare space or time to obtain extra revenue from properties held for their own use by letting off unused parts, perhaps even whole properties temporarily, or by granting a licence for out-of-hours use of their main premises. While the income from such minor commercial exploitation does not count as an investment return, SORP 2005 takes a stricter line than the original 1995 SORP in saying that it is only where 'the asset is wholly or mainly used for charitable purposes' that the whole property's classification follows that primary use. Conversely, where the charity itself occupies only a small part of an investment property, or even the whole of it only temporarily, that functional use is ignored and the whole property has to be accounted for as an investment property. This applies even if a property is subdivided to make the two parts self-contained. In all other cases, i e where the split is a more even one, paragraph 257(c) of the SORP requires the separately distinguishable, let part to be *apportioned* as 'investment properties'. The SORP is strangely silent about dual-use properties where neither use is clearly primary nor the two parts 'separately distinguishable', and where apportionment would again seem to be the only true and fair way to account for the asset in the balance sheet.

As regards what counts as an 'investment property', the SORP's Glossary defines it as:

> '... an interest in land and/or buildings (a) in respect of which construction work and development have been completed and (b) which is held for its investment potential, any rental income being negotiated at arm's length.'

> – *SORP 2005, Glossary GL 39*

The definition then seeks to clarify that this does not include:

> '(a)   a property which is owned and occupied by [the charity] for carrying out its purposes; and that
> (b)   a property let to and occupied by *another group company* is not an investment property for the purposes of [the letting charity's] own accounts or the group accounts.'

> – *SORP 2005, Glossary GL 39*

The trouble with (b) is that the text has not been properly adapted from commercial accounting to meet the needs of *charity* accountability: it speaks of the reporting charity letting to 'another group company' as its tenant and says this is a functional (i e non-investment) use for both the charity's entity accounts and the group accounts. While that is a logical consequence upon consolidation it is invalid for the charity's own entity accounts, which cannot properly ignore charity law constraints on its activities, whose discretionary limits are thus too narrow to permit an FRS5-style 'substance over form' reporting of all transactions.

Even if the property is used by the group member wholly or mainly for activities *within the letting charity's own (functional) purposes* it could only be classified in the charity balance sheet as a *social investment* asset (see chapter 9) – not as a functional, thus non-investment asset.

If wholly or mainly used for non-charitable trading or commercial letting by the (separately accountable) group member, thus outside the charity's own charitable Objects, it would surely have to be classified in the charity balance sheet as an *investment* asset, just as the rental income from it would have to be classified as investment returns in the SoFA. The definition really ought to be expanded to make that distinction clear. The SORP does not dwell on the point, but it should be noted here that 'own use' or 'occupied by the charity' also covers staff housing, i e residential properties held for personal use or occupation under an employment contract – as distinct from a tenancy agreement negotiated at arm's length. The difference and its implications are not always fully understood by those involved in the preparation of charity accounts.

Thus even where, as a short-term measure, such staff housing is let out in the market for lack of qualifying staff to occupy it, so long as it is still reasonably retained for staff (or other operational) use you do not have to reclassify it as an investment property despite the temporary change of use.

CAPITALISATION THRESHOLDS

8.5   In practice, assets considered financially immaterial may always be excluded from capitalisation. This applies where the asset is below a 'reasonable' cost threshold. Many charities have so far set thresholds that are far too low, unaware that the administration costs of capitalising a multitude of small assets and tracking their depreciation properly for conformity with FRS15/11 could be a considerable unnecessary burden to them. Not so long ago, a very large charity sought their auditors' agreement to the raising of their capitalisation threshold from £250 to £500, when the net book value of assets held was close to £4m. The response was that they should only consider capitalisation of assets for amounts of £5,000 or more.

It is common practice in accordance with accounting standards to group together for threshold purposes assets acquired for use in 'sets'. For example, the bulk purchase of ten networked computers for £1,000 each would be capitalised as representing a single set exceeding the £5,000 threshold, whereas the (separate) bulk purchase of three printers for stand-alone use at a cost of £1,500 each would not.

Trustees have a duty to ensure that financial systems allow for proper control over all assets as regards location, safe-keeping and proper use, in order to guard against loss to the detriment of the charity and its work – whether or not they are capitalised. It is therefore good practice, where assets are numerous, to maintain some kind of Fixed Assets register, containing a sub-section for assets retained for use but not capitalised. The latter need is to be able to track assets above a relatively low cost threshold, and is quite separate from the need to set a reasonably high level for capitalising fixed assets in the financial accounts.

ACCOUNTING POLICY DISCLOSURES

8.6   The generally accepted accounting policy for fixed assets held for a charity's own use must, in view of the disciplines imposed by FRS15/11, be to carry them at cost, spreading their depreciable value evenly over their *currently* anticipated useful working life (see below). In practice, many charities used to account for these assets only where purchased with their own money, thus not for donated assets.

However, the Charities SORP provides comprehensive rules to show how the latter should be dealt with in the SoFA and balance sheet – see chapters 5 and 6. Historically, some charities may even have had a general policy not to capitalise any assets at all, but such a practice has always been incorrect.

Applying the Charities SORP's requirements has long ago resulted in charities having to review and re-align their accounting policies, to formulate them anew, to arrive at reasonable amounts to be included in the accounts, to determine appropriate depreciation policies and to explain the effect of prior years' adjustments.

The impact of the SORP due to the advent of FRS15 (or the current 'FRSSE', for those charities adopting it as their accounting policy) entailed further changes for most charities – even if only through slight but significant adjustments to the wording of their existing accounting policies, particularly where (as was mostly the case) the depreciable life/amount had not previously been reviewed and adjusted in line with *current* expectations as required under FRS15/11 and reflected in the SORP.

Thus even where charities have chosen the 'least cost' option by avoiding the intricacies of 'current value' accounting under the rules of FRS15, carrying values nevertheless do need to be reviewed annually for depreciation adequacy – and in some cases also for possible 'impairment'. (Under the FRSSE, only 'regular' (rather than annual) reviews of residual values and useful economic lives are required, with revisions only 'when necessary', and the disciplines of 'impairment' reviews are largely relaxed.)

The decisions this can involve for non-FRSSE charities are summarised in the following flowchart.

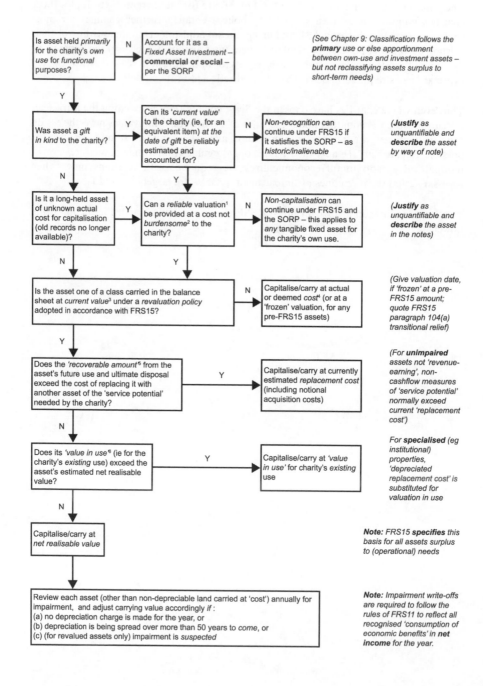

NOTES

(1)   Paragraphs 17 and 18 of FRS15 allow non-capitalisation of [donated heritage and other 'own use' fixed assets which] 'present measurement difficulties where conventional valuation approaches lack sufficient reliability'.

(2)   Non-capitalisation is also allowed by FRS15/SORP where *significant* costs of valuation 'are onerous compared with the additional benefit derived by users of the accounts in assessing management's stewardship of the assets'.

(3)   Defined by FRS15 as the lower of *replacement cost* (ie 'the least cost of purchasing the remaining service potential of the asset') and *recoverable amount* (of future economic benefits, including ultimate disposal proceeds, expected to be derived from the asset).

(4)   The initial valuation on capitalising a gift in kind or a long-held asset of unknown cost (FRS15, paragraph 43 footnote).

(5)   Defined by FRS15 as the higher of *value in use* (also known as 'existing use value' (EUV), as defined by FRS11) and *net realisable value* (ie net of selling costs on immediate disposal).

(6)   Defined by FRS11 as 'the present value of the future cashflows obtainable as a result of an asset's continued use, including those resulting from its ultimate disposal' – subject to paragraph 20:

> 'If a fixed asset is not held for the purpose of generating cash flows either by itself or in conjunction with other assets, for example certain fixed assets held for charitable purposes, it is not appropriate to measure the asset at an amount based on expected future cash flows. In such cases it may not be appropriate to write down the fixed asset to its recoverable amount – an alternative measure of its service potential may be more relevant.'

A typical accounting policy for fixed assets to comply with the SORP here might read as follows:

Fixed assets for the charity's own use

Except as set out below, all fixed assets acquired for the charity's own use are capitalised at their purchase cost or cost of production/improvement. Gifts in kind are capitalised at their estimated value to the charity at the time of gift.

Costs of fixed assets incurred prior to 1980 have not been capitalised, as the amounts are immaterial. Gifts in kind where the gift value cannot be reliably estimated (or only at undue cost outweighing the benefit of the information to users of the accounts) have not been capitalised.

Costs of maintaining properties occupied by the charity are written off as incurred.

Items of furniture and equipment costing less than £2,000 each are treated as an expense on acquisition.

No depreciation is provided on freehold land, or on heritage or inalienable assets expected to last in use longer than another 50 years, subject to annual impairment reviews.

In other cases, depreciation is provided at rates calculated to write off the excess of cost over estimated residual value (at prices ruling at the time of acquisition) evenly over the currently estimated useful working life of the asset, which for the following classes of asset is initially assessed as: ➡

Freehold buildings	50 years
Leased property (or: lease-term, if shorter)	50 years
Improvements to leased property	10–20 years
Furniture and equipment	3–10 years
Motor vehicles	4 years

DEPRECIATION AND IMPAIRMENT

8.7   The cost or value of all capitalised assets that wear out in use, or otherwise lose value over time, clearly needs to be recognised as expenditure in the SoFA, thus charged as an expense spread over the asset's useful working life. The Companies Act Regulations refer to 'provisions for depreciation calculated to write off that amount systematically over the period of the asset's useful economic life', while the Charities SORP 2005, reinforced by its related Regulations, builds on the work of FRS11/15 in summarising their rules for 'charging depreciation' (paragraph 259).

Thus, all capitalised tangible assets which are considered to have a limited useful working life should be depreciated over that life in accordance with *current* (ie up-to-date) expectations. The amount to be depreciated will be the historical cost or subsequent revaluation (the asset's 'carrying value' in the balance sheet) less any anticipated eventual sale proceeds ('residual value') – discounted for inflation back to the asset's acquisition date, where material. (Under FRS15, those proceeds are to be estimated by reference to the purchasing power of money *at the time of acquisition/revaluation.*)

This is summarised by the SORP by saying that:

> 'The useful economic lives and residual values of fixed assets should be reviewed at the end of the accounting period and, where there is a material change, the value of the asset should be depreciated over its remaining useful life.'
>
> *– SORP 2005, paragraph 260*

To be more specific, FRS15 requires both the life-expectancy and (if material) the ultimate disposal value to be reassessed each year and the calculation of depreciable amount and term revised for any *material* change 'prospectively', ie without retroactive effect – except for two special cases: 'impairments' and *revalued* assets:

> 'If a tangible fixed asset is carried in the balance sheet at a revaluation (particularly if valued using depreciated replacement cost), a reassessment of useful economic life may necessitate a revaluation of the asset ... The revalued amount should be depreciated over the revised useful economic life.
>
> A change in its estimated residual value should be accounted for prospectively over the asset's remaining useful economic life, except to the extent that the asset has been impaired at the balance sheet date.'
>
> *– FRS15, paragraphs 94–95*

In practice, however, apart from buildings on valuable land, it is quite rare for residual values to be allocated to assets that are not frequently replaced (eg cars), and for depreciation to be charged at a rate that does not eliminate the capitalised cost (or value). FRS15 retains this principle, whereas the FRSSE does so only where the effect is 'significant'.

The rate of depreciation used should be disclosed in the accounting policy note, as indicated at **8.6**. This may be done by reference either to the initially estimated life of each class of asset (as illustrated there) or by, for example, a percentage rate applied each year. It is most usual in current practice to apply a straight-line depreciation rate. This method writes off the depreciable amount evenly over time. The usual alternative is the reducing balance (or WDV) method, where the stated percentage is calculated on the written down balance – ie after deducting all previous depreciation. The latter is usually considered preferable where maintenance costs increase significantly with the age of the asset, as with older properties, motor vehicles and equipment retained for use well past their normal 'sell-by' date.

A change from one method to another has no retroactive effect:

> 'A change from one method of providing depreciation to another is permissible only on the grounds that the new method will give a fairer presentation of the results and of the financial position. Such a change does not, however, constitute a change of accounting policy; the carrying amount of the tangible fixed asset is depreciated using the revised method over the remaining useful economic life, beginning in the period in which the change is made.'
>
> – *FRS15, paragraph 82*

Thus the normal rule is that the trustees should choose whichever method seems most appropriate to each type of asset – and stick to it.

Note 1(a): Accounting policies –
Tangible fixed assets
Tangible fixed assets excluding land, held by the Group and the Trust are stated at cost less accumulated depreciation. Land is stated at cost. Depreciation is calculated using the straight-line method ... The useful lives for depreciation purposes for the principal categories of assets are: ... buildings 50 years ...

The Wellcome Trust – 2007/08 Accounts

Normal practice in the commercial sector for many years used to be to assess the anticipated useful economic life of a structurally substantial freehold building – such as the Trust's old headquarters opposite London's Euston Station – at a notional 50 years and to depreciate it over that period with no allowance for residual value, thus on the assumption that the building will have to be replaced. Since 2000, however, FRS15 has imposed a rather more refined practice of 'fair value' balance sheet accounting, though without any discernible effect on this giant charity so far.

Assets which do not normally depreciate or are considered to have an indefinitely long useful life, such as land, are not subjected to such a charge – in the absence of special factors, of course, such as population migration or toxicity leading to a permanent diminution in value. This can bring practical difficulties when considering freehold land and buildings, for it is often not easy to allocate the cost reliably between the land and the buildings standing on it. The conundrum arises where the sum of the parts appears to be greater than the whole.

When buying or revaluing such property, or on reviewing it for possible impairment, the trustees should therefore consult their advisers as to a reasonable allocation. When considering the advice received, trustees should be aware of two conflicting approaches. It is possible to allocate full value to the land, and treat the balance as attributable to the buildings. This may understate the cost to the charity of using the buildings. On the other hand, to attribute full value to an existing building by reference to rebuild costs may well understate the amount attributable to the land. If the building purchased was built some years previously, a reasonable 'second-hand' value needs to be assessed. This difficulty is less likely to arise with a new building.

Other assets which are not depreciated are those in course of construction. It is a basic principle that assets are only depreciated once they are made available for use, and not while they are still being prepared or constructed. As with other costs, depreciation should be allocated in the SoFA within the relevant expenditure headings, principally 'charitable activities' and 'costs of generating funds', according to the use made of the various assets that are being depreciated.

Thus the depreciation of assets used solely for or in support of furthering the charity's Objects – for example, beds in a residential home/hostel/hospice – should be treated as part of the costs of 'charitable activities'. Likewise, the depreciation of furniture and equipment used in the fundraising department should be treated as part of the 'costs of generating funds', whereas depreciation on buildings used partly for both kinds of activity should be apportioned between them on a fair and reasonable basis – for example, according to floor space occupied. When this is done there is no need to make special disclosure of the total depreciation charged in the SoFA, as this will be apparent from the fixed assets movement note supplementing the balance sheet.

In the not so distant past, it was common (and incorrect) practice for many charities not to capitalise assets at all. Somewhat paradoxically, others have not depreciated capitalised buildings used for charitable purposes, arguing that their expenditure on repairs and maintenance, in particular of the 'fabric' or 'structure', was of such a high standard that there was no actual 'wearing out' in use – that their useful working life was always 'indefinite' (if not quite perpetual).

After a long-overdue re-examination of accounting practices in this area, the ASB eventually issued FRS11 to lay down new rules on accounting for 'impairment' of an asset's carrying value and, later on, FRS15 covering the wider issues of capitalisation, carrying values, revaluation, anticipated residual values and the basis of recognition of annual depreciation.

As explained earlier in this chapter and more precisely in the FRS15 Decision Tree Flowchart above, FRS15 as reflected in the SORP considerably tightened the rules concerning the basis of any revaluation of fixed assets held for a charity's own use. By constraining the assessment of residual values, the FRS makes it almost impossible to avoid charging depreciation in respect of 'wasting' assets.

The ASB also took the view that 'in the longer term' the residual values of fixed assets held for 'own use' will *invariably* be less than initial capitalisation values – measuring these anticipated residual values (which, together with the asset's anticipated useful economic life, must be *annually* reassessed under FRS15) by reference to *prices ruling at the time of acquisition or revaluation*.

Thankfully, FRS15 itself – and therefore the SORP – does not take quite such a hard line as that indicates: there is *no* exclusion of the *appreciation* that can arise from changes in *supply and demand* – for example 'heritage' value; 'alternative use' potential, etc. Instead, FRS15 imposes an FRS11-type 'impairment' review on an *annual* basis if little or no depreciation is being charged. This is required even where depreciation is ignored as immaterial, also where the asset is not a 'revalued' asset. It is required in any case where charities wish to continue spreading depreciation over more than 50 years ahead on what may, for example, be a substantial and impeccably maintained institutional property used for carrying out their charitable purposes.

The traditional argument that depreciation charges at such low rates as 1% or 2% are 'immaterial' is severely constrained by FRS15's insistence on the potential materiality of the *accumulated* charge needed to reflect the ratio between the currently anticipated remaining life and the total life of such a property.

The FRSSE greatly simplifies the FRS15/11 rules for those charities allowed by the SORP to adopt it. But it does not relax the rule that while it is acceptable not to depreciate assets of indefinite life or whose currently anticipated *inflation-discounted* ultimate residual value is no less than their initial capitalisation value or subsequent revaluation, it is not acceptable to adopt such a policy (ie of non-depreciation) just because the asset's current market value happens to exceed book value. In the SORP's own words:

> 'The only exceptions to charging depreciation arise where any of the following conditions apply:
>
> (a)   the asset is freehold land which is considered to have an indefinitely long useful life;
> (b)   both the depreciation charge and the accumulated depreciation are not material because:
>   (i)   the asset has a very long useful life; or
>   (ii)   the estimated residual value (based on prices at the time of acquisition or subsequent revaluation) of the asset is not materially different from the carrying amount of the asset.
>   If depreciation is not charged because of immateriality, FRS 15 requires that the asset is subject to an annual impairment review (except for charities under the threshold for following the FRSSE); or
> (c)   the assets are *heritage assets* and have not been included in the balance sheet (see paragraphs 279 to 294).' (emphasis added)
>
> – *SORP 2005, paragraph 259*

(The FRSSE reference is just a reminder that under that Standard 'impairment' reviews are not unconditionally *annual* but only 'where necessary'.)

The apparent restriction here to *heritage assets,* as highlighted above, is an interesting one, as it can't be implying that FRS15's non-capitalisation rules apply *only* to heritage assets (which they don't), but it is also stating the obvious: you can't 'depreciate' a 'nil' value in the balance sheet!

Where the trustees do feel that no depreciation is required, an appropriate policy might be worded as follows:

Properties for charitable use
It is the policy of the Trustees to maintain buildings held for charitable use in such condition that their useful economic life is indeterminate. In the opinion of the Trustees, the favourable location of those properties, combined with this policy, results in the residual value of the properties (by reference to prices ruling at the time of their acquisition or revaluation) being not less than their present carrying value in the accounts. Consequently no depreciation is charged on these properties.

The great variety of situations and circumstances involved make it impossible to illustrate here all aspects of accounting for fixed assets held for a charity's own use, but the following extracts from the annual accounts of Help the Aged do seem to cover most of the issues that normally have to be considered:

NOTE 12: TANGIBLE FIXED ASSETS	Freehold and long leasehold properties	Gifted Housing	Short leasehold shops	Motor vehicles	Equipment fixtures and fittings	Total
	£'000	£'000	£'000	£'000	£'000	£'000
CHARITY AND GROUP						
Cost or donated valuation						
At 1 May 2007	2,094	6,369	8,104	3,580	997	21,144
Additions	-	216	47	297	153	713
Transfer	(100)	(117)	-	-	-	(217)
Disposals	–	(136)	-	(536)	-	(672)
At 30 April 2008	**1,994**	**6,332**	**8,151**	**3,341**	**1,150**	**20,968**
Depreciation						
At 1 May 2007	203	608	7,741	2,313	506	11,371
Charge for year	22	100	236	510	181	1,049
Transfer	(47)	(26)	-	-	-	(73)
Eliminated on disposal	–	(20)	-	(530)	-	(550)
At 30 April 2008	**178**	**662**	**7,977**	**2,293**	**687**	**11,797**
Net book value						
At 30 April 2008	**1,816**	**5,670**	**174**	**1,048**	**463**	**9,171**
At 30 April 2007	*17891*	*5,761*	*363*	*1,267*	*491*	*9,773*

During 2008 the Charity transferred from freehold properties and Gifted Housing portfolio assets with a net book value of £53K and £91K respectively (total £144K) to investment properties as shown in Note 13
...

NOTE 1. ACCOUNTING POLICIES

...

(f) Tangible Fixed Assets and Depreciation
Tangible fixed assets costing more than £2,000 are capitalised and included at cost including any incidental expenses of acquisition. Depreciation and any impairment is provided on all tangible fixed assets at rates calculated to write off the cost on a straight line basis over their expected useful economic lives as follows:

> Freehold land – nil
> Freehold and long leasehold properties and gifted housing – over 50 years

...

(j) Gifted Housing Scheme
Gifted houses are accounted for as income when donated at market valuation. A qualified surveyor carries out the valuations. When an individual donates a house to the Charity, the Charity is committed to caring for that individual. An actuarial valuation of the total cost of care for individuals who have gifted their house is made and the sum is included within provisions for liabilities and charges
...

Help the Aged – 2007/08 Accounts

Comment

No matter how detailed the analysis of the year's movements in value by class of tangible fixed assets held for 'own use', if those classes are too broad you could still be in the dark about some key aspect – as used to be the case here for the relationship between these 'gifted properties', where the elderly donor continues to reside in the house until in need of non-domiciliary care, and the more usual use of institutional properties as residential/care homes for the elderly – until the charity began treating these as two different classes, as above.

Furthermore, to comply with FRS15 upon its implementation, the charity's depreciation basis for freehold and long leasehold properties was changed in the 1999/2000 accounts (see second edition) to the minimum rate needed (as set out above) in order to avoid automatic impairment reviews in future. But instead of just validating the existing carrying values by reference to their 'service potential' as allowed by the Standard (and later by SORP 2000), all the properties seemed to have been revalued – yet with the resultant £1m write-down being accounted for as additional depreciation rather than as a reduction of the gross carrying value, which apparently had not changed from cost. This was presumably done to avoid any commitment to a 'current value' accounting policy for the future under FRS15 if the new valuation had been adopted as the gross carrying value on or after implementing that Standard. At the time, it was also disclosed in the accounts that Gifted Houses had been valued at open market value by firms local to each property, which also seemed to be reflected in the Accounting Policies disclosure that 'Fixed assets are stated at cost or donated valuation'. As there is no such accounting policy disclosure in these accounts for Gifted Housing, even though the figure is clearly a material item, we must assume that their gross carrying value is as required by the SORP: open market value at the date of gift, as their 'deemed cost' for FRS15 purposes.

'Service potential' as a charity-specific measure of 'impairment'

8.7.1   FRS11 tightened up the old SSAP12 rules for recognising the consumption or 'wearing out' of an asset in use or in the course of time as a charge against income.

This tightening was taken even further by FRS15's introduction of annual reviews for possible 'impairment' under the rules of FRS11 in respect of *non-depreciated* capitalised assets, as well as of those being *depreciated* over more than 50 years – which will normally mean permanent buildings rather than other kinds of asset.

But the SORP makes it quite clear that for assets used primarily to provide *charitable* (ie free or subsidised) benefit (rather than primarily to generate funds – where cash returns must be the obvious consideration), an impairment review does not have to be a complex and burdensome exercise:

> 'Many charities have fixed assets that are not held for the main purpose of generating surplus cash flows either by themselves or in conjunction with other assets. In these cases it is not appropriate to measure the value in use of the asset at an amount based on expected future cash flows. Instead an alternative measure of its service potential will be more relevant, such as the intrinsic worth of the service delivery or the replacement cost of the asset. Each charity can determine its own measure of service delivery but this must be reasonable, justifiable and consistently operated.'

> *– SORP 2005, paragraph 268*

As suggested in previous editions of this book, it would be more helpful, however, if the SORP could go on to explain what 'service potential' means in practice, perhaps by including an example or two of a 'measure of service delivery'. Instead, it just lists a selection of possible causes, based on commercial life:

> 'Events or changes which may indicate an impairment include:

> (a)   physical deterioration, change or obsolescence of the fixed asset;
> (b)   social, demographic or environmental changes resulting in a reduction of beneficiaries for a charity;
> (c)   changes in the law, other regulations or standards which adversely affect the activities of a charity;
> (d)   management commitments to undertake a significant reorganisation;
> (e)   a major loss of key employees associated with particular activities of a charity;
> (f)   operating losses on activities using fixed assets primarily to generate incoming resources.'

> *– SORP 2005, paragraph 268*

This could become a major issue for those charities with substantial elderly properties held for their own use. Such situations are more common in the charity sector than in the commercial world. Unlike their commercial counterparts, even charities that *charge* at a market rate for their public-benefit services still cannot be said to be holding the fixed assets they use to achieve this mainly for 'generating surplus cashflows', since that would be incompatible with their charitable status, which dictates that 'making money' out of a primary-purpose trading activity must take second place to providing the public benefit for which the charity is established. Subtle as the distinction may seem at first sight, it points to a fundamental difference in motivation and therefore *public* accountability, which is why the charity is given greater latitude here than its commercial counterpart, as explained in the SORP paragraph quoted above.

Here is an example taken from a seminar on this subject:

> A hospice or other residential care establishment may be able to continue servicing 40 beds from year to year on a charitable basis to meet community needs where perhaps the same unit operating on a more commercial basis would be shut down as uneconomic. '40 beds' may then be taken as the measure of 'service potential' of the assets in question to show that their 'value in use' *to the charity* remains undiminished. In that case, although of uncertain 'recoverable amount', the present carrying value (net book value) of these assets need not be reduced for impairment.

It is also unhelpful that (apart from the special case of heritage properties, discussed earlier) the SORP makes no mention of how charities should apply the provisions of FRS15 concerning the valuation of *specialised* properties, with a *charity* accounting requirement for interim 5-year valuations. This omission fails to recognise that properties used for the functioning of service-providing charities (eg schools, hospices, residential care homes, etc) do often have to be highly specialised. The valuation of these 'institutional' properties for their existing use can be difficult enough to require a special approach to be explained in the SORP itself.

The SORP does at least make clear, in the public interest, the fact that charities do not necessarily have to spend money on such 'accounting valuations':

> 'Independent formal professional valuations are not mandatory in the case of a charity, which instead may obtain a valuation from a suitably qualified person who could be a trustee or employee.'
>
> – *SORP 2005, paragraph 265*

GAINS AND LOSSES

On disposal

8.8.1   When assets for the charity's own use are eventually sold at the end of their useful life, the proceeds may differ from the depreciated amount brought forward. The treatment of the realised gain or loss on such sales differs between the SoFA and the income and expenditure account of a company. In the SoFA, any excess of proceeds over carrying amount (ie, a gain) is treated as an incoming resource, not as an item reducing expenditure (see the Charities SORP, paragraph 218(b)), except insofar as the gain clearly arises from excessive depreciation due to underestimation of asset lives or over-estimation of the rate of depletion, and is not simply a reflection of market changes. Losses are treated as an additional expense, in the same way as the depreciation charge, and should be allocated to the appropriate expense heading. In an income and expenditure account, it is usual practice to treat the gain or loss on disposal (unless exceptional) as an adjustment to the overall depreciation cost. This treatment, however, is not a valid reason for the separate production of a summary income and expenditure account (see chapter 7). Charitable companies accounting under company law should therefore follow the requirements and presentation recommended in the Charities SORP. Where the gain or loss is exceptional in size it should be included in the normal heading in the SoFA and explained in the notes to the accounts. If, however, it is so large that not to show it separately would lead to the accounts being unable to show a true and fair view, then under FRS3, any such gain or loss is to be shown separately after the operating result on ordinary activities. It would not be at all unusual for a charity to show an exceptionally large gain on disposal of a functional asset, but this cannot be grounds for excluding the incoming resource from the top section of the SoFA. FRS3 segregates non-operational results in the net income statement, but for charities, even a disposal of, say, a valuable painting from the collection of an art gallery (or an independent school) could be said to be part of its operational activities.

Or on revaluation

8.8.2   Where assets for the charity's own use are revalued *upwards*, their depreciation will have to be recalculated, with the resultant increase being reported in the SoFA on the special revaluation gains/losses line for these assets, and in the column relevant to the fund to which the asset belongs – except to the extent that it needs to be recognised as *negative expenditure* reversing any previously charged 'impairment' loss(es) in that section:

> 'Revaluation gains or losses (which are not considered to be impairment losses ...) on assets held for the charity's own use should be included in the section on gains and losses on revaluations of fixed assets for the charity's own use.'

> *– SORP 2005, paragraph 218(c)*

Where the revaluation is *downwards*, it will represent 'impairment' to the extent that the resultant charge in the SoFA exceeds any previously recognised *revaluation gains* on that asset, but the treatment of that excess can vary in the case of a charitable company accounting under company law.

For *non-company* charities and wherever else accounts are prepared under the 1993 Act (eg, a charitable company's *consolidated* accounts for a 'small' group as defined by the Companies Act 2006), the excess (being a reduction of carrying value below the level of the properly depreciated historical/deemed cost) is charged in the expenditure section of the SoFA, in the column relevant to the fund to which the asset belongs:

> 'Impairment losses of assets held for the charity's own use (ie not investments) should be regarded as additional depreciation of the impaired asset and included appropriately in the resources expended section of the Statement of Financial Activities.'

> *– SORP 2005, paragraph 218(a)*

To fulfil this requirement, your accounting records obviously have to be complete and detailed enough to be able to track the original cost of each asset, the amounts of all subsequent annual revaluations and all depreciation charges.

For a *charitable company accounting under company law*, revaluation movements on assets that are its own *corporate* property – whether upwards or downwards – should technically be taken to 'revaluation reserve' (whose balance must by law be distinguished in the balance sheet), and this can include impairment charges. The 2006 Companies Act does continue to allow the corporate revaluation reserve to become negative – though this obviously cannot be allowed to go so far that it then apparently compromises *trust* funds, if possible liability for breach of trust is to be avoided. Where, however, the impairment is considered 'permanent', the resultant loss is chargeable to the income and expenditure account under the Companies Act and will thus go to the expenditure section of the SoFA.

Each asset must be considered individually in measuring any valuation adjustment.

ACCOUNTS ON THE RECEIPTS AND PAYMENTS BASIS

8.9 Where a small *non-company* charity (ie below the new £250,000 (previously £100,000) 'gross income' threshold, as discussed in chapter 16) opts out of accruals accounting, under English law it is not required to account for asset *values* other than the net change in its year-end cash balances. This means that annual accounts on such a basis cannot recognise *non-monetary* changes caused by the depreciation or revaluation of fixed assets. Instead of a balance sheet, in England and Wales the charity is required simply to list and describe all significant assets and liabilities in a memorandum Statement, indicating to which fund (if the charity has any endowed or other restricted funds) each listed item belongs. The only 'linking' item will be the year-end cash balance(s) carried forward in the annual receipts and payments account(s) reporting all money movements on each of its funds. (In Scotland it is slightly different: the SORP's related 2006 Regulations also specify the contents of any 'Receipts and Payments Account' and the year-end 'Statement of Balances' that must accompany it and which therefore includes book values for all non-cash assets.)

The list will include a narrative description of the tangible and other assets used by the charity, which if they are numerous could usefully be listed by class of asset as already described. As with accruals accounts, the list will need to include assets held on finance leases or hire purchase (but not operating leases, because these are not (yet) regarded as resulting in 'ownership' for annual accounting purposes). To be helpful to the reader it should also distinguish any heritage or inalienable assets.

In addition to the description of the assets held, the charity should include an indication of the age and condition (ie its usability or state of repair) of each major asset.

Chapter 9

INVESTMENT ASSETS

INTRODUCTION

9.1 This chapter covers the balance sheet valuation of securities, properties and other assets of a charity that are held wholly/primarily for either commercial or 'social' (ie charitable) investment purposes, their classification as long-term or short-term – thus as fixed or current assets – and the accounting treatment of gains and losses arising on their annual revaluation and ultimate disposal. It highlights the differences between Companies Act and Charities Act requirements, and also deals with the little-understood problem of accounting for 'investment pooling'.

DEFINITIONS

9.2 It is important to start by defining what we mean by 'investment' if charities are to be able to account properly for using their resources in such a way. This is so because concepts of charity and civil society continue to evolve under the pressure of social conscience, and so do our ways of 'investing in the future'. In line with SORP 2005 and its related 2008 Regulations under the Charities Act 2006, we therefore need to recognise that investment by charities may be either:

(a) **commercial** – ie primarily with a view to securing either (i) the best possible investment return obtainable in the capital markets *unconstrained* by any ethical, social or environmental considerations (the traditional legal obligation) or (ii) the best possible return within any such *constraints of the investing charity's declared Objects* (in line with prevailing concepts of 'socially responsible' investing); or

(b) **charitable** – ie primarily as a means of delivering public benefit either through soft loans to individuals in need or through the loan-funding of or equity participation in a charitable project undertaken by a third party. This is actually a hybrid form of charitable activity standing somewhere between grant-making and investing – depending on the circumstances and expectations of both parties and the commitments they agree to make to each other in respect of the transaction.

Investment properties

SORP 2005 explains that:

> '... investment assets are generally held with the overall intention of retaining them long-term (ie as fixed assets) for the continuing benefit of the charity in the form of income and capital appreciation.'

> – *SORP 2005, paragraph 295*

That 'assets' here means both securities and properties (among other things of value that count as 'qualifying' investments for charity and tax law purposes) is made clear by the previous sentence of that paragraph, dealing with the balance sheet classification:

> 'Investment assets (including investments and investment properties ... and cash held for investment purposes) should be classified as a separate category within fixed assets except where the intention is to realise the asset without reinvestment of the sale proceeds. In such a case, it should be reclassified as a current asset.'
>
> *– SORP 2005, paragraph 295*

The 'fixed assets' of charities are defined by the SORP's related 2008 Regulations in the following terms:

> '*"fixed assets"* means the assets of a charity which are intended for use or investment on a continuing basis.'
>
> *– SI 2008/629, reg 2*

Perhaps because the topic is covered in some depth on the Charity Commission website, SORP 2005 seems to refrain from defining 'investment' more closely, leaving its 'investment properties' definition looking almost circular:

> '... an investment property is an interest in land and/or buildings:
>
> ...
>
> (b)   which is held for its investment potential, any rental income being negotiated at arm's length.'
>
> *– SORP 2005, Glossary GL 39*

For the avoidance of doubt, SORP 2000 had explained more fully what are and are not to be regarded as investment properties for charity accounting purposes:

> '"investment property" is an interest in land and/or buildings which is held *primarily* for the purpose of producing an income for the charity, any rental income being negotiated at arm's length. It does not include:
>
> (a)   land acquired primarily with a view to resale at a profit, whether or not after development; or
>
> (b)   property which is owned and *mainly* occupied by the charity for carrying out its purposes.' (emphasis added)
>
> *– SORP 2000, Glossary GL 18*

The above two words, *primarily* and *mainly* (as emphasised by us), should be especially noted. SORP 2005 instead refers to a property being used 'wholly or mainly' for investment or own use – which in our view renders essentially the same meaning. Much of the confusion about accounting for freehold and leasehold properties as investment assets – apart from the special case where they are let out only temporarily, whilst not needed for immediate operational use – concerns *dual-use* (or 'mixed use') properties, partly for the charity's own activities and partly let out for investment purposes. See **8.4.1**, where this is explained in detail from the 'own use' side.

However, it must be clear from the wording of paragraphs 168–169, dealing with cost attribution, allocation and apportionment to activity-based expenditure headings, and paragraph 257(c), quoted below, that SORP 2005, too, does not want trustees to flounder at this point:

> 'Land and buildings which contain clearly distinguishable parts which are held for different purposes ie partly functional and partly investment and [are not primarily one thing or the other] should be apportioned and analysed in the balance sheet between functional and investment assets.'
>
> – *SORP 2005, paragraph 257(c)*

Unless the *primary* purpose for which the property is being retained is dictated by the terms of trust of the (restricted) fund to which it belongs, or by operational circumstances, such an allocation or apportionment may need to be supported by clarification of the trustees' declared policies for the furtherance of the charity's Objects in the longer term. Clearly, however, any allocation according to a property's *primary* use must also imply the adoption of an appropriate accounting policy – one that similarly avoids apportioning the property's running costs in the SoFA.

Commercial investment

9.2.1 Thus the SORP and its related Regulations base their requirements on the duty that charity law imposes on trustees to 'apply' all resources in furtherance of the charity's Objects – subject to any specific constitutional powers/restrictions governing the manner in which this is to be achieved. This makes it a fundamental necessity to distinguish all investment assets between:

(a)   'charitable' and 'commercial' investment use; and

(b)   long- and short-term use.

If the primary objective is not charitable in a *positive* sense (to provide some particular public benefit within the investing charity's Objects), a commercial objective will be assumed – even where the investment performance is constrained by ethical, social or environmental considerations to avoid conflict with the furtherance of the charity's Objects (thus a *negative* charitable objective).

Company law starts from a different position, with the assumption that corporate assets are normally held for 'own' (ie operational) use. 'Investments' are then separated out as assets clearly surplus to the reporting entity's own operational needs; and because they are normally of a longer-term nature they are then required to be shown immediately below 'fixed assets' – unless forming part of current assets.

'Social investment'

9.2.2 'Social' or 'programme-related' investing for some charitable purpose or other is simply a means of recycling, instead of expending, a charity's perhaps over-stretched financial resources in the course of providing the public benefit it has been set up for. As such, this kind of investing has been with us for a long time already – especially in the form of soft loans to beneficiaries by the charitable benevolent funds set up as 'poverty relief' charities by many commercial organisations and some government departments as a staff welfare measure. The relief of poverty, hardship, etc, has the peculiarity of being the only class of charitable purpose which could have a closed set of beneficiaries (which can even be restricted to members of one's own family) rather than an open section of the general public as is normally required for any purpose to be recognised as charitable.

But also many charities now invest in the form of equity or loan financing to further charitable projects that are within their own Objects but are undertaken by some other entity. The only real difference between that and an outright grant is the charity's expectation of a return on its investment – if only in part, but in some cases even at a profit. This hybrid use of resources, *charitable* investing, is accorded a special accounting treatment under SORP 2005, which says of it:

> 'Charities also further their objectives by investing in tangible fixed assets to provide services or by making investments of a programme or social related nature. Such applications are charitable but do not decrease the funds of a charity.'

> – *SORP 2005, paragraph 242*

SORP 2005's Glossary expands on that in its definition:

> 'Programme related investments (also known as social investments) are made directly in pursuit of the organisation's charitable purposes. Although they can generate some financial return (funding may or may not be provided on commercial terms), the primary motivation for making them is not financial but to further the objects of the funding charity. Such investments could include loans to individual beneficiaries (eg for housing deposits) or to other charities (for example, in relation to regeneration projects).'

> – *SORP 2005, Glossary GL 47*

The Charity Commission's website guidance on investment also highlights the use of shareholdings in commercial enterprises whose activities impact significantly in some way (usually negatively) on the investing charity's own aims, as a means by which some major charities use their voting power to influence management policies for the furtherance of their own charitable objectives, pointing out that this is another example of 'programme-related' investment. If so, it would seem that the SORP's prescribed accounting treatment for social investment (see below) must then allow such a holding to be shown at historical cost (less any capital repayments/disposals to date) instead of current market value – as long as that is supported by an analysis note showing the type of asset and the charitable purpose for which it is (primarily) being held and used. Any 'impairment' write-down or (ultimately) disposal loss will then need to be expensed as 'charitable' expenditure in the SoFA – presumably as a cost of service-provision to mitigate beneficiary needs through the investee company's adoption of socially responsible operational policies less in conflict with the charity's Objects. Strange as that may seem, it is not unlike the SORP's 'grant' treatment of impairment where the investment is an equity interest in a company directly carrying out a charitable project. And whereas a disposal loss, like impairment, will count as grant expenditure, a disposal gain (less any impairment losses recognised as grant expenditure in prior years) will have to be accounted for in the SoFA's Incoming Resources section as a gain on disposal of fixed assets for the charity's own use instead of in the 'Other Recognised Gains/Losses' section.

CLASSIFICATION AND ANALYSIS

9.3 The various headings or categories under which investment assets are to be classified are set out in the Companies Act 2006 and its accounting Regulations, which for charitable companies accounting under company law is then further amplified by the requirements of the Charities SORP, while the latter stands alone for the accounts of 'small' groups headed by a charitable company and for the accounts of all *non-company* charities, supported by its related 2008 Regulations. The two lists are set out below.

The Companies Act uses different lists for fixed and current assets – both of which must distinguish any investment in *listed* companies (as is also required by the SORP). These lists are based on the Formats contained in the EC Fourth Council Directive on Company Law 78/660 EEC (Official Journal L222 14.8.78). The Act's 2008 Regulations (SI 2008/409 for 'small' companies; SI 2008/410 for large or medium-sized companies/groups) require fixed asset investments to be disclosed in the accounts under the following headings:

'1.   Shares in group undertakings
2.   Loans to group undertakings
3.   Participating interests
4.   Loans to undertakings in which the company has a participating interest
5.   Other investments other than loans
6.   Other loans
[7.   Own shares]'

– SI 2008/409, Reg 8(1)/(10) and Sch 6, Part I: Balance Sheet Format 1 – B III; and

– SI 2008/410, Reg 3(1) and Sch 1, Part I, Section B, Balance Sheet Format 1 – B III

A 'participating' interest here, while clearly referring to FRS9 (as distinct from FRS2), seems also to catch programme-related or 'social' investment holdings described at 9.2.2, perhaps as an unintended consequence of company law. In the *commercial* context it means:

'... an interest held by an undertaking in the shares of another undertaking which it holds on a long-term basis for the purpose of securing a contribution to its activities by the exercise of control or influence arising from or related to that interest.'

– SI 2008/409, Reg 13 (Interpretation) and Sch 8, para 8(1); and

– SI 2008/410, Reg 13 (Interpretation) and Sch 10, para 11

The schedule in each case continues with further details about the application of this definition.

Current asset investments are required to be listed under the following three headings:

'1.   Shares in [group undertakings]
[2.   Own shares]
3.   Other investments'

– SI 2008/409, Reg 8(1)/(10) and Sch 6, Part I: Balance Sheet Format 1 – C III; and

– SI 2008/410, Reg 3(1) and Sch 1, Part I, Section B, Balance Sheet Format 1 – C III

Paragraph 303 of the SORP requires fixed asset investments to be analysed in the notes under the following categories '*as a minimum*':

'(a)   investment properties;
(b)   investments listed on a recognised stock exchange or ones valued by reference to such investments, such as authorised unit trusts (AUTs) and open-ended investment trusts (OICs), common investment funds (CIFs), etc.;
(c)   investments in subsidiary or associated undertakings or in companies which are connected persons ...;
(d)   other unlisted securities;
(e)   cash and settlements pending held as part of the investment portfolio;
(f)   any other investments.'

– SORP 2005, paragraph 303

For the fixed assets of a charitable company accounting under company law, this means item (c) must be sub-divided to show categories (1) to (4) above; similarly category (5) – along with every other category – must distinguish item (b) from (d), while item (f) must be used to show the 'other loans' of category (6) and item (a), for investment properties, has to be extracted from the Companies Act's 'tangible fixed assets' category. Small wonder that accounts preparers and auditors coming from the corporate sector have a hard time adjusting to charity accountability!

Also, the lumping together with *group* companies of 'companies which are connected persons' seems to be an unmodified continuation of the wording used in the 1995 SORP, where the category did not include (ii) below but did include 'major donors' now excluded unless they have retained significant 'founders' powers' and are then caught by (ii). It now refers to the SORP's Glossary definition GL 50 to mean companies not wholly under charity control and in which either:

'(i)   the charity trustee has [or the trustees and their close family and the trustees of any non-charitable trusts in which any of them have a personal interest, and any business partners of any of them, taken together have] a participating interest; or
(ii)   the related person has, or the related person and any other related parties of the charity, taken together, have a participating interest.'

– SORP 2005, Glossary GL 50 (Related Parties)

The extension to (ii) is unfortunate in view of the practical difficulties that must arise from any attempt at compliance-monitoring, inevitably leading to complete disregard as a result of its unworkability: for many an investing charity peopled by the wealthy, it would need an unacceptable level of administrative effort and commitment to track and aggregate the investment holdings of all the charity's related parties as defined by Glossary definition GL 50 in order to determine whether for any particular investee the 20% threshold for a participating interest has been reached. And how else is the preparer of the annual accounts to know whether such a situation might have arisen? Even if the investee's registrars were willing to do the work, they would still need to be provided with a regularly updated list of the names of all related parties.

There is also a specific requirement in the SORP to sub-analyse *current asset* investments in the same way:

'Where investments are held as current assets the same disclosure is required as for fixed asset investments ...'.

– SORP 2005, paragraph 316

In this connection, it is important to note that the SORP's requirement for *commercial* investment assets generally to be carried in the balance sheet at their current open market value remains unaffected by their classification as fixed or current assets. This follows from the essential difference between the charity sector and the profit sector, in that the profit motive must always remain subservient to the overriding altruism of the *public benefit* purpose for which the charity is established – a purpose that precludes all but incidental private benefit (including the distribution of profits/gains as such – whether 'realised' or 'unrealised').

In addition, paragraph 142 of the SORP requires the charity's investment *income* to be analysed in the notes on the same basis as the investments themselves are analysed.

Charitable (ie 'social' or 'programme-related') investments

When it comes to the question of how to fit the Charities SORP's newest category of investment asset into the above sub-analysis, the obvious answer would seem to be to sub-divide (c) investment in subsidiaries/associates into 'commercial' and 'social' categories for all financing of such 'connected institutions' and similarly (d) for all other shares, securitised debt, etc, and the same for any other loans (including soft loans to individuals) under (f), other investments.

It is also possible for land and buildings to be held as a social investment – by a charity for urban regeneration, for example. In that case category (a), investment properties, would have to be similarly sub-divided.

Apart from also requiring disclosure of the *charitable objective* for which the social investment has been made, the SORP itself just skates over the above details, merely saying:

'The investment asset note to the accounts should disclose separately:

(a)   investments held primarily to provide an investment return for the charity; and
(b)   programme related investments ... that the charity makes primarily as part of its charitable activities.'

'The notes should also analyse programme related investments held between equity, loan and other investments and indicate the charitable objectives, programmes or projects the investment supports.'

– SORP 2005, paragraphs 299 and 312

Equity investment in subsidiaries/associates

9.3.1   The typical situation where the subsidiary/associate is set up to carry out *non-charitable* trading activities on a larger scale than the charity itself is permitted to undertake directly, so that the reporting charity's interest in it must obviously be accounted for as an 'investment' asset, is not the only one. We consider the accounting requirements for both kinds of equity investment here.

Any *loan*-financing (whether or not securitised) would follow the same principles, bearing in mind that the cost and market value of all recoverable loan capital will be the same, and that unless it is restricted to charitable use the loan must be for a fixed term at a market rate of interest and fully secured for it to be regarded by the authorities as a 'qualifying investment' by the charity.

Where instead the financing remains on current account, unless it can be shown that normal commercial terms of settlement have been applied the authorities tend to see that as *informal* loan-financing.

Commercial investment use (to finance non-charitable activities)

To comply with the SORP's general rule, any material equity interest in such an undertaking must clearly require annual revaluation to 'current value' in the open market. In practice, this is often impractical, as the 'trading preferences' usually accorded to such controlled undertakings (in the charity's own best interests) are such that an easier and more comfortable treatment is to carry the investment at cost – discounted for any known diminution in that carrying value, of course. In any case, if the consolidated accounts include the subsidiary/associate, etc, its underlying net assets value within the group will automatically be correctly shown there.

Added to this is the fact that for tax reasons these companies are mostly empty shells anyway, so that properly adjusted valuations will normally tend towards historical cost – as has been recognised and provided for in the SORP, as explained later in this chapter.

'Social' investment use (to finance charitable projects)

The use of non-charitable subsidiaries and associates (also corporate joint ventures) to carry out *charitable* activities is on the increase as charity trustees become more aware of the need to 'ring-fence' and mitigate risk. Shareholdings in such companies may be just for control purposes (e g two shares of £1 each, fully paid), as is normal for the financing of non-charitable activities through trading subsidiaries, with no significant reserves retained in them – though that is optional and therefore not always the case, since the use of the charity's funds to finance them is then no less a 'proper application' under charity law than any other method of providing public benefit. Their classification in the balance sheet will therefore usually – but not always – be immaterial.

SORP 2005 requires them to be shown separately in the balance sheet, as a special class of investment – though this, too, must remain subject to materiality. Also, their carrying values are to be cost-based or, where the equity has been gifted to the charity, the original gift-value as the 'deemed' cost – reviewed annually for any impairment in the investment's recoverability and with any write-off being treated as *charitable project* expenditure (grants) in the SoFA.

Mixed use

To the extent that their use is partly for activities *outside* the charity's Objects (as is often the case to some degree, perhaps involving a variable mix of charitable and non-charitable trading), any funding provided by the charity and not specially ring-fenced for charitable projects can only be justified as a *commercial* investment. This is usually presumed in any case whenever the authorities look at the use of charitable funds for a subsidiary/associate, etc, that is not itself a charity. They will then need to have the precise situation carefully and patiently explained to them if the purpose of any part of the funding provided by the charity is to finance *charitable* activities within its own Objects – for which their permission or consent will not then be needed as long as that funding can be shown to be properly protected (eg, under a 'control agreement') for its intended purpose and not at 'undue risk of loss' through being diverted for other (ie, non-charitable) purposes.

The investment asset itself will then be a *mixed-use* one, so that unless one or other is the primary use its carrying value will need to be apportioned between the two categories – similar to the rules for mixed functional/investment use properties.

Thus where the primary use is non-charitable this will determine the basis of the classification of the asset as a *commercial investment* – and also the carrying value, unless the historical cost option permitted by the SORP is adopted (and disclosed as an accounting policy).

Portfolio structure

9.3.2 The Companies Act Regulations require that for each of the amounts shown under fixed or current asset investments the company should also disclose how much is ascribable to *listed* investments, as well as the aggregate stock exchange value where materially different from market value. The Charities SORP, at paragraph 304 also calls for further analysis in the accounts notes for 'items in categories (a) to (f) of paragraph 303' (see the start of **9.3**) to show the split of investment assets within and outside the UK, though this is usually taken to mean only in aggregate. In this, *indirect* investment – ie by the investee – is to be disregarded.

The SORP also requires further details to be given in respect of any material holdings within the portfolio – but this is nowadays with no mention of the old 5% 'rule of thumb' to define immateriality:

> 'Further details should be given in the notes to the accounts of any particular investment that is considered material in the context of the investment portfolio.'

> 'In the rare case where the size or nature of a holding of securities is such that the market is thought by the trustees not to be capable of absorbing the sale of the shareholding without a material effect on the quoted price, the trustees should summarise the position in the notes to the accounts. If they are able to do so, the trustees should give an opinion in the notes to the accounts on how much the market price should be adjusted to take this fact into consideration.'

> *– SORP 2005, paragraphs 306 and 301*

Since the coming into force from 1 February 2001 of the Trustee Act 2000 ('TA 2000'), repealing the Trustee Investments Act 1961 ('the 1961 Act'), and bestowing 'absolute' investment powers on all trustees (subject to certain statutory safeguards – see chapter 5), there is no longer any requirement to maintain the old distinctions between investments belonging to 'narrower', 'wider' and 'special' range.

Fund-ownership

9.3.3 The original 1995 SORP's requirement to distinguish the investing funds where 'an investment is held within more than one of the charity's funds' (a vestigial reference to the common practice of putting money from a variety of endowed/other restricted funds, as well as general-purpose funds, into a CIF or else into a 'private' Investment Pooling Scheme – though it can equally well apply to a single direct investment, of course) has since been modified to say:

> 'The notes to the accounts should indicate the value of investments held in each category of fund. This may be included in the overall analysis of assets held in the different category of funds ...'.

– SORP 2005, paragraph 307

This refers to the funds-based analysis of the charity's assets and liabilities that is important for demonstrating 'proper application' of invested endowment and other restricted funds, by showing the necessary compliance with charity law concerning the separate interests of each distinct charitable trust fund, which must not be mixed together unless so authorised. Although that authority is now a statutory one under the TA 2000, it is still necessary to account properly for its exercise by means of *unitised* 'investment pooling' (see the end of this chapter).

It became common practice under the 1995 SORP to analyse only the total of investment assets across the individual funds or fund-types, and this has clearly been endorsed in the above paragraph.

Investment pooling is considered only at the end of this chapter, but we should note here that where the pool is constituted as a separate legal entity (eg the various kinds of 'collective investment' vehicle, such as unit trusts and investment trusts, operated by professional investment houses, as well as the CIFs and pool charities set up by the Charity Commission to overcome the limitations of the old 1961 Act) rather than an informal arrangement (whether or not managed by agents for the charity) the accounting treatment will follow accordingly. In the former case, all investment in it will count as a single asset in the balance sheet for each of the investing funds, while in the latter case each fund will have part-ownership of each investment asset directly.

Unlike pooling under the statutory power bestowed by the TA 2000, pooling under Charity Commission authority involves the Commission creating a separate charity comprising the pooled investments. This will be internal to the reporting charity unless one or more of the participating funds is 'external' (publicly accounted for elsewhere). The whole portfolio will then belong to the pool charity, and only the unitised interests (or percentages) in it of each investing fund will need to be shown in the notes.

Analysis of movements and asset classes

9.3.4 The following is an example of an accounts note analysing *commercial* investment assets in accordance with the requirements of the Charities SORP. The same sort of analysis will also be required for *social* investment assets, if material – see the end of this section. This illustration shows both the movements in the year and the required analysis by type of investment. It is noteworthy that the SORP's 'mark-down' for placement difficulties where the size of a substantial holding could affect market prices on a disposal seems to have been taken rather literally here: a 100% write-down for all those hard-to-place AIM shares!

[Note] 12 Investments	Group and Charity	
	2008	**2007**
	£'000	*£'000*
Market value at 1 April	75,751	64,362
Purchases at cost	27,693	32,326
Disposals at carrying value	(27,699)	(21,179
Write-down of donated shares	-	(939)
(Decrease)/Increase in market value (excluding movement in value of donated shares)	(2,567)	1,181
Market value at 31 March	**73,178**	**75,751**
Historical cost as at 31 March	69,428	*72,427*

The listed investments include shares in seven companies quoted on the Alternative Investment Market (AIM) of the London Stock Exchange and the Channel Islands Stock Exchange, which the charity accepted as donations under the condition that they would not be sold until various dates up to March 2007. At 31 March 2008 the total quoted value of these shares was £504,000 (2007: £889,000). Recognising the lack of any effective market for the quantity of the shares held, the board of trustees decided in 2007 that the difficulties in trying to establish a market value outweighs any benefit and since they were received at no cost and not part of the NSPCC's investment strategy, no amount has been included in the financial statements.

At the balance sheet date, the portfolio was invested as follows:	**2008**	**2007**
	£'000	£'000
UK equity shares	18,395	20,510
UK fixed interest bonds and deposits	45,897	49,964
Overseas fixed interest bonds and deposits	200	207
Money market instruments	4,916	-
UK high interest bank accounts	3,297	4,008
Cash instruments	473	1,062
Market value at 31 March	**73,178**	**75,751**

At 31 March 2008 the following investments represent more than 5% of the portfolio by market value:	%	**£'000**
Legal & General CAF UK Equitrack Fund	25.1%	18,392
HBOS Fixed Interest (maturing May 2008)	6.8%	5,000
HBOS Fixed Interest (maturing August 2008)	6.8%	5,000
HBOS Fixed Interest (maturing August 2008)	6.8%	5,000
HBOS Fixed Interest (maturing March 2009)	6.8%	5,000
RBS Fixed Interest (maturing November 2008)	6.8%	5,000
RBS Fixed Interest (maturing November 2008)	6.8%	5,000
RBS Fixed Interest (maturing November 2008)	6.8%	5,000
HBOS Fixed Interest (maturing July 2008)	6.0%	4,400

For a simple charity with few investments, the following is an example of the analysis of investments accompanied by the analysis of their income yields as recommended at paragraph 113 of the SORP:

11	FIXED ASSET INVESTMENTS			
			2008	**2007**
			£000s	*£000s*
	Market value at beginning of year		4,331	3,128
	Purchases at cost		1,455	1,837
	Disposals at book value (Proceeds – £978,000)		(978)	(760)
	(Decrease)/Increase in market value		(72)	144
	Decrease in cash held for reinvestment		(379)	(18)
	Market value at end of year		**4,357**	**4,331**
	Historical cost at end of year		*4,274*	*4,157*
	[Analysed by type:-]			
	Investments			597
	– Listed unit trusts/OEICs		597	885
	– Listed bonds fund		424	
	- Total Return funds		1,808	
	Investment Securities total		**2,829**	**2,824**
	Cash held within investment portfolio		1,528	1,907
		Total	**4,357**	**4,331**
	[Geographical analysis:-]			
	In the United Kingdom		2,005	2,424
	Outside the UK		824	-
		Total	**2,829**	**2,424**
			2008	**2007**
3	**ANALYSIS OF INVESTMENT INCOME**		*£000s*	*£000s*
	Distributions on listed unit trusts and OEICs		17	13
	Interest on Bond Funds (OEIC)		14	12
	Interest on Total Return funds		39	32
	Interest on cash held within investment portfolio		117	73
	Bank interest		244	172
		Total	**431**	**302**

United Response – 2007/08 accounts

Similarly, for its special category of *social investment* assets, SORP 2005 says:

> 'Where the use of programme related investments forms a material part of the work of the charity, or the amounts form a material part of the investment assets of the charity, the notes to the accounts should show all changes in carrying values of programme related investments, including any impairment losses, and reconcile the opening and closing carrying values of such investments.'

– SORP 2005, paragraph 311

Because comparative figures are not required for any fixed assets movements analysis, charities may find it convenient to use a columnar format within a single analysis note to distinguish between their commercial and social investment assets in compliance with the above, accompanied by separate commentary on the respective asset classes, etc.

VALUATION BASIS

9.4 Under the Companies Act, any asset or group of assets may be carried at historical cost or a 'fair value' current valuation. Since 1981, most reporting entities have been required to carry investment *properties* at [such a] valuation. The reason was explained in paragraph 2 of SSAP19, which stated that a treatment different from 'cost less depreciation' is applicable:

> '... where a significant proportion of the fixed assets of an enterprise is held not for consumption in the business operations but as investments, the disposal of which would not materially affect any manufacturing or trading operations of the enterprise. In such a case the current value of these investments, and changes in that current value, are of prime importance rather than a calculation of systematic annual depreciation. Consequently, for the proper appreciation of financial position, a different accounting treatment is considered appropriate for fixed assets held as investments (called in this standard "investment properties").'

> *– SSAP19, paragraph 2*

Interestingly enough, an explicit exclusion was to be found in paragraph 9, stating that SSAP19 'does not apply to investment properties owned by charities' – simply because the then Accounting Standards Committee did not wish to burden charities with the extra costs of valuation. The ASB therefore considered this disapplication only *permissive* rather than prohibitive at the time, so that there was in fact no conflict for charities following the 1995 SORP in this respect.

More recently, the original version of the FRSSE repeated the SSAP19 disapplication simply because the ASB felt that the FRSSE mandate did not allow anything else. However, that all changed with the introduction of FRS15 on accounting for tangible *non-investment* fixed assets, superseding SSAP12 (Accounting for Depreciation) in 2000 (see chapter 5). In the process, the opportunity was taken to remove the long-standing disapplication to charities by deleting paragraph 9 of SSAP19. This at least went some way towards ASB endorsement of the SORP's approach to the valuation of charities' investment properties.

Since SSAP19, views have changed concerning the information charities should disclose about their investment assets. Prior to the 1995 SORP, some charities brought them into account at market value, others at cost, many of them at least disclosing market value by way of note. In formulating the 1995 SORP, the committee's view was that it was essential for charities to disclose the value of all the investment assets at their disposal or under their control, and to account for changes in value as they arise year by year.

This was felt to be more informative than accounting for only the total change in value that had accrued over the whole period during which an investment had been held (the 'historical' gain/loss) once it was sold. One reason was so that the accounts could disclose the total return for the year on the investment portfolio (ie income plus gains or minus losses), comparable with the data normally provided by investment managers when reporting on investment *performance* during a period.

Exceptions to the 'market value' rule

Apart from the special mention of what is now the most notable exception to the general rule, paragraph 296 of SORP 2005 simply reiterates the original 1995 SORP here in saying that:

> 'All investment assets other than programme related investments ... should be shown in the balance sheet at market value or at the trustees' best estimate of market value ... Market value best represents a true and fair view of the value of these assets to the charity, given the duty of the trustees to administer the portfolio of investment assets so as to obtain the best investment performance without undue risk.'
>
> – *SORP 2005, paragraph 296*

This also reflects the view expressed in the old SSAP19, quoted above. For the special case of *social investment* assets, the SORP elsewhere prescribes a **historical cost** basis:

> 'Programme related investments should generally be included in the balance sheet at the amount invested less any impairments (in the case of equity or loans) and any amounts repaid (in the case of loans).'
>
> – *SORP 2005, paragraph 309*

For shares in subsidiaries/associates, and also for other 'hard-to-value' investments, where the SORP's 'reasonable approach' cannot yield a reliable enough estimate of the open market value, the SORP allows them to be carried at historical cost instead (see **9.4.1**).

Market value

'Market value' is defined in the Glossary to the Charities SORP, where the wording is clearly an abbreviation of the company law requirements, as:

> '... the price at which an asset could be, or could be expected to be, sold or acquired in a public market between a willing buyer and willing seller. For traded securities in which there is an established market, the market value basis that is to be used in the valuation for the balance sheet is defined as the midpoint of the quotation in the Stock Exchange Daily Official List or at a similar recognised market value. For other assets it is the trustees' or valuers' best estimate of such a value.'
>
> – *SORP 2005, Glossary GL 41*

Where any investments have been sold since the year-end or are likely to be sold 'in the short term', under company law the actual or estimated realisation costs must be deducted from the valuation – a refinement not mentioned in the SORP (presumably because the difference is normally below the threshold of materiality). Market value is also mentioned, but not defined, in the context of 'current value' for company law purposes, in para 50 of Sch 1 to SI 2008/409 and para 32 of Sch 1 to SI 2008/410, which deal with the 'alternative accounting rules' allowing companies to include assets at a valuation instead of historical cost. Where there is no ready market valuation, the Companies Act's Regulations permit investment (or other) assets to be valued less frequently as long as the following information is disclosed:

'(a)   the years ... in which the assets were severally valued and the several values, and

(b)   in the case of assets that have been valued during the financial year, the names of the persons who valued them or particulars of their qualifications for doing so and (whichever is stated) the bases of valuation used by them.'

– para 49, Sch 1 to SI 2008/409; para 52, Sch 1 to SI 2008/410

For charitable companies' individual and group accounts more generally under company law, the Regulations allow the market value of any asset other than a listed investment to be estimated:

'(b)   at a value determined on any basis which appears to the directors to be appropriate in the circumstances of the company;

but in the latter case particulars of the method of valuation adopted and of the reasons for adopting it shall be disclosed in a note to the accounts.'

– para 32, Sch 1 to SI 2008/409 and 410

By following the requirements of the Charities SORP, charitable companies accounting under company law can therefore comply with Companies Act requirements in this respect – as long as any materially lower *stock exchange* value is disclosed (in aggregate) as required by para 50 of SI 2008/409 or para 54 of SI 2008/410, presumably for comparison with the market value at which all 'listed' investments must, for SORP compliance, be carried. (That, of course, is the converse of the disclosure required by the SORP where a holding is so large that its disposal en bloc would be likely to depress the market price.)

The following illustration may or may not be of a material example (it is hard to tell):

Note 12: Investments held as fixed assets

...

Over the years Tearfund has been given a total of 108,000 £1 ordinary shares in the Southsea Mortgage and Investment Co Ltd, an unquoted company.

... as there are restrictions on Tearfund's ability to sell these shares they continue to be held as an investment.

The Directors have considered the market value of the investment and are of the opinion that it is not significantly different to the book value [ie £1,000].

Tearfund – 2007/08 accounts

Methods/frequency of valuation

9.4.1   Apart from listed investments, as mentioned above, and other assets (presumably including residential housing) for which there is a readily available market price, *'a reasonable approach'* is allowed under the Charities SORP. This recognises the obvious fact that charities have special needs justifying a more relaxed approach than that required by SSAP19 for 'investment properties'.

The following suggestions are therefore offered by the SORP for typical investment valuation problems.

(a) Shares in unlisted companies held for investment purposes

'... by reference to underlying net assets or earnings or the dividend record, as appropriate.'

– *SORP 2005, paragraph 297(a)*

Annual revaluation is required, as for listed investments.

(b) Shares in subsidiaries/associates

SORP 2005 takes a more general line than its predecessor here, which specifically cited the example of a trading subsidiary, whereas the SORP now only says:

'Where the cost of obtaining a valuation by one of the methods in (a) above outweighs the benefit to the users of the accounts, or lacks reliability, the investment may be included at cost.'

– *SORP 2005, paragraph 297(b)*

In the case of a subsidiary or associate (including a corporate joint venture), except in respect of any *charitable* trading undertaken through it, the net assets will usually be insignificant anyway, due to the constraints of tax/charity law. Where an earnings-based valuation method is used, however, it may also need adjustment to reflect the value of the premium that would be payable in the market for the continuation of any special relationship such as a preferential trading position (often on the charity's own premises). Again, unless the 'cost' option is used, annual revaluation would be required, as for listed investments.

What is specially noteworthy from the above quotation is that *other* (non-land) assets considered too difficult or too expensive to put a valuation on can *also* be carried at cost on the above basis – subject to (c), below, for assets other than shares and securities.

(c) Investment property and non-securitised investment assets

'For investment assets other than shares or securities (e g property), the trustees may use any reasonable approach to market valuations which must be done at least every five years, subject only to obtaining advice as to the possibility of any material movements between individual valuations. If there is a material movement the assets must be revalued. Where a charity has a number of such assets it will be acceptable for valuations to be carried out on a rolling basis over a five year period.'

– *SORP 2005, paragraph 298*

That this does not have to be as formal as going to the expense of an *independent* professional valuation is made clear in paragraph 265:

'Independent formal professional valuations are not mandatory in the case of a charity, which instead may obtain a valuation from a suitably qualified person who could be a trustee or employee ...'.

– SORP 2005, paragraph 265

The SORP also calls for further information to enable the reader to gauge the reliability of such calculations and opinions:

'Where values are determined other than by reference to readily available market prices ... the notes to the accounts should disclose who has made the valuation, giving:

(a) the name and qualification (if any) of the valuer and whether they are a member of staff or a trustee or external to the charity; and

(b) the basis or bases of valuation.'

– SORP 2005, paragraph 300

Gains and losses

9.4.2 *Unrealised* gains and losses are the differences between:

– the market value of a holding at the beginning and end of the year, for investments held throughout the year; and

– the cost of an investment acquired during the year and its market value at the end of the year, where it is still held.

They are to be included in the lower section of the SoFA: in the 'investment gains and losses' section, but since SORP 2000 they no longer have to be segregated from any 'realised' (ie disposal) gains/losses – except by a charitable company, for the sake of FRS3 compliance (see chapter 6).

The juxtaposition was actually a relatively late change in the development of the 1995 SORP, recognising that – for charities – realised and unrealised gains/losses are not entirely dissimilar, insofar as their permitted uses under charity law are really no different – unlike the position in the profit sector.

Realised gains and losses are the differences between:

– the sale proceeds, and

– market value at the beginning of the year and/or the costs of any later acquisition.

Being bound by FRS3, 'Reporting Financial Performance', it is not really possible for a *charitable company accounting under company law* (unless it were to be acting as a dealer by *trading* in investments – see below) to treat all investment movements in value during the year as unrealised, as is prescribed by the SORP and its related Regulations for the *non-company* charity's entity/consolidated SoFA, as well as for the consolidated SoFA for a 'small' group under the 1993 Act. This is because paragraph 21 of the Standard requires the movement between value at the beginning of the year (or later acquisition) and disposal proceeds to be accounted for 'in the profit and loss account'. The SORP's special requirements for charitable companies in this respect are explained more fully in chapters 6 and 7.

Opinions vary as to what must be disclosed in respect of investment gains and losses and how they should be presented, also as to how to calculate realised and unrealised gains/losses. For example, because FRS3 requires the asset's existing 'carrying value' to be used to calculate a realised gain/loss, some have chosen to revalue immediately before sale – as SORP 2005 carefully notes (though of course without endorsing it):

> 'Realised and unrealised gains and losses may be included in a single row on the Statement of Financial Activities ... where a charity adopts a "marking to market" or continuous revaluation approach in relation to its investment portfolio.'

> '... where charities adopt a policy of continuous revaluation of investments ... there may be no realised gains to report and all the revaluation movements will be classified as unrealised gains.'

> – *SORP 2005, paragraphs 219 and 423*

The problem that the SORP does not seem to address is that this does not actually meet the requirement of FRS3, because the new value has not yet been *published* and thus *established* as the new carrying value in the *accounts*. Although quite acceptable for a *dealer* 'marking to market', it is a somewhat artificial accounting method when used by an *investor*.

However, for charities' accounts prepared under the 1993 Act, all that has been irrelevant ever since SORP 2000 was issued. For charitable companies accounting under company law, any way of eliminating realised gains/losses from their 'net result for the year' would above all need to be justified within the meaning of FRS3 not by adopting an inappropriate accounting policy as noted by the SORP but by pointing to the fact that charity law makes *all* their corporate funds undistributable 'reserves', to which all corporate gains belong immediately and unconditionally, so that where investment sales proceeds are being fully reinvested as a matter of policy (eg to build up a designated fund for some particular purpose) the distinction between realised and unrealised becomes irrelevant for annual reporting.

Accounting for individual investments

9.4.3 To track the information needed to calculate the figures to be reported in the annual accounts, all movements in value of each investment holding need to be logged and analysed in the accounting records. A possible form of accounting record is shown on the following page.

Ordinary Shares in X Co plc

£

Date	Action	Nominal	Cost	Market Value	MV less cost	Proceeds	Gain in year	PY gain realised	Total HC gain
2009			£		£	£	£	£	£
January 1	Balance	1,000	2,500	3,000	500				
March 1	Bonus	100							
		1,100							
June 30	Rights	22	22	22					
		1,122	2,522	3,022	500				
September 30	Sold	(500)	(1,124)	(1,346)	(222)	1,750	404	222	626
	Transfer								
		622	1,398	1,676	278	1,750	404	222	626
December 31	Revalue			346	346				
	Balance	622	1,398	2,022	2,022	1,750	404	222	626

This method is clearly quite complex. Providing the charity can get all the above information from its investment managers, it may be appropriate to continue to hold investments at historical cost in its books (as it has probably always done), and adjust annually for changes in the market value, by the use of an investment valuation 'suspense' account supported by the investment manager's detailed reports of portfolio changes within and for the year.

Alternatively, a spreadsheet can be used as the link between the two, if necessary. The problem that can result from relying only on the in-house accounting/reporting systems of investment managers worsens the more the trustees delegate day-to-day investment management decisions to them. With their computer systems increasingly geared to reporting gains/losses either on the previous year-end valuation or on historical cost – but not both – there is a tendency to argue that charity clients must bear the full cost of providing such a dual reporting facility, on the basis that it is not required by non-charity clients.

Needless to say, such arguments are vigorously rejected by both charities and the Charity Commission, but – even on the total return basis of investing – the problem remains and could certainly contribute to cost/benefit reasons for trying to avoid the kind of additional disclosure called for by FRS3 in the case of a charitable company.

But until the ASB's 'fair value balance sheets' agenda can make it a *requirement* for investment fixed assets to be shown at current value by all companies, it will remain necessary for inter-company comparability purposes to be able to see the historical cost of these assets in the accounts – even if by the sleight of hand described above the disposal gains/losses figure were to be reduced to nil.

IMPACT OF THE TRUSTEE ACT 2000

9.5   On 1 February 2001, the TA 2000 superseded the old 1961 Act. The new Act, which covers wider ground than the old one, bestows 'absolute' powers of investment on *all* trustees (charities included), but subject to any specific contrary provisions that may be contained in an extant *post*-August 1961 governing document of a charitable trust fund, and subject also to some common-sense safeguards.

Being of universal application, this new statutory power is subject to a general duty of care which requires trustees to review their investments, take proper advice and have regard to the TA 2000's 'standard investment criteria' of:

–   *suitability* for the trust, thus permitting 'ethical' investment;

–   *diversification* to mitigate market risk; and

–   *even-handedness* as between different classes of beneficiary – which for charities means *present* and *future* beneficiaries where the trust fund is *endowed*.

Up to then, trustees without the necessary constitutional powers for modernisation had to go 'cap in hand' to the Charity Commission or the courts if they wanted to use some of the newer and more esoteric investment concepts not even contemplated in 1961, for example, 'ethical' investment, 'hedge funds' and 'derivatives', especially the 'total return' investment approach popularised by the withdrawal of charity tax relief on dividends. The position was the same for the 'pooling' of investment assets belonging to endowed or other restricted funds under common administration – see **9.6**.

'Suitability'

Restricted funds are a feature of most charities' accounts, and – even if not endowed – funds may in some cases need to be invested for years until the time comes for spending them on this or that project. The TA 2000 requires the investment of trust funds to be 'suitable' to the particular trust, which also includes its 'spending profile' – long, medium or short term as the case may be.

'Ethical' investment policies

Suitability must logically also refer to the Objects of the particular trust fund, and thus the TA 2000 now provides statutory ratification of 'ethical' investment – albeit strictly by reference to the ethics of the (trust) charity, not those of its trustees. More recently, in line with the increasing public awareness of the influence of such factors on all our lives, this has been extended in both the SORP and its related Regulations by requiring the larger charities' annual reports to disclose under investment policy/performance 'the extent (if any) to which social, environmental or ethical considerations are taken into account' – see chapter 4.

Apart from that, the multiplicity of restricted funds that characterises the sector can so fragment investment decision-making that many charities long ago resorted to investment pooling for more effective management. Trustees therefore still need to be aware of the accounting and reporting requirements for such (informal) pools even under the TA 2000.

'Diversification'

Because any specific terms of trust imposed by a donor from August 1961 (but not before that) override the TA 2000 as well as the general requirements of trust law, trustees need no *special* power to be able to accept and retain gifts of shares on the condition, for example, that they are to be retained permanently as they are – ie *un*diversified. Thus the TA 2000's statutory duty to consider diversifying is subject to any contrary wishes imposed by the founder of the trust. Where the wish of the donor is that the investment be retained unchanged, there is no duty to act against that wish by diversifying.

A well known example of this is The Wellcome Trust as originally endowed by the will of Sir Henry Wellcome in 1936 with an inalienable gift of the equity in his highly successful pharmaceutical company – also how the trustee-company then went to the High Court several times over the decades, obtaining gradual relaxation of the founder's share-disposal restrictions to enable them to diversify completely, and finally obtained a Scheme from the Charity Commission in February 2001, under which the trust fund is not only fully diversified in its investments but also completely unified as regards its capital and income components, yet with the trustee company having absolute discretion over all allocations between the two, subject only to the specific duty of *even-handedness*.

As can be seen from the following extract from that highly unusual legal Scheme, this even includes the use of derivatives for hedging purposes.

Portfolio management

(1) The Trustee may only enter into or acquire an investment that may be characterised as creating or having the potential to cause the Trust to incur an unlimited financial obligation or liability ... if either:

(a) it enters (at substantially the same time) into a matching investment that limits the financial obligation or liability of the Trust in respect of the first such investment to an ascertained or ascertainable amount; or

(b) it does so for the purpose of efficient portfolio management or protection in circumstances where the purpose of the transaction is to manage risk rather than to take advantage of risk.

The Wellcome Trust – Cl 3(1), Sch C, Charity Commission Scheme (2000)

'Even-handedness'

For charities, this statutory duty means striking the right balance between the needs of capital and income where the trust is an *endowment*. The need of permanent capital is clearly long-term growth – at least to keep pace with monetary inflation, which has been known at times to decimate funds within a decade or two. The need of income is normally for an assured level of ready money for spending in the short to medium term (an exception being where essential and expensive equipment has to be funded out of income, perhaps over decades).

This can present practical problems in formulating a proper investment policy for:

–   a permanent endowment with insufficient income to meet annual expenditure; or

–   an expendable endowment with surplus income but no legal power to 'accumulate' that surplus as capital.

Generally speaking, a charitable trust fund can always be invested for high income at the expense of capital – if that is what is needed to meet the needs of its beneficiaries; or it can go for capital growth at the expense of income if longer-term needs are more pressing. But the more extreme the investment policy, the more necessary it will be for it to be seen as based on 'appropriate advice' – ie by an investment expert, whether internal or external to the trustee-body.

Even for a *permanent* financial endowment, however, one that has been set up 'in perpetuity', with no power to expend capital, the trustees are under no legal obligation to maintain its 'real' value (ie in terms of the spending-power of money); in these inflationary times, 'permanence' does not necessarily mean forever – and that is official.

What was new with the advent of the TA 2000 was the Charity Commission's readiness to use its statutory powers to override the standard capital/income rules of trust law wherever expedient in the interests of a particular charity or its beneficiaries *when requested by the trustees*. That was made clear in the Commission's public consultation at the time on the subject of the 'total return' concept of investment.

INVESTING ON THE 'TOTAL RETURN' BASIS

9.6   To be able to invest, administer and account properly for endowed funds on this basis, the policy adopted by the trustees must not only satisfy the TA 2000 concerning 'even-handedness' and the other standard investment criteria. Going beyond that, it must also not infringe what the Charity Commission's guidance for the sector refers to as the 'standard' trust law rules regulating the respective rights of income and capital beneficiaries of trusts generally.

Under these normal rules, which apply automatically except where the trust's founder or the court/Commission has provided otherwise, income returns on an endowed investment can never be added to capital – even if (for good reason) they are retained unspent. In the same way, capital returns form part of the endowment and therefore cannot be diverted or converted to income without special legal authority. The TA 2000 does not set aside or change those rules in any way.

Being charities in their own right, Pooling Scheme charities set up by the Charity Commission can already achieve the required returns through appropriate investment policies designed to yield the desired mix of income distribution and capital accumulation for their participating funds. Under the TA 2000, however, charities may be able to achieve the same end-result for their trust funds with a policy of using other suitable investment vehicles, for example, authorised unit trusts or open-ended investment companies, which informal pooling for direct investment may not be able to do.

Thus investing under the TA 2000 does not of itself set you free from the existing *trust law* constraints on the *application* of income and capital returns. The *corporate* funds of a charitable company can certainly be invested for a required 'total return' (TR) regardless of capital/income distinctions, but its *trust* funds remain bound by trust law (ie common law and statute). Special authority is needed to break free from the constraints of the law.

Unless contained in the investing fund's *trust deed*, this authority will normally have to come from the Charity Commission. Following a public consultation on the subject, the Charity Commission published Operational Guidance (OG83) on this for its staff in 2001, setting out the rules and procedures for authorising charities to override the standard trust law rules governing the application of capital and income returns. This explains how the Commission's policy in this area is applied for the benefit of any particular charity, and can be freely downloaded from their website.

OG83 gently suggests that trustees may feel safer relying on a formal order from the Commission to authorise them to administer the fund's investments on the TR investment basis – even in cases where they already have a constitutional power to amend the administrative provisions of their trust deed for that purpose. This is because of the extra legal protection afforded by such an official order.

It is also made clear in the OG that if there is a likelihood of objections being raised by the trust's founder or its supporters, the trustees will be required to give due notice (in the appropriate form) of their intention to switch to TR.

Chapter 6 discusses how this is likely to affect investment accounting *in the SoFA*. In this chapter we are mainly interested in the impact on the balance sheet and notes.

OG83 is based on the concept of extracting annual spending money from the *cumulative* balance of the UTR in accordance with a policy that must be designed to be even-handed as between the perceived needs of present and future beneficiaries. That means giving *formal consideration* ('proper advice', board minutes, etc) to the adequacy of the capital balance for the furthering of the trust's Objects in the long term each time the decision is being taken to extract money for spending. All such annual extractions are then 'held on a trust for application (TFA) for the purposes of the charity' – ie they must be dealt with as *income*, which will include explaining any reserves retained out of such monies.

To get started with TR, the trustees must choose a 'base-date' in the past from which to start measuring. The deemed 'gift-value' of the permanently endowed trust is then *frozen* as at that date (any later gifts being added at their gift-value at the time, of course), and all 'realised' (ie income/capital distributions received, also disposal gains/losses calculated by reference to the base-date) as well as 'unrealised' (ie upon annual revaluation) investment returns will accrue to the UTR. The gift-value of the permanent endowment thus remains static except for adding further gifts received on the same trusts.

This means that all *investment growth/shrinkage* will take place *only* within the UTR, which (legally speaking) is kept in limbo as a kind of supplement to the permanent endowment. You can best envisage the relationship as an interest-free loan between the two parts, just as if the UTR immediately borrows and invests the *money value* of all gifts to the permanent endowment. Although the distinction need only be made clear in the accounts note analysing all assets and liabilities across the charity's funds, the UTR will therefore be represented in the balance sheet by the investment portfolio as *its* asset and the permanent endowment loan as its liability, while the permanent endowment itself will have the loan to the UTR as *its* sole asset. Referring back to chapter 6, the year 1 balance carried forward on the permanent endowment illustrated at **6.4.3** comprises:

	PE Gift	UTR	PE Total
Investment portfolio value	–	175	175
PE – UTR loan	150	(150)	–
PE – Total value	**150**	**25**	**175**

But since these two parts remain lawfully inseparable components of a single 'trust for retention', distinguishable only for the purposes of the trustees' use of their new legal power to make discretionary allocations into a 'trust for application', it is only accountants who need to be clear about this virtually invisible loan relationship between the two parts, so that – especially in the SoFA – we can account properly for the results.

As the OG makes clear, this base-date can be any date you choose – subject to the necessary records being still available, of course! The further back you start, the larger can be the UTR 'pot' available in case the charity suffers from a downturn in the investment market or, perhaps, poor investment advice.

OG83 emphasises the principle that although annual extractions out of the UTR can continue to be made even in a year when the total return is negative (*unrealised* losses on annual revaluation exceed *realised* returns), *they cannot be made beyond emptying out the*

UTR pot, nor to create or increase a negative balance (thus in anticipation of future growth). This means that as soon as the UTR is exhausted, the power to allocate anything at all to the TFA is suspended until the UTR again achieves a positive balance. This is more or less equivalent to the position under the standard trust law rules, where no income means no spending money. What it means for the balance sheet, however, is that whenever the UTR is negative its deficit will be visible only in the accounts note analysis, since the PE-UTR loan remains constant. We can see this more clearly by referring back to chapter 6 again, where by the end of year 3 the UTR part of the permanent endowment illustrated at **6.4.3** has fallen into deficit, so that the two parts now comprise:

	PE Gift	UTR	PE Total
Investment portfolio value	–	195	195
PE – UTR loan	200	(200)	–
PE – Total value	**200**	**(5)**	**195**

The Charity Commission order for the use of this basis of administering a permanent endowment's investments therefore requires certain information to be given in the accounts notes each year. In particular, the accounts note must:

– analyse the year's movements in the UTR;

– distinguish the amount of the actual or deemed historical gift value of the related permanent endowment *and the base date used*; and

– disclose the name of the investment adviser currently being relied on.

In other cases the accounting guidance from the Commission – as also summarised in SORP 2005 to cover this little-known area of charity accounting – requires not only the above information but also an explanation of how the UTR is being administered (in order to satisfy the statutory and other trust law requirements) and under what authority.

As further reading, the Commission's 11-page summary of the implications of the TA 2000 for charities, entitled 'Investment of Charitable Funds', can be freely downloaded from the website for a more detailed review of what the law requires and permits. The main point here is that a Charity Commission order authorising the use of the *total return* investment basis is on offer only for *permanent* endowments – as distinct from what is known as an expendable or 'discretionary' endowment, where the power to convert capital into income makes it unnecessary to seek special authority to switch to the TR basis. Nor is it available for *unendowed* trust funds, since their capital and income components are indistinguishable by trust law in the first place – which in any case does not allow a trust for expenditure as distinct from retention to remain unspent in the longer term except in extenuating circumstances.

MULTI-FUND INVESTMENT POOLING

9.7   A further problem confronting many charities once the TA 2000, in effect, ratified unofficial investment pooling (albeit without retrospective effect) has been the need to undertake a comprehensive review of their administration of *pooled* investment portfolios for multiple trust funds that are accounted for either within, or separately from, the reporting charity's own accounts.

Here, we may note in passing that investment pooling arrangements have more often than not been set up unofficially instead of officially, usually due to trustees' ignorance of the legal requirements, but in all such cases leaving the trustees at risk of personal liability if things ever went wrong through their own (de)fault, to the extent that spent funds could no longer be recouped for redistribution on the proper basis.

Prior to the TA 2000, charity law compliance needed an 'official' pooling arrangement to be formally established by Charity Commission Scheme, which also provides for the pool to be separately registered as a main or subsidiary charity (see chapter 14). One of the conditions of the Scheme setting up such an *external* Investment Pool (ie one with two or more 'main charities' participating) is normally that all participating charities must be administered by the same body of trustees, who are therefore appointed trustees of the Pool charity.

This need for a Pool charity as such was superseded by the TA 2000, whose statutory powers and safeguards for the investment of charitable trust funds also enable trustees to set up their own pooling arrangements without the need for any further authority.

Under the TA 2000, investment selection, etc, for *any* number of trusts under common trusteeship can now safely be delegated to professional fund managers – but only if a written investment policy is issued by the trustees, against which the actual investment performance will then have to be reviewed by them in order to fulfil their statutory duty of care.

But although the need for a formal Scheme to be made by the Charity Commission to authorise such pooling has gone, the trustees' *charity law accountability* for the rights of each of the participating trust funds in accordance with the strict apportionment rules applicable to 'unitised' funds has not. Despite this, the two different methods of accounting for 'internal' and 'external' investment pooling were not to be found at all in the Charities SORP until 2005, with the main administrative point about them still not being covered there (the intrinsic 'unitisation' principle involved).

> 'Some charities may operate a pooling scheme ... for the investments under the control of a single body of trustees common to the investing charities. Sometimes such arrangements are governed by a formal Charity Commission scheme but the pooling of investments may also be an informal arrangement under the Trustee Act 2000. This SORP does not provide details on how to operate or manage pooling schemes where underlying investments funds are apportioned between the investing charities or their funds on a similar basis to that adopted by unit trusts.'
>
> *– SORP 2005, paragraph 450*

The Unit Trust, or *aliquot*, method of apportionment, whereby all investment returns accrue pro rata to each investor's existing interests at the beginning of the distribution period, is explained in the Charity Commission's comprehensive website Operational

Guidance on the creation of Pooling Scheme charities. Investment pooling under such a formal Scheme made by the Charity Commission thus provides for investment and withdrawal of funds by participators to be only at *specified dates* (eg month- or quarter-ends) immediately following a revaluation of the pool, so as to ensure that the respective interests of existing participators are determined and protected. In this way their income and capital entitlements arising from existing investments are not distorted by new investment/divestment.

For any investment pooling arrangement entered into under the TA 2000, the trustees would need to be able to show that they are applying the same rules. Special care needs to be taken to ensure that the interests of participating charitable funds having different legal restrictions are not prejudiced by incorrect allocations or inappropriate investment policies. These rules therefore need to be set up by the trustees themselves, if operating their own pool, or else by their appointed professional fund-managers operating a kind of private unitised investment pool for them – akin to commercial unit trusts and other collective investment vehicles.

'Internal' v 'external' investment pooling – the accounting rules

For accounting purposes, there are two different kinds of Pool charity, whose proper accounting treatment by the reporting charity, and when to use it, therefore needs to be clearly understood:

(a) where *separate accounts* have to be prepared for the Investment Pool itself as a 'main' charity because two or more of the participating charities are separately accountable main charities (in which case the Pool charity itself still has to follow the *Charities SORP*, as the Regulations covering compliance with the more specialised *Authorised Funds SORP* of the Investment Management Association – see below – will not be applicable to it) each participating main charity's annual report and accounts should disclose the Pool charity as a 'connected' charity, showing its investment in the Pool charity in the same way as it would for an investment in one of the public CIFs; and

(b) where the Investment Pool, as a *subsidiary charity*, is *internal* to the reporting charity (ie accounted for as a 'charity branch'), when the Pool charity itself will be invisible in the SoFA because its activity will be fully apportioned among the participating funds, whereas in the balance sheet the Pool's portfolio will be shown as a fixed asset investment, analysed in the notes, with the percentage/unitised interest of each fund in the pool portfolio shown in the notes there or within the assets/funds analysis note.

For any *other* kind of investment pooling arrangement, one that does not involve such a 'pool charity', common sense suggests that it should be properly described somewhere in the required accounts notes:

(i) analysing the reporting charity's investment assets, and

(ii) summarising the assets and liabilities of its major funds.

For the trustees' own protection, if their annual accounts on public record are to evidence the proper discharge of their duties as trustees, such a description should identify the pool and say how and by whom it is managed. It should also table the respective interests of all participating (distinct) charitable funds belonging to the reporting charity, as well as indicating the extent of any external interests in the pool, particularly where the other participators include 'connected' charities with separate public accountability.

The disclosure should aim to enable the reader to appreciate the implications of the pooling arrangement for the proper administration of the reporting charity. Where the pool is one operated by a reputable professional fund-manager for charities that are otherwise unconnected, it may be enough just to say so.

Where pooling takes the form of joint participation in quoted investment vehicles, the disclosure becomes minimal.

Such a 'minimalist' line was taken by the 1995 SORP in requiring only the disclosure of each fund's interest where an investment is owned by more than one fund. But apart from a passing reference in paragraph 9 it said nothing specifically about *accounting* for investment pooling. (This has nothing to do with the few dozen fairly large registered CIFs set up as charities under Charity Commission Schemes since the Charities Act 1960 to act as authorised investment vehicles for charities having *different* trustees. CIFs are required under the 1993 Act further to follow the Authorised Funds SORP issued by the Investment Management Association in any case, so the Charities SORP could not cater for their accounting needs.)

> 'Where a pooling scheme holds investments for the separate funds of a single reporting charity, the scheme will form a restricted fund of the reporting charity. The assets of the pooled fund are the investments held and its liabilities are the share of these investments due to the funds of the reporting charity which have invested through the pooling arrangements. Its income and costs will accrue to the funds investing in the pool. Therefore, when accounts are prepared for the reporting charity, the assets, investment income and related costs of the pooling scheme fund will appear in the funds investing in the pool. The notes to the accounts simply disclose the pooling of investments with the underlying investments, income and costs being disclosed as part of the investment disclosures of the reporting charity. Thus to the reader of the accounts the pool will not be visible as a separate fund.'
>
> *– SORP 2005, paragraph 451*

Although not specifically mentioned in the SORP, the obvious sub-analysis category for the disclosure of all forms of investment pooling arrangement is the one indicated by paragraph 303(b):

> '... investments listed on a recognised stock exchange *or ones valued by reference to such investments*, such as common investment funds, open-ended investment companies and unit trusts; ...'. (emphasis added)
>
> *– SORP 2005, paragraph 303(b)*

Reference should also be made to chapter 6, where the SoFA-accounting implications of investment pooling are discussed.

Chapter 10

THE BALANCE SHEET AND CHARITY RESERVES

INTRODUCTION

10.1 The Charities SORP requires few modifications to the form and contents and their methods and principles for commercial balance sheets, which have long since been standardised by company law – except to highlight heritage assets (chapter 8), to carry investment assets (with certain exceptions) at their current open market value and highlight any 'social investments' (chapter 9) and to summarise the charity's unspent funds according to *charity law* requirements, since these must take precedence for charities.

These are the *endowed* and other *restricted* funds and the *unrestricted* funds that we considered in chapter 6, showing how to account for all *movements in their values* between the two year-end balance sheets, the SoFA being the *primary accounting statement* for a charity to be able to demonstrate a 'proper application' of its funds in compliance with charity law and in doing so to reconcile its fund-balances from one year-end to the next.

We therefore review first the SORP's broad requirements for the presentation of a charity's *funds* in the balance sheet as something specific to the charity sector, followed by the presentation of its *assets and liabilities* and their analysis by fund, before moving on to look more closely at the calculation, explanation and presentation of *charity reserves* – the main theme of this chapter.

There, we will also consider the different legal requirements for *non-company* charities and *charitable companies*, as well as for *designated funds* – and especially the impact of *pension scheme* over-funding/under-funding for those charities required under FRS17 to show this as a notional asset/liability in their annual balance sheet.

STRUCTURED PRESENTATION

10.2 The Charities SORP requires all funds to be grouped together in the balance sheet according to their type. This will normally require their separation into at least the three main groups that are characterised by the two fundamental kinds of charity law restriction on the spending of charitable funds.

In *consolidated* balance sheets, and also (under FRS9) even in the absence of group accounts, there can also be a fourth type to cater for group funds held for purposes falling outside those categories: *non-charitable trading* funds.

Charity law distinction of fund-types

10.2.1   The *primary* possible distinction is that of 'trust capital', which for charities must be separated from all other, ie, non-capital funds and accounted for as 'endowment(s)' given *on trust for retention* rather than for immediate spending. *Endowments* are thus gifts for retention as capital, in the form of money or other assets either to facilitate activities, or else to provide an investment return to finance those activities – in both cases on a continuing basis. This return will normally take the form of (i) expendable *income* and (ii) non-expendable *capital* gains (less losses) arising on asset disposals and annual revaluations – or it may, if specially so authorised, be an undivided 'total return' out of which *discretionary* allocations are made from capital to income.

Either way, the capital must not be spent without first converting it into income on proper authority – which can come only from the gift's terms of trust or from the Charity Commission or the High Court. The primary restriction on endowments as such is therefore a total ban on spending them as income – though there may in addition be restrictions on the *purpose(s)* for which the capital and/or the income can be used. This restriction of purpose can also apply to unendowed funds, and is thus the other fundamental distinction in charity accounting.

Any legally binding restriction that uniquely narrows down the purposes for which a *gift* made to a charity (including a charitable company) can be used makes it a separate trust fund within that charity. Charity law then protects the donor's requirements so that the trust fund must be separately administered and only for its intended purpose(s). Prior to the Trustee Act 2000 ('TA 2000') this also precluded its investment assets being mixed with those of any other funds of the charity or of other charities – except as specially authorised by its terms of trust or by the Commission or the Court.

For the sake of simplicity and clarity in annual reporting, the Charities SORP requires the accounts to split the charity's funds into endowed and unendowed and the latter into restricted and unrestricted (otherwise known as 'income funds' – though that is strictly incorrect for the unrestricted fund of a charitable company, which is not a *trust* fund at all but is just an undivided 'corporate' fund of its own *absolute* property to be retained or spent at will – within reason). The greater latitude this allows is obliquely acknowledged (the emphasis is ours) in the Charity Commission's published 'Operational Guidance' to case-working staff when looking at charity reserves:

> 'Company law does not impose an explicit duty on the directors of a charitable company to apply its corporate property within a reasonable time of receipt ... But that does not mean that a company is entitled to retain income indefinitely. Potential beneficiaries are entitled to expect that the charity's property *will* be applied to further its objects unless there are good operational reasons against this ... Charitable companies will therefore need to have a reserves policy in relation to their corporate property, and we recommend that they disclose that policy in their annual report.'
>
> – *OG43/C1*

Although not required by the SORP, it can often be helpful to the user of the accounts to make a further split, either in the SoFA or (more usually) the balance sheet, or even in both, as a way of highlighting a particularly important *designated* fund – for example, for fixed assets for the charity's own (ie functional) use, or a self-financing charitable trading activity, as in the case of the independent schools sector, or (in consolidated accounts and/or under FRS9, where the figures are likely to be more significant) subsidiary/associated undertakings' *non-charitable* trading activities (the separate presentation of these funds being a SORP requirement anyway).

What is important in all cases is to show for the endowed and other restricted funds the same amounts as are disclosed at the foot of each column of the SoFA, whereas most of the fund-by-fund sub-analysis can usually be relegated to the notes required by the SORP in order to explain the nature and purpose of the individual funds and to summarise their movements and their constituent assets and liabilities. This is subject to one important proviso, however:

> '... expenditure may be incurred in anticipation of the receipt of restricted income, possibly leading to a negative balance on a specific fund. Where such balances are material they should be shown separately as negative balances and not simply be netted off against positive balances on the fund category in the balance sheet. Therefore the balance sheet may show both positive and negative balances on restricted funds.'
>
> – *SORP 2005, paragraph 251*

On the other hand, for commonsense reasons, where, for one of the three main categories, the year-end balances or the movements are considered *immaterial*, it need not be segregated in the SoFA and/or balance sheet respectively but can be grouped with the most similar of the other two categories, the necessary sub-analysis then being relegated to the notes – provided the grouped funds containing it in the SoFA and balance sheet are suitably re-titled and cross-referenced to show this. Thus the Restricted Funds column could contain immaterial endowments, or the Unrestricted Funds column could contain immaterial restricted funds – as long as a footnote to the SoFA discloses the fact and the amounts involved.

Fund-analysis of assets and liabilities

10.2.2 The SORP's structural requirements for the balance sheet are derived from those of the Companies Act 1985 ('the 1985 Act'), now rewritten as the Companies Act 2006 and its 2008 accounting/reporting Regulations (SI 2008/409 for the 'individual' accounts of 'small' companies and SI 2008/410 for the accounts of larger companies and groups), so paragraph 249 calls for the familiar sub-totals of:

- fixed assets;

- net current assets;

- total assets less current liabilities;

- other liabilities (ie, those not payable within one year); and

- net assets.

In addition, there is a specific option in the SORP – but not a requirement – to use a columnar approach in the balance sheet in order to show the spread of the charity's assets and liabilities across the three fund-types:

> 'Charities may choose to adopt a columnar presentation of ... assets, liabilities and funds in the balance sheet. Such a presentation shows the asset and liability categories analysed in

columns between each fund group in a similar way to the Statement of Financial Activities showing incoming resources and resources expended by type of fund ...'.

– SORP 2005, paragraph 248

Few charities seem to have favoured this option so far, as it can clutter up the balance sheet, and it also highlights any inter-fund loans – which would otherwise be relegated to the accounts notes. Where instead the normal (non-columnar) kind of presentation is used, the SORP requires the fund-analysis as an accounts note.

'The notes to the accounts should provide information on the structure of the charity's funds ... as well as identifying any material individual funds among them. In particular:

(a)   The assets and liabilities representing each type of fund of the charity should be clearly summarised and analysed (eg investments, fixed assets, net current assets) between those funds unless this information is presented in a columnar balance sheet.'

– SORP 2005, paragraph 75

However, the actual balance sheet presentation of assets and liabilities is required to be rather fuller than that cryptic summary of asset-types would seem to imply. Taking each of the main categories in turn.

'Own use' fixed assets

10.2.3   The balance sheet treatment of tangible and intangible fixed assets held for a charity's own (ie 'functional') use, as well as the sub-division of the former to show those that are or are not 'heritage', and also its more detailed sub-analysis in the accounts notes, are all covered in chapter 8.

Investment fixed assets

10.2.4   Again, we have already covered the balance sheet treatment for all types of investment assets (commercial and 'social' (ie charitable), fixed and current), as well as their sub-analysis in the accounts notes, in chapter 9.

Current assets, including long-term debtors

10.2.5   The SORP treatment here does not differ markedly from that of commercial accounting – except for specifying *current open market value* for any investment assets reclassified from fixed assets to this heading where the intention is to sell them and spend the proceeds rather than to retain them for reinvestment. Therefore these assets are required by the SORP to be summarised in the usual way to show:

–   stocks and work-in-progress;

–   debtors;

–   investment assets; and

–   cash at bank and in hand.

With charities, the debtors figure often includes components foreign to a commercial enterprise, so before the sub-analysis headings are specified paragraph 314 says that 'where there are debtors ... which do not fit into any of the following categories, the headings may be added to or adapted as appropriate to the type of debtor ... and nature of the charity'. With that proviso, the SORP's headings are:

> 'Debtors should be analysed in the notes to the accounts between short term and long term (above one year) giving amounts for the following:
>
> (a)   trade debtors;
> (b)   amounts due from subsidiary and associated undertakings;
> (c)   other debtors;
> (d)   prepayments and accrued income.'
>
> *– SORP 2005, paragraph 314*

To illustrate its more general requirement for the analysis of all assets and liabilities 'in a way that enables the reader to gain a proper appreciation of their spread and character', the SORP says that:

> '... long-term debtors should, where the total is material, be separately stated in the balance sheet – otherwise their total amounts by category ... should be analysed in the notes to the accounts.'
>
> *– SORP 2005, paragraph 249*

This could be particularly important where a charity provides substantial financing, commercially, ie other than for 'social investing' purposes (see below), on terms extending beyond the one year implied by classification as 'current' (in contrast the balance sheet distinction is more strictly enforced for liabilities – see below). One perhaps obvious example of this is where customers (other than a subsidiary or associated company, of course) are offered extended credit terms of any kind for commercial reasons rather than as a charitable benefit.

Any kind of financing on a continuing basis (ie 2 years or more) for charitable purposes, however, is likely to come within the newly recognised class of fixed assets called 'social investments' (see chapter 9) – for example, staff housing loans, benevolent fund loans to individuals in need or soft loans to other charities or for the charitable activities/projects of subsidiaries/associates, etc.

Current liabilities; long-term creditors and provisions

10.2.6 Again, the SORP's requirements are the familiar ones of commercial accounting:

–   creditors: amounts falling due within one year;

–   creditors: amounts falling due after more than one year;

–   provisions for liabilities and charges.

The same as for debtors, with charities the figure for creditors can often include components foreign to a commercial enterprise, so paragraph 318 of the SORP says that 'where there are ... creditors which do not fit into any of the following categories the headings may be added to or adapted as appropriate to the type of creditor and nature of the charity', after which proviso it goes on to prescribe the usual sub-analysis headings:

'The totals for both short-term and long-term creditors should each be separately analysed in the notes giving amounts for the following:

(a)   loans and overdrafts;
(b)   trade creditors;
(c)   amounts due to subsidiary and associated undertakings;
(d)   other creditors;
(e)   accruals; and
(f)   deferred income.'

– SORP 2005, paragraph 318

In accordance with the original, 1995 SORP's as yet unchallenged accounting concept derived from the commercial sector, time-restricted *general-purpose* grants intended for future activities will normally be included under 'deferred income' as current liabilities, but where the restriction defers their use for more than one year ahead, that part of the grant will then have to be treated as a 'long-term creditor'. An alternative treatment, which the SORP Committee rejected on a majority vote at the time, would have been to account for such grants/gifts as *temporarily restricted* funds, and to use the inter-fund transfers line of the SoFA to show the de-restriction once the required time has elapsed.

The SORP no longer makes the clear distinction contained in the original, 1995 SORP for the sake of preserving full accountability under trust law in respect of all restricted funds administered. We should therefore note here that the short-term time-restricting (as distinct from longer-term or even fixed-term endowing) of a special-purpose grant or gift of any kind which is intended by the donor for spending on some particular future activity or other (ignoring for the moment the performance-related grants identified by SORP 2005, which are actually a special case – see chapter 6) cannot logically justify non-recognition of the grant/gift as restricted income in the SoFA. (In passing, it is also worth mentioning that as long ago as 1993 the USA's FASB standards on gift-accounting (SFAS116/117) had worked out an appropriate accounting treatment for this kind of 'voluntary contribution' by recognising it as a fixed-term or temporary endowment.)

This is because the nature of such a use-restriction is not a denial of the charity's legal ownership of the asset nor of the benefit it can and should derive from its retention until spent. After all, the interest to be earned from putting such money on deposit until it becomes spendable does belong and accrue to the charity, albeit as part of the same restricted fund. As such, it must certainly be recognised as income as soon as it is earned, not just carried forward as deferred income like a kind of hidden reserve. Similarly, deposited covenants, although now marginalised by the introduction of the more spontaneous GiftAid Scheme in 2000, involved 'soft loans' to the charity extending over 4 years or more. As a popular extra, many donors used to sign a repayment waiver to cover premature death, thus securing the charity's future funding to that extent. Any such donor-prepayment would also require splitting between short- and long-term creditors.

We have already covered the principles for the accrual or non-accrual of charitable commitments under SORP 2005 in chapter 6 – see **6.7.1**. The only thing to add is that these, too, must be split between short- and long-term creditors in the same way.

CHARITY RESERVES

10.3 Charity Commission guidance/requirements on this subject as set in its Leaflet CC19 can be summarised in the two words: *explain* and *justify*. The principle is simple and easy, but in practice it can be difficult to apply until you have been able to confirm the legal status of any endowments and other restricted funds the charity may have or may have been assumed to have.

SORP 2000 had built on the success of CC19 by requiring a *policy* statement in the annual report, though this was mandatory only if the trustees already had one. That must be right, because such a policy can only be meaningful where actual or prospective reserves are significant enough to influence future plans/strategy. Where, as with many charities, funding is in such short supply in relation to expenditure needs that 'reserves' are but a pipe dream, policy statements about them can have no practical application except perhaps to weaken public confidence.

In other cases, it is obviously good management to establish minimum and maximum levels for reserves within which planned future activities can be budgeted for, and outside which remedial action can be considered. For example, maintaining adequate reserves can be crucial for survival in the 'contract culture' in which many local community-based charities have to operate, where the usual safety net provided by a charity's supporters may not exist, or else cannot counterbalance the erosion caused by competing to take on service-provision agreements that turn out to be inadequately funded.

As explained in chapter 4, the disclosures now required by the SORP on the subject of reserves must address the adequacy or deficiency of the charity's actual reserves in relation to the policy adopted, as well as the nature and purpose of any designated funds excluded in arriving at the reportable level of existing 'free reserves'. Although the SORP requires this as part of the trustees' annual report, some of the information could equally well be given in the accounts notes, with suitable cross-referencing.

Where reserves are considered inadequate, there will clearly be a funding need to be addressed and therefore an opportunity to invite further support for the charity's work. Where they seem to be over-adequate, for charities liable to statutory audit the Commission's monitoring system (in theory) kicks in – see **10.5**.

Only a charity's 'freely available' funds (ie free from legal/operational constraints preventing their being spent *now* on its general purposes) can count as its free reserves for Charity Commission purposes. In SORP-compliant accounts that show adequately designated funds (this distinction can be, but does not have to be, made in the balance sheet), properly explained and justified in the accounts notes, this will normally mean only the undesignated unrestricted funds. 'Normally', because in theory a restricted fund, too, can have free reserves, for example, if the funding has outstripped the demand for the public benefit for which it has been given – even if that is only temporarily so. The converse scenario, where it has 'negative reserves' due to spending in advance of the special-purpose funding available, is a sensitive one where the SORP requires special disclosures in the annual report as well as the highlighting of any such deficits in the balance sheet or the accounts notes – see chapter 3 on Fund-accounting, where at **3.3.6** we discuss both the disclosures and the charity law constraints on the trustees.

The balance sheet presentation of *all* restricted funds, both capital and income in nature, together with the supporting notes listing them and indicating the purposes for which the major funds are being held, the movements on them in the year and their constituent assets and liabilities at the year-end, must engender public confidence that these resources are being properly administered in compliance with the strict requirements of charity law concerning their respective terms of trust.

Such analysis and explanation also facilitates the proper appreciation of the nature of these *special-purpose* funds as being quite separate from the charity's *general* 'reserves' – subject to the special case of convertible *general-purpose* endowments, as discussed below. 'General', because reserves can also arise within special trusts and other distinct charities included in the accounts under the Charities Act's branch-accounting rules.

Significance of general-purpose endowments

10.3.1 Endowments as such are restricted trust funds of a *capital* nature, as already explained – even where the *purposes* for which they are to benefit the charity are *un*restricted. But the SORP also requires the accounts notes to distinguish the year's incoming *permanent* endowments from any that are *expendable* (convertible) or 'discretionary' according to their terms of trust, as well as citing the authority for doing so where any amounts are converted into income in the year (including any allocations from the 'unapplied total return' of a permanent endowment invested on that basis on special authority – see chapters 6 and 9).

Such 'internal' income, as with 'income' yields on the 'old' basis of investing, must increase the charity's reserves – except where the donor of the capital has restricted it to some special-purpose *activity*, when *all* income derived from the endowment will then belong to a separate restricted fund instead. Nevertheless, even where it would be available for the charity's *general* purposes upon conversion, *unconverted* capital does not count as part of the charity's reserves – and it is just because the law does not allow the Charity Commission to 'second-guess' the trustees' management decisions that such endowments are becoming increasingly popular.

Sinking funds v Charity Commission 'recoupment' orders

10.3.2 A charity with a permanent financial (ie invested) endowment may be able to borrow internally from it rather than having to go to outside sources to finance, say, a new building for its own use – a not uncommon situation. Once upon a time, *capital* expenditure on 'wasting' assets always entailed setting up a 'sinking fund' to provide for the asset's eventual replacement out of the revenues generated by its utilisation. But inflation and technology have long since made 'capital maintenance' lose its point when nobody can foresee what kind of replacement will be needed and when – or even what its cost might then be.

The Charity Commission 'Recoupment Order' that provides for the replacement of capital borrowed from such a permanent endowment could in fact be the last remnant of the abandoned concept of capital maintenance. The Commission will normally make such an order part of its terms of authorisation for using permanent endowment monies to build on either endowed or unendowed 'functional' land, for example, the grounds of a school, hospice, etc. This is because that kind of use of permanent endowment is officially seen as 'expenditure' – not as investment – thus as 'not in keeping' with the concept of permanence. It therefore cannot lawfully be done without special authority.

The Commission's preference is to authorise only a borrowing, so that the reduction of capital is temporary (though normally lasting decades, in order not to prejudice the charity's operational viability), to be covered by the Commission's 'Recoupment' Order obliging the trustees to build up a special internal fund (the recoupment fund) out of reserves by setting aside specified annual sums out of income to reach the target figure. The Order may or may not include special directions concerning the use of the investment income earned on the recoupment fund during these years. The Commission will normally take note of the trustees' preference here – again for the sake of the charity's continuing viability. The options are to roll up the investment income along with the investment gains, in order to reach the target figure earlier, or else to spend the annual income if the need to finance current activities is more pressing.

Upon maturing to that target figure, the special fund is automatically merged with the permanent endowment to discharge the Order by reimbursing capital on a 'pound-for-pound' basis – thus *without compensating for inflation*, which is thus officially ignored. Until then, although not yet endowed, the special fund must clearly be accounted for as a 'restricted fund' and disclosed as such in the accounts, in recognition of the official constraints on its use.

Recoupment periods can vary from 10–50 years or even longer, depending on how much the charity can afford. They can also be amended by the Commission or waived altogether, if the charity falls on hard times and cannot afford the set repayments.

The best presentation of such a recoupment fund and its associated inter-fund loan is still not specified in the Charities SORP, and may be affected by the materiality of the original borrowing and any uncertainties involved. It now includes at paragraph 350 'loans from permanent endowment' in requiring disclosure in the accounts notes of the terms of all inter-fund borrowing (see chapter 12), but that is all. One case encountered not so long ago was of some £500,000 borrowed from permanent endowment for building works nearly two decades before, under a 60-year Recoupment Order for a specified annual sum, in this case (as an exception to the general rule) requiring the accumulation of all income earned by the recoupment fund. The only certainties were the 60-year recoupment period and the annual sum, the amount actually borrowed never having been recorded (it was stated in the Order as the cost of carrying out certain works specified in the application for the Order). In the circumstances, it was the first of the two alternative treatments suggested below that was found viable – not the second.

Strictly speaking, the amount borrowed should be shown in the SoFA for that year as an inter-fund transfer, being the authorised conversion of permanent endowment into unrestricted income to be used for 'capital expenditure' (in the truest sense of the word). The notes to the accounts should then explain that the transfer is authorised under a Charity Commission Recoupment Order, and should outline its terms as required by paragraph 350. The internal borrowing will not increase the charity's reserves if the capital expenditure results in a corresponding increase in the fixed assets fund – thus preserving the right to avoid a kind of 'back-door' automatic conversion of reserves into permanent endowment in the event of the property's disposal.

Each year's recoupment should then be shown in the SoFA as a transfer from unrestricted to restricted funds, supported by the accounts note explaining the terms of the Recoupment Order. In the funds-analysis of assets and liabilities each year, the recoupment fund (represented by its own investment assets) will be seen as a restricted fund that builds up to the target figure. In the final year, the discharge of the Order upon merging the recoupment fund with the permanent endowment for which it was originally set up should be shown in the SoFA as a transfer of the total amount recouped to endowment funds out of the restricted funds column in which it will have been shown each year while the Recoupment Order was in force.

An alternative and perhaps more elegant treatment does not affect the SoFA at all. Instead, it just shows the original borrowing as an inter-fund loan in each year's funds-analysis of assets and liabilities, supported by the same kind of explanatory note, but describing the internal loan as an asset of the permanent endowment capital fund and a corresponding liability of the unrestricted funds. The annual sums taken out of free reserves and invested in accordance with the Order will then build up within a *designated* recoupment fund that always offsets the ring-fenced investment asset in the balance sheet.

As the capital expenditure has been financed by the loan, it cannot result in an increase in the fixed assets fund, and reserves remain unaffected by the borrowing transaction. The only difference to be seen where the investment income is to be rolled up as capital is that the recoupment fund will increase (and reserves will decrease) by both the recoupment sum and the rolled-up income each year. The internal loan itself, of course, will disappear when automatically extinguished upon the merging of the matured recoupment fund with the permanent endowment, which is reflected in the merging of their two investment portfolios.

Internal v external borrowing for 'temporary' reserves

10.3.3   For charities having no recourse to such a permanent financial endowment of their own, thus with no such 'soft option', the increasing competition for funding nowadays is making *temporary* financing from *external* sources a more attractive proposition – especially where this means 'soft loans' being offered by friends and supporters, by *charity-friendly* financial institutions like Unity Trust Bank, or major charities like CAF with its banking arm – or even by the big commercial banks and other corporate sponsors. Often the external loan will be secured on the fixed assets provided out of the reporting charity's reserves. Alternatively, a substantial 'draw-down' facility may be negotiated with the charity's bankers, to be used as a temporary buffer whenever the charity's own 'working capital' (where reserves are minimal) is insufficient.

The effect of using such an external borrowing facility is to release (even if only on a temporary basis) a corresponding part of the charity's otherwise locked-up general reserves by reducing the amount of the designated fund needed to represent those fixed assets. It can also sometimes provide vital protection against any suggestion that restricted funds might have been wrongly used to cover 'negative' reserves where unrestricted funds are fully designated – see chapter 3 where fund-deficits are covered in depth.

Definition of 'charity reserves'

10.3.4 The sector guidance provided for administrative purposes in CC19 defines 'reserves' as 'income which becomes available to the charity and is to be expended at the trustees' discretion in furtherance of any of the charity's objects, but is not yet spent, committed or designated'. This has made it clear that in practical terms *capital* funds – even those that are freely convertible into income at the trustees' own discretion – are excluded. The reason is that the law does not allow the regulator to 'second-guess' charity trustees' own decisions as to how best (and when) to provide the public benefit for which their charity has been set up.

It also clearly excludes all other restricted funds, funds tied up in assets held for the charity's own use or needed to cover unaccruable expenditure commitments already made, and also any other funds justifiably 'earmarked' as set aside (designated) to cover the costs of specific activities (projects) planned but not yet committed even only internally – as exemplified by this Armed Forces charity.

BALANCE SHEETS at 31 March 2008

		GROUP		CHARITY	
	Notes	2008	2007	2008	2007
		£000	£000	£000	£000
...		...	...	...	...
NET ASSETS	20	**40,258**	**40,980**	**40,269**	**41,001**
Represented by:					
CAPITAL FUNDS					
Endowment Funds	4	46	46	46	46
INCOME FUNDS					
Restricted Funds	3,22	5,895	6,638	5,895	6,638
Unrestricted Funds:					
– Designated Funds	2, 21	1,043	483	1,043	483
– General Funds	23	33,274	33,813	33,285	33,834
		40,258	**40,980**	**40,269**	**41,001**

CONSOLIDATED STATEMENT OF FINANCIAL ACTIVITIES
for the year ended 31 March 2008

	General Funds	Designated Funds	Restricted Funds	Total 2008	Total 2007
	£000	£000	£000	£000	£000
...	...	...	...	...	...
TOTAL INCOMING RESOURCES	6,481	799	205	7,485	7,565
...					
Costs of Generating Funds	2,246	47	–	2,293	3,105

CONSOLIDATED STATEMENT OF FINANCIAL ACTIVITIES
for the year ended 31 March 2008

	General Funds	Designated Funds	Restricted Funds	Total 2008	Total 2007
	£000	£000	£000	£000	£000
Charitable Activity Costs	3,919	227	747	4,893	4,841
Governance Costs	70	–	–	70	47
Total expenditure	**6,235**	**274**	**747**	**7,256**	**7,993**
Net Incoming/(Outgoing) Resources	**246**	**525**	**(542)**	**229**	**(428)**
(Loss)/Gains on investments	(735)	(15)	(201)	(951)	2,082
Net Movement in Funds	**(489)**	**510**	**(743)**	**(722)**	**1,654**

NOTES TO THE ACCOUNTS at 31 March 2008

1. ACCOUNTING POLICIES

Accounting convention

The accounts have been prepared under the historical cost convention as modified by the revaluation of investments, and in accordance with the Statement of Recommended Practice (SORP 2005) 'Accounting and Reporting by Charities', published in March 2005, applicable accounting standards, the Charities Acts 1993 and 2006 and the Charities (Accounts and Reports) Regulations 2005.

TRUSTEES' REPORT

...

RESERVES

The Trustees have also determined that, for reserves policy management purposes, the General Fund Reserves should be separated into Strategic Reserves and Contingency Reserves. As at 31 March 2008 the General Fund Reserves of £33.3 million are made up of Strategic Reserves of £27.0 million (2007: £26.0 million) and Contingency Reserves of £6.3 million (2007: £7.8 million).

There are a number of factors which determine the appropriate level of Strategic Reserves: ... It is considered prudent for the Fund to hold in reserve an amount equivalent to between 18 and 24 month's Unrestricted Funds benevolence grants for individuals and to other charities ... and this requires a reserves holding of around £7 million.

The Fund acts as a strategic reserve for other Army benevolent funds including those of Regiments and Corps, who currently make benevolence grants in excess of £5 million a year. It also has an obligation to support the Army Dependants' Trust (ADT), where it has been agreed that if that organisation's net outgoing resources in any one year exceed £3 million then the Army Benevolent Fund will, if necessary, make available a loan of up to £4 million. It is considered that the Fund should hold in reserve an amount equivalent to between 18 and 24 month's Regimental and Corps benevolence grants, and combined with the obligation to the ADT this requires a reserves holding of around £13 million.

In addition the Fund needs to ensure that it can maintain the appropriate infrastructure to make benevolence payments on its own behalf and also on behalf of Regiments and Corps for a period of up to two years. The reserves required to satisfy this obligation are around £3.6 million. Taking all of these factors into account the level of Strategic Reserves required is around £24 million.

The Contingency Reserves have arisen largely as a result of investment gains and are held to absorb investment losses which may arise in the future ...

The Trustees feel that in current circumstances the level of the Strategic and Contingency Reserves are prudent and appropriate.

The Army Benevolent Fund – 2007/08 Annual Report and Accounts

Comment

Against the Charity Commission's original 1995 'benchmark' level of 3 years, as published in its website Operational Guidance, the apparent free reserves here equate to nearly 5 years' total expenditure (or, if ignoring fundraising activities, 7 years' charitable expenditure) in hand. It thus needs a reasoned reserves policy to show that this is no excessive retention of unspent income. The declared intention here to retain the whole of the Fund's £39m investment portfolio to finance annual grant-making implies a capital-retention power not supported by the accounts disclosures. By declaring a policy of holding all reserves intact as either 'strategic' or contingent on falling investment markets, nothing at all is left as 'free reserves' to be explained and justified. This is an area of trust law and public accountability that still remains something of a mystery to most trustees – simply because until now nobody has felt it right to question the legal basis for their decisions if based on long-standing custom and practice.

For accounting and reporting purposes, the SORP provides a very carefully reasoned and objective definition of reserves in its Glossary at GL 51:

'The term "reserves" has a variety of technical and ordinary meanings, depending on the context in which it is used. In this SORP the term "reserves" (unless otherwise indicated) describes that part of a charity's income funds that is freely available. This definition of reserves therefore normally excludes:

(a)   permanent endowment funds;
(b)   expendable endowment funds;
(c)   restricted funds;

and any part of unrestricted funds not readily available for spending, specifically:

(d)   income funds which could only be realised by disposing of fixed assets held for charity use and ["social"] investments.

Individual charities may have more or less reserves available to them than this simple calculation suggests for example:

(a)   Expendable endowments may be readily available for spending or
(b)   Unrestricted funds may be earmarked or designated for essential future spending and reduce the amount readily available.'

– *SORP 2005, Glossary GL 51*

The second paragraph above challenges trustees to defend their position here on what SORP 2000 opened up for further consideration (now to be found only in the Charity Commission's own website guidance on the subject) by extending the definition to say:

'There is an argument[1] for saying that expendable endowment and designated income funds ought to be counted as reserves. The argument is that in each case the trustees are free to regard the funds, if they so choose, as available for general purpose expenditure. There are no

---

[1]   The old SORP's suggested 'argument' here has not been taken further, but in any case would raise practical objections. Some expendable endowments are for restricted purposes. In some cases the spending of an endowment depends wholly/partly on non-discretionary factors, such as time, or the useful economic life of the fund's asset if held on trust for the charity's own use on a continuing basis. Designated funds representing fixed assets already provided for the charity's own use or either 'social investment' or 'capital expenditure' commitments could possibly be regarded as potential reserves only to the extent that such an asset could be dispensed with entirely or else pledged as a source of temporary funding – the implications for

legal restrictions preventing trustees treating those two types of funds as free, general purpose funds. But there are practical reasons, why the funds should not normally be regarded as free (though there are exceptions). A charity will not be justified in creating, or transferring resources to, a designated fund where the main purpose of doing this is to allow the charity to show a reduced level of reserves.

By contrast, restricted funds can never be regarded as general purpose funds. Restricted income funds do not fall within the scope of reserves as the term is used in this SORP. Nevertheless, the legal principles on the retention of income apply to restricted income funds, as do the principles of justifying and explaining any retention. For the purpose of applying the principles in this SORP it is suggested that trustees treat each restricted income fund as if it were a separate charity. Thus, each material restricted income fund could have its own "reserve", which should be justified and (if practicable) explained in its own right.'

– SORP 2000, Glossary GL 27

The regulator's argument for requiring the explaining and justifying of any continuing retention of significant amounts of *restricted* income (e g on special-purpose trust funds) is more subtle than the above, backed up as it is by the Commission's legal powers to deal with *unreasonable* delay by trustees in meeting their charity law obligation to apply all income funds for their proper purposes. Even though the matter is not highlighted in SORP 2005, charities should therefore review the operation of any *special trust* fund balances still being carried forward unused after some years, in order to explain and justify any material retentions in the same way as for *unrestricted* reserves.

Calculating reserves levels

10.3.5   The starting point for this is the total funds on the charity's balance sheet, from which you must first eliminate the endowed and other restricted funds, as already indicated. This includes *expendable* endowments because until the power to expend capital as income is actually exercised, they must be retained as capital and therefore to treat them as part of the reserves would be incorrect. However, since such funds can be spent following a decision by the trustees to do so, they cannot be entirely eliminated from any consideration of *funding needs* when justifying the existing level of reserves held, so that they are not without a certain significance where reserves are high.

Restricted funds of a non-capital nature are those held on trust for *donor-specified activities* that are *narrower* than the reporting charity's declared Objects, so the funds cannot lawfully be used for any wider or different purposes. However, because these restricted funds must by law be spent within a reasonable time, entailing their proper management in the meantime, the trustees' spending policy in respect of each restricted fund held can – as indicated above – have a 'reserves' aspect, albeit only in relation to each individual fund and without normally impacting on general reserves.

'Fixed assets', 'social investments' and other designated funds

10.3.6   As we saw from the SORP's definition, the elimination of *designated funds* in calculating the amount of the charity's year-end reserves may be open to question by the purists, but in practice the Commission does accept that, properly maintained, such

---

the charity's operational efficiency being in each case a matter of judgment that is not normally open to question by the Commission. A similar counter-argument would apply to funds designated for future charitable activity projects.

funds are already spoken for and are therefore not as *freely available* as they would have to be to count as *general* 'reserves' – even though, at a pinch, they could be made available.

In particular, funds which could only be realised by disposing of 'social investments' or dispensing with fixed assets acquired out of the charity's *general-purpose* funds for its own use (e g buildings or equipment), must be respected as 'committed' funds to the extent that the trustees still regard these assets as needed for operational purposes, thus to further its charitable objectives. The only basis for their realisation or sale (without some form of replacement) would be the curtailment of some of those activities – or ultimately of all of them, thus the termination of what the charity now does to provide public benefit as a 'going-concern' – when such a basis can no longer be used as the carrying value of the assets in question unless there was no question of a forced sale of assets at undervalue in order to meet pressing demands from creditors.

Of course, fixed assets acquired out of *endowed* funds belong to capital – already eliminated from the calculation (see above) – and must therefore be ignored here to prevent their being eliminated twice over!

The standard way to make the need for continued retention of such 'locked up' funds clear is to set up a designated 'fixed assets' fund that serves to 'ring-fence' each class of committed reserves so that they will not be mixed up with the free reserves to be disclosed and reported on.

SORP 2000 dealt only with the fixed assets fund ('social investment' had not yet been recognised by then for accounting purposes), recommending that it should be shown separately from other designated funds in the balance sheet and adjusted annually to reflect the year's increases and decreases – and with an accounts note to explain any material effect on the charity's reserves (thus implying the same funds-based analysis as in the SoFA, of course):

'Note of Changes in Resources Applied for Fixed Assets for Charity Use

Where resources expended during the year on the acquisition of functional fixed assets is material, this fact should be explained in a note to the accounts to help the reader understand the impact on the more liquid funds of the charity. It may be useful for this note to follow on immediately after the reconciliation of funds at the bottom of the Statement of Financial Activities. The format should, where necessary, show:

(a) net movement in funds for the year (from the Statement of Financial Activities);
(b) resources used for net acquisitions (or obtained from net disposals) of fixed assets for charity use (ie the increase or decrease in the net book value of functional fixed assets);
(c) net movement in funds available for future activities (ie those not held in functional fixed assets).'

– SORP 2000, paragraph 180

SORP 2005 expands this analysis to include reserves committed to 'social investment', but sees no need for the note to be given the special prominence it was accorded by SORP 2000. While recognising that *'charities also further their objectives by investing in tangible fixed assets to provide services or by making investments of a programme or social related nature'* and that *'such applications are charitable but do not decrease the funds of a charity'*, it goes on instead to observe that *'information on such charitable applications and sources can be ascertained from a charity's cash flow statement (when prepared)'*. Therefore – in deference to the ASB, which was never comfortable with the note's closeness to the SoFA – the SORP no longer gives it any special prominence.

The Cashflow Statement, of course, cannot include such assets coming to the charity as a *gift in kind*, since no cash is involved, just as it cannot include depreciation and impairment – which also affect the *spendable funds* figure that interests the public. And as long as the SoFA is the *audited* primary statement referred to in the auditor's report (rather than Cashflow – which normally is not even mentioned there), the public will understandably tend to look to the former rather than the latter.

As for the note's format, SORP 2005 abandons the funds-based analysis that enabled it to be linked to the SoFA. It recommends instead a charity-total format that fails to distinguish between restricted and unrestricted funds. It also omits the all-important final line intended to inform the public *how much new unrestricted money is available for spending on future activities*:

> 'Where relevant a charity may choose to provide in the notes to the accounts the following information:
>
> (a)   total net movement in funds for the year;
> (b)   net endowment receipts for the year ...;
> (c)   net expenditure on additions to functional fixed assets ... for the year; and
> (d)   net investment in programme related investments ... for the year.'

– SORP 2005, paragraph 243

We would therefore suggest a necessary enhancement here by replacing line (c) with SORP 2000's more appropriate wording for the year's *net movement on functional fixed assets*, and adding a fifth line (e) as the resultant 'net movement in funds available for future activities', including a columnar analysis of these charity-total figures to match the SoFA (in which case line (b) should be dropped as it then becomes redundant) and either making the note a footnote to the SoFA or cross-referencing to it the SoFA's 'net movement in funds' line.

SORP 2000 had to give up the latitude allowed by the 1995 SORP in respect of forward charitable commitments, which meant that only truly 'internal' commitments could be ring-fenced from reserves by setting aside the amounts required as designated funds – all non-conditional 'external' commitments being required to be accrued as *expenditure of the year*, as even if not legally binding they now count as 'constructive obligations' according to the rules of FRS12. The SORP's interpretation of those rules was then refined in SORP 2005, since commitment-accounting problems of this kind are common among the larger grant-making charities funding longer-term external research projects, and also in the education sector where scholarships and bursaries (disregarding those to subsidise the charity's own, as yet unearned, fee-based service-provision) need to cover several years ahead. The assurance of future funding needed by the beneficiary then has to be weighed against the uncertainty needed by the grant-making charity so that the future commitment will not be an immediate liability under SORP 2005. Chapter 6 goes into all this in some detail for SoFA purposes.

But there are often good reasons for setting up designated funds for *other* purposes. Even the unaccrued 'capital expenditure' commitments familiar in the commercial world are valid here – though these are more properly added to the fixed assets designated fund. Similarly, any material commitments to further social investing should be added to the social investments designated fund. For example, the board of trustees may decide to expand/extend into other lines of charitable activity within the charity's Objects, or perhaps to embark on a fundraising project, in both cases by committing 'start-up' funding to carry the project through the early years of its resource-expenditure or 'outlay' before future revenues can make it self-funding.

Whatever the project, if the board think it needs funding out of reserves, and if it is a genuine intention at the time (and also a proper application of the charity's resources, of course), such is the trustees' freedom of decision under charity law that the funds so earmarked can no longer be regarded by others as 'freely available' and should therefore be eliminated in calculating the year-end reserves figure.

But there is yet another kind of designated fund to be considered as a possibility here, not to finance future projects but to cover existing *non-accruable contingencies* which if they were to 'crystallise' would materially reduce reserves. One obvious example would be where a substantial claim of some kind has been made against the charity. A commercial organisation would merely note the contingent liability (if unaccruable). However, a charity with high reserves might instead find it expedient to ring-fence the possible liability in a *'contingent claims'* fund – under a suitable name, of course, in order not to prejudice the charity's position in the eyes of the claimant!

Another example, one that could mitigate a problem for *charitable companies* (*not* trusts) with high reserves but dependent to some extent on unendowed investment returns to finance current activities, might be an *'investment contingencies'* fund to ring-fence the extent of the portfolio's exposure to market risk. This would be the directors' quantification (on advice) of the proportion of the corporate portfolio value that, due to this dependency, should be held back as a matter of prudent management and therefore could not really form part of its 'freely available' reserves for spending on future activities without prejudicing the level of those activities.

This is not at all the same as the idea some have put forward of treating the corporate revaluation reserve (see **10.4**) as a designated fund – for which there would be no possible charity law justification, since the portfolio's 'unrealised gain' is clearly affected by the 'churn' frequency (sales/purchases), whereas the market risk is not. (The error here is even compounded for any charity adopting the 'marking to market' rule now permitted by SORP 2005 (and sanctioned by the ASB in conflict with its own FRS3 rules) as a way of eliminating all investment disposal gains from the SoFA.)

The Charity Commission's case-working staff are given the following guidance about how to determine whether a designated fund is acceptable or not:

'Purposes for which designated funds are *clearly acceptable* include:

- provision for a grant which the charity is not legally bound to pay but which it has a clear intention of paying;
- a repairs and renewals fund where there is an asset or group of assets clearly identified and the amount is reasonable in relation to the expected repairs account. (There may, for example, be a five yearly property inspection to which the fund builds up.) Such a fund may even have been set up on our advice – for example, an Emergency or Cyclical Repair Fund for an almshouse charity that is neither required nor authorised

by the charity's governing document. (Where trustees are required or authorised by the charity's governing document to set up a fund for a particular purpose, it is *restricted* not designated);

- a fund to save for an event which takes place every so often – for example, a conference taking place every ten years;
- money put aside for a building project that is planned to be carried out in the future but for which the resources needed cannot be found all at once;
- a fund to cover the future expenses of current life members. Such a fund balance might even be actuarially assessed;
- a fund to provide for the winding down of a project where there is a strong possibility that this might happen though the exact timing is not known. Such a fund may need to take account particularly of possible redundancy costs.

Items which might need to be challenged include:

- provision for some extremely unlikely event;
- a fund set aside to generate income to cover future expenditure (rather than to spend as income). This is because, had the money been intended for this, it would have been sought or given as an endowment;
- a sum clearly in excess of the amount required for the intended purpose, e g a repair fund which greatly exceeds the rebuilding cost of the building.'

– OG43/C1

The following illustration shows how the proper presentation of designated funds can clarify the charity reserves position rather than – as is often done – masking it by their relegation to the Notes.

BALANCE SHEET

Year Ended 31 March 2008		Charity		Group	
	Note	**2008**	**2007**	**2008**	*2007*
		£'000	*£'000*	*£'000*	*£'000*
...					
FUNDS					
Unrestricted Funds:					
General Funds		10,449,681	*12,343,127*	10,449,681	*12,343,127*
Designated Funds	8	62,209,972	*62,113,403*	62,209,972	*62,113,403*
		72,659,653	*74,456,530*	72,659,6534	*74,456,530*
Permanent Endowment Fund	7	50	*50*	50	*50*
		72,659,703	*74,456,580*	**72,659,703**	*74,456,580*

STATEMENT OF FINANCIAL ACTIVITIES

For the year ended 31 March 2008		**Unrestricted Funds**		**2008**	**2007**
		General	**Designated**	**Total**	*Total*
		£000	*£000*	*£000*	*£000*
...					
Total Incoming Resources		3,228,228	11,433,132	14,661,360	*21,930,280*
...					
Total Resources Expended	16	2,000,642	11,907,788	13,908,430	*16,346,947*

Net Incoming Resources before transfers		1,227,586	(474,656)	752,930	5,583,333
Transfers between funds	8	(3,121,032)	3,121,032	–	–
Net Incoming Resources before other recognised gains/losses		(1,893,446)	2,646,376	752,930	5,583,333
Investment gains/(losses)		–	(2,549,807)	(2,549,807)	1,276,991
Net movement in Funds		(1,893,446)	96,569	(1,796,877)	6,860,324

Poor Servants of the Mother of God – 2007/08 Accounts

Evaluating reserves adequacy/deficiency

10.3.7   Having calculated the year-end level of *free* reserves as above, the next step is for the trustees to evaluate their adequacy or otherwise in relation to any contingencies with serious enough implications for the charity's future activities to make it advisable to retain *'buffer-funds'* against them. This will identify the *minimum* level of reserves needed in readily available form (but suitably invested in the meantime) for viability. The use of 'sensitivity analysis' to evaluate 'best-case' and 'worst-case' scenarios will enable a *maximum* level to be derived in much the same way as strategic and business plans are evaluated to see how robust they are and what management action is safe to base on them. Some of the more obvious contingencies are discussed below.

'Working capital'

Any organisation needs to maintain 'cashflow' to allow it to continue its operations on a going concern basis, since (although not as harshly as in the commercial sector) 'cash is king' here too. Ready money is needed to pay for operating expenditure, for example, staff salaries, buildings maintenance, purchase of stationery, utilities, telecommunications, etc. But *charity* cashflow planning/control must make due allowance for immediate payment needs and any lag in the flow of the *right kind of funds* to meet them, and then retain sufficient *unrestricted* cash in reserve to avoid running out unexpectedly and being forced into emergency action to bridge the gap.

The funding needs for *day-to-day* activities cannot be fully appreciated by looking at the balance sheet figures for net current assets on unrestricted funds from year to year in relation to their cash/bank balances/borrowings. Fluctuations during the year, due to buying for stock, leads and lags in paying for other supplies and services, staff costs, etc, and receiving funds from donors/customers, etc, the timing of which cannot always be precisely controlled, will normally result in cashflow 'peaks and troughs' that need 'smoothing' for good financial management.

From the *fund-by-fund* daily/weekly/monthly cashflow forecasts used (depending on volatility) the deepest of these troughs on *unrestricted* funds, after filling any troughs on *restricted* funds, is the indicator of the minimum level of cash reserves needed as 'working capital' – subject to any overdraft facilities and other sources of temporary funding, some of which can be seen in the balance sheet where the net current assets figure is negative.

However, be warned that Charity Commission staff looking at working capital needs are given very specific Operational Guidance here – even if it is hedged around with the usual caveats to prevent anyone jumping to premature conclusions:

'The amount of working capital that can be justified will vary from charity to charity. As a *very general guide*, few people would take issue with working capital levels representing three to four months' gross expenditure. More than this could probably be justified if, say, grant income arrived in six-monthly or twelve-monthly amounts. But this is a matter for consideration by the trustees. There is no "norm": many charities have very little working capital and some will rely on loans to provide this.'

– OG43/C1

The 'safety net'

The 'going concern' basis of accounting implies the continuing viability of the charity to adapt its activities from time to time to cope with changing circumstances which cannot always be reliably foreseen and anticipated. This means retaining sufficient reserves as a kind of safety net in case of the unexpected. For example, membership charities are usually dependent on subscription income. Should a rival organisation be set up with similar aims, the effect could be to divert part of the charity's main source of funds. Another example is of a charity dependent on its appeals income if changes in public sympathies result in a sudden and unexpected drop in its 'donor-appeal'. Any such occurrence will invalidate existing cashflow forecasts, constraining future and perhaps also current activities, and may therefore need to be guarded against as a contingency by carrying correspondingly larger reserves.

Opportunities

Trustees should also, however, consider whether there is a need for funds to expand the charity's activities (within current or long-term plans) or to exploit new areas of opportunity. An example would be how to fund a project where it had been hoped full governmental funding would be available, but where only partial funding was achieved. In the case of an *endowed* charity, in formulating these plans the trustees also have to maintain the right balance in meeting the needs of current and future beneficiaries. All these factors make it advisable to retain sufficient reserves to be able to make the best use of opportunities as they arise.

Trustees' duty to 'apply' trust income

The general duty imposed by charity law requires all *unendowed trust* funds (ie excluding those that are of a 'capital' nature under trust law) to be used (ie spent) in furthering the charity's Objects within a 'reasonable' time from when they are received – subject to any specific requirements or powers in the governing document of that trust. Therefore such trust funds must not be unreasonably retained as reserves that are not actually needed to maintain viability, even in some cases being invested as a kind of pseudo-endowment that then becomes self-perpetuating through the myth that it cannot be spent without prejudicing future activities. This applies equally to the trust funds of charitable companies – hence the Commission's internal instructions on reserves-monitoring:

'Where a charitable company is a trustee of material charitable funds (normally reported as restricted funds in the company's accounts) the reserves policy in relation to those funds should also be produced.'

– OG43/C1

Prior to the 1995 SORP and the clarification it brought for *fund-based* management and accountability, many charities had reinvested for long-term retention substantial unspent income funds without any thought of justifying or explaining such action – contrary to this duty. On realising that they had been sitting on such unendowed trust funds instead of spending them, the trustees obviously needed to review the position and adopt a new strategic plan to put the charity back into the correct position by eliminating all excess reserves. Clearly, this did not mean their immediate expenditure at all costs but rather their use to finance *accelerated* project-development plans aiming to deliver the *immediate* public benefit (as distinct from long-term) for which they were intended in the first place.

Care is always needed to ensure that there is proper authority in place for any charity income so far accumulated as capital (or just retained as reserves in excess of obvious needs) and that the purpose of doing so is clear. Since that authority may be a constitutional one, OG43 reminds Charity Commission staff:

> 'You will also need to look at the charity's governing document to ensure there is no provision which expressly prohibits the holding of reserves or, alternatively, which expressly allows this for specified periods.'

– OG43/C1

Some trust deeds expressly empower the trustees to retain income at their own discretion within any limitations imposed by law, thus authorising reserves retention beyond the normal limit of 'a reasonable time after receipt'. In such a case, the trustees might well be able to argue that even a pseudo-endowment is being properly retained if that seems to be the best way to ensure continuity of service. In some cases, however, there may be only an *implied* power by reference to donors' known but unexpressed wishes, or to the nature of the purpose for which the charity is established – for example, to provide *temporary* assistance to a certain class of persons in need, for which substantial reserves may need to be maintained. Where this includes the making of repayable grants, however, the funding for it can be ring-fenced under SORP 2005 in the form of a social investment fund.

In other cases the trustees may be *required* to carry out the *founder's* wish to build up a permanent endowment out of annual income – subject to the trust law 'rule against perpetuities', though this can in fact run for quite a long time: terminating as much as 21 years after the date of the trust deed, or even later if specified as 21 years after the death of a named person living at the time.

If doubts remain, Charity Commission help may be needed to regularise the position once and for all.

One other factor that can easily be overlooked because it is not often encountered in practice is whether there are any constitutional powers/restrictions affecting reserves retention. In practical terms, the power would be to *retain income* (either as 'reserves' or by conversion into capital), whereas the restriction would have to be a *requirement to capitalise unspent income* each year, usually by adding it to the related permanent endowment – thus 'zeroising' all reserves from the outset.

You will also need to look at the charity's governing document to ensure there is no provision which expressly prohibits the holding of reserves or, alternatively, which expressly allows this for specified periods.

Charitable companies' corporate reserves

While the *trust funds* of a charitable company are subject to the above requirements in just the same way as any other trust, their *corporate* funds are different: as mentioned above, these are not held on charitable trusts at all, but are owned absolutely. (These reserves also include the statutory 'revaluation reserve', for which there are special disclosure requirements – we discuss these at **10.4**.) That gives the company the right to do what it likes with these funds – as long as that is in accordance with the powers bestowed, and obligations imposed, by the Memorandum and Articles of Association, of course – one of these obligations being to aim to provide the public benefit intended by the company's charitable Objects and not to fail to do so.

The company, though a legal 'person' in its own right, can act only via its executive officials, its directors, who themselves must act in accordance with the proper wishes of the membership, the latter being somewhat akin to trust-founders, but with a statutory reserved power to be able to amend the company's constitution at any time – subject to Charity Commission veto under Part VIII of the Charities Act 1993 ('the 1993 Act') if any such amendment might detract from the public benefit that is intrinsic to charity status, of course.

Within the rigorous framework of company law, therefore, underpinned by the supervisory powers of the Charity Commission as the general sector regulator, the particular constraints of the company's own constitution operate to achieve much the same end as does charity law in the case of a trust or unincorporated association. For the directors would not be acting with the propriety required by law if they were not to take all reasonable care to administer their *corporate* reserves with due regard to the needs of the intended beneficiaries. In practice, this means that spending must not be unreasonably delayed – though that does, of course, allow greater latitude than the *positive duty* to spend unendowed trust funds within a reasonable time.

Tools for financial evaluation/control

Clearly, some form of budgetary control is needed to make proper use of the available financial information to obtain a clear assessment of the need for funds in monetary terms. The minimum requirements for this are:

–   a 'strategic' plan (normally derived from a published 'mission statement') for the direction to be taken by the charity in the longer term, say the next 10 years, in order to further its Objects in the way the trustees deem best in the circumstances;

–   a 'business plan' – to translate the strategic plan into action in the medium term, usually taken as 3–5 years nowadays;

–   an 'incoming funds' forecast for the current and following year in detail;

–   expenditure forecasts for each distinct charitable fund on the same basis (matched with available funding to achieve planned activity levels within the range set by the charity's reserves policy – thus tending to the ideal of a 'balanced budget');

–   cashflow forecasts for fund-by-fund day-to-day management control of revenues, of expenditure on activities and of 'capital expenditure' – each on the same basis.

The following table shows how to calculate the charity's actual free reserves.

Calculation/evaluation of the charity's free reserves:

	This year £'000	Last year £'000
Total funds per balance sheet	X	*x*
Deduct:		
Permanent Endowments (note xx)	(x)	*(x)*
Expendable Endowments (note xx)	(x)	*(x)*
Restricted Funds (note xx)	(x)	*(x)*
Designated project funds (note xx)	(x)	*(x)*
Social Investment Fund (reserves used plus new commitments)	(x)	*(x)*
Fixed Assets Fund (assets for own use, provided from reserves)	(x)	*(x)*
Total deductions	(x)	*(x)*
Undesignated Unrestricted Funds at year-end: charity reserves	X	*x*
Evaluation of reserves needs:		
'Working capital' needs	(x)	*(x)*
'Safety net' needs	(x)	*(x)*
'Free' reserves above the minimum level*	X̲	*x̲*

(* 'Appeal Needs' – if negative)

Note the separation of the fixed assets fund, usually shown in the balance sheet or accounts notes as a separate designated fund in view of its special nature (which should include any outstanding commitments to *planned* capital expenditure to be made out of existing reserves), and also nowadays the social investment fund under **SORP 2005**.

The Commission's guidance specifically excludes these *fixed assets* funds from the definition of free reserves.

The advantage of segregating material designated funds on the face of the balance sheet is the avoidance of any misunderstandings arising from a too superficial 'quick glance' review by accounts-users, which may only notice the figure of 'unrestricted' or 'general' funds as the apparent 'charity reserves'. The difference this can make is graphically illustrated by the following example.

BALANCE SHEET	Without designation A £'000	With designation B £'000
Fixed assets held for charity use	500	500
Social Investment fixed assets	250	250
(Other) Investment fixed assets	100	100
Net current assets	400	400

BALANCE SHEET	Without designation	With designation
	A	B
	£'000	£'000
	1,250	**1,250**
Funds		
Endowment funds	100	100
Restricted income funds	150	150
Unrestricted funds		
– Designated: Fixed Assets Fund (held for the charity's own use)	–	500
– Designated: Social Investment Fund	–	250
– Undesignated (apparent 'charity reserves')	1,000	250
	1,250	**1,250**

Explaining and justifying charity reserves

10.3.8   As an overall measure, free reserves should be reviewed against unaccrued contingent liabilities not specially covered by designated funds, in order to ensure that any likely impact on reserves can be absorbed. However, it is not suggested that a specific amount should necessarily be designated for all these contingent liabilities, since by definition the amounts are only possibilities, to be covered by the 'safety net' of the charity's free reserves.

Charity Commission case-working staff are given the following Operational Guidance here, where OG43 says:

'... a charity may need to maintain reserves at a certain level in order to:

-   protect against a decline or interruption of future sources of income – discretionary grants, for example, may cease, or be reduced, and new sources of revenue have to be found;
-   provide for regular fluctuations in income and expenditure – incomings and outgoings are unlikely to coincide exactly. Money may need to be set aside to meet regular quarterly or annual bills. Income may peak at a particular time of the year – perhaps as a result of a regular and successful annual appeal – and need to be set aside to cover leaner months;
-   ensure continuity in its provision of a service. The service provided by many charities is an integral and essential part of the lives of beneficiaries. To have to withdraw or cut back with little or no notice could cause very real hardship;
-   assimilate a large legacy or donation which cannot be spent all at once – it would be unreasonable to insist that a charity spend immediately a one-off windfall out of all proportion to its regular income. ([Where there is circumstantial evidence of capital intentions] ... it might be appropriate to treat such a gift as endowment);
-   assimilate an abnormally large dividend (one which perhaps just fell short of being capable as treated as a partial return of capital investment ...).'

– OG43/C1

Trustees need to decide what designated and undesignated (ie freely available) reserves are reasonable and appropriate for their charity and to keep that decision under regular review. While that does not mean they have to distinguish between designated and undesignated funds within unrestricted funds in the balance sheet, a sub-analysis showing the free reserves will clearly assist public understanding of the more extensive reserves disclosures in the annual report under SORP 2005 to highlight the nature and purpose of material designated funds (also the timescale for their use/spending) deducted in arriving at the reported level of *freely available* reserves. For in this context SORP 2005 specifically observes:

'The objective of the balance sheet is to show the resources available to the charity and whether these are freely available or have to be used for specific purposes because of legal restrictions on their use. It may also show which of the resources the trustees have designated for specific future use ...'.

– SORP 2005, paragraph 245

Referring back to the calculation table shown above, the following specimen wording shows how the charity's free reserves might then be explained and justified in the context of the trustees' policy.

Explanation/justification of reserves level by reference to the trustees' policy:

The charity needs reserves to protect its current activities, in order to allow the trustees to meet their day-to-day responsibilities and to ensure that it continues to operate on a going concern basis. The trustees have examined the needs, risks and challenges faced by the charity in both the short and medium term, along with relevant financial forecasts, and have formulated a policy to meet those needs, which are satisfied by the level of reserves at the Balance Sheet date. Designated general purpose funds include £x to cover the charity's need for fixed assets already held for its own use (as shown in the Balance Sheet) or to be acquired over the next 2 years; £x to cover existing and planned social investments to cover projects expected to be completed within the next 3 years and £x to finance the launching of new services planned for next year. Undesignated general purpose funds as shown in the Balance Sheet represent 'x' months of total expenditure at current levels.

The trustees consider that, in view of the level of commitment needed to provide reasonable assurance to beneficiaries of the continuation of the charitable services they depend on, the minimum level of free reserves would be 'y' months.

In order to achieve this level without cutting back on the number of beneficiaries being helped, the trustees have adopted a reserves policy of budgeting for annual spending of 90% of available income. It is estimated that this will raise the charity's reserves level to 'y' months within 'z' years.

This can be achieved all the more quickly if the need to build up the charity's reserves attracts additional voluntary support, perhaps by galvanising further fundraising efforts by the appeals committee network.

In relation to *major* funds, confirmation is in any case required in the accounts notes that the assets of individual funds are sufficient, and available in readily usable form as and when needed, to meet the liabilities of those funds.

'An indication should also be given as to whether or not sufficient resources are held in an appropriate form to enable each fund to be applied in accordance with any restrictions. For example, if a charity has a fund which is to be spent in the near future, it should be made clear in the notes whether or not the assets held (or expected to be received) in the fund are liquid assets.'

– SORP 2005, paragraph 75(b)

Where assets do exceed liabilities in each fund (ie there are no deficits), such confirmation can be stated merely in aggregate, as long as it is clear that the financial viability of each material fund has been reviewed.

In the first of the following illustrations the presentation of a single charitable fund that was originally entirely permanent endowment, but is now totally discretionary as between capital and income in *either* direction, has recently been achieved by one of the world's wealthiest and most innovative of charities.

Consolidated Statement of Financial Activities	2008	2007
For the year to 30 September 2008	£m	£m
...		
Incoming resources	258.1	293.7
...		
Total resources expended	742.3	559.8
Net outgoing resources before gains/(losses) on investments	(484.2)	(266.1)
Gains/(Losses) on investment assets [in total]	(1,817.5)	1928.7
Actuarial gains/(losses) on defined benefit schemes	(16.7)	9.4
Net movement in Fund	(2,318.4)	1,672.0
Fund at start of year	14,243.5	12,571.5
Fund at end of year	11,925.1	14,243.5
Notes to the Financial Statements		
1. Accounting policies		
Fund accounting		
All the funds of the Group are unrestricted funds with the exception of certain grants receivable that are not considered material to the Financial Statements of the Trust and the Group.		
Trustee's Annual Report		
...		
Reserves policy		
The Trust's spending policies are set at a level intended to maximise sustainable spend through time and preserve, at least, the real purchasing power of the investment bases.		
		...

The Wellcome Trust – 2007/08 Annual Report and Accounts

Comment

The Charity Commission Scheme dated 20 February 2001 for the restructuring of this charity's hitherto inalienably *permanently* endowed charity, which Scheme was published on the Commission's Website in view of the great public interest in the Trust as (then) the world's largest charity, actually seemed designed to preserve the nature of the above Fund as *expendable* endowment, but with a power to treat income as capital at any time, subject to what is now a statutory duty of 'even-handedness' as between present and future demands on the Trust's resources. This meant the charity had no longer any need of a quantified reserves policy, since none of its funds count as retained income – hence the somewhat cryptic but quite adequate reserves policy disclosure here. Prior to the Scheme, a trust law distinction was always made in the annual accounts between income and capital gains and losses arising from the investment portfolio. These were taken to the Distribution and Capital Funds respectively, which were shown in separate columns in the Statement of Financial Activities. Subsequently, the relevant Accounting Policies Note disclosed that *'the Trustee no longer considers this distinction to be relevant, and accordingly the funds of the Trust are now in a single column format'*. Since that is clearly a capital column under trust law, this SoFA reports all expenditure as if directly charged to capital, as a simpler and more elegant way of dealing with the prior conversion into income of the minimum amount of capital needed to fund the year's activities.

The second illustration, below, is of a major charity that achieves an astonishing simplification of the complexities of a nationwide collection of hundreds of heritage properties worth billions of pounds, many of them with onerous maintenance obligations. Special disclosures in the annual report point to statutory provision authorising the trustees to avoid accounting fully in the normal way for the liabilities arising from the charity's Objects of heritage preservation, while the presentation of a unique 'funding requirement' statement contrives to limit attention to the annual funding deficit by comparing 'ordinary' revenues against total annual spending.

Consolidated Balance Sheet				
As at 29 February 2008		2008		2007
	£'000	£'000	£'000	£'000
Endowment Funds	427,640		439,774	
Restricted Funds	325,084		319,432	
Total tied funds		**752,724**		**759,206**
Designated Funds	202,653		199,283	
General Fund	38,390		30,888	
Total Unrestricted Funds before Pension Scheme Surplus/Deficit	241,043		230,171	
Add/Deduct Pension Surplus/(Deficit)	6,340		(46,102)	
Total Unrestricted Funds		**247,383**		**184,069**
TOTAL FUNDS		**1,000,107**		**943,275**

Consolidated Statement of Financial Activities

For the year ended 29 February 2008

	Unrestricted Funds £'000	Restricted Funds £'000	Endowment Funds £'000	Total 2008 £'000	Total 2007 £'000
...					
Total Incoming Resources	294,415	82,705	11,381	388,501	357,166
...					
Total Resources Expended	266,025	84,110	1,234	351,369	312,758
[Net incoming before transfers]	28,390	(1,405)	10,147	37,132	44,408
[Inter-fund transfers]	(9,373)	13,214	(3,841)	–	–
Net incoming resources	19,017	11,809	6,306	37,132	44,408
Investment (loss)/gain (net)	(2,420)	(6,157)	(18,440)	(27,017)	35,452
Actuarial gain/(loss) on Defined Benefit pension scheme	46,717	-	-	46,717	(369)
NET MOVEMENT IN FUNDS	63,314	5,652	(12,134)	56,832	79,491
Fund balances at 1 March	184,069	319,432	439,774	943,275	863,784
Fund balances at 29 February	247,383	325,084	427,640	1,000,107	943,275

Accounts Note 2

Departure from the requirements of FRS15 – Tangible Fixed Assets

The reporting requirements set out for charities within the Statement of Recommended Practice (revised 2005) refer to a category of assets termed 'Heritage Assets'. Heritage assets are defined as assets a charity holds in pursuit of preservation or conservation objectives. The National TrustConsiders its inalienable properties and other properties held for preservation to fall within this definition of heritage assets. Financial Reporting Standard 15 (FRS15) first applied to the financial statements for the year ended 28 February 2001. Under FRS15, the Trust would be required to capitalise heritage assets if acquired after 1 March 2000.

The Trustees of the National Trust considered the position carefully and concluded that, in the Trust's particular circumstances, the application of FRS15 to heritage assets would result in a distorted view of the Trust's financial position. As explained in the Board of Trustees' Report – Financial Review, these properties are not 'assets' in the normal sense, as any value placed on them would be more than offset by the obligation to maintain them in perpetuity. The Trust has therefore excluded these properties from the balance sheet and they are not included among the tangible fixed assets disclosed in Note 20.

This position was specifically recognised by the National Trust Act 1971 which permitted the Trust to exclude from the financial statements assets held for preservation and any long-term obligation for their future maintenance. However, the Trustees have been advised that this permission does not override the requirements of FRS15. The auditors note this departure in their report ...

The National Trust – 2007/08 Annual Report and Accounts

Comment

The accounts note for earlier years used to go on to disclose that these excluded heritage properties were insured for some £5bn in reinstatement costs, though that figure might seem irrelevant to the Trust's unaccrued and unfunded total commitment in respect of outstanding maintenance (dilapidations) in respect of these properties. The open question here must be whether the Trust's stated reserves can cover such unaccrued maintenance obligations, or whether there is actually a funding deficit – temporary or permanent.

COMPANY REVALUATION RESERVES

10.4 Five standard headings are required to be used in describing any company's funds in accounts prepared under company law, as listed under 'Capital and Reserves' within the balance sheet format options specified in Sch 1 to each of the 2008 Regulations (SI 2008/409 and SI 2008/410) made under the Companies Act 2006. These are to be shown on the face of the balance sheet:

(1)   called up share capital;

(2)   share premium account;

(3)   revaluation reserve;

(4)   other reserves;

(5)   profit and loss account.

These headings clearly do not at all fit the reporting needs of *charitable* companies, though of course (1) will cover the issued capital in the unusual case of a charitable company limited by (non-equity) shares rather than membership guarantees. It is also possible but unlikely for (2) to apply, since any premium over and above the face value of the shares in a *charitable* company must represent a *gift* by the subscribing member, who cannot lawfully receive back more than that face value anyway (usually, but not necessarily, £1). As such, (1)/(2) are the only *corporate* capital a charitable company could have, but the fact is that they are virtually unknown as funding options, so easy is it to give endowments and other restricted funds *on trust*.

The Companies Act requires that any net gain or loss arising from a valuation of corporate assets:

> '... must be credited or (as the case may be) debited to a separate reserve ("the revaluation reserve").'
>
> *– para 35(1), Sch 1 to SI 2008/409 and 410*

and that:

> 'The amount of the revaluation reserve must be shown in the company's balance sheet under a separate sub-heading in the position given for the item "revaluation reserve" in Format 1 or 2 of the balance sheet formats set out in Part I of [Sch 1], but need not be shown under that name.'
>
> *– para 35(2), Sch 1 to SI 2008/409 and 410*

However, charity law constraints on the use of *trust funds* do not allow this to be done for gains/losses on those funds, so that the third heading can apply only to *corporate* gains/losses – though even then to no avail. This is recognised in the way the SORP refers to the lack of significance that revaluation reserves have for *charity* financial reporting as such:

> 'Where fixed assets are revalued upwards, a revaluation reserve will arise being the difference between the original depreciated cost or valuation of the asset and the revalued amount. Separate reporting of the reserve is not significant for charities as they do not distribute profits, but a revaluation reserve will, nevertheless, arise. This will form part of the funds in which the revalued assets are held ...'.

– SORP 2005, paragraph 427

Clearly, the fourth heading can and must be expanded under the Companies Act to accommodate any charitable *trust* funds for which the company is accountable:

> 'The balance sheet or profit and loss account may include an item representing or covering the amount of any asset or liability, income or expenditure not otherwise covered by any of the items listed in the format adopted ...'.

– para 3(2), Sch 1 to SI 2008/409 and 410: Part I, Section A (General Rules)

Strictly speaking, it is also under the fourth heading that *all* of a charitable company's 'corporate reserves', comprising its 'designated' funds as well as the undesignated balance on its unrestricted funds, must be included, since the fifth heading is restricted to 'distributable profits' – which cannot lawfully apply to a *charitable* company at all.

It is thus the *undesignated* part of corporate reserves that is equivalent to the 'charity reserves' with which CC19 and OG43 are concerned, since that part represents the 'unrestricted' funds that are *freely available* – but not, of course, for making any kind of distribution to members by way of private benefit.

Therefore, for true comparability with *non-charitable* companies, the fifth heading should really be eliminated by transferring any undesignated, unrestricted net income for each year to '*corporate charitable reserves*'. This is one of those finer points of company/charity law still not specifically addressed by the SORP Committee, but which the authors consider might be best covered by specific legislation – if ever charitable companies, being part of a regulated sector, do get a special Schedule of their own in the Companies Act 2006 and are not perhaps outlawed one day, now that an alternative form of corporate charity with limited liability is available under provisions contained in the Charities Act 2006.

Of course, the problem would not exist at all for that new legal form of corporate charity, called a 'Charitable Incorporated Organisation' (CIO) – as the official alternative to company law incorporation to achieve limited liability for charities. This concept was one of the recommendations for reform emerging from the old DTI's massive review of company law some years ago.

Under the Companies Act, where an amount is transferred to or from any reserves and the reserves are shown as separate items in the balance sheet prepared under company law, the following information must be given:

> '(a) the amount of the reserves ... as at the [beginning and end] of the financial year ...;
> (b) any amounts transferred to and from the reserves during that year; and

(c)   the source and application ... of any amounts so transferred.'

– para 54(2), Sch 1 to SI 2008/409; para 59(2), Sch 1 to SI 2008/410

This clearly equates to the SORP's requirement to itemise and explain *inter-fund transfers* – this being *mandatory* where a transfer is to/from an endowed or other restricted fund in the case of a *non-company* charity, under the SORP's related Regulations. While para 10(2) of Sch 1 to each SI as above permits departure from the accounting principles set out in paras 10–15 of that Schedule, there is no provision in the Companies Act for departure from the required main *headings* in the formats it stipulates as options, other than those described above.

A charitable company cannot be another charity's 'special trust' as defined by s 97(1) of the 1993 Act because it is not a trust in the first place. Corporate property belongs to the company *absolutely* and not *on trust*. Nevertheless, the company can administer both capital and income *trust funds* that are within its own Objects. Many charitable companies are held publicly accountable for such *special trusts* – and in some cases also for one or more related charitable trusts administered by independent trustees, who are then accountable for that trust to the company alone as its 'main' or 'reporting' charity and must therefore provide it with the necessary 'branch returns' for the preparation of the company's accounts each year.

However, it is only the *corporate* funds of a charitable company that are its 'reserves' under company law – as distinct from any 'special trusts' it may have (its *trust* funds). As a *charity*, however, any corporate funds it needs to retain for properly *designated purposes* do *not* count as freely available 'charity reserves' under trust law, while these corporate reserves are in any case not available for any purpose other than *charitable* use/distribution in accordance with the stated Objects of the company. Changes to those Objects are regulated by the Charity Commission's power under the 1993 Act, s 64 to prevent non-charitable use (e g distribution by way of profit/gain to members) of a charitable company's corporate funds – *realised and unrealised*.

Nevertheless, the SORP has to point out that, just like any other company:

> 'Charities that are companies are required to report, in respect of their unrestricted funds, the difference between the historic cost of fixed assets (including investment assets) and their revalued amount as a revaluation reserve.'

– SORP 2005, paragraph 334

Regardless of how it may be described in the balance sheet, this corporate revaluation reserve – as can be seen below – is a redundant sub-division cutting across lawful designations made out of corporate funds in furtherance of the company's charitable purposes, one that can have no legal application whatever in the administration of the company and therefore provides no useful information to accounts users. It could even mislead the reader into thinking this company has 'negative' free reserves for charitable activity purposes.

	SORP 2005	(Say:)	(Say:)
	Fund totals	**Realised**	**Unrealised**
	£'000	**£'000**	**£'000**
Corporate funds:			
– Fixed Assets designated fund	1,000	400	600
– Designated charitable projects funds	1,500	1,100	400
– Reserves	500	500	–
Total corporate funds	**3,000**	**2,000**	**1,000**
[Revaluation Reserve]	*[1,000]*		
Trust funds	**4,000**		
Total charity funds	**7,000**		

The proper administration of the company as a (non-exempt) *charity* is subject to the regulatory powers of the Charity Commission, and this implies that the directors (as the charity trustees) must have the power to designate corporate funds to be retained for *special charitable purposes* at their own discretion. The exercise of that power should not be made to appear to be subject to a constraint that cannot even apply to the company *as a charity*.

The constraint is only imposed by the Companies Act to regulate 'distributable reserves', a concept that simply does not exist for a charitable company, because its members cannot legally have any equity interests or 'rights' to such distributions – other than the pound-for-pound return of any share capital contributed in the rare case of a non-guarantee company.

The *non-corporate* funds of a charitable company are its *trust* funds, of course. These do not really form part of the charity's own 'capital and reserves' as envisaged by the Companies Act in line with EU Directives, but are simply *additional* reserved funds *also* not available for distribution as profits/gains. As such, these trust funds do need to be shown separately, distinguishing between income and capital as required by the Charities SORP, if the balance sheet is to be able to show a true and fair view for the company *as a charity*, which can certainly be done by showing them, suitably described, as 'other reserves' within the chosen format prescribed by the Companies Act.

SORP 2005 does bring out this distinction between corporate and trust funds, and also allows the disclosure's disruptive effect to be minimised by recommending that it be made merely in the form of an inset note on the face of the balance sheet:

> 'To comply with the Companies Act 1985 charitable companies must separately disclose the revaluation reserve in respect of their unrestricted funds within the relevant funds section on the face of the balance sheet but may change the heading as appropriate. This may be best effected by use of a prominent inset.'
>
> – *SORP 2005, paragraph 428*

Actually, most of the sub-headings under 'Capital and Reserves' as prescribed in the Companies Act are inappropriate for showing a true and fair view in the case of charities. The various charitable trust funds are not covered by the statutory headings, and hence a charitable company should account for them as recommended in the Charities SORP.

Summing up, charitable companies should classify all their funds other than share capital under the general heading of 'reserves' according to the nature and purpose of each fund in accordance with the Charities SORP, which will also mean that their corporate funds are grouped together and kept separate from their trust funds. And if splitting their *corporate* funds between 'revaluation reserve' and 'other' in order to satisfy the letter of company law would obscure the true and fair view of their *designated* funds (because these will have been set up out of total corporate funds without regard to revaluations), then the analysis by fund-designation should obviously prevail in the public interest, with the revaluation figure shown as inset information as recommended by SORP 2005.

The following illustration shows how easily this can be achieved:

Group Balance Sheet (extract)	Notes	£'000
[Corporate] Funds:		
– Unrestricted Funds		5,944
– Designated Funds		5,181
- Total Unrestricted Funds – includes Revaluation Reserve of £49,000 (2007: £174,000)	16	11,125
[Trust] Funds:		
– Restricted funds	17	606
- Restricted Property Fund	18	238
- Total Restricted Funds		844
Total funds	15	**11,969**

United Response – 2007/08 Accounts

Comment

The anomalous and (for charities) potentially misleading *segregated* disclosure of the company's 'revaluation reserve', which is <u>required</u> (for Companies Act compliance) *on the face of the balance sheet* presents no particular problem if tucked away from the columns of figures as an **inset note**, as illustrated here, to accord with the preferred treatment recommended in SORP 2005 – but which surprisingly few of the major charitable companies with material *trust fund* investments now seem to favour. (The comparative figure, of course, is also needed within the brackets.)

THE CHARITY COMMISSION AND RESERVES

10.5   Following the original publication of CC19: 'Charity Reserves', the Commission made it quite clear at the time that charities' reserves levels were to be monitored via the computerised Annual Returns evaluation system at their Liverpool Office. Based on research into charities' existing reserves levels, an unpublished 'benchmark' figure of 3 years' total annual expenditure was established as a pragmatic threshold to use for any action to be considered where a charity's reserves appeared from its accounts to be excessive. This was the basis on which Guide Dogs for the Blind, with some 4 years' reserves at the time (in the nineties), was told by the Commission that this was thought to be excessive for a fundraising charity and should be reduced to a more appropriate level, which they duly did by expanding activity levels accordingly.

Then, in November 2000, the Commission published its long-awaited Operational Guidance on the monitoring of charity reserves, from which it was seen that this rough 'rule of thumb' (carefully hedged about with the usual caveats, of course, when offered for public consumption) had since been expanded to catch 'under-spending' *permanent endowments*, and also other situations where a build-up of excessive reserves is masked in the accounts by fund-designations, perhaps, in addition to an investment policy geared to 'capital gains' at the expense of income.

In the Commission's own words:

> 'The following are indicators that reserves may be excessive. But, again, these figures are not "norms" – trustees cannot avoid the need to consider and justify their position merely by ensuring their reserves are within these limits:
>
> – reserves in excess of three years' gross expenditure;
> – the expected income return[2] on unrestricted investments is significantly above the charity's current gross annual expenditure – say, more than twice as much.
>
> As indicated above, this guidance should be treated with extreme caution. These are a guide to what you might expect to see, not hard and fast rules. Reserves set at these levels are by no means right for every charity. You will need to consider reserves that are much less than this to ensure they are not excessive. (Conversely, reserves that are higher may well be justified and prudent.) You must always take into account the circumstances of the particular charity you are dealing with, and the considered views of its trustees, and recognise that what is reasonable for one charity can never be assumed to be reasonable for another.'

– *OG43/C1, paragraph 6.4*

In this connection it is interesting to note from the views of professional investment managers that in today's (longer-term) investment climate a portfolio invested for the best total return commensurate with the charity trustees' statutory duty to avoid undue risk and with a requirement to maintain its 'real value' against inflation would normally allow some 4% (on average) of the portfolio value to be taken out for spending each year – thus providing a possible benchmark quantification for 'expected income return' or its equivalent. This is in the same ball park as the minimum annual spend of 5% by value of a private charitable foundation in the USA for donations to it to be deductible in personal tax returns filed with the IRS.

Reserves monitoring against such criteria can normally apply nowadays only to registered charities above the current statutory audit threshold of £500,000 gross income, as the Commission no longer requires smaller charities to complete the relevant boxes in the monitoring information section (Part B) of its statutory Annual Return.

However, this reserves-monitoring must always be done without any attempt at 'second-guessing' the charity trustees by the regulator, since the Commission has no

---

[2]   In the event of a 'total return' approach to investment being adopted any allocation of capital growth on grounds of even-handedness should be added into this figure.

legal power to intervene in the administration of a charity where not invited – other than in its supervisory capacity for the purpose of enforcing restitution in the event of misuse or for the prevention of undue loss. This constraint has been explicitly confirmed in the Commission's above-mentioned OG for its case-working staff, published on the website in November 2000:

> 'Bear in mind that it is not for us to substitute our own judgements for those of reasonable trustees who know the business of their charity, who have taken care to plan properly, and who have justified their plans. It is very important for us to interfere as little as possible with the trustees' discretion to run the charity.'
>
> – *OG43/C1*

The income/expenditure and funds analysis questions for charities below the statutory audit threshold were dropped from these Annual Returns some years ago, so that the monitoring of such a charity's reserves levels and any monitoring of the charity's solvency requires – unlike the case with larger charities, where the relevant data extracted from Parts B and C of the Annual Returns facilitate automated research studies – a special exercise of evaluating any discernible trends in the relationship between total income and expenditure levels in the light of data on fund-movements/-balances, investments and yields, all of which data would have to be picked up manually from the (SORP-compliant) annual accounts. Where this relationship appears to indicate grossly excessive/deficient free reserves, further information and explanation must then first be sought in the charity's statutory annual report, supplemented if need be by raising queries directly with the charity trustees.

This is where there can be an immediate benefit from having carefully complied with the *reserves* disclosure requirements of SORP 2005 – quite apart from the obvious publicity value of such clarity wherever funding is dependent on appeals to donors.

This also brings in another point where SORP-compliance can become critical, in that the required note to the accounts showing how the charity's funds are deployed in relation to its total assets and liabilities is clearly intended to enable the trustees to demonstrate the viability of these funds for the purposes for which they are being held – which must inevitably involve assessing the adequacy (or any deficiency) of its 'free reserves'.

THE FRS17 PENSION-FUNDING ASSET/LIABILITY

10.6 The balance sheet and reserves impact of this Standard was being felt in many cases long before the Standard's full implementation for a charity's first financial year commencing in 2005 (or, under the FRSSE, year-*end* after 22 June 2006). Even so, apart from the special case of voluntary (ie charitable) staff-retirement benefit provision, it can only affect a charity operating a 'defined benefit' staff pension scheme (or one promising a 'guaranteed return') in which (if other employers are involved) it can identify its own share of the Scheme's assets and liabilities and thus how much of any under-funding (or over-funding – though that can be ring-fenced as a designated fund to avoid inflating apparent free reserves) is attributable to itself.

However, it has now become clear that (despite ASB assertions to the contrary) there is a marked potential for volatility in the amount of the notional asset or liability that the

Standard requires to be shown on the face of the balance sheet. Charities with vulnerable reserves therefore need special guidance on the possible implications of an FRS17 deficit and how best to cope with them. That was in due course provided by the Charity Commission as part of its website guidance on charity administration and accountability in support of charity trustees.

FRS17 justifies its requirement for this notional asset/liability to be shown on the face of the balance sheet by pointing to the employer's *control* over the use of any ultimate Scheme surplus and its *liability* (legal/constructive) to make good any ultimate deficit:

> '31 ... Usually the employer's obligation under the trust deed is to pay such contributions as the actuary believes to be necessary to keep the scheme fully funded but without building up a surplus. When a surplus arises, it is unlikely that the employer can be required to make contributions to maintain the surplus. In addition, the award of benefit improvements is also usually in the hands of the employer. Thus, in general, the employer controls the use of a surplus in the scheme ...
>
> 39 Conversely, the employer has a liability if it has a legal or constructive obligation to make good a deficit in the defined benefit scheme. In general, the employer will either have a legal obligation under the terms of the scheme trust deed or will have by its past actions and statements created a constructive obligation as defined in FRS 12 "Provisions, Contingent Liabilities and Contingent Assets". The legal or constructive obligation to fund the deficit should be assumed to apply to the deficit based on assumptions used under the FRS.
>
> 40 In a scheme where employees as well as the employer make contributions, any deficit should be assumed to be borne by the employer unless the scheme rules require members' contributions to be increased to help fund a deficit. In this case, the present value of the required additional contributions should be treated as reducing the deficit to be recognised by the employer.'

– FRS17, paragraphs 31, 39 and 40

What FRS17 requires for the balance sheet presentation is very specific:

> '... The defined benefit asset or liability should be presented separately on the face of the balance sheet:
>
> (a)   in balance sheets of the type prescribed for companies in Great Britain by the Companies Act 1985, Schedule 4, format 1: after item J *Accruals and deferred income* but before item K *Capital and reserves*; and
> (b)   in balance sheets of the type prescribed for companies in Great Britain by the Companies Act 1985, Schedule 4, format 2: any asset after ASSETS item D *Prepayments and accrued income* and any liability after LIABILITIES item D *Accruals and deferred income*.'

– FRS17, paragraph 47

Two tables graphically illustrate how this can swing from one extreme to the other in charity balance sheets:

Table 1: Notional Asset	£'000s
Net Assets *excluding pension scheme*	7,500
Pension Scheme asset: estimated over-funding	5,000
Net Assets including Pension Scheme notional asset	12,500
Funds:	
Endowment(s)	1,000
Restricted Funds	250
Unrestricted Funds:	
Fixed Assets fund	2,000
General funds (free reserves)	4,250
Total Funds excluding Pension Reserve	7,500
Pension Reserve fund	5,000
Total Funds including Pension Reserve	12,500

If, rather than a £5m notional asset, there is a £5m notional liability as at the year-end, the free reserves (undesignated unrestricted funds) will appear to become negative, which cannot be, thus calling into question the validity of the fixed assets fund, as shown below.

Table 2: Notional Liability	£'000s
Net Assets *excluding pension scheme*	7,500
Pension Scheme liability: estimated under-funding	(5,000)
Net Assets including Pension Scheme notional funding deficit	2,500
Funds:	
Endowment(s)	1,000
Restricted Funds	250
Unrestricted Funds:	
Fixed Assets fund	2,000
General funds (free reserves)	4,250
Total Funds excluding Pension Reserve	7,500
Pension Reserve – notional funding deficit	(5,000)

Table 2: Notional Liability	£'000s
Total Funds including Pension Reserve notional funding deficit	2,500

Charities will always need to proceed carefully where the recognition of the pension scheme liability implies a negative balance on free reserves (undesignated unrestricted funds). In such a case it would be advisable where possible to release to free reserves part/all of an existing designated fund, or even of all designated funds (in the extreme position). This is because fund-designations are optional, even for fixed assets retained for the charity's own use, and the cardinal rule under the Charities SORP is that no designations should be made which would result in a deficit on free reserves.

In such a case, especially where a deficiency of free reserves in the balance sheet is implied, the charity would be well advised to combat the apparent financial vulnerability shown in the accounts by tabling[3] the projections needed to show that this deficit is a mere accounting fiction that has no adverse implications for:

(i)   any permanent endowment or other restricted funds held; and

(ii)   the going concern basis on which the accounts will be presumed to have been prepared except as stated otherwise under Accounting Policies.

In doing so, two points should be emphasised. First, that the 'liability' shown in the balance sheet will only result in additional future payments to the extent that actuarial valuations of the Scheme's liabilities do continue to outpace the expected long-term return on its investment portfolio (subject to the prevailing volatility of the capital markets). And, secondly, that any extra payments to be made as a result will, in the absence of a special arrangement to the contrary (ie for *accelerated* payment to keep the transient funding deficit within bounds), be financed out of future income and spread over the remaining anticipated years of service of employees now in the Scheme. It is therefore to that extent just something of a possible future funding need that could just as easily vanish again – certainly not an actual deficiency of the charity's existing funds.

In our hypothetical funding-deficit example above, therefore, the 'fixed assets fund' figure would need to be reduced by the £750,000 (ie, £5m less £4.25m) in order to avoid inferring that the charity has 'negative reserves' to that extent – no matter in what order the items are shown in the balance sheet. Indeed, it may have been with this sort of problem in mind that the SORP allows the FRS17 deficit to be shown after sub-totalling all the real funds of the charity – even though it can normally relate only to the undesignated unrestricted funds figure! As for how the deficit may affect your free reserves, paragraph 447 of the SORP says either the accounts notes or the trustees' annual report *'should explain the impact, if any, on resources available for general application'*. In the converse situation, paragraph 448 says you should indicate the timescale for a Scheme surplus to benefit the charity through planned reductions in future contribution rates.

---

[3]   Even if, for audit reasons, this clarification takes the form of an accounts note, it will also need to be reflected in the trustees' annual report, where the charity reserves position and policy are disclosed.

Beyond the SORP itself, the Charity Commission's website guidance makes it quite clear that reserves policy, which (or else the fact that the charity has none) must be disclosed in the annual report, can properly ignore an FRS17 deficit *except to the extent of any accelerated cashflow commitments in the form of agreed extra contributions out of existing reserves in order to reduce the transient notional funding deficiency to an 'acceptable' level.*

That won't solve the balance sheet presentation problem, however. It may therefore be advisable to cross-reference the reserves figure there to an explanatory comment within the FRS17 supporting accounts note to clarify for interested readers to what extent the balance sheet reserves figure is or is not affected by the FRS17 deficit.

In this connection, at **6.7.6** we took a critical look at FRS17's assertion of 'stability' in the calculation of long-term investment returns, in that the projection of current market yields is supposed to counterbalance temporary fluctuations in the current open market value of the scheme's investments. We also discussed the need for charities to be allowed to restrict their annual assessment of scheme liabilities as if 'closed' by termination of employment one year hence, to avoid burdening inadequate reserves with a notional 'under-funding provision' that can only arise if the charity continues as a 'going concern' beyond the following year-end as the minimum requirement for FRS18 purposes.

One further aspect that could need careful thought is the possible impact a pension scheme 'liability' could have on restricted funds if they have borne significant (relevant) staff costs for the period(s) to which the liability is attributable, particularly if that liability ever exceeds the charity's unrestricted funds. In theory at least, it seems there could be a right of recourse pro rata for any *actual* additional contributions (as and when) paid over to cover such a pension fund deficit. In practice, the annual amounts recoverable from restricted funds might be too slight in all but the extreme case – given the employer's normal right to spread deficit-funding payments prospectively over the remaining service life of scheme members. The SORP provides detailed guidance on this somewhat rarified fund-accounting aspect of FRS17, saying in effect that any allocation or apportionment of a funding surplus or deficit under FRS17 to restricted funds, and therefore of the year-on-year changes to such figures, must be in line with the staffing costs of the funds involved.

Chapter 11

THE CASHFLOW STATEMENT

APPLICABILITY

11.1   The Charities SORP 2005 requires the accounts of all charities that are larger than what the Companies Act 2006 defines as 'small' to include a Cashflow Statement, purely for FRS1 compliance, as a *primary* accounting statement ranking alongside the SoFA and (for charitable companies otherwise unable to comply with FRS3) the Summary Income and Expenditure Account. It should therefore be given equal prominence in the accounts, normally done by positioning it immediately after the balance sheet.

The SORP follows the Standard by *requiring* this only where the charity has exceeded two of three limiting figures (used by the Companies Act 2006, s 382 and s 383, as amended by SI 2008/393,[1] to define 'small' for financial years from 6 April 2008 onwards) in its last financial year* and two again this year – except that FRS1's 'turnover' threshold is replaced in the SORP by 'gross income':

(a)   gross income in the year in excess of £6.5m (previously £5.6m);

(b)   a balance sheet total (ie fixed and current assets – or funds plus liabilities) in excess of £3.26m (previously £2.8m);

(c)   more than 50 employees.

*As a transitional provision, reg 2(3) of SI 2008/393 applies the new thresholds to the prior financial year (2007/8) for eligibility as a 'small' company/group for 2008/9.

But the Standard *also* requires it if the charity *group* is not 'small' on the same basis (or the equivalent figures before statutory consolidation adjustments under the 1985 Act – see below):

'The FRS applies to all financial statements intended to give a true and fair view ... except those of:

...

(f)   companies incorporated under companies legislation and entitled to the exemptions available in the legislation for small companies when filing accounts with the Registrar of Companies.

---

[1]   Companies Act 2006 (Amendment) (Accounts and Reports) Regulations 2008, SI 2008/393.

(g)   entities that would have been in category (f) above if they were companies incorporated under companies legislation.'

– FRS1, paragraph 5

'A parent company qualifies as a small company in relation to a financial year only if the group headed by it qualifies as a small group.'

– Companies Act 2006, s 383(1)

Group size can be assessed either net or gross of the statutory adjustments to turnover and assets (to eliminate any 'unrealised' profits, etc) required by the Act in preparing consolidated accounts, and on the latter basis the turnover and gross assets figures are uplifted by 20% to:

(a)   £7.8m; and

(b)   £3.9m.

USEFULNESS

11.2   However, if it were not for the fact that its format as recommended by SORP 2005 suppresses the all-important gross cash figures of gifts/grants, etc, to a charity and payments by it for charitable activities, fundraising, etc, and governance, not to mention the constraints imposed by trust law on the cashflows of *restricted* funds, *any* charity that is dependent on voluntary funding either from the public or from funding bodies/agencies could find it helpful to include a Cashflow Summary in the statutory accounts as *additional* information. It would then be necessary, of course, to ensure that the audit report refers to 'gross cashflows' as well as the now familiar 'incoming resources' and 'application of resources' (and, in the case of a charitable company, 'income and expenditure').

The SORP does in fact start off here with the right intention by declaring:

'The object of the cash flow statement is to show the cash received and used by the charity in the accounting period.'

– SORP 2005, paragraph 351

But in its present emaciated form, by starting from *net* instead of *gross* operational cashflows, and without distinguishing any material restricted funds, this extra 'primary accounting statement', with its strictly commercial orientation and utility, is just a compliance burden that the larger charity cannot ignore even though it hardly rates even a mention in charity audit reports – see chapter 17.

The anomaly has now become plain for all to see, ever since the charity-specific 'Summary Information Return' (SIR) (see chapter 15) for financial years ending after 14 February 2005 entered the public domain. For the SIR is a far more interesting and equally freely available dataset that is simple enough for the *non-accountant* to see what the larger registered charity (those above a threshold of £1m gross income) has been doing with its financial resources.

FORMAT

11.3   Like the Summary Income and Expenditure Account under FRS3, the Cashflow Statement under FRS1 – not being intrinsic to charity law requirements (unless preparing statutory accounts on a receipts and payments basis – when the charity is, in any case, outside the scope of FRS1) – does not distinguish between the funds of the reporting charity (or its group) according to their respective restrictions, other than capital/income distinctions. The Statement therefore presents only charity-totals (group-totals, if presented in *consolidated* accounts) – so that adequate supporting notes will need to explain any significant fund-accounting features for the reader.

FRS1 defines 'cash' as including cash in hand and deposits repayable on demand or at not more than one day's notice, less overdrafts repayable on demand. Having said that, however, there are certain features that could require special attention in the charity context, as discussed below.

Cashflow Statements turned out to be an aspect of the updating of the original 1995 SORP that was of considerable interest to the sector at the time, as reported on the Charity Commission website following its Autumn 1998 launch of the public consultation phase for SORP 2000:

> 'There was a general desire for increased guidance (with some suggesting alternative formats) particularly on reconciling the cashflow to the SOFA while still meeting the requirements of existing accounting standards. Opinion was split on the usefulness of the statement – varying from making it compulsory to seeking to remove it altogether.'

This realisation makes it necessary to take a closer look at the detailed requirements of FRS1 than we find in the rather brief summary provided in SORP 2005, where the headings used could have been made much more specific to charity accounting needs without conflicting with the Standard, thus furthering the standardisation of 'simplified' financial reporting across the sector and perhaps even pre-empting the development of the SIR itself.

Gifts in kind

11.3.1   *Charitable gifts* are (for obvious reasons) not contemplated at all by the FRS, which is content to start with net incoming cash *from* 'operating activities'. That would logically imply the exclusion from the latter not only of *capital* gifts of money – as has been recognised in the SORP – but even of incoming cash directly from *voluntary* sources, thus all 'pure income' monetary grants, donations and bequests, since these are not 'economic benefits' flowing *from* the charity's operating activities. Rather, they are the starting-point from which those operating activities arise.

In contrast, *investment income returns* are quite another matter: by analogy with the reasoning followed in FRS1, these inflows should perhaps be included in the 'operating' section if the charity's operational activities are mainly being financed by them – as is certainly the case for non-trading charities. Even for the latter, however, it may be more informative to include them in their own section in the normal way specified by the FRS and the SORP.

Clearly, by definition a Cashflow Statement must not include any *non-cash* transactions. What this means in practice is that not only the accruals, revaluations and depreciation mentioned by the SORP but also any *gifts in kind* (whether for use as fixed assets or, if 'operating' inflows and outflows were (for the sake of a proper understanding of the reporting entity as a *charity*) to be shown gross, as 'donated services and facilities' ('intangible income' in SORP 2000) – see chapter 6) must therefore be eliminated:

> 'Material transactions not resulting in movements of cash of the reporting entity should be disclosed in the notes to the cash flow statement if disclosure is necessary for an understanding of the underlying transactions.'
>
> – *FRS1, paragraph 46*

The SORP therefore requires that:

> 'transactions which do not result in cash flows should not be reported in the cash flow statement (e g depreciation, revaluations, accruals) but may need to be disclosed ...'.
>
> – *SORP 2005, paragraph 354(d)*

> 'major transactions not resulting in cash movements should be disclosed in the notes if necessary for an understanding of the underlying transactions. For instance the release of expendable endowment; ...'.
>
> – *SORP 2005, paragraph 355(a)*

What it should *not* exclude (contrary to paragraph 355(a)'s very specific 'for instance') is the transfer of cash between an endowed and unendowed fund consequent on a duly authorised conversion of capital into income or vice versa – because such movements are between different *sections* of the Cashflow Statement: the 'operating' and 'financing' sections. Even though these are internal to the charity and so ignored by the FRS, their full disclosure must be considered intrinsic to charity financial reporting in view of the strict rules of trust law governing the proper administration of capital as distinct from income.

However, FRS1 does require any *restrictions* affecting internal cashflows to be *noted* on the face of the Statement, which would certainly apply in the presence of either endowed funds or any *un*endowed restricted funds – though this point has not been taken up by the SORP, perhaps because 'part' has not been equated with 'fund':

> **'Restrictions on remittability**
>
> A note to the cash flow statement should identify the amounts and explain the circumstances where restrictions prevent the transfer of cash from one part of the business or group to another.'
>
> – *FRS1, paragraph 47*

For an *entity* Cashflow Statement, this note therefore needs to deal with charity law restrictions on *unauthorised* transfers out of any constituent fund that is permanently endowed or otherwise legally restricted, whereas for a *group* Cashflow Statement the note should *also* deal with charity law restrictions on inter-company transfers for purposes outside the parent charity's Objects.

'Operating' activities

11.3.2 SORP 2005 provides a special section dealing with Cashflow Statements, basically continuing the original 1995 SORP's recommendations apart from one or two matters that could be very significant for some charities. For practical reasons, the most important of these is the abbreviated presentation of 'operating' cashflows already mentioned at the beginning of this chapter – thus the first section of the Statement. The more meaningful 'direct method' (formerly called 'gross basis') of presenting 'operating' cashflows is no longer recommended, perhaps because it involves more work in making the necessary adjustments for accruals, etc, than the easier 'indirect method' ('net basis') that starts with 'net incoming resources' in the SoFA and eliminates non-cash movements. The 1995 SORP said:

> 'the analysis of the cash movements should accord with the charity's operations as reported in its Statement of Financial Activities, and be given in appropriate detail (the "gross basis" for reporting "operating activities" may be the most suitable approach for many charities).'
>
> *– 1995 SORP, paragraph 212(b)*

In SORP 2000, and currently also SORP 2005, this vital preference has been reversed, so that the easier method is now the only one recommended, though FRS1 does allow the use of either method:

> 'Operating cash flows can be presented by either the direct method (showing the relevant constituent cash flows) or the indirect method (calculating operating cash flows by adjustment to the operating profit reported in the profit and loss account).'
>
> *– FRS1, paragraph 7*

> 'The analysis of the cash movements should accord with the charity's operations as reported in its Statement of Financial Activities, and be given in appropriate detail. The starting point will normally be "net incoming/outgoing resources before other recognised gains and losses".'
>
> *– SORP 2005, paragraph 353*

This then requires an explanatory note to reconcile that figure in the SoFA to the Cashflow Statement's starting point of 'net operating cash inflow/outflow', as provided by paragraph 355(c) of the SORP.

Inter-fund transfer restrictions

11.3.3 The special treatment of *endowment* cashflows, as distinct from 'operating' cashflows, is carefully explained in paragraph 354, which says:

> 'Movements in endowments should not be included in cash flows from "operating activities" but should be treated as increases or decreases in the financing section. This is achieved as follows:
>
> (a) cash donations to endowment should be treated as additions to endowment in the "financing" section;
>
> (b) the receipts and payments from the acquisition and disposal of investments should be shown gross in the "capital expenditure and financial investment" section of the cash flow statement. A single row should then be included in this section showing the net movement in cash flows attributable to endowment investments. A corresponding row

should be included in the "financing" section for the same amount. The row in the "financing" section should reflect the cash into/(cash out of) the endowment fund whereas it will be the opposite direction in the "capital expenditure and financial investment" section; ...'.

– SORP 2005, paragraph 354

Reconciliation of changes in 'net debt'

11.3.4   Paragraph 355(b) of the SORP enigmatically requires that:

'cash (and any financing) movements should be reconciled to the appropriate opening and closing balance sheet amounts ...'.

– SORP 2005, paragraph 355(b)

This is the equivalent of the requirement in FRS1 to reconcile the year's net cash inflow/outflow to the movement in 'net debt' between the two balance sheets. What the Standard means by 'net debt', and why it is important to relate movements in this figure to the cash inflow/outflow, is explained in its definition of 'net debt' (called, somewhat confusingly for charities, 'net funds' where positive):

'The objective of the reconciliation of cash flows to the movement in net debt is to provide information that assists in the assessment of liquidity, solvency and financial adaptability. Net debt is defined to include borrowings less liquid resources because movements in net debt so defined are widely used as indicating changes in liquidity, and therefore assist in assessing the financial strength of the entity. The definition excludes ... debtors and creditors because, while these are short-term claims on and sources of finance to the entity, their main role is as part of the entity's trading activities.'

– FRS1, paragraph 53

'The changes in net debt should be analysed from the opening to the closing component amounts showing separately, where material, changes resulting from:

(a)   the cash flows of the entity;
(b)   the acquisition or disposal of subsidiary undertakings;
(c)   other non-cash changes; and
(d)   the recognition of changes in market value and exchange rate movements.'

– FRS1, paragraph 33

'The definition of liquid resources is expressed in general terms, emphasising the liquidity of the investment and its function as a readily disposable store of value rather than setting out a narrow range of investment instruments. Depending on the entity's policy (which should be disclosed), term deposits, government securities, loan stock, equities and derivatives may each form part of that entity's liquid resources, provided they meet the definition. Short-term deposits would also fall within the definition, though the requirement that they should be readily convertible into known amounts of cash at or close to their carrying amounts would tend to exclude any that are more than one year from maturity on acquisition.'

– FRS1, paragraph 52

What all this means in practice is that you should show how much of (a) was derived from or absorbed by any changes in the level of external *borrowings* (including any finance leases) and the book value of *'investments held as liquid resources'* (ie those belonging to all the charity's *income* funds – even where, as is mostly the case, they are classed as fixed assets), *between the two balance sheets.*

Layout of a charity-specific and more meaningful format

11.3.5 The SORP does not set out the actual format required to comply with FRS1, so to see what the Charity Commission considers acceptable in this area you will need to go through the worked examples published as website companions for SORP 2005. In view of the need to use headings that follow the SoFA format as closely as possible, the following modified format for more informative charity/group cashflow statements in the case where any cashflows for restricted funds are only immaterial and therefore not an audit issue is offered here as also showing how you might wish to use the 'direct method' for reporting the 'operating' cashflows that must surely be of essential interest to the donating public, in this case with a sub-section for income returns on investment assets:

Operating Activities

    Gross cash inflow from

        – Charitable Activities *(ie those primarily to further the (parent's) Objects)*

            – Less: Charitable Expenditure payments (direct/support costs)

    Gross cash inflow from

        – Other (trading) Activities undertaken (primarily) to generate funds

            – Less: Payments for such activities *(not: investment asset management)*

    Gross cash inflow from Voluntary Sources *for* activities *(not: endowments)*

        – Less: Payments to raise such funds *(not: 'trading' activities)*

        – Less: Payments for charity management/administration

    Add: Amounts converted/borrowed from endowed funds *(see below)*

    – Less: Authorised transfers/conversions from income into endowment

    = Net inflow/outflow *of* **(i e** *for* **and** *from***) operating activities**

Income returns of investment assets

    Gross investment earnings *(this means gross rents, dividends/interest)*

    – Less: Payments for investment-management *(ie revenue-related costs)*

Servicing of finance

    Interest payable on borrowings

Non-operational cashflows:

Capital expenditure and financial investment

    Receipts (gross) from disposals of fixed assets for own *(ie functional)* use

    – Less: Payments to provide such fixed assets

    Receipts (gross proceeds) from disposals of investment assets

    – Less: Payments to acquire investment assets

Deduct: Net cashflows attributable to endowed fixed assets *(see below)*

Receipts (gross) from disposals of (operational) undertakings*

– Less: Payments to acquire (operational) undertakings*

(for a **group** statement, this would include subsidiaries/associates, etc)*

Financing

Endowment receipts and amounts legally capitalised out of income

– Less: Endowment funds converted/borrowed as income *(see above)*

Net cashflows attributable to endowed fixed assets *(see above)*

Cash borrowed (externally)

– Less: Instalments repaid to those external sources

= Net cash inflow/outflow for the year

Chapter 12

NOTES TO THE ACCOUNTS

OVERVIEW OF THE REGULATORY REQUIREMENTS

12.1 For *charitable companies*, the accounts notes required by the SORP can best be regarded as the *charity-specific* 'best practice' overlay onto the more general statutory requirements of the Companies Act 2006 and its 2008 accounting Regulations (SI 2008/409 and 410) – an overlay that, while not actually mandatory, is normally no less unavoidable for a true and fair view of the company *as a charity*. This is because non-compliance in any material respect must inform the auditor's opinion on the accounts, in conformity with professional auditing practice, the increasingly strict regulation of which through the FRC's Audit Inspection Unit (for 'public interest' audits) and in other cases the Quality Assurance Directorates run by the Recognised Supervisory Bodies like the ICAEW and other CCAB members aims to stamp out poor audit quality which, if it comes to the notice of the Charity Commission, may be seen as *cause for concern*, with possibly unpleasant regulatory consequences in the end for the directors themselves.

For those companies larger than 'medium-sized' as defined by the Companies Act 2006 and preparing accounts under that Act, the Act continues to require disclosure (as did the 1985 Act) of any departure from accounting and financial reporting standards, effectively anchoring into the law FRS18's specific SORP-compliance disclosure requirements. (For the *exemption* see reg 4(2) of SI 2008/410.)

For *non-company* charities and 'small' groups (again, as defined by the Companies Act 2006) headed by a charitable company preparing 'regulated' accounts under Part VI of the 1993 Act, the SORP's requirements are more immediately binding – even for the smaller ones not subject to statutory audit (up to £500,000 gross income). Thus unlike charities preparing accounts under company law they are *obliged* by para 1(v) of Sch 2 to the SORP's related 2008 Regulations – no matter how small the charity – to disclose and explain (though not to evaluate) any material departures from SORP/Standards – see **12.2.1**.

Those Regulations simply say:

> 'There shall be provided by way of notes to the accounts the information specified in Schedule 2 [to these Regulations].'
>
> – *SI 2008/629, reg 8(10)*

There are, of course, *no* such statutory disclosure requirements for accounts prepared on the alternative (i e receipts and payments) basis except that such accounts are required in respect of *each distinct charitable trust fund* for which the charity trustees are publicly accountable under the Charities Act 1993 ('the 1993 Act') – see chapter 16.

On comparing SORP 2005 with the said Schedule, it can be seen that the Regulations impose unconditional compliance with SORP 2005 for its key 'best practice' disclosures – thus making the Charities SORP more or less a Statement of *Required* Practice, as a notable departure from the normal meaning of a SORP. For other requirements of SORP 2005, only part-compliance is made mandatory – and in some cases there is no statutory underpinning at all. The table below summarises the SORP 2005 accounts notes that are *mandatory* for *non-company* charities' entity accounts and for *all* group consolidated accounts prepared under the 1993 Act. These fall into four broad categories, grouped together in this chapter (and supplementing the other chapters indicated below) as:

–   the applicable *accounting framework* (policies, assumptions, bases, legislation);

–   *funds*-related (see chapter 3) and *SoFA*-related (see chapter 6) notes, including trustee-transactions and other '*related party*' or public interest disclosures;

–   notes in support of the *balance sheet(s)* (see chapters 8–10); and

–   information about *group undertakings* (see chapter 14 on consolidated accounts).

Except for items indicated as dealt with in the other, more relevant chapters as noted above, these key information requirements are considered in detail in the remainder of this chapter:

Note	Statutory disclosure imposed by Sch 2 to the SORP's Regulations 2008 under reg 8(10) for entity accounts or reg 15(5)(a) for group accounts	Chapter
	Accounting policy, etc, disclosures	
1(b)/(c)	Accounting policies *'and estimation techniques'*, if material, including	12
	• description,	
	• any material changes therein,	
	• the reason for such change, and	
	• its effect (if material) on the accounts,	
	as per the SORP	
1(x)	For any 'true and fair override' departure under reg 8(4)(d):	12
	• particulars of the departure,	
	• reasons for it, and	
	• its effect	
1(v)	For *all* charities (ie, not just those exceeding the prevailing audit threshold, as was required by the 2005 Regs):	12
	• statement of compliance with SORP(s) and accounting standards,	
	• particulars of any material departure(s), and	
	• reasons for such departure	
1(w)	Reasons for any change (beyond +/- 7 days) of financial year under reg 3(4)(b)	12
1(a)/(u)	Comparative figures, and any material adjustments made to them	(various)
1(y)	Any additional information needed:	12
	• for reg 8 compliance, or	

Note	Statutory disclosure imposed by Sch 2 to the SORP's Regulations 2008 under reg 8(10) for entity accounts or reg 15(5)(a) for group accounts	Chapter
	• as 'reasonably' assisting the user to understand the accounts	
	Restricted funds: SoFA-related disclosures	
1(d)	Nature and purpose of all material funds of the charity, *as per the SORP*	3; 12
1(h)	Distinction between permanent and expendable incoming endowments	3; 12
1(q)	Charitable activities expenditure analysis, *as per the SORP*	
1(r)	Support Costs analysis, *as per the SORP*	
1(i)	Inter-fund transfers affecting any restricted fund:	6; 12
	• itemisation of all material transfers,	
	• explanation of the nature and purpose of both funds affected	
1(m)	Details of any fund in deficit at the year-end	10; 12
	Other SoFA-related disclosures	
1(o)/2	Grants (except those made out of trust funds whose founder or any spouse or civil partner remains alive) to institutions/individuals, *as per the SORP*	6; 12
1(f)/(g)	Staff **employment** costs and executive pay-bands, *as per the SORP* (= **all** charities – not just auditable charities only, as under the 2005 Regs)	12
	Trustee-transactions and other 'related party' or public interest disclosures	
1(e)	'Related Party' transactions of	12
	• the charity, and also of	
	• its [charitable/non-charitable] subsidiary/associated undertakings,	
	• *as per the SORP (which can also bring in some 'charity branches' here)*	
1(n)	Auditor's or independent examiner's remuneration (i) for such work and (ii) for any *other* services rendered to the charity	12
1(p)	'Ex gratia' payments/asset-surrenders made	12
	Balance Sheet notes	
1(s)	Analysis *as per the SORP* of the figures for	8; 9
	• fixed assets,	10
	• debtors, creditors and provisions	
1(t)	Analysis of all material *movements* on fixed assets, *as per the SORP*	8; 9
1(l)(i)	Outstanding loans *to* the charity where expressly secured on any of its assets	12
1(k)	Guarantees under which the charity still has a potential liability	12
	Group undertakings	
1(j)	For each [non-charitable subsidiary/associated undertaking]:	14
	• its name, and also the nature of the relationship,	
	• its activities, including, where material,	
	• its turnover and net profit/loss for its corresponding financial year, and	
	• any qualification expressed in an auditor's report on its accounts	
1(l)(ii)	Outstanding loans *by* the charity to any [charitable/non-charitable] subsidiary or associated undertaking	14

ACCOUNTING POLICY DISCLOSURES

12.2   Accounting policy disclosures seem to have grown considerably in length and prominence in line with the continuing development of accounting standards and the consequent need to clarify more and more precisely the accounting rules followed in any particular case. Where the 1995 SORP devoted just a single paragraph (35) to the subject, subsequent versions in 2000 and now 2005 – taking their cue from FRS18 – have gone to town on it, as you can see from the following sections detailing what you now have to disclose under this heading alone – never mind actual sub-analysis and explanation of SoFA and balance sheet items themselves.

The basic idea under FRS18 is that the accounting policies and 'estimation techniques' (previously: assumptions) adopted and, if material, to be disclosed must be the ones considered *most appropriate to the reporting charity's own circumstances* to enable a 'true and a fair view' to be shown in the accounts. It is therefore up to you to decide which of these extended SORP disclosure requirements you can safely omit where the items themselves are immaterial for a proper understanding of the accounts – or whether just to copy them all in from year to year 'for safety's sake', as most seem to do.

Above all, such policies must be based on the two remaining[1] fundamental accounting concepts or 'principles' said by FRS18 to have a 'pervasive' role in accounts intended to show a true and fair view – and therefore for the selection of accounting policies:

(a)   the 'going concern' concept; and

(b)   the 'accruals' concept.

Observance of these two principles is to be presumed unless stated otherwise.

In addition, the appropriateness of the individual accounting policies and estimation techniques adopted is to be judged by how well they enable the charity's accounts to achieve four specific objectives as set out in FRS18:

(c)   relevance;

(d)   reliability (which brings in the old concept of 'prudence' to resolve uncertainty);

(e)   comparability (which now subsumes the concept of 'consistency'); and

(f)   understandability.

In particular, the Accounting Policies note should also indicate how the relevant accounting standards and recommendations have been applied in respect of any *material items* in the accounts.

These requirements may seem much stricter than the original, 1995 SORP, but in reality they are merely more detailed. The Charities SORP, being 'tailor-made' for the charity sector, had already provided for all six of them even in its original form.

---

[1]   It seems the other two, prudence and consistency, are no longer quite so fundamental as they used to be – see below.

Nowadays the note on accounting policies, etc, nearly always comes first. Some charities even present it as a separate statement prefacing the SoFA and balance sheet.

Compliance declarations

12.2.1　A brief and concise 'overview' statement is normally all you need to provide here, as long as in doing so you are identifying the particular framework of accountability, in terms of law, standards and any sector-specific set of practices (ie the Charities SORP 2005 here), within which the trustees/directors are reporting. The overarching requirement of the SORP's Regulations 2008 is to give:

> 'a description of each of the accounting policies ... adopted ... [which] are material in the context of the accounts ... and the estimation techniques adopted ... which are material to the presentation of the accounts ... [and] of any material changes ... the reason for such change and its effect (if material) on the accounts, *in accordance with the methods and principles set out in the SORP* ...'.

– SI 2008/629 Sch 2, para 1(b)/(c)

What the SORP itself requires of *all* charities for a 'true and fair view' is that:

> 'The notes regarding the basis of preparation of the accounts should state that the accounts have been prepared in accordance with:
>
> (a)　this SORP and accounting standards or with this SORP and the FRSSE ...;
> (b)　the Charities Act or the Companies Act or other legislative requirement; and
> (c)　the historic[al] cost basis of accounting except for investments (and if applicable, fixed assets) which have been included at revalued amounts.'

– SORP 2005, paragraph 358

Eligibility for FRSSE adoption is discussed in chapter 5. As regards (c), whose perpetuation seems to be in deference to the Companies Act option of current value instead of cost for *fixed* assets, for strict FRS15 compliance 'revalued amounts' now means 'current value' for the whole class of any 'own use' fixed assets not being accounted for on the basis of their 'historical costs' – that term having been widened to include actual/deemed cost and also any pre-FRS15 'frozen' valuations, as explained in chapter 8. Therefore, as apart from social investments the Charities SORP requires you to carry *all* investment assets (whether shown under fixed or current assets) at their open market value (see chapter 9), with other current assets at the lower of cost and realisable value, you will only need to say something extra under (c) if (i) you opt out of the customary 'historical cost' basis for *non-investment* assets or (ii) you have social investments whose cost and current value are now materially different, since these will be stated under SORP 2005 at cost less any impairment write-offs.

Alternatively, that point could just as well be clarified in the subsequent more detailed description of the particular accounting policies adopted, and 'estimation techniques' used (previously: 'assumptions made'), for 'material items' in the accounts. We deal with those in the next section.

A typical compliance declaration here for FRSSE-based accounts prepared under the SORP's related Regulations might therefore preface the accounting policies note by saying:

'These accounts have been prepared under the Charities Act 1993 in accordance with the Charities SORP 2005 and the current FRSSE [on the basis of historical cost modified by the adoption of current value for certain fixed assets as indicated below].'

The phrase in square brackets is often seen, even though it may be considered redundant where more detail is given further on in the note on accounting policies and estimation techniques.

Although for a *charitable company's* accounts that have to be prepared under company law, the SORP has no statutory underpinning at all, the statutory audit achieves much the same result in terms of compliance enforcement via the Financial Reporting Council's quality-control monitoring of the auditing profession – especially for 'public interest' entities (which for charities means those above £100m gross income) – through official interpretation of the 'true and fair view' requirement, for as the SORP observes:

'The requirement to show a true and fair view and to adapt the accounts for the special nature of charity means that there is a strong presumption that charitable companies will, in all but exceptional circumstances, have to comply with this SORP in order to meet the requirements of company law ...'.

– SORP 2005, paragraph 422

Wherever consolidated accounts are *also* required of any charity, because the charity *group* is not 'small' by reference to the 1993 Act's statutory audit threshold (see chapter 14 for this, and also chapter 11, where the size-criteria under company law are discussed in a different context) and so does not qualify for the *general* exemption from consolidation under SORP 2005, it will be necessary to make the same disclosures in respect of the consolidated accounts as well:

'Where consolidated accounts are prepared the policy notes should state the method of consolidation and which subsidiaries or associated entities are included and excluded from the consolidation.'

– SORP 2005, paragraph 399

Since the FRSSE ignores consolidated accounts for the sake of its own brevity and simplicity, their inclusion along with the entity accounts would then make it necessary to add:

'supplemented by applicable accounting standards for the consolidated accounts.'

Reason for any change of financial year-end

12.2.2   In the exceptional event of a permissible shortening/lengthening (by more than 7 days) of any *non-company* charity's financial year, para 1(w) of Sch 2 to the SORP's 2008 Regulations requires an explanation of the reasons for making the change. This is all the more important for *non-company* charities because the 1993 Act's various administrative provisions based on size-bands does not flex them pro rata to a charity's accounting periods longer or shorter than the normal 12 months – unlike the 1985 Act. Therefore the Regulations prohibit them from making any such change of greater than 7 days either way any more frequently than once every 3 years – and even then only allows such a change where there is good reason.

But this disclosure would also catch a charitable company that has to prepare consolidated accounts under the 1993 Act for a 'small' group, in the rare event that the parent's financial year has changed.

Treatment of 'material items'

12.2.3 The SORP contains a long list of specific accounting policy disclosures that *may* need to be made – ie to clarify the treatment of any 'material' items. This surely implies that the chosen accounting method must be one of a number of materially different alternatives, each of which would fully comply with the SORP – otherwise what would be the point of explaining it?

> 'Trustees should explain in the notes to the accounts the accounting policies they have adopted to deal with material items. Explanations need only be brief but they must be clear, fair and accurate.'
>
> *– SORP 2005, paragraph 361*

Such explanations should not be overdone – unless you like writing reports for their own sake. If the SORP *specifies* it already, and without options, repetition in your accounts notes must weary the reader as well as burdening you with unnecessary work. Rather than confirming in detail exactly how you have done what the SORP says you should (or, in effect: *must?*) do, the real need is for you to highlight here what – if anything – is unusual and different enough for it to mislead the reader on something *significant* unless specially explained.

First and foremost comes what the authorities must always hope will be a rarity: the reporting entity's use of the saving 'true and fair override' facility to depart from the more particular requirements of the relevant accounting legislation, SORP or accounting standard.

This comes to a head with the need to explain the unusual treatment of some 'material item' due to special (ie unusual) circumstances that will then also have to be explained. It is mandatory for *any* charity departing from a specific requirement of the relevant accounting *legislation* to disclose the particulars, the reasons and the (material) financial effect of the departure on its accounts.

Non-company charities, however small, as well as parent charitable companies preparing consolidated accounts under the 1993 Act for a 'small' group, also have to make this disclosure of particulars and reasons (but not of financial effect) wherever an accounting policy or the treatment of a material item differs significantly from that required by the SORP's Regulations other than (i) the *basic* requirement under reg 8(4)(a)/(b) for the SoFA and balance sheet to show a true and fair view and (ii) the *supplementary* requirement under reg 8(4)(c) for any *extra* disclosures needed for a true and fair view. Thus they have to explain any material departure from the SORP's 'methods and principles' or any material omission of the accounts notes information called for by Sch 2 to the 2008 Regulations.

However, as we have seen already, para 1(c) of that Schedule (from which there is also no exemption) does require disclosure in *all* cases of the **effect** on the accounts of any material **change** of an accounting policy and/or estimation technique, while reg 8(5) requires that:

'the statement [of accounts]—

(a)   shall be prepared in accordance with the methods and principles set out in the SORP ...'.

– SI 2008/629, reg 8(5)

The effect of the latter is to make SORP/Standards compliance in that respect *a requirement of the legislation*, with any material departure being a mandatory disclosure for all *non-company* charities, while the effect of the former is to make a nonsense of any description of a material change in 'accounting policies and estimation techniques' that fails to disclose material non-compliance with the SORP's 'methods and principles'.

Appendix 5.3.1 of SORP 2005 explains that a certain latitude is allowed by the SORP in the reporting of expenditure and disclosure of supporting information by small charities up to the statutory audit threshold (£500,000 gross income), but pointedly does *not* do the same in respect of the SORP's general requirement for compliance disclosures:

'If the accounts depart from accounting standards in any material respect, this should be stated in the accounting policies giving the reason and justification for the departure and the financial impact. Similarly the following details should be given for any material departure from this SORP:

(a)   a brief description of how the treatment adopted departs from this SORP;
(b)   the reasons why the trustees judge that the treatment adopted is more appropriate to the charity's particular circumstances; and
(c)   an estimate of the financial effect on the accounts where this is needed for the accounts to give a true and fair view.'

– SORP 2005, paragraph 359

In addition, there is para 1(a) of Sch 2 to the 2008 Regulations, requiring explanation of any 'material adjustments' made to *comparative figures* for the previous financial year to ensure their year-on-year comparability. Again, such adjustments are unlikely to arise other than as a follow-on from the special treatment adopted for a material item in *this* year's SoFA or balance sheet.

Fund-accounting policies

12.2.4   Fund-accounting is intrinsic to the Charities SORP, and the rules for strict compliance with charity law are therefore spelt out there in some detail. Despite this, paragraphs 368 and 369 still ask you to describe 'the different types of fund held by the charity, including the policy for any transfers between funds and allocations to or from designated funds' and 'the policy for determining each designated fund'.

To avoid repetition here, you could perhaps just cross-refer to the accounts note required by paragraph 75 to explain the 'reasons' for the fund balances being carried forward, where sub-paragraph 75(b) (and also para 1(d) of Sch 2 to the SORP's 2008 Regulations) requires you to describe the 'nature and purpose' of each material fund – with the SORP (but not the Regulations) also calling for disclosure of the fund's *origin*.

Some inter-fund *transfers* may be imposed or authorised by charity law – for example, a Charity Commission order to recoup out of unrestricted revenues (income) specified annual instalments to repay an interest-free loan from the charity's permanent general-purpose financial endowment, or the donor-authorised transfer of the surplus on a restricted fund. Others may result from the lawful apportioning of overhead costs to calculate total expenditure on each of the charity's general-purpose and special-purpose activities. The *use* (but not the proper, ie true and fair, *accounting*) of restricted funds held for the latter can be constrained by donors – for example, a specified limit of 6% of an EC-funded project's direct costs to cover the 'core' costs of administering the charity, which if the 'true and fair' rate for the year is 10% would then necessitate a deficit-funding transfer from unrestricted funds to cover the unfunded 4%, so that the SoFA figures will not be misleading in that respect. Failure to recognise the need for such a 'purist' approach in overhead-spreading to avoid material detriment to some other restricted fund(s) is not uncommon in the sector even among professionals – thus putting the charity trustees at unnecessary risk of personal liability for breach of trust if the mistake can no longer be rectified when it comes to light.

Where an inter-fund transfer is material and the amount is based on an accounting policy or estimate, or on a trust law *assumption* you have had to make, for that matter (see below), you may wish to cross-refer from the accounting policies note to the accounts note required by paragraph 75(d) of the SORP:

> 'Material transfers between different funds and allocations to designated funds should be separately disclosed, without netting off, and should be accompanied by an explanation of the nature of the transfers or allocations and the reasons for them.'
>
> – *SORP 2005, paragraph 75(d)*

For a *non-company* charity's accounts, or for any charity's *consolidated* accounts prepared under the 1993 Act, a material transfer affecting any endowed or other restricted fund must in any case, under para 1(i) of Sch 2 to the SORP's 2008 Regulations, be covered by:

> 'an itemised analysis … together with an explanation of the nature and purpose of each of those funds.'
>
> – *SI 2008/629, Sch 2, para 1(i)*

Fund-accounting assumptions

It is also here that you will need to explain any *assumptions* the trustees are relying on (in the absence of documentation in support of the necessary legal authority) for their treatment of any significant *trust funds* included in the SoFA and balance sheet as either permanent or expendable endowment or else as restricted or unrestricted income. Such assumptions are part of the FRS18 concept of 'estimation techniques' as a pragmatic way of resolving uncertainties. Many charities – and their auditors – still have unresolved doubts (uncertainty) as to the precise legal status of such trust funds. Even today, after more than a decade of regulated charity accountability under the Charities SORP, new examples of such uncertainty keep on coming to light.

For example, the capital grant-funding for the new Academies being set up all over the country by the Department for Children, Schools and Families (DCSF) is carefully ring-fenced by the terms and conditions imposed in the Master Funding Agreement. The intended use of this funding is safeguarded by the Agreement's stringent clawback provisions in respect of any disposal proceeds of the fixed assets it provides. That clear intention of 'own use on a continuing basis' of the capitalised assets thus provided for each Academy out of such government grants must, in the absence of any express clause in the Funding Agreement to the contrary, *endow* the recipient charity under trust law.

The DCSF's 'Academies Financial Handbook' points out that the funded charities' annual accounts must comply with company and charity law, but then calls this capital funding simply a 'Restricted Fixed Assets Fund' to be shown in the SoFA and Balance Sheet, but without acknowledging the Fund's 'endowment capital' status under trust law. The accounting error this perpetuates is the inclusion of each year's capital funding as if it were 'restricted income' in the Summary Income & Expenditure Account that the Handbook recommends for compliance with FRS3 and the Companies Act 2006. Not only would that materially mis-state the year's 'net income' for inter-company comparison by the DBIS (previously: DBERR), but it would also not comply with SSAP4, which requires such government grants to be taken to income in line with the related asset-depreciation – not immediately and in full! To be fair to those involved, it must be acknowledged that such errors in trust-accounting are bound to follow from the SORP's strange coyness in burying its very clear and unequivocal guidance on this subject in an appendix, instead of making it part of the text of the SORP.

If after researching all available records the trustees have drawn their own conclusion on 'best evidence', supporting this with a suitable minute in their records of trustees' meetings, but without the benefit of official endorsement (preferably in the form of written advice from the Charity Commission under the power provided in s 29 of the 1993 Act), then that would count as an important 'assumption' on which the accounts as drawn have been based.

SoFA policies and estimates – incoming resources

12.2.5   Suggestions for the kind of incoming resource for which further details of your accounting policies and 'estimation techniques' may be required are set out in paragraph 362(a)–(g) of the SORP. These are characterised as unusual in some respect or other that may make it necessary to spell out the accounting rules actually followed. Here, we take a look at each kind in turn. In each case, though, it is only worth saying something about the policy and/or calculation basis for the SoFA figure if:

(i)   the item/category really is 'material' (likely to influence the reader); and

(ii)   the further details you provide really will add value for the reader over and above what is said in the SORP itself, for example by removing ambiguities or saying which of two or more recommended options you have taken.

For example, the obvious category of *trading activities*, whether primarily 'to further the charity's Objects' or 'to generate funds', is not even mentioned here – even though charitable trading turnover has been estimated to account for some 45% of the aggregate gross income of all registered charities. The implication is that if you follow the normal commercial accounting rules for trading revenues (including long-term contracts) there will be nothing further to add to what the accounting standards say.

An example of an unusual treatment of trading activities would be the grossing up in the charity's SoFA (perhaps by means of an inset note there) of the profit-stripping GiftAid donation from a subsidiary from trading (usually 'on a shoestring' for lack of working capital) outside the charity's own Objects (and in excess of the Finance

Act 2000 'de minimis' limit for charities), in order to dispense with consolidated accounts for such an insubstantial or 'shell' company on the ground of its immateriality.

Such grossing up may be seen as the inverse of the normal SORP rule against 'netting off'. By separately disclosing the subsidiary's turnover as 'activities [of subsidiary undertakings] to generate funds' within the incoming resources section[2] of the charity SoFA and linking this through the accounts notes to the separate disclosure of the subsidiary's operating costs under the SoFA heading of 'costs of generating funds', it can be made clear that while the legal form of the transaction is just the donation, the *substance* (FRS5) of the transaction is the non-charitable trading activity undertaken for the benefit of the charity, at its behest and under its ultimate control.

In the case of donations coming in as *money*, whether unsolicited or in response to fundraising appeals (including the *cash collections* highlighted in the original 1995 SORP), and whether or not under GiftAid, SORP 2005 seems to dismiss their accounting treatment as self-evident. Paragraph 362 says only that the policy for *all* incoming resources 'will normally be on a receivable basis but may need further details in some cases'.

Prior to the 1995 SORP, the prevailing practice had been to disclaim responsibility for 'donated income' until actually received by the charity, taking the convenient audit view that voluntary resources generally were not susceptible to any effective control system until that point had been reached. But in accounting for donation income only on a 'received' basis instead of the 'receivable' basis implied by their charity law obligations, charity trustees then found they had to put up with auditors reserving their opinion on such income – to the point where the reservation became almost standard wording in audit reports, threatening discredit to the trustees and thereby also loss of public confidence in the charity.

Having outlawed the disclaimers, charity accountability has moved on in its further development, in common with other and wider issues of environmental responsibility, social conscience, the 'open government' code and the ever greater need for transparency and 'good governance' in public life as the pace quickens. So the SORP now leaves it to the trustees to come to terms with their auditors over the practical problems of their accountability for (and control over) the stream of donated money flowing into their charity as a result of their efforts. If they still want to adopt a cash-accounting policy for this kind of incoming resource, they must disclose the fact and clear its audit implications, as it is no longer acceptable to adopt a do nothing policy 'until the cheque hits the deck'.

It may be practical in normal circumstances to disclose particular accounting policies and valuation bases/methods only where the resource concerned exceeds a threshold of, say, 5% of total incoming resources, in which case the kind of question to be answered here will be as follows.

---

2   Paragraph 141(c) of the SORP requires it to be treated as *investment income* in the SoFA, on a line of its own if material, which can thus facilitate using an inset note.

Legacies – SORP 2005, paragraph 362(a)

What precise accounting rules have you used? (These must be in compliance with the three basic recognition criteria[3] set by paragraph 94 of the SORP, as illustrated by examples of legacy situations in paragraphs 123–127 – but you will hardly need to repeat all of those in your accounts.) Do your rules suffice to determine *what to bring into the SoFA*, describing in the accounts notes those entitlements that on this basis you cannot yet accrue, as required by paragraph 128 of the SORP? (See also **6.3.1** where we discuss those rules.)

Gifts in kind and donated services/facilities (intangible income) – SORP 2005, paragraph 362(b)

How have the amounts of all such *non-purchased* resources included in the accounts been *valued* for major items (if any) with no published market price (and/or any provisional estimates subsequently adjusted) and what sort of *financially significant* items (if any) have you excluded? (See also **6.3.2** and **6.3.3** where we discuss the SoFA recognition rules in detail.)

(Where there *is* a readily available market value (as in the case of those major gifts of quoted securities for which the donor can claim a deduction from taxable income under the Finance Act 2000), there is surely no need to state the obvious – that you have complied with the SORP – even if the item happens to be the largest incoming resource for the year.)

Grants receivable for fixed assets or for activities – SORP 2005, paragraph 362(c)

In what column/category have they been shown in the SoFA (see **6.3.4**), and on what basis have you assumed trust or contract law to apply to a major grant for activities if the applicable law has not been specified by the grantor? (See also **6.3.4** where we discuss the difference this can make in the SoFA.)

Deferred income – SORP 2005, paragraph 362(d)

Other than contract income received/invoiced in advance, and *performance-related* grant monies subject to as yet unsatisfied pre-conditions for entitlement to the money *as income* (see also **6.3.4**), both of which (if material) the reader only needs to be able to discern in the SoFA and related accounts notes, since a *standard* accounting treatment is involved, what is the justification for the deferral and how is the amount calculated?

(Apart from the most obvious situation provided as a special case in the SORP, ie where a funding body or other donor imposes a timing condition that postpones to some future accounting period the *benefit* of the gift, the next example illustrates what the SORP means by this.)

---

[3] These require that (a) the will must have 'matured' (ie the donor died) by the year-end, giving rise to 'entitlement'; furthermore that – unless the amount to be recognised in the SoFA has already been received as money or other assets after date – the charity's entitlement must have become legally enforceable against the executors, with (b) its ultimate receipt a reasonable certainty and (c) the assessment of its monetary value sufficiently reliable.

Life-membership commuted subscription income – SORP 2005, paragraph 362(e)

How have the amounts deferred to future years been calculated? (See also **6.2.1** where we discuss possible accounting bases for this.)

(The 1995 SORP suggested amortising the income over the commutation period – e g 10 years – but where substantial membership *benefits* are involved (professional membership associations, for instance) it may be more prudent to assess the 'future years' income element actuarially, by analogy with 'defined benefit scheme' pension fund liabilities. This disclosure must also be seen in the context of paragraph 114, which requires an analysis note reconciling all changes from last year-end to this year-end. (The National Trust takes all life membership subscriptions to an Equalisation Account disclosed in its accounts notes, and from there credits them to the SoFA evenly over the 10 years.)

Endowment income – SORP 2005, paragraph 362(f)

How was the attribution of the income to unrestricted or restricted funds decided?

(Any legally binding restriction of the use of income from a financial endowment will normally only be one imposed by the donor of that endowment – except that in setting up any charitable trust the founder can instead give the trustees a discretionary power to impose this or any other kind of restriction at any time, either as a revocable act or an irrevocable one.)

Income shown net of costs – SORP 2005, paragraph 362(g)

From what source, and why was it necessary to net off the costs?

Investment returns

In view of the requirement elsewhere to report actual investment performance against the investment policy (if any) set by the trustees, paragraph 142 requires the income for the year to be analysed over the investment categories specified by paragraph 303.

In chapter 6, we discussed the impact of 'total return' investment accounting, as well as investment pooling, on the SoFA; here, you may wish not only to cross-refer to the *investment assets* analysis note, where the operation of the total return basis (and/or any inter-fund pooling arrangements) will need to be disclosed and explained, but also to explain here how the *total return* is accounted for in the SoFA, adding that this includes a supporting analysis over the investment categories used for the balance sheet note. Similarly, the method of accounting for *pooled* investment returns for multiple trust funds included in the accounts (if applicable) will need to be explained here.

SoFA policies and estimates – expenditure

12.2.6 SORP 2005 devotes a lengthy section (paragraphs 148–213) to accounting for charity expenditure, from 'liability' recognition under the rules of FRS12 to the revised *purpose-related* activity-based (as distinct from the 'functional' analysis favoured by SORP 2000) presentation of resources shown in the SoFA as 'consumed' (rather than in the balance sheet as 'capitalised'), and the supplementary information and explanations needed to facilitate the reader's understanding of the impact and implications of the application of the charity's financial resources in this way. The policies and estimating methods/bases that are required to be disclosed in this connection include not only 'the policy for the recognition of liabilities including constructive obligations' but the basis of any estimates made in making provision for *longer-term* liabilities. As the SORP puts it, pointing especially to grant-making activities:

> '... the point at which the provision is considered to become binding and the basis of any discount factors used in current value calculations for long term commitments should be given.'
>
> – *SORP 2005, paragraph 363(a)*

The SORP's requirements for the disclosure of expenditure have always been more extensive than those of the corporate/commercial sector, for the obvious reason that the 'bottom line' in charity accountability is not a profit figure but the particular *public benefit* for which the charity is established and/or aiming to provide. Charity law imposes a strict duty of care on the trustees to *apply* the resources of their charity 'properly' – either by spending them to provide such public benefit (charitable expenditure) or by investing (without 'undue' risk) any funds not immediately needed for that purpose.

While not itself a *charitable* purpose, the reasonable (ie expedient) use of a charity's resources for *fundraising* and even for other, more overtly commercial 'activities to generate funds' is also acceptable to the eye of the law. Under the Finance Act 2000, charities enjoy a statutory concession permitting them to trade 'for profit' (ie outside their Objects) directly – with a 'turnover' ceiling of up to £50,000 per annum, depending on the size of charity by reference to its gross income. What is not acceptable, of course, is for a charity's resources to provide unauthorised private benefit to its trustees or their 'connected persons', and charity law therefore makes the trustees personally liable for restitution to their charity of any loss arising from their own default in such cases.

As explained later in this chapter, the extended requirements of the SORP for FRS8 compliance in disclosing *related party* transactions can be optimised where internal controls are in place to manage potential conflicts of interests, so that the constraints of charity law can be relied on to enable the trustees to modify their disclosure policy accordingly.

Paragraph 363(b) requires detailed policy disclosures wherever the following kinds of expenditure include 'items' regarded as 'material' – for which, while the SORP no longer offers such useful tips, you could again take a threshold of 5% of total expenditure as practicable in normal circumstances. If you really want to be helpful to the accounts user, this should *not* confirm the obvious (eg *'the policy is to treat fundraising and permissible non-charitable trading expenditure as part of the costs of generating funds'*). Instead, it should identify the activity-costs that would not be included there had it not been for the fact that the *primary* purpose of the activity was to generate funds.

Here are the categories, which – as you can see – do not leave you much scope for minimising expenditure-accounting policy disclosures:

–   grants of money or goods and services provided (primarily) to further the charity's Objects, and also the support costs of providing such benefits – *SORP 2005, paragraph 363(b)(ii)*;

–   'governance' costs (ie the management and administration of the charity) – *SORP 2005, paragraph 363(b)(iii)*;

–   the costs of activities (primarily) to generate funds – *SORP 2005, paragraph 363(b)(i)*;

–   the methods and principles followed for the allocation and apportionment of all costs between the above categories – *SORP 2005, paragraph 363(c)*.

Paragraph 363(c) goes on to add:

> 'This disclosure should include the underlying principle ie whether based on staff time, staff salaries, space occupied or other. Where the costs apportioned are material, then further clarification on the method of apportionment used is necessary, including the proportions used to undertake the calculations.'
>
> *– SORP 2005, paragraph 363(c)*

Balance sheet policies and estimates

12.2.7   Fixed assets is the only significant issue here for most charities – apart from the fund-accounting already covered at **12.2.4**. Even this is only where *major items* have to be accounted for. Unfortunately, policy declarations in this area seem to have become commonplace and 'boiler-plate', even where inconsequential for lack of major items – which is regrettable, as the practice devalues the disclosures needed to highlight situations of real significance for the (informed) general public as the *primary* (general-purpose) user of charities' annual accounts and reports. What is vital here under SORP 2005 is to review the wording of the charity's existing accounting policy note on fixed assets capitalisation and depreciation so that you can ensure it complies with the very strict requirements of FRS15, as already explained in chapter 8.

Having said that, we also need here to look at the relatively new addition of *heritage assets* accounting policy (derived from the inalienable/historic category under SORP 2000), in particular the requirement that:

> 'The policy for capitalisation of fixed assets for charity use should be stated including ... whether or not heritage assets are capitalised and if not, the reason why (eg, lack of reliable information, cost/benefit reason, etc. ...) specifying the acquisition and disposal policies for such assets; ...'.
>
> *– SORP 2005, paragraph 364*

The requirement here could be misleading, as you only really have to disclose the actual grounds relied on for any *non*-capitalisation – of this or, indeed, any other kind of *donated* asset that the charity is obliged under trust law to retain for its own use on a continuing basis. It is only there that you can have any kind of option. In all other respects, the requirements of SORP 2005 are singular and mandatory.

Looking at the more general class of *all* fixed assets for the charity's own use, SORP 2005 simply echoes FRS15/11, in requiring that:

> 'The policy for capitalisation of fixed assets for charity use for capitalisation of fixed assets for charity use should be stated including:

(a)   whether each class of asset is included at cost, valuation or revaluation and the method of valuation where applicable;

(b)   the value below which fixed assets are not capitalised;

...

(d)   the rates of depreciation applying to each class of fixed asset; and

(e)   the policy with respect to impairment reviews of fixed assets.'

– SORP 2005, paragraph 364

What this also means in practice is that, having taken advantage of FRS15's transitional provisions ever since 2000 (see chapter 8) to 'freeze' an asset's *pre-FRS15* accounting valuation as the only way to avoid being forced to keep updating it to 'current value' (meaning 'value in use', of course) every year, you must continue to disclose the fact that 'its value has not been updated', as well as the date and amount of the old valuation.

Investment assets

For most charities, apart from mentioning their 'social investments' (see chapter 9) as part of their more general 'accounts basis' declaration, there will be nothing to add to what the SORP already *requires* by way of an accounting policy for investment assets – except where these include *material* items in one of the three categories below, since for readily marketable assets (other than those social investments) the SORP allows no options. On the other hand, for a select few the option under SORP 2005 to revert to cost for what has perhaps always (for them) been a highly successful commercial trading subsidiary (albeit for tax reasons a mere shell with little or no working capital) is also covered here:

'The policy for including investments in the accounts should be given. This should be at market value but may need to be modified for the valuation of ...

...

(c)   investments in subsidiary undertakings.'

– SORP 2005, paragraph 365

Other material items

Seemingly by way of a catch-all, the SORP ends up with the following set of 'other policy notes' that you *might* have to consider, saying that:

'These could include policies for the recognition of the following:

(a)   pension costs and any pension asset or liability;

(b)   foreign exchange gains and losses;

(c)   treatment of exceptional items;

(d)   treatment of finance and operating leases;

(e)   treatment of irrecoverable VAT.'

– SORP 2005, paragraph 370

In the same way here also, unless the *policy* you have adopted to account for items of such a class either differs from the SORP's requirement or is an option within the SORP, any further statement of the obvious (in addition to your more general SORP-compliance declaration) must surely be redundant. What FRS18 really contemplates is therefore not unnecessary repetition here but simply a specific disclosure of how you have arrived at any financially significant *estimates* within the class of item concerned – on the basis that if there are generally accepted alternative estimation techniques yielding a materially different result then the reader needs to know which one you have adopted.

Changes and corrections

12.2.8 Accounting policies are *changed* when it is considered that another policy is more suitable to the matter than the one followed to date, or when a new/revised FRS or a revised version of the SORP is issued, requiring a change of policy. FRS18 sets out precise rules to determine whether it is the *accounting policy* that has changed, requiring disclosure of the effects of the change on the current year's 'results' and, where the change affects the brought forward figures, the effect on last year's 'results', or whether it is just the *'estimation technique'* that has changed. The latter should not be made retrospectively unless it corrects a fundamental error or is given retrospective effect by law/standards:

'The following information should be disclosed in the financial statements:

...

(c)   details of any changes to the accounting policies that were followed in preparing financial statements for the preceding period, including:
    (i)   a brief explanation of why each new accounting policy is thought more appropriate;
    (ii)   where practicable, the effect of a prior period adjustment on the results for the preceding period, in accordance with FRS 3 "Reporting Financial Performance"; and
    (iii)   where practicable, an indication of the effect of a change in accounting policy on the results for the current period.

Where it is not practicable to make the disclosures described in (ii) or (iii) above, that fact, together with the reasons, should be stated.'

– FRS18, paragraph 55

'When an entity changes the way it presents a particular item in the balance sheet or in the profit and loss account, that is a change of accounting policy.'

– FRS18, paragraph 12

'Care is needed when an accounting change involves both a change of presentation and a change of estimation technique. The former will be treated as a change of accounting policy but the latter will not.'

– FRS18, paragraph 13

'... where there is uncertainty over the monetary amount [to be calculated on the estimation] basis [adopted under an accounting policy], the amount will be arrived at by using an estimation technique.

Estimation techniques include, for example:

(a)   methods of depreciation, such as straight-line and reducing balance, applied in the context of a particular measurement basis, used to estimate the proportion of the economic benefits of a tangible fixed asset consumed in a period;

(b)   different methods used to estimate the proportion of trade debts that will not be recovered, particularly where such methods consider a population as a whole rather than individual balances.'

– FRS18, paragraph 4

'A change to an estimation technique should not be accounted for as a prior period adjustment, unless

(a)   it represents the correction of a fundamental error, or

(b)   another accounting standard, a UITF Abstract or companies legislation requires the change to be accounted for as a prior period adjustment.'

– FRS18, paragraph 54

One of the few examples the SORP gives of a *change* of accounting policy is the now obsolete one of the change needed for FRS15 compliance when bringing into the balance sheet for the first time fixed assets still used for the charity's own purposes but which prior to SORP 2000 had previously been excluded as inalienable or historic under paragraph 186 of the 1995 SORP:

'... where [tangible fixed assets for the charity's own use] are capitalised some time after being acquired, for example as a result of a change in accounting policy, they should be included at original cost or at the value at which the gift was included in the Statement of Financial Activities less an amount for depreciation.'

– SORP 2005, paragraph 255

This is to be distinguished from adopting a new policy for the first time to deal with a newly commenced *activity*, or where a new requirement is issued calling for a new approach, or where there is a decision to change the basis of accounting, say from historical cost to current value. For instance, some accounting standards when issued clearly state that they only apply to future accounting periods; others require adjustment to previously reported performance.

In fact, the SORP only mentions *significant* changes of *specific* accounting policies, which it then goes on to exemplify in paragraphs 361–370, saying that such changes should be disclosed in detail:

'Specific Policies

Trustees should explain in the notes to the accounts the accounting policies they have adopted to deal with material items ... Changes to any of the policies that result in a material adjustment to prior periods should be disclosed in detail ...'.

– SORP 2005, paragraph 361

However, this is then made mandatory by para 1(c) of Sch 2 to the SORP's related 2008 Regulations – for the accruals accounts of all *non-company* charities but also for *any* charity's consolidated accounts prepared under the Charities Act, which in the case of a charitable company will be only where it heads a 'small' group as defined by the Companies Act 2006 and the 2008 Regulations made thereunder.

An example of the kind of change that, where the amount involved is material, will need disclosure here is the *accounting policy* that must be newly adopted for the purpose if related interest costs are to be included as part of capitalised expenditure, instead of being expensed as normal in the SoFA:

> 'Tangible fixed assets should initially be included in the balance sheet using the following bases.
>
> (a)   The cost of acquisition including costs that are directly attributable to bringing the assets into working condition for their intended use. This can include costs of interest on loans to finance the construction of such assets but only where the charity has adopted this as a policy for all tangible fixed assets and capitalisation should cease when the asset is ready for use. This applies whether assets are bought outright or through hire purchase or finance leasing ...'.

– SORP 2005, paragraph 255

Change in accounts preparation basis

As a special case, a small *non-company* charity may switch between accruals and cash-based accounting from year to year, when previous versions of the SORP pointed out that:

> 'For each year in which the charity changes from accruals accounts to receipts and payments accounting or vice versa, the corresponding amounts for the previous financial year should be restated on the basis of the new accounting policy.'

– SORP 2000, paragraph 357

SORP 2005 has been so thorough in restricting itself to accruals-based accounting by cutting out all the cash-based accounting recommendations that had been added into SORP 2000 that it no longer includes the above guidance, which remains pertinent from whichever side of the option you approach it. A faint allusion to remind practitioners about this point is all that now remains in the SORP:

> 'The corresponding figures for the previous accounting period should be provided in the accounts in accordance with generally accepted accounting practice ...'.

– SORP 2005, paragraph 31

Accounting policies – Decision tree for the adoption of FRSSE 2008

12.2.9   Ever since the FRSSE 2000, SORP-issuing bodies have been allowed by the FRSSE itself *to restrict its scope*, and the underpinning of the Charities SORP by its related Regulations applicable to *non-company* charities for their accruals-based accounts (and also to charitable companies for their consolidated accounts if the group is 'small') gives it legislative authority to override the Standards in any case. Appendix 5.2.1 of SORP 2005 therefore says:

> 'Any charity (whether or not it is a company) which is under the thresholds for small companies as described in the Companies Acts (Appendix 4), can follow the ... FRSSE in preparing its financial accounts except where it conflicts with this SORP in which case this SORP should be followed.'

– SORP 2005, Appendix 5.2.1

However, there may be a small snag here that could catch thousands of charities with little enough trading 'turnover' to meet the criteria as set out in the Companies Acts, but which may be dismayed to find that Appendix 4 offers an amendment by asserting that for charities 'turnover' means 'gross income'! While that was certainly true for the *company audit exemption regulations*, until the 1985 Act's special regime for charitable companies was abolished for financial years starting after March 2008, the SORP cannot of itself amend the Companies Act's current size criteria for the various *accounting reliefs* enjoyed by 'small' entities and groups – which is what FRSSE eligibility is based on. Therefore we suggest that when using the decision tree that follows, you stick to the SORP's *text* here and ignore Appendix 4 – or else argue things out with your auditors. See also chapter 5, where this point is discussed in further detail at **5.3**, dealing with the FRSSE. The SORP itself says:

> 'Appendix 5 explains how the Financial Reporting Standard for Smaller Entities (FRSSE) can be applied by charities (whether or not they are companies) which are under the thresholds for small companies as described in the Companies Acts ...'.

– SORP 2005, paragraph 62

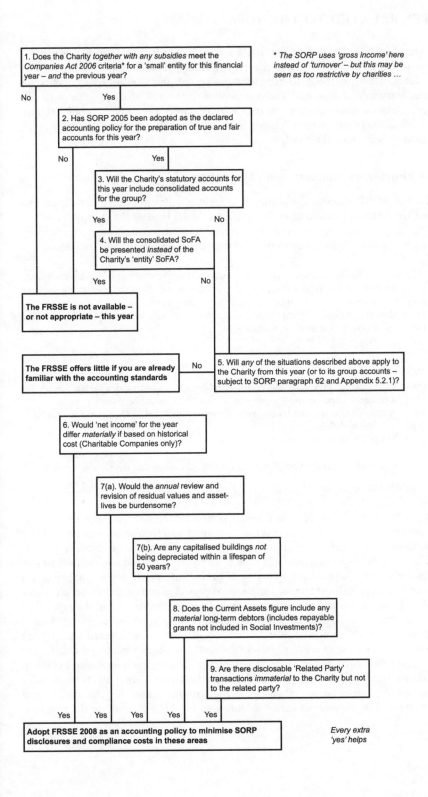

1. Does the Charity *together with any subsidies* meet the *Companies Act 2006* criteria* for a 'small' entity for this financial year – *and* the previous year?

* The SORP uses 'gross income' here instead of 'turnover' – but this may be seen as too restrictive by charities ...

No   Yes

2. Has SORP 2005 been adopted as the declared accounting policy for the preparation of true and fair accounts for this year?

No   Yes

3. Will the Charity's statutory accounts for this year include consolidated accounts for the group?

Yes   No

4. Will the consolidated SoFA be presented *instead* of the Charity's 'entity' SoFA?

Yes   No

The FRSSE is not available – or not appropriate – this year

The FRSSE offers little if you are already familiar with the accounting standards

No

5. Will *any* of the situations described above apply to the Charity from this year (or to its group accounts – subject to SORP paragraph 62 and Appendix 5.2.1)?

6. Would 'net income' for the year differ *materially* if based on historical cost (Charitable Companies only)?

7(a). Would the *annual* review and revision of residual values and asset-lives be burdensome?

7(b). Are any capitalised buildings *not* being depreciated within a lifespan of 50 years?

8. Does the Current Assets figure include any *material* long-term debtors (includes repayable grants not included in Social Investments)?

9. Are there disclosable 'Related Party' transactions *immaterial* to the Charity but not to the related party?

Yes   Yes   Yes   Yes   Yes

Adopt FRSSE 2008 as an accounting policy to minimise SORP disclosures and compliance costs in these areas

Every extra 'yes' helps

NOTES RELATED TO THE SOFA

12.3   In chapter 3, we studied the SORP's *fund-accounting* requirements, which are intrinsic to charity accountability. In chapter 6, we looked at each section of the SoFA in some detail. Here, we need to remind ourselves of the various requirements for supplementary information and analysis mentioned there so that, together with this chapter's detailed consideration of the 'related party' and other 'public interest' disclosures required under the Charities SORP, we can have a useful overview of all these *activity-related* accounts notes.

Funds movements summary and explanation

12.3.1   The SORP requires the accounts to include a description of the nature and purpose (ie declared Objects) of each significant (trust) fund of the charity, as well as distinguishing between permanent and expendable (also called 'discretionary' or 'convertible') endowments, other restricted funds, designated funds and free reserves:

> 'The notes to the accounts should provide information on the structure of the charity's funds so as to disclose the fund balances and the reasons for them, differentiating between unrestricted income funds (both general and designated), restricted income funds, permanent endowment and expendable endowment, as well as identifying any material individual funds among them. In particular:
>
> ...
>
> (b)   Disclosure of how each of the funds has arisen (including designated funds), the restrictions imposed and the purpose of each fund should be provided ...
> (c)   Any funds in deficit should always be separately disclosed ... Designated funds should never be in deficit.
> (d)   Material transfers between different funds and allocations to designated funds should be separately disclosed, without netting off, and should be accompanied by an explanation of the nature of the transfers or allocations and the reasons for them ...'.

– SORP 2005, paragraph 75

On the other hand, provided it is adequately covered by reserves or a temporarily designated fund, which is really an *informal* inter-fund 'soft loan' arrangement, so that it can be clearly seen that no misuse of other restricted funds is involved, it is quite permissible for an *unendowed* restricted fund to be shown in the accounts to have run up a deficit for a time – for example, spending in advance of appeal monies (or, perhaps, a grant) known to be forthcoming for some special project would result in a deficit on the appeal or project fund, and the situation would then need explaining in the notes. The unusual alternative would be to make a transfer in the SoFA by way of a formal *inter-fund loan* (such an arrangement, which would need to be minuted as a trustee decision, is the converse of a Charity Commission Recoupment Order – see chapter 10) to 'neutralise' the deficit, but this loan would then need to be clearly explained as such in the accounts notes in order to avoid problems in a later year when – unless the transfer is reversed by repayment(s) shown on the transfers line of the SoFA and cross-referenced to the original loan – an unusable surplus will result on the restricted fund.

In any case, as already noted above, any material inter-fund transfers affecting an endowed or other restricted fund must be disclosed item-by-item and their nature and purpose explained. This would, of course, include any *inter-fund* loans and their authority and any terms of repayment.

The following illustration comes from the consolidated accounts of a charitable company without trust funds and financed almost entirely from the profits and research activities of its trading subsidiaries – among them being the highly successful *Which?* magazine. Although its treatment of the statutory *corporate revaluation reserve* as if it were a separate *charitable* fund looks at odds with the spirit and intention of the SORP, yet in other respects it is fairly typical of prevailing practice in analysing movements for the year on individual funds as required by the SORP.

18. Movement of funds during the year	Unrestricted charity funds	Revaluation reserve	Accumulated deficit of trading subsidiaries	Group funds
	£'000	£'000	£'000	£'000
Balance at 1 July 2007	34,588	6,064	(3,794)	36,858
Net outgoing resources before gift aid payment	(6,710)	–	–	(6,710)
Revaluation of investment assets (Note 10)	–	(3,722)	–	(3,722)
Realised gains on investments	1,436	–	–	1,436
Trading profit before gift aid	–	–	9,826	9,826
Gift aid payments from subsidiaries to Charity	9,767	–	(9,767)	–
Actuarial gains on defined benefit pension schemes	(200)	-	-	(200)
Balance at 30 June 2008	**38,881**	**2,292**	**(3,735)**	**37,438**

Consumers' Association – 2007/08 Accounts

Incoming resources sub-analysis

12.3.2 The SORP seems to require numerous supplementary disclosures in support of the SoFA here:

–   analysis of movements in the balance sheet figure of 'deferred income' (meaning from *voluntary* as well as any contractual sources) between amounts deferred from the current year and amounts released from previous years, grouping together 'incoming resources of a similar nature'– *SORP 2005, paragraph 114*;

–   details of 'the types of activities undertaken to generate' any material 'voluntary income' (if not shown in the SoFA along with their respective costs) – *SORP 2005, paragraph 122*;

–   particulars of any material legacies notified but excluded from the SoFA 'because the conditions for recognition have not been met', with estimates, where possible, of the amounts receivable – *SORP 2005, paragraph 128*;

–   the basis of any valuation (of gifts in kind) – *SORP 2005, paragraph 131*;

–   a general description of any stocks of gifts in kind *received for distribution* and an estimate of their value, if material – *SORP 2005, paragraph 132*;

–   analysis to show any major components, such as 'seconded staff, loaned assets, etc', of donated services and facilities (ie what the SORP used to call 'intangible income') in the SoFA – *SORP 2005, paragraph 136*;

–   analysis of 'gross investment income' by investment category – *SORP 2005, paragraph 142*.

In addition to all that, SORP 2005 also requires information to enable the accounts user to relate charitable activity costs to the income derived from (or for) each one (and presumably also the 'net result' of each activity – even though, by definition, that must surely be the last thing on the minds of the trustees for external financial reporting in deciding to undertake such a *public benefit* activity in the first place):

> 'An analysis of incoming resources from charitable activities should be given in the notes to the accounts to supplement the analysis on the face of the Statement of Financial Activities. It should be sufficiently detailed so that the reader of the accounts understands the main activities carried out by the charity and the main components of the gross incoming resources receivable for each material charitable activity. As far as possible, incoming resources should be analysed using the same analysis categories as used for resources expended on charitable activities.'
>
> – *SORP 2005, paragraph 146*

This requirement is discussed in chapter 13, where we cover 'Operating Activities'.

Expenditure sub-analysis

12.3.3   In addition to showing all expenditure in the SoFA under *objective-based* headings, the larger charities (ie above the statutory audit threshold) must provide supporting sub-analysis for all these SoFA categories by function to distinguish any material grant-making included within charitable activities and also any support costs included. Quite apart from the familiar analysis of all the charity's staff costs (for which, see below), all its 'support costs' are to be cross-analysed by cost-centre in terms of the 'back office' functions they provide (eg management, finance, IT, HR, etc) for each category of SoFA cost reported – ie charitable activities, fund-generating activities and their respective sub-categories, and governance. Furthermore, an expense-type analysis of any major components of those support costs (but not for any of the direct costs) is to be provided.

This evolutionary change in the way the SORP requires expenditure to be explained is yet another step along the way to a fully purpose-related presentation that can better support the new performance-reporting, since the old SORP's expense-type sub-analysis is now almost universally interpreted as requiring only a division between total staff costs (because these average nearly two-thirds of charities' total expenditure) and some other significant kinds of cost, such as consumables or other *bought-in* supplies/services – perhaps highlighting cost-types that are special to the charity or type of charity (eg schools, churches, hospices, etc).

Charitable activity costs

The SORP offers a pro forma table (at paragraph 194) to show how each objective-category of cost as shown in the SoFA can be split into its three main components of service-provision, grant-making (meaning their direct costs in each case) and any support costs. The figure for grants payable (which of course means grants of money – not of *money's worth*, ie the value of any charitable [goods or] services provided, for which there is no further analysis required by type of beneficiary) is now the only link figure with the further split the SORP requires between individuals and institutions – see 12.3.4.

Support costs

Again, the SORP offers a pro forma table (at paragraph 167) to show how all the charity's non-direct costs should be analysed by function across each of the SoFA's reported activities, for which purpose it defines 'support costs' and the functions involved as follows:

> 'In undertaking any activity there may be support costs … incurred that, whilst necessary to deliver an activity, do not themselves produce or constitute the output of the charitable activity. Similarly, costs will be incurred in supporting income generation activities such as fundraising, and in supporting the governance of the charity. Support costs include the central or regional office functions such as general management, payroll administration, budgeting and accounting, information technology, human resources, and financing.

> 'Support costs do not, in themselves, constitute an activity, instead they enable output-creating activities to be undertaken …'.

> 'The notes to the accounts should provide details of the total support costs incurred and of material items or categories of expenditure included within support costs.'

> *– SORP 2005, paragraphs 164 to 166*

Paragraph 167 of the SORP then requires this tabular analysis to be supported by a description of the method used for calculating the amount (or percentage, if preferred) of each functional category of support cost shown in the table as included in each of the SoFA categories in addition to the direct costs of that activity – see chapter 6, where we discuss the cost-spreading methodology envisaged for this purpose by the SORP.

Governance costs

The SORP requires you at least to 'explain the nature of costs' reported in this category of expenditure, but paragraph 212 further suggests that this 'may' include an expense-type sub-analysis for *'the main items of expenditure … where it is considered to provide useful information to the users of the accounts'*.

Costs of generating funds

Similar to that for charitable activities, the SORP now asks for an activity-type rather than expense-type sub-analysis here for activities to generate (i) voluntary funds and (ii) trading profits:

> 'Where the costs of generating voluntary income are material, details of the types of activity on which the costs were expended should be shown in the notes to the accounts. Types of activity could include collections (e g street and house-to-house collections), sponsorship, legacy development and direct mail. As far as possible the analysis provided here should match the detailed analysis of voluntary incoming resources ...'.
>
> – *SORP 2005, paragraph 183*

> 'Where the costs associated with fundraising trading are material, details should be given in the notes to the accounts to distinguish the cost of separate trading activities in a way that matches the analysis of income.'
>
> – *SORP 2005, paragraph 186*

Charities below the statutory audit threshold

As mentioned above, all this *activity-based* expenditure analysis is only obligatory for 'larger' (ie, auditable) charities. All the others, being of insignificant public interest financially (even in aggregate), can still go their own way in deciding how best to report their expenditure in the SoFA and therefore also in the notes:

> '... concessions for smaller charities that are not subject to a statutory audit ... cover the Statement of Financial Activities and notes to the accounts:
>
> (a)   In relation to the Statement of Financial Activities, smaller charities do not need to analyse either resources expended or incoming resources by activity categories within the Statement of Financial Activities. They may instead choose resource classifications to suit their circumstances.
>
> (b)   Where a small charity adopts an alternative approach to analysis within the Statement of Financial Activities certain note disclosures may no longer be necessary, for example, where these disclosures relate to the constituent costs of an activity category or where relevant information is provided on the face of the Statement of Financial Activities.'
>
> – *SORP 2005, Appendix 5.3.1*

SORP 2000 was more specific here, saying:

> 'They may choose expenditure classifications to suit their circumstances (e g salaries and wages, office costs, repairs and maintenance, etc).'
>
> – *SORP 2000, paragraph 348*

Grants to institutions/individuals

12.3.4   Regardless of how the total expenditure for the year is presented in the SoFA, the SORP's disclosure requirements here recognise the special regulatory and public interest in charities with significant grant-making activities, as gifts of *money* do need the most careful control to ensure their proper application for public benefit. That duty can be safely and quickly discharged simply by obtaining a valid written receipt for it if the money is going to another charity (within the meaning of English law) rather than to an individual for personal (charitable) benefit or to a non-charitable body for charitable application. However, the SORP itself makes no such distinction. In tightening the grants-disclosure rules, SORP 2000 had set a materiality threshold (to include grant-making to *individuals*) of *5% of total expenditure* below which further information did not have to be provided except where 'the value of grants to an institution ... is material compared to the total institutional grants in that year and information regarding such grants could be useful to the users of the accounts and should be disclosed'.

That was a refinement of the 1995 SORP, under which grants of £1,000 or more per institution per year were to be considered 'material' unless the total of all such grants for the year was *immaterial* (5% of total expenditure or less), when no disclosures at all were required.

As a further narrowing of options, the SORP 2005 text makes no reference at all to any such numerical 'rule of thumb', leaving it to you and your auditors to assess whether an item is or is not 'material' in *all* the circumstances. Where further disclosure does have to be made, ie unless *'grant-making activities in total are not material in the context of a charity's overall charitable activities'*, paragraph 198 requires it to *'provide the reader with a reasonable understanding of the nature of the activities or projects that are being funded'*. First, paragraph 203 requires this to comprise a split of the year's total between grants to individuals and those to institutions, disclosing in each case *'the total amount of the grants'* and then *'an analysis ... by nature or type of activity or project being supported'*. Paragraph 199 explains how you can distinguish between a grant to an individual and one to an institution:

> 'An individual grant is one which is made for the direct benefit of the individual who receives it, for example to relieve financial hardship or for an educational bursary. All other grants should be regarded as institutional. For example, a grant which is made to an individual to carry out a research project should be regarded as a grant to the institution with which the individual is connected rather than as a grant to the individual.'
>
> *– SORP 2005, paragraph 199*

Paragraph 204 explains what is meant by 'the nature of the activities or projects being funded', saying that these should 'relate to the charity's objectives', with a few examples:

> 'For example, categories may be social welfare, medical research, the performing arts, welfare of people in financial need, help to people seeking to further their education, depending on the nature of the charity. Some charities may decide that it is appropriate to provide further levels or alternative levels of analysis, perhaps for example showing a geographical analysis of the value of grants made.'
>
> *– SORP 2005, paragraph 204*

Although SORP 2005 makes no special distinction here to highlight *impairment* write-offs in respect of a *social investment* project, despite classifying such costs as 'grant-making', these would clearly be a further helpful alternative or extra level of analysis of the kind suggested by paragraph 204 – for example, for a perhaps costly urban regeneration project being funded through equity or loan investment in another institution.

Paragraph 203 requires this analysis to show *'amounts that reconcile with the total of grants payable'* within the SoFA figure for the costs of charitable activities – and now discernible only in the accounts note sub-analysing that figure, as noted above.

In the case of accrued provisions that later turn out to be excessive, perhaps because the grant has had to be withdrawn or curtailed:

> 'Where later events make the recognition of a liability no longer appropriate, the liability should be cancelled by credit against the relevant expenditure heading in the Statement of Financial Activities. The credit should mirror the treatment originally used to recognise the expenditure for the liability and should be disclosed separately.'
>
> – *SORP 2005, paragraph 163*

Grants to institutions

Within the total figure for grants to institutions, for any material amounts going to particular institutions the total must, subject to a new overriding statutory exemption for grant-making *trusts* (see below), be analysed to show:

(a)   the name of the recipient institution, and

(b)   the aggregate amount of grants made to that institution for the year *'for each activity or purpose'* (at a minimum this must be taken to mean each charitable objective disclosed in the SoFA and in the annual report),

for a sufficient number of institutional grants to provide a reasonable understanding of the range of institutions' that have been supported by the reporting charity's grant-making activity (paragraph 206).

With effect from 1 April 2008 the Charities Act 2006 has now introduced a blanket exemption from this disclosure requirement by amending both Part VI of the 1993 Act and also the SORP's related 2008 Regulations. This amendment gives *unconditional total exemption* from the above disclosures for any *charitable trust* during the lifetime of its founder or that person's spouse or 'civil law partner':

> '[The SORP's related] regulations may, however, not impose on the charity trustees of a charity that is a charitable trust created by any person ("the settlor") any requirement to disclose, in any statement of accounts prepared by them ... (a) the identities of recipients of grants made out of the funds of the charity, or (b) the amounts of any individual grants so made, if the disclosure would fall to be made at a time when the settler or any spouse of civil partner of his was still alive.'
>
> – *s 42(2A), Charities Act 1993 (as amended)*

> 'The charity trustees of a charity that is a charitable trust created by any person ("the settlor") are not required to disclose [as required by the SORP any particulars of grants made by the charity] if the disclosure of that information would fall to be made at a time when (a) the settlor, or (b) the spouse or civil partner of the settlor, is still alive.'
>
> – *para 1(2), Sch 2 to SI 2008/629*

What may be less obvious here at first glance is that, subject only to this statutory concession being highlighted in the next version of the Charities SORP, it should also (if only by analogy) enable a *charitable company* to claim equivalent exemption for institutional grants made out of any *special trust* it administers and includes within its own statutory accounts.

This statutory exemption can certainly be relied on for the *consolidated* accounts of a 'small' group headed by a charitable company above the Charities Act audit threshold of £500,000 gross income for financial years starting after March 2008, since the SORP's related 2008 Regulations are automatically applicable in such a case.

Apart from that, even though the matter is not specifically covered within the 2008 edition of PN11: *'The Audit of Charities'*, a common-sense interpretation should ensure that the SORP's general 'best practice' requirement here is not imposed for any *trust funds* shown within a charitable company's accounts prepared under company law.

All this further analysis and explanation, where required, can instead be provided in the trustees' annual report or even a separate publication – as long as the accounts notes cross-refer to it in the trustees' report or separate publication:

> 'Where the analysis is contained in a separate publication, it should be made available by the charity to the public on request. The notes to the accounts should identify the publication and state how copies of it can be obtained.'

– SORP 2005, paragraph 206

Apart from the blanket exemption noted above for grant-making *trusts*, charities can only withhold information on those particular grants where the trustees consider that the disclosure *'could seriously prejudice the furtherance of the purposes either of the recipient institution or of the charity itself'* (paragraph 208), in which case the SORP stipulates that the charity should in such circumstances:

> '(a) disclose in the notes to the accounts the total number, value and general purpose of those grants the details of which have not been disclosed;
> (b) give in writing to the charity's regulatory body (i) the full details of any grants not disclosed, and (ii) a full explanation of the reasons why those details have not been disclosed in the accounts;
> (c) state in the notes to the accounts whether or not those details have been given to the charity's regulatory body ...'.

– SORP 2005, paragraph 209

'Client-confidentiality' was at first claimed in its accounting policies note to justify non-compliance with the SORP's requirement to give identifying particulars of the most material grants to institutions by *Charities Aid Foundation* (CAF). That rather debatable reason has since been dropped in favour of the equally fragile argument that grants made via CAF's 'donor-chequebook' system were *'not representative of CAF's own grant-making policies'*, because the founder of each of CAF's numerous 'special trust' funds (or 'Trust Account' funds, as they are described in CAF's annual accounts) is enabled by the terms of trust to 'direct' the application of that fund by CAF. At 30 June 2008 these trust funds stood at £515m in aggregate, after deducting nearly £81m in grants made by CAF that year to honour donors' instructions. In another category of what look like trust funds donated by individuals, £75m was held in 'Individual Charity Accounts' at that date after grant payments of £73m for the year, plus £39m and £25m respectively in 'Company Accounts' and 'GAYE Charity Accounts' after grants payments of £72m and £32m. As an essential basis for their tax claims on donors' gifts

to these funds, however, CAF can veto such a grant by refusing to honour 'cheque-vouchers' made out in favour of questionable recipients, though it seems they are almost invariably made in favour of <u>other charities</u>. Such ownership of these trust funds does not quite square with referring to their donors as 'clients' (see below)! All of which makes for an interesting interpretation of the SORP phrase: *'seriously prejudice the furtherance of the purposes ... of the charity itself'* – ie of CAF in its laudable aspiration to be 'banker to the charity sector'.

It remains to be seen whether CAF's future annual accounts will rely instead on the much firmer ground of the Charities Act's blanket exemption for trusts, as a valid reason for continuing not to make any such institutional grants disclosures. Meanwhile there is nothing else to be found in the 2007/08 report and accounts than the following explanatory statement:

Accounts Note 1

Accounting Policies

...

Charitable activities expenditure

Tax efficient giving principally represents donations to charities by CAF clients.
...

...

Accounts Note 17

17.2 Restricted Funds

Trust Accounts

Trust Accounts consist of capital gifted to CAF plus the related income. The capital is held in accordance with CAF's investment policy for Trust Accounts and investment gains or losses are credited or charged to the funds. These funds may only be used to make payments to other charities as instructed by the donor.

Other restricted funds

Individual Charity Accounts, Company Accounts and GAYE Charity Accounts represent amounts gifted to CAF by individual and corporate donors which are held in accounts until disbursed to charities on behalf of the donor. ...

Charities Aid Foundation – 2007/08 Accounts

So *did* CAF send the Charity Commission the required full particulars of all the undisclosed, material 'donor-directed' institutional grants within the above £258m paid out by CAF at the direction of its numerous founders of 'special trust' funds, and did

CAF get the Commission's agreement to the non-disclosure? CAF's Annual Report and Accounts have never yet said anything about that – but perhaps for next year they won't need to anyway.

Repayable grants ('soft loans')

This kind of charitable activity, common to staff benevolent funds operated by both the public and corporate sectors, seemed to fall between two stools until elevated to 'social investment' status (see chapter 9) under the Charities SORP. On the accruals basis of accounting, the charity's SoFA must make it seem relatively inactive, since hardly any of its grant-making will qualify as 'expenditure' from year to year – at least, insofar as each grant is still considered 'good and recoverable'. This is because, as a way of furthering the charitable Object of 'poverty relief', it is hard to beat for sheer economic efficiency.

Most of the repayable grants made by such a charity will sooner or later replenish the fund set up for the purpose, which then only needs topping up by further donations from the employer of the beneficiary staff in order to maintain viability. After all, staff members who fall on hard times and have to seek temporary relief from such a fund will hardly want their careers to suffer by being seen as unreliable debtors.

As 'soft loans' to beneficiaries, all amounts regarded as recoverable as at the year-end and intended for recycling as a social investment should now be accounted for as such in the balance sheet. Because such assets are clearly not readily available for spending on other charitable purposes, they should be ring-fenced by means of a designated Social Investment Fund/Reserve (see chapter 10).

The notes to the accounts should disclose the grant-making policy adopted, including the repayment conditions imposed and any interest rates applying. Only to the extent that each loan is assessed as unlikely to be recovered and therefore needing to be converted into an outright grant should corresponding provision for impairment be made against it and recognised in the SoFA under the heading of 'charitable grants' expenditure.

Staff costs and executive pay-bands

12.3.5   The SORP makes it clear that the basis for disclosure of the average number of employed staff is their estimated *'full-time'* equivalents:

> 'The total staff costs should be shown in the notes to the accounts giving the split between gross wages and salaries, employer's national insurance costs and pension costs (those pension costs included within resources expended excluding pension finance costs) for the year. The average number of staff during the year should be provided and where material to the disclosure, e g due to the number of part-time staff, an estimate of the average number of full time equivalent employees for the year may be provided in the notes to the accounts, providing sub-categories according to the manner in which the charity's activities are organised.'
>
> *– SORP 2005, paragraph 235*

The SORP requires this 'staff costs' figure to include seconded staff, agency staff (temps) and any contract staff employed by connected or even independent companies – but this is *not* underpinned by the related 2008 Regulations, where the requirement is only for directly *employed* staff. The *reasons* for resorting to staff not directly employed by the charity are also required by the SORP:

> 'It is important that the accounts disclose the costs of employing staff who work for the charity whether or not the charity itself has incurred those costs ... Where such arrangements are in place and the costs involved are material (in relation to the charity's own expenditure) there should be disclosure by way of note which outlines the arrangement in place, the reasons for them and the amounts involved.'

– SORP 2005, paragraph 234

The disclosure for *higher-paid* employees (meaning their *'emoluments ... including taxable benefits in kind but not employer pension costs'*), which parallels the same kind of disclosure by government bodies generally and was built into the 1995 SORP to cater for the continuing public interest in what charities pay their senior executives, is now in bands of £10,000 above a threshold* of *£60,000* (with a 'nil' disclosure only required if there are none at all above that threshold), and with disclosure also of their *pension benefits*, as follows:

> 'In addition the following pension details should be disclosed in total for higher paid staff ...:
>
> (a)   contributions in the year for the provision of defined contribution scheme [benefits] (normally money purchase schemes); and
> (b)   the number of staff to whom retirement benefits are accruing under defined contribution schemes and defined benefit schemes respectively.'

– SORP 2005, paragraph 237

*Some charities use a lower threshold for this disclosure so that the reader can get a feel for staff pay at the higher levels, not just a spotlight only on the most senior – of whom there may be just one or two!

Although, according to the wording of Definition GL 50 of the SORP's Glossary, any 'employee of the charity having authority or responsibility for directing or controlling the major activities or resources of the charity' is classed as a 'related party' (see **12.3.7**), paragraph 229(c) normally exempts them from the disclosure as such:

> 'Some related party transactions are such that they are unlikely to influence the pursuance of the separate independent interests of the charity. These need not be disclosed unless there is evidence to the contrary. Examples are:
>
> ...
>
> (c)   contracts of employment between a charity and its employees (except where the employees are the charity trustees or people connected with them).'

– SORP 2005, paragraph 229

Therefore no personal disclosure is required for 'related party' transactions where the only 'connection' arises from such a bona fide employment contract in the case of a senior member of staff (e g the education of a teacher's children at the same independent school). However, with the introduction of corporate governance concepts into charity administration to bring staff representatives onto the trustee board (somewhat akin to beneficiary-representation on the board as 'user-trustees'), their employee-remuneration – along with any other 'related party' transactions, of course, subject to the exemptions mentioned at **12.3.6** – *will* then become individually disclosable under the related party disclosure rules of the SORP as a *trustee-benefit*, being also subject to the same need for legal authority as is any other benefit accruing to a charity trustee *directly/indirectly* out of the charity's resources. This is still rather sensitive charity information, although the Charities Act 2006 does now provide statutory authority for remunerating a *minority* of the trustees for *non-trustee* services (but not under any kind of *employment contract*, as the Act specifically rules that out), with the SORP disclosure here cutting across the normal confidentiality of employee-earnings.

For a *charitable company*, a greater degree of anonymity is possible within the statutory requirement (as distinct from full SORP-compliance as 'best practice'), as not only can directors' emoluments[4] be disclosed *in aggregate* (unless any of them exceeded £200,000!), but there is also no specific requirement for the sometimes 'sensitive' disclosures that could spotlight higher-paid staff above the £60,000 level – although this way of 'obeying the letter of the law' does admittedly fall short of strict compliance with the Charities SORP, with the risk of a 'non-standard' audit report if the accounts are then considered 'misleading'.

Staff pension scheme disclosures (FRS17)

12.3.6 FRS17, which replaced SSAP24 on full implementation for financial years from 1 January 2005 (or those ending after 22 June 2006, if accounting under the FRSSE), has made the cost and adequacy (or deficiency!) of employers' provision for retirement benefits for employed staff through 'defined benefit' pension schemes very much a 'public interest' issue as the average lifespan increases and with it anxiety about personal financial security in retirement.

The SORP's disclosure requirements here are (for **all** *non-company* charities' accruals accounts and now also for the consolidated accounts of an auditable parent charitable company if these are prepared under the 1993 Act for a 'small' group for which group accounts are not 'required' by company law) underpinned by its related Regulations 2005, requiring:

> 'such particulars of the cost to the charity of employing, and providing pensions for, staff as may be required by the SORP to be disclosed.'
>
> – *SI 2008/629, Sch 2, para 1(f)*

SORP 2005 devotes a special section to this topic in view of its complexity, with paragraphs 443–448 summarising FRS17's detailed disclosure requirements for 'defined benefit' (otherwise known as 'final salary') schemes where the employer retains participatory rights and obligations in scheme surpluses and deficits respectively *and can identify its own share of them.*

---

4   Where the 1993 Act disclosure catches *all* benefits (regardless of what they are for) for each trustee separately, the 1985 Act disclosure is in total and only in respect of 'qualifying services' – thus ignoring, for example, the earnings of non-managerial staff representatives appointed to the Board other than any additional pay for such service:
  '"qualifying services" in relation to any person, means his services as a director of the company, and his services while director of the company—(a) as director of any of its subsidiary undertakings; or (b) otherwise in connection with the management of the affairs of the company or any of its subsidiary undertakings.'– *Companies Act 1985, Sch 6, para 1(5).*

Before looking at them we should note that, for 'defined contribution' (otherwise known as 'Money Purchase') schemes, paragraph 75 of FRS17 requires nothing further than to disclose *'any outstanding or prepaid contributions at the balance sheet date'*.

For a 'multi-employer' defined benefit scheme that qualifies for FRS17's 'default' treatment as a defined contribution scheme, for lack of any reliable and consistent figures on which the reporting charity's share of scheme surpluses/deficits could be recognised in its annual accounts, but where its share of scheme liabilities is not defined solely by reference to the current period of service of its own staff, paragraph 77 of the FRS imposes *additional* disclosures as set out in paragraph 9(b)(i) and (ii), quoted below:

> 'Where more than one employer participates in a defined benefit scheme the employer should account for the scheme as a defined benefit scheme unless:
>
> (a)   the employer's contributions are set in relation to the current service period only (ie are not affected by any surplus or deficit in the scheme relating to past service of its own employees or any other members of the scheme). If this is the case, the employer should account for the contributions to the scheme as if it were a defined contribution scheme;
>
> (b)   the employer's contributions are affected by a surplus or deficit in the scheme but the employer is unable to identify its share of the underlying assets and liabilities in the scheme on a consistent and reasonable basis. If this is the case, the employer should account for the contributions to the scheme as if it were a defined contribution scheme but, in addition, disclose:
>
>   (i)   the fact that the scheme is a defined benefit scheme but that the employer is unable to identify its share of the underlying assets and liabilities; and
>
>   (ii)   any available information about the existence of the surplus or deficit in the scheme and the implications of that surplus or deficit for the employer.'

– FRS17, paragraph 9

To qualify under paragraph 9(a), the employing charity will need to be able to show:

> '... clear evidence that the employer cannot be required to pay additional contributions to the scheme relating to past service, including the existence of a third party that accepts that it has an obligation to fund the pension payments should the scheme have insufficient assets.'

– FRS17, paragraph 10

For the remaining defined benefit schemes, FRS17's requirements are for the 'controlling employer(s)' to disclose and recognise in the annual accounts certain specified components of the changes in net fund-value[5] of that employer's 'interests' in the fund from one year-end to the next – that is, to the extent that such changes impact on the employer's own rights and obligations under that scheme – as adjusted to reflect any *additional* liabilities arising from 'constructive obligations' for *non-scheme* staff retirement benefits, within the meaning of FRS12.

In chapter 10 we looked at the segregated presentation required in the balance sheet, and how this 'notional' asset/liability could seem to impact on charity reserves, making it

---

5   'Net fund-value' here means the currently expected long-term return on the year-end 'open market' value of the Scheme's total assets *less* the net present value of its total liabilities in the long term (actuarially assessed, and discounted for inflation at the currently assumed long-term rate): 'The fair value of the scheme assets, the present value of the scheme liabilities based on the accounting assumptions and the resulting surplus or deficit should be disclosed in a note to the financial statements.'– *FRS17, paragraph 88.*

necessary to explain (either in the accounts notes or the trustees' annual report) its *cashflow* implications. Similarly, in chapter 6 we considered the effect on the SoFA of the FRS's detailed requirements for recognition of the annual movement in this figure. In this chapter we are concerned with the detailed *disclosures* designed to facilitate the inclusion of those figures in the annual accounts for a proper understanding by the accounts user. Here is the full set of disclosures and how it was suggested they be displayed in the accounts note on pensions costs for a June 2006 year-end (the figures below are a modified version of those given by way of illustration in the FRS itself at the time, but adapted here for use in the charity sector):

The charity operates a defined benefit scheme in the UK. A full actuarial valuation was carried out at 30 June 2005, updated to 30 June 2006 by a qualified independent actuary.

The major assumptions used by the actuary were:

	30/6/06	30/6/05
Rate of increase in salaries	4.0 %	5.5 %
Rate of increase in pensions in payment	2.0 %	3.0 %
Discount rate	4.5 %	7.0 %
Inflation assumption	2.5 %	4.0 %

The assets in the scheme and the long-term expected rate of return (LTR) were:

	LTR at 30/6/06	Value at 30/6/06	LTR at 30/6/05	Value at 30/6/05
		£m		£m
Equities	7.3%	111.6	8.0%	72.1
Bonds	5.5%	29.8	6.0%	19.2
Property	6.0%	7.4	6.1%	4.9

The surplus in the Scheme as at 30 June 2006 is derived as follows:

	30/6/06	30/6/05
	£m	£m
Total [long-term] market value of assets	148.8	96.2
Scheme liabilities at their present value (p.v.)	(100.9)	(75.8)
	47.9	20.4

Contributions made to the Scheme for the year were £2.5m (8% of pensionable pay). It has been agreed with the Scheme Trustees that contributions for the next 3 years will remain at that level.

History of the Pension Scheme's experience gains and losses

		2005/06	2004/05	2003/04	2002/03	2001/02
Actual less expected return on Scheme assets	£m	48.0	13.8	(0.6)	9.4	(7.3)
% of scheme assets		32%	14%	(1%)	16%	(26%)
Experience gains/losses on scheme liabilities	£m	(5.8)	(0.6)	3.4	2.5	(2.3)
% of scheme liabilities at p.v.		(6%)	(1%)	5%	2%	(2%)
Actuarial gains recognised	£m	27.6	9.1	0.1	6.6	(15.8)
% of the scheme liabilities at p.v.		27%	12%	0%	5%	(14%)

The FRS requires you to disclose the fact if the Scheme valuation was by *'an employee or officer'* of the charity or group.

Paragraph 76(d) of the FRS also requires you to state:

> 'for closed schemes and those in which the age profile of the active membership is rising significantly, the fact that under the projected unit method the current service cost will increase as the members of the scheme approach retirement.'
>
> *– FRS17, paragraph 76(d)*

Finally, paragraph 445(g) of the SORP calls for analysis of the amounts included in the SoFA (see chapter 6), which the FRS requires to be shown here in some detail:

> '82   The following amounts included within operating [net income/expenditure] (or capitalised with the relevant employee remuneration) ...:
>
> (a)   the current service cost;
> (b)   any past service costs;
> (c)   any previously unrecognised surplus deducted from the past service costs;
> (d)   gains and losses on any settlements or curtailments; and
> (e)   any previously unrecognised surplus deducted from the settlement or curtailment losses.
>
>   ...
>
> 84   The following amounts included as other finance costs (or income)...:
>
> (a)   the interest cost; and
> (b)   the expected return on assets in the scheme.
>
> 85   The following amounts included within the statement of total recognised gains and losses ...:
>
> (a)   the difference between the expected and actual return on assets;
> (b)   experience gains and losses arising on the scheme liabilities; and
> (c)   the effects of changes in the demographic and financial assumptions underlying the present value of the scheme liabilities.'
>
> *– FRS17, paragraphs 82–85*

With the FRSSE 2005 also having been extended to include the requirements of this Standard, smaller charities have since been unable to escape these complicated new accounting and reporting requirements by adopting the current FRSSE, thus removing a significant advantage and further marginalising the benefits of FRSSE adoption.

Trustee-transactions and other 'related party' disclosures

12.3.7   The much stricter disclosure requirements of the SORP here since the original 1995 version form a special section of their own, now at paragraphs 221–229, headed 'related party transactions', followed by the *charity-specific* paragraph 230: 'trustee remuneration and benefits' (this includes *any* private benefit going to 'trustee-connections' – see below) and then 231–232: 'trustees' expenses'. The SORP's related 2008 Regulations make *all* those disclosures mandatory for *non-company* charities and for the consolidated accounts of any 'small' group headed by an auditable charitable company, saying that the accounts must give:

> 'such particulars of the related party transactions of the charity, or of any institution or body corporate connected with the charity, as may be required by the SORP to be disclosed.'

> – *SI 2008/629, Sch 2, para 1(e)*

Where the 1995 SORP spoke only of 'connected persons', the SORP has since had to encompass a wider class to comply with FRS8's 'related party' requirements to put all material transactions with such parties into the public domain whether or not any actual private benefit did in fact result from them.

So where the 1995 SORP's definition of *trustee-connections* in the context of regulating trustee-benefits and disclosing their legal authority, and also the definition used in the 1993 Act's accounting regulations, were derived from the 1993 Act's Sch 5, to do with Part V's restrictions on selling charity land to the trustees or persons closely connected with them, SORP 2005 seeks to fit that into the FRS8 definition – in the process leaving out any non-custodian 'trustee *for* the charity'.

Instead of a 'child, parent, grandchild, grandparent, brother or sister of the charity trustee' and a 'spouse'/'civil partner' of any of these, the SORP definition therefore specifies 'members of the same family or household of the charity trustee ... *who may be expected to influence, or be influenced by, that person in their dealings with the charity'*.

The intention here seems to be to *distance* charity accounting from the explicit regulatory regime of the 1993 Act, pulling back into the Standard's broader but *unregulated* regime of 'possible self-dealing implications' for the reader to sort out.

The definition is therefore extended to include:

–   an *employer* (e g other than central/local government, of course) of a *seconded trustee* or 'representative' trustee – thus whoever *'makes available to the charity the services of [that trustee]'*; and also

–   the *directors* (or their equivalent) of a *corporate trustee* of the charity.

The SORP's definition in Glossary GL 50 of 'related parties' includes as *'persons related to the charity'* all the previously mentioned 'trustee-connections' and also:

–   custodian ('holding') trustees, but *not* mere nominees nor any other 'trustees *for* the charity' (rather than *of* it) – this strange exclusion being of a class of 'related party' who must be named in the trustees' annual report but with no specific accounts note to identify the asset(s) they hold nor how and why. The term is defined in the SORP's Glossary at GL 59, and would clearly include third parties (such as fundraising 'friends' groups') holding money or other assets that belong to the charity, but would seem to include also *anyone* making unauthorised profits/gains out of a fiduciary relationship with the charity, even if not caught by the next two categories;

–   persons entitled to appoint *or* remove a 'significant' proportion of the trustees (and therefore perhaps in practice able to wield significant influence for ulterior purposes over the trustees – however, this is typically a power reserved by a founder, perhaps with succession-rights, ostensibly for supervisory purposes, and also by any kind of supervisory board or electoral college, whose members could be numerous);

–   persons 'whose consent is required' or who are 'entitled to give directions' to 'the exercise of any of the discretions of [the charity trustees]' (thus catching founders as well as the above-mentioned supervisory boards and electoral colleges and even external authorities (eg the Bishop; but surely not also the Charity Commission itself?) instead of the major donors previously included);

–   not only all subsidiaries and associates, etc, but also all their directors;

–   other [reporting] charities most of whose trustees are also trustees of this charity ('common control'), but only if one party 'subordinates its interests to the other charity in any transaction because of this relationship' – a *breach of trust* if not done in furtherance of the subordinate charity's Objects as a 'connected charity';

–   pension funds for the charity's employees or for 'any other person who is a related party of the charity';

–   only those officers, agents and employees 'having authority or responsibility for directing or controlling the major activities or resources of the charity'.

'Related to the charity' thus includes not only the original 1995 SORP's:

–   trustees and their own close family/business and private trust connections, as well as all the charity's *non-charitable* subsidiary interests, as defined by charities legislation in order to enforce the trustees' accountability to their charity for any unauthorised 'private benefits' arising from their office; but also (from FRS8)

–   any *other* body that is (a) under the direct/indirect control of any of the above and (b) has had dealings with the charity during the financial year.

You will need to note the requirement to disclose transactions with related parties that are subsidiaries/associates or consortium undertakings (corporate JVs) *and are not included in the reporting charity's accounts*. Furthermore, while *contributions* to a staff pension fund (and also any refunds, presumably) are specifically exempted from disclosure under this heading by paragraph 229(d) of SORP 2005, being partially disclosable elsewhere (see **12.3.5**) the fund itself still counts as a related party, as do its trustees as such, and so any *other* transactions are disclosable (eg payments in respect of the costs of any administrative services provided by the charity to its pension fund).

The practical problems arising from all this are:

(i)   how to confirm that you really have identified all the persons who must be regarded as the charity's 'related parties'; and

(ii)   how to identify which of all the perhaps voluminous transactions of the year might be disclosable as 'related party transactions' involving one of these persons.

The problem faced by *charity auditors* here is how to avoid putting the client through the kind of hoops outlined below. The answer may lie in being able to demonstrate that:

(a) the charity has effective 'conflicts-of-interest' identification and management protocols (formal procedures) at board level; and that

(b) therefore the only possible transactions that could emerge from trawling the records would be inconsequential.

One early idea for this was to set up a Register of Personal Interests (trusteeships, directorships, beneficiary interests, investor-interests, etc) to be kept up to date by notifications from the trustees and senior staff – but that approach was soon discarded as unworkable. An alternative possibility was for the charity's own finance staff to extract from the accounting records each year a master-listing of all transacting parties and the total amount of supplies to and by each one. Not a long job for a competent computer-based accounting program. Trustees and senior executives could then be asked to mark the names of any of their 'related parties' so that the disclosure implications could be considered by the Board.

Whatever your approach (and these were only two among many), the work involved in trying to provide positive assurance that everything disclosable has in fact been duly identified and disclosed does seems quite daunting when you think how slight is the benefit to the user of such information (whoever that might be), and that if at the end of the day it does not seem likely to produce anything significant to disclose there will probably be nobody willing to take it on!

Charity law constraints

The trouble is that the SORP's list now casts a 'related parties' net so wide that accountants and auditors will need to contain the work involved, by assessing 'materiality' for disclosure purposes not only by reference to the financial amounts themselves *but also to the public interest (if any)* in the information to be considered for disclosure – bearing in mind that all these transactions are regulated by charity law under the watchful eye of the Charity Commission and, in terms of professional audit regulation for quality control more generally, the Financial Reporting Council.

For, as the SORP explains in its Glossary:

> 'Materiality is the final test of what information should be given in a particular set of financial statements. An item of information is material to the financial statements if its misstatement or omission might reasonably be expected to influence the economic decisions of users of those financial statements, including their assessments of stewardship. Immaterial information will need to be excluded to avoid clutter which impairs the understandability of other information provided.
>
> Whether information is material will depend on the size and nature of the item in question judged in the particular circumstances of the case. Materiality is not capable of general mathematical definition as it has both qualitative and quantitative aspects. The principal factors to be taken into account are set out below. It will usually be a combination of these factors, rather than any one in particular, that will determine materiality.
>
> (a) The item's size is judged in the context both of the financial statements as a whole and of the other information available to users that would affect their evaluation of the

financial statements. This includes, for example, considering how the item affects the evaluation of trends and similar considerations.

(b)　Consideration is given to the item's nature in relation to:

  (i)　the transactions or other events giving rise to it;
  (ii)　the legality, sensitivity, normality and potential consequences of the event or transaction;
  (iii)　the identity of the parties involved; and
  (iv)　the particular headings and disclosures that are affected.

If there are two or more similar items, the materiality of the items in aggregate as well as of the items individually needs to be considered.

Trustees are responsible for deciding whether an item is or is not material. In cases of doubt an item should be treated as material.

This process may result in different materiality considerations being applied depending on the aspect of the accounts being considered. For example, the expected degree of accuracy expected in the case of certain statutory disclosures e g trustees' remuneration, may make normal materiality considerations irrelevant.'

– SORP 2005, Glossary GL 42

The final paragraph in the SORP's definition was the only change from the 2000 to the 2005 version. It highlights a point that should not be overlooked: that these 'related party' disclosure requirements of FRS8 are so much more onerous than was originally envisaged for the public accountability of the regulated charity sector because they are based on the (comparatively unregulated) profit sector's company law concept of 'control' as always giving access to some kind of financial or other benefit which includes contractual and other arrangements/situations involving 'dominant influence' over the operating policies of the other body to the point where it is 'inhibited from pursuing its own separate interests'. This is, of course, unlawful in the case of a charity if the connection prevents the trustees of that charity from acting in its own best interests.

The 'related parties' concept is therefore capable of extremely wide interpretation, whereas the constraints of charity law on the activities of charities, and of their trustees in relation to them, would tend to narrow down any such interpretation. Hence in the SORP's definition of that term the inclusion of other *charities* under the trustees' control must be a reference to 'connected charities' (definition GL 9 in the SORP's Glossary) not already accounted for within the charity's own accounts. Reference to any other body under the control of the charity and/or persons connected with the charity trustees would not normally yield additional material transactions requiring disclosure under FRS8. This is either because the Charities SORP requires consolidated accounts in such cases or else because the transactions would be disclosable as trustee-benefits, etc. The exception (rare in practice in the sector, apart from special cases like consortium charities and certain Investment Pool charities) is the FRS8 requirement to disclose material intra-group transactions in those cases where an outside minority interest of more than 10% exists – even where consolidated accounts are prepared.

Furthermore, like other accounting and financial reporting standards the application of FRS8 to *charity* accounts must be conditioned by the requirements of the particular legislation under which those accounts are prepared. For all *non-company* charities and for charitable companies' 'small' group consolidated accounts, this means Part VI of the 1993 Act and its detailed accounting regulations in the first place – but also the other administrative provisions of that Act, in that Part VI compliance also discharges the trustees' charity law duty to account to the general public for the *proper administration* of all charitable resources under the reporting trustees' control.

Although *charitable companies'* accounts (other than consolidated accounts for a 'small' group, where company law does not 'require' them) are prepared under the general provisions of the Companies Act 2006, which are modified only to recognise their 'not-for-profit' nature but not their special nature as companies *regulated by charity law*, these accounts also have to fulfil the same function under Part VI, namely to discharge the directors' accountability under *charity* law. Part of that accountability is the liability to make restitution to their charity in respect of any unauthorised private benefit arising from their office of charity trustee.

The protection afforded by charity law has in fact been duly acknowledged in paragraph 223 of the SORP:

> 'Any decision by a charity to enter into a transaction ought to be influenced only by the consideration of the charity's own interests. This requirement is reinforced by legal rules which, in certain circumstances, can invalidate transactions where the charity trustees have a conflict of interest. This does not necessarily mean that all transactions with related persons are influenced by the consideration of interests other than the charity's nor that they are liable to invalidation.'
>
> – *SORP 2005, paragraph 223*

Unfortunately, in the very next paragraph the SORP itself seems to have succumbed to dominant influence here – by the ASB. It subordinates the interests of charity accounting to those of the larger commercial sector. Instead of selectively modifying FRS8's disclosure requirements to cut out information superfluous to the needs of the charity sector it imports them more or less wholesale, justifying this by saying:

> 'Transparency is particularly important where the relationship between the charity and the other party or parties to a transaction suggests that the transaction could possibly have been influenced by interests other than the charity's. It is possible that the reported financial position and results may have been affected by such transactions and information about these transactions is therefore necessary for the users of the charity's accounts.'
>
> – *SORP 2005, paragraph 224*

Having taken a preliminary canter round the field for a survey of the wider FRS-based disclosure requirements of the Charities SORP, we can take a closer look at the requirements and exemptions for the essential accounts note concerning 'trustee-transactions'.

Remuneration and other trustee-benefits

Charity law makes trustees accountable for *any* unauthorised financial benefit derived (regardless of what 'hat' they may be wearing at the time) *directly or indirectly* from the funds of the charity – which includes the funds of a non-charitable subsidiary/associate, to the extent of the charity's financial interest in it.

In the accruals-based accounts of *non-company* charities, the *accounting regulations* of the 1993 Act therefore require disclosure of *all* benefits to trustees and connected persons either directly or indirectly from the charity's funds. Trustee-name and total benefit for the year must be disclosed, mirroring the SORP requirement for all charities – companies included – which not only says at paragraph 226 that, subject only to a special exemption for 'beneficiary-trustees' (see below), *'trustee remuneration or other benefits should always be regarded as material'* but also that the *authority* for the benefits must be disclosed – which if constitutional is easily overlooked.

---

7. Staff Costs

... The Chief Executive received remuneration and benefits for his service in that office which amounted to £150,549 (2007: £117,150).

Annual Report: Administrative Information

The Committee of the Council

Trustees

...

Derek Twine, CBE, Chief Executive

...

Scout Association – 2007/08 Annual Report and Accounts

Where there are no such benefits, a 'nil' disclosure is required – unlike the situation for related parties generally, where no such 'nil disclosure' is required.

Trustee-expenses and other 'related party' transactions/arrangements

SORP 2005 continues the pre-existing requirement for *aggregated* disclosure of the number of trustees claiming (or a 'nil' disclosure) and the total amount (and nature) of all *personal* trustee-expenses, however borne by the charity:

> 'Where a charity has met individual expenses incurred by trustees for services provided to the charity, either by reimbursement of the trustee or by providing the trustee with an allowance or by direct payment to a third party, the aggregate amount of those expenses should be disclosed in a note to the accounts ...'.

– *SORP 2005, paragraph 231*

To make this clearer, there is a specific exemption where the trustee pays for a third party to supply goods/services to the charity that are not personal to him and is reimbursed by the charity, as for any other agency transactions undertaken.

Similarly, the SORP normally requires no disclosure of the trustee-body's *collective* expenses – ie those that do not relate to any particular individual(s):

'... there is no need to disclose routine expenditure which is attributable collectively to the services provided to the trustees, such as the hire of a room for meetings or providing reasonable refreshment at the meeting.'

– *SORP 2005, paragraph 232*

On the other hand, paragraph 230(b) of the SORP requires *individual* disclosure of each type of 'contract, arrangement', etc, in which trustees or persons connected with them have/had an interest (ie a personal one) – regardless of 'materiality' – including such information as amounts outstanding, written off, etc.

Transaction-types

The SORP provides a list of transaction types:

'Related party transactions potentially include ...:

(a) purchases, sales, leases and donations (including donations which are made in furtherance of the charity's objects) of goods, property, money and other assets such as intellectual property rights to or from the related party;

(b) the supply of services by the related party to the charity, and the supply of services by the charity to the related party. Supplying services includes providing the use of goods, property and other assets and finance arrangements such as making loans and giving guarantees and indemnities;

(c) any other payments and other benefits which are made to trustees under express provisions of the governing document of a charity or in fulfilment of its charitable objectives.'

– *SORP 2005, paragraph 225*

Where the related party is *not* a trustee-connection, the SORP limits the disclosure to 'material' transactions – ie material to the charity or, unless the FRSSE is adopted, to the related party. The disclosure can normally be given in aggregate by class of transaction and of related party – except where the individual particulars would be needed for a proper understanding of the impact on the accounts.

Professional advisers as trustees

Many charity trustee boards include one or more professional specialists, such as solicitors, accountants, medical experts, etc, needed to help manage and administer the charity – rather than just to advise. Although they themselves are normally unpaid for acting as a charity trustee, like almost all charity trustees, in some case they or their own firm (or a company under their control) may, independent of and quite apart from their trustee duties, be providing professional services to the charity, the charges for which must then be disclosed – citing the legal authority for any trustee-benefit this entails.

Where *no* charges are involved, under SORP 2005 there is the question of recognising in the SoFA (see chapter 6) the value to the charity of the free service thus provided, which then raises the question here of disclosure of the trustee-transaction itself. Although the SORP is silent about that, the *principle* is quite clear from paragraph 229's exemption of donations where '*the donor has not attached conditions which would, or might, require the charity to alter significantly the nature of its existing activities if it were to accept the donation*' and (although to a lesser extent in this context) for '*minor or routine unremunerated services provided to a charity by people related to it*'.

Strictly speaking, the disclosure of any actual charges can come under this 'trustee-expenses' heading alone only where they are limited to strict cost-recovery by the firm/company concerned, so that they do not include the benefit of any 'remuneration' or profit/gain for a person (ie a partner) or a body corporate 'connected' with the trustee in the way defined by charity law. This may be seen as over and above the immediate implications of a professional charging clause in the charity's governing document to authorise the trustee's own remuneration.

Charity law constrains trustee-benefits by making trustees accountable to the charity for any unauthorised benefits to themselves or 'connected persons'. Relief from this personal liability in any particular case will normally require an approach to the Charity Commission (except where the trustee-benefit is authorised by the Charities Act 2006 and complies with the safeguards set out therein).

This is unlikely to be a problem for transactions entered into with good faith, and which can be accepted as justified and reasonable in the circumstances – especially where the amount of benefit is immaterial to the charity and the trustee personally.

Nevertheless, the Charities SORP's declaration that all trustee-transactions are to be considered 'material' to a reader of the accounts clearly makes it necessary for the board of trustees (directors, in the case of a charitable company) to inquire into the charging basis of 'related party' transactions so that they can be sure to include any material profit element in their disclosure of trustee benefits for each of them.

Regardless of any profit element, the trustee-transaction itself remains disclosable under the Charities SORP, FRS8 and, for *non-company* charities and also for auditable parent charitable companies heading a 'small' group as defined by company law, the SORP's related 2008 Regulations. A typical form of words for this would be along the following lines: '*Legal costs included fees amounting to £3,500 payable to the firm of Jones & Co, in which Andrew Jones (a trustee) is a partner'*. Where no actual fees are involved, ie the professional services are provided free ('pro bono'), the grossing up of their value in the SoFA does *not* entail any disclosure here as long as acceptance of such a donation has not, in the words of paragraph 229(a) of the SORP, subjected the charity to '*conditions which would, or might, require the charity to alter significantly the nature of its existing activities*' – normally a somewhat unlikely scenario.

Transactions exempted

It seems clear that paragraph 223 of the SORP also supports the first-mentioned ground for non-disclosure in the opening sentences of paragraph 229:

'Some related party transactions are such that they are unlikely to influence the pursuance of the separate independent interests of the charity. These need not be disclosed unless there is evidence to the contrary. Examples are:

(a)   donations received by the reporting charity from a related party, so long as the donor has not attached conditions which would, or might, require the charity to alter materially the nature of its existing activities if it were to accept the donation (but any material grant by the reporting charity to a charity which is a related party should be disclosed);

(b)   minor or routine unremunerated services provided to a charity by people related to it;

(c)   contracts of employment between a charity and its employees (except where the employees are the charity trustees or people connected with them);

(d)   contributions by a charity to a pension fund for the benefit of employees ...;

(e)   the purchase from a charity by a related party of minor articles which are offered for sale to the general public on the same terms as are offered to the general public;

(f)   the provision of services to a related party (including a charity trustee or person connected with a charity trustee), where the related party receives the services as part of a wider beneficiary class of which he is a member, and on the same terms as other members of the class ...; and

(g)   the payment or reimbursement of out-of-pocket expenses to a related party (including a charity trustee or person connected with a charity trustee ...).'

– SORP 2005, paragraph 229

That being so, paragraph 223 can be cited as justifying the non-disclosure of *all* normal (arm's length) transactions between two *charities* connected by having one or more trustees in common – especially where the respective Boards of trustees have taken the trouble to minute the fact of this connection, so that it can be seen to have been duly noted and taken into consideration.

Among these disclosure exemptions, we should take special note of the following:

–   *immaterial* transactions are exempted by paragraph 226 *unless they involve private benefit for a trustee or his/her close connections*;

–   *volunteers* (although not specifically mentioned at paragraph 229(b), this must logically include all unremunerated trustees and trustee-connections) are covered by the minor/routine 'unremunerated services' exemption above.

Thus many religious order/society charities have trustees who are required to be members of the Order chosen from among its live-in volunteer workforce. As (materially) impoverished beneficiaries of the Order's charitable activities, all these live-in members are equally dependent on it for bed and board, clothing, etc, as a consequence of the vows of poverty required to join the Order. Provided the 'benefit' is no greater for the trustee than for the non-trustee member of the Order, the specific exemption contained in paragraph 229(f) of SORP 2005 (and therefore the SORP's related 2008 Regulations) will apply, avoiding the need to disclose each trustee's annual living costs borne by the charity. Even so, some still prefer transparency here by disclosing those living costs – albeit only in aggregate for *all* resident members of the Order, as illustrated below.

	Unrestricted funds	Total funds	2006
	£	£	£
Sisters' living and personal expenses	1,298,361	1,298,361	*1,043,091*
Premises	1,508,178	1,508,178	*1,007,785*
Staff costs	1,052,207	1,052,207	*1,228,446*
Spiritual renewal	210,234	210,234	*144,079*
Other costs	114,953	114,953	*117,734*
Support costs	108,794	108,794	*126,577*
	4,292,727	**4,292,727**	*3,667,712*

Sisters of Charity of St Vincent de Paul Charitable Trust – 2007 Accounts

As a further example, a school's pupils will be its immediate beneficiaries, while their education has hitherto also been *presumed by law* (at least, as things stood for more than 400 years until the abolition of that presumption with effect from 1 April 2008 under the Charities Act 2006) to benefit the public at large if the school is set up as a charity. So a school governor's children/grandchildren being educated at the school will fall within this exemption – so long as the fee-paying basis for this is 'at arm's length', of course.

Many independent schools will from time to time have governors who, as trustees of the charity, at the same time are paying full fees for a son or daughter, or perhaps a grandchild, to be educated there. In some cases the fees payable may be abated or covered by a scholarship award won by the child in open competition. Provided the terms of the arrangement are no more favourable than the normal terms for children attending that school, the SORP exempts the arrangement from disclosure as a related party transaction.

The same holds good for the school's head (as for any other senior executive carrying substantial delegated trustee-powers), in that teachers enjoy an industry-wide 'marginal costing' basis agreed with HMRC for calculating the notional fees they normally pay for their children to attend the same school.

Aggregated disclosure

'Aggregated' disclosure by:

(a)   transaction-class; and

(b)   class of related party

is allowed for all transactions except that for (b) those involving the reporting charity's trustees and their connected persons – *SORP 2005, paragraph 230(b)*.

That means naming the trustee concerned, but it allows all disclosable transactions for that trustee to be aggregated by transaction-class. This specifically includes any outstanding indebtedness between the parties – either way – and also, for any pension provision arrangements, amounts contributed and benefits accruing.

On the other hand, aggregated disclosure for the whole of the board is specifically allowed for trustee-expenses, as already mentioned.

6(d) [Governance Costs]

Resources Expended include ... Trustees' expenses reimbursed: 2008 £35,000 (2007: £53,000).

During the year 22 (2007: 23) trustees were reimbursed for their out of pocket expenses arising from attending meetings and carrying out their duties. The Association provided accommodation for the Chief Scout and others while they were on Scout business.

Scout Association – 2007/08 Accounts

8d. Related Parties

Sir Trevor Chinn is chairman of the Automobile Association (AA). During 2006 Motability Operations undertook a competitively tendered process to obtain best value for driving lessons and a contract was awarded to the AA. The maximum value of driving lessons awarded to the AA in the year was £939,000 (£815,000 in 2007) of which £835,000 (£83,000 in 2007) was paid during the year. Sir Trevor took no part in the negotiations.

Motability paid Motability Operations £13,029,000 (£8,461,000 in 2007), in respect of grants awarded to customers, to fund advance payments on vehicles provided under the contract hire or hire purchase schemes.

Motability received from Motability Operations £3,812,000 (£3,283,000 in 2007) in respect of a levy on the leases to defray Motability's administration costs in processing charitable grant applications and support for the Scheme. A further £2,041,000 (£733,000 in 2007) was received from Motability Operations as rebates, in respect of grant awards towards advance payments, where customers have terminated their hire agreements.

Motability – 2007/08 Accounts

Impact of the FRSSE on FRS8 disclosures

For charities adopting the FRSSE, the 'materiality' of related party transactions for disclosure purposes (other than 'trustee-transactions' – which the SORP says can never be considered immaterial) need be considered only in relation to the reporting charity/group, thus *disregarding the related party*. This should greatly reduce the volume of information called for.

A 'trustee-disclosures' declaration form

The following template was designed to satisfy the need for a simple form of personal declaration that trustees could be asked to complete and lodge with their Board in order to facilitate this 'relevant audit information' aspect of their annual accounts.

The set of explanatory notes, if in small print as below, should fit on the back of a single A4 sheet, thus making the actual declaration look disarmingly simple and easy.

To the Board of .... [Charity Name]

I hereby confirm that, to the best of my knowledge and belief, and after making such enquiries as seemed reasonable in my capacity as a charity trustee, I am not aware of any financial transactions of the Charity for the financial year ended .... 20xx.... [*other than those already made known to the Board as identified below] that would be required under the Charities SORP 2005 [*and in accordance with Schedule 2 to the Charities (Accounts and Reports) Regulations 2008, SI 2008/629] to be disclosed in the annual accounts as either 'trustee-benefits' or 'related party' transactions in connection with myself. ➡

[* delete as appropriate – see explanatory notes on the reverse of this form]

....   (signed)

....   [Name of Trustee]

....   (Dated)

Charity transactions to be disclosed in this year's accounts in connection with myself and persons connected with me:

...

...

...

Explanatory Notes (References in Notes 2–4 are to the Charities SORP 2005)

1. Under SORP 2005, it is *mandatory* for non-company charities to disclose:

   'such particulars of the related party transactions of the charity, or of any institution or body corporate connected with the charity, as may be required by the SORP to be disclosed.'

   – SI 2008/629, Sch 2, para 1(e)

2. The following persons all count as 'related parties':

   – the charity trustees
   – any custodian trustee(s) of the charity
   – anyone entitled to exercise dominant influence over the
       – composition of the trustee-body, or
       – exercise of the trustees' discretionary powers (ie giving directions, consent/ veto)
   – the charity's *subsidiary/associated* undertakings and their directors
   – any other *charity* with which the reporting charity is 'commonly controlled' (see 5 below)
   – a *pension fund* for the charity's staff or for any of its related parties
   – any officer/agent/employee with *delegated responsibility* for major activities/resources.

   And the following 'connected persons' *also* count as 'related parties':

   – family/household members likely to influence or be influenced by any of the above in their dealings with the charity
   – a business partner of any of the above
   – the trustees of a non-charitable trust of which any of the above is or could be a beneficiary
   – a company (not under charity control) in which any of the above collectively have a 'participating interest' (defined as 20% of the equity or of the voting rights in it)
   – a 'seconded' trustee's employer.

   – SORP 2005, Glossary GL 50

3. However, the following categories of *personal* disclosure are exempted by SORP 2005:

(a) Beneficiary-benefits on the same basis as for any non-Trustee in that beneficiary-class:

'the provision of services to a related party (including a charity trustee or person connected with a charity trustee), where the related party receives the services as part of a wider beneficiary class of which he is a member, and on the same terms as other members of the class ...'.

– SORP 2005, paragraph 229(f)

(b) Trustee-donations:

'donations received by the reporting charity from a related party, so long as the donor has not attached conditions which would, or might, require the charity to alter materially the nature of its existing activities if it were to accept the donation ...'.

– SORP 2005, paragraph 229(a)

4. Transactions with a 'connected charity' are also exempted provided that *each* charity is being properly administered (as is required by charity law) in its own best interests:

'A charity is not necessarily related to another charity[6] simply because a particular person happens to be a trustee of both. It will only be related if one charity subordinates its interests to the other charity in any transaction because of this relationship.'

– SORP 2005, Glossary GL 50.1(d)

5. 'Common control' is defined by SORP 2005 as where the same person(s):[7]

– has/have the right to appoint a majority of the charity trustees of both charities, or
– hold(s) a majority of the voting rights in the administration of both charities

6. 'Control' is defined by SORP 2005 as being able to secure that the affairs of the other body are conducted in accordance with the controller's wishes.

We observed earlier that the SORP's related 2008 Regulations require *individual* disclosures for the trustees of *non-company* charities and for the directors of any auditable parent charitable company in respect of its consolidated accounts where the group is 'small' under company law. And, while paragraph 229(c), above, specifically excludes '*contracts of employment between a charity and its employees*' from disclosure as transactions with 'persons connected with the charity', it must be emphasised that this can only apply so long as the employee is not a trustee or 'connected' with a trustee.

Officers/agents as 'related parties'

It should also be noted here that in the case of a charitable company the Companies Act 2006 requires certain (aggregated) disclosures in respect of any credit facilities

---

6 Defined as follows: Charity A is the trustee of Charity B; or A is entitled to appoint or remove a 'significant' proportion (i e amounting to dominant influence over B) of B's trustees; or A and B are under common control (e g mostly the same trustees) or a trustee of B is A's agent or a senior executive with major responsibilities.

7 Treating family/business relationships – see above – as one person for this purpose.

provided for non-director managers (including the company secretary, if any) in excess of a value of £2,500 per person for the year.

Similarly, *auditors' remuneration* has long been a disclosable item in company accounts, and also under the Charities SORP – in line with the Companies Act requirement, as you can see from the wording:

> 'The notes to the accounts should disclose separately the amounts payable to the auditor, independent examiner or reporting accountant in respect of:
>
> (a)   the costs of their respective external scrutiny; and
> (b)   other financial services such as taxation advice, consultancy, financial advice and accountancy.'
>
> – *SORP 2005, paragraph 239*

Ex gratia transactions

12.3.8 'Ex gratia' situations are peculiar to charities, special legal authority being needed to protect the trustees from personal liability if they give away, renounce or sacrifice valuable resources belonging to their charity instead of fulfilling their legal obligation to spend those resources in furtherance of its Objects or else to retain them for the charity's own benefit. The legal term used is 'ex gratia payment', but the term actually covers any kind of waiver (e g of part of a contested legacy entitlement) and also benefits in kind. The disclosure of 'particulars' of all such transactions is made mandatory for non-company charities by para 1(p) of Sch 2 to the SORP's related 2008 Regulations, which also contain the following definition:

> '"*ex gratia payment*" means any such application of the property of a charity, or any such waiver by a charity of any entitlement to receive any property, as may be authorised under section 27(1) of the 1993 Act.'
>
> – *SI 2008/629, reg 2*

The SORP itself also requires any official *authority* for the transaction to be disclosed:

> 'The total amount or value of any:
>
> (a)   payment; or
> (b)   non-monetary benefit; or
> (c)   other expenditure of any kind; or
> (d)   waiver of rights to property to which a charity is entitled,
>
> which is made not as an application of funds or property for charitable purposes but in fulfilment of a compelling moral obligation should be disclosed in the notes to the accounts. Where trustees require and obtain the authority of the court, the Attorney General or the Charity Commission, the nature and date of the authority for each such payment should also be disclosed.'
>
> – *SORP 2005, paragraph 240*

The legacy example given above is the most obvious one, where in order to be able to surrender part of a legacy in order to settle a dispute with, say, relatives of the testator, Charity Commission authorisation will normally be needed to make the surrender as an 'ex gratia payment' out of the charity's legal entitlement. This is because such a transaction is legally considered an *adverse* one for the charity – even in cases where it is obvious that it can save money for the charity simply by reducing the two sides' legal costs, which have been known to dwarf a hotly contested legacy, perhaps leading to a 'pyrrhic victory' for the winner.

Another example might be the payment of some kind of 'honorarium' to a retiring unpaid trustee who may have put in a lifetime of serving the needs of the charity over and above the normal call of duty and may now be facing hardship in retirement yet be ineligible as a beneficiary. The trustees' implied power, highlighted in paragraph 241 of the SORP (see below), to remunerate *staff* and provide for their retirement does not include remunerating a trustee, for which special authority is needed. If the charity's governing document does not contain any such trustee-benefit authority, application to the Charity Commission will be needed to authorise the honorarium payment as 'ex gratia', so that the trustees will not be at risk of personal liability for the unauthorised application of the charity's resources.

> 'Payments which the trustees reasonably consider to be in the interests of the charity (more than a moral obligation) should not be treated as ex-gratia, even though there is no legal obligation to make them. For example, the trustees may think that it will motivate retained staff and hence benefit the charity if they make redundancy payments over and above the minimum legally required.'
>
> *– SORP 2005, paragraph 241*

BALANCE SHEET NOTES

12.4   This section is just for completeness, and to remind you where else this book deals with the *main* topic for which these disclosures are merely supplementary.

Fixed and current assets; liabilities

12.4.1   Like the Companies Act 2006 and its 2008 Regulations on annual accounts, the Charities SORP – as also its related 2008 Regulations – requires *tangible* fixed assets held for the charity's own use, and of course *heritage* assets, to be analysed by class to show all movements in value for the year. The detailed requirements for this are covered in chapter 8.

Likewise, in chapter 9 we discussed the detailed accounts note needed in support of the balance sheet figures for investment assets, fixed and current.

Similarly, chapter 10 deals with the analysis of other current assets and of creditors, both short-term and long-term, as well as any provisions for liabilities and charges. There, we noted that in paragraph 314 of the SORP it is made clear that the *indebtedness* of any subsidiaries/associates must be shown separately in each accounts note. Here, we need to note that as part of that figure:

> 'Loans made to trading subsidiaries ... should be disclosed as a separate item in the notes to the accounts.'
>
> *– SORP 2005, paragraph 350*

In addition, paragraphs 326–328 of the SORP require special disclosure in the accounts notes to show *'particulars of'*, and also the year's movements (including total SoFA charges and write-backs) in, all:

–   material 'provisions for liabilities and charges accrued ... as liabilities', and (separately)

–   material [unaccrued] 'commitments in respect of specific charitable projects', as well as

–   'other material binding commitments ... (e g operating leases)'.

The note should also disclose for **all** *charitable* commitments (i) *'the reason'* (separately, for any material charitable projects) and for each of the above three categories (ii) their totals and (iii) when the outstanding obligations *'are likely to be met'*, distinguishing between amounts within and beyond the following year. For the *charity-specific* content here, see also **12.4.6**. There, we discuss the movements analysis required by the SORP for *non-accrued* charitable commitments, while here we need only note in passing that exactly the same analysis is required for *accrued* commitments.

Analysis of assets and liabilities by fund

12.4.2   The SORP's requirement here is usually interpreted as calling for a summary showing to what fund-*group* each *class* of asset and liability belongs, and this is what most charities provide by way of note – though some go further and segregate major individual funds within the analysis table. In chapter 10 we also noted (see **10.2.2**) what the SORP offers as an alternative: a *columnar* presentation of the balance sheet to include a fund-type analysis, though it is hard to see how that can appeal to more than a handful of charities, what with all those extra columns. Otherwise what the SORP calls for is that:

> 'The notes to the accounts should provide information on the structure of the charity's funds ... in particular:
>
> (a)   The assets and liabilities representing each type of fund of the charity should be clearly summarised and analysed (e g investments, fixed assets, net current assets) between those funds unless this information is presented in a columnar balance sheet.
> (b)   ... An indication should be given as to whether or not sufficient resources are held in an appropriate form to enable each fund to be applied in accordance with any restrictions. For example, if a charity has a fund which is to be spent in the near future, it should be made clear in the notes whether or not the assets held (or expected to be received) in the fund are liquid assets.'
>
> – *SORP 2005, paragraph 75*

Tucked away near the end of the SORP, there is yet another requirement that may well be relevant here for your charity at some time or other:

> 'The amounts and interest and repayment terms of all inter-fund loans (including any loans from permanent endowment and summarised, if necessary) should be disclosed in the notes

to the accounts. Loans made to trading subsidiaries, the security provided, the interest payable and the repayment terms should be disclosed as a separate item in the notes to the accounts.'

– SORP 2005, paragraph 350

The mention of loans from a permanent financial endowment, which was new in SORP 2005, is simply to highlight best practice, since the Charity Commission has always been able to achieve this result within the terms of the 'Recoupment Order' (see chapter 10) that the charity needs to apply for as its borrowing authority – except in those rare cases where the founder included a borrowing power within the original terms of endowment (or more generally a power of variation of trust), in which case trust law compliance would still require these disclosures.

The following illustration is typical of current practice in sub-analysing assets and liabilities where the charity is accounting for a multiplicity of funds.

22. Analysis of Group net assets between funds	Unrestricted				
	General	Designated	Restricted	Endowment	Total
	£'000	£'000	£'000	£'000	£'000
Fund balances at 31 March 2008 are represented by:					
Tangible fixed assets	3,814	24,992	6,493	–	35,299
Investments	71,801	–	–	1,377	73,178
Current assets and liabilities	(17,712)	1,437	9,120	29	(7,126)
Long-term liabilities excluding pension reserve	(3,921)	–	–	–	(3,921)
Provisions	(5,000)	-	-	-	(5,000)
Total funds excluding pension provision	**48,982**	**26,429**	**15,613**	**1,406**	**92,430**
Pension provision	(5,239)	–	–	–	(5,239)
Total net assets	**43,743**	**26,429**	**15,613**	**1,406**	**87,191**

NSPCC – 2007/08 Accounts

Assets pledged to secure loans and other liabilities

12.4.3 Wherever charity assets are pledged as security for a loan, in addition to complying with the 'advice' requirements of s 38 of the 1993 Act before each such legal charge can lawfully be entered into, particulars of the pledge must be disclosed in the accounts. Also where any other kind of actual or contingent liability is secured by pledging assets of the charity. This would include not only any secured guarantee given by the charity but (under the Charities Act 2006) also the legal charge now being required by some grant-makers like the Millennium Commission to cover the contingent repayment liability arising on non-compliance with their terms of grant.

These pledge-disclosures are also specified in the FRSSE 2008, based on those contained in the relevant Companies Act Regulations (for SORP purposes, the FRSSE's reference to a *company* must also be taken to include a *non-company charity*):

'2.26   For each item shown [in the balance sheet] under creditors, the aggregate amount of any debts included where any security has been given by the company must be disclosed.' *(Small Companies and Groups (Accounts and Directors' Report) Regulations 2008, Sch 1, para 55(2))*

'11.9   Details must be provided where any valuable security has been provided by the company in connection with a contingent liability and if so, what.' *(Companies Act 1985, Sch 8, para 46 wording now superseded by fuller provision under the 2006 Act – see *)*

'11.11   Particulars must be given of any charge on the assets of the company to secure the liabilities of any other person, including where practicable, the amount secured.' *(Small Companies and Groups (Accounts and Directors' Report) Regulations 2008, Sch 1, para 57(1))*

– FRSSE 2008

* 'The following information must be given with respect to any ... contingent liability [other than para 57(1) above] not provided for – (a) the amount or estimated amount of that liability, (b) its legal nature, and (c) whether any valuable security has been provided by the company with that liability and if so, what.'

(Small Companies and Groups (Accounts and Directors' Report) Regulations 2008, Sch 1, para 57(2))

For *non-company* charities and for a parent charitable company's consolidated accounts where the group is 'small' under the Companies Act 2006, the disclosure in respect of charity *borrowings* is mandatory under para 1(l) of Sch 2 to the SORP's related 2008 Regulations, but is no longer specified there in respect of *contingent liabilities* (other than for any outstanding guarantee, where para 1(k) requires 'particulars' of it) – their disclosure being considered unavoidable under the accounting standards and the SORP in any case.

The requirement of the SORP itself is:

'If any specific assets (whether land or other property) of the charity are subject to a mortgage or charge given as security for a loan or other liability, a note to the accounts should disclose:

(a)   particulars of the assets which are subject to the mortgage or charge;
(b)   the amount of the loan or liability and its proportion to the value of the assets mortgaged or charged.'

– SORP 2005, paragraph 349

Contingent liabilities (and assets)

12.4.4   FRS12 requires material *contingent* liabilities (because they are not accrued in the accounts) to be explained in terms of their legal nature and the amounts involved unless so remote as to be improbable and thus inconsequential. Material *guarantees* given by the charity also have to be disclosed – however remote the contingency. (The disclosures required in respect of 'derivatives' are a special case – see **12.4.5**.)

This disclosure must include the uncertainties involved, though for third party claims against the charity that must clearly be tempered by caution where over-disclosure could prejudice the charity's interests. The relevant requirements of the SORP here, which now also specifically cover related contingent *assets*, as well as allowing similar contingencies to be aggregated, but also requiring cross-linking to any accrued provisions under the liabilities note, are:

> 'Material contingent assets and liabilities should be disclosed in the notes to the accounts unless the probability of a future transfer of resources (to or from the charity) is extremely remote – in which case no disclosure is necessary.'

> 'The accounts should disclose the nature of each contingency, the uncertainties that are expected to affect the outcome, and a prudent estimate of the financial effect where an amount has not been accrued. If such an estimate cannot be made, the accounts should explain why it is not practicable to make such an estimate.'

> *– SORP 2005, paragraphs 345 and 346*

> 'All material guarantees given by the charity, and the conditions under which liabilities might arise as a result of such guarantees, should be disclosed in a note to the accounts.'

> *– SORP 2005, paragraph 336*

As noted above, these disclosures for outstanding guarantees are mandatory under the SORP's related 2008 Regulations at Sch 2, para 1(k) for *non-company* charities and also for a parent charitable company's consolidated accounts where required to be prepared under the 1993 Act because the group, though 'small' under the Companies Act 2006, is above the Charities Act audit threshold of £500,000 gross income.

Derivative financial instruments for risk-mitigation

12.4.5 SORP 2005 had to include a new sub-section here for the disclosure of a charity's use of 'derivatives', since these not only affect investment performance or reduce borrowing costs, but also in some cases could have implications for the future financial viability of the reporting charity/group. Charity Commission guidance for the sector points out that derivatives as such are not investments, but that their use '*may be authorised by the general power of investment [the Trustee Act 2000], when that use is "ancillary" to the investment process*', before going on to outline the conditions to be satisfied for that purpose:

> 'There must be an investment transaction or intended transaction to which the use of derivatives is ancillary ...

> If the related investment transaction is one which is proposed for the future, but the proposal is then changed or abandoned, the derivative transaction may, as a consequence, cease to be "ancillary". In such a case the charity should normally "close out" or withdraw from the derivative transaction as soon as it is economically sensible to do so ... In other instances it may be necessary to enter into a new derivative transaction, or to terminate or restructure an existing one, if the nature of the related intended investment transaction itself changes ...

> The intention must be to manage risk, or to manage transaction costs (or both) within the investment process ...

> The derivative transaction must be "economically appropriate". This means that trustees, when entering into and reviewing it, should be satisfied that its value is such that the transaction can fairly be regarded as related to the objective of managing risk, or of managing transaction costs in the investment process. The economic appropriateness of the transaction will be determined by the relationship between the size of the payments which

are to be made or received under it, and any fluctuations in the value of the investment transaction(s) to which it relates. The amount of the capital on which the derivative transaction is based should not significantly exceed the capital of the investment transaction ...'.

– 'Investment of Charitable Funds' (February 2003), paragraph 16

The SORP itself explains that because charities cannot properly hold derivatives except as a means of reducing risk (certainly not speculatively – ie as a gamble – nor in the course of any substantial taxable business as an investment dealer) there is normally no need to value such holdings separately from the *'underlying investment or debt'*, but that:

'The notes to the accounts should indicate what derivative products are in use by the charity and indicate their impact on the risks of the underlying asset or liability to which they relate. The description of the products held should be in sufficient detail so that the reader of the accounts can understand what the charity's position would have been with, and without the derivatives, and should give an indication of the costs and benefits of the derivative products.'

– SORP 2005, paragraph 339

Charitable and other financial commitments

12.4.6 As noted at **12.4.1**, charitable and other financial commitments *not provided for* can be disclosed en bloc by category. While the disclosure of *uncontracted* 'capital expenditure' commitments (regardless of whether made out of capital or income funds) should not present any particular difficulty, prior to the issue of FRS12 it could sometimes be problematical to decide what disclosures were needed for certain kinds of outstanding *charitable* commitment, depending on whether they were accrued as liabilities or not.

For *accrued* charitable commitments payable by instalments, the 1995 SORP had required a time-based summary in the notes (including the movement since last year's reported figure) to show the pattern of instalment payments. As can be seen from **12.4.1**, this has since been widened to cover *unaccrued* commitments as well under SORP 2000 and now 2005:

'Particulars of all material provisions for liabilities and charges accrued in the balance sheet as liabilities should be disclosed in the notes. Similarly, particulars of all material commitments in respect of specific charitable projects should be disclosed if they have not been charged in the accounts.'

'These particulars should include the amounts involved, when the commitments are likely to be met and the movements on commitments previously reported ...'.

– SORP 2005, paragraphs 326 and 327

The SORP then calls for details of the year's movements in *charitable* commitments:

'The notes should distinguish between those commitments included on the balance sheet as liabilities and those that are intentions to spend and are not included but in both cases should detail:

(a)   the reason for the commitments, giving separate disclosure for material projects;

(b)   the total amount of the commitments, including amounts already charged in the accounts;

(c)   the amount of commitments outstanding at the start of the year;

(d)   any amounts charged in the Statement of Financial Activities for the year;

(e)   any amounts released during the year due to a change in the value in the commitments;

(f)   the amount of commitments outstanding at the end of the year and an indication as to how much is payable within one year and over one year.'

– *SORP 2005, paragraph 328*

Where a designated fund has been set up out of free reserves in order to ring-fence amounts being put aside to meet unaccrued charitable commitments (whether these be for grants or services), items (d) and (e) will instead comprise inter-fund transfers to and from general (undesignated) funds respectively – which, unless designated funds (as an exception) are segregated in the SoFA and/or Balance Sheet, will be visible only in a supporting accounts note summarising the movements on major individual funds of the charity), and similarly for any such commitments made out of restricted funds.

Where it is a matter of 'provisions' made in the accounts for liabilities in respect of charitable awards (ie those of uncertain amount or timing), FRS12's more general requirements also call for the following:

'For each class of provision, an entity should disclose:

...

(c)   amounts used (ie incurred and charged against the provision);

...

(e)   the change in the discounted amount arising from the passage of time and the effect of any change in the discount rate.'

– *FRS12, paragraph 89*

'... the entity should give:

...

(b)   an indication of the uncertainties about the amount or timing of those outflows ...'.

– *FRS12, paragraph 90*

In the case of non-corporate 'joint arrangements' (eg charity 'partnerships'), the SORP requires the accounts notes to provide:

'... appropriate details of the charity's commitments in the arrangement.'

– *SORP 2005, paragraph 418*

For commitments other than the above, the SORP requirement is as follows:

'Particulars of all other material binding commitments should also be disclosed (eg operating leases).'

– *SORP 2005, paragraph 327*

'Custodian trustee' holdings and other assets held outside the accounts

12.4.7 The requirements of SORP 2005 for this information to be disclosed are somewhat scattered according to the nature of the relationship:

> 'Where a charity is, or its trustees are, acting as custodian trustees, the following matters should be disclosed in the [trustees' annual] report:
>
> (a)   a description of the assets which they hold in this capacity;
> (b)   the name and objects of the charity (or charities) on whose behalf the assets are held and how this activity falls within their own objects;
> (c)   details of the arrangements for safe custody and segregation of such assets from the charity's own assets.'
>
> *– SORP 2005, paragraph 59*

And again:

> 'Some incoming resources do not belong to the charity, for instance where it receives the resources in circumstances where the trustees acting as agents (and not as custodian trustees) are legally bound to pay them over to a third party and have no responsibility for their ultimate application. In these circumstances the transaction is legally a transfer of resources from the original payer (who remains the principal) to the specified third party. If the original payer retains the legal responsibility for ensuring the charitable application of the funds, the intermediary charity should not recognise the resources in the Statement of Financial Activities or the balance sheet (see paragraph 319).'
>
> *– SORP 2005, paragraph 112*

> 'Where a charity has held resources for a third party which have not been included in the Statement of Financial Activities, the notes to the accounts should analyse the movement of these resources during the year relating to each party or type of party where material. Where resources have been held for related parties the required disclosure of paragraphs 227 to 228 should be given.'
>
> *– SORP 2005, paragraph 115*

And also:

> 'Where a charity is acting as an intermediary agent (as opposed to a custodian trustee) for another organisation as described in paragraph 112, then any assets held and the associated liabilities should be separately identified in the notes to the accounts but not included in the balance sheet. The notes to the accounts should provide sufficient detail so that the reader of the accounts understands the relationship and nature of the transactions between the charity, the funding organisation and the recipient of the funds.'
>
> *– SORP 2005, paragraph 319*

INFORMATION ABOUT GROUP UNDERTAKINGS

12.5   There are three separate statutory requirements here for *non-company* charities and for the consolidated accounts of parent *charitable companies* where the group is 'small' under the Companies Act 2006. The main one is under para 1(j) of Sch 2 to the SORP's related 2008 Regulations, which requires them to disclose for each subsidiary and associated undertaking:

– its name and the nature of the charity's relationship with it (this would include particulars of the control rights through shares, votes, or however);

– its activities;

– (if material) its turnover and profit/loss for its financial year; and

– any qualification expressed in an auditor's report on its accounts.

In addition to that information, for *subsidiaries* the SORP requires you to say how each one's activities relate to those of the charity (with *charitable* subsidiaries' activities summarised in terms of their gross incoming resources, the key components of their total expenditure: costs of generating funds, of charitable activities and of governance and the net result of these, but also surely their 'other recognised gains/losses') and also to disclose:

'... the aggregate amount of the total investment* of the charity in its subsidiary undertakings and, unless the subsidiary is not material, in relation to each one:

...

(d)   the aggregate amount of its assets, liabilities and funds;

...

Similar details should be provided relating to any minority interest external to the charity held in the subsidiary undertakings, including any restrictions that may be placed on the group's activities.'

– SORP 2005, paragraph 401

*For a *charitable* subsidiary (except where it is an Investment Pool charity, as a special case) only *non-equity* investment can be included here, for example loans – including any securitised debt. However, the disclosure requirement itself poses the general question of whether 'subsidiary' charities for this purpose catches those included in the reporting charity's *entity* accounts or only those included in its *consolidated* accounts. That is not an issue for FRS2/9, neither of which focus on the charity sector at all, while a strict reading of the relevant definitions in the SORP and its Regulations reveals that these are based on 'control', which the SORP itself defines in terms that clearly do not exclude 'special trusts' not specifically disunited by Direction of the Charity Commission nor other connected charities accounted for within the reporting charity's entity accounts under a Uniting Direction issued by the Commission, thus:

'"Controlled" means that the charity is able to secure that the affairs of the institution are conducted in accordance with its wishes. A charity will control another if it is trustee of that charity or has power to appoint or remove a significant proportion of its trustees.'

– SORP 2005, Glossary GL 50.1(c)(i), 'Related Parties'

'"Connected charities" are those which have common, parallel or related objects and activities; and either:

(a)   common control; or

(b)   unity of administration (eg shared management).'

– SORP 2005, Glossary GL 9, 'Connected Charities'

'"Common control" exists if:

(i)   the same person, or persons have the right to appoint a majority of the charity trustees of both or all the charities; or

(ii)   the same person, or persons, hold a majority of the voting rights in the administration of both or all of the charities.'

– SORP 2005, Glossary GL 50.1(d), 'Related Parties'

We must therefore conclude that although the point is not specially highlighted by the SORP, and so has gone completely unnoticed up to now, the disclosure here is meant to catch *all* subsidiary charities, whether or not included in the reporting charity's entity accounts, as well as the obvious *non-charitable* subsidiaries and associates defined by FRS2 and 9 respectively. Thus it has become established custom and practice for charities to give these particulars only for *self-accounting* group members, but not for the perhaps numerous registered (and in many cases even more numerous unregistered) subsidiary charities included in the reporting charity's own entity accounts.

To cater for the modern tendency to proliferation, however, paragraph 403 of the SORP provides that:

'If a charity has a large number of subsidiary undertakings such that the disclosure in paragraph 401 would result in information of excessive length being given, the information need only be given in respect of those undertakings whose results or financial position materially affected the figures shown in the charity's annual accounts. The full disclosure must be made available (in the same way as the accounts) to any member of the public upon request.'

– SORP 2005, paragraph 403

If *consolidation exemptions* are claimed (other than the SORP's general exemption for small groups up to the statutory audit threshold, currently £500,000 gross income, of course), then paragraph 317 requires that for *each subsidiary*:

'... the trustees should explain the reasons in a note to the charity's accounts ...'.

– SORP 2005, paragraph 404

The second statutory requirement is under paragraph 1(s), which in requiring debtors and creditors to be analysed *'according to the categories set out in the SORP'* thus requires separate disclosure of those in respect of group undertakings; while the third, under para 1(l), as already noted above requires disclosure of any outstanding *loans* made to them by the charity. The SORP, however, requires rather more:

'Loans made to trading subsidiaries, the security provided, the interest payable and the repayment terms should be disclosed as a separate item in the notes to the accounts.'

– SORP 2005, paragraph 350

Finally, for corporate joint ventures and consortium undertakings, as well as for all other associated undertakings, apart from the statutory disclosures set out at the beginning of this section the SORP also requires for each one:

'(d) the charity's interest in the results showing separately its share in:
  - (i)   gross incoming resources by type;
  - (ii)   costs of generating funds;
  - (iii) expenditure on charitable activities;
  - (iv)   expenditure on governance;
         (these first four items may need to be adapted in the case of associates or joint ventures that are not charities)[8]
  - (v)   the net results (where tax is payable, the share of the results pre and post tax and the share in the tax should be shown);
  - (vi)   gains or losses on investments and the share in unrealised gains on other fixed assets;
  - (vii) fixed assets;
  - (viii) current assets;
  - (ix)   liabilities under one year;
  - (x)   liabilities over one year;
  - (xi)   the different funds of the charity;[9]
  - (xii) contingent liabilities and other commitments ...'.

– SORP 2005, paragraph 417

And lastly the SORP requires the notes to any consolidated accounts to:

'... give the position of the group as well as the parent undertaking ...'.

– SORP 2005, paragraph 400

---

[8]   This compensates for the SORP's failure to adapt FRS9's consolidation method so as to ensure that the Charity Group SoFA properly *integrates* the group's share of the charitable and non-charitable activities of these undertakings (which can even include *charitable* consortium undertakings) in the same way as it automatically does for non-charitable subsidiaries.

[9]   This looks like just another little 'typo' where it really means 'entity'.

Chapter 13

ACCOUNTING FOR 'OPERATING ACTIVITIES' FOR THE PUBLIC BENEFIT OR FOR THE CHARITY'S OWN BENEFIT

INTRODUCTION

13.1 As society's demands on the resources of the charity sector rise, yet voluntary giving to charities wanes despite the Government's remarkably generous tax incentives on offer in recent years, the sector is becoming increasingly dependent on funds raised through trading and other revenue-generating 'operating' activities of such a similar nature that they need to be grouped together for accounting purposes. Taking *charitable* trading alone, it has been estimated that 45% of the nearly £50bn aggregate gross income of *registered* charities is from this source.

Charities are also having to be ever more inventive in their more commercially oriented fundraising activities: charity shops, corporate sponsorship, affinity cards, catalogues and charity lotteries are commonplace. In addition there is the 'contract culture' of local authority-funded community care services, where it is often difficult to distinguish grant-aid from contracting.

For the Charity Commission, a prime concern in the updating of the Charities SORP to the 2005 version was the need to ensure that the revenues and costs of 'economic' and 'similar' activities are properly presented in charities' accounts to highlight their *performance* in a more standardised way than hitherto. For although SORP 2000 provided some guidance with that in mind, this had not led to the desired consistency in the way trading and similar activities as a source of funding are presented in the published accounts of the larger charities in the face of the complexities involved. This chapter is therefore devoted to the special aspect of how to achieve the required consistency of presentation of the income and costs of 'operating activities' whose common feature is that they 'generate' funds (or aim to) – as distinct from absorbing them – either in the course of furthering the charity's Objects for the public benefit as their primary/ancillary purpose or else primarily to raise funds for that purpose.

TRADING AND 'SIMILAR' OPERATING ACTIVITIES

13.2 Other than the limited statutory power given in the Finance Act 2000 to raise funds through *non-charitable* trading activities up to the *de minimis* turnover level (maximum: £50,000) specified there, the law does not allow charities to carry out *trading* activities on a permanent basis – except in the course of directly furthering their Objects as their primary aim ('primary-purpose' trading). This is because charity law requires charitable resources to be applied only for their declared purposes, either directly to deliver public benefit or indirectly by investing them prudently (ie, without putting them at undue risk) to provide financial benefit for the charity itself.

SORP 2005 takes a step back again to group the latter with voluntary contributions and investment income under the heading of 'Incoming Resources from Generated Funds' as distinct from the former, now reported under its own heading of 'Income from Charitable Activities'.

Nevertheless, the same principle has been followed within the constraints of trust law where applicable: to achieve a linked SoFA presentation of the revenues and costs of all operating activities undertaken either primarily to further the charity's Objects for the public benefit or (separately presented) primarily to generate funds for the charity's own benefit.

What is 'trading'?

13.2.1   The Charities SORP no longer requires the separate identification of charities' *trading* activities as such – which in any case, to the purist, can smack of self-interested commercialism, seemingly at odds with the whole idea of charity and its ideal of selfless altruism. Putting aside that controversial issue, the SORP highlights as the main thing not the trading itself but only the difference between:

–   trading and similar revenue-generating activities undertaken primarily to deliver public benefit, thus as their essential purpose or 'aim'; and

–   the other kind of both activities, where the primary motivation is to raise funds,

thus relegating to second place the tax implications that were a deciding factor for annual accounting under the original 1995 SORP.

Whilst this need to identify for tax purposes the primary *reason* for undertaking any trading activity is clear, defining what is or is not trading is not so easy. Thankfully, that issue no longer decides where the revenues are to be shown in the SoFA – though it can still leave us with accruals problems in deciding whether to account on a contract or grant basis for the income and costs of some of the more ambivalent service-provision agreements charities may have to enter into with local authorities or central government departments, if the activity spans two or more year-ends. In such situations, the question of 'what is trading' must still be answered.

Some activities will be instantly recognised by most people as being the sort of 'value-for-value' commercial venture that must be accounted for as trading. However, other activities undertaken by charities are hard to pigeon-hole in this way. In these circumstances, some of the tests set out in tax case-law are helpful, though it should be noted that the definitions of trading for income tax and value added tax purposes are not quite the same.

Income tax law has established what are termed the 'badges of trade'. These are common features by which trading can be recognised, thus where the activity has some or all of the following characteristics or their equivalent (eg, selling not goods but a service):

(a)   has a profit-seeking motive;

(b)   is connected to an existing trading activity;

(c)   is carried on continually and repetitively;

(d)   is undertaken through a selling organisation;

(e)   involves the purchase of goods with a view to selling them on, particularly if there is a short interval of time between the acquisition and disposal;

(f)   is financed in a commercial manner such as through a bank loan;

(g)   involves the changing or modifying of an asset prior to its disposal;

(h)   relates to transactions involving the sort of assets that by their inherent nature are usually associated with trading.

The existence of any single badge of trade will not be an indication that a trade is being carried out. However, if several badges can be recognised in the activity then there will be a strong presumption of trading. It is important to recognise that charities can gain exemptions from tax on the profits of trading activities in a number of situations. These include trading directly in furtherance of the charity's primary purpose(s), and also situations where the trading is only ancillary to the primary purpose or is not exclusively primary-purpose but the non-charitable element is not significant, and where fundraising trading events are only on a small scale. In addition, as already mentioned, there is also the specific statutory tax exemption under the Finance Act 2000 for a *de minimis* level of non-charitable trading.

Although tax definitions of trading are helpful, they are not conclusive: even though an activity undertaken by the charity may be accepted as not chargeable to tax, its income and costs may still have to be accrued under the rules of contractual rather than trust law in certain situations. Nevertheless, the SORP does provide a conclusive set of definitions of its own for this purpose in its Glossary:

> 'In a strict legal sense trading activities are those carried out under contract, whether at the point of sale or otherwise, where goods and services are provided in return for consideration for those goods or services. Normally, trading activities are carried out on a regular basis with a view to making profits, though it is possible that some one-off activities could be regarded as trading.
>
> However, in an economic sense trading can be regarded as the provision of goods and services in return for a payment whether or not this payment is in fact under contract. Therefore, certain incoming grants which are, in a legal sense, donations, but which have specific terms attached to them such that a charity *becomes entitled to the payment on the provision of specified goods or services*, are in the context of this SORP recognised on the same basis as trading income (see Performance Related Grant: GL 45). This is because the charity has an obligation to provide the specific services or goods in the same way that it would have to provide them under contract. If it fails to provide the goods or services, then if the funds are by way of grant this will be a breach of trust, but if they are by way of contract this will be ... breach of contract. The legal remedies of the funding body are different depending upon the circumstances.

Similarly, the sale of donated goods is in a legal sense regarded as the realisation of a donation. However, in the context of this SORP it is regarded as trading, and recognised as an activity for generating funds ... because it is so similar to the sale of bought in goods as to be indistinguishable in the actual processes involved except for the legal distinction.'

– *SORP 2005, Glossary GL 57: 'Trading'*

'The term "performance-related grant" is used to describe a grant that has the characteristics of a contract in that:

(a)   the terms of the grant require the performance of a specified service that furthers the objectives of the grant maker; and
(b)   where payment of the grant receivable is *conditional on a specified output* being provided by the grant recipient.'

– *SORP 2005, Glossary GL 45: 'Performance Related Grant'*

'A payment made to a charity for the purpose of providing goods or services may be by way of grant or contract. The main distinction is that grant payments are voluntary whereas contracts are normally legally binding between the payer and the charity: the payment is not then voluntary and is not a grant. The distinction is important because:

(a)   a contractual payment will normally be unrestricted income of the charity, but a grant for the supply of specific services will normally be restricted income;
(b)   the nature of the payment may be relevant to its VAT treatment.

It is not always easy in practice to decide whether a particular arrangement is or is not intended by the parties to be a legally binding contract for the supply of services. If, under the arrangement, the payer, rather than the recipient charity, has taken the lead in identifying the services to be provided, or if the arrangement provides for damages to be paid in the case of a breach of its terms, rather than, say, for total or partial refund of the payment, it is more probable that there is a contract for the supply of services. If there is no such contract, the rights and obligations of the parties will depend primarily on the law of trusts and conditional gifts, rather than on the law of contract.

Certain grant arrangements may not be contractual in law but nevertheless have the characteristics of a contract, in that the conditions attaching to the grant *only give entitlement to the recipient of the funding (and a liability to the grant provider) as the goods or services specified in the grant terms are provided.* Such arrangements are termed performance related grants (see GL 45 Performance-related Grants).'

– *SORP 2005, Glossary GL 30: 'Grants and/or Contract Income'*

The emphasis in the above definitions is ours, to highlight the subtle and extremely careful distinction being made in SORP 2005 here to achieve strict compliance with trust law as well as accounting standards.

In our view this can at last resolve the vexed question of how to account for central and local government-funded service-provision agreements (and similar situations) where the law governing the agreement is not specified and cannot readily be identified. Even if trust law does apply, if by the above means the discharge of the trust created by the gift (grant) is made a *precondition* for entitlement to it as income (as distinct from mere accountability for it as a loan or advance), then the 'perfection' of that gift has left no money on trust at all, and it becomes clear that the grant and the costs it is funding must be matched in the SoFA in the same way as for a trading contract.

'Primary purpose' trading

13.2.2 The argument that the net profits will all be applied to further the charity's Objects does not make a trading activity itself 'charitable' – as distinct from one that is undertaken *primarily* as a way of delivering the charitable public benefit for which it was established (primary-purpose trading) or else to facilitate that delivery (ancillary trading).

Primary-purpose trading has been defined by the Charity Commission as:

> 'a trade that is exercised in the course of the actual carrying out of a primary purpose of the charity, or a trade in which the work in connection with the trade is mainly carried out by beneficiaries of the charity.'
>
> – *CC35: 'Charities and Trading'*

Examples of this are the provision of educational services by a school or college in return for course fees, the provision of residential accommodation by a community care charity in return for payment, or the sale of tickets for a theatrical production staged by a performing arts charity.

'Ancillary' trading

13.2.3 A charity may also undertake trading activities that are 'ancillary' to its primary purposes in that, although not part of the actual charitable benefit provided, they directly support or facilitate its delivery – but not just by making a profit, though that is, of course, a further help. Typical cases are the provision of accommodation to students in a school or college in return for rent, the sale of food and drink in a restaurant or bar to members of the audience of a theatre, or the sale of confectionery, toiletries and flowers to patients/visitors in the case of a hospital or hospice, etc.

The Charities SORP still provides a useful checklist of these two basic kinds of *charitable* trading (direct and ancillary):

> 'Incoming resources from charitable activities should include:
>
> (a) the sale of goods or services as part of the direct charitable activities of the charity (known as primary purpose trading);
> (b) the sale of goods or services made or provided by the beneficiaries of the charity;
> (c) the letting of non-investment property in furtherance of the charity's objects;
> (d) contractual payments from government or public authorities where these are received in the normal course of trading under (a) to (c) eg fees for respite care;
>
> ...
>
> (f) ancillary trades connected to a primary purpose in (a) to (e).'
>
> – *SORP 2005, paragraph 145*

By adding in an obviously *non-trading* (even if in some cases seemingly revenue-'earning') category of *special trust* funding here, the SORP broadens the list to the point where it could have been called 'charitable operating activities' because it effectively sub-divides the SORP 2000 heading – instead of which SORP 2005 less helpfully calls all these income sources 'incoming resources from charitable activities' because they include:

> '(e)   grants ... specifically for the provision of goods and services as part of the directly charitable activities or provided by the beneficiaries; ...'.

– SORP 2005, paragraph 145

What the SORP is referring to here, but which is clearly and unambiguously expressed only by the term 'performance-related' grants (see **13.2.1** for the Glossary definition), is:

> '... those grants (although legally donations) which have conditions which make them similar in economic terms to trading income ...
>
> This category will not include grants which are for core funding or do not have particular service requirements or are in response to an appeal ...'.

– SORP 2005, paragraphs 143–144

'Non-charitable' trading

13.2.4   The SORP requires a fully grossed-up presentation of the income and costs of all 'operating' activities in the SoFA – even where, as here, only the trading profit is of interest to the charity (as a source of funding) and the activity itself (turnover and related costs) is therefore only 'a means to that end'. This is only an issue for small charities, however, since for tax-exemption reasons any substantial non-charitable trading (beyond a turnover range of £5,000–£50,000 it must not exceed 25% of the charity's gross income) cannot be carried out by the charity itself, so the activity is normally hived down into a subsidiary/associate whose annual profits are then donated to the charity under the GiftAid Scheme.

SORP 2005 says, at paragraph 141(c), that in the charity's entity SoFA all such GiftAid donations or (more rarely) dividends passed to the charity from the subsidiary/associate must be shown (separately, if material) under *investment income*. An explanatory note is then needed under paragraph 401 of the SORP to summarise the trading results for each subsidiary – even where these are consolidated.

The original 1995 SORP had specified for non-charitable trading results a 'single-line' accounting treatment in the SoFA that was specifically agreed with the ASB at the time, serving the sector well since then until outlawed by SORP 2000 for a closer alignment with the (commercial) accounting standards. It provided a neat way of avoiding consolidation where only 'shell' subsidiary/associate companies are used for trading outside the reporting charity's Objects – as is nearly always the case, due to the constraints of tax and charity law on financing them out of charity funds. Although immaterial for balance sheet consolidation and for the consolidation of their *net* results, many of these fundraising trading undertakings now have to be seen as having a material *turnover* in the context of the charity's incoming resources, making it difficult to justify their exclusion from consolidation.

Strangely enough, the one place where the SORP still does require a single-line presentation is in the consolidation of interests in the net results of 'associated undertakings' – regardless of whether these are used for charitable or non-charitable purposes. It remains to be seen whether to any great extent the *inverse* of the 1995 SORP treatment will be used under SORP 2005 or any successor to justify *not* consolidating the results of non-charitable trading carried on through such 'shell' non-charitable subsidiaries/associates. This could perhaps by done by using an inset note on the face of the charity SoFA to show their grossed up turnover and costs, plus memorandum adjusted sub-totals for:

– income of 'activities for generating funds'; and

– costs of generating funds.

The Charities SORP gives examples of some of these non-charitable activities often carried on by charities directly, such as:

'(a) fundraising events such as jumble sales, firework displays and concerts (which are legally considered to be trading activities);
(b) those sponsorships and social lotteries which cannot be considered as pure donations;
...'.

– SORP 2005, paragraph 137

Thus care is needed to distinguish between the soliciting of *monetary gifts* (as distinct from gifts in kind for conversion into cash to fund activities – as the proceeds of *these* are to be accounted for like trading turnover, e g of 'charity shops' and the like), and the sale of goods/services by way of trade.

However, other kinds of fundraising activity that can easily be seen as non-charitable trading are becoming increasingly common:

'Activities for generating funds ... will include:
...
(c) shop income from selling donated goods and bought in goods,
(d) providing services other than for the benefit of the charity's beneficiaries,
(e) letting and licensing arrangements of property held primarily for functional use by the charity but temporarily surplus to operational requirements.'

– SORP 2005, paragraph 137

'Whilst selling donated goods is legally considered to be the realisation of a donation in kind ... in economic terms it is similar to a trading activity and should be included in this section.'

– SORP 2005, paragraph 138

'It may be possible to segregate the incoming resources and resources expended for each different component of an activity (this may have to be done for tax purposes) but often these will be viewed as a single economic unit. Charity trustees should consider the balance of the activities being undertaken to determine the most appropriate place to include the incoming resources from such enterprises but having done this the components of incoming resources need not be analysed further. For example a shop may mainly sell donated and bought in goods, but it may also sell a small amount of goods made by its beneficiaries and incidentally provide information about the charity. It would be acceptable to class all the incoming resources from the shop as "shop income" under "activities for generating funds".'

– SORP 2005, paragraph 139

Particular care is needed when setting up 'commercial sponsorship' arrangements, as reviewed in the following extract from published Charity Commission guidance:

'Common types of agreement between charities and commercial companies:

8.   Agreements between charities and companies vary in their detail, but most fall into one of three main types:

–   *Licensing agreements*
Under this type of agreement the charity gives the company a licence to use the charity's name and or/logo in selling a product or service. The company will promote sales of the product with a promise to the consumer that the charity will benefit financially from the sales of that product. Such promotions will usually act as a buying incentive to the consumer and so help to boost sales of that product. A wide range of commercial products, the best-known being Christmas cards, is commonly marketed under this type of agreement. The charity typically takes no active part in the product marketing – it is simply selling to the company, in return for payments, a limited right to the use of the charity name.

–   *Joint promotional agreements*
In this type of agreement the image of the charity plays an integral part in the marketing of the company's image, product or service. This is the basis of cause-related marketing. The agreement often envisages the building up of a long-term relationship between the charity and the company. The company's aim is to build an image of it as a socially responsible organisation. It seeks to achieve this by creating, through marketing and publicity, a link in people's minds between itself and the cause the charity represents. Its underlying aim is still, of course, to improve its financial performance for shareholders. The benefits for the charity might again include sales-linked payments from specific promotions, but it also hopes to benefit from the raised awareness of itself, its work and its funding needs that can result from increased exposure in the media. As part of the agreement the charity might also receive specified benefits in kind – goods, services, facilities or expertise provided to it by the company.

–   *Sponsorship agreements*
Under this type of agreement a company is in effect paying a charity to publicise the company and the fact that it has contributed to the charity. The company agrees to meet some or all of the costs of, for instance, one of the charity's publications, fundraising events or projects. In return the charity will publicly acknowledge the company's contribution. The company again hopes that its visible association with, and financial support for, a charitable cause will improve its image, or promote and sell its products. The charity benefits from the sponsorship payments and, it hopes, from increased exposure of its name and cause in the company's own advertising of its support for the charity.

...

12. ... A charity that does not already have a power to enter into fundraising agreements may be able to introduce such a power into its governing document, if it has a power of amendment. If trustees are in doubt about whether they have the power to enter into fundraising agreements or to alter their governing documents to introduce this power they should contact the Commission for advice or take their own legal advice.

13. Once satisfied that they have the necessary power to enter into the agreement trustees must then consider whether Part II of the Charities Act 1992 and the Charitable Institutions (Fund-raising) Regulations 1994 apply to the venture or any element of it. These provisions

protect charities against misuse of their name, by prohibiting professional fundraisers and commercial participators from using a charity's name in a fundraising venture or promotion without the charity's permission.

The law includes requirements for:

–   a written agreement, in a prescribed form, between the charity and the professional fund-raiser or commercial participator;
–   a statement to be given to inform potential donors what proportion of their donation will be used to pay the costs of the fund-raiser;
–   the public to be informed how the charity will benefit from its involvement with a commercial participator; and
–   the transfer of funds raised by professional fund-raisers or commercial participators to the charity.

14.   These provisions are likely to apply to many licensing agreements and joint promotion agreements as described above. Any charity in doubt about complying with or enforcing the legal requirements applying to particular types of joint venture should take legal advice. Some agreements fall outside the Regulations mentioned at point 13 above. Part II of the 1992 Act and the 1994 Regulations do not apply to fund-raising agreements between commercial companies and charities' subsidiary trading companies (rather than the charity). Neither do they apply to agreements between a commercial company and a charity, if the payment made to the charity by the commercial company is not a donation (ie it is a payment for goods or services provided by the charity to the commercial company, or payments by the company for the use of the charity's name or logo).

...

Considering the benefits to the charity

16.   The endorsement of commercial products or services by a charity has the potential to increase sales of, or add value to, those products or services. Is the charity confident (having taken independent professional advice if necessary) that the benefits it is being offered under the agreement reflect its full and fair share of that added value? Is any information available to the charity about the terms and benefits that other charities have managed to negotiate in similar deals? If so, has the charity drawn on this to ensure that it does not agree terms that are less than the best it could reasonably hope to negotiate? What arrangements will the charity make for regular reviews of the costs and benefits of the venture? We would expect a charity to keep the cost/benefit balance of any joint venture with a company under regular review and, if the balance turns against the charity, to have the ability to withdraw from the venture.'

– Charity Commission website guidance: 'Charities and Commercial Sponsorship – Fund-raising through partnerships with companies' (updated September 2005)

Three types of trading activity

13.2.5   It can be seen, therefore, that trading activities can take three different forms, namely activities:

(a)   to provide the charitable goods and services that are the primary purpose of the charity but without using up its financial resources in doing so; or

(b)   that are ancillary to that primary purpose; or

(c)   carried out by the charity primarily as a way of raising funds.

In the first two cases, the trading activity could either be carried out by the charity itself or by a trading subsidiary (usually done to ring-fence the trading risks), but the third kind can lawfully be carried out on a permanent or regular basis by the charity itself only up to the maximum turnover permitted under the Finance Act 2000. This is in addition to any occasional and relatively insignificant trading events that are not undertaken on a continuing basis, of course.

Charity shops, etc

13.2.6   While the sale of donated goods to fund the charity's activities is not regarded by HMRC as a trade, for accounting purposes under the SORP it is treated just as if it was. As a result, the gross proceeds of such sales are to be shown under the heading of 'Income from Activities to Generate Funds' in the financial year in which the gift is sold. What this means in practice, as noted above, is that you do not need to split out the 'turnover' of charity shops arising from adding bought-in lines of goods (which has long been common practice) but can treat them both (ie, donated and bought-in goods) as part of a single 'business' in the SoFA.

Any associated costs are to be shown under 'Costs of Generating Funds' – regardless of whether the use of High Street shop premises, perhaps, or of more temporary venues such as car boot sales, fairs, etc, as sales outlets for this type of activity is merely the result of the charity's popularity or represents serious fundraising efforts by the charity.

The following illustrations taken from the accounts of two major fundraising charities highlight the problem that this can bring for a proper appreciation of the charity's (or the group's) fundraising efforts – especially where charity shops or more expensive activities are involved.

The standardised columnar format specified by the SORP requires the gross incoming resources of all funds to be reported in the first section of the SoFA, followed by a section for all the costs of activities (primarily) to generate funds, which is then followed by the costs of (primarily) charitable activities and then of the 'governance' of the charity (its management and administration, in old terminology) before arriving at total expenditure and then net incoming resources subject to inter-fund transfers and gains and losses on revaluations and investment disposals.

For some charities, strict compliance with this format without careful explanation of the mix of activities involved, and especially of long-term trends and results, can make it difficult for the reader of the accounts to appreciate the overall efficiency of the fundraising approach used.

SoFA extract – year to 30 April 2008	Unrestricted	Restricted	£'000
INCOMING RESOURCES			
Incoming resources from generated funds			
Voluntary income:			
- Donations and gifts	6,235	11,378	**17,613**
- Legacies	10,616	1,925	**12,541**

SoFA extract – year to 30 April 2008	Unrestricted	Restricted	£'000
- Grants	588	1,140	**1,728**
Activities for Generating Funds:			
– Merchandising and Retail	31,385	-	**31,385**
- Other trading income	2,525	81	**2,606**
- Events	702	19	**721**
- Sale of services by joint venture	1,629	-	**1,629**
Investment income	1,121	186	**1,307**
Incoming resources from charitable activities:			
- Combating poverty	21	291	**312**
- Reducing isolation	113	1,928	**2,041**
- Defeating ageism	-	-	**-**
- Challenging neglect	280	65	**345**
- Preventing future deprivation	466	282	**748**
- International	170	-	**170**
Other incoming resources:			
- Exceptional item: VAT refund	-	-	**-**
- Gain on disposal of fixed assets	390	-	**390**
Total incoming resources inc. share of jt. venture	**56,241**	**17,295**	**71,907**
Less: Share of joint venture	(1,629)	-	**(1,629)**
Total incoming resources	**54,612**	**17,295**	**71,907**
RESOURCES EXPENDED			
Costs of generating voluntary income:			
- Fundraising	4,517	3,588	**8,105**
- Legacies	954	16	**970**
- Grants	174	17	**191**
Activities for generating funds:			
- Cost of selling donated/bought-in goods	27,016	246	**27,262**
- Merchandising and commission costs	6,440	9	**6,449**
- Event costs	679	-	**679**
Investment management costs	113	-	**113**
	39,893	**3,876**	**43,769**
Net income available for charitable activities	*14,719*	*13,419*	*28,138*
Charitable Activities			
- Combating poverty	3,155	1,556	**4,711**

SoFA extract – year to 30 April 2008	Unrestricted	Restricted	£'000
- Reducing isolation	5,306	3,625	8,931
- Defeating ageism	2,369	590	2,959
- Challenging neglect	3,136	613	3,749
- Preventing future deprivation	3,259	4,027	7,286
- International	3,182	6,501	9,683
Total charitable spend	20,407	16,912	37,319
Governance costs	329	–	329
Total expenditure before jt. ventures & transfers	60,629	20,788	81,417
Net outgoing resources before joint venture & transfers	(6,017)	(3,493)	(9,510)

Help the Aged – 2007/08 Accounts

The above extract shows what a dramatic impact the SoFA format must have on this famous charitable company's annual reporting as regards its apparent operating efficiency.

While the charity shows up well on *restricted fund* activities, with over 80% of funds raised available for its Aid programme, only 25% of its *general-purpose* funds raised are now seen as available for core charitable activities – not a very appealing picture.

Thus the 14% profit generated by the 'charity shops' activities (a creditable result for a *trading* business) can all too easily be viewed as 86% of donors' gifts in kind swallowed up in procuring and converting them into cash, leaving only 14% available to provide the promised public benefit – unless such shops happen to be staffed and run primarily by elderly beneficiaries, of course. But that would then require the entire operation to be grouped with the charity's public benefit programme instead, as a *charitable* activity.

SoFA extract – year to 31 March 2008	Unrestricted	Restricted	Total
	£'000	£'000	£'000
INCOMING RESOURCES			
Income from generated funds:			
Voluntary income:			
- Donations & Gifts	30,230	27,626	57,856
- Legacies	15,288	33	15,321
- Gifts in kind	–	8,602	8,602
- Institutional grants	6,400	59,042	65,442
Retail income	7,639	–	7,639
Investment income	2,780	616	3,396
Income from charitable activities:			
- Overseas programme income	535	462	997

SoFA extract – year to 31 March 2008	Unrestricted	Restricted	Total
	£'000	£'000	£'000
Other income	1,421	103	1,524
Total income	**64,293**	**96,484**	**160,777**
RESOURCES EXPENDED			
Cost of generating funds			
Costs of raising voluntary income	15,748	355	16,103
Retail costs	6,594	–	6,594
Investment management fees	148	–	148
Total cost of generating funds	**22,490**	**355**	**22,845**
Income available for charitable application	*41,803*	*96,129*	*137,932*

Save the Children – 2007/08 Accounts

Here again, SCF's way of generating its own general-purpose funding looks somewhat expensive at first sight, with costs of £22m accounting for 35% of all general-purpose income – until we notice that this includes SCF's charity shops ('retail' operations) as a special case. However, when legacies (whose associated costs – also known as 'fundraising for the future' – but which are not identified here) are taken out of the calculation the ratio moves the other way, from which the more thoughtful reader will conclude that the SORP has not yet found a way to account to the public for charity fundraising efficiency at all, which must therefore still be seen as work-in progress for the SORP Review Committee.

Charitable service-provision trust agreements v trading contracts

13.2.7 By grouping grant-aided operating activities under service-performance agreements of a *special-purpose* nature together with those of a contractual (and therefore general-purpose) nature under the heading of 'Activities to Further the Charity's Objects', SORP 2000 neatly resolved one dilemma – but not the accounting problem itself! It is only in SORP 2005 that a definitive solution has been provided.

For arrangements spanning 2 years or more, you still have to choose between trust-accounting and contract-accounting for the proper recognition of income and costs, whereupon similarities of wording can again make it difficult to distinguish between:

(a) a funding agreement with a statutory body requiring certain services provided by the charity to comply with specified service-level/performance conditions as part of the terms of trust on which the grant is provided; and

(b) a trading contract providing for specified services to, or to the order of, such a body.

While under (a) any surplus *grant* monies will normally have to be repaid, any *contract profits* under (b) will normally be retained – except as otherwise provided for in the terms of agreement/contract, of course. For as the SORP's Glossary explains:

> 'It is not always easy in practice to decide whether a particular arrangement is or is not intended by the parties to be a legally binding contract for the supply of services. If, under the arrangement, the payer, rather than the charity, has taken the lead in identifying the services to be provided, or if the arrangement provides for damages to be paid in the case of a breach of its terms, rather than, say, for total or partial refund of the payment, it is more probable that there is a contract for the supply of services. If there is no such contract, the rights and obligations of the parties will depend primarily on the law of trusts and conditional gifts, rather than on the law of contract.'
>
> *SORP 2005, Glossary GL 30: 'Grants and/or Contract Income'*

Even for legal experts, it can sometimes be difficult to decide from the wording of the documentation whether the charity has entered into a type (a) or a type (b) agreement. Type (a) regulates the use of a *grant* to fund specific charitable services that is then subject to charity law, where the terms agreed between the parties will usually specify the nature and extent of the work to be done, the standard of performance required and the financial adjustments to be made in the event of any shortfall, perhaps also the time-scale for the work and even the method of calculating the allowable costs.

But these experts may conclude that the agreement is regulated by contract law. It must then be *accounted for* as type (b). This accords with the fundamental commercial accounting principle that for each financial year the costs to be recognised in the accounts as 'incurred' must be 'matched' with the revenues 'earned' by those costs to show a prudently anticipated surplus/deficit on the contract.

Those revenues and costs will then belong to the charity's *unrestricted* funds (except to the extent of any surplus/deficit accruing to the other party under the agreement terms, of course). This requires a (post-) year-end assessment of the likely outcome of the agreement in terms of surplus/deficit.

Once the ultimate outcome can be foreseen with reasonable certainty, the full contract revenues (less any *unearned* surplus on work yet to be done) can be recognised as income. Against this will be matched an accrual of the remaining costs to completion of the contract.

In the early stages, however, subject to providing for any ultimate loss already seen as unavoidable, an excess of contract revenues to date over costs incurred to date will be kept out of the SoFA and just carried forward as deferred income.

By contrast, in the case of grant-funded activities, the SORP requires immediate recognition of the full amount of the grant (less any part carried forward either as deferred income until the expiry of donor-imposed timing restrictions prohibiting the *use* (spending) of a general-purpose grant or as cash advances that cannot be recognised as special-purpose grant income until, the related expenditure having been incurred, output (performance) has satisfied certain donor-imposed *pre-conditions*) against the accrual of all project costs either actually incurred or operationally unavoidable by the year-end.

The grant will constitute a restricted fund if the agreement *limits the purposes* for which it can be used so that it cannot be described as 'core funding' – where there must be no narrowing down of purpose.

Some agreements provide only partial funding for the project to be undertaken, which may be outside the charity's 'core' activities and/or subject to a precondition of 'matched funding' being provided by the charity or some other party.

Agreements may include a formula limiting the grantor's contribution to the charity's general administration costs, leaving a deficit to be met out of unrestricted funds. Any unspent balance of grant will remain as a fund of the charity on the same terms of trust – unless repayable under the agreement, when it will be a liability.

This accounting problem will be familiar to unendowed charities set up to provide community care services of the kind traditionally undertaken by local authorities and now 'outsourced', as under the Government's 'care in the community' initiative.

The following example shows how the recognition of income and expenditure in the SoFA is affected each year – depending on how the income has to be accounted for, either as a normal charitable grant (whether 'unrestricted' or for some *specified* public benefit) or as what SORP 2005 defines as a 'performance-related' grant (which will normally be on such specific terms, including its purpose, that it has to be accounted for as *restricted*) or else as a trading contract in the *unrestricted* funds column of the SoFA:

	Grant-funding to provide services	Performance-related Grant for service-provision	Contracted sale of services
Case 1 – Costs turn out to be 25% lower than funding (no clawback if work all done)			
	£'000	£'000	£'000
Year 1 Income in SoFA	1000	188	250
Costs (25% of work completed)	(188)	(188)	(188)
Net income recognised for year	812	-	62
Add: Unspent Fund B/F	-	-	-
Balance Sheet:			
- Unspent Fund C/F	812	-	62
- Liability for any cash in advance	-	(812)	(750)
(Note: Contract-accounting matches income (including any profits earned to date) against costs, but there is no 'profit' in a performance-related grant.)			
Year 2 Income in SoFA	–	562	750
Costs to completion	(562)	(562)	(562)
Net income recognised for year	(562)	-	188
Unspent Fund B/F	812	-	62
Unspent Fund C/F	*250	-	250

	Grant-funding to provide services	Performance-related Grant for service-provision	Contracted sale of services
Liability for repayment to Grantor	*if repayable per terms of trust	(250)	-

Case 2 – Costs turn out to be 25% under-funded (any grant-deficit irrecoverable)				
Year 1	Income in SoFA	1000	313	250
	Costs (25% of work completed)	(313)	(313)	(313)
	Provision for unavoidable costs/loss	–	(187)	(187)
	Net income recognised for year	687	(187)	(250)
	Unspent Fund B/F	–	–	–
	Unspent Fund C/F	687	(187)	(250)
	Liability for any cash in advance	–	(687)	(750)
	(Note: Contract-accounting must provide in full for any <u>unavoidable loss</u>, and trust-accounting must include any <u>unavoidable costs</u> under a grant-agreement – but these funding deficits need to be fully covered out of unrestricted funds.)			
Year 2	Income in SoFA	–	687	750
	Costs to termination/completion	*(687)	(750)	(750)
	Net income recognised for year	(687)	(63)	–
	Unspent Fund B/F	687	(187)	(250)
	Unspent Fund C/F (for deficit-funding)	–	(250)	(250)
	(*Note: Grant-funded work can normally be terminated if the money runs out – but not if it is a performance-related grant, as income-entitlement is for duly meeting targets!)			

For a *'performance-related'* grant, however, there is no such problem under trust law: because the grant-control agreement specifically *denies the recipient charity any entitlement to grant monies as income* until it has provided the promised charitable services to the satisfaction of the funding body, any monies advanced to it before then must be accounted for as liabilities (loans) so that, in effect, all grant monies are accounted for as income in line with (qualifying) expenditure – exactly like a trading contract!

SOFA REQUIREMENTS

13.3.1   SORP 2005 requires the revenues and related costs of all 'operating activities' as shown in the SoFA to be clearly linked – primarily through the use of similar descriptions within the SoFA or else in the accounts notes sub-analysis. Also, the supporting analysis in the notes to the accounts must be sufficiently detailed to provide a proper understanding of the *'main activities'* and the *'main components'* of the charity's revenues, with the new *objectives-based* analysis of costs being consistent with this. Whether you should also highlight the surplus or deficit arising on each of these main activities, the SORP carefully does not say. A deficit on furtherance of the Objects can properly go without comment here, but could have implications for the trustees' policy on 'free reserves' as disclosed in the annual report.

The SoFA under SORP 2005 fundamentally divides income from a charity's 'operating activities' between those undertaken primarily:

(a)   to further the charity's Objects; or

(b)   to generate funds.

Which you should then describe in such a way as to 'mirror' your description of the related activity-costs as categorised by the type of purpose-related *objective* involved. However, care is needed so that such analysis does not make you lose sight of the vital distinctions for charity law and tax purposes:

Income to be recognised	SoFA treatment	Legal status
Local Authority grant income for:		
– specified community services – *or* with required service standards	'Charitable Activities' income	Depending on terms, contract income or *restricted* grant
– general (core) activities with *no* service-performance conditions	Voluntary income	Depending on terms, contract income or *unrestricted* grant
'Charity Shop' income from:		
– goods donated to the charity for sale	'Activities to Generate Funds' income	Donation income (usually – but not necessarily – unrestricted)
– bought-in goods for sale (not as part of a 'primary purpose' trade – such as workshops for the disabled)	'Activities to Generate Funds' income	Taxable trading income (subject to 'de minimis' exemptions)
Sales of uniforms, sports clothing and so on, to pupils at a school:		
– to maintain dress standards	'Charitable Activities' income	Ancillary trading, tax-free
– to subsidise school fees	'Activities to Generate Funds' income	Ancillary trading, tax-free
Corporate sponsorship income from licensing the use of the charity logo:		
– as Objects-related brand-marking of *qualifying* products of the company	'Charitable Activities' income	Primary purpose trading income (non-taxable)
– as a means of fundraising through *suitable* products of the company	'Activities to Generate Funds' income	Taxable/non-taxable trading if not pure donation income

The SORP does not specify the format or contents of the analysis note it requires to relate the respective costs and revenues of the two categories of mutually exclusive 'operating' activities it requires to be shown in the SoFA: charitable or fund-generating. Regardless of which category it falls into, however, it would seem appropriate to show for each 'revenue-generating' activity its turnover or other gross proceeds, its operating costs and net operating result. Where any of these activities are carried out through a subsidiary, then it is the donation/dividend (if any) from the subsidiary that must be shown (separately, if material) in the charity SoFA, whereas instead the gross trading income/costs will be shown in the consolidated SoFA – unless the special presentation suggested above is used to qualify for consolidation exemption on grounds of immateriality.

Public Benefit vs Other Operating Activities

13.3.2 Neither does SORP 2005 specify any sub-analysis of charitable activities to distinguish between those undertaken to primarily further the charity's public benefit aims and those which are only ancillary thereto in meeting other needs of the charity's beneficiaries. In the Charity Commission's statutory guidance on meeting the Public Benefit test an interesting example of the latter is given as the restaurant/bar for patrons attending a performing arts charity's theatre/concert or other performance. Thus while both kinds of charitable activity can qualify for HMRC purposes as non-taxable trading (subject to the possible test of 'commmerciality' if HMRC were now to take the view that for there to be public benefit in charitable service-provision at a fee the pricing must be substantially below competitive market rates), only the former will enable the charity to satisfy the Public Benefit test to be administered by the Charity Commission in England and Wales or OSCR in Scotland. It is at this point that the SORP's 2008 Regulations have overtaken it, for without a clear distinction of Operating Activities in the SoFA between what is or is not undertaken primarily for the public benefit, the required narrative reporting disclosures in the Trustees' Annual Report may lack credibility, being unsupported by the accounts – albeit deemed 'consistent' with them for audit report purposes.

It remains to be seen whether the next version of the SORP will specify such a distinction in the SoFA, or whether in England and Wales the regulator will instead require this to be clarified in the Summary Information Return that has to be filed by all the largest registered charities.

SUMMARY INCOME AND EXPENDITURE ACCOUNT

13.4 Certain charitable companies must prepare a summary income and expenditure account in addition to the SoFA, as explained in chapters 6 and 7. Where such a summary is prepared it will be necessary to separate trading turnover from other gross income and cross-reference both to the SoFA.

However, if trustees wish to make use of the summary's 'commercial' format to highlight significant trading activities and their net results (as an alternative to using a separate column for this in the SoFA, or else relegating information to the accounts notes) one way of doing so might be to adopt a columnar format, for example, as below:

	Trading Fund 'A'	Trading Fund 'B'	Voluntary Activities	2009 Total	2008 Total
	£'000	£'000	£'000	£'000	£'000
Voluntary income:					
– restricted	–	–	3,650	3,650	3,250
– unrestricted	–	–	3,720	3,720	1,855
Trading turnover:					
– from charitable activities	3,630	–	–	4,130	3,000
– from activities to generate funds	–	1,950	–	1,450	1,200
Total income	**3,630**	**1,950**	**7,370**	**12,950**	**9,305**

	Trading Fund 'A' £'000	Trading Fund 'B' £'000	Voluntary Activities £'000	2009 Total £'000	2008 Total £'000
Expenditure:					
– on charitable activities	3,950	–	5,750	9,700	8,300
– on activities to generate funds	–	1,230	–	1,230	1,000
– on charity governance	–	–	120	120	100
Total expenditure	**3,950**	**1,230**	**5,870**	**11,050**	**9,400**
Net operating income	(320)	720	1,500	1,900	(95)
Investment disposal gains/losses	–	–	(650)	(650)	(500)
Net income for the year	**(320)**	**720**	**850**	**1,250**	**(595)**

BALANCE SHEET REQUIREMENTS

13.5 The balance sheet presentation of funds used for trading and similar operating activities follows the requirements of charity law, in that:

– *trading* funds as such cannot be restricted funds, and therefore must form part of the charity's free reserves, except insofar as they have been designated for their own particular purpose – ie the 'working capital' needed to keep that trading activity going; and

– unused *restricted-purpose*[1] grant-funding must be shown as part of restricted funds.

The proceeds of donated goods received on trust for sale and use of the proceeds for activities must follow the purpose for which they have been donated. Although this will normally be unrestricted, if the terms of an appeal for such contributions were to indicate that the need was for some special purpose, then the proceeds would belong to restricted funds.

Where a *subsidiary* is used primarily to carry out *non-charitable* trading activities, the reporting charity's interest in it must obviously be accounted for as an 'investment' asset, while in the *consolidated* balance sheet all funds retained in the subsidiary but *not available for charitable purposes* (a reference to its 'working capital' of reserves tied up in assets used for non-charitable trading to generate profits for the charity) must be segregated from those of the charity:

---

[1] In contrast to the 'deferred income' treatment of *time-restricted* general-purpose voluntary funding – as explained in chapter 6.

> 'In consolidated accounts, funds or reserves retained by subsidiary undertakings other than funds available to be used in carrying out the charity's objects should be included under an appropriate separate fund heading in the balance sheet (e g funds retained within a non-charitable subsidiary).'

– SORP 2005, paragraph 406

SORP 2000 was clearer here: it simply distinguished as 'non-charitable trading funds' all reserves actually used for non-charitable purposes, whereas now the requirement is to distinguish only those 'not available' for charitable use – with no clear description of their actual or intended use!

The SORP does not otherwise have anything much to say on trading activities in relation to the balance sheet, and you are therefore left to interpret for yourself how to apply its special accounting rules for *social investment* in charitable projects – which could also be undertaken within the reporting charity's own group instead of by some independent third party. See chapter 9 about that.

Thus a related situation that is increasingly common with charity trustees' awareness of the need to 'ring-fence' and thus contain trading risks, is where some sort of controlled undertaking – usually a subsidiary but often a 'corporate joint venture', a consortium undertaking or an 'associate' – is used *primarily to carry out trading activities within the charity's Objects*. There, the retained funds clearly form part of the group *charitable* reserves – as is implied by the above quotation.

But actually they may more properly be shown as a designated social investment fund rather than as reserves, since they are already spoken for. Indeed, in view of the restrictions imposed by charity law, it may be argued that they must be so shown in order not to mislead the reader as to the nature of the group's funds and their proper use.

An obvious difficulty arises where the subsidiary carries out both primary purpose and non-charitable fundraising trading activities. In this case, retained reserves would need to be analysed between those arising from charitable and from non-charitable activities – which may be difficult to establish with any reliability. It may even be argued that the charity has sufficient control over the subsidiary (certainly if wholly owned) to require it to pay over reserves that have arisen from fundraising activities, to be applied by the charity on its charitable purposes.

Until that day comes, however, the subsidiary's reserves will, as indicated, need to be split for consolidation purposes between charitable and non-charitable trading funds of the group, in order not to lose sight of the charity law constraints within which the charity parent has to operate.

Chapter 14

BRANCH-ACCOUNTING VERSUS CONSOLIDATED ACCOUNTS

PRECEDENCE AND STATUS

14.1 This is the *first* question that confronts the reporting charity with separately constituted *branch-charities* – especially where the main charity itself is a *charitable company*, even more so if it also uses *non-charitable* subsidiaries, joint-venture/consortium or 'associated' undertakings (where these are themselves corporate bodies) to further its charitable purposes. They can only be accounted for properly in any given situation when you know the precise legal status of each connected legal entity that appears to be subordinate to the reporting charity, so that you can ask yourself whether it is to be treated as a *charity branch* or a *group member or a part-controlled body*.

Branch-accounting before consolidation

14.1.1 In short, the answer is that branch-accounting under the Charities Act 1993 ('the 1993 Act') always takes precedence for a *charity's* public accountability. Confirmation of this can be seen in the way the Charities Act 2006 has now made provision for group-accounting by *non-company* charities as well as by parent charitable companies of 'small' groups not required to prepare consolidated accounts under company law, in line with the SORP and similar to the Companies Act requirements for parent charitable companies of larger groups. That still leaves the question of how a charitable company of such a larger group is to reconcile its statutory accounting obligations under Part 15 of the Companies Act 2006 (or previously under Part VII of the 1985 Act) with its public accountability under Part VI of the 1993 Act (as amended), as the former legislates only for *corporate* funds and is silent about *trust* funds. The 1993 Act provides for *special trusts* and deemed 'subsidiary' charities to be aggregated within the entity accounts of the reporting charity as its 'restricted' funds, thus as charity branches – but specifically excludes charitable companies to the extent of their accounting *obligations* under company law.

To bridge the gaps between the two accounting regimes, the charity sector had already achieved a pragmatic consensus since the issue of the original, 1995 SORP. *Charitable companies* are expected to account for all their *trust* funds within their entity accounts before consolidating all their *non-trust* group interests, while *non-company* charities must by law in any case account for all *subsidiary charities* in their *entity* accounts, adding *consolidated accounts* to this as an 'extra', in order also to deal with any *non-charitable* group interests in accordance with the Charities SORP. In this way, a practical solution to the disparity between the two regimes had been achieved as a matter of generally accepted accounting practice. That consensus has now been endorsed by the SORP's related 2008 Regulations for financial years starting after 31 March 2008 (or upon earlier voluntary adoption), where Part 3, under s 49A and Sch 5A of the 1993 Act, governs the preparation of consolidated accounts for all groups whose aggregate gross income exceeds £500,000 (the Charities Act audit threshold) wherever this is not *required* by company law.

The basic requirement is set out in para 3 of Sch 5A:

'(1) This paragraph applies in relation to a financial year of a charity if—

(a) the charity is a parent charity at the end of that year; and
(b) (where it is a company) it is not required to prepare consolidated accounts for that year under section 227 of the Companies Act 1985 (duty to prepare group accounts), whether or not such accounts are in fact prepared.

(2) The charity trustees of the parent charity must prepare group accounts in respect of that year.

(3) "Group accounts" means consolidated accounts (a) relating to the group, and (b) complying with such requirements as to their form and contents as may be prescribed by regulations made by the Minister. ...'.

– Charities Act 1993, Sch 5A, para 3

Groups below the £500,000 threshold are then exempted by para 4(2) of Sch 5A and the SORP's related 2008 Regulations:

'The requirement in paragraph 3(2) does not apply to the charity trustees of a parent charity in relation to a financial year if the aggregate gross income of the group for that year does not exceed such sum as is specified in regulations made by the Minister.'

– Charities Act 1993, Sch 5A, para 4(2)

'The sum specified for the purposes of paragraph 4(2) ... is £500,000.'

– SI 2008/629, reg 18

Finally, this is subject to para 1(4) of Sch 5A, which excludes from the definition of a 'subsidiary undertaking' for group-accounting purposes (because they are 'charity branches' to be included in the reporting charity's *entity* accounts):

'(a) any special trusts of a charity,
(b) any institution which, by virtue of a direction under section 96(5) of this Act, is to be treated as forming part of a charity for the purposes of [Part VI), or
(c) any charity to which a direction under section 96(6) of this Act applies for those purposes.'

– Charities Act 1993, Sch 5A, para 1(4)

What *is* a 'charity branch'?

14.1.2 The public accountability imposed by the 1993 Act on all 'main' charities for all their *controlled* charities treats them as *charity branches* in certain circumstances (see below) – necessitating 'branch returns', which must by law be provided even where the other charity is administered by a separate body of trustees. The Register of Charities contains nearly 170,000 'main' charities plus nearly 30,000 'subsidiary' charities that have to be accounted for as 'restricted funds' (either income or capital in nature) in the relevant main charity's 'entity' accounts where possible – otherwise in its consolidated accounts, eg, in the exceptional case where both are charitable companies. Before looking to see what constitutes a charity branch, therefore, it would be useful to start with what the SORP means by a 'charity' in the first place:

> 'A "charity" is any institution established for purposes which are exclusively charitable*. Where the institution is involved in more than one activity, operates more than one fund, or is not centralised into one unit of operation, the term is used in this statement to include all those activities, units and funds which fall within the scope of either a single governing instrument (or instruments supplemental to the main instrument) or for which the trustees are otherwise legally liable to account (eg branches …).'
>
> – *SORP 2005, Glossary GL 6*

*To this, of course, we must now add the proviso 'and for the public benefit' from the Charities Act 2006!

The local branch of a national charity is the kind of 'branch' most frequently encountered in practice, but in legal terms this kind is normally only an 'internal division' of the national charity itself. Only where the local branch has its own *separate constitution* (this must normally be in writing, and is often in a standard form agreed between the national charity and Charity Commission), is it then (unless it is *autonomous* enough for the Commission to direct that the local charity is to be self-accounting under Part VI of the 1993 Act) the national charity's 'charity branch' (or 'branch-charity') – to be accounted for as such. But there are other kinds as well, and these are reviewed in the rest of this section.

Accounting for local branches

The basic rule is that these *non-autonomous* local branches must be included in the accounts of the national charity. All branch transactions should be accounted for gross within the national charity's accounts wherever restricted funds are involved. All their assets and liabilities should also be included in the national charity's balance sheet. In so doing, due regard must be had to charity law restrictions governing the permissible uses of all these local branch funds according to any legally binding wishes – express or implied – of the donors.

The effect of this treatment is to include branches as parts (divisions) of the whole. Many charities operate divisions or departments concerned with specific areas or activities within the charity's overall Objects. To ensure their finances are properly monitored, *divisional* budgets and management accounts are normally prepared. A similar approach needs to be adopted for branches of all kinds.

Practical difficulties for branch-accounting – the problem of identification

There is often a degree of confusion when it comes to identifying charity branches for entity-accounting (as distinct from group-accounting) purposes. The characteristics described in the SORP's Glossary (see below) will help to ensure the proper identification of all charity branches. Often the key lies in whether the local organisation has its own established legal identity and separate trustees. If it does, it is more likely that it is a separately accountable charity in its own right. Each individual case, however, needs careful assessment.

In addition to applying the various SORP 'tests' to establish whether there is or is not a charity branch, charities with locally managed activities should also establish procedures to ensure they are kept informed about everything being done in their name locally. It frequently occurs that self-appointed supporter groups have set up activities to fundraise in the name of the main charity, and the charity has only become aware of their existence at a much later date.

This has often involved the opening of bank accounts in the main charity's name, a common difficulty for the larger *multi-cellular* national charities in this country. Such charities should try to establish closer working links with the local branches they have set up, and to look out for any organisations appearing to be operating in their name in the localities in which they work. This could ensure that the charity's integrity is not compromised, and that the trustees have proper control over any funds given for the charity or raised in its name and held by others.

'Known as branches'

In some cases, separate legal entities are set up and referred to as branches of the founding charity. However, because they have their own legal identity and do not meet the definition of a branch (or a special trust of the main charity), they may be liable to prepare their own annual report and accounts – certainly if they are either companies or 'connected charities' – see below.

Separate incorporation as a limited company

Some local branches have a separate legal identity or 'personality' of their own, for example, where the branch has been set up as a limited company. For branch-accounting purposes, it should be noted that a charitable company as such cannot, under s 97(1) of the 1993 Act, be a 'special trust', and the Charity Commission will normally be reluctant to unite ('link') it with a parent charitable company under s 96(5) or (6) of the 1993 Act, since *charitable company* entity accounts as such are prepared not under Part VI but under the Companies Act, thus losing one of the main benefits of such an arrangement: savings in accounts preparation and audit. For financial years starting after 31 March 2008 any such subsidiary charitable company must then be included in the parent charity's statutory group consolidated accounts, as long as it meets the 'control plus benefit' test, which is the same under Charities and Companies Acts – see below.

Funds not remitted to the main charity at the balance sheet date

Funds may be collected by a branch but not remitted to the main charity at the balance sheet date. This is less often seen nowadays, as many charities organise bank 'sweeps' to ensure funds are passed to the main bank account, usually at the month end. Where funds are collected, but not remitted, they should of course be included in the main charity's balance sheet.

Fund-accounting requirements

Care is also needed to ensure that the proper division of funds between unrestricted, restricted and endowment is maintained at the branches. Branches may themselves receive funds to be spent in a specific area, and when these funds are included in the main charity balance sheet they must fall within restricted funds. The same situation usually applies where the branch is a separate legal entity.

How to get the information

Due to the administrative difficulties involved, until forced to do so in the mid-1990s by the SORP and its related Regulations many charities had not included the activities and funds of branches in their accounts at all. They may also have been reliant on the goodwill of local volunteers and treasurers to organise these local branches and activities to raise funds. There is always a delicate balance to be maintained in making sure that the required information is received whilst not overburdening such people or being too overbearing about it. The result can all too easily be a loss of their goodwill and perhaps of substantial future funding for the charity's work in that locality.

The most effective way of ensuring that branch organisations understand the need to provide the necessary accounting information is to organise meetings of branch treasurers at which to explain the reporting requirements and the regulatory regime to which all are subject under the 1993 Act. With their assistance, standard return-forms for branch-reporting can be drawn up. This method ensures proper consultation and allows problems to be resolved at the earliest possible stage. In this connection the specific trustee-duty imposed on both parties by the new Sch 5A (Group Accounts) inserted into the 1993 Act is worth citing:

> **'Accounting records**
>
> 2(1)   The charity trustees—
>
> (a)   of a parent charity, or
> (b)   of any charity which is a subsidiary undertaking,
>
> must ensure that the accounting records kept in respect of the charity ... are such as to enable the charity trustees of the parent charity to ensure that, where any group accounts are prepared by them under paragraph 3(2), those accounts comply with the relevant requirements.'
>
> *– Charities Act 1993, Sch 5A*

Materiality

As with all other areas of the Charities SORP, it is necessary to bear in mind that if the activities of branches are immaterial to the charity as a whole, they need not be included. This removes the potential for high cost, low return situations where only a few small branches or supporter groups operate.

Branches generally

Although (apart from the special case of a charity for investment pooling, legally known as a CIF) charity law does not permit *equity* interests (ie proprietary participation) in a charity, there are a number of ways in which two charities can be so closely related that the consolidated accounts requirements of the Charities Act 1993 or the Companies Act 2006 will apply – unless of course either the 1993 Act itself or the Charity

Commission as empowered by that Act already requires the subordinate charity, in the public interest, to be accounted for as a 'charity branch' of the 'main' reporting charity – thus in its *entity* accounts.

The control relationship for this purpose is defined by paragraph 390 of the SORP in one of two possible ways:

(a)   *[trustee-control]* 'the charity trustees and/or members and/or employees of the parent charity are, or have the right to appoint or remove, a majority of the charity trustees of the subsidiary charity';

(b)   *[founder's rights]* 'the governing document of the subsidiary charity reserves to the parent charity's trustees and/or members the right to direct, or to give consent to, the exercise of significant discretions by the trustees of the subsidiary charity'.

– SORP 2005, paragraph 390

SORP 2005 qualifies what SORP 2000 defined as a third kind of control relationship (one peculiar to the charity sector), and which it had described in the following terms:

'(c)   *[objects-control]* 'the objects of the subsidiary charity are substantially or exclusively confined to the benefit of the parent charity.'

The SORP no longer uses the words 'subsidiary' and 'parent' in this situation, where at paragraph 392 it says you must first look for *'dominant influence being exercised'* if a relationship for *consolidated accounts* is to be established – though of course that will be quite unnecessary where a *non-company* charity is a 'special trust' of another charity under s 97(1) of the 1993 Act, in which case it will be treated as a charity branch (see above) unless the Charity Commission directs otherwise in the public interest.

For administrative convenience, the 1993 Act provides for the whole set of such closely related charities to be accounted for as distinct parts ('restricted' funds) of what has come to be known as a 'multi-cellular' charity. Hence the fund-accounting provisions of the Charities SORP, which take precedence over the group consolidation requirements of the Charities Act 1993 for parity with company law. As already mentioned, nearly a sixth of the charities on the Register are accounted for as charity branches by this means.

The SORP's Glossary definition offers a number of criteria to help determine 'when is a branch not a branch' for charity accounting purposes:

'"Branches" ... may also be known as supporters' groups, friends' groups, members' groups, communities or parishes which are part of a common trust etc ... They may or may not be legal entities which are separate from the reporting charity. For the purpose of this SORP a "branch" is either:

(a)   simply part ... of the reporting charity; or
(b)   ...
  (i)   a ["special trust" under Charities Act 1993, s 97(1) – see below]; or,
  (ii) [a "deemed" subsidiary charity under a s 96(5)/(6) "uniting" direction made by the Charity Commission – see below] ...

...

Some of the characteristics of a branch are:

(i)   it uses the name of the reporting charity within its title;

(ii)   it exclusively raises funds for the reporting charity and/or for its own local activities;

(iii) it uses the reporting charity's registration number to receive tax relief on its activities;

(iv) it is perceived by the public to be the reporting charity's local representative or its representative for a particular purpose;

(v)   it receives support from the reporting charity through advice, publicity materials, etc.

If the branch exists to carry out the primary objects of the charity, typically it will receive funds from the reporting charity for its work and may be staffed by employees of the reporting charity.

If the branch is not a separate legal entity, all funds held by a branch will be the legal property of the reporting charity, whether or not the branch has a separate bank account.

Organisations which are not branches

Some charities may be known as "branches" ... but if their ... administrative autonomy ... as determined by their constitutions ... requires them to be treated as separate accounting entities, then they should not be regarded as "branches" for accounting purposes ... Such "branches" may also be subsidiaries.

Other examples of organisations which are not "branches" for the purpose of these recommendations include:

(a)   groups of people who occasionally gather together to raise funds for one or a number of different charities, and

(b)   special interest groups who are affiliated to a particular charity, but do not themselves undertake charitable activities (including fundraising for the charity).'

– *SORP 2005, Glossary GL 4*

'Main' and 'linked' charity status for branch-accounting

14.1.3 The 'reporting charity' is the actual (or else deemed) 'main' charity, while its 'linked' charities (as determined by the Charity Commission) are its 'charity branches' that have no public accountability of their own under the 1993 Act even though they will also have their own statutory accounts in the case of a controlled charitable company. Most linked charities are *trusts* declared during the founder's lifetime or by will, or by a corporate *founding* body of some kind, or even perhaps by the reporting charity itself – if constitutionally empowered to do so. However, it is equally possible for them to be societies or associations. These may be unincorporated or (more rarely) incorporated as a charitable company. (Charities constituted by Royal Charter or Act of Parliament will invariably be 'main' charities.)

Since the introduction of charity regulation in the mid-1990s, Charity Commission policy has been to harmonise (where possible) the registration and accounting status of each charity on the Register. The branch or 'linked' charity will then usually carry the same registration number as its main (controlling) charity, but with the addition of a unique suffix, and its governing document(s) will be kept on the public record file of the main charity that accounts for it. This makes it easier for the Commission to limit its Annual Return forms to *main* charities only, and to avoid collecting unnecessary separate accounts from linked charities already included as branches in their main charity's statutory accounts.

In practice, however, many old registrations – some going back to the early 1960s – still retain their original numbering, which has not been changed after all to reflect the Commission's current policy for branch-accounting. To confuse things further, experience to date suggests that thousands of registered charities have taken on subsidiary charitable trusts over the years without ever realising that the duty to register applies to these as well, so as they have never notified them to the Commission these do not appear on the Register at all.

Although Part VI of the 1993 Act makes the 'main' charity's trustees publicly accountable for its branch charities, thus requiring any *independent* body of trustees separately administering such a branch charity to report via 'branch returns' to the main body of trustees for annual accounting purposes and not directly to the public, this obligation does not in any way reduce the administrative legal powers and responsibilities of the subsidiary charity's trustees, nor does it constrain the exercise of their discretion in deciding how best to use their charity's resources within the bounds of its declared Objects.

SORP compliance

To summarise, the Charities SORP basically requires:

(a)   *entity accounts* to include *all* (material) charity branches and controlled charities that are deemed to be branches on the above basis; *and*

(b)   *group accounts* to consolidate the reporting charity's interests in *all other* material subsidiary undertakings, distinguishing (for the subsidiaries – but not, strange to say, for the reporting charity's interests in any joint venture, consortium and associated undertakings, which we discuss below) between activities primarily:
   (i)   to further the reporting charity's Objects for the public benefit; or
   (ii)   to generate funds;
   – except that 'small' groups (gross income up to the statutory audit threshold of £500,000) are exempted under SORP 2005 and the 1993 Act from any requirement to prepare consolidated accounts, since they will not normally be of any great public interest even in the charity sector, where the threshold of public interest is nowhere near as high as it is in the profit sector.

In this, priority must always be given to the charity's *entity* accounts, with any consolidated accounts required by the legislation and the SORP *added* – not substituted. But there are some special cases to be noted, as below.

'Special trusts' and other connected charities under the Charities Act 1993

14.1.4   'Special trust' is an example of terminology peculiar to charity accounting. The definition in s 97(1) of the 1993 Act is:

> 'property [funds] ... held and administered by or on behalf of a charity for any special purposes of the charity, and ... so held and administered on separate trusts relating only to that property [those funds] ...'.

The sub-section goes on to declare that:

'... a special trust shall not, by itself, constitute a charity for ... Part VI of this Act.'

– *Charities Act 1993, s 97(1)*

This means that a 'special trust' cannot be a *main* charity unless for public interest reasons its trustees were (exceptionally) to be made publicly accountable for it under a 'Disuniting' Direction from the Charity Commission under s 96(5) of the 1993 Act. It therefore *automatically* follows that it must normally be accounted for as a *restricted fund* (endowed or unendowed according to its terms – see below) by the main charity to which its Objects point.

Where the special trust has different trustees, their *independence* and *control* over it is unaffected by this 'non-public' or branch accountability.

The founding of a 'restricted' fund

Whereas *un*restricted (ie general-purpose) funds may arise from:

(i)   voluntary sources; or

(ii)   the investment income of the charity's general-purpose capital funds; or

(iii) the investment income/gains of its *un*restricted funds; or

(iv)   trading with the latter,

'*restricted*' funds can normally only arise from *voluntary* sources in order to recognise the legally binding wishes or intentions of a *founding donor* – meaning one whose gift cannot except on special authority be merged with any existing fund of the charity, because the uniqueness of its terms of trust necessitate its separate administration.

Such a gift is then said to have a different 'foundation' from that of any other fund of the charity, and does in fact constitute a distinct charitable institution – even when administered as a restricted fund within the larger charity. Legally speaking, it will be its 'branch charity' for accounting purposes, as explained above. Whatever else is then earned from the use of any such restricted fund, or added to it by subsequent donors, will normally be subject to those same restrictions.

English law allows the founder of any new charitable trust the greatest possible latitude to be able to determine how the founding gift and everything subsequently added to it may be used – but only to the extent that the rules for this have been declared at the outset, meaning before the gift is 'perfected' (made). Once that takes place, the newly executed trust deed or other governing document stands on its own, and any legal powers not already reserved to the founder can no longer be claimed under charity law.

The members for the time being of a charitable association (unincorporated or incorporated) are somewhat akin to founders – but with one big difference. Except where provided otherwise (eg a charter body or an association governed by a founding trust), and subject to the constraints of Part VIII of the 1993 Act for charitable companies, they normally enjoy undiminished legal power to make their own rules and regulations.

Others are better placed to expand on this fascinating aspect of charity creation and administration (eg, Tudor, Picarda, Luxton). Here, we only need to note that, as an infrequent exception to the normal rule, the trustees of a charitable trust may have been empowered at the outset by the *founder* to set up their own special-purpose funds out of unrestricted funds by declaring irrevocable legal restrictions on their use. Such changes then have to be recognised as inter-fund transfers in the SoFA and explained accordingly in the notes.

The endowing of a charitable company

'General-purpose' endowments do not meet the above definition, so cannot be special trusts – except where they are given to a charitable company, of course. They merely constitute the capital part of the (non-company) charity's general-purpose funds (their distinction *as capital* being their only restriction) – the income part being its *un*restricted funds. This applies regardless of how the charity so endowed has been constituted – even if as a charitable company, though in that case the capital part will, as noted, be a special trust, whereas the income part will not (it counts as *corporate* funds).

Very few charitable companies are incorporated with a *share capital*. For obvious reasons, this will always be 'non-participating', meaning that the shareholder can only be reimbursed the capital originally subscribed. Somewhat like the old system of pre-paying covenanted donations, such capital is really akin to an interest-free permanent loan from the members, and must not be confused with the *charity capital* with which the company may be <u>endowed</u> by donors as part of its *trust* funds.

'Connected charities' that the Commission may deem charity branches under s 96(5)–(6)

These sub-sections of the 1993 Act empower the Charity Commissioners to 'direct that for all or any purposes' of the Act:

s 96(5)	an institution established for any special (charitable) purposes
	of or in connection with a charity …
	shall be treated as forming part of that charity, *<Uniting Direction>*
	or as forming a distinct charity;*<Disuniting Direction>*
s 96(6)	two or more charities having the same trustees
	shall be treated as a single charity. *<Uniting Direction>*

'Subsidiary undertaking' for consolidation purposes

14.1.5   Wherever the reporting charity has 'subsidiary' undertakings, all interests in the *non-charitable* undertakings can *only* be accounted for in *consolidated* accounts, which are covered at the end of this chapter.

Regardless of whether consolidated accounts are prepared, however, any material interests in *associated* undertakings, charitable *or* non-charitable (meaning those under externally *shared* control), must at present be accounted for in accordance with the completely unmodified commercial requirements of FRS9 – also covered there.

The SORP defines all such interests by reference to the reporting charity's exercise of 'dominant influence' – which, in line with EC Directives, UK company law (and therefore FRS2/9) and now charity law, it now uses instead of the old concept of 'participation' (thus a 'participating interest') enabling the reporting entity to obtain economic or other benefit for itself from its exercise of such influence either alone (a 'subsidiary') or with others (an 'associate').

Paragraph 388 of the SORP says:

> 'Subsidiary undertakings can be identified by the measure of control (Glossary GL 44) exercised by the parent charity. FRS 2 outlines how such control can be determined in the context of:
>
> (a)   voting rights (mainly stemming from share ownership) and/or
> (b)   dominant influence over the board or activities of the subsidiary.'

– SORP 2005, paragraph 388

This is amplified in the Glossary definition as 'Control requires that the parent can both direct and derive benefit from the subsidiary'. What is implicit here is surely that the deriving must be active, ie, through subordination – not merely passive as with a charity beneficiary. As a 'public interest' case in point here, new guidance on the Charity Commission website ('Maintaining independence' – guidance for corporate trustees and trustee bodies managing NHS charitable funds, 27 August 2009) reminds charity trustees that independence from government control is intrinsic to charitable status, so that it would not expect NHS *charities* as such to be included in the group consolidated accounts of an NHS body, as that would imply administration of the charity under Ministerial instructions, which would be misleading. The same argument must logically deny consolidation in respect of the many land-holding charities under trustee-control by their Local Authority, either as a sole corporate trustee or through its Councillors being a majority of the charity trustees, of course.

Surprisingly, the SORP continues to ignore the case where a charity above the £500,000 statutory audit threshold but with *no* eligible subsidiaries for consolidation nevertheless has interests in corporate joint ventures or consortium/associated undertakings – see **14.3**. The exceptional case, as provided for in paragraph 48 of FRS9, requires that such a charity:

> '... should present the relevant amounts for associates and joint ventures, as appropriate, by preparing a separate set of financial statements or by showing the relevant amounts, together with the effects of including them, as additional information to its own financial statements.'

– FRS9, paragraph 48

The SORP definitions of 'subsidiary undertaking' and 'participating interest' seek to bridge across to that commercially oriented definition:

'Parent Undertaking and Subsidiary Undertaking

In relation to a charity, an undertaking is the parent undertaking of another undertaking, called a subsidiary undertaking, where the charity controls the subsidiary. Control requires that the parent can both direct and derive benefit from the subsidiary.

(a)   Direction is achieved if the charity or its trustees:
      (i)   hold or control the majority of the voting rights, or

(ii)   have the right to appoint or remove a majority of the board of directors or trustees of the subsidiary undertaking, or

(iii) have the power to exercise, or actually exercise, a dominant influence over the subsidiary undertaking, or

(iv)   manage the charity and the subsidiary on a unified basis.

For a fuller definition, reference should be made to sections 258 and 259 Companies Act 1985.

(b)   Benefit derived can either be economic benefit that results in a net cash inflow to the charity or can arise through the provision of goods or services to the benefit of the charity *or its beneficiaries*.' (emphasis added)

– SORP 2005, Glossary GL 44

This is now reinforced by the 1993 Act's Sch 5A, where parent and subsidiary status are defined by reference to the 1985 Act:

'(2)   A charity is a "parent charity" if it is (or is to be treated as) a parent undertaking in relation to one or more other undertakings in accordance with the provisions of section 258 of, and Schedule 10A to, the Companies Act 1985.

(3)   Each undertaking in relation to which a parent charity is (or is to be treated as) a parent undertaking in accordance with those provisions is a "subsidiary undertaking" in relation to the parent charity.'

– Charities Act 1993, Sch 5A, para 1

The SORP's definition was considerably widened from that in SORP 2000 for the sake of a closer fit with company law and commercial accounting standards, partly by changing the legal *right* to exercise dominant influence in (iii) to any situation where it either could be or in practice is exercised, but also by adding in at (iv) the *management in common* that is also one of two criteria for the Glossary definition of 'connected charities' (GL 9) but cannot apply to a charity's use of a *non-charitable* subsidiary, due to charity law constraints.

In (b), inserted in order to explain how a charity '*can … derive benefit from the subsidiary*' in order to qualify as its 'parent', the words we have emphasised could be problematical because they stretch the meaning of self-interested 'economic benefit' on which commercial accounting standards are predicated to make it include the altruism that is intrinsic to the charity sector but foreign to the profit sector. They are redundant unless the subsidiary is a charity, which if used by the parent charity for the furtherance of its own Objects to provide public benefit is classed here as providing *self-benefit* – thus the very opposite of the public benefit test to be applied under the Charities Act 2006.

Furthermore, '*participating interest*' as a factor in defining an associated undertaking has been eliminated. It is now used only as part of the SORP's 'related parties' definition:

'"**Participating interest**" means that the charity:

(a)   is interested in shares comprised in the *equity* share capital of the body of a nominal value of more than one fifth of that share capital; or

(b)   is entitled to exercise or control the exercise of more than *one-fifth of the voting power* at any general meeting of that body.' (emphasis added)

– SORP 2005, Glossary GL 26

Having been drawn from the commercial sector, these definitions all presuppose the usual ulterior motive of exploiting another entity for one's own economic benefit – so that in cases where some legal or operational impediment makes that impossible the reporting charity must logically be able to claim exemption, as explained below. But it can also happen that *charitable* undertakings have to be accounted for in the same way under the SORP's revised definition.

Consolidation is the only way if subsidiary and parent are charitable companies

In this case, although the subsidiary company could well be dealt with as a charity branch (if so required by the Commission) within a single *annual report* prepared and filed under s 45 of the 1993 Act, the *entity accounts* of the parent, as a company, are *excluded* from ss 41–44 of the 1993 Act. Under the 1985 and 2006 Companies Acts, each company must prepare statutory accounts in any case, but these can only be required for filing with the Commission from the parent – not from the subsidiary, if registered as a branch charity. To bridge the gap, the Commission can only look for the subsidiary's accounts to be *consolidated* (as a statutory requirement, if the group exceeds the charity audit threshold) with those of its parent company as the 'main' charity, since it has no power to require branch-accounting in such a case. This situation is covered by paragraphs 383(d) and 386–387 of the SORP.

Consortium (joint-venture) charitable undertakings – unless 'united' under Charities Act 1993, s 96(5)

Charities may work together for a time on charitable projects too large for any one of them to work on alone. For *ongoing* situations of this kind where there is no intention of merging, the projects are often best undertaken by a separate but *connected charity* (e g as a limited company). This will normally be set up for loan financing (now to be accounted for under SORP 2005 as a 'social investment' by the reporting charity – see chapter 9) and/or deficit-funding by grants from the consortium members, with control being shared (ie, in common rather than by any one of them individually) – though for charity registration reasons it may be much quicker and easier to set it up as a *non-charitable* company.

Unfortunately, the rules of FRS9 as interpreted by the Charities SORP for including in the consolidated (or else the entity) SoFA all interests in corporate joint ventures (*charitable* as well as *non-charitable* ones – see the end of this chapter) are totally inadequate for a true and fair view in respect of the *charitable* projects.

Where the figures cannot be ignored as immaterial, it may therefore be preferable to argue that, given the necessary absence of any beneficial proprietary interest in their consortium undertaking if it happens to be a *charity*, FRS9 cannot apply[1] to it, and that in any case its *consolidation* or equivalent treatment in the way required by the Charities

---

[1]   FRS9's inapplicability to charitable undertakings that are registered as 'main' charities (and as such are required by charity law to be independently administered in their own best interests) can be seen from the following quotations from the relevant paragraphs of FRS9:

'11 Joint control, like control itself, is a relationship that has a benefit aspect. The venturers exercise their joint control for their mutual benefit, each conducting its part of the contractual arrangement with a view to its own benefit.

12 The effect of the requirement in the definition for consent to high-level strategic decisions of joint control is to give each venturer a veto on such decisions. This veto is what distinguishes a joint venturer from a

SORP would actually *impair* a true and fair view of the totality of their respective charitable activities in the accounts of each of the consortium members.

For a solution that would clearly be more appropriate to the charity sector, even though not mentioned in the Charities SORP, the consortium members could agree to ask the Charity Commission for a s 96(5) uniting direction under which the consortium *charitable* undertaking will be 'linked' on the Charities Register with (ie treated as a *subsidiary charity* in the entity accounts of) a designated consortium member (the lead charity). All the others can then treat it as a 'connected charity', to be disclosed by way of note in their accounts.

Thus the SORP basically requires consolidated accounts where the charity has non-charitable subsidiary undertakings, but branch-accounting where the subsidiary undertaking is a charity – unless both are charitable companies, when consolidated accounts are the only solution. If the group then becomes too complex to monitor properly, the Charity Commission can always unravel it by issuing a 'dis-uniting direction' under s 96(5) of the 1993 Act to separate the two charities whose activities it cannot otherwise discern for regulatory purposes.

'CONNECTED CHARITIES'

14.2   The definition offered in the SORP's Glossary is:

> '"Connected charities" are those which have common, parallel or related objects and activities; and either:
>
> (a)   common control; or
> (b)   unity of administration (eg, shared management).
>
> Within this category may be charities which come together under one umbrella organisation or are part of a federal structure ...'.
>
> *– SORP 2005, Glossary GL 9*

The reader is then referred to the 'related parties' definition at GL 50, which explains that:

> '*Common control* exists if:
>
> (i)   the same person or persons have the right to appoint a majority of the charity trustees of both or all the charities; or
> (ii)   the same person or persons hold a majority of the voting rights in the administration of both or all of the charities.

---

minority [shareholder] ...
13 One of the conditions for an investment to qualify as an associate is that its investor should have a participating interest.
14 For an investment to be an associate, its investor must exercise significant influence over the investee's operating and financial policies.'

> Persons who are related with each other through family or business relationships should be treated as the same person for the present purposes.'

– *SORP 2005, Glossary GL 50.1(d)*

Connected charities as such may or may not have to be accounted for as branches by the reporting charity. Branch-accounting applies (in England and Wales) only where they are 'special trusts' of it or, as explained above, for so long as they are deemed controlled (ie, unable to break away from the connection unilaterally) and therefore linked to it on the Charities Register by means of a Charity Commission 'uniting direction' under s 96(5) or (6) of the 1993 Act for accounting purposes (and therefore also normally for registration purposes). Under the Scottish charity accounting regulations, branch-accounting is optional for connected charities – see **14.3.8**, below.

Often the existence of a connection with an 'umbrella charity' is easy to confirm, since the close liaison between them will make it clear that an association or affiliation of some kind exists. Such connections only need to be noted in the accounts.

It is less clear when there is an indirect connection, particularly where the connection is established through family membership or business. Trustees must investigate and establish such connections and ensure that the correct treatment is applied.

The question of whether the connected charity is subordinate and must therefore be included in the accounts of the reporting charity can also be problematical, but trustees must examine the way in which the charity operates, and what the consequences of the decisions of the trustees in respect of that charity are:

–   Do they refer to the main charity?

–   Are the trustees the same people?

–   Are all the decisions made with the needs of the main charity in mind?

Identification of the precise legal status of old charitable trusts

The statutory regime of *regulated* public accountability since the mid-1990s has resulted in many situations where old charitable trusts are being accounted for as part of the charity (often where previously excluded) without any clear knowledge of the different restrictions that might still attach to them under charity law and must therefore be observed and accounted for.

Full compliance with charity law in such cases, including the proper segregation of the assets of these trust funds, entails researching the charity's old records – certainly for the last 6 (3, for a limited company) complete financial years, more if available. Solicitors' records pertaining to these charitable trusts, as well as the public records of the Charity Commission and also the Land and Probate Registries, etc, should also be consulted for any available indications of the donors' intentions at the time.

Any remaining uncertainties as to the precise nature of the restrictions attaching to assets known to have been acquired from voluntary sources can then be resolved by taking the most sensible decision in the best interests of the charity and its beneficiaries and recording this as a trustees' minute.

Where the financial values are significant, for charities in England and Wales this decision should be supported and protected by a request for formal advice from the Charity Commission under the 1993 Act, s 29. It is interesting to note that such statutory help and support for charity trustees is not available for Scottish charities.

CONSOLIDATED ACCOUNTS

14.3   The SORP's requirements for the consolidation of subsidiaries in accordance with FRS2 and also (whether or not consolidated accounts are required by law) for adding in the group's share of the activities and net assets of associates, etc, in accordance with FRS9, are collected together as paragraphs 381–418. The main effect on the SoFA is simply and automatically to enforce the *line-by-line* consolidation of the charitable and non-charitable activities of the group in respect of *subsidiaries* – but unfortunately not of corporate joint-ventures, consortium undertakings and other associates, as explained below.

However, it is important to note from the outset that SORP 2005, and now the Charities Act 1993 with effect for all financial years starting after 31 March 2008, provides a 'blanket' exemption for all groups below (in aggregate) the charity gross income threshold (currently £500,000) for statutory audit – a considerable relaxation of the stringent consolidation rules of the original 1995 SORP, which had allowed no such general size-based exemption.

Thus, the SORP and the 1993 Act override the Companies Act consolidation exemptions for small groups here in the public interest by setting a lower threshold (£500,000 gross income instead of what is now £6.5m turnover for companies).

For most charities, with only one such subsidiary, usually a 'shell', wholly owned and donating all its taxable profits to the charity, (slightly more) careful structuring of the SoFA may still allow consolidated accounts to be avoided where – as is nearly always the case – the balance sheets of the charity and group are virtually identical. That is an administrative saving still largely unnoticed by the accountancy profession, with most auditors turning a blind eye to the preparation of group consolidated accounts that are materially no different from the charity's entity accounts!

Omission of the entity SoFA in consolidated accounts for a charitable company

Since charitable companies' own accounts are prepared not under Part VI but under the 1985 Act (or now its successor, the Companies Act 2006), which also governs their publication, Charity Commission policy has always been not to reject their *statutory* consolidated accounts if submitted for filing without an 'entity' activity statement – provided the activities of the parent company *as a charity* are clearly discernible in the consolidated SoFA and/or the notes. This is not too difficult to achieve where profit-stripping donations remit substantially all the *non-charitable* trading subsidiaries' net profits for the year to the parent charity, but it is rather more involved where *charitable* activities are carried out by *non-charitable* subsidiaries as well.

The Commission's policy and practice here, as embodied in the SORP, has now been tightened up by specifically requiring the key (charity total) figures from the entity SoFA of the *parent* to be set out in the consolidated accounts' notes. By 'key' figures the Charity Commission means gross incoming resources, costs of generating funds, costs of charitable activities and of governance, the net result of these, net gains/losses and total funds movement for the year. However, this can't be instead of equivalent information on subsidiaries – especially where the parent is a charitable company, as it then has to comply with the Companies Act disclosure requirements for subsidiaries in any case.

One other way to make the necessary distinction for the Commission would be to devote a column of the SoFA to either the parent charity or the rest of the group – unless both have restricted funds, when an accounts note will be needed.

Wherever the consolidated accounts *'obscure information about the different undertakings and [their] activities'*, then paragraph 405 of the SORP says that:

> '... segmental information may need to be provided ... It is important that the presentation adopted and disclosure in the notes is sufficiently detailed to distinguish the key results of the charity from those of its subsidiary undertakings. Examples of those items that should be separately disclosed include the costs of generating funds, management and administration and the costs of charitable activities.'
>
> – *SORP 2005, paragraph 405*

Omission of the entity SoFA in consolidated accounts for a non-company charity

Under Part VI of the 1993 Act and its 2005 accounting and reporting Regulations, ie, for financial years starting before April 2008, only the entity SoFA and related balance sheet have had *statutory* validity, with the consolidated SoFA being only a *'best practice'* add-on for a wider true and fair view of the charity group's financial resources and their utilisation.

The lack of any provision at all for consolidated accounts prior to the SORP's 2008 Regulations taking effect was the natural consequence of the 1993 Act's overriding concern prior to the Charities Act 2006 to ensure that anybody administering a charity can be called to account *personally* for the proper application of its resources for their declared purpose of providing public benefit.

For that purpose, the 1993 Act had already made full and adequate provision via *branch-accounting* as described above for the accountability of all controlled *charitable* undertakings, and therefore had had no need to make provision for group accounts dealing with the reporting charity's *non-charitable* interests, since these were seen as adequately supervised as investment vehicles – for which there are special rules to minimise risk to the charity – or else they were regarded as just another means of furthering the charity's Objects through a third party. The fact that this is some kind of 'controlled' third party actually makes no difference to the personal liability of the trustees under charity law for the 'proper application' of any resources of their charity made available to this third party (as a non-charity) other than by way of investment.

Nevertheless, long before the Charities Act 2006 added provision for consolidated accounts to Part VI of the 1993 Act, the SORP has committed the ever-pragmatic

Charity Commission to a conditional acceptance of such a substitution (which had already become common practice in the sector) regardless of whether or not the accounts are for a charitable company:

> '... consolidated accounts are often filed with the Commission omitting the Statement of Financial Activities for the parent charity. The Commission is prepared to accept these accounts as long as the gross income/turnover and results of the parent charity are clearly disclosed in the notes. The group accounts must still contain the entity balance sheet of the parent charity. The Commission retains the power to require the production and filing of any individual charity Statement of Financial Activities and similarly members of the public have a legal right to request this statement.'
>
> – *SORP 2005, paragraph 397*

For that purpose, it is necessary here, too, to distinguish *the financial activities (ie incoming resources, expenditure, gains/losses) of the reporting charity* from those of the rest of the group – also especially where subsidiaries/associates, etc, are used to carry out *mixed* activities that are partly charitable and partly non-charitable, as is frequently the case.

General exemptions under the Charities SORP

14.3.1 Where the original 1995 SORP had imposed a blanket requirement to consolidate without regard to the size of the group, SORP 2000 replaced the FRS2 exemption for 'small' groups with a much lower one geared to the 1993 Act threshold for compulsory audit: then £250,000 gross income but now £500,000. This level effectively restricts the consolidation requirement to the top 9,000[+] charities currently on the Charities Register.

'Quasi-subsidiaries' (if you can find one)

Paragraph 389 of the SORP mentions what to many in the charity sector must seem a hypothetical requirement, by reference to FRS5 (Substance over Form), to consolidate the accounts of any 'quasi-subsidiaries' – defined as those where the relationship is such that *'all the risks and rewards of the transactions remain with'* the reporting charity.

The example given in the SORP is of a transfer of the ownership of assets that are to remain subject to the transferor's own exclusive use and to maintenance at the transferor's own expense. It is difficult to imagine what advantage such a transfer could bring to the transferor as a *charity*, regulated as an institution set up to serve the public interest, so that one cannot help wondering why such an esoteric and unusual arrangement merits even a mention.

Non-charitable associates and 'corporate joint ventures'

14.3.2 By analogy with the consolidation of non-charitable subsidiaries, one would have expected the Charities SORP to require the consolidation of the charity group's share of *non-charitable* associated and consortium undertakings (or *corporate joint ventures*) to distinguish in the SoFA between funds and activities that are wholly or mainly (ie primarily):

(a)   to further the reporting charity's own Objects; or alternatively

(b)   to raise funds for its benefit.

The constraints imposed on charities by charity law would surely justify modifying the application of FRS9 to require the SoFA to include the group's (or charity's) share of the gross revenues and costs of *charitable activities* (those under (a) above) using the line-by-line method (even if, in deference to the purist argument that the net of these figures, being in respect of *non-controlled* entities (ie, those where control needs external consent) must first be taken out from the group 'net result' for the year before adding it back in below that line in the SoFA), while keeping to FRS9's equity and gross equity methods respectively in the balance sheet.

Unfortunately, paragraph 413 of SORP 2005 instead applies FRS9's 'net equity' method to the SoFA consolidation without regard to the nature of the reporting charity and the activities of its associates. Such a treatment clearly conflicts with the rest of the SORP. It inappropriately constrains the charity sector with the commercial logic of ring-fencing profits earned but not yet distributable until brought under direct control – instead of catering instead for the fundamentally different motivation of charities, in which profit-distribution plays no part. This would have meant modifying the application of FRS9 to make it easy to present, in the public interest, the *wider picture* of all the charity's direct and indirect public benefit activities (ie those under sole *and* shared control) for charitable purposes as well as for the purpose of generating funds for itself (whether or not through non-charitable trading). Specifically, it calls instead for a 'single-line' SoFA presentation (*below* the line for [group] net incoming/outgoing resources) of the reporting charity's interest in the net results of *all* the trading activities (charitable and non-charitable alike) of these *associates*.

A *consistent* treatment would distinguish (a) and (b) above by showing separately for the charity group's share of the associates' charitable and other activities the:

(i)   turnover for inclusion in the 'incoming resources' section; and

(ii)   costs for inclusion in the relevant sub-sections of 'expenditure'.

Where the objectives-based classification of expenditure has to be used in the charity's entity SoFA, which means *all* auditable charities, the relevant sub-sections in the consolidated SoFA will obviously be 'costs of generating funds', 'costs of charitable activities' and expenditure on 'governance' as appropriate.

Much the same thing is done in paragraph 414, dealing with the charity/group's share of the turnover of the two possible kinds of trading activities (ie to further charitable Objects or to generate funds) through *corporate joint ventures* (consortium undertakings). Only the turnover is consolidated on a line-by-line basis as you would expect, but not the related costs – which are not included at all.

In particular, the fourth and fifth sentences of paragraph 414 again conflict with the SORP's 'transparency' principle by specifying:

(1)   a special line to eliminate the consolidated turnover figures for these ventures from group incoming resources; and then

(2)   the inclusion (lower down in the SoFA, as for associates) of the group share of total net results for this source.

Instead of (1) and (2), for consistency's sake this paragraph should have called for the line-by-line inclusion of the group share of the *costs* of these ventures so as to present a 'true and fair' view of *the grouping together of all the reporting charity's interests as if they were contained in a single entity*. The SORP compensates for not doing this by instead requiring more detailed analysis in the accounts notes – see **12.5**.

In the group (or else charity) balance sheet, whereas 'simple investment' interests in entities used for *non-charitable* purposes (ie to generate funds) must be shown at market value, interests in those used for undertaking *charitable* activities qualify for special treatment as 'social investment' assets (see chapter 9). Their recognition as such means that they can be shown on a historical cost basis plus the charity/group share of their retained income as recognised in the SoFA.

'Immaterial results' exemption

14.3.3 Paragraph 383(b) of the SORP recommends that where the '*results*' of subsidiary undertakings are not material to the group they need not be consolidated. Despite this, a great number of auditors and charity accountants still misread the SORP as requiring them to continue producing consolidated accounts that differ very little from the entity accounts.

That may be simply because 'results' for this purpose cannot be adequately judged only by reference to the subsidiary's net trading profit/loss. The SORP does make it clear that testing for materiality will normally involve comparing the charity's entity accounts with its proposed group accounts in respect of the 'result' of including in the latter the subsidiary's:

(i)   turnover;

(ii)   operating costs;

(iii)   assets; and

(iv)   liabilities.

It is only where *each* of these make little difference to the overall picture that an auditor can safely conclude that the 'results' are 'immaterial'. Where, as is often the case, it is only (i) that is material, by showing that figure (plus the related costs to derive the figure of net profit donated to the parent charity) as a prominent inset on the face of the SoFA, it is possible to rely on this ground to dispense with consolidated accounts entirely.

'Insolvent liquidation' exemption

14.3.4 Paragraph 385 of the SORP, in line with FRS2, only exempts an insolvent subsidiary company that has already been put into insolvent liquidation, but a far more common and equally deserving situation is where the subsidiary would be insolvent without the continuing financial support of the reporting charity.

If the promise of that support for the ensuing year is relied on by the subsidiary's auditors as justifying the preparation of its accounts on the going concern basis, then it could be argued that this exemption can hardly be invoked. For financial years starting after 31 March 2008 (or earlier adoption of the SORP's related 2008 Regulations) this is conditioned by a special disclosure under reg 41(2)(e), which says that the group report to be prepared by the parent charity's trustees must:

> 'where the total of capital and reserves in any of the parent charity's subsidiary undertakings was materially in deficit at the beginning of the financial year, contain particulars of the steps taken by the relevant undertaking or undertakings to eliminate that deficit'

– SI 2008/629, reg 41(2)(e)

To bridge the gap between these two situations, the SORP should (but doesn't) at least extend the exemption to include a subsidiary in or about to go into insolvent administration, thus without having to wait for the actual winding up decision. The obvious indicator for consolidation purposes is that its accounts are not prepared on the going concern basis, so that any unsecured interests in it will already have been written down in the reporting charity's own balance sheet and its inclusion would not materially change the group balance sheet.

'Incompatibility' and similar consolidation exemptions

14.3.5 The SORP is also unhelpful at paragraph 385 in merely commenting that the FRS2 consolidation exemption on grounds of 'incompatible activities' requires something more significant than just the difference between 'for-profit' and 'not-for-profit' undertakings. Apart from other 'incompatibility' situations, which experience shows are not quite as rare as the SORP suggests, there must also be reservations about the argument for consolidation where a charity has been placed in control (normally by endowment) of a substantial non-charitable trading company primarily as:

(a) an investment asset with the charity's policy being to refrain from any exercise of 'dominant influence' over the subsidiary's operating and financial management policies in case that might be to the detriment of other interested parties (employees; other investors) – which in other countries would be seen as a 'conflict of loyalties' in the extreme case requiring divestment action; or else

(b) a *social investment asset* (see chapter 9) the voting control over which facilitates or protects the furtherance of the charity's own Objects but in which the charity has little or no beneficial financial (equity) interest.

Situation (a) was exemplified by the Wellcome Foundation prior to the Glaxo-Wellcome merger in the late 1990s. Here, the parent charity typically regarded itself as merely a major investor and dealt at arm's length with its subsidiary, carefully refraining from influencing its management and operating policies – thus balancing its legal right to exercise dominant influence against its social responsibilities as a charity. In such circumstances, it is difficult to justify subjecting the charity parent to consolidation rules whose primary aim remains to regularise the profit-accounting of multi-national conglomerates and other major for-profit institutions!

The immateriality of the financial interest in case (b) and the special status it now has as a social investment (ie carried at historical cost less any 'impairment'), make it difficult to argue that consolidation of the subsidiary in question (as distinct from adequate disclosures) will in fact result in a truer and fairer view! It is therefore to be hoped that a future review of the Charities SORP will expand its guidance here to cover such charity-specific situations, which the FRS itself can hardly be expected to refer to.

'Severe long-term restrictions' exemption

14.3.6   Paragraph 384 of the SORP deals with the consolidation relief in the case where *'severe long-term restrictions substantially hinder'* the parent's control over its subsidiary to its own advantage or 'benefit' – such control being exercised either through membership voting rights or in some other way (eg a legal right to act in its own interests (regardless of those of the other entity) in appointing/removing the entity's directors or their equivalent, contractual exclusivity, etc). Again, the SORP unhelpfully dismisses this relief, asserting that *'it is unlikely that these exclusions will generally apply to a charitable group'.*

We should note here that the ground-rules for the parent/subsidiary relationship (as now inserted by the Charities Act 2006 into the 1993 Act as Sch 5A) were changed in recent years by company law reforms – principally by the Companies Act 1985 (International Accounting Standards and Other Accounting Amendments) Regulations 2004, SI 2004/2947, dated November 2004, affecting company accounts for financial years from January 2005. In particular, reg 12 of that SI amended s 258(4)(a) of the 1985 Act by deleting the criterion that along with legal control the parent *'has a participating interest in the undertaking'* and inserting instead the criterion that it either *'has the power to exercise, or actually exercises, dominant influence or control over [the undertaking]'* or (as an alternative) has legal control. This is the 'control plus benefit' test as now contained in Part 15 of the Companies Act 2006 as well as in Part VI of the Charities Act 1993.

This amended definition could fatally undermine the 'severe long-term restriction' argument hitherto relied upon by many a charity to justify its non-consolidation of a substantial family trading company where the charity has voting control but only a minority participating (usually – but not necessarily – equity) interest (if any) in it.

Quite apart from the general charity law duty of all charity trustees to administer only in the best interests of their own charity and *its* beneficiaries, what is not really explained properly and fully in the SORP is that the requirement to consolidate must exclude a 'controlled' *charity* within the meaning of paragraph 390(a) or (b) (ie where its trusteeship (a), or its discretionary power (b), is in some way governed by the reporting charity – as summarised at the end of **14.1.2** above) but where the controlled charity's Objects do **not** allow it to be used *to its own detriment* to benefit preferentially the parent charity itself or even to further the Objects of the parent charity more directly.

Here, the SORP ambiguously just comments in passing, without differentiating the lawful exercise of a controlling charity's discretionary power to give preference to itself as a member of the controlled charity's beneficiary class, or to its own Objects as a sub-set of the controlled charity's Objects, that:

> 'Where (unusually) a subsidiary charity's Objects are substantially different from the parent charity, the benefit test of control will not be met and so no consolidation should take place.'

– SORP 2005, paragraph 386

Instead, the SORP ignores these charity law constraints and requirements in order to focus in paragraph 390 on FRS2's exclusively commercial view of consolidation of a charity of any kind *'where the parent charity has the power to exercise, or actually exercises, dominant influence or control over the subsidiary or the parent and subsidiary are managed on a unified basis'*, hinting only at the end of paragraph 391 that *'where one of the relationships described in the previous paragraph exists ... trustees may, in a particular case, be able to produce evidence to the contrary'*.

Similarly, paragraph 408 says that where a charity has FRS9 entities 'consolidated accounts should be prepared subject to the exemptions in paragraph 383'. This does not mean quite what it says! The logic of the sentence is that if – and only if – you *do* prepare consolidated accounts (ie for a non-excluded subsidiary whose gross income brings the group figure over the £500,000 threshold), then you should also include these FRS9 entities, subject to those and FRS2's other exemptions – but not otherwise. However, the reporting charity's interest in the gross income of FRS9 entities does not count towards the threshold for a statutory audit or for consolidated accounts preparation. Moreover, FRS9 says they should all be included in the reporting entity's own accounts if no consolidated accounts are prepared in respect of it. And as the SORP has studiously avoided modifying the application of FRS9 in any way, the intention must be that a charity above the Charities Act's statutory audit threshold of £500,000 gross income should include its FRS9 interests either in its consolidated accounts or else in its own entity accounts. And furthermore if the whole set of exclusions is equally applicable to FRS2 and FRS9 entities, it must logically also, in this case, include immateriality due to 'severe long-term restrictions' of the same kind.

Disclosures required for subsidiaries, associates and consortia

14.3.7 The extensive disclosures called for by paragraph 417 of the SORP contrast sharply with the smaller set of disclosures required for (material) subsidiaries at paragraphs 401/403, being designed to supplement the accounts without any regard to the inclusion or exclusion of the particular associated or consortium (corporate joint-venture) undertaking, etc. If this is in consequence of paragraph 383(b), permitting non-consolidation for 'small' groups up to the charity audit threshold of £500,000 gross income, it may be possible to avoid at least the duplicate disclosures mentioned below if the undertaking is in fact consolidated.

The disaggregated disclosures called for by paragraph 417(d)(i)–(iv) in respect of its financial/trading activities and (vii)–(x) in respect of its assets and liabilities, funds (or reserves) and commitments clearly ought to be able to exclude those FRS9 undertakings – or at least the minor ones (by analogy with the SORP's disclosure requirement only for *major* individual funds and sub-analysis of the year's movements on them) – in respect of which the charity group's interests *are* included in the consolidated accounts or (where there are no material subsidiaries for consolidation) in the parent charity's entity accounts. It is so obviously burdensome for a charity with multiple undertakings of this nature, particularly where they are used for charitable projects or are even charities themselves, first to have to consolidate them along commercial lines and then also to have to provide an accounts note detailing for each of them *individually*:

'(d)   the charity's interest in the results showing separately its share in:
      (i)   gross incoming resources by type;
     (ii)   costs of generating funds;
    (iii)   expenditure on charitable activities;

(iv)   expenditure on management and administration ...'.

– SORP 2005, paragraph 417

Finally, as we noted in chapter 13, paragraph 406 requires a segregated presentation in the group balance sheet for 'working capital' retained in the subsidiary:

> 'In consolidated accounts, funds or reserves retained by subsidiary undertakings other than funds available to be used in carrying out the charity's objects should be included under an appropriate separate fund heading in the balance sheet (eg funds retained within a non-charitable subsidiary).'

– SORP 2005, paragraph 406

Identifying the amount, however, is not always simple and straightforward, as it can, for example, be affected by consolidation adjustments to eliminate deferred tax liabilities in the subsidiary's accounts. These may represent timing differences arising on capital allowances, so that the provision can be eliminated in the group accounts in recognition of the mitigating effect of a profit-stripping covenant (or other binding commitment made by the subsidiary's Board to continue donating to the parent charity under the GiftAid scheme) on the subsidiary's future taxable profits.

The Scottish regulatory regime for charities

14.3.8   The accounting Regulations that became effective for financial years from 1 April 2006 onwards for Scottish charities, indeed for all charities in Scotland, under the *Charities and Trustee Investment (Scotland) Act 2005* set the same threshold as the English/Welsh regime for cash-based accounting (raising it from £25,000 under Scotland's 1990 Act and 1992 Regulations to £100,000), and also for <u>mandatory</u> consolidated accounts to comply with the SORP for groups above £500,000 gross income. In other respects (eg in allowing only 9 months, instead of the Charity Commission's 10, for annual filing with OSCR, also in providing no size-based exemption from registration or from independent examination) the Scottish regulatory regime differs from that in force or to be provided for south of the Border.

The group-accounting requirement to be imposed by the Regulations was described in the Scottish Executive's 2005 public consultation as:

> 'A charity which has one or more subsidiary undertakings (whether charitable or not) must produce group accounts, except where FRS2 provides for the exclusion of the subsidiaries, the gross income of the group is below £250,000, [or] the results or assets or liabilities of the subsidiary are not material to the group. All according to the methods and principles of the SORP.'

In the event, that threshold was raised to £500,000 (net of any consolidation adjustments) under reg 6 of SSI 2006/218, which simply requires the consolidated accounts to comply with the 'methods and principles' in the Charities SORP 2005. It also allows an option of a consolidated trustees' annual report complying with the SORP, enabling each subsidiary charity to omit its own trustees' annual report as long as its 'statement of account' says where the reader can obtain the consolidated one.

Like the SORP, the Scottish Regulations define 'connected charities' as 'charities having common or related charitable purposes, or charities which have common control or unity of administration'. Regulation 7 allows the trustees of such charities an option for their accounts to be 'collated into a single document to send to OSCR'. Similarly, it allows a combined trustees' annual report to be prepared covering all the connected charities.

The rule under this Regulation is that the size of the largest charity determines the accounting, reporting and audit options (if any) available for all the connected charities.

The Scottish regime thus provides as an *option* an equivalent public accountability framework to that of the English and Welsh regime in respect of special trusts and other connected charities.

At the time of writing, the Scottish Government is running a public consultation on proposed new 2009 Regulations to update and replace those of 2006.

ACCOUNTING FOR CHARITY RESTRUCTURING

14.4 The 'restructuring' of charities can mean merging, combining or even fragmenting them – with or without terminating at least one of them – or more frequently a conversion into a limited company, or (as a special case where a change of public accountability can also affect the charity's annual accounts) the replacement of the trustee-body itself. In fact, each of these different kinds of structural change will involve some kind of transfer, either of:

– charity *funds* (net assets) as a gift/grant – ie for no financial consideration; or

– charity *trusteeship* – which in the case of a permanent endowment does not normally (unless it is very small – see below) involve a gift/grant at all but only a change of *public accountability*, usually from one 'main' charity to another.

Some restructuring changes are wholly internal to one publicly accountable charity, while others involve two or more such charities.

Where the change goes beyond what is permitted by the constitution of the charity concerned, or by the amending powers given to trustees by the 1993 Act, special authority will be needed from the Charity Commission, the High Court, the Privy Council or Parliament, depending on the kind of constitution the charity has. The accounting consequences will vary according to whether the transfer is one of trusteeship or else of charitable funds (all or part).

The SORP only briefly refers to these accounting consequences in its Appendix 2 on the application of accounting and financial reporting standards to charity accounts, but without clarifying the rules any further. This may be because it is immediately obvious that a gift or grant of charitable resources will normally have to be accounted for in the 'Incoming Resources' section of the SoFA by the transferee charity at its current value (ie the gift is akin to an acquisition under FRS7), and in the 'Expenditure' section by a transferor charity at its existing carrying value, since no disposal proceeds are involved. Thus there can be no question of aligning the values at which each charity accounts for the transfer. What may be less obvious, since the nearest parallel in the commercial world would be a true merger in the sense of a voluntary pooling of interests, is that acquisition-accounting would be inappropriate where it is the *charity trusteeship* that is being transferred, not just the charitable resources – see **14.4.3**.

Transferring *trusteeship* of a subsidiary charitable trust fund

14.4.1 The 1993 Act's accounting rules treat the transfer of an existing subsidiary charity in its entirety by a *continuing* main charity to another main charity as merely a change of public accountability for the administration of the transferred charity as a restricted fund. Such a transfer of legal responsibility and accountability is not regarded as an '*application*' of the charity's funds, which remain unaffected.

Unlike a transfer of assets out of general funds or, more rarely, a part-transfer out of a restricted fund, the transfer of a charity's *trusteeship* therefore cannot be accounted for as a 'grant' by either the outgoing or the incoming trustees in the respective accounts of their charity. This difference is only alluded to, but without going into its accounting consequences, in the SORP's Appendix 2 commentary on the relevance of FRS6 among other standards:

> '... where funds are merely transferred from one charity to another this may constitute a gift or in the case of a restricted fund simply the administrative transfer of the restricted fund from one set of trustees to another.'
>
> *– SORP 2005, Appendix 2: Application of Accounting Standards, FRS6*

In the latter case, where the transfer of its trusteeship results in the restricted (trust) fund (or, for that matter, a previously self-accounting charity) becoming a subsidiary charitable fund (in the sense of s 97(1) or 96(5)/(6) of the 1993 Act) of an existing main charity, that requires restating the reporting charity's comparative figures by adding in those for the transferred charity, supported by a suitable accounts note explaining the transfer of trusteeship. This maintains the required continuity in public accountability for the respective charities. It equates to how FRS6 requires a merger to be accounted for.

Conversely, the comparative figures will need to be restated by eliminating any restricted (trust) fund hived off by way of transfer of trusteeship (whether to another main charity's trustees or to become self-accounting as a main charity itself). This latter is one way of enfranchising locally autonomous charities developed out of a national charity's branches, in order to form a federated charity network, for example.

For FRS3 compliance by a charitable company, this sort of event needs to be carefully distinguished from the acquisition/disposal of a business when presenting company annual net income/expenditure figures comparable with those of companies in the profit sector as required by the DTI. This becomes obvious from the fact that the transferred charity trusteeship must be accounted for by the new main charity not from the date of transfer, like an acquisition, but from *the transferred charity's previous year-end*, the same as in merger-accounting – thus maintaining continuity in financial reporting for both charities. Similarly, the old main charity needs to eliminate from its comparative figures those relating to the charity for whose trusteeship it is no longer publicly accountable.

Transfers to a successor charitable company for limited liability

14.4.2 Estimates have shown that nearly three-quarters of all the largest registered charities are now charitable companies, usually – but not necessarily – limited by membership guarantees (normally £1 to £10 per member). These are generally allowed by law to omit the 'limited' from their name. A few are limited by share capital just like any commercial company but with this difference: any shares in a charitable company must by law be 'non-participating' – ie with no right to any distribution by way of profit or gain out of its corporate funds). Normally the share will have only voting rights and entitlement to the return of the amount paid upon it.

Some years ago, with the announcement of Government intentions to provide for a new legal form of limited-liability charity (the Charitable Incorporated Organisation (CIO), now provided for in the Charities Act 2006, with also a Scottish equivalent – the SCIO – in their 2005 legislation), with quick and easy conversion to CIO status from all other forms of charitable institution, many trustees pondered whether to wait for this rather than convert to charitable company status for limited liability, with the significant professional costs that can be involved. The short answer must still be that as long as the option remains available the CIO may well be the lesser one – unless the charity law constraints on retained income, which do not apply to the corporate reserves of a charitable company but do apply to those of a CIO, are of only academic interest, for lack of any substantial reserves (actual or prospective) in your charity. At the time of writing, the long-delayed detailed CIO Regulations are being finalised by the OTS following their public consultation in 2008 and the CIO option is expected to become available from April 2010.

Setting up the new 'successor' charity

The conversion process normally involves incorporating and registering with the Charity Commission (there is now a fast-track procedure for this, together with an even faster online application facility more generally – see the Commission's website) a 'shell' charitable company having the same or similar enough Objects to permit it to continue the same charitable activities and to receive the existing unrestricted funds (preferably) as its own *corporate* funds. Any existing restricted funds will become its *trust* funds, upon transferring the old charity's assets and liabilities to it accordingly under the authority of either:

(i)   a funds-transfer power (if any) contained in its governing document (this may be a general grant-making power or else part of a dissolution/cessation clause – if there is one); or

(ii)   a Charity Commission Scheme in all other cases.

Terminating the old charity

Unless the old charity is *permanently* endowed or the trustees prefer to leave its restricted funds where they are and just change its trusteeship, the old charity, once it has no funds left and so no activity, will qualify to be 'removed' from the Register of Charities as having 'ceased to exist'. Any formal dissolution procedures required by its governing document will still have to be followed, of course, including filing the final year's accounts up to the date of closure, together with the trustees' formal notification of the charity's cessation, requesting its removal from the Register.

The SORP is largely silent on charity succession, but the final year's accounts for the old charity to the date of transfer of all its funds must include a 'nil' balance sheet, while the last line of the SoFA can, in recognition of the exceptional nature of the transaction, show the closing funds balances as transferred to the successor charitable company instead of carried forward, and cross-referring to a supporting accounts note confirming the authority for the transfer. Thus the assets and liabilities are all transferred out to the successor charity at their existing *book values*, without any need or requirement for revaluations of any kind, because they are all, even the investment assets, being transferred by way of gift – not by way of sale. Final-year accounts, like those of the start-up year, or of any year of change, must by law be for at least 6 months and not more than 18 months – or else they will be invalid.

Charity Mergers Register

Another common reason for keeping the old charity alive on the Register has been legacy succession: the risk of losing a legacy that might already have been made long ago in favour of the old charity but which the testator perhaps never gets round to updating in favour of the successor charity. For the future, the Charities Act 2006 now enables the Commission, if you ask, to enter particulars of your charity-restructuring (even if it took place before the passing of the Act) on a 'Charity Mergers Register', whereupon it will qualify for *automatic* transfer of entitlement of such legacies even though the old charity is marked as 'removed' on the Register of Charities as having 'ceased to exist'. It should be noted here that this provision of the 2006 Charities Act cannot take effect where the testator has made alternative provision in case the chosen charity has ceased to exist by the date of death. In that case the Mergers Register cannot help and the old charity will need to be kept alive.

Permanently endowed charities

Many ancient, and some newer, charities are trusts endowed in perpetuity, some with land for their own 'functional' use, while others may have a permanent endowment of investment assets for the benefit of their work. Transferring all the trust's activities to the successor charitable company then increases the separation between the capital fund and the income fund, with implications for administration costs. Unless the endowment is small enough for its assets to be transferred to the company under the 'small charities' restructuring powers given to trustees by s 74/75 of the 1993 Act (as amended by the 2006 Act), the Commission will normally have to insist on its retention in the old charitable trust. Instead, they will usually be able to agree to a *transfer of trusteeship* of the endowment so that either:

(i)   the successor charitable company is the endowment's sole corporate trustee; or

(ii)   the company's directors become trustees of the old charity (or vice versa).

In either case, the Commission will usually follow this up by changing the status of the old 'main' charity to show it on the Register as a 'linked' (ie subsidiary) charity of the company, the latter being its new 'main' charity now publicly accountable for it. Such a change must then be accounted for as a *change of trusteeship* as described above, and not as a grant from one charity to another – which in legal terms it clearly is not.

In the first year's accounts of the successor charitable company, the incoming corporate funds representing the old charity's unrestricted trust funds (plus any *non-permanent* restricted funds – its unspent restricted income and its expendable endowment capital, both of which are transferred to the company *on trust*) can in practice be shown as a special external transfer equating to 'Funds Brought Forward', and cross-referring to a supporting accounts note detailing the funds so transferred and citing the authority for the transfer.

If they are to be considered as a gift, then the SORP's normal gift-accounting rules would seem to dictate that those transferred funds must be brought into the new company's SoFA at *current value* as at the date of transfer, and not at the 'book value' at which the transfer out (representing assets neither sold nor scrapped) has to be shown in the old charity's SoFA.

On the other hand, FRS6 itself makes the point (which we have emphasised below) that the use of a new legal vehicle for business combination purposes (restructuring for limited liability in this case) is to be regarded as secondary to the overall objective to be reached (which in substance is clearly no acquisition (or gift) here, as in principle the same persons will be the charity trustees both immediately before and after the conversion):

> '14   Where a combination is effected by using a newly formed ... company ... the accounting treatment depends on ... whether a combination of the [charities] other than the new parent company would have been an acquisition or a merger. If the combination would have been an acquisition, one [charity] can be identified as having the role of an acquirer. This acquirer and the new parent company *should first be combined by using merger accounting* ... On the other hand, where the substance of the business combination effected by a new parent company is a merger, the new parent company and the other parties should all be combined by using merger accounting.'
>
> – *FRS6: Accounting for Acquisitions and Mergers*

That puts accounting for conversion of a charitable trust/association to a successor charitable company on the same 'merger' footing as accounting for the *transfer of trusteeship* of any permanent endowment(s) or other restricted funds retained in the old charitable trust.

In the latter case, for strict compliance with charity law concerning the respective trustees' public accountability, the *same* balance must be shown as 'Funds Brought Forward' in the endowments column of the company's SoFA as was carried forward in the endowments column in the transferor charity's published SoFA for the previous financial year. The continuity of public accountability for the old charity is then maintained by taking as the company's comparative (trust funds) figures the old charity's total figures for all funds as shown in that previous year's published accounts.

The elegant result thus obtained for the charitable company's first annual accounts is a 'seamless' transition from the last annual accounts of the old unincorporated charity, with no loss of historical data (e g accumulated depreciation) and year-on-year comparability at all. In fact it can make the restructuring virtually invisible, were it not for the necessary narrative disclosures to explain the restructuring that has taken place.

Merger-accounting in principle and practice

14.4.3   The SORP's Appendix 2 simply notes that '*the principles of merger accounting are applicable to charities where two or more charities merge*'. That entails combining the respective assets' existing 'book values', but if any of FRS6's three applicable criteria for merger accounting are not met by the two charities then their combination will have to be accounted for as an acquisition of one by the other – ie at current values under FRS7. FRS6 observes that true mergers are rare (in the profit sector), where acquisitions (some of them quite predatory) tend to be the rule rather than the exception, but the very opposite applies in the charity sector. Here, charity law inhibits any 'takeover' mentality by generally prohibiting proprietary interests in charities and by requiring the trustees to administer only in their charity's own best interests and those of its beneficiaries. Yet experience shows that most charity merger approaches still fail for lack of synergy between the parties, making the accounting issue a rarity here, too.

The three criteria from FRS6, translated into charity sector terminology, are:

– Neither charity is portrayed by either side as 'acquirer' or 'acquired'.

– Both charities participate in establishing the management structure for the combined charity and selecting the management personnel, with such decisions being made by consensus rather than through voting power.

– The relative sizes of the combining charities are not so disparate that one of them dominates the combined charity by virtue of its relative size.

The FRS's explanatory notes amplify how these criteria are to be applied, saying:

> '63 ... if decisions can be reached only by the exercise of majority voting rights against the wishes of one of the parties to the merger, or if one party clearly dominates this process, this indicates that the combination is not a genuine pooling of interests. However, this does not preclude the possibility of all, or most, of the management team of the combined entity coming from only one of the parties, provided that this clearly reflects the wishes of the others.
>
> ...
>
> 66 ... it is necessary to consider only the [management] decisions made in the period of initial integration and restructuring at the time of the combination; but both the short-term effects and expected long-term consequences of decisions made in this period need to be considered.
>
> ...
>
> 68 A party would be presumed to dominate if ... more than 50 per cent larger than each of the other parties to the combination ... However, this presumption may be rebutted if it can be clearly shown that there is no such dominance; other factors ... can mean that a party to the combination has more influence, or conversely less influence, than is indicated by its relative size. Circumstances that rebut the presumption of dominant influence based on relative sizes would need to be disclosed and explained.'
>
> – *FRS6: Accounting for Acquisitions and Mergers*

In the charity sector, considerations of public accountability and the trust law duty of care leave very little possibility for an independent charity to be lawfully subordinated through the exercise of 'dominant influence' by another charity's trustees, so that apart from the special case where one of the merging charities has Objects that fall within those of the parent charity, which alone could permit the latter to dominate the merger and thus turn it into an acquisition, any charity merger approach can generally only be one of consensus in combining their resources in the public interest, but not of dominance, thus making it a true merger regardless of any size disparity.

Chapter 15

SUMMARISED ACCOUNTS AND THE 'SIR'

SCOPE OF SUMMARISED ACCOUNTS

15.1   Many of the larger charities have always found it necessary to prepare simplified financial summaries, sometimes known as 'summarised accounts', each year for the public, in addition to their statutory annual accounts, which for a charity with numerous branches, subsidiaries, special trusts and operational activities can be a little indigestible unless the reader happens to be a trained accountant. These summarised accounts (unless for a *charitable company* – see **15.2**) do not have the legal standing of the charity's statutory accounts, but – as published information purporting to represent (or even symbolise) the latter in whole or in part – their content must be of great interest to the charity's auditors.

Although the Charities SORP provides no detailed guidance on the actual form and essential content of summarised accounts, nor on their uses, since they must vary considerably according to their intended purpose, it does recommend as basic principles that they should:

(a)   contain information on both the SoFA and balance sheet;

(b)   be consistent with the statutory accounts; and

(c)   not mislead through *'either omission or inappropriate amalgamation of information'*.

As a special case to be carefully distinguished from the above, see **15.3**, where we review the impact of the statutory *Summary Information Return* ('SIR') which registered charities with at least £1m gross income must provide for *public domain* use (ie not for the Commission's monitoring of 'auditable' charities, the data for which have to be provided in Part B of the Return) as Part C of their Annual Return to the Charity Commission. This innovation of *mandatory simplified financial reporting* on public record since 2004/05 could revolutionise charity accountability and its regulation in due course, once the public and the media begin to make serious use of its potential for self-regulation.

SORP recommendations – *non-statutory* use

15.1.1   Even so, paragraphs 377–378 of SORP 2005 continue to make a number of general recommendations from the original 1995 SORP, concerning the production and use of any kind of *non-statutory* summarised accounts or 'financial statements' by a charity.

–   They can only be additional to and not instead of the full annual report and accounts.

–   They should not portray only the charity's financial activities without reference to its financial position (or vice versa), but should include information relating to both the statement of financial activities and the balance sheet of the charity (or its branch, in which case both branch and charity should be named), and also to the report of any auditor, independent examiner or reporting accountant (as appropriate) – in particular as to whether or not that report was qualified in any way and, if it was qualified, including enough details to enable the reader to appreciate the significance of the reservations it expressed.

–   They should also be accompanied by a statement of opinion obtained from the charity's auditor, independent examiner or [for years starting before April 2008 only] reporting accountant as to whether the summarised accounts are consistent with the charity's full annual accounts. Clearly, this will have to be an extra-statutory opinion, but should not be a problem unless the summarised accounts are thought to give such a misleading impression that having them linked with the statutory accounts could be an embarrassment.

–   An accompanying statement 'signed on behalf of the trustees' should make it clear that the summarised accounts are only a summary of information extracted from the annual accounts and say when the trustees approved the full accounts, whether or not they were independently audited or examined and whether or not they have been filed with the Charity Commission or other appropriate regulatory authority.

–   Details should be given of how the reader can obtain a copy of the trustees' annual report and accounts together with the report of the charity's auditors, independent examiner or reporting accountants (as appropriate).

Their use in appeals and annual reviews

15.1.2   Summarised accounts are usually included in annual reviews explaining the work of the charity and frequently appealing for financial or other support, and in order to achieve the greatest possible impact are often presented in pictorial form – usually some kind of graph or pie chart. Here are just a few of the more popular topics singled out for such treatment in annual reviews and appeals/fundraising literature which on their own are unrepresentative and could be highly misleading:

–   how each pound of your donation has been (/will be) spent (/used);

–   how our work and your financial support have grown over the years;

–   where our income came from;

–   where we spend our resources;

–   how our resources are deployed.

The following examples from recent publications are typical of the slightly hesitant approach often adopted in trying to make financial summaries interesting and easily readable yet 'representative' within the setting of an annual review or an appeal flyer.

SoFA summary – year to 31 July 2008	Income	Costs	Net
	£'000	£'000	£'000
Fundraising [activities]			
Donations	2,670	699	1,971
Events	1,118	835	283
Legacies	19,890	624	19,266
Shops	2,178	2,256	(78)
Mail Order and Trading	447	420	27
	26,303	**4,834**	**21,469**
Other [income]			
Intellectual property	4,527	–	4,527
Investment	2,959	182	2,777
Other income	161	–	161
Gains from sale of fixed assets	6	–	6
	7,653	**182**	**7,471**
Total [income and related costs]	**33,956**	**5,016**	**28,940**
Charitable expenditure			
Research grants		20,236	
Research Institutes		6,727	
Education		1,562	
Governance		153	
Total*			**28,678**
Net income for the year			**262**
Increase/(Decrease) in value of investments			(5,105)
Net movement in funds for the year			**(4,843)**
Balance Sheet summary – 31 July 2008			
Assets		94,911	
Liabilities		(47,321)	
			47,590
Reserves			
Committed:			
– Restricted		987	
– Designated		6,203	
Uncommitted:			
– General reserve		32,675	
– Revaluation reserve		7,725	

SoFA summary – year to 31 July 2008	Income	Costs	Net
	£'000	£'000	£'000
			47,590
*Charitable expenditure – year to 31 July 2008			
Disease analysis:			
- Bone disease		1,692	
- Connective tissue disease		2,485	
- Inflammatory arthritis		11,196	
- Osteoarthritis		7,290	
- Soft tissue disorder and back pain		3,447	
- Surgical techniques		358	
- General research support		989	
- Education and educational research		113	
Other ARC costs		1,108	
Total*		**28,678**	
*Funding target			
Developing & improving treatment/diagnosis	6,012		
Disseminating research results	24		
Promoting best practice / education	2,606		
Understanding causation & aetiology	13,284		
Building academic strength	5,644		
Other ARC costs	1,108		
	28,676		

Arthritis Research Campaign – 2007/08 Annual Review

The following example is a somewhat simplistic form of summarised accounts stipulated by the Regulator with a view to promoting public understanding and inter-charity comparability. It comes from the new-style Charity Commission website, where all the registered charities above the £500,000 gross income audit threshold are graphically summarised on an 'overview page' constructed from the data they provide in Part B of the charity's Annual Return to the Commission. What is noteworthy here is the suppression of the trust law distinctions that are designed to protect and uphold the wishes of donors but which are so foreign to commercial accountability.

Income & Expenditure summary for 2007-8	
	£m
Charitable activities	21.63
Voluntary income	3.49
Trading to raise funds	1.61
Investment income	.54
Total Income	**27.27**
Charitable activities	23.84

Income & Expenditure summary for 2007-8	
	£m
Trading to raise funds	.87
Generating Voluntary Income	.37
Governance of the Charity	.53
Total Spending	**25.61**
Summary Balance Sheet extract as at 31 March 2008	
Fixed Assets (for own use)	**.92**
Current Assets	15.25
Liabilities	(7.69)
Net Assets	**8,484**

Motability – Charity Overview 2007/08 (Charity Commission website)

Some charities give only a simple summary of their income and expenditure within a non-statutory and often very attractive and interesting illustrated Annual Review, but with nothing at all about their financial position – no doubt because their website offers ready access to both the Review and the full Annual Report and audited Accounts. This may be on the basis that the SORP's 'best practice' recommendations here, intended to cover non-statutory 'summarised accounts', are not applicable to such *partial* summarised information, of which this is a typical example from a well-known public fundraising charity's website:

Where our money came from ...	£m	%
Christian Aid Week	14.6	17
Emergency appeals	11.5	13
General donations	30.3	35
Legacies	9.8	11
Government and other grants	17.6	21
Other income	2.7	3
Total income	**£86.5m**	
... and how we spent it		
Charitable activities		
– Long-term development projects	39.0	47
– Emergencies	15.0	18
– Campaigning, advocacy and education	12.2	15
	66.2	**80**
Other expenditure		
Fundraising	15.6	19
– Governance	0.7	1
Total expenditure	**£82.5m**	

Christian Aid – 2007/08 Annual Review

Whole charity or special trust, charity branch, etc?

15.1.3 'Summarised accounts', as defined in the Charities SORP, can also include segmental accounts of individual parts of the 'accountable charity' (as defined for Part VI purposes) – such as subordinate charities, local branches, operating divisions, etc – as long as the same rules are followed (see above).

It will be obvious that where such a part is a corporate body accountable under the Companies Act 2006, its statutory accounts as a company – or any non-statutory summary made of them for external use by the charity – should also comply with the SORP recommendations on summarised accounts if they are not to become misleading to the reader. At the very least, this should include disclosure of its relationship with the charity as a whole.

The relevant requirements of SSAP25 (see below) concerning the provision of segmental information in large companies' accounts can be useful as a guide to the disclosures needed in the accounts of the part-charity in relation to the whole.

Segmental reporting (SSAP25)

15.1.4 The rules of SSAP25's *segmental reporting* can never be more than partially – if at all – applicable to charities, and even then only as a requirement for the very largest of charities. The Standard requires the full accounts to include analysis of the reporting entity's trading turnover and results between any 'significant' activities that are either substantially different from each other or attributable to different geographical areas.

The threshold of significance is 10% of total turnover. A 'large' company* as a reporting entity for this purpose for financial years from 6 April 2008 is defined as one that is ten times the size of a medium-sized company under s 465 (and s 466 for groups) of the Companies Act 2006 – thus any reporting entity exceeding two out of the three size-thresholds of:

– £259m (previously £228m turnover (this would taken as meaning gross income** for a charity);

– £129m (previously £114m gross assets; or

– 2,500 (paid) employees.

*For group consolidated accounts, adding 20% to the above two financial thresholds gives you the gross figures for the group before 'consolidation adjustments'.

**However, such an interpretation must be open to challenge on the basis that the Standard itself does not include voluntary income and investment income in operating activities – nor therefore in the trading turnover and 'results' of those activities. While the SORP's related 2008 Regulations do use gross income instead of trading turnover to measure a charity's size for audit and other regulatory threshold purposes, the SORP itself only uses this substitution in an appendix, in reminding us that only a reporting entity that is 'small' within the meaning of company law is allowed to adopt the current FRSSE as an accounting policy.

'Large' reporting entities are thus required to analyse:

– net assets employed (multiple-fund charities of all sizes already provide this information in their analysis of net assets by fund-type – distinguishing any major charitable funds, of course);

– inter-segment turnover (this would mean gross income** including charitable turnover for each designated trading fund);

– geographical origin of turnover (in the case of a charity with overseas trading activities);

– geographical segment result (this is considered not relevant to charities, since profit cannot lawfully be their primary purpose).

Where such segmental information is provided, it should also include the reporting entity's share of the trading results (for non-charitable activities) and net assets of any significant 'associated' undertakings.

Trustees' statement on *non-statutory* summarised accounts

15.1.5 The SORP recommends the inclusion of separate statements by the trustees and the auditor(s) or independent examiner of the statutory accounts for that year. However, to minimise costs and the length of the text, we would advocate that these are normally best combined into a single composite statement.

A suitably brief 'pro forma' for this is suggested below.

[The square brackets enclose text to be excluded or modified as may be appropriate to the accounting and reporting obligations of the particular charity.]

[The italicised text at (1) and (2) is only for guidance: it does not form part of the text to be printed. It merely reminds you to delete the whole of the first of these two alternative forms of wording if your charity's accounts had an independent examination report instead of an audit report – or else to delete the whole of the second alternative instead.]

These summarised accounts [for] [name of special trust or charity branch if only part of the charity is being summarised] are [only] an extract from the statutory [annual report and] accounts of [charity name] for the financial year ended [(date)] and which have been

[1. In the case of an audited charity, or for a charitable company partially exempt from audit:]

[audited [/examined] by (auditor's[/reporting accountant's] name), who gave an unqualified audit [exemption] report [or: an audit [exemption] report qualified as set out below] on (date)].

*[2. Alternatively, for a **non-company** charity that chose **independent examination** in lieu of statutory audit:]*

[examined by (name), whose independent examination report on (date) contained no [or: only the following] matters to be brought to the attention of the reader]. ➡

The auditors [reporting accountants*/independent examiner] have/has confirmed to the trustees that these summarised accounts are consistent with the full annual accounts of the charity for the year ended [date].

The full annual accounts [and trustees' report] of the charity were approved by the trustees and signed on their behalf on [date]. [They will be [have been] submitted to the Charity Commission [on (date)].

Copies of the charity's full annual accounts [and the auditor's [/(other)] report on those accounts] [and the trustees' report] may be obtained from [(name and address)].

Signed on behalf of the trustees

....

[Date]

(* for years starting before April 2008 only)

STATUTORY SUMMARISED ACCOUNTS (CHARITABLE COMPANIES)

15.2   Company law has long included statutory requirements regulating the form and content of summarised accounts for distribution to members of *public* companies in place of their audited accounts, but in August 2005 this was extended by removing the old restriction to 'listed' companies in s 251 of the 1985 Act in order to make the same (regulated) facility available to all private companies, thus also charitable companies. To that end, the DTI issued *The Companies (Summary Financial Statement) (Amendment) Regulations 2005*, SI 2005/2281, updating *The Companies (Summary Financial Statement) Regulations 1995*, SI 1995/2092 ('the Companies Regulations 1995').

Since 1 October 2005 these Regulations have allowed charitable companies to provide the specified statutory form of summarised accounts instead of their full audited accounts to members and others entitled to receive them (once this has been agreed with each recipient). They are superseded by SI 2008/374, made under the Companies Act 2006 and saying essentially the same thing, for financial years from 6 April 2008.

Among the statutory requirements to be satisfied is, at reg 6(2) of SI 2008/374, the inclusion of:

'(a)   ... a statement by the company's auditor of his opinion as to whether the summary financial statement—

(i)   is consistent with the company's annual accounts and, where information derived from the directors' report is included in the statement, with that report, and

(ii)   complies with the requirements of section 427 of the 2006 Act ... and of these Regulations,

(b)   [a statement as to] whether the auditor's report on the annual accounts was unqualified or qualified.'

This is reinforced by a prohibition inserted as reg 4(2) in these 2008 Regulations, so that if a company claims total exemption from audit under the Companies Act it cannot distribute any kind of summarised accounts in place of its full accounts:

> '... a company may not send a summary financial statement to [an entitled] person [instead of copies of its full accounts and report] in relation to any financial year where ... no auditors' report has been made ... under section 495 ... of the 2006 Act . . .'

> *– SI 2008/374, reg 4(2)(a)*

The same prohibition applies if the statutory filing period (now 9 months) has expired or the summary financial statement does not have Board approval and the full financial statements have not been signed by a director on the Board's behalf.

Prior to SI 2005/2281, as noted by paragraph 373 of the SORP, charitable companies only had to comply with the requirements of s 240 of the 1985 Act, as now restated in s 435 of the 2006 Act (which the SORP itself has mirrored from the outset as best practice for *all*) concerning publication of *'non-statutory accounts'* in relation to the statutory ones:

> '(1) If a company publishes non-statutory accounts, it must publish with them a statement indicating—

> (a)   that they are not the company's statutory accounts,
> (b)   whether statutory accounts dealing with any financial year with which the non-statutory accounts purport to deal have been delivered to the registrar, and
> (c)   whether an auditor's report has been made on the company's statutory accounts for any such financial year, and if so whether the report–
>   (i)   was qualified or unqualified, or included a reference to any matters to which the auditor drew attention by way of emphasis without qualifying the report, or
>   (ii)   contained a statement under section 498(2) (accounting records or returns inadequate or accounts ... not agreeing with records and returns), or section 498(3) (failure to obtain necessary information and explanations).

> (2)   The company must not publish with non-statutory accounts the auditor's report on the company's statutory accounts.

> (3)   References in this section to the publication by a company of "non-statutory accounts" are to the publication of—

> (a)   any balance sheet or profit and loss account relating to, or purporting to deal with, a financial year of the company, or
> (b)   an account in any form purporting to be a balance sheet or profit and loss account for a group headed by the company relating to, or purporting to deal with, a financial year of the company, otherwise than as part of the company's statutory accounts. ...'.

> *– Companies Act 2006, s 435*

Where statutory summarised accounts are published, s 427 of the 2006 Act (restating s 251(3) of the 1985 Act) says they must:

> '(1)   ... —

> (a)   be derived from the company's annual accounts and
> (b)   be prepared in accordance with this section and regulations* made under it.'

and that:

'(2)   The summary financial statement must be in such form, and contain such information, as the Secretary of State may specify by regulations. The regulations may require the statement to include information derived from the directors' report.

...

(4)   The summary financial statement must—

(a)   state that it is only a summary of information derived from the company's annual accounts

(b)   state whether it contains additional information derived from the directors' report and, if so, that it does not contain the full text of that report;

(c)   state how a person entitled to them can obtain a full copy of the company's annual accounts and the directors' report;

(d)   contain a statement by the company's auditor of his opinion as to whether the summary financial statement (i) is consistent with the company's annual accounts and, where information derived from the directors' report is included in the statement, with that report, and (ii) complies with the requirements of this section and regulations made under it;

(e)   state whether the auditor's report on the annual accounts was unqualified or qualified and, if it was qualified, set out the report in full together with any further material needed to understand the qualification;

(f)   state whether, in that report, the auditor's statement under s 496 (whether directors' report consistent with accounts) was qualified or unqualified and, if it was qualified, set out the qualified statement in full together with any further material needed to understand the qualification;

(g)   state whether that auditor's report contained a statement under—
      (i)   s 498(2)(a) or (b) (accounting records or returns inadequate or accounts not agreeing with records and returns); or
      (ii)   s 498(3) (failure to obtain necessary information and explanations),
      and if so, set out the statement in full.'

– Companies Act 2006, s 427

*Unlike the SORP, the Companies Act's 2008 Regulations, as cited above, specify in detail the information to be provided in summarised accounts – albeit only where distributed in place of the full audited accounts. Separate requirements are listed for (a) the entity accounts and (b) the group accounts (if applicable) in Sch 1 and Sch 4 respectively, in respect of:

(i)   the summarised FRS3-compliant SoFA or its equivalent, as the charity sector's version of a company profit and loss account; and

(ii)   the summarised balance sheet.

Thus for a charitable company with no consolidated accounts, the summarised SoFA, in a case where full audited accounts are (by agreement) not provided to anyone entitled to a copy, is required by para 1 of Sch 1 to these Regulations (SI 2008/374) to show:

'(1)   ... in so far as they may be derived from the full [FRS3-compliant SoFA], the items ... listed in sub-paragraph (3), in the order set out in that sub-paragraph.

(2)   The items or combinations of items listed in sub-paragraph (3) may appear under such headings as the directors consider appropriate.

(3)   The items ... referred to in sub-paragraph (1) are:

(a)   Turnover ...
(b)   Income from shares in group undertakings and participating interests ...
(c)   Other interest receivable and similar income and interest payable and similar charges ...
(d)   [Net income from] ordinary activities [before any taxation][1] ...
      ...
(g)   Extraordinary income and charges [net after tax][2] ...
(h)   [Surplus/Deficit] for the financial year ...'.

For a *consolidated* SoFA summary instead of the full version, the above requirements are modified by para 1 of Sch 4 to the same Regulations (SI 2008/374) as follows:

'(3)(a) in place of [Income from shares in group undertakings and participating interests], there shall be shown, under such heading as the directors consider appropriate, the item 'Income from interests in associated undertakings' ...;
(b)   between ... [Net income from ordinary activities] and ... [Extraordinary income and charges] there must in addition be shown, under such heading as the directors consider appropriate, the item ... "minority interests" ...; and
(c)   [Extraordinary income and charges] shall be shown after ... "minority interests" ...'.

Also, for a charitable company with no consolidated accounts, the summarised balance sheet where the full audited accounts are not provided is required by para 3 of Sch 1 to the same Regulations to show:

'(2)   subject to sub-paragraphs (3) and (4) ... in so far as it can be derived from the full balance sheet and under such heading as the directors consider appropriate, a single amount for each of the [main] headings ... used for the full balance sheet ... and ... in the order set out in the full balance sheet.

(3)   Where an alternative position is permitted for any item in the balance sheet format used, the summary balance sheet shall use the position used by the full balance sheet.

(4)   ... in the case of ... "Liabilities", two figures must be shown, one figure for amounts falling due within one year and one for amounts falling due after one year.'

For the consolidated balance sheet summary, in addition to the above requirements para 2 of Sch 4 to the same Regulations requires the addition of the item for 'minority interests' – as is required to be inserted in the full balance sheet by para 17(2) of Sch 6 to the 2006 Act's respective accounting regulations for small and large/medium-sized companies.

As with the full audited accounts, para 7 of Sch 1 and para 3 of Sch 4 to the Summarised Accounts 2008 Regulations requires comparative figures to be shown after 'any adjustments to corresponding amounts made in the full accounts and reports' [to ensure comparability for the financial year in question].

---

[1]   Normally not applicable in the case of a charity.
[2]   Normally not applicable in the case of a charity.

Although all this appears to exclude endowment capital movements, the Summarised Accounts 2008 Regulations do permit such items to be included as additional information contained in the full audited accounts and therefore pertinent to the summarised accounts:

> 'Nothing in this section or regulations made under it prevents a company from including in a summary financial statement additional information derived from the company's annual accounts or the directors' report.'

– para 427(3), Companies Act 2006

The following example is of strict compliance with the SORP's recommendations and is of special interest because it looks like the sort of information a charitable company's statutory 'summarised financial statements' would have to show, though as a charter body not registered under the Companies Act this charity has no need to comply with DBIS (previously DBERR) regulations.

Summary statement of financial activities – the year ended 30 June 2008	2008	2007
	£'000	£'000
Incoming resources		
Charitable activities		
To advance the management and development of people through:		
Education and membership services	16,367	*15,332*
Research, innovation and dissemination of expertise	109	*57*
Branches	1,539	*1,320*
Generating funds		
Commercial income	20,315	*17,464*
Investment income	1,107	*1,072*
Total incoming resources	**39,437**	***35,245***
Resources expended		
Charitable activities		
To advance the management and development of people through:		
Education and membership services	(10,085)	*(8,734)*
Research, innovation and dissemination of expertise	(6,638)	*(5,772)*
Branches	(4,163)	*(3,393)*
Cost of generating funds		
Commercial expenditure	(17,378)	*(15,227)*
Investment management costs	(53)	*(75)*
Governance costs	**(195)**	***(164)***
Total resources expended	**(38,512)**	***(33,365)***
Net incoming resources	**925**	***1,880***
Other recognised gains and losses		
Actuarial (losses)/gains on pension scheme	(4,869)	*2,591*

Summary statement of financial activities – the year ended 30 June 2008

		2008	2007
		£'000	£'000
Net (losses)/gains on investment assets		(1,086)	1,782
Net movement in funds		**(5,030)**	*6,253*
Fund balances brought forward		33,894	*27,641*
Fund balances carried forward		**28,864**	*33,894*

Summary balance sheet at 30 June 2008

		2008	2007
Tangible assets		11,832	*12,262*
Investments		20,095	*18,403*
Total fixed assets		**31,927**	*30,665*
Current assets			
Stocks of goods for resale		284	*652*
Debtors		5,277	*4,840*
Cash at bank and in hand		11,393	*12,730*
Total current assets		**16,954**	*18,222*
Creditors: Amounts falling due within one year		(12,965)	*(12,930)*
Net current assets		**3,989**	*5,292*
Net assets excluding pension liability		**35,916**	*35,957*
Defined benefit pension scheme liability		**(7,052)**	*(2,063)*
Net Assets		**28,864**	*33,894*
FUNDS			
General fund		**31,541**	*31,408*
Pension liability		(7,052)	*(2,063)*
Net general fund		**24,489**	*29,345*
Designated funds:			
Building fund		1,355	*1,485*
Information technology fund		436	*789*
New learning fund		575	*325*
Research and development fund		665	*764*
Strategic initiatives fund		1,344	*1,186*
Total designated funds		**4,375**	*4,549*
Total Funds (all unrestricted)		**28,864**	*33,894*

Summary statement of cash flows

	2008	2007
Net cash inflow from operating activities	**558**	*416*
Returns on investments	**1,093**	*1,057*
Capital expenditure and financial investment	**(2,988)**	*(1,091)*
(Decrease)/increase in net funds	**(1,337)**	*382*
Movement in funds placed on long term deposit	**(1,470)**	*670*

Summary statement of financial activities – the year ended 30 June 2008

	2008	2007
	£'000	£'000
Increase/(Decrease) in cash and bank	**133**	*(288)*

The summary financial statements were approved by the directors on 15 September 2008 and [signed, etc.].

Summary directors' report

CIPD is established to advance the art and science of the management and development of people for the public benefit. It is the leading professional body in the United Kingdom and Republic of Ireland for all those specialising in the management and development of people.

The document in which this summary report is published contains an overview of the Institute's key activities and achievements during the year, including: membership growth; new research, guidance and online resources for our members and the wider public; a greater profile and impact for our research and other work; and our contribution to public policy.

This financial statement and directors' report gives a summary of the information contained in the directors' report and financial statements for the year ended 30 June 2008. The full statutory report and financial statements have been prepared in accordance with the Statement of Recommended Practice 'Accounting and reporting by charities' (SORP 2005). The report and financial statements were approved by the directors on 15 September 2008, have been audited and received an unqualified audit report and will be sent to the Charity Commission.

The summary financial statement is not the Institute's statutory accounts. For a full understanding of the results of the group you can access the annual review, statutory directors' report and financial statements on the web …

[Signed, etc.]

Independent auditors' statement to the members of the Chartered Institute of Personnel and Development

We have examined the summarised financial statements of the Chartered Institute of Personnel and Development. This statement is made solely for its members and to the fullest extent permitted by law we do not accept or assume responsibility to anyone other than its members for this statement.

Respective responsibilities of the Directors and Auditors

The Directors are responsible for preparing the summarised annual report in accordance with the applicable law. Our responsibility is to report to you our opinion on the consistency of the summarised financial statements with the full financial statements. We read the other information contained within the annual report and summary financial statements and consider the implications for our report if we become aware of any apparent misstatements or material inconsistencies within the summarised financial statements.

Basis of Opinion

We conducted our work in accordance with Bulletin 1999/6 'The auditors' statement on the summarised financial statement' issued by the Auditing Practices Board for use in the United Kingdom.

Opinion

In our opinion the summarised financial statements are consistent with the full financial statements of the Chartered Institute of Personnel and Development for the year ended 30 June 2008.

[Signed, etc.]

Chartered Institute of Personnel and Development – 2007/08 summarised financial statements

STATUTORY SUMMARY INFORMATION RETURNS: THE 'SIR'

15.3   Government plans for the introduction of this radical simplification of annual reporting for easier inter-charity comparability were numbered 18–22 and 34 in the Cabinet Office Strategy Unit's 2002 Report, *Private Action, Public Benefit*, and were taken forward in the Home Office 2003 publication, *Charities and Not-for-Profits: A Modern Legal Framework*. The original idea here was for charities with at least £1m gross annual income to be required to include a 'Standard Information Return' of key performance data in their annual report and accounts.

Instead, it was found more practical in the interests of public access and data reliability and comparability for the Charity Commission to use its regulation-making powers to specify the SIR as a special section (Part C) of the statutory Annual Return for larger registered charities (though that could not then cover the exempt charities and the largest excepted charities, of course).

As 'public domain', rather than confidential monitoring, information each charity's SIR is intended for publication, primarily on the Charity Commission's website database of registered charities, but is also fed through along with other public Register data to the Guidestar UK (originally Treasury-funded) free public access charity database launched in December 2005. The Commission originally indexed as a special page on its website the thousands of completed SIRs received from charities filing their Annual Returns for 2005 year-ends onwards, but of late this facility seems to have been discontinued and the only way to access a charity's SIR is via its homepage on the Commission's website.

The SIR highlights key data on charities' operational, fundraising and campaigning activities in relation to their strategic planning and annual objectives, as well as on the quality and effectiveness of their governance, including trustee-recruitment/training. It pulls together many of the key SORP-based performance-related annual reporting disclosures, having dropped the original 'impact/outcomes' focus that had racked some of the best brains in the sector to little avail. Its standardised format asks about:

–   the charity's 'aims', the medium-to-long-term strategy and its 'success-indicators', and how it is affected by the year's results;

–   achievements against last year's objectives to further the charity's Objects;

–   next year's main objectives;

–   how the charity's beneficiaries can influence its development;

–   the year's income and expenditure, sub-analysed to show the main income sources, but not for 2009 year-ends onwards, since the advent of the Commission's new-look website, the costs of the year's 'most significant' activities and the costs/proceeds of the main kinds of fundraising activities;

–   comment on the charity's state of 'financial health' at the year-end;

–   how effective 'governance' is achieved (eg selection-criteria, recruitment, induction, training of trustees; protocols to manage any conflicts of interests; etc).

This comparatively bland set of disclosures certainly increases the charity sector's transparency in the interests of maintaining public confidence, since absolutely no accountancy training is needed to be able to read and understand the SIR, thus making it accessible to the 99.9% of the public who can't or won't make use of a charity's audited accounts and annual report – but it is nothing like as demanding as the SIR originally proposed by the Prime Minister's Strategy Unit. But its significance for the future of charity regulation my be seen in an open letter of July 2006 on the Cabinet Office website, where Hilary Armstrong, as Chancellor of the Duchy of Lancaster and Minister for the Cabinet Office and Social Exclusion (including the charity sector) said:

> 'I believe that in many areas of public and private sector activity, the promotion of better consumer information about services and providers can empower citizens and can also reduce the need for traditional regulation.'

Key 'Performance Indicators' in the SIR

The data for this simplified, *standardised* statutory performance-reporting by all the major players in the (registered) charity sector come from various sources:

Item	Disclosure	Correlation	Data-set/-source
1	The trustees' *'aims'*	Annual Report	Current Strategic Plan
2	How *beneficiaries* can influence the charity's development	Annual Report/ Board Minutes	Identification of each beneficiary class; User-group relationships; Customer-satisfaction monitoring; Policy on identifying beneficiary needs
3	Medium/long-term *strategy* and its *success-indicators*	Annual Report/ Board Minutes	Strategic Plan
4	The year's Objects-related *objectives* and *achievements*	Annual Report/ Board Minutes	Management accounts; Business Plan; Strategic Plan
5a/b	*Fundraising* efficiency analysis	Annual Report/ SoFA	For 3 main + sundry other types of fundraising activity/event/project: Costs and Proceeds for this year
5c/d	*Expenditure* analysis	SoFA	Costs of 3 'most significant' Objects-related activities + all other expenditure
6	*Financial state of health at the year-end*	Annual Report; Balance Sheet	Short-term and long-term solvency-assessment; year-end free reserves and Business Plan sensitivity including any voluntary funding dependencies
7	*Next year's main objectives and any change of Strategy*	Annual Report/ Board Minutes	Current annual budget/forecast in the context of the current Business Plan
8	*Governance effectiveness*	Annual Report/ Board Minutes	Trustee-selection criteria; induction and training arrangements; competence monitoring (skills-audits); formal Board protocols on conflicts of interests

Group basis

There has been a 'group' focus from the outset in this relatively new development in charity reporting, in contrast to the entity focus of the Charities Act 1993 ('the 1993 Act') itself prior to enactment and implementation of the Charities Act 2006. The 1993 Act up to then could only regulate the group's charity members, which meant monitoring those above the audit threshold through the Charity Commission's

Regulations for completion of Part B of the Annual Return, as well as inspection where necessary of their individual statutory annual report and accounts as filed with the Commission.

The 1993 Act used to see each charity's interests in its *non-charitable* undertakings purely as investment assets, the continued retention and use of which had to be justified in terms of either the investment return (if used primarily to generate funds) or the public benefit achieved (if used primarily as a vehicle for 'social' (programme-related) investing) for the reporting charity's beneficiaries. Such a 'disaggregated' approach to charity regulation, necessitated by the *exclusivity of purpose* required for charitable status, had for some time been at odds with the Commission's ever-pragmatic but nowadays increasingly commercial approach of aggregating the entire group's activities for charity reporting and monitoring purposes (an approach that can all too easily blur the strict boundaries set by trust law). Hence the need for the group-accounting provisions of the Charities Act 2006 which effectively validate the Commission's policy and practice and are now to be found in the 1993 Act as s 49A and Sch 5A thereto.

Annual Return Regulations

New Regulations are made each Spring by the Charity Commission to determine the content of that year's Annual Returns. Thus the 2005 Regulations, for 2005 year-ends after February of that year, introduced the SIR as Part C of the Annual Return – but with a strange twist for logistical reasons that has since persisted: Part C is mandatory if the charity's gross income for the *previous* financial year has exceeded £1m – even if the gross income fell below that level for the reporting year. Conversely, no SIR data may be demanded by the Commission's computer system unless the charity was above that threshold for its *previous* year. If at the boundary line here, the charity may have to resort to the Commission's Annual Returns helpline to resolve the problem.

Board approval

As the data needed for completing much of the SIR (as Part C of the statutory Annual Return for charities above the £1m gross income threshold set by the Regulations) are the same data needed for making a number of key disclosures in the annual report and/or accounts, the SIR clearly needs to be checked for consistency with those published documents – meaning the group consolidated figures, where relevant – before being tabled for discussion and formal approval by the board.

Although not itself an *audited* document, this fact and the public record status of the SIR make it advisable to clear a draft with the charity's auditors beforehand.

A strong incentive to do so is to be found in the following statutory warning and declaration above the signature of the board member who must be authorised to sign the completed Annual Return for an auditable charity on the Board's behalf:

> 'Those who give answers that they know are untrue or misleading may be committing an offence.
>
> I certify that the information I have provided in this form is correct to the best of my knowledge and has been brought to the attention of all the charity trustees.

I further confirm that there are no serious incidents or other matters which they should have brought to the Commission's attention and have not done so already.'

– *Charity Commission Annual Return form, AR2008*

Chapter 16

ACCOUNTS OF THE SMALLER NON–COMPANY CHARITY

INTRODUCTION

16.1   In this chapter we look at the Charity Commission's website guidance and pro forma packs CC16 and CC17, respectively, for the accounts of charities small enough to opt out wholly or partly from the fully regulated form of annual accounts prescribed by SORP 2005 and (for *non-company* charities) underpinned by its related 2008 Regulations under the Charities Act 1993 ('the 1993 Act'), Part VI.

Although smaller *charitable companies* are excluded from the relevant accounting and audit provisions of Part VI to the extent of their equivalent obligations under the Companies Act 2006, preparation of their accruals accounts can still benefit from the guidance described here if used as an adjunct to the more general Companies House guidance available for them and provided they can satisfy the other criteria specified in the guidance notes for charities using the CC17 Accruals Accounts Pack, which is designed for charities which are below the statutory audit threshold and whose accounts do not have to include either:

–   material subsidiary undertakings, joint venture/associated trading undertakings; or

–   permanently endowed trust funds invested on a [duly authorised] 'total return' basis.

Neither does CC17 cater for the accounting and disclosure requirements of FRS17 in respect of 'Defined Benefit' (or 'Final Salary') staff pension schemes, nor the SORP's special requirements for either 'heritage' or 'social investment' assets (including longer-term charitable loans to beneficiaries).

So if your smaller charity has any of these five kinds of 'special situation' you will need to look up how SORP 2005 itself says you should account for it – as covered elsewhere in this book.

The statutory threshold for compulsory accruals accounting by *non-company* charities was £100,000 gross income for financial years ending before April 2009, but has been increased to £250,000 for financial years ending on or after 1 April 2009 by Ministerial Order made by the OTS (SI 2009/508).

More generally, for charities below the statutory audit threshold under the Charities Act 1993 (ie, those up to the £500,000 gross income ceiling – this becomes £250,000* if their gross assets exceed £3.26m* – for *Charities Act* audit exemption) *all* accruals-based accounts can still use the optional expense-type expenditure analysis in the SoFA, thereby obviating much supporting sub-analysis in the accounts notes, as well as preparing only the 'brief' form of trustees' annual report outlined in the SORP's Appendix 5, 'Accounting for Smaller Charities' and discussed in detail in chapter 4 of this book. (*These are the new thresholds under S.I.2009/508 for financial years ending after March 2009. For earlier years the old thresholds were £100,000 and £2.8m respectively.)

In chapter 5 we discussed a rather larger kind of 'small' that defines over 99% of all registered charities, qualifying them to adopt the current FRSSE. (That was the 2007 version for financial years starting before 6 April 2008, or the 2008 version thereafter – the only difference being that the later version is cross-referenced to the Companies Act 2006 and its Regulations instead of to the 1985 Act.) Appendix 4 to the SORP reinterprets the FRSSE's eligibility criteria as referred to in paragraph 62 of the SORP itself and also in its Appendix 5 (see below) by saying that the *gross income* ceiling for that purpose is £6.5m (£5.6m for financial years starting before 6 April 2008), though there are other size criteria as well. You should go to chapter 5 if you want to know more about where and how you can benefit from following the FRSSE instead of having to explore and comply with all the other accounting standards and ASB pronouncements as and where relevant, but the important point to note here is the unequivocal precedence claimed by the SORP in Appendix 5:

> 'Any charity (whether or not it is a company) which is under the thresholds for small companies as described in the Companies Acts ... can follow the Financial Reporting Standard for Smaller Entities (FRSSE) in preparing its financial accounts except where it conflicts with this Charities SORP, in which case this SORP should be followed.'

– SORP 2005, Appendix 5.2.1

ACCRUALS ACCOUNTING OPTION

16.2   The Charity Commission's original free booklet CC55 on this subject, entitled *Accruals Accounting for the Smaller Charity* (October 1995), came to be known as a kind of mini-SORP for the tens of thousands of simple, straightforward charities with a gross income of less than £100,000 a year where the trustees wished to report annually in accordance with best practice rather than opting out of the SORP entirely. That was hardly surprising. CC55 was, in effect, a précis of what was left of the 1995 SORP after eliminating all the recommendations on investment-accounting, trading, charity branches and non-charitable subsidiaries.

A computerised version was subsequently developed by the Commission's in-house accountants and published in 1998. It comprised a handy set of accounting and reporting document-formats that you could tailor to your own needs by just filling in the boxes, deleting those not needed and adding any extra information desired. Coded CC58, the 'Accruals Accounts Pack' could be freely downloaded from the Charity Commission website.

Both packs, together with their guidance notes, were later updated to SORP 2000, and in turn superseded by newer versions available on the Commission's website for use by smaller charities for financial years from April 2005 onwards.

The great advantage of downloading and completing the CC17a accounts pack – as long as you take careful note of the difference between the 'should' of the SORP's 'best practice' requirements on which CC17a is based and the 'must' of the statutory minimum requirements contained in the SORP's related 2008 Regulations – is that:

> 'These pro forma accounts are designed to help smaller charities prepare and present accruals accounts. They provide a format for such accounts and set out the key disclosures in Accounting and Reporting by Charities: Statement of Recommended Practice (the Charities SORP) 2005. The pro forma accounts and notes to the accounts (CC17a) when fully completed will include all the information necessary for smaller charities preparing accruals accounts.'
>
> *– CC17 Guidance Notes*

For example, reg 8(11) says *'the balance sheet shall be signed by at least one of the charity trustees of the charity, each of whom has been authorised to do so'*, whereas CC17 says:

> 'The charity trustees must approve the accounts and at least one (but we recommend two) of them should sign the balance sheet as evidence of approval.'
>
> *– CC17 Guidance Notes*

Accounting rules (policies)

16.2.1 The charity accounting rules – especially those for restricted funds – are actually the same no matter how small the charity, but there is really no need to go into lengthy explanations about them in your accounts where the figures involved are not material to the public interest. You do always need an explanatory note to clarify what 'accounting policies' the accounts follow to 'show a true and fair view' as required by law, but not to detail how the various kinds of income, endowment, expenditure, asset and liability have been treated except where an individual item is large enough to be 'material' in its own context and therefore 'likely to influence the reader' in coming to a proper understanding of your charity's financial position and activities.

However, the 'model' accounting policy descriptions offered in CC17a do include some useful clarifications of interest even to the larger charity. Two prime examples are the following 'standard' texts for where the charity receives or makes the kind of 'performance-related' grant described by SORP 2005 as *denying entitlement to the grant as income* until the work done by the recipient to qualify for grant-aid has met the donor's specified 'output' requirements as 'pre-conditions' – see chapter 6. The accounting policy here is needed to clarify the basis of any material accrual or non-accrual of outstanding grant monies, including prepayments/advances received or made within the year:

> 'Contractual income and performance related grants: This is only included in the SoFA once the related goods or services have been delivered.
>
> Grants with performance conditions: Where the charity gives a grant with conditions for its payment being a specific level of service or output to be provided, such grants are only recognised in the SoFA once the recipient of the grant has provided the specified service or output.'
>
> *– CC17a: pro forma Accounting Policies*

Another useful standard text on offer in CC17a is that for governance costs, saying what kind of expense this includes:

> 'costs of the preparation and examination of statutory accounts, the costs of trustee meetings and cost of any legal advice to trustees on governance or constitutional matters.'
>
> *– CC17a: pro forma Accounting Policies*

Yet another is on 'capitalisation', depending on your preferred threshold level:

> 'Tangible fixed assets for use by the charity: These are capitalised if they can be used for more than one year, and cost at least £500. They are valued at cost or a reasonable value on receipt.'
>
> *– CC17a: pro forma Accounting Policies*

Prior to the SORP's 2008 Regulations, you did not even need to mention the SORP itself, nor (unless choosing the FRSSE) the accounting standards, as you can see from the following extracts from the SORP's 2005 Regulations, which provided 'small charity relief' from the general requirement for the notes to include:

> 'a statement as to whether or not the accounts have been prepared in accordance with any applicable accounting standards and statements of recommended practice and particulars of any material departure from those standards and statements of practice and the reasons for such departure.'
>
> *– SI 2005/572, Sch 1, para 1(v)*

> 'Sub-paragraph ... (v) of paragraph 1 above shall not apply in the case of any financial year of a charity which is not an auditable charity.'
>
> *– SI 2005/572, Sch 1, para 2*

That de-regulatory relief was quietly withdrawn in harmonising the regulatory regime across the charity sector, being absent from SI 2008/629. Thus where reg 3 of SI 2005/572 automatically invoked both the SORP and any applicable standards by requiring the SoFA and balance sheet to be prepared in accordance with the SORP but did *not* made any compliance statement here mandatory for the smaller *non-company* charity, the SORP's general requirement to disclose any material non-compliance with accounting standards or the SORP itself is now mandatory for *all* accruals-based accounts of charities (other than 'exempt charities') prepared under the 1993 Act:

> 'If the accounts depart from accounting standards in any material respect, this should be stated in the accounting policies giving the reason and justification for the departure and the financial impact. Similarly ... details should be given for any material departure from this SORP ...'
>
> *– SORP 2005, paragraph 359*

To complement this further statutory disclosure requirement thus imposed by the SORP's 2008 Regulations on *non-company* charities below the audit threshold, by analogy with the equivalent requirement of reg 25(1)(g)(iii) for all *charitable company audit reports* under the 1993 Act, ie, where company audit exemption is claimed for financial years from April 2008, any independent examination report on the accounts of such a 'small' charitable company is required by reg 31(i)(iv)(bb) to state:

'whether or not any matter has come to the examiner's attention in connection with the examination which gives him reasonable cause to believe that in any material respect ... in any case whether [the charitable company's] accounts state they have been prepared in accordance with the SORP, have not in fact been prepared in accordance with the methods and principles set out in the SORP;'

> – *SI 2008/629, reg 31(i)(iv)(bb)*

Still, it does focus the mind of the reader for the charity to have to name the SORP it must or should comply with, so your accounting policies statement in all cases will need to say something to the effect that 'these accounts are prepared in accordance with the current FRSSE as modified by the Charities SORP 2005 within the requirements of [the relevant accounting legislation – i e Charities Act or Companies Act]'.

The current FRSSE only needs mentioning because, within its self-imposed limitations (e g it stops short of accounting for 'controlled' entities*, for which FRS2/9 provide authoritative accounting rules – subject to the SORP, as usual), it is clearly easier for charities to use it in preference to the other accounting standards because of its relative simplicity – in which case the FRSSE itself requires its adoption to be explicitly stated.

(*This means other than charities that are required under the 1993 Act to be treated as part of the reporting entity itself, rather than only being included in group consolidated accounts.)

In addition, to put the matter beyond doubt you might – like a company, which must say whether current costs or historical costs are being used – add that the accounts are on the 'historical cost basis, modified by current value for investment assets [other than social (programme-related) investments]'.

Incoming resources and expenditure in the SoFA and notes

16.2.2 Charities in England and Wales opting for accruals accounting under s 42(1) of the 1993 Act (as distinct from the 'receipts and payments' accounting basis, described below, under s 42(3) of the 1993 Act) must all comply with reg 8 of the SORP's related 2008 Regulations (SI 2008/629), no matter what their size. Regulation 8 binds them to the whole of SORP 2005's requirements for the SoFA, including its title, making the old income and expenditure account as such unacceptable. The statutory requirements do not seem to permit anything in between the s 42(1) and (3) options except by carefully reading between the lines of the SORP.

SORP 2005 clearly does have statutory relief in mind to excuse smaller charities from the general requirement to follow its prescribed SoFA format for incoming and expended resources:

> 'The classification of incoming resources and resources expended by activity is encouraged for all charities preparing accruals accounts. Smaller charities may be excused from adopting this approach by legislation[1] recognising that such information is likely to be less relevant to the users of small charity accounts. Where a small charity adopts an alternative approach to

---

[1]   The reference to 'legislation' is intriguing: in the absence of specific 'small charity' relief in reg 3, it needs to be taken as a pointer to reg 8(5), which says *'the statement [of accounts] shall be prepared in accordance with the methods and principles set out in the SORP'* – whose specific relief (see below) seems to be obliquely authorised by the legislation in this way.

analysis within the Statement of Financial Activities certain note disclosures may no longer be necessary ... These concessions for smaller charities are summarised in Appendix 5.'

– SORP 2005, paragraph 93

Furthermore, the SORP explains that any SoFA *'category headings'* for which *'there is nothing to report'* (meaning that there are no material items for this year or last year) should be excluded, and says that:

'A charity may also vary the order in which it presents activity categories within the incoming resources and resources expended sections of the Statement of Financial Activities to meet its own presentational needs.'

– SORP 2005, paragraph 91

As for the *categorisation* of incoming and expended resources for presentation in the SoFA, the SORP says:

'The Statement of Financial Activities may be adapted to give a true and fair view, but disclosure requirements should always be met and the underlying structure should not be changed.'

– SORP 2005, paragraph 86

This is clearly subject to further clarification as provided in paragraph 93 as set out above, but also in the Small Charities Appendix, in particular at 5.3.2, where the SORP says of its various reliefs for smaller charities:

'These concessions are intended to reduce the detail of reporting requirements placed on smaller charities, though any such charity wishing to follow the full recommendations of the SORP is encouraged to do so.'

– SORP 2005, Appendix 5.3.2

In this way SORP 2005, like previous versions, relieves the smaller charity of its general requirement to follow the prescribed SoFA format for incoming and expended resources, though it does not prescribe a 'best practice' alternative format for either section:

'... smaller charities do not need to analyse either resources expended or incoming resources by activity categories within the Statement of Financial Activities. They may instead choose resource classifications to suit their circumstances.'

– SORP 2005, Appendix 5.3.1(a)

Nevertheless, the CC17b guidance notes do include the following suggested alternative SoFA line-headings (to which we have added [clarifications] where needed) that you can insert into the inset boxes provided for that purpose in the pro forma SoFA in CC17a, instead of the standard ones from the SORP, wherever they seem more appropriate to your charity:

'Incoming resources

–   Donations, legacies and grants [meaning for assets, or else for activities unless *performance-related*]
–   Fundraising events e g concerts, raffles, jumble sales etc.
–   Shop sales

- Interest and dividends [and presumably any rental income]
- Fees for charitable services
- Grants for [charitable] services [if *performance-related*]

Resources expended

- Wages, salaries, pensions and NI [contributions]
- Cost of fundraising events
- Rent, rates and insurance
- Repairs and maintenance
- Light and heat
- Telephone, postage and stationery
- Grants and donations
- Legal and professional fees
- Bank charges and interest'

It goes without saying that whatever the classification adopted it does need to enable the annual report and accounts to demonstrate to the world that the charity's resources have been 'properly applied' within its declared Objects with the aim of providing public benefit, as required by charity law.

Although you can avoid splitting the costs of staff, premises and bought-in supplies, utilities and other services between charitable service provision, trading, fundraising, charity governance, etc, any *charitable grants*, as you can see from the above, will still be in a separate category in their own right – for obvious reasons.

CC17a also provides pro forma tables to be used for sub-analysing income and expenditure (under the same objectives-related activity headings prescribed for the SoFA by the SORP in the case of a larger charity) *'if this would help the reader of the accounts'*, just as it also includes a pro forma analysis table to split 'Support Costs' across fundraising, charitable activities and governance *'if the charity has analysed its expenses using activity categories [in the SoFA] and has support costs'*.

The balance sheet

16.2.3 The only noticeable difference for smaller charities here is normally the size of the figures and the fewer categories of assets and liabilities – such as the absence of an FRS17 notional asset or liability. It is therefore noteworthy that CC17a offers only a *columnar* form of balance sheet rather than the simpler kind of format specified in company law and therefore so familiar to the commercial world that it is almost universally preferred by charities. True, the latter necessitates a separate accounts note analysing the charity's assets and liabilities by fund type, which the use of a columnar balance sheet makes unnecessary, but one might have expected the Commission at least to offer alternative formats.

There is also no great difference in most of the accounts notes supporting the balance sheet, where the pro forma tables in CC17a are nevertheless particularly useful.

RECEIPTS AND PAYMENTS ACCOUNTING OPTION

16.3   When the earliest precursor of the original 1995 Charities SORP was published in 1988 as No 2 in a series of advisory SORPs formulated by the Accounting Standards Committee to cater for sectors of the economy that were seen as having special needs, with SORP2 came a small companion guide, a kind of unofficial tract on the traditional 'receipts and payments' basis, with example accounts illustrating its common usage in this country.

Following publication of the 1995 SORP and its related Regulations, the Charity Commission was left with the task of updating that old booklet for use as guidance on how best to interpret the rather minimalist requirements of the 1993 Act, s 42(3). The result was its popular free guidance leaflet CC54 – *Accounting for the Smaller Charity*. This contained a completely reworked version of the Commission's old standard form of fund-by-fund receipts and payments account and accompanying statement of assets and liabilities annotated to show the fund to which each item belongs, in line with the strict charity law requirements underlying the 1992 and 1993 Charities Acts.

CC54, too, could be downloaded from the Commission's website. Like CC55, it was subsequently turned into a computer-based accounts pack, CC57, the 'Receipts and Payments Accounts Pack', which was also available for downloading and reformatting to suit individual needs.

While both CC54 and CC57 were kept under review, along with the updating of all the other Charity Commission guidance on annual accounting, the continuing absence of changes in the statutory requirements governing accounts prepared under s 42(3) makes it unlikely that in this respect new editions will be able to vary in substance from the old cash-based accounting guidance and computerised work-pack as originally published on the Commission's website – nowadays available as CC16a (as with CC17, you can choose either an Excel spreadsheet or an Acrobat PDF version) and CC16b (guidance notes).

General principles

16.3.1   Where the trustees of a charity in England or Wales opt out of accruals accounting, s 42(3) of the 1993 Act requires an 'account and statement' every year, simply specifying 'receipts and payments' for the content of the one and 'assets and liabilities' for the other. Nothing is said about formats, methods or principles either in Part VI of the 1993 Act itself or in the SORP-related Regulations made thereunder.

CC16 therefore offers guidance on these matters. It suggests separate receipts and payments accounts for endowed, other restricted and unrestricted funds. Interestingly, it does not advise the preparation of a total receipts and payment account for the charity. Of course, the charity law obligation to account separately for distinct restricted funds of the reporting charity can equally well be satisfied by a columnar form of receipts and payments account for the year, rather than a separate account for each fund. Similarly, the required listing of assets and liabilities can be simply annotated in the year-end statement to show their respective fund-ownerships, as an alternative to preparing separate lists for each fund.

On the 'receipts and payments' accounting basis, as the name implies, only the cash (ie money) movements are extracted from the accounting records and reported as the transactions of the year, so gifts in kind to (or by) the charity are not reported as such in the 'account'. Their presence (or absence) will, of course, be picked up by comparing the descriptions of assets in the 'statement' from one year-end to another where they are of the more enduring kind – such as land and buildings, vehicles, equipment, stocks and shares, etc. Where 'material', all such transactions should be featured in the trustees' (brief) annual report as a matter of best practice.

The guidance emphasises the need for consistent treatment of items of the same class within and between each accounting year, and also defines 'materiality' as: 'an item should be regarded as material unless the trustees of the charity can justify its omission from the accounts or annual report on the grounds that it is too trivial to influence the reader'.

An example set of annual accounts prepared on this basis, together with an acceptable form of trustees' annual report derived from the minutes of the members' annual general meeting, will be found in Appendix 8 on the CD-ROM.

The rules for financial years commencing before April 2006 are slightly different for Scottish charities. In Scotland, the Charities Accounts (Scotland) Regulations 1992 remained in force until their repeal by new Regulations made on 24 April 2006. The old rules allowed a 'recognised charity' to prepare a 'receipts and payments account' for a particular financial year and a 'statement of balances' at the year end if the year's gross receipts did not exceed £25,000 (under the 2006 rules this was raised to £100,000, as in England). The contents of the account and statement are currently prescribed by reg 9 and Sch 3 of the 2006 Regulations in place of Part II of Sch 1 to those 1992 Regulations – subject to proposals for new 2009 Regulations currently undergoing public consultation.

The receipts and payments account – receipts

16.3.2 The Charity Commission acknowledges the great diversity of charities and refrains from being too prescriptive as to the headings required here. The basic need is to show the nature and sources of money received, without unnecessary detail and preferably with comparative figures for the previous year.

On the basis that the account must obviously explain changes in total cash resources from year-end to year-end, as well as other 'ins and outs' of money during the year, immaterial items cannot just be omitted but should be included in 'other' or 'sundry' figures as the counterpart of the more significant and therefore specially identified items or headings. Trustees are free to devise their own headings, but the following suggestions offer *general* guidance:

–   covenanted, GiftAid and other donations, also legacies, grants and similar receipts of a *voluntary* nature from external sources (ie excluding trading revenues);

–   GiftAid/covenanted profits donated to the charity by a trading subsidiary (if any);

–   dividends and interest from investment securities;

–   rents from property held as an investment – or from sub-letting or room-hire, etc;

–   interest received on loans and deposits;

–   gross proceeds received from revenue-generating activities by or for the charity, preferably distinguishing between:
  –   charitable trading, ie primarily to promote the charity's Objects;
  –   events/activities to raise 'voluntary' funds (including sales of donated goods);
  –   value-for-value trading primarily to generate profits (fundraising-trading);[2]

–   HMRC receipts from income tax claims;

–   other (occasional) receipts that do not fit in with any of the above (eg money *repaid* to the charity, the sale of an investment or of an asset previously held for the charity's own use, an insurance claim).

The guidance goes into some detail on each of these items, emphasising in the case of voluntary sources that *all* receipts of money have to be included. For gifts other than money, the asset will need to be included in the statement of assets and liabilities (see below) and can only be included in the receipts and payments account for the year when it is sold (converted into money).

Where gifts are received to be passed on 'in kind' to beneficiaries, or where 'intangible' benefits such as free accommodation, supplies, publicity, printing or other free services are received, then they will never be converted into money. Where these are of some significance, such incoming and outgoing gifts should therefore be mentioned in the trustees' annual report. The same goes for volunteer help.

For trading and other fundraising activities, it is the gross proceeds (ie before deduction of costs) as received by the charity (or on its behalf – eg by somebody acting as agent for it) that must be accounted for, thus bringing the cash receipts and cash payments into line with the standard practice required in the Charities SORP.

Income tax claims should of course be accounted for when the cash is received – not when the claim is made (which creates an asset, nevertheless, for inclusion in the year-end statement – see below). Where, for example, donations under GiftAid have been received but the tax claimed on the gift has not yet been received from HMRC, there is a difference from the SORP treatment because the latter 'accrues' the tax claim as arising at the date of gift.

The receipts and payments account – payments

16.3.3   Again, it is up to the trustees and their advisers to devise appropriate headings. In line with Charity Commission guidance, the general suggestions here would be:

---

2   Charities are nowadays allowed by law to undertake this kind of ongoing 'non-charitable' trading activity within prescribed limits without being taxed on the profits, but for any turnover in excess of that the trading activity must be 'hived down' into a trading subsidiary or consortium company that, for tax efficiency, can then donate its annual profits to the charity/charities under GiftAid. Or it could just as easily be 'outsourced' to a parallel trading company set up by the charity's supporters and financed by soft loans from them, as the same tax benefit (though without the nine-month grace period allowed for a profit-stripping GiftAid donation to be paid over by a wholly owned subsidiary) is then available without the hassle of official restrictions designed to constrain the use of the charity's own resources for this purpose.

–   grants of money paid to/for beneficiaries (individuals and institutions) in furtherance of the charity's Objects;

–   loans made to beneficiaries in accordance with the charity's Objects ('recoverable grants');

–   money spent in publicising the charity and educating the public about its work;

–   payments made for bought-in goods/services provided to or for beneficiaries – including the dedicated costs of supporting the provision of these goods/services (eg employed staff, premises (rent, heating, lighting, cleaning), etc);

–   payment of other costs such as solicitors', accountants' and other professional fees; bank charges and interest; any costs of holding trustees' meetings and/or annual general meetings of members (of a charitable association), etc;

–   payments made for fundraising activities/events (and any related publicity) – this would also include any payments made for goods/expenses of a trading activity that falls outside the charity's Objects and must therefore be to raise funds by generating profits (see fundraising trading under 'receipts', above);

–   payments for:
    –   assets such as land/buildings, furniture, vehicles or equipment (eg a wheelchair or a photocopier) which are intended for use by the charity for a number of years; and, separately,
    –   assets which are intended to be retained for investment purposes (eg a payment of cash to purchase shares or other securities);

–   other payments (eg under hire-purchase agreements; repayment of part or the whole of a loan; or an amount transferred to another fund that is being separately accounted for).

The statement of assets and liabilities

16.3.4   The guidance sensibly suggests that assets should be listed in order of their ready availability for spending or use by the trustees. Thus the first item should be the cash and bank balances 'on current account' – ie other than money on fixed or long-term deposit (at notice of more than 7 days), which is more usefully shown separately as an 'investment' asset. The year-end cash/bank balance on each fund of the charity can be checked by adding the net receipts for this year (as shown on the fund's receipts and payments account) to the year-end figure for the previous year (or deducting the net payment).

After that comes the listing of other monetary assets such as debts and all other sums of money owed to the charity, including income tax claims made but not yet received.

Investment assets should be listed next. Securities should be named and the charity's holding described, preferably with either a note of their cost and date of acquisition or perhaps indicating what they are now worth. The market value of quoted stocks and shares can easily be ascertained, although this is not a requirement. However, for other kinds of asset a market value can be more problematical, so a note of the insured value might be helpful instead. A suitable description should be included where this is helpful – such as: *'agricultural land subject to tenancy and currently used for grazing'*. For properties in general, it is clearly helpful to indicate the original cost to the charity and briefly to describe the age and condition of the buildings.

Fixed assets held by the charity mainly for their own use, rather than as investments, need to be included as the next category. The important point here is to get across to the reader a clear idea of the nature and significance of these assets. Age, condition and original cost, perhaps also disposable value or insured value of each significant asset, could usefully be given by way of note. All such assets should be included even though they may be still be on hire-purchase terms as long as the ownership rights are, or will be, ultimately with the charity itself.

Another nicety is the recognition of legacies. Obviously, the money received must be included in the account along with all other income or capital receipts (as the case may be) of the year. Until then, as soon as it becomes legally enforceable against other parties the *right* to a legacy is an asset of the charity and should therefore be included in the year-end statement of assets and liabilities. Such assets are better described as *'the right to a bequest/legacy of £x (or whatever the asset)'* rather than just listing the £x or the asset itself. For further information, it is helpful to indicate the circumstances under which the right has arisen – for example 'under the will of Mr X', and the date of probate (if known) granted to the executors by the court to empower them to gather in and administer the estate.

Liabilities should be listed as current where the charity is due to settle them in the course of the following financial year, but as 'future liabilities' if thereafter. For this purpose, future liabilities and commitments would include outstanding hire-purchase instalments and leasing/rental payments under any kind of legally binding agreement – for example *'the charity is committed to paying rent of £1,000 pa for a further 7 years under the existing lease of its premises'*.

Any legally binding commitment to pay over an already awarded charitable grant (other than by way of charitable loan or 'repayable grant' – which by its very nature is not expected to deplete the charity's resources but only to recycle them) would also come into this category.

Conditional or contingent liabilities (such as guarantees and indemnities) need to be clearly disclosed as such, so that they cannot be confused with actual liabilities.

Chapter 17

THE KEY ROLES OF AUDIT AND INDEPENDENT EXAMINATION

BACKGROUND AND CURRENT POSITION

17.1 The concept of 'audit' is ancient, but people's interpretation or expectation of the concept has changed over the years. To the layman, it is nowadays defined as:

> 'an official inspection of an organisation's accounts, typically by an independent body.'
>
> – The Oxford Dictionary of English (OUP, 1998 edn – current edn 2005).

There would, in general, be an expectation that accounts should be produced and audited when anybody delegates control to another to look after their financial affairs. This would normally require a third person to be assigned to report on the activities of the person to whom such control has been delegated.

This traditional view of audit reflects a triangle formed between 'owner', 'steward' and 'auditor'. During the last half-century in particular, 'audit' has developed almost entirely within the constraints of company law and the production of 'true and fair' accounts mainly of companies trading 'for profit' for the benefit of their shareholders. Indeed, *Chambers Encyclopaedic English Dictionary* (1994) has defined an audit more precisely as 'an official inspection of an organisation's accounts by an accountant'.

Audits are now defined by statute and governed by international auditing standards developed by the auditing profession originally as part of a self-regulatory regime to meet government requirements for greater reliability in the interests of public confidence. To some small companies, these provisions have proved onerous by requiring them to do things that are not suited to their particular situation. The aforementioned requirements, however, have also caused the current professional 'audit' to become onerous to many other types of activity, such as private societies and small charities. Furthermore, as a result of EU concerns over the international ramifications of Enron, WorldCom and other major corporate failures in the USA in recent years, companies legislation now provides for statutory audit regulation through the Public Oversight Board (POB), a subsidiary of the Financial Reporting Council (FRC), the 'unified' independent regulator exercising delegated powers under the Companies Acts. The POB monitors the quality of all independent professional audits in the UK under auditing, accounting and actuarial standards issued by its sister-subsidiaries of the FRC, whose other subsidiaries include the Financial Reporting Review Panel and the Accountancy Investigation and Discipline Board. It is thus responsible for regulatory oversight of the work of accountants and actuaries through their respective professional bodies.

Audit quality regulation for 'public-interest' entities

For major audits – those of public companies and other 'public interest' entities (ie those exceeding £100m turnover, or gross income, for charities – at which level there are only a few dozen charities) – this is achieved directly, through a regime of independent compliance inspections by the POB's Audit Inspection Unit. (For smaller audits the POB relies on an updated version (Quality Assurance Directorates) of the self-regulatory (Joint) Monitoring Units set up and run by those professional accountancy bodies that are now Recognised Supervisory Bodies under the legislation.)

This is now being enhanced through further regulation to provide for 'transparency reports' (detailing the firm's structure, governance and 'network arrangements', its 'processes and procedures' to maintain independence and audit quality, and how partners in the firm are remunerated) by all auditors of 'public-interest' entities, in compliance with Art 40 of a revised EU 8th Company Law Directive which took effect on 29 June 2006 with a two-year timescale for implementation by member states. Putting such information in the public domain will *'provide an incentive for all within the firm to live up to both the spirit and letter of what the firm has promised publicly'*, to quote the POB's director.

International Standards of Auditing (ISAs)

A parallel development in the wake of national and international concerns over the rise of 'money-laundering' and terrorist activities, and especially the risk of charities and the wider voluntary sector being misused for such clandestine purposes, has been the Auditing Practices Board's replacement of its UK Statements of Auditing Standards (SASs) by International Standards on Auditing (ISAs) for the UK and Ireland.

ISAs are more detailed and prescriptive than the old UK/SASs for auditing procedures and documentation, whatever the charity's size, and leave less room for professional judgment. This can only increase audit costs as auditors demand more extensive explanations of a charity's policies and procedures, and in greater depth than hitherto, to enable them to document the more rigorous audit approach needed under ISAs.

Three ISAs in particular, those on audit risk and fraud, have additional requirements to those in the SASs they replaced – ie SAS110: Fraud and Error, SAS210: Knowledge of the Business and SAS300: Accounting and Internal Control Systems, by reference to their ISA equivalents.

ISA240 requires the auditor to understand the charity's process for identifying and responding to fraud risks and how such risks are mitigated by its internal controls. The APB also expects auditors to look out for unusual/unexpected relationships that could increase risk, and to review Board and Committee meeting minutes to evaluate risk factors – such as the use of volunteers and/or inexperienced staff, unpredictable patterns of giving to the charity, branches/operations not under the direct control or supervision of central management, etc.

ISA315 requires the auditor to understand the charity and its regulatory *'environment, including its Internal Control'*. That includes trust law compliance, as well as the special audit reporting requirements where the charity is a Non Departmental Public Body (NDPB) (reporting any losses arising from Internal Control failures, etc), the need for audit information on connected (perhaps non-subsidiary) charities managed and controlled by a *non-company* charity, and even whether any ultra vires activities invalidate the true and fair view required in the accounts. It also includes *'an understanding of the measurement and review of the charity's financial (including investment, fundraising, cost-spreading, reserves-setting – but not: operational) performance'*, its risk-mitigation systems/procedures (including risk-registers), controls over the use of volunteers (especially for fundraising), etc. Obtaining an 'understanding' means evaluating the design and operation of controls (including the use of 'walk-through' tests) to determine whether they can be relied on as effective for preventing, or at least detecting and correcting, material misstatements in the annual accounts.

ISA330 addresses the difficult areas of 'completeness' of incoming resources, overseas operations and restricted funds, as likely to be *'significant risk areas'* for misstatement in annual accounts, and which can thus require special audit procedures for the year's transactions. The APB guidance makes the point that *'the trustees of a charity cannot be held responsible for the security of money or other assets which are intended for its use until that money or assets are, or should be, within the control of the charity'*, and that *'where informal fundraising groups raise money or other resources for charitable purposes on a voluntary basis ... even if a legal entitlement ... may arise under trust law, it would normally be inappropriate for the charity to account for income from such sources since its ultimate cash realisation, so far as the charity itself is concerned, cannot be determined with sufficient certainty'*.

ISAs also call for extra audit procedures to evaluate the risk of 'management override' of controls on journal entries, estimates and accounting for non-routine transactions. These are also areas of particular concern to charity trustees, especially where delegation to executive staff or to agents leaves them with limited involvement in key decision-making or monitoring, needing careful design/documentation of information systems to help them meet their responsibilities – and the auditors to meet theirs.

ISAs impose a specific requirement for auditors to obtain audit evidence for the accuracy and completeness of information produced by the charity when they use it in their audit work. Being able to rely on information produced for the management and governance of the charity is vital to the charity trustees, especially where they have to manage by 'remote control' of operational activities, for example, charities with complex organisational management structures, with large-scale and/or widespread operations.

Charity trustees must then establish, maintain and monitor comprehensive controls over the systems that generate information for them, also over general IT and manual operations as well as specific procedures. Where the trustees are able to demonstrate the reliability of the information generated by the charity, the auditors will be able to save time in obtaining audit evidence to support their use of that information.

Whilst the Bulletin addressed those aspects of auditing standards that changed most significantly due to the introduction of ISAs, the APB pointed out that other aspects of PN 11 also needed to be revised, and said it planned to revise the whole Practice Note in due course, which with hindsight clearly meant in line with the implementation of the 2006 Charities Act, with PN11's revised version being delayed accordingly and finally issued only in December 2008. Richard Fleck, APB Chairman, said at the time:

> 'Following the publication of the ISAs (UK and Ireland) in December, there is a need to update most of the APB's industry-specific Practice Notes currently in issue to provide

relevant guidance, not least on the new requirements relating to audit risk and fraud (ISAs (UK and Ireland) 315, 330 and 240). Due to forthcoming changes in the regulation of charities, PN 11 (Revised) is due to be updated towards the end of 2005. Given this timing, the APB is issuing a transitional Bulletin at this stage setting out guidance for auditors of charities on the areas of audit risk and fraud, which I hope auditors will find useful when planning their 2005 audits.'

Exempt charities

Charities that are 'exempt' under the Charities Act 1993 ('the 1993 Act') are subject to their own overriding law or regulations here. Those requirements may or may not require the kind of audits described in this chapter, and might permit some alternative form of examination. To the extent that they are similar, the rest of this chapter may provide a guide.

Alternatives to full professional audit

In recent years, the law has been changed to permit certain (smaller) regulated organisations to adopt a form of independent scrutiny of their annual accounts that satisfies the original general concept of 'audit' without having to meet all the detailed professional and legal requirements for the audit of larger companies in particular. As far as *non-exempt charities* are concerned, this means that for financial years starting after 31 March 2008 we now have the following progression from total exemption to full professional audit:

Statutory audit or other report on the accounts	Size criteria – Charitable Companies[1]	Size criteria – Other charities
None	Gross income ceiling: £10,000*	Gross income ceiling: £10,000[2]
Report by an independent examiner – suitably qualified if the charity exceeded £250,000 gross income	Gross income ceiling: £500,000	Gross income ceiling: £500,000
Full statutory audit report: Charities Act 1993 (as amended)	Gross income over £500,000 (£100,000* if book value of gross assets over £2.8m*) or else no 'company audit exemption' claim	Gross income of charity or group over £500,000 (£100,000* if book value of gross assets over £2.8m*)
Full statutory audit report: Companies Act 2006 (in succession to the 1985 Act**)	Thresholds: turnover £6.5m; gross assets £3.26m; 50 staff (or 'audit exemption' unclaimed)	Not applicable

*As already noted in chapter 2, for financial years ending after March 2009 the above £10,000, £100,000 and £2.8m thresholds have been increased by the Office for the Third Sector to £25,000, £250,000 and £3.26m respectively, as recommended by the Charity Commission in the light of responses to its 2007 public consultation on a range of proposed changes to the sector's regulatory thresholds to make the regime more 'proportionate'.

[1]   For *company audit* exemption, the claim must be made on the face of the signed balance sheet, confirming that an audit is not demanded by the membership (10% or more; one month's notice given before the year-end) and that the company/group qualifies as 'small' for the year.

[2]   For *parish church councils* below this level, some form of independent examination is a statutory requirement (though without having to conform to the secular legislation), as provided for by *Church Accounting* Regulations made from time to time by the General Synod of the Church of England in the best interests of local congregations.

**Note that the 1985 Act's 'small companies' regime thresholds would apply (instead of the new thresholds shown above) if the company's financial year began between 1st and 5th April 2008 (inclusive): ie, £5.6m turnover, £2.8m gross assets (Balance Sheet value) and 50 staff.

Where a charitable company is the 'parent' of a group for Companies Act purposes, however, for audit exemption to be claimable by any member of the group, including a non-charitable trading subsidiary, apart from other considerations both it and the charity group of which it is a member must be 'small': only one of the above three size criteria can be exceeded for the reporting year and similarly for the previous financial year for this claim to remain valid.

Thus charities preparing accounts under either the 1993 Charities Act or the 2006 Companies Act may have to have a statutory report by a registered auditor or else one by an independent examiner (who must be suitably qualified, as well as experienced, if the charity's gross income was above £250,000 for the year) working to Charity Commission Directions. Exceptionally, they may have no statutory report at all, if below the threshold for independent examination.

Even if not constrained by some kind of audit provision in the charity's governing document, the trustees (or the members, in the case of a charitable company or an unincorporated association) can always choose to procure a more rigorous form of external scrutiny report on their accounts than the minimum laid down by statute.

Conversely, where a charity can otherwise opt out of statutory audit, the trustees may not be able to do so if the constitution (company: memorandum and articles or a statutory notification by 10% of the voting membership; others: trust deed or other 'governing document') states that the accounts are to be audited or otherwise refers to 'audited accounts'.

Charitable companies can amend such an audit provision without further ado by following the procedures laid down in the 1985 Act or its successor, the Companies Act 2006. Charity Commission consent is no longer required for this, because with effect from 18 March 2008 the Charities Act 2006 has restricted the need for such consent to situations where a constitutional amendment affects a provision:

'(b)   ... directing the application of property of the company on its dissolution [or]
(c)   ... where the alteration would provide authorisation for any benefit to be obtained by directors or members of the company or persons connected with them.'

– Charities Act 1993, s 64(2)(b)l(c), as amended with effect from 18 March 2008

For other charities, the constraint can usually be removed where the charity was constituted a long time ago before 'audit' acquired its present meaning. If there is no existing constitutional amendment power, it will need the Charity Commission to effect the change, which it will readily do if satisfied that this is in the public interest. In other cases the Commission's formal consent may be needed.

For certain special situations, charities (other than for an audit under companies legislation) can seek dispensation under reg 34 of the SORP's related 2008 Regulations, but such situations will be the exception rather than the rule.

Apart from charities audited by the National Audit Office (or its Welsh equivalent) or the Audit Commission, which are given ongoing dispensation by reg 34(2)(a) and (b), or for group accounts reg 34(4)(a) or (b), the Charity Commission's dispensation powers are meant to relieve charities where circumstances make the statutory audit or examination unnecessarily burdensome. This may be where the charity is administered by a trust corporation audited under statute, for example.

The rest of this chapter considers the types of report applicable to each situation described in the table above, the work the reporting person will need to do, and who can be appointed to undertake such work.

STATUTORY REPORTS ON THE ACCOUNTS

17.2   There are now just two different forms of statutory report on the accounts, depending on the size of the charity.

Very small *non-company* charities

17.2.1   As long as they make use of their statutory right to remain unregistered, these charities, having no more than £5,000 a year gross income, will remain fully exempt from audit and so do not have to have any form of external scrutiny report on their accounts.

Whether or not registered, those below an annual gross income ceiling of £25,000 for years ending after March 2009 (£10,000 for earlier years) are not required to have a statutory independent examination.

In any of these cases, the trustees are free (subject to constitutional constraints) to commission any kind of review of their accounts and records. This can be an internal or external one, independent or not, and professional or volunteer, as they wish. The form and credibility of the reviewer's report would, of course, depend upon what they want done and upon that person's own knowledge, skill and experience.

If the trustees do not wish to incur the cost of a statutory audit, or even of a statutory independent examination as laid down by the Charity Commission, they should word their instructions accordingly.

Very small *charitable companies*

17.2.2   Again, no statutory report on the accounts is required below a ceiling of £25,000 (£10,000 for years ending before April 2009) gross income, but in this case the directors would normally be well advised not to obtain any non-statutory form of report for attaching to the accounts. They will of course have to include on the balance sheet the form of statement mentioned at **17.2**.

If they have the accounts prepared for them by an independent accountant, they can ask that accountant to report to them on the work done, but this report is non-statutory, it should be addressed to the directors, not to the company's members, and it should not be attached to accounts provided to the public or to the charity's members.

Small charitable companies: 'audit exemption' report – for financial years starting before April 2008 only

17.2.3 The form of report known as a 'reporting accountant's report', as specified in the 1985 Act, s 249C, until that Act's special provisions for charitable company audits were repealed by the Companies Act 2006, was less reliable than that of the independent examiner from the regulator's (Charity Commission/OSCR) viewpoint. The reporting accountant was required to express an opinion only on the following matters:

(a)   whether the accounts were in agreement with the accounting records;

(b)   whether the accounts had been drawn up in a manner consistent with the relevant provisions of the 1985 Act; and

(c)   that the company had satisfied the conditions exempting it from audit.

Note that in (c) above the opinion had to be expressed positively. There was no scope for a negative opinion. In other words, if the reporting accountant considered that the company was not entitled to the exemption, he could not properly complete the report, and therefore the accounts had to be audited. Opinions (b) and (c) were expressed 'having regard only to, and on the basis of, the information contained in' the accounting records mentioned in opinion (a). This clearly precluded all possibility of expressing any kind of opinion on whether or not the accounts showed a true and fair view, for which a full professional audit would have been required.

Small charities subject to an independent examination

17.2.4 Independent examiners, like auditors, may have to report on either receipts and payments accounts or full 'true and fair' accruals accounts. In the latter case, the examiner does not express an opinion on whether the accounts are in fact true and fair, because such an opinion can lawfully only be expressed by a qualified auditor. The reporting requirements in detail are set out in the SORP's 2008 Regulations, in particular reg 31 (or reg 32 in the case of an English or Welsh NHS charity). The form of the report depends on whether it is on receipts-and-payments-based accounts or on full 'true and fair view' accruals accounts. When reporting on accounts (regardless of their basis), the independent examiner has to state the facts:

–   Fact 1: that the report is in respect of an examination carried out under s 43 of the 1993 Act made in accordance with any applicable Directions (see CC31 (June 2008) on the Commission's website: Independent Examination of Charity Accounts issued by the Charity Commission (reg 31(g));

–   Fact 2: whether or not any matter has come to his attention in connection with the examination which gives him reasonable cause to believe that in any material respect accounting records have not been properly kept in respect of the charity as required by the Charities or Companies Act (as applicable) or similarly that the accounts do not accord with those records, or (reg31(h)(i), (ii)); and

–   Fact 3: whether or not any matter has come to his attention in connection with the examination to which in his opinion attention should be drawn in the report in order to enable a proper understanding of the accounts to be reached (reg 31(i)).

The examiner also has to state the fact (where this has become apparent to him during the course of the examination) if, but only if:

–   Fact (i): there has been any material expenditure or action which appears not to be in accordance with the trusts of the charity (reg 31(j)(i)); and

–   Fact (ii): any information to which he is entitled under reg 33 has not been afforded to him (reg 31(j)(ii)).

Additional requirements for the examination of accruals accounts

17.2.5   When reporting on accounts prepared on the accruals basis, the examiner has to make all the above statements and also state whether or not any matter has come to his attention in connection with the examination which gives him reasonable cause to believe that, in any material respect:

–   Fact 4: the statement of accounts does not comply with any of the requirements of the Charities or Companies Act (as applicable) regarding the contents of the accounts, or for a charitable company adopting the Charities SORP any non-compliance with the SORP's 'methods and principles' (but note that in all cases the 'true and fair view' requirement is outside the scope of the independent examiner's report) (reg 31(h)(iii)/(iv)).

Finally, he must also give particulars if, but only if, during the course of the examination it has become apparent to him that:

–   Fact (iii): any information contained in the statement of accounts is inconsistent in any material respect with the trustees' report or the directors' report (in respect of Companies Act disclosures) (reg 31(j)(iii)/(iv)).

Non-company charities and 'small' charitable companies/groups subject to a Charities Act audit

17.2.6   Auditors may also have to report on either receipts-and-payments-based accounts or full 'true and fair' accruals-based accounts. In the SORP's 2008 Regulations, reg 24 or 26 for non-company charities, reg 25 for charitable companies and reg 30 for groups headed by a charitable company require auditors in all cases to state the fact that:

(a)   their report is in respect of an audit carried out under s 43 (or for groups: para 6 of Sch 5A) of the 1993 Act and in accordance with regulations made under s 44 (for groups: as modified by para 8 of Sch 5A) of that Act;

(b)   when reporting under reg 26 on receipts and payments accounts and the accompanying statement of assets and liabilities, auditors must include their opinion as to whether the account and statement *properly present* the receipts and payments of the charity for the financial year in question and its assets and liabilities as at the end of that year (reg 26(1)(f)(i); and

(c)   whether the account and statement adequately distinguish any material special trust or other restricted fund of the charity (reg 26(1)(f)(ii).

Further, auditors are required in all cases (regardless of the basis of the accounts) to include their opinion, and the grounds for it, if in their opinion:

(i)   accounting records have not been kept in respect of the charity* in accordance with Charities or Companies Act requirements (as applicable); or

(ii) the [entity] accounts of the charity* do not accord with the accounting records; or

(iii) any information or explanation to which the auditors are entitled under reg 33 has not been afforded to them.

*This reporting requirement does not apply to the audit of a charity's group accounts – the intention of the Charities Act 2006 is that group consolidated accounts are additional to the parent charity's own entity accounts, not in substitution for them. The audit report on charity accounts published as group consolidated accounts combined with the entity accounts of the parent charity but omitting the entity SoFA (as is customary) must therefore comply with both reg 24 or 26 (for the entity accounts) and reg 30 (for the group accounts).

Special requirements for accruals accounts

17.2.7   When reporting on accruals accounts, auditors must include their opinion (and the grounds for that opinion) on whether the entity accounts comply with the requirements of reg 8 (for ordinary charities), or reg 6 (for common investment funds or common deposit funds) or reg 7 (for non-exempt charities that are either RSLs or higher/further education institutions), and for any group accounts reg 15 or 13/14 respectively, and give a true and fair view of the state of affairs of the charity/group at the end of the financial year in question and of the incoming resources and application of the resources of the charity in the case of a SoFA (as well as of the income and expenditure, in the case of a charitable company) and of the movements in total resources of the group, for any group accounts, in that year.

For the accounts (entity or group) of a charitable company, the audit report must confirm that a Companies Act audit was not required. It must also (unless, exceptionally, there is no declaration in the accounts that they have been prepared in accordance with the Charities SORP) say whether in the auditor's opinion the SORP's 'methods and principles' have been followed.

Finally, the auditors also have to include their opinion (and the grounds for it) if – but only if – in their view any information contained in those accruals accounts is inconsistent in any material respect with matters stated in the trustees' report for that year.

Charitable companies subject to a Companies Act audit

17.2.8   A full Companies Act audit report is required for an incorporated charity unable to claim company audit exemptions, so s 43(9) of the 1993 Act states that the audit provisions of the Charities Act do not apply to a charity which is a company required to be audited under the Companies Act. Under the Companies Act 2006, s 495 (in the 1985 Act, s 235), auditors give their opinion as to whether the accounts give a true and fair view of the financial position and the profit for the year, and whether the accounts have been properly prepared in accordance with that Act. The Auditing

Practices Board's Practice Note PN 11, 'The Audit of Charities', prepared in close collaboration with the Charity Commission, provides the necessary guidance on how to modify this by replacing the inappropriate reference to 'profit'.

That is done by reporting the charity auditor's opinion as to whether the accounts show a true and fair view of the charity's 'incoming resources for the year and application of resources in the year' – thus all its capital and income funding and all its expenditure.

This is reinforced, in recognition of the need for inter-company comparability, by adding 'including its income and expenditure' – thus covering the narrower requirements of company law as well as the special nature of charities.

Auditors also have to report by exception if in their opinion:

(a)   proper accounting records have not been kept by the company;

(b)   proper returns adequate for their audit have not been received from branches not visited by them;

(c)   the balance sheet and income and expenditure account are not in accordance with the accounting records and returns; or

(d)   they have failed to obtain all the information and explanations which to the best of their knowledge and belief are necessary for the purposes of their audit.

The auditors are also required to provide certain information about directors' remuneration if it has not been given in the accounts. This is likely to be an audit issue affecting mainly those charities with directors (being the charity trustees) receiving fees or other remuneration from the company under the new authority provided in the Charities Act 2006 in respect of contracts for non-trustee services to their charity. (Note that employment contracts as such are specifically excluded from this new statutory authorisation. These would have to be authorised by a suitable remuneration clause in the company's Memorandum and Articles – for which consent from the Charity Commission is needed.)

The 'propriety' of charity expenditure is a special feature of the larger registered charities' annual returns to the Charity Commission (ie those with more than £500,000 gross income), where all the key figures from the SoFA and Balance Sheet must be entered in numbered boxes for use by the Charity Commission for regulatory purposes – and also for publication on its website as public domain information. The Charities SORP defines what needs to be included in the accounts of a charity in order to give a true and fair view, and this then – as PN11 explains – requires charity auditors to embrace the SoFA in their report. This will be the case whether the SoFA includes all the information required of an income and expenditure account or whether a separate summary income and expenditure account is prepared. It will normally be achieved by including reference to the charitable company's 'incoming resources and application of resources' as well as its income and expenditure, as required by the APB, and as explained above.

The Companies Act 2006, s 496 (in the 1985 Act s 235(3)) also requires a *positive* opinion as to whether the *statutory* information (ie under the Companies Act, as distinct from the Charities Act) given in the directors' report – see chapter 4 – is consistent with the audited accounts.

OTHER INFORMATION IN REPORTS

17.3   The SORP's related Regulations, the Companies Act and also the auditing standards require certain other information to be included in the above reports. Their requirements are similar, and taken together mean that the reports should:

(a)   be addressed to the charity trustees (or to the members, if a company);

(b)   state the name of the charity;

(c)   identify the constituent parts (SoFA, balance sheet, cashflow statement, if applicable, accounting policies and other accounts notes) of the accounts being reported on, including stating the financial year in respect of which the accounts have been prepared – as well as clarifying (within the audit opinion) the particular *accounting framework* (for all charities this will be UK, as distinct from EU or even international, Generally Accepted Accounting Practice or GAAP) under which those accounts were prepared;

(d)   state the name, address and qualifications of the person reporting. For an independent examiner the latter includes any relevant professional qualifications or membership of any relevant professional body. Auditors have to state that they are registered auditors;

(e)   be signed and show the actual date of signature.

TRUSTEES'/DIRECTORS' RESPONSIBILITY FOR THE ACCOUNTS

17.4   Under statute, the trustees are only required to acknowledge their responsibility for the accounts where they are the directors of a company claiming exemption from audit. That apart, the board must authorise one or more directors to sign the balance sheet to indicate that they as a body have formally approved the accounts, and the date on which that happened.

The APB, however, requires auditors generally to ensure that a fuller statement is included in respect of true and fair accounts. This will be either in the audit report itself, or cross-referenced in the audit report to a separate statement provided by the charity trustees as part of the annual report and accounts.

In the case of the Scout Association (see the illustration below) the responsibilities statement is contained within the auditors' report. As is generally done for safety's sake, the statement more or less follows the standard wording suggested by the APB in the Auditing Standard and PN11 – which unfortunately still does not make any special mention of the perhaps blindingly obvious: the trustees' responsibility under charity law for ensuring the proper application of all the charity's resources – surely something no auditor would like to be thought even partly responsible for. Similarly, it does not acknowledge that the accounting policies must be those considered *most* suitable – as specifically required by FRS18. (In the case of a 'small' charitable company (as defined by the Companies Act) the disclosure obligation under the third bullet point is subsumed by, and would need to be restricted to, departures from *company accounting principles*, as now set out in the legislation.)

Respective Responsibilities of the Trustees and Auditors

Charity law requires the Trustees to prepare financial statements in accordance with applicable law and United Kingdom Generally Accepted Accounting Practices, for each financial year which give a true and fair view of the state of affairs of the charity and of the results for that period. In preparing those financial statements, the Trustees are required to:

- select suitable accounting policies and then apply them consistently

- make judgements and estimates that are reasonable and prudent

- comply with applicable accounting standards subject to any material departures disclosed and explained in the financial statements; and prepare the financial statements on the going concern basis unless it is inappropriate to presume that the charity will continue in operation.

The Trustees are responsible for maintaining proper accounting records which disclose with reasonable accuracy the financial position of the charity and to enable them to ensure that the financial statements comply with the Charities Act 1993. They are also responsible for safeguarding the assets of the charity and hence for taking reasonable steps for the prevention and detection of fraud and other irregularities.

Scout Association – 2007/08 Accounts: Audit Report

This professional audit requirement of the APB (suitably adapted) applies equally to auditors' reports on receipts and payments accounts. Consequently, it would be good practice for professional independent examiners to ensure that the respective responsibilities of the trustees and examiners are made clear by a similar statement.

WORK DONE IN EXAMINING ACCOUNTS

17.5   It is not the role of this book to cover charity audit or independent examination in detail, but just to provide an outline for charity trustees of what needs to be done so that they can appreciate how this impacts on the preparation of annual reports and accounts. This chapter therefore does not discuss the way in which the work itself is managed.

The very smallest charities

17.5.1 As stated above, the very smallest charities which are fully exempt from any statutory reporting requirement may nevertheless commission their own form of independent scrutiny of the accounts. This may often be done orally with little specific direction as to the areas to be looked at, or the form of report required. The work done will be at the scrutineer's discretion within the terms of engagement agreed beforehand with the trustees, but is likely to include checking documentation to the accounts, seeing that the accounts reflect the decisions of the trustees, checking additions and summaries, and perhaps checking completeness of income where that is possible. An example would be reconciling membership income to membership records. The scrutineer may also wish to check bank statements and any material assets, but is unlikely to seek independent confirmation of any matters.

Independent examiners

17.5.2 The work required to be done by independent examiners in carrying out an independent examination is laid down and explained in the 'General Directions' and guidance notes issued by the Charity Commission as CC31: Independent Examination of Charity Accounts, the June 2008 version of which can be downloaded from the Commission's website. Reg 33 of the SORP's related 2008 Regulations (SI 2008/629) gives examiners a right of access to the books, documents and other records of the charity and entitles them to require information and explanations from past or present trustees, officers or employees.

CC31 sets out its 10 statutory Directions and explains their minimum requirements for the procedures which the examiner must fulfil in order to be able to report on the accounts of the charity as required by the Regulations. The first six Directions apply to the examination of all accounts, whether they are 'receipts and payments' based or 'true and fair'. Three apply only to 'true and fair' accounts (those containing a SoFA and balance sheet), and the last one covers the examiner's reporting responsibilities.

Procedures for all accounts

17.5.3 The six procedures governing the examiner's work on all accounts cover understanding the charity, the form of the accounts and exemption from audit, examining the underlying records, making an overall review of the accounts and checking these back to the records, use of 'analytical review' procedures where considered necessary and documenting all examination procedures as evidence of the work done and the basis for all conclusions reached.

Understanding the charity (Direction No 3) requires the examiner to:

(a)   obtain a copy of, and understand the charity's trust deed or other constitutional document;

(b)   know who the trustees are and the people they have authorised to undertake the charity's business;

(c)   understand the intention of the charity and how it is organised;

(d)   identify its beneficiaries, the nature of its transactions and its assets and liabilities;

(e) review the minutes of trustee meetings, and hold discussions with trustees to obtain further information about the actions, decisions and the planned activities of the charity and any problems of which the trustees are aware.

To ensure that the form of the accounts is appropriate and independent examination is a valid option (Direction No 1), the examiner will need to:

(a) check that the trust deed or other governing instrument does not include an audit requirement;

(b) check that the total income (on the permissible accounting basis) of the charity including any 'charity branches' is within the audit exemption limits (ie, between £10,000*/£25,000 and £500,000 gross income – or £100,000*/£250,000 if gross assets at their book value under the SORP exceed £2.8m*/£3.26m) and that if the charity has subsidiaries that would have to be consolidated where group aggregate gross income is above £500,000 after 'consolidation adjustments', that this threshold has not been exceeded (*for years ending before April 2009 or the new, higher threshold thereafter).

For this purpose it should be noted that certain 'capital' movements have always been excluded from the Charity Commission's definition of gross income, such as incoming permanent endowments, any purchases and sales of investments, any gains or losses arising on disposal of fixed assets, and also all loans, whether made, received or repaid.

The examination of the accounting records and review of the accounts prepared from them, including any necessary 'analytical review' procedures (Directions No 4 to 6) should be sufficient to support the examiner's opinion, but it is not necessary to check every item in the accounts with the underlying records.

As a minimum the independent examiner would usually:

(a) check all large amounts back to the underlying records, particularly where several detailed trust accounts have been combined to produce the accounts being examined;

(b) check or perform bank reconciliations;

(c) check any control accounts and list of balances on subsidiary ledgers;

(d) test the underlying records in sufficient detail to ensure that all material errors and any major failures to keep the records correctly are identified and corrected;

(e) review major assets and liabilities for consistency with the level and kind of activity undertaken and the latter's appropriateness in relation to the charity's Objects for the public benefit.

Particular attention should be paid to any areas where the examiner suspects there may be weaknesses in bookkeeping or control. The examiner should carry out analytical review procedures to help identify any unusual items, disclosures or omissions. This is mainly done by comparing the current and preceding year's accounts for changes in trends, and by comparing the accounts against budgets or forecasts and what the examiner would expect to see from his knowledge of the charity's activities.

Where the examiner is not satisfied with the information, or does not understand the amounts disclosed, he should discuss the points with the trustees. In addition, the examiner might decide to undertake some verification work, such as physically inspecting a major tangible asset or obtaining third-party verification of it, checking for subsequent settlement of an outstanding debt, etc, but this extra work is outside the General Directions.

The above work is designed to enable the examiner to satisfy himself that the accounting records are *reliable*, or whether there is 'reasonable cause to believe that in any material respect the accounting records have not been kept' *in accordance with* s 41 of the 1993 Act (or with s 386 Companies Act 2006 (s 221 in the 1985 Act), in the case of a charitable company). If there is reasonable cause, the examiner would normally attempt to persuade the trustees to provide further information, or to correct the accounts where appropriate. If the accounts are adjusted, the 'reasonable cause' might be removed and the examiner would not have to draw attention to the problem in the report on the accounts. However, if the accounts remain uncorrected the examiner may still have to highlight it in the report.

Procedures for 'true and fair' accounts only

17.5.4 Procedures applicable only to 'true and fair' accounts cover the form and content of the accruals accounts, compliance with the SORP's 'methods and principles (disregarding whether or not this results in the accounts showing a 'true and fair view' as required by law), the key to this being the Accounting Policies disclosure note, any post-balance sheet events and the need for consistency between accounts figures and the trustees' report. In examining the form and content of the accounts, the examiner has to carry out such detailed procedures as (the examiner) considers necessary to provide a reasonable basis on which to decide whether or not the accounts comply with the regulations (or with Companies Act requirements, in the case of a charitable company) as to the form and content of the accounts (Direction No 7).

In practice, this means *understanding* the form and content of accounts required by the legislation. It also involves ensuring that all relevant headings, fund analyses and notes relevant to the charity's affairs have been included in accordance with the specifications in Sch 2 to the SORP's related 2008 Regulations.

The Charity Commission will also expect the accounts to follow those 'best practice' recommendations for small charities below the audit threshold as summarised in Appendix 5 of the Charities SORP that are not made mandatory by its related 2008 Regulations. The use of an appropriate checklist is recommended (see Appendix 7 on the CD-ROM).

The requirement for accruals accounts to include a statement of the accounting policies and estimation techniques adopted is one of the most crucial in the SORP's 2008 Regulations (or the Companies Act requirements, in the case of a charitable company), as, in conjunction with the 'true and fair view' requirement[3] of the relevant legislation, it effectively applies accounting standards, as well as underpinning the application of the Charities SORP, to the accounts.

The examiner must therefore *review* the accounting policies and assumptions disclosed (or not) in the accounts notes (Direction No 8). Consideration must be given to their *conformity* with the two fundamental accounting concepts or 'principles' described in FRS18 as having a 'pervasive' role in accounts intended to show a 'true and fair' view, and which for this reason are normally left unsaid:

(1)   the assumption that the charity will continue to be a 'going concern' for the next financial year; and

(2)   the 'accrual', in full, of all assets and liabilities.

In particular, consideration must be given to the extent to which those policies and assumptions enable the accounts to meet FRS18's four key 'objectives' of:

(3)   relevance;

(4)   reliability (which includes the concept of prudence in cases of uncertainty);

(5)   comparability (which includes consistency); and

(6)   understandability,

within the constraints imposed by the need for these four different objectives to be weighed against each other and for the cost of providing accounts information not to outweigh the benefit to the user.

The accounting policies and assumptions must also be reviewed as to whether they have been applied consistently from year to year and within the same set of accounts, and how appropriate they are to the charity's activities. This includes considering the appropriateness, or reasonableness, of any significant estimates or judgments made by the trustees – even though this must stop short of any conclusion as to whether or not the accounts do in fact show a true and fair view as required by law, since that would require an audit.

Particular areas of interest might for the examiner include:

(a)   cost allocations between expenditure headings;

(b)   significant transfers to or from designated funds;

(c)   transfers between restricted funds and/or from there to unrestricted funds (Charity Commission approval is normally needed for any variation of the purposes for which endowed or other restricted funds are held, unless donor-authority has been previously obtained);

---

[3]   It should be noted here that although the examiner is to disregard the 'true and fair view' requirement in its entirety, this does not in any way lessen the statutory obligation of the trustees themselves to prepare accounts showing a true and fair view.

(d)   the valuation of major gifts of land, buildings and listed/unlisted investments or other assets that are required to be recorded in the accounts, where not done by a qualified valuer.

Reporting procedures

17.5.5   Even though independent examiners are not required to form an opinion on the view given by the accounts, they do need to see that relevant facts are reported. They may therefore need to consider, in reviewing the accounts (see above) any significant events occurring after the balance sheet date and before the date of their report, to see whether and to what extent these may affect the amounts included in the accounts, or whether they need to be mentioned in the accounts notes or in the trustees' report.

The independent examiner compares 'accruals' accounts with the trustees' annual report. This is to see if there are any major inconsistencies that would have any significant effect on a proper understanding of the charity's accounts (Direction No 9), and which would therefore need to be mentioned in the examiner's report (Direction No 10) whose detailed contents are specified in the SORP's 2008 Regulations.

Whatever the extent of the independent examiner's work, it should be recorded in sufficient detail for another experienced examiner to be able to understand it and the grounds for the conclusions reached (Direction No 2).

The examiner should therefore retain documentary evidence of all important matters affecting the examination report. Such records should include, inter alia:

–   notes of extracts from the governing document and trustees' minutes;

–   notes of discussions with trustees;

–   the tests done on the areas examined;

–   notes about any areas of concern and action taken to resolve them or leading to comments in the report; and

–   copies of the final accounts and report, and any supporting summaries linking the accounting records to the accounts.

Certain matters are required to be reported in writing direct to the Charity Commission as regulator (see **17.8**). These are now the same for auditors and examiners, and are now set out in s 44A inserted into the 1993 Act by the Charities Act 2006.

AUDITORS

17.6   In simple terms, the work of the auditors includes all that the independent examiner has to do, plus many other aspects, including those specifically excluded from the work of the independent examiner (as mentioned above). Auditors have to comply with all international auditing standards for the UK and Ireland, which require them, amongst other things, to:

(a)   obtain an adequate 'knowledge of the business' of the entity which they are auditing;

(b)   design their tests to have a reasonable chance of detecting all material errors (whether or not caused by fraud) and of breaches of laws and regulations affecting the entity;

(c)   consider whether the entity is a going concern;

(d)   review other information to be issued with the audited accounts;

(e)   understand and document the accounting and control systems so far as relevant to their audit;

(f)   obtain independent evidence supporting the entries in the accounting records, of the existence, value and ownership of assets and liabilities, and of completeness of income and expenditure; and

(g)   obtain written confirmation from the trustees or directors of any information supplied affecting the accounts which cannot be verified by third-party evidence.

For the last requirement, under the new ISAs, auditors are not allowed to place reliance on any unsupported confirmations, and must therefore look beyond the traditional 'management representations' letter from the Board for the corroborating audit evidence needed for compliance with standards. This ties in with the company law requirement for a special statement in the directors' report – see chapter 4 – to confirm that each of the current directors has taken all necessary steps to ensure they are fully informed on all relevant audit matters and that the auditors also have such information.

WHO CAN BE APPOINTED?

17.7   The 1993 Act has been amended by the 2006 Act to specify who may undertake the work of independent examiner and auditor.

'Qualified' independent examiners

17.7.1   Only a 'qualified' independent examiner may act for any charity above the old audit threshold of £250,000 gross income, charitable companies included, whereas for all smaller charities the trustees can lawfully appoint as independent examiner anyone they reasonably believe to be competent – even if unqualified professionally. The 1993 Act (as amended by the Charities Act 2006) defines what is meant by 'qualified' here to include those who used to be eligible to act as 'reporting accountant' for a charitable company under the 1985 Act until the special audit exemption regime for charitable companies was abolished by the 2006 Companies Act for financial years starting after March 2008. This was a person who is either entitled to engage in public practice (provided they were independent of the directors in accordance with s 27 of the Companies Act 1989), or who is eligible for appointment as a company auditor. As specified in the 1985 Act and its successor of 2006, the person may be an individual, a body corporate or a partnership.

The 1985 Act's list, now set out in s 43(3A) and (3B) of the 1993 Act, has also been extended to include fellows of the Association of Charity Independent Examiners. In all other cases the person must be a member, and eligible under the rules, of one of the 'recognised supervisory bodies' as listed at **17.7.3** (for company and charity audits) or one of the following:

–   Association of Accounting Technicians;

–   Association of International Accountants;

–   Chartered Institute of Management Accountants;

–   Institute of Chartered Secretaries and Administrators;

–   Chartered Institute of Public Finance and Accountancy.

Other independent examiners

17.7.2   Trustees are in any case duty bound to exercise due care to ensure that they obtain a competent and independent examination of their accounts. In doing this they should take all reasonable steps to satisfy themselves as to the suitability of an appointee. The 1993 Act defines an independent examiner as:

> 'an independent person who is reasonably believed by the trustees to have the requisite ability and practical experience to carry out a competent examination of the accounts.'
>
> – *Charities Act 1993, s 43(3)(a)*

This definition is expanded on in the Directions issued by the Charity Commission (CC31):

> *Independence* is important because this means that the examiner is not influenced, or perceived to be, by either close personal relationships with the trustees or by day to day involvement in the administration of the charity. For an examiner to be independent that individual should have no connection with the charity trustees which might inhibit the impartial conduct of the examination. An examiner cannot independently review his or her own work and so the person who is the charity's book-keeper cannot be the charity's examiner. However this does not mean an examiner cannot be a member or supporter of the charity, and often some involvement brings an added quality of personal enthusiasm and familiarity to the role of examiner.

> [To be *competent* the examiner] must be familiar with accounting methods, but he need not be a practising accountant ... people such as bank or building society managers, local authority treasurers or retired accountants [would all have this competence, according to views expressed at the time in the House of Lords whilst debating the 1991 Charities Bill].

To this, the Commission's Directions add:

> Whether receipts and payments accounts or accruals accounts are prepared, the examiner needs some familiarity with certain basic principles, including the different types of income

funds (unrestricted and restricted) and capital funds (permanent and expendable endowment), the nature of trusts, the responsibilities of trustees and the role of the charity's governing document.

To have *practical experience* of, for example, previous financial administration of a charity of similar size and/or nature, or previous experience of acting as independent examiner or relevant practical accounting or commercial experience, is considered an essential adjunct to the above competence.

Persons who would not be considered suitable include:

(a)   the trustees themselves;

(b)   other persons closely involved in the administration of the charity;

(c)   major donors to, or dependent beneficiaries of, the charity;

(d)   any close relative, business partner or employee of any of the above; and

(e)   anyone who has no experience of charities or other kinds of institution giving them the necessary practical experience of financial management, review and reporting.

The 1993 Act uses the word 'person' here, which is normally understood to embrace individuals, partnerships and corporate bodies. The Interpretation Act 1978, Sch 1, applies this use of the word 'person' in any Act of Parliament or subordinate legislation made after 1 January 1979 except where the contrary intention is apparent.

It is therefore of some interest to note the distinction between the references in the SORP's 2008 Regulations to an auditor and an independent examiner. Sub-para (1)(b) of reg 24 for a non-company charity's accruals-based accounts, reg 25 for a charitable company's accounts, reg 26 for a non-company charity's cash-based accounts and reg 30 for group accounts in each case requires the report of the auditor to be signed by him:

'... or, where the office of auditor is held by a body corporate or partnership, in its name by a person authorised to sign on its behalf ...'.

– *SI 2008/629, reg 24(1)(b), reg 25(1)(b), reg 26(1)(b) and reg 30(1)(b)*

In contrast, reg 31(b) and (e) simply require the independent examiner's report to be signed by him and to specify:

'... any, or any other, relevant professional qualifications or professional body of which he is a member ...'.

– *SI 2008/629, reg 31(e)*

Consolidated accounts below the audit threshold

CC31 also points out that where consolidated accounts are prepared for a 'small' group, ie, one below the Charities Act audit threshold, these would be *non-statutory*, and that their independent examination would also be non-statutory – ie, not subject to the Commission's ten Directions to examiners. By the same token, in respect of the group accounts the examiner would not be subject to the whistle-blowing duty imposed by s 44A – although that duty would certainly apply in respect of the parent charity's own entity accounts if its gross income exceeded the £25,000 (or £10,000 for years ending before April 2009) gross income threshold for a statutory independent examination.

This odd situation seems to have resulted from the fact that although para 6 of Sch 5A makes provision for regulations to set a lower income threshold for the audit of small groups with assets above a specified threshold (like the *non-company* charity's lower accruals-accounting threshold of £250,000 (previously £100,000) gross income if the SORP-based book value of gross assets exceeds £3.26m (previously £2.8m)) no such regulations have yet been made:

Preparation of group accounts

3.—(1) This paragraph applies in relation to a financial year of a charity if—

(a) the charity is a parent charity at the end of that year; and
(b) (where it is a company) it is not required to prepare consolidated accounts for that year under ... the Companies Act ... whether or not such accounts are in fact prepared.

(2) The charity trustees of the parent charity must prepare group accounts in respect of that year.

Exceptions ... to requirement to prepare group accounts

4.— (2) The requirement in paragraph 3(2) does not apply to the charity trustees of a parent charity in relation to a financial year if the aggregate gross income of the group for that year does not exceed such sum as is specified in regulations made by the Minister.

Audit of accounts of larger groups

6.—(1) This paragraph applies where group accounts are prepared for a financial year of a parent charity under paragraph 3(2) and—

(a) the aggregate gross income of the group in that year exceeds the relevant income threshold, or
(b) the aggregate gross income of the group in that year exceeds the relevant income threshold and at the end of the year the aggregate value of the assets of the group (before deduction of liabilities) exceeds the relevant assets threshold.

(2) In sub-paragraph (1)–

(a) the reference in paragraph (a) or (b) to the relevant income threshold is a reference to the sum prescribed as the relevant income threshold for the purposes of that paragraph, and
(b) the reference in paragraph (b) to the relevant assets threshold is a reference to the sum prescribed as the relevant assets threshold for the purposes of that paragraph. "Prescribed" means prescribed by regulations made by the Minister.

– Charities Act 1993, Sch 5A

Exceptions ... to requirement to prepare group accounts

18. The sum specified for the purposes of paragraph 4(2) of Schedule 5A to the 1993 Act is £500,000.

Audit of accounts of larger groups

29. The sum prescribed as the relevant income threshold for the purpose of paragraph 6(1)(a) of Schedule 5A to the 1993 Act is £500,000.

– SI 2008/629, reg 18 and reg 29

This is consistent with chapter 4 of the SORP's 2008 Regulations, where reg 31 and, for NHS charities, reg 32, provide for independent examination not of groups but only of individual charity accounts, thus in the case of a parent charity its entity accounts. The relevant audit thresholds for this are prescribed in the primary legislation as:

Annual audit or examination of charity accounts

43.—(1)   [The accounts must be audited for] a financial year of a charity if–

(a) the charity's gross income in that year exceeds £500,000; or

(b) the charity's gross income in that year exceeds the accounts threshold and at the end of the year the aggregate value of its assets (before deduction of liabilities) exceeds £2.8 million*.

"The accounts threshold" means £100,000* or such other sum as is for the time being specified in s 42(3) ...

– Charities Act 1993, Part VI

(*for financial years ending after March 2009 these thresholds were raised by SI 2009/508 to £3.26m and £250,000 respectively.)

As a solution to this problem, CC31 goes on to suggest that its 'principles could be applied by a contractual arrangement between the charity and the examiner'.

An alternative might be for the trustees of a charity preparing *non-statutory* group accounts to take up the kind of non-audit assurance service recently launched by the Institute of Chartered Accountants (E&W) to fill the gap that has been left in the profit sector for non-charitable companies below the £6.5m turnover threshold for company audit exemption.

Auditors

17.7.3   Section 43 of the 1993 Act states that an auditor must be a person who:

(a)   would be eligible for appointment as auditor of the charity under Part 2 of the Companies Act 1989 if the accounts of the charity were required to be audited in accordance with ... the Companies Act ...; or

(b)   is a member of a body for the time being specified in regulations under s 44 ... and is under the rules of that body eligible for appointment as auditor of the charity.

At the time of writing, only (a) applies since no regulations have been issued under s 44. The Companies Act 1989 states that:

'(1)   A person is eligible for appointment as a company auditor only if he—

(a)   is a member of a recognised supervisory body, and
(b)   is eligible for the appointment under the rules of that body.

(2)   An individual or a firm may be appointed a company auditor.'

– Companies Act 1989, s 25

The recognised supervisory bodies are:

–   Institute of Chartered Accountants in England and Wales;

–   Institute of Chartered Accountants of Scotland;

–   Institute of Chartered Accountants in Ireland;

–   Association of Chartered Certified Accountants;

–   Association of Authorised Public Accountants.

A person is 'eligible for appointment' if he is already recognised by the relevant body as a 'registered auditor'. If in doubt, the trustees should consult the registration department of the relevant body to confirm the status of the proposed auditor.

REPORTING TO THE REGULATOR

17.8   Whereas reg 7(5) of the SORP's 2005 Regulations made under Part VI of the 1993 Act imposed a statutory duty on charity auditors to report certain matters in writing to the Charity Commission as regulator and an equivalent, if somewhat simplified, statutory duty was imposed on independent examiners by the Charity Commissioners' General Directions at the time, the Charities Act 2006 has instead brought the charity auditor's duty into the primary legislation as s 44A, at the same time imposing exactly the same duty on independent examiners as well – thus enabling the Commission to drop the old Direction No 12 for its revised Directions, which are now set out in CC31: Independent Examination of Charity Accounts (June 2008). The harmonised whistle-blowing duty is now:

Duty of auditors etc to report matters to Commission

(1)   This section applies to ... a person acting as an auditor or independent examiner appointed ... under s 43 ...

(2)   If, in the course of acting in [that] capacity ..., [the auditor or examiner] becomes aware of a matter—

(a)   which relates to the activities or affairs of the charity or of any connected institution or body, and

(b)   which he has reasonable cause to believe is likely to be of material significance for the purposes of the exercise by the Commission of its functions under s 8 or 18 above,

he must immediately make a written report on the matter to the Commission.

(3)   If, in the course of acting in [that] capacity ..., [the auditor or examiner] becomes aware of any matter—

(a)   which does not appear to him to be one that he is required to report under s 44A(2) above, but
(b)   which he has reasonable cause to believe is likely to be relevant for the purposes of the exercise by the Commission of any of its functions,

he may make a report on the matter to the Commission.

(4)   Where the duty or power under s 44A(2) or (3) [respectively] has arisen [for the auditor or examiner], [it] is not affected by his subsequently ceasing to act in that capacity.

(5)   Where a person makes a report as required or authorised by s 44A(2) or (3), no duty to which he is subject is to be regarded as contravened merely because of any information or opinion contained in the report.

(6)   In this section "connected institution or body", in relation to a charity, means—

(a)   an institution which is controlled by, or
(b)   a body corporate in which a substantial interest is held by,

the charity or any one or more of the charity trustees acting in his or their capacity as such.

(7)   Paragraphs 3 and 4 of Sch 5 to this Act apply for the purposes of s 44A(6) above as they apply for the purposes of [s 36 (disposal of charity land)].

– Charities Act 1993, s 44A

Meaning of "connected person" ...

3.   ... a person controls an institution if he is able to secure that the affairs of the institution are conducted in accordance with his wishes.

4.—(1)   ... [a] connected person ... has a substantial interest in a body corporate if the person or institution in question—

(a)   is interested in shares comprised in the equity share capital of that body of a nominal value of more than one-fifth of that share capital, or
(b)   is entitled to exercise, or control the exercise of, more than one-fifth of the voting power at any general meeting of that body. ...

– Charities Act 1993, Sch 5

As the APB's PN 11 'The Audit of Charities' makes clear, while under the 1993 Act auditors (like independent examiners, as explained above) must report directly to the Charity Commission anything coming to notice during their work that gives them reasonable cause to believe that a *breach of trust or of legislative requirements, maladministration* or other cause (such as gross carelessness/neglect on the part of the trustees) of actual or potential *loss of charity funds* may be of *material significance* to the exercise by the Commissioners of their supervisory powers (s 8 (inquiries) and s 18 (intervention by the Commission) of the 1993 Act), prior to the implementation for financial years starting after March 2008 of the above-mentioned 'whistle-blowing' provision as s 44A of the 1993 Act, auditors of *charitable companies* used to have no legal *duty* but only a legal *right* to do the same 'in the public interest'. It was in fulfilment of the old DTI's (now DBIS, in succession to the DBERR) 'level playing field' commitment during the setting up of the present regulatory regime for charities in the early nineties, that this right has now been made a duty under the Charities Act 2006 in tandem with the equivalent duty simultaneously imposed on the auditors of larger charitable companies by s 33 of the Charities Act 2006 by the insertion of a new s 68A into the 1993 Act:

> *Duty of charity's auditors etc. to report matters to Commission*
>
> (1)   Section 44A(2) to (7) above shall apply in relation to a person acting as ... an auditor of a charitable company appointed under [the Companies Act], ... as they apply in relation to [a charity auditor acting under s 43].
>
> (2)   For this purpose any reference in section 44A to a [charity auditor] is to be read as a reference to his acting [unde the Companies Act].
>
> (3)   In this section "charitable company" means a charity which is a company.
>
> *– Charities Act 1993, s 68A*

No additional work seems to be required for this purpose, and charity auditors and examiners can draw comfort from the assurance that the law protects against claims of breach of client confidentiality in such cases. However, in 2002 PN 11 abandoned the line (taken originally by the Charity Commission in 1996 for fear of being swamped by inconsequential audit notifications) that these situations will always be *extreme* cases; cases characterised by trustees appearing to be unable/unwilling to fulfil their personal duty of care in protecting their charity's assets and ensuring their proper application as required by law – the care normally taken by a 'prudent man of business'.

In such cases the Commission's supervisory action to protect the charity would seem to be unavoidable once the facts come to light. The list of actually or potentially notifiable situations is set out in Appendix 5 to PN 11, broadly in line with the 'Serious Incidents Reporting' regime imposed on charity trustees under the Annual Returns regulations for all registered charities exceeding £25,000 annual gross income, with the seriousness with which these situations are perceived by the Commission being based on the materiality or 'significance' of the loss or risk to the charity or the sector.

The Commission's Annual Return guidance notes for the charity trustees say:

> 'All trustees should provide information about serious incidents as soon as possible after they become aware of them. If your charity has an income over £25,000 you must, as part of the Annual Return, confirm that there are no serious incidents or other matters relating to your charity over the previous financial year that you should have brought to our attention but have not. Failure to confirm this will be regarded as a breach of legal requirements. ...
>
> ... if it is just an allegation or suspicion ... you should still report this to us if you have received information that leads you to believe or suspect that a serious incident has happened

and you have reasonable grounds for the suspicion. Trustees are responsible for taking appropriate action in response to a suspicion and we will expect to know what you have done.

What is serious or significant?

This is for you to decide in the context of your charity. ... We have ... identified several 'zero tolerance' issues ... that we will always deal with ... as a priority. These issues are, in no particular order:

- Connections to proscribed (banned) organisations
- Charity links to or support for terrorism, financial or otherwise
- Misuse of a charity to foster criminal extremism
- Fraud and money laundering
- Abuse of vulnerable beneficiaries
- Not having adequate measures in place to protect vulnerable beneficiaries
- Sham charities, set up for illegal or improper purposes

Fraud, theft or significant loss of funds or other property

You should report to us any actual or suspected fraud or theft (or loss due to any other actual or suspected criminal activity) regardless of the scale of funds or value of other property involved. You should report to us any significant loss due to other causes. As a guide, we would expect you to report any loss of funds or other property with a value of 20% or more of the charity's income, or £25,000, whichever is the smaller amount. ... This does not include the value of investment funds lost in the ordinary course of investment business.

Significant sums of money or other property donated to the charity from an unknown or unverified source

This could mean an unusually large one off donation or regular smaller donations from a source that you cannot identify or cannot check. Donations may take forms other than money, e g shares or goods. ... Here, we would expect you to report . . . [anonymous donations of/adding up to at least] £25,000 ...

The charity (including individual staff, trustees or volunteers) has any known or alleged link to a proscribed (banned) organisation or to terrorist or other unlawful activity

If this comes to your attention, or you suspect that another trustee, member of staff, volunteer or anyone associated with the charity has any such links, you should immediately inform the police and us. ...

A person disqualified from acting as trustee has been or is currently acting as a trustee of the charity

Some people are disqualified by law from acting as trustees, including anyone described in section 72(1) of the Charities Act 1993. ...

It is normally an offence to act as a trustee while disqualified unless we have given a waiver under section 72(4) of the Charities Act 193 (some special provisions apply to the administration of charitable companies). ...

The charity does not have a policy in place for safeguarding its vulnerable beneficiaries (e g children and young people, people with disabilities and the elderly/old people)

We do not administer legislation on safeguarding children and vulnerable adults, but we are concerned to protect public confidence in the integrity of charities. ...

You must make CRB checks if these are legally required. In addition we advise you to make CRB checks if you are legally entitled to do so; this will ensure you fulfil your trustee duties. CRB checks on continuing trustees should be carried out regularly. ...

The charity has <u>no vetting procedure</u> to ensure that a <u>trustee</u> or member of <u>staff</u> is <u>eligible</u> to act in the position he or she is being appointed to

The law does not require charities to ask prospective new trustees to sign a declaration of their eligibility to act but it is best practice to do so. ... There are legal restrictions on who can be a trustee. We would have serious regulatory concern if you ahd failed to put systems in place to vet trustees or to protect vulnerable beneficiaries. You should ensure that you have suitable vetting procedures for staff and volunteers. These could include CRB checks where appropriate ...

Suspicions, allegations and incidents of abuse or mistreatment of beneficiaries

You should report this if ... there has been an incident ... and/or allegations have been made that this may be the case (irrespective of when ...) and/or you have grounds to suspect that this may be the case.

The charity has been subject to a criminal investigation, or an investigation by another regulator or agency; or sanctions have been imposed or concerns raised by another regulator or agency (eg, Health & Safety Executive; Ofsted)

You should inform us [of] any criminal investigation or ... formal sanction [imposed on your charity.] ...

Questions the Charity Commission may ask:

For any incident, it would be helpful if you told us:

- Whether the incident has happened or whether there have been serious allegations/suspicions that it has happened
- When the incident happened and who was involved, including his or her position in the charity
- If this person is still involved with the charity
- The effect of the incident on the charity and/or its beneficiaries
- What action, if any, has been taken since the incident
- If there has been any publicity about the incident
- If the charity has conducted its own inquiry into the incident and what was the outcome
- If another regulator or law-enforcement or government agency is involved and what action it has taken, if any ...'.

From a risk perspective, if auditors were able to obtain independent evidence – perhaps by seeking direct confirmation through the use of a standard form of protective 'whistle-blowing notification' to the Commission in terms pre-agreed with the client – to satisfy themselves that the Commission is already aware of any 'situation' as above that the trustees considered likely to be of concern to it, whether or not that situation has or may come to light in the course of the particular audit, and that no supervisory action of any kind is currently in hand or under consideration by the Commission at the time of the audit, it may then be enough for audit purposes to include an appropriate statement as part of the usual management representations to be obtained from the charity trustees in order to cover the audit risk posed by the APB's tough stance in this area.

Appendix 1

ACCOUNTING AND REPORTING BY CHARITIES: STATEMENT OF RECOMMENDED PRACTICE (REVISED 2005)[1]

STATEMENT BY THE ACCOUNTING STANDARDS BOARD ON THE SORP 'ACCOUNTING AND REPORTING BY CHARITIES: STATEMENT OF RECOMMENDED PRACTICE'

The aims of the Accounting Standards Board (the ASB) are to establish and improve standards of financial accounting and reporting, for the benefit of users, preparers, and auditors of financial information. To this end, the ASB issues accounting standards that are primarily applicable to general purpose company financial statements. In particular industries or sectors, further guidance may be required in order to implement accounting standards effectively. This guidance is issued, in the form of Statements of Recommended Practice (SORPs), by bodies recognised for the purpose by the ASB.

The Charity Commission has confirmed that it shares the ASB's aim of advancing and maintaining standards of financial reporting in the public interest and has been recognised by the ASB for the purpose of issuing SORPs. As a condition of recognition, the Commission has agreed to follow the ASB's code of practice for bodies recognised for issuing SORPs.

The code of practice sets out procedures to be followed in the development of SORPs. These procedures do not include a comprehensive review of the proposed SORP by the ASB, but a review of limited scope is performed.

On the basis of its review, the ASB has concluded that the SORP has been developed in accordance with the ASB's code of practice and does not appear to contain any fundamental points of principle that are unacceptable in the context of accounting practice or to conflict with an accounting standard or the ASB's plans for future standards.

Dated 28 February 2005

STATEMENT BY THE CHARITY COMMISSION FOR ENGLAND AND WALES

The Charity Commission is pleased to publish this revised edition of the Charities SORP.

The accounting recommendations of this SORP are based on Financial Reporting Standards currently in issue and have been developed in conjunction with the Charities SORP committee, an advisory committee made up of charity finance directors, charity auditors, academics, charity advisers and charity regulators. The committee is also structured to reflect the different charity jurisdictions of the UK.

Sector involvement has been a central part of producing this SORP. The research, input and feedback provided by the sector and the SORP Committee has informed each stage of its development. The resulting document provides a platform for transparent and consistent reporting by charities. The Commission would like to thank the SORP Committee, and all those who responded to the consultation on the exposure draft as well as all those who prepared research papers and publications that have informed this SORP's development.

This revision creates a new focus for charity reporting, building on existing SORP principles and recommendations. It provides a framework that enables charities to explain what they aim to do, how they go about it and what they achieve. It does so in a way that pulls together narrative and financial reporting into a coherent package focused on activities undertaken.

We, in the UK, are fortunate in benefiting from a dynamic and energetic charity sector that encompasses a huge diversity in terms of size of charity and the activities they undertake. Retaining and enhancing the high reputation of the sector is a responsibility that we share with the sector. This SORP has a key role to play in this respect by assisting charities in providing financial information about their activities and resources that is of interest to many people and to meet legal requirements that such accounts give a "true and fair" view.

Dated 4 March 2005

THE CHARITIES STATEMENT OF RECOMMENDED PRACTICE: SMALL CHARITIES AND SORP 2005

Introduction

This guidance is intended to provide a brief introduction to what the Charities Statement of Recommended Practice (the SORP) is, the options available to small charities in preparing their accounts and annual report and signposts further sources of help and advice.

The Charities Statement of Recommended Practice: Small Charities and SORP 2005

This section is designed to help trustees and executive staff in charities who are responsible for preparing their charity's annual report and accounts, who are not fully familiar with the rules governing charity accounts. The types of accounts that can be prepared and sources of help are summarised below to help you.

The Statement of Recommended Practice (commonly referred to as the SORP) is issued by the Charity Commission and the Office of the Scottish Charity Regulator (OSCR) and basically gives instructions as to how charities are expected to report their activities, income and expenditure and financial position in their annual report and accounts.

Your charity's annual report and accounts not only help you manage your charity well by recapping on the achievements of the past year but can help you attract money from organisations or people who are interested in what you do. The annual report and accounts together form a package that provides accountability to stakeholders in the widest sense.

The whole purpose of your charity's annual report and accounts is to demonstrate to your funders, donors, beneficiaries and suppliers in an open and transparent way, how you have spent the money you have received, how what you have spent supports your work and the resources available to you at the end of your financial year.

Every registered charity is expected to produce an annual report and accounts that explains where your money came from and what you did with it. However, the SORP only applies if your charity reports its income and expenditure on the basis of when the activity happens, rather than when you receive and spend the cash. The income and expenditure basis is called accruals based accounting.

Not all charities are required to report their financial information in exactly the same way. What you have to do depends on the size of your charity's income in your accounting year and the assets held at the end of the year. If your charity is not required by law to have an audit then you can prepare a simple annual report and a simpler presentation can be used for your accounts. If your charity is larger in size and is required by law to have an audit then you should follow the recommendations set out in the SORP.

In England and Wales the audit threshold has been increased for accounts starting on or after 27 February 2007 and you will not usually need an audit until your income in a year is more than £500,000 or your total assets are £2.8m or more. In Scotland these same thresholds apply for non-company charities and the changes to bring charitable companies in line with these thresholds took effect from 1 April 2008.

Charities that are required by the law to be audited by a qualified accountant must follow the SORP in full for both the annual report and accounts. If you are unsure if you require an audit, look at Appendix 4 of the SORP which sets out the various thresholds in full or view the advice on the Commission and OSCR websites, detailed at the end of this section. Your charity's governing document may also require your charity's acounts to have an audit.

If your charity is not set up under company law and its income is £100,000 or less, then you do not have to prepare accruals accounts. You then have the option of preparing your accounts simply on the basis of the cash you receive and spend, and you do not have to comply with the SORP. This is called receipts and payments accounting and is explained later.

If you are unclear as to whether you do, or do not, need to prepare accruals based accounts, or comply with the SORP, look at the advice on the Commission and OSCR websites, detailed at the end of this section.

Receipts and payments accounts

As noted above if your charity's income is £100,000 or less then provided your charity is not a company you can prepare receipts and payments accounts. If you prepare receipts and payments accounts then the accounting recommendations of the SORP do not apply to your accounts at all.

Receipts and payments accounts are basically a statement of the cash you received and what you spent it on. You do not have to summarise the income and expenditure according to the activities that you undertook during the year, you may summarise your receipts and payments in any way you feel is helpful to those using the information. However, you do need to say what assets (things that you own or sums of money owed to your charity) and liabilities (money that you owe to others) you have and these should be listed in what is called a Statement of Assets and Liabilities (Statement of Balances in Scotland). If you have land, property or other assets used by the charity in its work, you do not have to value them if that is difficult provided you describe them in your statement of assets and liabilities unless the charity is registered with OSCR in which case values for assets and liabilities must be provided within the Statement of Balances.

If your charity is registered in Scotland, your receipts and payments accounts must be set out in a particular way. For more information on the layout please refer to the OSCR website detailed at the end of this section.

For small charities preparing receipts and payments accounts, both the Commission and OSCR provide guidance on the form and content of the trustees' annual report via their websites which are detailed at the end of this section. As explained above, the annual report for a small charity need not be as detailed as those of larger charities who are expected to follow the recommendations of the SORP in full.

Accruals accounts and small charities

If you are preparing accruals accounts, whatever type of charity you are (a trust, an association, or a company), you are required to prepare, in accordance with the SORP, what are called 'primary' financial statements.

These are:

1.   A Statement of Financial Activities (SOFA) which describes all of your sources of income and expenditure.

2.   A balance sheet which tells readers what cash you have in the bank and what other assets and liabilities you have.

In addition, notes to the accounts should be given which explain in more detail how your income and expenditure is made up, and gives extra information about particular assets and liabilities or particular payments, for example on payments to trustees.

The SORP allows small charities considerable freedom in how they set out their SOFA and Appendix 5 of this SORP sets out the simpler requirements applying to small charities.

The Trustees' Annual Report and small charities

In addition to the financial information provided by accounts, the SORP also requires you to produce a written explanation of what activities and plans your charity had for the year in question and how you did against what you planned to do. This information is to help those people who read your annual report and accounts (who may be donors, funders, beneficiaries or suppliers) to understand your work and to be reassured that you are managing your charity well. Your written explanation should expand on some of the detail contained in your accounts. This narrative information is contained in a report which accompanies the accounts and is known as the trustees' annual report.

If you are a small charity, which for the trustees' annual report purposes means your charity is below the audit threshold, the information you provide in the written section will not need to be detailed. You are allowed to keep it simple and easy to understand. All you need to do is provide a summary of the activities you undertook during the year and how they help to support your charity's objectives (particularly your charitable objects which you will have defined in your governing document).

To help people understand the financial aspects of your charity when they are reading your report and accounts, you need to explain what your reserves policy is (ie what money you have set aside for a 'rainy day' and why); whether there is any aspect of your finances where you are in deficit, why that deficit arose and what, if anything, you are doing to deal with the deficit.

However the annual report is designed to help people understand what you do and how you do it. So it makes sense for small charities to follow as many of the recommendations contained in the SORP as is reasonable depending upon the size of your charity. If you wish to provide more information because you believe it will help the readers of your annual report and accounts, then you are free so to do, but you do not have to provide extra information.

A checklist for the simplified annual report for small charities is set out in table 11 of Appendix 5 of this SORP.

If your charity is also registered as a company with Companies House then you also need to ensure that your annual report and accounts comply with company law. For more information about these requirements see the Companies House website: http://www.companieshouse.gov.uk

Further sources of advice

Whether preparing accruals accounts or receipts and payments accounts, the Charity Commission provides model packs with model accounts formats, trustees' annual report and independent examiner's report templates and additional advice. The Office of the Scottish Charity Regulator provides a model pack for receipts and payments accounts including trustees' annual report and independent examiner's report templates as well as accounts formats and example accounts.

Access to resources is via the home pages on the internet for:

The Charity Commission http://www.charitycommission.gov.uk

The Office of the Scottish Charity Regulator http://www.oscr.org.uk

The Charity Commission Direct facility also offers help line support for charities in England and Wales to do with the SORP, accessible via the home page or by telephone 0845 3000 218 or for hearing impaired callers 0845 3000 219.

INTRODUCTION

Effective Date of Commencement

1 This Charities Statement of Recommended Practice (SORP) is applicable to all accounting periods beginning on or after 1 April 2005. Early adoption is encouraged.

The Objectives

2 The objectives of publishing these recommendations include:

(a) improving the quality of financial reporting by charities;

(b) enhancing the relevance, comparability and understandability of information presented in accounts;

(c) providing clarification, explanation and interpretation of accounting standards and of their application in the charities sector and to sector specific transactions; and thereby;

(d) assisting those who are responsible for the preparation of the Trustees' Annual Report and Accounts.

Scope

3 The accounting recommendations of this SORP apply to all charities in the United Kingdom that prepare accounts on the accruals basis to give a true and fair view of a charity's financial activities and financial position regardless of their size, constitution or complexity.

4 Each accounting recommendation should be considered in the context of what is material (Glossary GL 42) to the particular charity.

5 Where a separate SORP exists for a particular class of charities (eg SORPs applicable to Registered Social Landlords and to Further and Higher Education institutions), the charity trustees of charities in that class should adhere to that SORP and any reporting requirements placed on such charities by charity law.

6 The accounting recommendations of this SORP do not apply to charities preparing cash-based receipts and payments accounts, though such charities are encouraged to adopt the activity approach provided in this SORP (see paragraph 93) to the analysis of their receipts and payments (see Appendix 5). In Scotland the form and content of receipts and payments accounts is governed by Regulations.

7 The SORP recognises that particular accounting disclosures and the activity basis for the analysis of income and cost within the SoFA may not be relevant information for the users of accruals accounts prepared by smaller charities. The concessions for smaller charities are summarised in Appendix 5.

8 Whilst charities in the Republic of Ireland do not fall within the scope of this SORP they may choose to comply with its recommendations. If charities based in the Republic of Ireland choose to adopt this SORP's recommendations they are encouraged to disclose that fact.

9 Charity accounts are accompanied and complemented by information that does not form part of the financial statements. Within the United Kingdom such accompanying information is primarily provided by charities through a Trustees' Annual Report. As is explained in paragraph 24, the legal requirements for an annual report and its contents differ according to the charity reporting frameworks that apply within the separate legal jurisdictions of the UK. The SORP recognises that such accompanying information is of high importance for users of charity accounts in understanding the activities and achievements of a charity as a whole and therefore provides best practice recommendations for the content of such reports. In England and Wales and Scotland these best practice recommendations are underpinned by law, in Northern Ireland whilst the recommendations are considered to be consistent with the law they should be regarded as voluntary best practice recommendations supplementing legal requirements.

Purpose of Trustees' Annual Report and Accounts

10 The purpose of preparing a Trustees' Annual Report and Accounts is to discharge the charity trustees' duty of public accountability and stewardship. This SORP sets out recommended accounting practice for this purpose but charity trustees should consider providing such additional information as is needed to give donors, beneficiaries and the general public a greater insight into the charity's activities and achievements. Accounts prepared on the basis of this SORP are not a substitute for management accounts required to run the charity on a daily basis, though both will draw on the same primary financial records.

11 Charities are highly disparate in character, so any comparison of the financial information they produce should be undertaken with care, even if the charities involved seem to be similar. Essentially the accounts should include all the money and other assets entrusted to the charity for whatever purpose, and show how they have been expended during the year and how the balance of each fund is deployed at the end of the accounting period.

12 The balance sheet is not necessarily a measure of the wealth of the charity but does show the resources available, what form those resources take and how they are held in the different funds, and provides information about the liquidity of assets and general solvency.

13 The Statement of Financial Activities provides information as to how a charity receives and applies its resources to meet its objectives. It is not intended to demonstrate a charity's efficiency.

14 Accounts focus on financial performance and in isolation do not give the reader a perspective of what has been achieved from the activities undertaken and the resources expended in their delivery. The SORP recognises these limitations and places significant weight on the Trustees' Annual Report to provide a necessary link between objectives, strategies, activities and the achievements that flow from them. Without this information the value of the accounts to the reader may be significantly diminished.

15 The Trustees' Annual Report and Accounts should therefore:

(a)   provide timely and regular information on the charity and its funds;

(b)   enable the reader to understand the charity's objectives, structure, activities and achievements; and

(c)   enable the reader to gain a full and proper appreciation of the charity's financial transactions during the year and of the position of its funds at the end of the year.

How to Use the SORP

16 This SORP recommends particular accounting treatments and provides guidance on the application of accounting standards (compliance with which is considered necessary, in all save exceptional circumstances, to meet the legal requirement to give a true and fair view) in a manner which takes account of the particular circumstances of charities. In all but exceptional circumstances, charities preparing accruals accounts should follow this SORP's accounting recommendations to assist in ensuring that their accounts give a true and fair view.

17 There will be few, if any, charities preparing accruals accounts to which all parts of this SORP apply since it caters for a wide variety of charity activities and transactions. Charities do not have to follow those sections which do not apply to them. For example, advice on how to account for gifts in kind and the proceeds of trading activities will not apply to all charities. Readers whose charity does not have receipts from those sources may safely pass over the sections dealing with them and any other sections which do not apply to their charity's own activities. However, there are several sections which will apply to all or nearly all charities.

18 The main text of the SORP deals with the normal accounting practice for those charities producing accruals accounts. Small charities that are not subject to a statutory audit requirement may choose to apply a number of concessions available under the SORP in relation to both reporting disclosures and presentation. These concessions are summarised in Appendix 5.

19   Certain charities will have to meet additional requirements due to the transactions undertaken or the legal or operating structures adopted. The following sections set out additional recommendations applicable for:

(a)   Consolidation of Subsidiary Undertakings – paragraphs 381–406.

(b)   Accounting for Associates, Joint Ventures and Joint Arrangements – paragraphs 407–418.

(c)   Charitable Companies – paragraphs 419–429.

(d)   Accounting for Retirement Benefits – paragraphs 430–448.

(e)   Common Investment Funds and Investment Pooling Schemes – paragraphs 449–451.

20   The accounting disclosure requirements have been separately identified throughout the SORP. Generally charities are only excused from a particular disclosure requirement where the item in question is not relevant to a charity or where disclosure would be immaterial for the user of the accounts. For example, investment disclosures are not required if a charity has no investments. Certain other disclosures, for example, remuneration of trustees, provide information of significance to the reader and require a "nil" disclosure in the event of no remuneration being paid. Where such a "nil" disclosure is required, this is specifically stated in the relevant disclosure recommendation.

21   The main obligation of charity trustees in preparing accruals accounts is to give a true and fair view of the charity's incoming resources and application of resources during the year and of its state of affairs at the end of the year. To achieve this, the charity trustees' judgement may dictate the disclosure of more information than specifically recommended in this SORP. Similarly charity trustees may occasionally find that following a recommendation is incompatible with the obligation to give a true and fair view. They should then use the alternative accounting treatment which gives a true and fair view and provide particulars within the accounting policy notes (in accordance with paragraph 359) of any material departure from the recommendations in this SORP. A departure from the SORP is not justified simply because it gives the reader a more appealing picture of the financial position or results of the charity.

The SORP and the Law

22   The SORP is compatible with the requirements of the law. The SORP clarifies how charity accounting is affected by legal requirements, including aspects of trust law. It provides the charity sector with an interpretation of accounting standards and principles and clarifies the accounting treatment for sector specific transactions. In so doing, applying the SORP enables the preparers of charity accounts to meet their legal or other reporting duties for their accounts to give a true and fair view.

23   Charity trustees should include any additional information which they are required by law to report and in order for the accounts to comply with current statutory requirements or the requirements of the charity's governing document to the extent that these exceed statutory requirements.

24   The legal requirements for a Trustees' Annual Report and its contents differ according to the charity reporting frameworks that apply within the separate legal jurisdictions of the UK. The SORP provides best practice recommendations that in England, Wales and Scotland are underpinned by law. In Northern Ireland, whilst the recommendations are considered to be consistent with the law they should be regarded a voluntary best practice recommendations supplementing legal requirements.

25   The charity trustees (see glossary GL 7) are jointly responsible for the preparation of the Annual Report and Accounts which should be approved by the charity trustees as a body in accordance with their usual procedures and both documents should be signed on behalf of the charity trustees by one of their number authorised so to do or as otherwise required by law. The date of approval should be stated.

26   Any audit, independent examination or other statutory report on the accounts should be attached to the accounts when they are distributed or made available to users of financial information.

27   The primary legislative sources as at 1 April 2008 that contain requirements relating to the form and content of charity accounts and reports prepared under this SORP include:

(a)   The Charities Act 1993 (as amended by the Charities Act 2006) and Regulations made thereunder;

(b)   The Companies Act 1985 and 1989 and 2006;

(c)   The Industrial and Provident Societies Acts 1965 to 2002;

(d)   The Charities and Trustee Investment (Scotland) Act 2005 and Regulations made thereunder.

28   Charitable companies governed by the requirements of the Companies Act 2006 should refer to paragraphs 419 and 429 that provide recommendations as to how the particular requirements of company law should be addressed within charity accounts.

29   Table 1 below summarises the legislative framework applying to the accounts of charities within the UK not reporting under company law.

Table 1. Legislative Framework for Charity Accounts in the United Kingdom

Country	Charity authority	Act(s) Governing Charities	Registration and Filing of Accounts	Preparation of Accounts
England and Wales	Charity Commission for England and Wales	Part VI Charities Act 1993 (as amended by the Charities Act 2006), and applicable Regulations	The Charity Commission is responsible for the supervision and regulation of charities that are not exempt and maintains a public register of charities that are not exempt or excepted. Trustees' Annual Report and accounts must be filed by all registered charities with gross income of over £10,000.	All charities required to prepare accounts. Registered and excepted charities follow Regulations. Exempt charities follow relevant legislation or governing documents or prepare income and expenditure account and balance sheet.
Scotland	Office of the Scottish Charity Regulator	Charities and Trustee Investment (Scotland) Act 2005 and applicable Regulations	The Office of the Scottish Charity Regulator is responsible for the supervision and regulation of all charities in Scotland. Trustees' Annual Report and accounts must be filed by all charities entered on the Scottish Charity Register.	All charities required to prepare accounts. Registered charities follow Regulations.
Northern Ireland	Department for Social Development	Charities Act (Northern Ireland) 1964 and the Charities (Northern Ireland) Order 1987	There is no register of charities for Northern Ireland, and no requirement for accounts to be filed with the Department except where this is specifically directed by the High Court of Justice in Northern Ireland or the Department acting under specific statutory powers.	Section 27 of the Charities Act (Northern Ireland) 1964 requires the trustees of a charity to keep proper accounts and preserve them for at least 7 years.

Accounts Structure

30   Charity accruals accounts should comprise:

(a)   a Statement of Financial Activities for the year that shows all incoming resources and all resources expended by it and reconciles all changes in its funds. The statement should consist of a single set of accounting statements and be presented in columnar form if the charity operates more than one class of fund;

(b)   an income and expenditure account where this is a legal requirement. In certain circumstances the Statement of Financial Activities will also meet the legal requirements for an Income and Expenditure Account. Where the two statements are combined this should be identified in the heading of the statement. Paragraphs 423 to 426 fully describe the circumstances in which a summary income and expenditure account is necessary for companies in addition to the Statement of Financial Activities;

(c)   a balance sheet that shows the recognised assets, the liabilities and the different categories of fund of the charity;

(d)   a cash flow statement, where required, in accordance with accounting standards; and

(e)   notes explaining the accounting policies adopted (as set out in paragraphs 356 to 370) and other notes which explain or expand upon the information contained in the accounting statements referred to above or which provide further useful information. This will include notes analysing the figures in the accounts and explaining the relationships between them.

31 The corresponding figures for the previous accounting period should be provided in the accounts in accordance with generally accepted accounting practice. The duration of the current and previous accounting periods should also be shown.

32 The Statement of Financial Activities, the income and expenditure account (or summary), the balance sheet and the cash flow statement (where required), are all considered to be "primary statements", and should therefore be given equal prominence in the accounts and should not be relegated to the notes to the accounts.

33 Where any charity is, or its trustees are, acting as custodian trustees, they should not include the funds they hold as custodian in their own balance sheet but should disclose them by way of a note to their accounts and provide the details, set out in paragraph 59 below, in their Trustees' Annual Report.

Summary Financial Information

34 Where summary financial information of any kind is prepared (including financial information contained in publicity or fundraising material and annual reviews), charity trustees are reminded that these accounts should always be fair and accurate. This is dealt with in paragraphs 371 to 379.

Trustees' Annual Report

35 Charity accounts alone do not meet all the information needs of users who will usually have to supplement the information they obtain from the accounts with information from other sources. Accounts also have inherent limitations in terms of their ability to reflect the full impact of transactions or activities undertaken and do not provide information on matters such as structures, governance and management arrangements adopted by a charity. The accounts of a charity cannot alone easily portray what the charity has done (its outputs) or achieved (its outcomes) or what difference it has made (its impact). This is mainly because many of these areas cannot be measured in monetary terms: indeed some areas are difficult to measure with any numbers at all. The Trustees' Annual Report provides the opportunity for charity trustees to explain the areas that the accounts do not explain.

36 Charity accounts should therefore be accompanied and complemented by information contained within the Trustees' Annual Report. The Trustees' Annual Report should be a coherent document that meets the requirements of law and regulation and provides a fair review of the charity's structure, aims, objectives, activities and performance. Good reporting will explain what the charity is trying to do and how it is going about it. It will assist the user of accounts in addressing the progress made by the charity against its objectives for the year and in understanding its plans for the future. Good reporting will also explain the charity's governance and management structure and enable the reader to understand how the numerical part of the accounts relates to the organisational structure and activities of the charity (see paragraphs 44 to 59).

As part of the report, or attached to it, a statement containing the reference and administrative details of the charity as described in paragraphs 41 to 43 will inform the reader who are the charity's trustees and its advisers and will provide other relevant legal or administrative information.

37 Responsibility for preparing the Trustees' Annual Report rests with the charity trustees. It provides important accompanying information to the accounts and should therefore be attached to the accounts whenever a full set of accounts is distributed or otherwise made available.

38 Legal requirements and this SORP do not limit the inclusion of other information within the Trustees' Annual Report or as additional information accompanying the accounts. Charity trustees may incorporate other material into their annual reporting, for example a chairman's report, environment report, impact assessment or an operating and financial review (see Glossary GL 43).

39 Charities may additionally use other means of providing information, outside of the accounting and reporting framework, about who they are and what they do. Such information is often tailored for the needs of particular audiences and presented through annual reviews, newsletters and websites. Whilst charity trustees might usefully refer to these other sources of information within their Trustees' Annual Report, such additional information should not be seen as a substitute for good statutory annual reporting.

40 Charitable companies must also prepare a Directors' Report (see paragraph 420) in order to meet the requirement of Section 415 of the Companies Act 2006 and applicable Regulations. A separate Trustees' Annual Report is not required provided that any statutory Directors' Report prepared also contains all the information required to be provided in the Trustees' Annual Report.

CONTENT OF THE TRUSTEES' ANNUAL REPORT

Reference and Administrative Details of the Charity, its Trustees and Advisers

41 The report should provide the following reference and administrative information about the charity, its trustees and advisers:

(a)   The name of the charity, which in the case of a registered charity means the name by which it is registered. Any other name by which a charity makes itself known should also be provided.

(b)   The charity registration number (in Scotland the Scottish Charity Number) and, if applicable, the company registration number.

(c)   The address of the principal office of the charity and in the case of a charitable company the address of its registered office.

(d)   The names of all of those who were the charity's trustees (Glossary GL 7) or a trustee for the charity (Glossary GL 59) on the date the report was approved. Where there are more than 50 charity trustees, the names of at least 50 of those trustees (including all the officers of the charity, e g chair, treasurer etc) should be provided. Where any charity trustee disclosed is a body corporate, the names of the directors of the body corporate on that date.

(e)   The name of any other person who served as a charity trustee (Glossary GL 7) or as a trustee for the charity (Glossary GL 59) in the financial year in question.

(f)   The name of any Chief Executive Officer or other senior staff member(s) to whom day to day management of the charity is delegated by the charity trustees.

(g)   The names and addresses of any other relevant organisations or persons. This should include the names and addresses of those acting as bankers, solicitors, auditor (or independent examiner or reporting accountant) and investment or other principal advisers.

42   Where the disclosure of the names of any charity trustee, trustee for the charity, senior staff member, or person with the power of appointment, or of the charity's principal address could lead to that person being placed in personal danger (e g in the case of a women's refuge), the charity trustees may dispense with the disclosure provided that (for charities in England and Wales), the Charity Commission has given the trustees the authority so to do. For charities in Scotland there is also provision (under charity law) for such information to be excluded. It is recommended that the reasons for non-disclosure should be given in the report. The directors of charitable companies should note that, with the exception of the details of the charitable company's auditor, there is no corresponding dispensation in relation to the disclosure requirements for the statutory directors' report.

43   Charities that are not subject to a statutory audit requirement may omit the disclosures in 41(f) and 41(g) above. However the disclosure of these items is encouraged as a matter of good practice.

Structure, Governance and Management

44 The report should provide the reader with an understanding of how the charity is constituted, its organisational structure and how its trustees are appointed and trained and assist the reader to understand better how the charity's decisionmaking processes operate. The level of detail provided in the report is likely to be dependent on the size and complexity of the charity and be proportionate to the needs of the users of the report. In particular, the report should explain:

(a) The nature of the governing document (eg trust deed; memorandum and articles of association; Charity Commission Scheme; Royal Charter; etc) and how the charity is (or its trustees are) constituted (eg limited company; unincorporated association; trustees incorporated as a body; etc).

(b) The methods adopted for the recruitment and appointment of new trustees, including details of any constitutional provisions relating to appointments, for example, election to post. Where any other person or body external to the charity is entitled to appoint one or more of the charity trustees this should be explained together with the name of that person or body (subject to paragraph 42 above – where disclosure of a person's name could lead to personal danger).

(c) The policies and procedures adopted for the induction and training of trustees.

(d) The organisational structure of the charity and how decisions are made. For example, which types of decisions are taken by the charity trustees and which are delegated to staff.

(e) Where the charity is part of a wider network (for example charities affiliated within an umbrella group) then the relationship involved should also be explained where this impacts on the operating policies adopted by the charity.

(f) The relationships between the charity and related parties, including its subsidiaries (see paragraphs 221 to 229 and Glossary GL 50) and with any other charities and organisations with which it co-operates in the pursuit of its charitable objectives.

45 A statement should be provided confirming that the major risks to which the charity is exposed, as identified by the trustees, have been reviewed and systems or procedures have been established to manage those risks.

46 Charities that are not subject to a statutory audit requirement may limit their disclosures within this section to those set out in paragraph 44 (a) and (b) above. The additional disclosures of this section are encouraged as a matter of good practice.

Objectives and Activities

47 The report should help the reader understand the aims and objectives set by the charity, and the strategies and activities undertaken to achieve them. The report may also, where relevant, explain how the objectives set for the year relate to longer term strategies and objectives set by the charity. Where significant activities are undertaken through subsidiary undertakings, these should be explained in the report. In particular the report should provide:

(a)   A summary of the objects of the charity as set out in its governing document.

(b)   An explanation of the charity's aims including the changes or differences it seeks to make through its activities.

(c)   An explanation of the charity's main objectives for the year.

(d)   An explanation of the charity's strategies for achieving its stated objectives.

(e)   Details of significant activities (including its main programmes, projects, or services provided) that contribute to the achievement of the stated objectives.

(f)   In England and Wales, the Charities (Accounts and Reports) Regulations 2008 specifically requires the report to address those activities undertaken to further a charity's purposes for the public benefit and a statement that the trustees have had regard to Charity Commission guidance on public benefit.

48   The details of significant activities provided should focus on those activities that the charity trustees consider to be significant in the circumstances of the charity as a whole. The details of activities should, as a minimum, explain the objectives, activities, projects or services identified within the analysis note accompanying charitable activities in the Statement of Financial Activities (see paragraphs 191 to 194).

49   Where the charity conducts a material part of its activities through grantmaking, a statement should be provided setting out its grantmaking policies.

50   Where social or programme related investment (Glossary GL 47) activities are material in the context of charitable activities undertaken, the policies adopted in making such investments should be explained.

51   Where a charity makes significant use of volunteers in the course of undertaking its charitable or income generating activities this should be explained. Whilst measurement issues, including attributing an economic value to such unpaid voluntary contributions, prevents the inclusion of such contributions within the Statement of Financial Activities (see paragraph 133), it is nevertheless important for readers to be provided with sufficient information to understand the role and contribution of volunteers. Such information may, for example, explain the activities that volunteers help provide, quantify the contribution in terms of hours or staff equivalents, and may present an indicative value of this contribution.

52   Charities that are not subject to a statutory audit requirement may limit their disclosures within this section to that set out in paragraph 47(a) above, together with providing a summary of the main activities undertaken in relation to those objects. The additional disclosures of this section are encouraged as a matter of good practice.

Achievements and Performance

53   The report should contain information that enables the reader to understand and assess the achievements of the charity and its subsidiary undertakings in the year. It should provide a review of its performance against objectives that have been set. The report is likely to provide both qualitative and quantitative information that helps explain achievement and performance. It will often be helpful to identify any indicators, milestones and benchmarks against which the achievement of objectives is assessed by the charity. In particular, the report should contain:

(a) A review of charitable activities undertaken that explains the performance achieved against objectives set. Where qualitative or quantitative information is used to assess the outcome of activities, a summary of the measures or indicators used to assess achievement should be included.

(b) Where material fundraising activities are undertaken, details of the performance achieved against fundraising objectives set, commenting on any material expenditure for future income generation and explaining the effect on the current period's fundraising return and anticipated income generation in future periods.

(c) Where material investments are held, details of the investment performance achieved against the investment objectives set.

(d) Comment on those factors within and outside the charity's control which are relevant to the achievement of its objectives; these might include relationship with employees, users, beneficiaries, funders and the charity's position in the wider community.

54 Charities that are not subject to a statutory audit requirement may limit their disclosures within this section to providing a summary of the main achievements of the charity during the year. The additional disclosures of this section are encouraged as a matter of good practice.

Financial Review

55 The report should contain a review of the financial position of the charity and its subsidiaries and a statement of the principal financial management policies adopted in the year. In particular, the report should explain the charity's:

(a) Policy on reserves (Glossary GL 51) stating the level of reserves held and why they are held.
    Where material funds have been designated, the reserves policy statement should quantify and explain the purpose of the designations and, where set aside for future expenditure, the likely timing of that expenditure.

(b) Where any fund is materially in deficit, the circumstances giving rise to the deficit and details of the steps being taken to eliminate the deficit.

(c) Principal funding sources and how expenditure in the year under review has supported the key objectives of the charity.

(d) Where material investments are held, the investment policy and objectives, including the extent (if any) to which social, environmental or ethical considerations are taken into account.

56 Charities that are not subject to a statutory audit requirement may limit their disclosures within this section to those set out in paragraph 55(a) and 55(b) above.

Plans for Future Periods

57   The report should explain the charity's plans for the future including the aims and key objectives it has set for future periods together with details of any activities planned to achieve them.

58   Charities that are not subject to a statutory audit requirement may omit this disclosure although disclosure of this matter is encouraged as a matter of good practice.

Funds Held as Custodian Trustee on Behalf of Others

59   Where a charity is, or its trustees are, acting as custodian trustees, the following matters should be disclosed in the report:

(a)   A description of the assets which they hold in this capacity.

(b)   The name and objects of the charity (or charities) on whose behalf the assets are held and how this activity falls within their own objects.

(c)   Details of the arrangements for safe custody and segregation of such assets from the charity's own assets.

GENERAL ACCOUNTING PRINCIPLES

Fundamental Accounting Concepts

60   Accounts intending to show a true and fair view must be prepared on the going concern assumption and the accruals concept and provide information that is relevant, reliable, comparable and understandable (see Appendix 2: FRS 18).

Accounting Standards

61   In meeting the obligation to prepare accounts showing a true and fair view (see paragraph 21) accruals accounts should follow the standards and principles issued or adopted by the Accounting Standards Board, or its predecessors or successors as set out in:

(a)   Statements of Standard Accounting Practice (SSAPs);

(b)   Financial Reporting Standards (FRSs);

(c)   Urgent Issues Task Force abstracts (UITFs);

And in addition take note of:

(d)   The Interpretation for Public Benefit Entities of the Statement of Principles for Financial Reporting (June 2007).

This SORP provides guidance and recommendations that supplement accounting standards in the light of the special factors prevailing or transactions undertaken with the charity sector and, as with the law, does not seek to repeat all of their requirements. Appendix 2 provides a summary of these accounting standards and of their general applicability to charities.

62 Appendix 5 explains how the Financial Reporting Standard for Smaller Entities (FRSSE) can be applied by charities (whether or not they are companies) which are under the thresholds for small companies as described in the Companies Acts (see Appendix 4).

63 UK accounting standards provide the financial reporting framework under which this SORP has been developed. In the UK, compliance with companies' legislation presently requires compliance with UK accounting standards as does charity legislation in England, Wales and Scotland through its adoption of the methods and principles of this SORP. Section 395 (2) of the Companies Act 2006 requires that a charity must prepare Companies Act individual accounts and section 403 (3) requires that where charities prepare group accounts they prepare Companies Act group accounts. Therefore charities cannot prepare their statutory accounts in accordance with international accounting standards.

64 Currently the Accounting Standards Board is undertaking a phased approach to convergence of UK accounting standards with IFRS. This includes new standards effective in 2005 and 2006 and thereafter a series of 'step changes' replacing one or more existing UK accounting standards with standards based on IFRS as their development is completed. This SORP will continue to be reviewed in line with the Accounting Standards Board's Policy and Code of Practice to reflect changes in UK standards, including those arising from the convergence process.

Accounting for Separate Funds

65 The main purpose of the accounts is to give an overall view of the total incoming resources during the year and how they have been expended, with a balance sheet to show the overall financial position at the year end. There are additional requirements for charities that have to account for more than one fund (Glossary GL 27) under their control. The accounts should provide a summary of the main funds, differentiating in particular between the unrestricted income funds, restricted income funds and endowment funds (see figure 1). The columnar format of the Statement of Financial Activities (and of the balance sheet, where the option is taken to use a columnar presentation of funds) is designed to achieve this. Depending on the materiality (Glossary GL 42) of each, the notes to the accounts should group the restricted funds under one or more heads.

66 Charities need to account for the proper administration of the individual funds in accordance with their respective terms of trust and accounting records must be kept in a way which will adequately separate transactions between different funds. Some charities may hold one or more restricted funds, some of which may be permanent or expendable endowment funds. Appendix 3 explains in detail the legal position as regards transactions involving these various funds. The position is summarised in the following paragraphs 67 to 76.

Figure 1 – The types of funds of charities

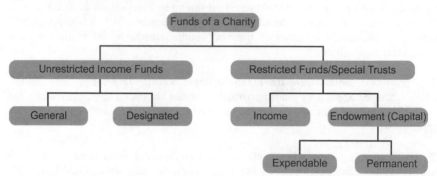

Unrestricted Income Funds (Including Designated Funds) (see also Appendix 3)

67 Nearly all charities have a fund which is available to the trustees to apply for the general purposes of the charity as set out in its governing document. This is the charity's "unrestricted" fund (sometimes called a "general" fund) because the trustees are free to use it for any of the charity's purposes. Income generated from assets held in an unrestricted fund will be unrestricted income.

68 The trustees may earmark part of the charity's unrestricted funds to be used for particular purposes in the future. Such sums are described as "designated funds" and should be accounted for as part of the charity's unrestricted funds. The trustees have the power to re-designate such funds within unrestricted funds. When a designation has been made at the balance sheet date, the amount of the designation may be adjusted subsequent to the year end if more accurate information becomes available (see Appendix 2 FRS 21).

Restricted Funds (see also Appendix 3)

69 Many charities hold funds that can only be applied for particular purposes within their objects. These are restricted funds and have to be separately accounted for. The restriction may apply to the use of income or capital or both. Income generated from assets held in a restricted fund (e g interest) will be legally subject to the same restriction as the original fund unless either:

(a)   the terms of the original restriction specifically say otherwise (for example, the expressed wishes of a donor or the terms of an appeal), or

(b)   the restricted fund is an endowment fund, the income of which is expendable at the discretion of the trustees.

Endowment Funds (see also Appendix 3)

70 One form of restricted fund is an "endowment", which is held on trust to be retained for the benefit of the charity as a capital fund. Where the trustees must permanently maintain the whole of the fund it is known as permanent endowment. Such a fund may consist of investment assets and/or assets that are used for the purposes of the charity. Such a fund cannot normally be spent as if it were income.

71 In some instances the trustees may have a power of discretion to convert endowed capital into income in which case the fund is known as expendable endowment.

72 The initial gift and subsequent increases and decreases in the amount of any endowment funds should be shown in the Statement of Financial Activities as part of those funds.

Gains and Losses

73 Realised and unrealised gains and losses on assets held in a particular fund form part of that fund.

Similarly, provisions for depreciation, or for a permanent fall in value of assets form part of the fund in which the asset is held.

Reconciliation of Funds

74 The Statement of Financial Activities should reflect the principal movements between the opening and closing balances on all the funds of the charity. It should be analysed between unrestricted income funds, restricted income funds and endowment funds (permanent and expendable combined).

Particulars of Individual Funds and Notes to the Accounts

75 The notes to the accounts should provide information on the structure of the charity's funds so as to disclose the fund balances and the reasons for them, differentiating between unrestricted income funds (both general and designated), restricted income funds, permanent endowment and expendable endowment as well as identifying any material individual funds among them. In particular:

(a) The assets and liabilities representing each type of fund of the charity should be clearly summarised and analysed (e g investments, fixed assets, net current assets) between those funds unless this information is presented in a columnar balance sheet (see paragraph 248).

(b) Disclosure of how each of the funds has arisen (including designated funds), the restrictions imposed and the purpose of each fund should be provided. An indication should also be given as to whether or not sufficient resources are held in an appropriate form to enable each fund to be applied in accordance with any restrictions. For example, if a charity has a fund which is to be spent in the near future, it should be made clear in the notes whether or not the assets held (or expected to be received) in the fund are liquid assets.

(c) Any funds in deficit should always be separately disclosed. An explanation should be given in the Trustees' Annual Report (see paragraph 55(b)). Designated funds should never be in deficit.

(d) Material transfers between different funds and allocations to designated funds should be separately disclosed, without netting off, and should be accompanied by an explanation of the nature of the transfers or allocations and the reasons for them.

(e)   Where, in relation to permanent endowment, a total return approach to investments has been adopted, the notes to the accounts should give particulars of the movements in the value of the unapplied total return for the financial year. The note should reconcile the balance held as unapplied total return at the beginning with that at the end of the financial year. (See Appendix 3 paragraphs 3(g) to 3(k).)

76   Separate sets of statements may be produced for each major fund and linked to a total summary. The trustees should decide on the most suitable form of presentation, bearing in mind:

(a)   the complexity of the fund structure,

(b)   the need for the total provided in the summary to agree to the primary statements (Statement of Financial Activities and Balance Sheet), and

(c)   the need to avoid confusion between the movements on the various funds.

An example of a suitable summary is given in Table 2:

Table 2.   Outline Summary of Fund Movements

Fund Name	Fund Balances brought forward £	Incoming Resources £	Outgoing Resources £	Transfers £	Gains and Losses £	Fund Balances carried forward £
Major Fund 1						
Major Fund 2						
Major Fund 3						
Other Funds						
Total Funds						

Branches

77   Before preparing accounts, trustees must be quite clear as to the legal structure of the charity. A charity may operate through "branches" to raise funds and/or carry out its charitable purposes. Branches as defined in the Glossary (GL 4) will be accounted for as part of the whole charity. But if both reporting charity and the "branch(es)" are companies, company law requires each entity to prepare its own accounts. In such a case, one Trustees' Annual Report should normally be prepared to cover both the reporting charity and its branch(es) and consolidated accounts should be prepared in accordance with paragraphs 381 to 406.

78   Separate legal entities which may be known as branches but do not fall within the definition of a branch in the Glossary should prepare their own Annual Report and

Accounts and, if they are connected charities, the relationship should be explained in the Trustees' Annual Report (see paragraph 44(f)).

79 All branch transactions should be accounted for gross in the reporting charity's own accounts excluding those transactions which net off eg. branch to branch transactions or those between the branches and the head office. Similarly all assets and liabilities of the branch including, for example, funds raised but not remitted to the reporting charity at the year end, should be incorporated into the reporting charity's own balance sheet. This provision need not apply where the transactions and balances of the branches in aggregate are not material to the charity's accounts.

80 Funds raised by a branch for the general charitable purposes of the reporting charity will be accounted for as unrestricted funds in the accounts of the reporting charity. Funds raised by a branch for specific purposes of the reporting charity will need to be accounted for as restricted funds in the accounts of the reporting charity. Funds held for the general purposes of a branch which is a separate charity should usually be accounted for as restricted funds in the accounts of the reporting charity.

81 Where a branch is not a separate legal entity, its accounts must form part of the accounts of the reporting charity, but it may be in the interests of local supporters and beneficiaries for additional accounts to be prepared covering only the branch.

STATEMENT OF FINANCIAL ACTIVITIES

Introduction

82 The Statement of Financial Activities is a single accounting statement with the objective of showing all incoming resources and resources expended by the charity in the year on all its funds.

It is designed to show how the charity has used its resources in furtherance of its objects for the provision of benefit to its beneficiaries. It shows whether there has been a net inflow or outflow of resources, including capital gains and losses on assets, and provides a reconciliation of all movements in the charity's funds.

Presentation of Information

Structure of the Statement

83 In the Statement of Financial Activities the charity's incoming resources and resources expended should be analysed so that the reader can see where its resources came from and what it spent its resources on during the year. As a minimum it must also distinguish between unrestricted income funds, restricted income funds and the endowment funds of the charity. All of the charity's incoming resources and resources expended can be categorised between these funds (see Figure 1), but a charity will not necessarily have funds of all three types.

84 If it has more than one type of fund, the statement should show, in columns, the movements in the different types of funds as well as the total movements of all the funds. Comparative figures for the previous financial year, given on the face of the statement will normally only be given for the row totals (eg voluntary income, investment income etc) rather than for the analysis of each row across the various categories of funds.

Adaptation of Formats

85 The structure, format and activity categories of the Statement of Financial Activities are shown in Table 3 below.

86 The Statement of Financial Activities may be adapted to give a true and fair view, but disclosure requirements should always be met and the underlying structure should not be changed. Trustees should balance the provision of information with clarity.

87 The three columns in the Statement of Financial Activities providing an aggregate total for unrestricted, restricted and endowment funds of a charity will often contain several individual funds which will be explained in greater detail in the notes to the accounts (see paragraph 76). If any one of these funds (or a group of these funds) is of particular materiality and the charity trustees wish to draw the attention of readers to it, they may add additional columns to the Statement of Financial Activities to display such funds on the face of the SOFA rather than in notes. For example a school may have two unrestricted fund columns, one containing the resource movement connected with teaching, another welfare and other costs. Similarly a charity engaged in collecting funds to acquire fixed assets may have two restricted fund columns, one including all funds related to fixed assets acquisition and another for other restricted funds. Any additional analysis of this type provided on the face of the Statement of Financial Activities should make clear the type of fund (unrestricted, restricted or endowment) in the title and not mix up different types of fund.

88 Some charities may also find it informative to their readers to insert additional subtotals. For example, after row B1c (investment management costs), an additional subtotal "net incoming resources available for charitable application" may be added.

89 Charities should expand the structure, where necessary using notes, in order to present a true and fair view and convey a proper understanding of the nature of all their activities. Charities should, where possible, have a clear link between the incoming and outgoing resources and in particular activity analysis. Two examples of this are:

(a)   a charity running a care home could use the sub-heading "Residential Care Fees" within row A2 (incoming resources from charitable activities) and "Residential Care Costs" in row B2 (resources expended on charitable activities);

(b)   a charity fundraising through a shop could use the sub-heading "shops" within row A1b (activities for generating funds) and row B1b (fundraising trading costs).

Thus incoming resources and resources expended can be linked together by using similar or identical headings in different parts of the Statement of Financial Activities.

Table 3.   Statement of Financial Activities

	Unrestricted Funds £	Re-stricted Funds £	Endow-ment Funds £	Total Funds £	Prior Year Total Funds £	Fur-ther De-tails £
A Incoming resources						
A1 Incoming resources from generated funds						
A1a Voluntary income						121–136
A1b Activities for generating funds						137–139
A1c Investment income						140–142
A2 Incoming resources from charitable activities						143–146
A3 Other incoming resources						147
Total incoming resources						
B Resources expended						
B1 Costs of generating funds						178–179
B1a Costs of generating voluntary income						180–184
B1b Fundraising trading: cost of goods sold and other costs						185–186
B1c Investment management costs						187
B2 Charitable activities						188–209
B3 Governance costs						210–212
B4 Other resources expended						213
Total resources expended						
Net incoming/outgoing resources before transfers						
C Transfers						
Gross transfers between funds						214–216

	Unrestricted Funds £	Re- stricted Funds £	Endow- ment Funds £	Total Funds £	Prior Year Total Funds £	Fur- ther De- tails £
Net incoming resources before other recognised gains and losses						
D **Other recognised gains/losses**						
D1 Gains on revaluation of fixed assets for charity's own use						217–218
D2 Gains/losses on investment assets						219
D3 Actuarial gains/losses on defined benefit pension schemes						220
Net movement in funds						
E **Reconciliation of Funds**						
Total funds brought forward						
Total funds carried forward						

90   In order to comply with FRS 3, where a charity has discontinued any of its operations or acquired new ones, the accounts should distinguish between continuing, discontinued and acquired operations. This will normally apply to the whole of a distinctive type of activity of a charity but not to the development or cessation of new projects within that activity.

91   Category headings should be omitted where there is nothing to report in both the current and preceding periods. A charity may also vary the order in which it presents activity categories within the incoming resources and resources expended sections of the Statement of Financial Activities to meet its own presentational needs.

92   Where, as a result of adopting the activity approach, the categories shown in the Statement of Financial Activities change from those used in the prior year, comparatives will also need to be restated in accordance with FRS 18 (Appendix 2).

93   The classification of incoming resources and resources expended by activity is encouraged for all charities preparing accruals accounts. Smaller charities may be excused from adopting this approach by legislation recognising that such information is likely to be less relevant to the users of small charity accounts. Where a small charity adopts an alternative approach to analysis within the Statement of Financial Activities certain note disclosures may no longer be necessary, for example, where these disclosures relate to the constituent costs of an activity category or where relevant information is provided on the face of the Statement of Financial Activity. These concessions for smaller charities are summarised in Appendix 5.

Incoming Resources

Recognition of Incoming Resources

General Rules

94 Incoming resources – both for income and endowment funds – should be recognised in the Statement of Financial Activities when the effect of a transaction or other event results in an increase in the charity's assets. This will be dependent on the following three factors being met:

(a)   entitlement – normally arises when there is control over the rights or other access to the resource, enabling the charity to determine its future application;

(b)   certainty – when it is virtually certain that the incoming resource will be received;

(c)   measurement – when the monetary value of the incoming resource can be measured with sufficient reliability.

95   All incoming resources should be reported gross when raised by the charity (or by volunteers working at the charity's direction) or its agents. However where funds are raised or collected for the charity by individuals not employed or contracted by the charity, the gross incoming resources of the charity are the proceeds remitted to the charity by the organisers of the event, after deducting their expenses.

96   Within the charity sector entitlement to incoming resources may arise from a wide variety of transactions varying from contractual (ie in exchange for goods or services of approximately equal value between a seller and a purchaser) to the receipt of unrestricted grants or donations (resources given to use on any of the charity's purposes).

97   This SORP seeks to provide guidance on how such differing transactions can be distinguished. However, judgement will still be required in deciding how any individual transaction fits into this framework and in identifying those factors that are likely to lead to different accounting treatments for their recognition. The recommendations provided below set out how accounting standards and principles should be applied in the context of transactions that are commonly undertaken within the charity sector. In order to understand how accounting standards apply to different funding arrangements, charity trustees need to determine for each source of funds:

•   What legal arrangements (eg contract or trust law) govern the terms of the arrangement and how any disputes arising are to be settled.

•   Whether entitlement to the funding requires a specific performance to be achieved (a contract or performance related grant).

•   Whether funds can be used for any of the purposes of the charity, or whether they can only be used for a specific purpose.

Contractual Arrangements

98   Some charities earn income by providing goods and/or services in return for a fee as part of their charitable activities. Such contractual income is recognised as incoming resources in the Statement of Financial Activities to the extent that the charity has provided the goods and/or services. Where such incoming resources are received in advance then a charity may not have entitlement to these resources until the goods or services have been provided. In this situation incoming resources received in advance should be deferred (Glossary: GL 15) until the charity becomes entitled to the resources.

99   Certain grant funding arrangements may contain conditions that closely specify the service to be performed by the charity. The terms of such funding may be set out in a service level agreement where the conditions for payment are linked to the performance of a particular level of service or units of output delivered, for example, number of meals provided or the opening hours of a facility used by beneficiaries. Entitlement to the incoming resources derived from such performance-related grants (Glossary GL 45) may be conditional upon the delivery of the specified level of service and in such circumstances should be recognised as incoming resources to the extent that the charity has provided the services or goods.

100   Simply because a grant is restricted to a particular purpose of the recipient charity does not mean it should necessarily be recognised as a performance related grant. For a performance related grant entitlement to the incoming resource only arises with the performance of a specific output identified as a condition for the grant. Entitlement to the grant in such cases only arises as the performance conditions are met. This can be contrasted with a restriction that whilst limiting how a charity may expend funds to particular purposes does not require a specific and measurable output to be delivered by the recipient charity as a condition of a charity's entitlement to the funds. Such restricted grants are recognised on the basis set out in paragraphs 104 to 111.

101   Where charities receive membership subscriptions, these may be in the nature of a gift, or they may effectively buy services or access to certain privileges. Where the substance of the subscription is that of a gift, the incoming resource should be recognised on the same basis as a donation. If the subscription purchases the right to services or benefits, the incoming resource should be recognised as the service or benefit is provided. If the subscriber receives rights to such benefits evenly over the period of membership then recognising such membership income on a pro-rata basis for the period of time covered by the subscription may be an appropriate estimation technique for income recognition.

102   Charities may also, on occasions, undertake activities under a long-term contract. Owing to the length of time taken to complete such contracts, it is appropriate to take credit for ascertainable incoming resources and the cost of any resources expended while contracts are in progress in accordance with the guidance given in SSAP 9.

103   Application Note G to FRS 5 provides specific guidance on revenue recognition under long-term contractual arrangements. A charity should recognise incoming resources in respect of its performance under a long-term contract when, and to the extent that, it obtains entitlement to consideration. This should be derived from an assessment of the fair value of the goods or services provided to its reporting date as a proportion of the total fair value of the contract. There will be contracts where costs incurred to date reflect the work performed and in such circumstances it would be appropriate to calculate incoming resources recognised at the balance sheet date based on the proportion of costs incurred to date in comparison with total expenditure. In the case of services, it may be appropriate to use the time spent as a proportion of the total time to be spent to fulfil the contract where this provides a reasonable estimate of a charity's performance and therefore entitlement. The incurrence of costs by the charity, does not, in itself, justify the recognition of revenue.

Grants and Donations Receivable

104 A pre-requisite of recognition of a promised grant or donation is evidence of entitlement. Evidence will normally exist when the grant is formally expressed in writing. Where entitlement is demonstrable, and no conditions are attached, such promises should be recognised as incoming resources once the criteria of certainty and measurability are met.

105 Charities often receive grants or donations with conditions attached that must be fulfilled before the entity has unconditional entitlement (control) of the resources. Meeting such conditions may be either within the recipient charity's control or reliant on external factors outside its control. Where meeting such conditions is within the charity's control and there is sufficient evidence that the conditions will be met, then the incoming resource should be recognised. Where uncertainty exists as to whether the recipient charity can meet conditions within its control, the incoming resource should not be recognised but deferred as a liability until certainty exists that the conditions imposed can be met.

106 For example, a grant may be conditional on a charity obtaining matched funding, or subject to a successful planning consent. Meeting the conditions attaching to such grants would not be either certain or wholly within the control of the recipient charity. The charity would not therefore have unconditional entitlement (control) of the incoming resource until these conditions were met. The incoming resource and corresponding asset should not be recognised until the conditions set have been met.

107 Conditions such as the submission of accounts or certification of expenditure can be seen as simply an administrative requirement as opposed to a condition that might prevent the recognition of incoming resources.

108 Incoming resources may also be subject to donor imposed conditions that specify the time period in which the expenditure of resources can take place. Such a pre-condition for use limits the charity's ability to expend the resource until the time condition is met. For example, the receipt in advance of a grant for expenditure that must take place in a future accounting period should be accounted for as deferred income and recognised as a liability until the accounting period in which the recipient charity is allowed by the condition to expend the resource.

109 Where the existence of a condition prevents the recognition of an incoming resource, a contingent asset should be disclosed where it is probable (but not virtually certain) that the condition will be met in the future (see paragraphs 340 to 348).

110 Charities are normally entitled to incoming resources when they are receivable. Recognition of a grant or donation without pre-conditions should not be deferred (Glossary GL 15) even if the resources are received in advance of the expenditure on the activity funded by the grant or donation. In such cases the charity has entitlement to the resource with the timing of the expenditure being within the discretion of the charity. Such incoming resources cannot be deferred simply because the related expenditure has not been incurred. Similarly, a condition that allows for the recovery by the donor of any unexpended part of a grant does not prevent recognition. A liability for any repayment is recognised when repayment becomes probable.

111 Where either incoming resources are given specifically to provide a fixed asset or a fixed asset is donated (a gift in kind), the charity will normally have entitlement to the incoming resources when they are receivable. At this point, all of the incoming resources should be recognised in the Statement of Financial Activities and not deferred over the life of the asset. As explained in paragraph 110 the possibility of having to repay the incoming resources does not affect their recognition in the first instance. Once acquired, the use of the asset will either be restricted or unrestricted (see paragraph 117). If its use is unrestricted the trustees may consider creating a designated fund reflecting the book value of the asset. The relevant fund will then be reduced over the useful economic life of the asset in line with its depreciation. This treatment accords with the requirements under accounting standards for the recognition of assets and liabilities and provides the most appropriate interpretation of SSAP 4 for charities (see Appendix 2: SSAP4).

Funds Received as Agent

112 Some incoming resources do not belong to the charity, for instance where it receives the resources in circumstances where the trustees, acting as agents (and not as custodian trustees), are legally bound to pay them over to a third party and have no responsibility for their ultimate application. In these circumstances the transaction is legally a transfer of resources from the original payer (who remains the principal) to the specified third party. If the original payer retains the legal responsibility for ensuring the charitable application of the funds, the intermediary charity should not recognise the resources in the Statement of Financial Activities or the balance sheet (see paragraph 319).

113 However, in some cases an intermediary charity may control the use of resources prior to their transfer to a third party and its trustees will act as principal and have responsibility for their charitable application. For instance, where the trustees of the intermediary charity may have applied for the grant of the resources or are able to direct how the grant should be used by the third party or both. Other forms of funding arrangements involving intermediary charities may need their trustees to accept the legal responsibility for the transfer of the grant to the third party (and for its charitable application, where the third party is not a charity). In all of these circumstances the resources should then be included in the intermediary charity's Statement of Financial Activities and balance sheet (see paragraph 320).

Disclosure

114 Where any incoming resources have been deferred, the notes to the accounts should explain the reasons for the deferrals and analyse the movement on the deferred account between incoming resources deferred in the current year and amounts released from previous years. Incoming resources of a similar nature can be grouped together in the notes as appropriate.

115 Where a charity has held resources for a third party which have not been included in the Statement of Financial Activities, the notes to the accounts should analyse the movement of these resources during the year relating to each party or type of party where material. Where resources have been held for related parties the required disclosure of paragraphs 227 to 228 should be given.

Incoming Resources Subject to Restrictions

116 The fact that a grant or donation is for a restricted purpose does not affect the basis of its recognition within the Statement of Financial Activities. There is an important difference for accounting purposes between restrictions placed on the purposes for which a particular resource may be used and conditions which must be fulfilled prior to entitlement or use by the charity. The existence of a restriction does not prevent the recognition of the incoming resource as the charity has entitlement to (control of) the resource and is simply limited by the restriction as to the purposes to which the resource can be applied.

117 Funds received for the restricted purpose of providing fixed assets should be accounted for immediately as restricted funds. The treatment of the fixed assets provided with those funds will depend on the basis on which they are held. The terms on which the funds were received may either require the fixed asset acquired to be held in a restricted fund or the fixed assets' acquisition may discharge the restriction and the asset will be held in the unrestricted funds (see also paragraph 111). There is no general rule and the treatment will depend upon the circumstance of each individual case (see Appendix 3). Where assets are re-allocated from one fund to another, this should be reflected as a transfer between the relevant funds.

A: Incoming Resources

118 Incoming resources should be analysed according to the activity that produced the resources. The analysis adopted should follow that given in Table 3, in particular grouping separately those resources generated by charitable activity from those activities aimed primarily at generating funds.

119 In most cases it will be clear which activity generated a particular resource. When the resources are generated from several activities then it is permissible to apportion the resources between the activities on a reasonable, justifiable and consistent basis.

Disclosure

120 Where any apportionment has taken place the method of apportionment should be disclosed in the accounting policy notes to the accounts.

A1: Incoming Resources from Generated Funds

A1a: Voluntary Income

121 Voluntary income (Glossary GL 61) includes incoming resources generated from the following sources:

(a) gifts, donations and any related gift aid claimed, including legacies (see paragraph 123), given by the founders, patrons, supporters, the general public and businesses;

(b)   grants which provide core funding or are of a general nature provided by government and charitable foundations but will not include those grants which are specifically for the performance of a service or production of charitable goods, for instance a service agreement with a local authority;

(c)   membership subscriptions and sponsorships where these are, in substance, donations rather than payment for goods or services;

(d)   gifts in kind (see paragraph 129) and donated services and facilities (see paragraph 133).

Disclosure

122   Where material, details of the types of activities undertaken to generate voluntary income should be provided either on the face of the Statement of Financial Activities or in the notes to the accounts. As far as possible the analysis categories provided here should match the detailed analysis provided for the costs of generating voluntary income.

Legacies

123   It is good practice to monitor a legacy from the time when notification is received to its final receipt. A charity should not, however, regard a legacy as receivable simply because it has been told about it. It should only do so when the legacy has been received or if, before receipt, there is sufficient evidence to provide the necessary certainty that the legacy will be received and the value of the incoming resources can be measured with sufficient reliability (see paragraph 94).

124   There will normally be sufficient certainty of receipt, for example, as soon as a charity receives a letter from the personal representatives of the estate advising that payment of the legacy will be made or that the property bequeathed will be transferred. It is likely that the value of the resource will also be measurable from this time. However, legacies which are not immediately payable should not be treated as receivable until the conditions associated with payment have been fulfilled (e g the death of a life tenant).

125   It is unlikely in practice that the entitlement, certainty of receipt and measurability conditions will be satisfied before the receipt of a letter from the personal representatives advising of an intended payment or transfer. The amount which is available in the estate for distribution to the beneficiaries may not have been finalised and, even if it has, there may still be outstanding matters relating to the precise division of the amount. In these circumstances entitlement may be in doubt or it may not be possible to provide a reasonable estimate of the legacy receivable, in which case it should not be included in the Statement of Financial Activities.

126   Where a charity receives a payment on account of its interest in an estate or a letter advising that such a payment will be made, the payment, or intended payment, on account should be treated as receivable.

127   Similarly, where a payment is received or notified as receivable (by the personal representatives) after the accounting year end, but it is clear that it had been agreed by the personal representatives prior to the year end (hence providing evidence of a condition that existed at the balance sheet date), then it should be accrued in the Statement of Financial Activities and the balance sheet.

Disclosure

128 Where the charity has been notified of material legacies which have not been included in the Statement of Financial Activities (because the conditions for recognition have not been met), this fact and an estimate of the amounts receivable should be disclosed in the notes to the accounts. Similarly, an indication should be provided of the nature of any material assets bequeathed to the charity but subject to a life tenancy interest held by a third party. Where material, the accounting policy notes should distinguish between the accounting treatments adopted for pecuniary and residuary legacies and legacies subject to a life interest held by another party.

Gifts in Kind

129 Incoming resources in the form of gifts in kind should be included in the Statement of Financial Activities in the following ways:

(a) Assets given and held as stock for distribution by the charity should be recognised as incoming resources for the year within "voluntary income" only when distributed with an equivalent amount being included as resources expended under the appropriate category of the Statement of Financial Activities to reflect its distribution.

(b) Assets given for use by the charity (e g property for its own occupation) should be recognised as incoming resources and within the relevant fixed asset category of the balance sheet when receivable (see paragraph 111).

(c) Where a gift has been made in kind but on trust for conversion into cash and subsequent application by the charity, the incoming resource should normally be recognised in the accounting period when receivable and where material, an adjustment should be made to the original valuation upon subsequent realisation of the gift. However in certain cases this will not be practicable and the incoming resources should be included in the accounting period in which the gift is sold. The most common example is that of second-hand goods donated for resale, which, whilst regarded as a donation in legal terms, is in economic terms similar to trading and should be included within "activities for generating funds".

130 In all cases the amount at which gifts in kind are included in the Statement of Financial Activities should be either a reasonable estimate of their gross value to the charity or the amount actually realised as in the case of second-hand goods donated for resale. Where gifts in kind are included in the Statement of Financial Activities at their estimated gross value, the current value will usually be the price that it estimates it would have to pay in the open market for an equivalent item.

Disclosure

131 The basis of any valuation should be disclosed in the accounting policies.

132   Referring to 129(a) above, where there are undistributed assets at the year end, a general description of the items involved and an estimate of their value should be given by way of a note to the accounts provided such value is material.

Donated Services and Facilities

133   A charity may receive assistance in the form of donated facilities, beneficial loan arrangements or donated services. Such incoming resources should be included in the Statement of Financial Activities where the benefit to the charity is reasonably quantifiable and measurable. The value placed on these resources should be the estimated value to the charity of the service or facility received: this will be the price the charity estimates it would pay in the open market for a service or facility of equivalent utility to the charity.

134   Donated services and facilities recognised in financial statements would include those usually provided by an individual or entity as part of their trade or profession for a fee. In contrast, the contribution of volunteers should be excluded from the Statement of Financial Activities as the value of their contribution to the charity cannot be reasonably quantified in financial terms. Commercial discounts should not be recognised as incoming resource except where they clearly represent a donation.

135   Where donated services or facilities are recognised, an equivalent amount should be included as expenditure under the appropriate heading in the Statement of Financial Activities.

Disclosure

136   The notes to the accounts should give an analysis of donated services or facilities included in the Statement of Financial Activities distinguishing appropriately between the different major items eg seconded staff, loaned assets etc. The accounting policy notes should also indicate the basis of valuation used. Where donated services are received but not included in the Statement of Financial Activities (eg volunteers) this should be disclosed in the Trustees' Annual Report if this information is necessary for the reader to gain a better understanding of the charity's activities.

A1b: Activities for Generating Funds

137   Activities for generating funds are the trading and other fundraising activities carried out by a charity primarily to generate incoming resources which will be used to undertake its charitable activities. The activities included within this category involve an element of exchange, with the charity receiving income in return for providing goods, services or an entry to an event. This category will include:

(a)   fundraising events such as jumble sales, firework displays and concerts (which are legally considered to be trading activities);

(b)   those sponsorships and social lotteries which cannot be considered as pure donations;

(c)   shop income from selling donated goods and bought in goods;

(d)   providing goods and services other than for the benefit of the charity's beneficiaries;

(e)   letting and licensing arrangements of property held primarily for functional use by the charity but temporarily surplus to operational requirements.

138 Whilst selling donated goods is legally considered to be the realisation of a donation in kind (see paragraph 129(c)), in economic terms it is similar to a trading activity and should be included in this section.

139 It may be possible to identify the incoming resources and resources expended for each different component of an activity (this may have to be done for tax purposes) but often these will be viewed as contributing to a single economic activity. Charity trustees should consider the balance of the activities being undertaken to determine the most appropriate place to include the incoming resources from such enterprises but having done this the components of incoming resources need not be analysed further. For example, a shop may mainly sell donated and bought in goods but it may also sell a small amount of goods made by its beneficiaries and incidentally provide information about the charity. It would be acceptable to classify all the incoming resources from the shop as "shop income" under activities for generating funds.

A1c: Investment Income

140 Investment income includes incoming resources from investment assets, including dividends, interest and rents but excluding realised and unrealised investment gains and losses.

141 Where a charity has subsidiary undertakings:

(a)   all payments to the charity by its subsidiary undertakings and all dividend entitlements from them, other than amounts receivable by the charity for the provision of goods and services to subsidiaries, should be separately recognised as incoming resources and appropriately described under investment income in the parent charity's accounts.

(b)   The exact amount of a gift aid payment from a subsidiary undertaking relating to a financial year can often only be precisely determined subsequent to the year end, for example with the calculation of taxable profits. Provided that a liability for the gift aid payment existed at the year end, the amount of the liability should be adjusted where calculations subsequent to the year end provide greater accuracy (see Appendix 2: FRS 21).

(c)   Gift aid payments from subsidiary undertakings should be separately disclosed in the charity's Statement of Financial Activities within investment income, or, if not material, in the notes to the accounts. The subsidiary undertakings themselves will only be accounted for by the charity in its consolidated Statement of Financial Activities of the group (see paragraphs 381 to 406).

Disclosure

142 The notes to the accounts should show the gross investment income arising from each class of investment shown in paragraph 303.

A2: Incoming Resources from Charitable Activities

143 This category includes any incoming resources received which are a payment for goods and services provided for the benefit of the charity's beneficiaries. It will include trading activities undertaken in furtherance of the charity's objects and those grants (although legally donations) which have conditions which make them similar in economic terms to trading income, such as service level agreements with local authorities.

144 This category will not include grants which are for core funding or do not have particular service requirements or are in response to an appeal. Such grants should be included in the section for voluntary income (see paragraph 121(b)).

145 Incoming resources from charitable activities should include:

(a) the sale of goods or services as part of the direct charitable activities of the charity (known as primary purpose trading);

(b) the sale of goods or services made or provided by the beneficiaries of the charity;

(c) the letting of non-investment property in furtherance of the charity's objects;

(d) contractual payments from government or public authorities where these are received in the normal course of trading under (a) to (c), eg fees for respite care;

(e) grants specifically for the provision of goods and services to be provided as part of charitable activities or services to beneficiaries;

(f) ancillary trades connected to a primary purpose in (a) to (e).

Disclosure

146 An analysis of incoming resources from charitable activities should be given in the notes to the accounts to supplement the analysis on the face of the Statement of Financial Activities. It should be sufficiently detailed so that the reader of the accounts understands the main activities carried out by the charity and the main components of the gross incoming resources receivable from each material charitable activity. As far as possible, incoming resources should be analysed using the same analysis categories as used for resources expended on charitable activities.

A3: Other Incoming Resources

147 Other incoming resources will include the receipt of any resources which the charity has not been able to analyse within the main incoming resource categories. This will be a minority of incoming resources and most charities will not need to use this category. Examples of items that fall within this category include a gain on the disposal of a tangible fixed asset held for the charity's own use (paragraph 218) and a gain on the disposal of a programme related investment (paragraph 310).

Expenditure and Costs

Recognition of Resources Expended

General Rules

148 Expenditure should be recognised when and to the extent that a liability is incurred or increased without a commensurate increase in recognised assets or a reduction in liabilities. In accounts prepared on the accruals basis, liabilities are recognised as resources expended as soon as there is a legal or constructive obligation committing the charity to the expenditure as described in Financial Reporting Standards 5 and 12. A liability will arise when a charity is under an obligation to make a transfer of value to a third party as a result of past transactions or events.

149 Just as charities may receive funds under a variety of arrangements (see paragraphs 96–97) so may charities expend their funds in a variety of ways ranging from meeting contractual liabilities to the payments of grants or donations. This SORP seeks to provide guidance on how such differing transactions can be distinguished. However, judgement will still be required in deciding how any individual transaction fits into this framework. The recommendations below set out how accounting standards and principles should be applied in the context of transactions that are commonly undertaken within the charity sector.

Contractual Arrangements

150 Where a charity enters into a contract for the supply of goods or services, expenditure is recognised once the supplier of the goods or services has performed their part of the contract, for example, the delivery of goods or the provision of a service.

151 Certain grants made may contain specific conditions that closely specify a particular service to be performed by the recipient of the grant. The terms of such grants may be set out in a service level agreement where the conditions for payment are linked to the performance of a particular level of service or units of output delivered, for example, number of meals provided or the opening hours of a facility used by beneficiaries. Often, in such cases, the grant maker will have negotiated the services to be provided to it or its beneficiaries. Expenditure on such performance-related grants (Glossary GL 45) should be recognised as resources expended to the extent that the recipient of the grant has provided the specified service or goods.

152 A grant that is merely restricted to a particular purpose of the recipient does not create a performance-related grant unless the grant also includes specific performance terms that meet the criteria set out above. Similarly, certain restricted grants may fund a programme of work to be undertaken over a number of years by the recipient. Again, this does not mean it should necessarily be recognised as a performance-related grant simply because of the period of the funding commitment or because the grantor is involved in monitoring or influencing the focus of the work as part of its grantmaking procedures.

153 For example, a grantmaking charity may fund a three year research programme enabling the recipient to undertake a programme of work identified by the recipient as necessary to meet its own objectives or that adds to the stock of knowledge on a topic. In order to provide funding, the work undertaken will need to be consistent with the legal objects of the grantmaker which may also, as part of its own grant approval processes, be involved in monitoring or influencing the focus of the work. Such an arrangement would not create a performance-related grant (see Glossary GL 45) if the funding is not directed at providing a specified service to the grantmaker or its beneficiaries as a condition of payment. Grants without such performance conditions that are directed at enabling the recipient to follow its own programme of work or increasing the pool of knowledge in an area of work should be recognised as a liability where a constructive obligation arises to make the grant payment (see Paragraph 155).

Grants Payable and Constructive Obligations

154   In the case of grants (other than performance-related grants) and certain other expenditure relating directly to charitable activities, an exchange for consideration does not arise. Such expenditure is incurred to further the charity's objects but without creating a contractual or quasi-contractual relationship with the recipient of the grant or the charity's beneficiaries. Nevertheless, the charity may still have a liability (Glossary GL 40) which needs to be recognised.

155   Liabilities may arise from a constructive or a legal obligation (Glossary GL 10). A constructive obligation arises under FRS 12 where events have created a valid expectation in other parties that the charity will discharge its obligations. Evidence that a valid expectation has been created might be provided by the charity's current and past practice in discharging such obligations and the specific communication of a commitment to the recipient. A constructive obligation always involves a commitment to another party that has been communicated to those affected in a sufficiently specific manner to raise a valid expectation on the part of the recipient that the charity will discharge its obligations. Because an obligation always involves a commitment to another party, it follows that a funding decision by a charity's trustees does not give rise to a constructive obligation at the balance sheet date unless the decision has been communicated before the balance sheet date to those affected in a sufficiently specific manner to raise a valid expectation in them that the charity will discharge its responsibilities.

156   Charities may on occasions make general or policy statements of their future intentions, for example, of an intention or aim of relieving famine in a particular location or to improve the quality of care provided to a particular group of people. Such statements can be communicated in a variety of ways including mission statements, setting out future plans in a Trustees' Annual Report or simply by making a general policy statement. Statements such as these do not create a constructive obligation as discretion is retained by the charity as to their implementation. A term in a grant agreement or offer that relieved a donor charity from a future obligation in the event of lack of funds at a future settlement date would not normally prevent the recognition of a liability by the donor charity. The liability would however be derecognised when an event requires the funding offer to be rescinded.

157   A constructive obligation is likely to arise where:

(a)   a specific commitment, or promise to provide goods, services or grant funding is given, and

(b)   this is communicated directly to a beneficiary or grant recipient.

In such circumstances, the charity is unlikely to have a realistic alternative but to meet the obligation. However, the recognition of any resulting liability will be dependent on any conditions attaching to such commitments.

158 A charity may enter into commitments which are dependent upon explicit conditions being met either by itself or by the recipient before payment is made or upon future reviews. A liability, and hence expenditure, should be recognised once such conditions fall outside the control of the giving charity. If the conditions set remain within the control of giving charity, then the charity retains the discretion to avoid the expenditure and therefore a liability should not be recognised.

159 By way of illustration, where a charity makes a specific commitment to grant fund a project over a three year period, the following situations may arise:

(a) If the multi-year grant obligation:
   (i)   is conditional on an annual review of progress that determines whether future funding is provided; and
   (ii) discretion is retained by the giving charity to terminate the grant;
   then provided evidence exists (eg from past review practice) that the discretion retained by the charity has substance, this amounts to a condition and an immediate liability arises only for the first year of the funding commitment.
   If the annual review process, although set out in the conditions of the grant, is not in practice used to determine whether funding is provided in the subsequent years of the commitment, then the review stipulation should not be interpreted as a condition and a liability for the full three years of the grant should be recognised.

(b) If there is no condition attaching to the grant that enables the charity to realistically avoid the commitment, the liability for the full three years of the funding should be recognised.

160 Commitments may contain conditions that are outside the control of the giving charity. For example, a charity may promise a grant payment on the condition that the recipient finds matching funding. As the condition falls outside the control of the giving charity, a liability arises and expenditure should be recognised.

General Issues

161 Where a liability is not accrued, because conditions have not been met, such a commitment should normally be treated as a contingent liability. The balance sheet treatment for both outstanding commitments and contingent liabilities is given in paragraphs 340 to 348.

162 The trustees may wish to designate some of the charity's income funds to represent contingent liabilities and other planned expenditure which may not have created a liability.

163 Where later events make the recognition of a liability no longer appropriate, the liability should be cancelled by credit against the relevant expenditure heading in the Statement of Financial Activities. The credit should mirror the treatment originally used to recognise the expenditure for the liability and should be disclosed separately.

Support Costs

164   In undertaking any activity there may be support costs (Glossary GL 54) incurred that, whilst necessary to deliver an activity, do not themselves produce or constitute the output of the charitable activity. Similarly, costs will be incurred in supporting income generation activities such as fundraising, and in supporting the governance of the charity. Support costs include the central or regional office functions such as general management, payroll administration, budgeting and accounting, information technology, human resources, and financing.

165   Support costs do not, in themselves, constitute an activity, instead they enable output-creating activities to be undertaken. Support costs are therefore allocated to the relevant activity cost category they support on the bases set out in paragraphs 168 to 174. This enables the total cost of an activity category to be disclosed in the Statement of Financial Activities and for the cost of the constituent sub-activities to be presented at a service, programme or project level within the notes to the accounts. There is nevertheless legitimate user interest in both the level of support costs incurred and the policies adopted for their allocation to the relevant activity cost categories that should be addressed through relevant note disclosures.

Disclosure

166   The notes to the accounts should provide details of the total support costs incurred and of material items or categories of expenditure included within support costs.

167   Where support costs are material, an explanation should be provided in the notes of how these costs have been allocated to each of the activity cost categories disclosed in the Statement of Financial Activities or the supporting notes to the accounts. The explanation may include percentages or amounts allocated, details of the methods of apportionment used or a table showing the detailed allocations such as that shown below in Table 4.

Table 4.   Example of Support Cost Breakdown by Activity

Support Cost (Examples)	Fundraising	Activity 1	Activity 2	Activity 3	Activity 4	Activity 5	Basis of allocation
Management	£x	£x	£x	£x	£x	£x	Text describing method
Finance	£x	£x	£x	£x	£x	£x	Text describing method
Information Technology	£x	£x	£x	£x	£x	£x	Text describing method
Human Resources	£x	£x	£x	£x	£x	£x	Text describing method

Support Cost (Examples)	Fundraising	Activity 1	Activity 2	Activity 3	Activity 4	Activity 5	Basis of allocation
Total	£x	£x	£x	£x	£x	£x	

Allocation of Costs

168 A reliable approach to cost allocation should be adopted but a charity should also consider the materiality of the amounts involved and the cost benefit advantages of the approach in that greater accuracy may on occasions only be achievable at a high incremental cost.

169 In attributing costs between activity categories, the following principles should be applied:

(a) Where appropriate, expenditure should be allocated directly to an activity cost category.

(b) Items of expenditure which contribute directly to the output of more than one activity cost category, for example, the cost of a staff member whose time is divided between a fundraising activity and working on a charitable project, should be apportioned on a reasonable, justifiable and consistent basis.

(c) Depreciation, amortisation, impairment or losses on disposal of fixed assets should be attributed in accordance with the same principles.

(d) Support costs may not be attributable to single activity but rather provide the organisational infrastructure that enables output producing activities to take place. Such costs should therefore also be apportioned on a reasonable, justifiable and consistent basis to the activity cost categories being supported.

170 There are a number of bases for apportionment that may be applied. Examples include:

(a) usage – eg on the same basis as expenditure incurred directly in undertaking an activity;

(b) per capita – ie on the number of people employed within an activity;

(c) on the basis of floor area occupied by an activity.

(d) on the basis of time (eg where staff duties are multi-activity).

171 The bases for apportionment adopted by a charity should be appropriate to the cost concerned and to the charity's particular circumstances and selected to enable its accounts to give a true and fair view. The bases adopted for apportionment will normally be consistent between accounting periods.

172 Particular issues arise where a charity provides information about its activities in the context of a fundraising activity. Information about the aims, objectives and projects of a charity is frequently provided in the context of mail shots, websites, collections and telephone fundraising. In determining whether a multi-purpose activity arises, and therefore a need to apportion costs, a distinction should be drawn between:

(a)   publicity or information costs involved in raising the profile of a charity which is associated with fundraising (costs of generating funds); and

(b)   publicity or information that is provided in an educational manner in furtherance of the charity's objectives (charitable expenditure).

173   In the context of a fundraising activity, for publicity or information to be regarded as charitable expenditure, it must be supplied in an educational manner. To achieve an educational purpose, information supplied would be:

(a)   targeted at beneficiaries or others who can use the information to further the charity's objectives; and

(b)   information or advice on which the recipient can act upon in an informed manner to further the charity's objectives; and

(c)   related to other educational activities or objectives undertaken by the charity. Where information provided in conjunction with a fundraising activity does not meet these criteria, it should be regarded as targeted at potential donors and therefore relating wholly to the fundraising activity.

174   For example, a health education charity that targeted high-risk beneficiary groups or the medical profession supplying information as to health risks or symptom recognition and advising on steps that should be taken. Such information would fall within charitable expenditure in that it is targeted at beneficiaries, advises on steps that can be taken and is likely to link to the charity's activities or objectives in health education. Therefore when such information is provided in the context of a fundraising activity, a joint cost would arise with costs apportioned between the fundraising and charitable activities.

Disclosure

175   The accounting policy notes should explain the policy adopted for the apportionment of costs between activities and any estimation technique(s) used to calculate their apportionment.

176   Where any fundraising activity is identified as meeting the criteria of a multi-purpose activity (see paragraphs 172 to 174) and part of the costs of the multi-purpose activity are allocated to charitable activities then the policy for the identification of such multi-purpose costs should be explained in the accounting policy notes together with the basis on which any allocation to charitable activities is made.

B: Resources Expended

177   The Statement of Financial Activities provides an analysis of the resources expended by a charity based on the nature of the activities undertaken. Resources expended are split into three main activity categories, being:

(a) the costs of generating funds (paragraph 178–187);

(b) the costs of charitable activities (paragraph 188–209); and

(c) the governance costs (paragraph 210 to 212).

The Statement of Financial Activities or the notes to the accounts should include an analysis of the sub-activities, services, programmes, projects or other initiatives that contribute to a particular activity category.

B1: Costs of Generating Funds

178 These are the costs which are associated with generating incoming resources from all sources other than from undertaking charitable activities. The main components of costs within this category are:

(a) costs of generating voluntary income (Glossary GL 13 and see paragraphs 180 to 184);

(b) costs of fundraising trading, including cost of goods sold and other associated costs (see paragraphs 185 to 186); and

(c) costs of managing investments for both income generation and capital maintenance (see paragraph 187).

179 Costs of generating funds should not include:

(a) costs associated with delivering or supporting the provision of goods and services in the furtherance of the charity's objects; nor

(b) the costs of any subsequent negotiation, monitoring or reporting relating to the provision of goods or services under the terms of a grant, contract or performance-related grant.

B1a: Costs of Generating Voluntary Income

180 Costs of generating voluntary income are defined in the Glossary (GL 13). All such fundraising costs, including agents' costs where fundraising agents are used, should be included within this category. In the case of consolidated accounts any such costs incurred by any subsidiary companies or other entities should be consolidated on a line-by-line basis.

181 Some fundraising costs may be incurred in starting up a new source of future income such as legacies, or in developing a supporter database.

(a) Start-up costs of a new fundraising activity should be treated in the same manner as similar costs incurred as part of a charity's ongoing activities. In most cases, it will be inappropriate to carry forward start-up costs as prepayments or deferred expenditure as the future economic benefits that may be derived are usually not sufficiently certain (see Appendix 2: UITF Abstract 24 – Accounting for Start-up Costs).

(b)   Data capture costs of internally developed databases may only be capitalised where future benefit can be demonstrated and the resulting database has a readily ascertainable value.

182   The start-up costs of a new fundraising activity may be material in the context of the overall fundraising activity and may, because of their exceptional size or incidence, require separate disclosure to explain performance.

Disclosure

183   Where the costs of generating voluntary income are material, details of the types of activity on which the costs were expended should be shown in the notes to the accounts. Types of activity could include collections (eg street and house-to-house collections), sponsorship, legacy development and direct mail. As far as possible the analysis provided here should match the detailed analysis of voluntary incoming resources (see paragraphs 121 to 122).

184   Exceptional costs that arise in the context of generating voluntary income should not be presented as a separate category of costs on the face of the Statement of Financial Activities but, rather, should be included as an exceptional item within the relevant activity cost category. The amount of each exceptional item, either individually or as an aggregate of items of a similar type, should be disclosed in the notes to the accounts or on the face of the Statement of Financial Activities (within the activity category to which the cost relates) if that degree of prominence is necessary to give a true and fair view. An adequate description should be given to enable its nature to be understood.

B1b: Fundraising Trading: Cost of goods sold and other costs

185   This category should include all those costs that are incurred by trading for a fundraising purpose in either donated or bought-in goods or in providing non-charitable services to generate income. This includes:

(a)   the cost of goods sold or services provided;

(b)   other costs related to the trade, including staff costs, premises costs and other costs incurred in the activity including allocated support costs; and

(c)   costs related to the licensing of a charity logo.

In consolidated accounts this category will include the costs incurred by both the charity and any subsidiaries or other entities consolidated on a line-by-line basis.

Disclosure

186   Where the costs associated with fundraising trading are material, details should be given in the notes to the accounts to distinguish the cost of separate trading activities in a way that matches the analysis of income.

B1c: Investment Management Costs

187 Investment management costs are defined in the Glossary (GL 38). Where investment management fees are deducted from investment income by investment managers, the charity should show as investment income the gross investment income before fees and report the fees within this cost category (see paragraph 140). As explained in Appendix 3, paragraph 3(c), investment management costs associated with endowment fund investments should generally be charged to the endowment fund in the Statement of Financial Activities.

B2: Charitable Activities

188 Resources expended on charitable activities comprise all the resources applied by the charity in undertaking its work to meet its charitable objectives as opposed to the cost of raising the funds to finance these activities and governance costs. Charitable activities are all the resources expended by the charity in the delivery of goods and services, including its programme and project work that is directed at the achievement of its charitable aims and objectives. Such costs include the direct costs of the charitable activities together with those support costs incurred that enable these activities to be undertaken.

189 Charities may carry out their activities through a combination of direct service provision and grant funding of third parties to undertake work that contributes to the charity's objectives or programme of work. In such cases, the total cost of the activity involves both costs incurred directly by the charity and funding provided to third parties through grantmaking activities.

190 Where incoming resources are received either under contract or by a restricted grant to provide a specified service, further analysis of charitable activities expenditure may be provided in the notes to the accounts to demonstrate the link between the incoming resource and the charitable activity that it funds.

Disclosure

191 Resources expended on charitable activities should be analysed on the face of the Statement of Financial Activities or in a prominent note to the accounts. This analysis should provide an understanding of the nature of the activities undertaken and the resources expended on their provision. This analysis may, for example, set out the activity cost of the main services provided by the charity, or set out the resources expended on material programmes or projects undertaken by the charity.

192 The note to the accounts should identify the amount of support costs allocated to charitable activities.

193 Where activities are carried out through a combination of direct service or programme activity and grant funding of third parties, the notes to the accounts should identify the amount of grantmaking expenditure using the note to explain the activity funded.

194 The disclosures required may, for example, be presented in a table such as Table 5 (with totals reconciling with the Statement of Financial Activities and other notes as appropriate).

Table 5.   Breakdown of Costs of Charitable Activity

Activity or Programme	Activities undertaken directly £	Grant funding of activities £	Support costs £	Total £
Activity 1				
Activity 2				
Activity 3				
Total				

Grantmaking

195   Costs associated with grantmaking activity include the grants actually made and the support costs associated with the activity. The term grant is defined in the Glossary (GL 29) and associated support costs are explained further at paragraph 164 above.

196   Support costs related to grantmaking will include:

(a)   costs incurred before grants are made (pregrant costs) as part of the decision making process;

(b)   post-grant costs eg monitoring of grants; and

(c)   costs of any central or regional office functions such as general management, payroll administration, budgeting and accounting, information technology, human resources, and financing.

197   Grantmaking charities may undertake their entire programme of work through grantmaking activities, whilst other charities may undertake their activities through a combination of direct service provision and grant funding of third parties. In either case, further analysis of grantmaking, where material, should be provided.

198   The further information provided in relation to grantmaking should provide the reader with a reasonable understanding of the nature of the activities or projects that are being funded and whether the financial support is provided directly to individuals or to assist an institution undertake its activities or projects. In the case of institutional grants, information as to the recipient(s) of the funding should be provided so that the reader can appreciate the type and range of institutions supported.

199   An individual grant is one that is made for the direct benefit of the individual who receives it, for example, to relieve financial hardship or for an educational bursary. All other grants should be regarded as institutional. For example, a grant which is made to an individual to carry out a research project should be regarded as a grant to the institution with which the individual is connected rather than as a grant to the individual.

200   Information provided in relation to grantmaking may be limited or excluded when:

(a)   grants are made to individuals – in which case details of the recipient are not required;

(b)   grantmaking activities in total are not material in the context of a charity's overall charitable activities – in which case no disclosures are required;

(c)   total grants to a particular institution are not material in the context of institutional grants – in which case the name of the recipient institution need not be disclosed;

(d)   disclosure of a particular institutional grant would seriously prejudice either the grant maker or the recipient;

(e)   where disclosure of grants made by a charity registered only in England and Wales would occur in the lifetime of the settlor, or any spouse, or civil partner of the settlor.

Disclosure

201   The analysis and explanation should help the reader of the accounts understand how the grants made relate to the objects of the charity and the policy adopted by the trustees in pursuing these objects.

202   The notes to the accounts should identify the amount of support costs associated with grantmaking activities.

203   The analysis and explanation in the notes should provide details, with amounts that reconcile with the total of grants payable of:

(a)   the total amount of grants analysed between grants to individuals and grants to institutions,

(b)   an analysis of the total amount of grants paid by nature or type of activity or project being supported.

This statement may, for example, be structured as shown in Table 6.

204   The analysis of grants should provide the reader with an understanding of the nature of the activities or projects being funded by the grantmaker. This analysis of grants should relate to the charity's objectives, for example, categories may be social welfare, medical research, the performing arts, welfare of people in financial need, help to people seeking to further their education, depending on the nature of the charity. Some charities may decide that it is appropriate to provide further or alternative levels of analysis perhaps for example, showing a geographical analysis of the value of grants made.

205   The trustees may give further analysis and explanation of the purposes for which grants were made as part of the Trustees' Annual Report or by means of a separate publication. Such further analysis does not excuse the trustees from providing sufficient detail in the notes to the accounts as is needed to provide a true and fair view.

Table 6. Analysis of grants

Analysis	Grants to Institutions Total amount £	Grants to Individuals Total amount £
Activity or Project 1		
Activity or Project 2		
Activity or Project 3		
Total		

206 If a charity has made grants to particular institutions that are material in the context of grantmaking, the charity should disclose details, as specified in paragraph 207, of a sufficient number of institutional grants to provide a reasonable understanding of the range of institutions it has supported. This information may be provided either in the notes to the accounts, or as part of the Trustees' Annual Report or by means of a separate publication. Where the analysis is contained in a separate publication, it should be made available by the charity to the public on request. The notes to the accounts should identify the publication and state how copies of it can be obtained.

207 The disclosure of institutional grants should give the name of the institution and total value of grants made to that institution in the accounting year. Where grants have been made to a particular institution to undertake different activities or projects, the total value of the grants made for each activity or purpose should be disclosed. For example, a charity may have made grants to different officers or departments of a particular university for different projects. Such grants should be treated as having been made to the same institution.

208 Very exceptionally, even though the grants to a particular institution are material, it is possible that the disclosure of the details of one or more of those grants could seriously prejudice the furtherance of the purposes either of the recipient institution or of the charity itself. Situations where serious prejudice is clearly indicated include those where disclosure could result in serious personal injury.

209 Where the circumstances amount to serious prejudice, a charity may withhold details of the recipient of any institutional grant concerned but should in such circumstances:

(a)   disclose in the notes to the accounts the total number, value and general purpose of those grants the details of which have not been disclosed;

(b)   give in writing to the charity's regulatory body:
    (i)   the full details of any grants not disclosed, and
    (ii)   a full explanation of the reasons why those details have not been disclosed in the accounts;

(c)   state in the notes to the accounts whether or not those details have been given to the charity's regulatory body.

It is unlikely in practice that all the material institutional grants of a charity would fall within this exception.

B3: Governance Costs

210 Governance costs (defined in Glossary GL 28) include the costs of governance arrangements which relate to the general running of the charity as opposed to the direct management functions inherent in generating funds, service delivery and programme or project work. These activities provide the governance infrastructure which allows the charity to operate and to generate the information required for public accountability. They include the strategic planning processes that contribute to future development of the charity.

211 Expenditure on the governance of the charity will normally include both direct and related support costs. Direct costs will include such items as internal and external audit, legal advice for trustees and costs associated with constitutional and statutory requirements e g the cost of trustee meetings and preparing statutory accounts. Where material, there should also be an apportionment of shared and indirect costs involved in supporting the governance activities (as distinct from supporting its charitable or income generation activities).

Disclosure

212 The accounting policy notes should explain the nature of costs allocated to the governance category, and an analysis may be provided within the notes to the accounts of the main items of expenditure included within this category where it is considered to provide useful information to the users of the accounts.

B4: Other Resources Expended

213 Other resources expended will include the payment of any resources which the charity has not been able to analyse within the main resources expended categories. This category should not be used for support costs which can be allocated to other activity costs.

C: Transfers

214 All transfers between the different categories of funds should be shown on the transfer row of the Statement of Financial Activities. The transfer row will be used for several purposes including:

(a) when capital funds are released to an income fund from expendable endowment;

(b) where a charity has authority to adopt a total return approach to investment (see Appendix 3 paragraph 3(g)) to record the release of funds to income from the unapplied total return fund held within the permanent endowment fund;

(c) where restricted assets have been released and reallocated to unrestricted income funds;

(d) to transfer assets from unrestricted income funds to finance a deficit on a restricted fund; and

(e) to transfer of the value of fixed assets from restricted to unrestricted funds when the asset has been purchased from a restricted fund donation but the asset is held for a general and not a restricted purpose.

215 Material transfers should not be netted off but should be shown gross on the face of the Statement of Financial Activities.

Disclosure

216 The notes to the accounts should provide an explanation of the nature of each material transfer between funds.

D: Other Recognised Gains and Losses

D1: Gains and Losses on Fixed Assets

217 Gains and losses arising on disposal, revaluation or impairment of fixed assets – whether held for the charity's own use or for investment purposes – will form part of the particular fund in which the investment or other asset concerned is or was held at the time of disposal, revaluation or impairment.

218 Such gains and losses should be recognised as follows:

(a) impairment losses of assets held for the charity's own use (ie not investments) should be regarded as additional depreciation of the impaired asset and included appropriately in the resources expended section of the Statement of Financial Activities;

(b) gains on the disposal of fixed assets for the charity's own use should be included under the heading "other incoming resources". Losses on disposal should be treated as additional depreciation and included appropriately in the resources expended section of the Statement of Financial Activities; and

(c) revaluation gains or losses (which are not considered to be impairment losses (see paragraphs 267–272)) on assets held for the charity's own use should be included in the section on gains and losses on revaluations of fixed assets for the charity's own use.

D2: Gains and Losses on Investment Assets

219 Any gains and losses on investment assets (including property investments) should be included under the gains and losses on the revaluation and disposal of investment assets. Realised and unrealised gains and losses may be included in a single row on the Statement of Financial Activities. In particular this approach will be necessary where a charity adopts a "marking to market" or continuous revaluation approach in relation to its investment portfolio.

D3: *Actuarial Gains or Losses on Defined Benefit Pension Schemes*

220 Actuarial gains or losses on defined benefit pension schemes should be separately disclosed in the gains and losses section of the Statement of Financial Activities (see paragraphs 430 to 448 – Accounting for Retirement Benefits).

Other Matters to be Covered in Notes to the Accounts

Related Party Transactions

221 Subject to paragraph 229 below, disclosure in a note to the accounts is required of any transactions which the reporting charity or any institution connected with it has entered into with a related party. Such transactions might inhibit the charity from pursuing its own separate interests.

222 Related parties are defined in the Glossary (GL 50).

223 Any decision by a charity to enter into a transaction ought to be influenced only by the consideration of the charity's own interests. This requirement is reinforced by legal rules which, in certain circumstances, can invalidate transactions where the charity trustees have a conflict of interest. This does not necessarily mean that all transactions with related persons are influenced by the consideration of interests other than the charity's nor that they are liable to invalidation.

224 Transparency is particularly important where the relationship between the charity and the other party or parties to a transaction suggests that the transaction could possibly have been influenced by interests other than the charity's. It is possible that the reported financial position and results may have been affected by such transactions and information about these transactions is therefore necessary for the users of the charity's accounts.

225 Related party transactions potentially include (exceptions in paragraph 229):

(a) purchases, sales, leases and donations (including donations which are made in furtherance of the charity's objects) of goods, property, money and other assets such as intellectual property rights to or from the related party;

(b) the supply of services by the related party to the charity, and the supply of services by the charity to the related party. Supplying services includes providing the use of goods, property and other assets and finance arrangements such as making loans and giving guarantees and indemnities; and

(c) any other payments and other benefits which are made to trustees under express provisions of the governing document of a charity or in fulfilment of its charitable objectives.

Required Disclosure

226 Trustee remuneration or other benefits should always be regarded as material (subject to paragraph 229(f)). Material transactions with related parties should be disclosed irrespective of whether or not they are undertaken on an arm's length basis.

227   The required disclosure is as follows (also see paragraph 303(c) re investments):

(a)   the name(s) of the transacting related party or parties;

(b)   a description of the relationship between the parties (including the interest of the related party or parties in the transaction);

(c)   a description of the transaction;

(d)   the amounts involved;

(e)   outstanding balances with related parties at the balance sheet date and any provisions for doubtful debts from such persons;

(f)   any amounts written off from such balances during the accounting year; and

(g)   any other elements of the transactions which are necessary for the understanding of the accounts.

228   The disclosure can be given in aggregate for similar transactions and type of related party, unless disclosure of an individual transaction or connected transactions:

(a)   is necessary for an understanding of the impact of the transactions on the accounts of the charity; or

(b)   is a legal requirement, for example, in relation to trustee remuneration (see paragraph 230(b)).

Disclosures not Required

229   Some related party transactions are such that they are unlikely to influence the pursuance of the separate independent interests of the charity. These need not be disclosed unless there is evidence to the contrary. Examples are:

(a)   donations received by the reporting charity from a related party, so long as the donor has not attached conditions which would, or might, require the charity to alter significantly the nature of its existing activities if it were to accept the donation (but any material grant by the reporting charity to a charity which is a related party should be disclosed);

(b)   minor or routine unremunerated services provided to a charity by people related to it;

(c)   contracts of employment between a charity and its employees (except where the employees are the charity trustees or people connected with them);

(d)   contributions by a charity to a pension fund for the benefit of employees; (also see paragraph 235);

(e)   the purchase from a charity by a related party of minor articles which are offered for sale to the general public on the same terms as are offered to the general public;

(f)   the provision of services to a related party (including a charity trustee or person connected with a charity trustee), where the related party receives the services as part of a wider beneficiary class, and on the same terms as other members of the class (for example, the use of a village hall by members of its committee of management, as inhabitants of the area of benefit); and

(g)   the payment or reimbursement of out-of-pocket expenses to a related party (including a charity trustee or person connected with a charity trustee – but see paragraphs 231 to 233).

Trustee Remuneration and Benefits

230   Unlike in the case of the directors of commercial companies, it is not the normal practice for charity trustees, or people connected with them, to receive remuneration, or other benefits, from the charities for which they are responsible, or from institutions connected with those charities. Detailed disclosures of remuneration and benefits are therefore required where the related party is a charity trustee, or a person connected with a charity trustee. The following points should be borne in mind when reporting on transactions, where the related party is a charity trustee or a person connected with a trustee.

(a)   Unless one of the exceptions in paragraph 229 applies, the transaction should always be regarded as material, and should therefore be disclosed regardless of its size.

(b)   Each type of related party transaction must be separately disclosed. This means, for example, that particulars of remuneration paid to each charity trustee or person connected with a charity trustee, should be given individually in the notes. Where the charity has made any pension arrangements for charity trustees or persons connected with them, the amount of contributions paid and the benefits accruing must be disclosed in the notes for each related party.

(c)   Where remuneration has been paid to a charity trustee or a person connected with a charity trustee, the legal authority under which the payment was made (eg provision in the governing document of the charity, order of the Court or Charity Commission) should also be given, as should the reason for such remuneration.

(d)   Where neither the trustees nor any persons connected with them have received any such remuneration, this fact should be stated.

Trustees' Expenses

231   Where a charity has met individual expenses incurred by trustees for services provided to the charity, either by reimbursement of the trustee or by providing the trustee with an allowance or by direct payment to a third party, the aggregate amount of those expenses should be disclosed in a note to the accounts. The note should also indicate the nature of the expenses (eg travel, subsistence, entertainment etc) and the number of trustees involved.

232   Sometimes trustees act as agents for the charity and make purchases on its behalf and are reimbursed for this expenditure, eg payment for stationery or office equipment. Such expenditure is not related to the services provided by a trustee and there is no need to disclose it. Likewise there is no need to disclose routine expenditure which is attributable collectively to the services provided to the trustees, such as the hire of a room for meetings or providing reasonable refreshment at the meeting.

233   Where the trustees have received no such expenses, this fact should be stated.

Staff Costs and Emoluments

234   It is important that the accounts disclose the costs of employing staff who work for the charity whether or not the charity itself has incurred those costs. This includes seconded and agency staff and staff employed by connected or independent companies. For instance, staff working for a charity may have contracts with and be paid by a connected company. Payments may also be made to independent third parties for the provision of staff. Where such arrangements are in place and the costs involved are material (in relation to the charity's own expenditure) there should be disclosure by way of note which outlines the arrangement in place, the reasons for them and the amounts involved.

235   The total staff costs should be shown in the notes to the accounts giving the split between gross wages and salaries, employer's national insurance costs and pension costs (those pension costs included within resources expended excluding pension finance costs) for the year. The average number of staff during the year should be provided and where material to the disclosure, eg due to the number of part-time staff, an estimate of the average number of full time equivalent employees for the year may be provided in the notes to the accounts providing sub-categories according to the manner in which the charity's activities are organised.

236   Where a charity is subject to a statutory audit then the notes should also show the number of employees whose emoluments for the year (including taxable benefits in kind but not employer pension costs) fell within each band of £10,000 from £60,000 upwards. Bands in which no employee's emoluments fell should not be listed.

237   In addition the following pension details should be disclosed in total for higher paid staff as defined in paragraph 236:

(a)   contributions in the year for the provision of defined contribution scheme (normally money purchase schemes); and

(b)   the number of staff to whom retirement benefits are accruing under defined contribution schemes and defined benefit schemes respectively. (Further information on accounting for Retirement Benefit Schemes is given in paragraphs 430 to 448).

238   If there are no employees with emoluments above £60,000 this fact should be stated.

Cost of Audit, Independent Examination or Reporting Accountant Services and other Financial Services

239   The notes to the accounts should disclose separately the amounts payable to the auditor, independent examiner or reporting accountant in respect of:

(a)   the costs of their respective external scrutiny; and

(b)   other financial services such as taxation advice, consultancy, financial advice and accountancy.

Ex-Gratia Payments

240   The total amount or value of any:

(a)   payment; or

(b)   non-monetary benefit; or

(c)   other expenditure of any kind; or

(d)   waiver of rights to property to which a charity is entitled,

which is made not as an application of funds or property for charitable purposes but in fulfilment of a compelling moral obligation should be disclosed in the notes to the accounts. Where trustees require and obtain the authority of the Court, the Attorney General or the Charity Commission, the nature and date of the authority for each such payment should also be disclosed. (The Charity Commission has provided further guidance on such payments, that is applicable to charities in England and Wales, in its publication (CC7) – Ex Gratia Payments by Charities).

241   Payments which the trustees reasonably consider to be in the interests of the charity (more than a moral obligation) should not be treated as ex-gratia, even though there is no legal obligation to make them. For example, the trustees may think that it will motivate retained staff and hence benefit the charity if they make redundancy payments over and above the minimum legally required.

Analysis of the Net Movement in Funds

242   The net movement of funds represents the increase or decrease in resources available to a charity to deploy in undertaking future activities. Unlike profit or loss in a commercial entity, it should not necessarily be regarded as an indicator of a charity's performance. Charities also further their objectives by investing in tangible fixed assets to provide services or by making investments of a programme or social related nature. Such applications are charitable but do not decrease the funds of a charity. Charities may also receive gifts of an endowed nature, which are identified separately in the primary accounting statements. Whilst endowments provide a source of income or service generation in future periods they are not available to finance expenditure.

243   Information on such charitable applications and sources can be ascertained from a charity's cash flow statement (when prepared). A note summarising these effects, when material, can provide valuable information to readers of accounts in interpreting net movements in funds and help the reader understand the impact of such transactions on the liquid funds of the charity. Where relevant a charity may choose to provide in the notes to the accounts the following information:

(a)   total net movement in funds for the year;

(b)   net endowment receipts for the year (value of endowment receipts less any release of expendable endowment to income funds);

(c)   net expenditure on additions to functional fixed assets (cost of additions less proceeds of any disposals) for the year; and

(d)   net investment in programme related investments (cost of additions less proceeds of any disposals) for the year.

BALANCE SHEET

Introduction

244   The balance sheet provides a snapshot of the charity's assets and liabilities at the end of its accounting year and how assets are split between the different types of funds. The balance sheet will not always include all of the assets and liabilities of a charity, nor attach an up-to-date valuation for all assets. Some heritage assets (see paragraphs 279 to 294), or contingent liabilities (see paragraphs 340 to 348) may be omitted. Where such assets or contingent liabilities exist and are not included in the balance sheet, details should be provided in the notes to the accounts.

245   The objective of the balance sheet is to show the resources available to the charity and whether these are freely available or have to be used for specific purposes because of legal restrictions on their use. It may also show which of the resources the trustees have designated for specific future use. It will normally be necessary to read the reserves policy and plans for the future in the Trustees' Annual Report (see paragraphs 55(a) and 57) to gain a fuller understanding of the availability and planned use of the charity's funds.

Structure of the Balance Sheet

246   Table 7 sets out the format and the asset, liability and fund categories of the balance sheet.

247   The assets and liabilities are analysed within the balance sheet according to the category of the asset or liability as set out in Table 7. The balance sheet should also distinguish, as a minimum, between the total funds held as unrestricted income funds, restricted income funds and as endowment funds. Distinctions between funds held as permanent and expendable endowment and held as designated funds may also be shown on the face of the balance sheet. The order in which the categories of funds are presented within the balance sheet (Section E of Table 7) may be varied to accommodate an individual charity's presentational preference.

248 Charities may choose to adopt a columnar presentation of its assets, liabilities and funds in the balance sheet. Such a presentation shows the asset and liability categories analysed in columns between each fund group in a similar way to the Statement of Financial Activities showing incoming resources and resources expended by type of fund. This presentation is not mandatory, but using it ensures charities present the required analysis of assets and liabilities by category of fund. Where a charity does not have funds of a particular category, the column related to that category of fund is omitted. If this columnar presentation is not adopted then the assets and liabilities (eg investments, fixed assets, net current assets) representing each category of fund should be summarised and analysed between those funds in the notes to the accounts (see paragraph 75(a)).

249 Further details of the assets and liabilities should be given in the balance sheet or the notes to the accounts. This analysis should enable the reader to gain a proper appreciation of their spread and character. For example, long-term debtors should, where the total is material, be separately stated in the balance sheet – otherwise the total amount of the category (see paragraph 314) should be analysed in the notes to the accounts.

250 If for any category of assets (row in Table 7 – the balance sheet) there are no amounts for the current and prior year then no entries need to be made on the balance sheet and the headings can be omitted.

251 As explained in paragraph 4(b) of Appendix 3, expenditure may be incurred in anticipation of the receipt of restricted income, possibly leading to a negative balance on a specific fund. Where such balances are material they should be shown separately as negative balances and not simply be netted off against positive balances on the fund category in the balance sheet. Therefore the balance sheet may show both positive and negative balances on restricted funds.

Table 7. Balance Sheet

		Total Funds £	Prior Year Funds £	Reference
A	**Fixed assets:**			
A1	Intangible assets			252
A2	Tangible assets			253 to 278
A3	Heritage assets;			279 to 294
A4	Investments:			
A4a	Investments			295 to 307
A4b	Programme related investments			308 to 312
	Total fixed assets			
B	**Current assets:**			313 to 316

		Total Funds £	Prior Year Funds £	Reference
B1	Stocks and work-in-progress			
B2	Debtors			314
B3	Investments			316
B4	Cash at bank and in hand			
	Total current assets			
C	**Liabilities:**			
C1	Creditors: Amounts falling due within one year			317 to 320
	Net current assets or liabilities			
	Total assets less current liabilities			
C2	Creditors: Amounts falling due after more than one year			317 to 320
C3	Provisions for liabilities and charges.			321 to 329
	Net asset or liabilities excluding pension asset or liability			
D	**Defined benefit pension scheme asset or liability**			330–332
	Net assets or liabilities including pension asset or liability			
E	**The funds of the charity:**			
E1	Endowment funds			
E2	Restricted income funds			
E3	Unrestricted income funds			
E3a	Share capital			333
E3b	Unrestricted income funds			
E3c	Revaluation reserve			334
	Unrestricted income funds excluding pension asset/liability			
E3d	Pension reserve			335
	Total unrestricted funds			
	Total charity funds			

Content of the Balance Sheet

A1: Intangible Fixed Assets

252 Intangible fixed assets should be included in the balance sheet in accordance with FRS 10 "Goodwill and Intangible Assets" (see Appendix 2 FRS 10).

A2: Tangible Fixed Assets (other than Investments)

253 FRS 15 "Tangible Fixed Assets" requires that:

(a) all tangible fixed assets should be capitalised on initial acquisition and included in the balance sheet at cost or valuation;

(b) tangible fixed assets may be periodically revalued;

(c) subsequent expenditure which enhances (rather than maintains) the performance of tangible fixed assets should be capitalised.

254 Within charities, tangible fixed assets (other than investments) fall into two categories, those held for charity use (including those used for the running and administration of the charity) and those classed as heritage assets (Glossary GL 32). Paragraphs 255 to 278 describe the general rules for inclusion of tangible fixed assets in the balance sheet. In principle heritage assets meet the definition of an asset and should be recognised and included within a charity's balance sheet. However, particular considerations arise where the cost or valuation of heritage assets can only be obtained at significant cost or where such information lacks sufficient reliability. Specific recommendations for the accounting treatment of heritage assets are set out in paragraphs 279 to 294.

General Rules for Tangible Fixed Assets

255 Tangible fixed assets should initially be included in the balance sheet using the following bases.

(a) The cost of acquisition including costs that are directly attributable to bringing the assets into working condition for their intended use. This can include costs of interest on loans to finance the construction of such assets but only where the charity has adopted this as a policy for all tangible fixed assets and capitalisation of interest should cease when the asset is ready for use. This applies whether assets are bought outright or through hire purchase or finance leasing.

(b) If a functional fixed asset is acquired in full or in part from the proceeds of a grant it should be included at its full acquisition cost (or in the case of a joint arrangement at the gross value of the charity's share in the asset (see paragraph 416)) without netting off the grant proceeds.

(c) Where functional fixed assets have been donated, they should be included in the balance sheet at their current value at the date of the gift and also included in the Statement of Financial Activities (see paragraph 111) as an incoming resource.

(d)   Where functional fixed assets are capitalised some time after being acquired, for example, as a result of a change in accounting policy, they should be included at original cost or at the value at which the gift was included in the Statement of Financial Activities less an amount for depreciation. However, if neither of these amounts is ascertainable, a reasonable estimate of the asset's cost or current value to the charity should be used. Such a valuation will be regarded as the asset's initial carrying amount and will not be regarded as a revaluation (see paragraphs 262 to 266).

256   Where the net book value of a fixed asset is higher than its recoverable amount, it will be impaired and should be written down to its recoverable amount. This is covered in more detail in paragraphs 267 to 272.

Rules for Mixed use of Fixed Assets (Functional and Investment)

257   Where land and buildings are held for mixed purposes, ie. partly as functional property and partly as investment, the balance sheet category in which they should be included depends upon the primary purpose for holding the asset and the extent to which they are separable. The following criteria for balance sheet analysis should be adopted:

(a)   Land and buildings held primarily for charity use of which a part is leased at a commercial rent should be regarded as functional fixed assets and included within tangible fixed assets provided the asset is wholly or mainly used for charitable purposes.

(b)   Land and buildings held primarily for investment purposes (Glossary GL 39) where the asset is wholly or mainly used for investment purposes should be included within the fixed asset investment category of the balance sheet.

(c)   Land and buildings which contain clearly distinguishable parts which are held for different purposes ie. partly functional and partly investment and do not fall under (a) or (b) above, should be apportioned and analysed in the balance sheet between functional and investment assets.

Depreciation of Tangible Fixed Assets (other than Investments)

258   Most tangible fixed assets depreciate; that is they wear out, are consumed or otherwise suffer a reduction in their useful life through use, the passing of time or obsolescence. Their value is thus gradually expended over their useful economic life. This expenditure should be recognised by means of an annual depreciation charge in the Statement of Financial Activities and shown in the balance sheet as accumulated depreciation deducted from the value of the relevant fixed assets.

259   Tangible fixed assets held for use by the charity which are included in the balance sheet should be depreciated at rates appropriate to their useful economic life. The only exceptions to charging depreciation arise where any of the following conditions apply:

(a)   the asset is freehold land which is considered to have an indefinitely long useful life; or

(b)   both the depreciation charge and the accumulated depreciation are not material because:

(i)   the asset has a very long useful life; or

(ii)   the estimated residual value (based on prices at the time of acquisition or subsequent revaluation) of the asset is not materially different from the carrying amount of the asset;

If depreciation is not charged because of immateriality, FRS 15 requires that the asset is subject to an annual impairment review (except for charities under the threshold for following the FRSSE); or

(c)   the assets are heritage assets and have not been included in the balance sheet (see paragraphs 279 to 294).

260 The useful economic lives and residual values of fixed assets should be reviewed at the end of the accounting period and, where there is a material change, the value of the asset should be depreciated over its remaining useful life.

261 Where a fixed asset for charity use comprises two or more major components with substantially different useful lives, each component should be accounted for as a separate asset and depreciated over its individual useful life.

Revaluation of Tangible Fixed Assets (other than Investments)

262 In accordance with FRS 15, tangible fixed assets (other than investment assets) do not need to be revalued unless the charity adopts a policy of revaluation. Where such a policy is adopted, whilst it need not be applied to all fixed assets it must be applied to entire classes of fixed assets. Therefore if an individual fixed asset is revalued, all other assets in that class must also be revalued. Classes of assets can be narrowly defined, within reason, according to the operations of the charity (see paragraph 273).

263 When an asset is donated or when it is capitalised as a result of the change in an accounting policy, its initial valuation will not be regarded as a revaluation and hence will not require the entire class of such assets to be revalued.

264 Similarly, where a charity was holding assets at a revalued amount at the date FRS 15 requirements first applied, (for accounting periods ending on or after 23rd March 2000) this will not be regarded as a revaluation and no requirement exists for such assets to be revalued periodically unless the trustees so choose.

265 Where there is a policy to revalue fixed assets, their value must be updated on a regular basis. The trustees may use any reasonable approach to valuation at least every five years, subject only to obtaining advice as to the possibility of any material movements between individual valuations. Where a charity has a number of such assets, it will be acceptable for valuations to be carried out on a rolling basis over a five-year period. Independent formal professional valuations are not mandatory in the case of a charity, which instead may obtain a valuation from a suitably qualified person who could be a trustee or employee (see Appendix 2 FRS 15).

266 In the case of assets other than properties, such as motor vehicles, there may be an active second-hand market for the asset, or appropriate indices may exist allowing a valuation to be made with reasonable certainty by an appropriate person (but not necessarily a qualified valuer) either internal or external to the charity. Where this method of valuation is used the assets' values must be updated annually. As an alternative to market value such assets can be recorded at depreciated replacement cost (see Glossary GL 18).

Impairment of Fixed Assets for Use by the Charity

267   On rare occasions a functional fixed asset may become impaired. This occurs if its carrying value (net book value, at cost or valuation) is higher than its recoverable amount. In such a case FRS 11 would require it to be written down to its recoverable amount. The recoverable amount is the higher of the net realisable value and the value in use.

268   Value in use is normally the present value of the future cash flows obtainable as a result of an asset's continued use. However many charities have fixed assets that are not held for the main purpose of generating cash flows either by themselves or in conjunction with other assets. In these cases it is not appropriate to measure the value in use of the asset at an amount based on expected future cash flows. Instead an alternative measure of its service potential will be more relevant, such as the intrinsic worth of the service delivery or the replacement cost of the asset. Each charity can determine its own measure of service delivery but this must be reasonable, justifiable and consistently operated.

269   Impairment reviews should only be carried out where there is some indication that the recoverable amount of a functional fixed asset is below its net book value. Such a review should, as far as possible, be carried out on individual assets or where this is not possible then categories of assets can be grouped (see FRS 11 paragraphs 24 to 28). Events or changes which may indicate an impairment include:

(a)   physical deterioration, change or obsolescence of the fixed asset;

(b)   social, demographic or environmental changes resulting in a reduction of beneficiaries for a charity;

(c)   changes in the law, other regulations or standards which adversely affect the activities of a charity;

(d)   management commitments to undertake a significant reorganisation;

(e)   a major loss of key employees associated with particular activities of a charity;

(f)   operating losses on activities using fixed assets primarily to generate incoming resources.

270   Where an impairment review is required, the charity should first determine the net realisable value of the asset. If this is lower than the net book value, the value in use will need to be considered. If the value in use is considered to be above the net book value, the asset should be valued at the net book value. If a decision is made to sell the asset, it should be valued at its expected net realisable value.

271   Value in use calculations should not be used to manipulate the write down of fixed assets. For instance when a new specialised asset is purchased, although it may have a low net realisable value, it is unlikely that it will suffer an impairment in service delivery within the first years after acquisition.

272   Where there is an impairment loss that needs to be recognised, charities should determine this in accordance with the requirements of FRS 11 (whilst being able to use alternative valuation methods for some assets). The loss should be treated as additional depreciation and included in the Statement of Financial Activities in accordance with paragraph 218. The revised carrying amount of the asset should be depreciated over its remaining useful economic life.

Disclosure

273   Tangible fixed assets for use by the charity should be analysed in the notes to the accounts within the following categories:

(a)   freehold interest in land and buildings;

(b)   leasehold and other interests in land and buildings;

(c)   plant and machinery including motor vehicles;

(d)   fixtures, fittings and equipment; and

(e)   payments on account and assets in the course of construction.

These are broad categories and any charity may, within reason, split the headings or adopt other narrower classes that meet the definition of a class of tangible fixed assets and are appropriate to its operations.

274   The notes should summarise all material changes in the values of each class of tangible fixed assets and reconcile the opening and closing balances. This may be achieved by using a table such as Table 8 below omitting any rows and columns that are not needed for a charity's particular circumstances:

Table 8.   Analysis of Movement of Fixed Assets

	Freehold land & Buildings	Lease-hold land & Buildings	Plant and Machinery	Fixtures, Fittings and Equipment	Payments on account & assets under construc-tion	Total
	£	£	£	£	£	£
Asset cost, valuation or revalued amount						
Balance brought forward						

	Freehold land & Buildings	Lease-hold land & Buildings	Plant and Machinery	Fixtures, Fittings and Equipment	Payments on account & assets under construc-tion	Total
	£	£	£	£	£	£
Additions						
Disposals						
Revaluations						
Transfers						
Balance carried forward						
Accumulated depreciation and impairment provisions						
Balance brought forward						
Disposals						
Revaluations						
Impairment charges						
Transfers						
Charge for year						
Balance carried forward						
Net Book Value						
Brought forward						
Carried forward						

275 The methods of depreciation used and useful economic lives or depreciation rates should be disclosed in the accounting policy notes (see paragraph 364).

276 There is often a considerable difference between the carrying value and market value of interests in land and buildings not held as investments. Where the trustees consider this to be so material that it needs to be drawn to the attention of the users of the accounts then the difference should be included, with such precision as is practicable, in the notes to the accounts. If it is not practicable to quantify the difference, a written explanation will suffice.

277 Where any class of tangible fixed assets of a charity has been revalued, the notes to the accounts should give:

(a)   the name and qualification (if any) of the valuer and whether they are a member of staff or a trustee or external to the charity;

(b)   the basis or bases of valuation;

(c)   where records are available, the historical cost less depreciation;

(d)   date of the previous full valuation;

(e)   if the value has not been updated in the reporting period, a statement by the trustees that they are not aware of any material changes since the last valuation.

278   The methods used in the impairment review to determine net realisable value and value in use should be disclosed in the notes to the accounts. This should include details required in paragraph 277.

A3: Heritage Assets

279   FRS 15 requires that all tangible fixed assets should be capitalised in the balance sheet (see paragraph 253). In principle this includes tangible fixed assets which are of historical, artistic or scientific importance that are held to advance preservation and conservation objectives of a charity.

280   However, charities will not necessarily need to capitalise such heritage assets (Glossary GL 32) that were acquired in past accounting periods and omitted from previous balance sheets when the circumstances in paragraph 283 below apply.

281   To fall within the definition of heritage assets, the charity must hold the relevant assets in pursuit of preservation or conservation objectives. The objective of the charity may be specifically of a preservation or conservation nature, or the heritage assets may be integral to a broader objective such as educating the public in history, the arts or science as in the case of museums and galleries.

282   Newly purchased heritage assets should be initially measured and recognised at their cost.

283   When heritage assets were acquired in past accounting periods and not capitalised, it may be difficult or costly to attribute a cost or value to them. In such cases these assets may only be excluded from the balance sheet if:

(a)   reliable cost information is not available and conventional valuation approaches lack sufficient reliability; or

(b)   significant costs are involved in the reconstruction or analysis of past accounting records or in valuation which are onerous compared with the additional benefit derived by users of the accounts in assessing the trustees' stewardship of the assets.

284   The assessment of the costs involved in establishing a cost or valuation for heritage assets and the benefits derived by users of accounts from this information will involve the separate consideration of any material sub-classes of assets held within the heritage asset category. Whilst the cost/benefit test may not be practical to apply on an individual asset by asset basis, it should considered in the context of particular parts or sub-classes of an overall collection. For example, in the context of a general museum valuing a fossil collection may be onerous but valuing its collection of vintage cars may not.

285 FRS 15 provides details of appropriate valuation bases. However, certain heritage buildings, structures or sites may present particular valuation issues. Whilst most specialised buildings can be valued using depreciated replacement cost (see Glossary GL 18), particular issues can arise in attempting to estimate the replacement cost of achieving the same service potential of certain historic buildings. The uniqueness of certain structures that are associated with particular locations, events, individuals or periods in history may be irreplaceable in terms of recreating the same service potential. The same service potential in terms of its heritage value or educational benefit to the public may only be achieved through the original structure or site.

286 Examples of heritage assets for which a cost or valuation may be difficult to attribute include:

(a)   museum and gallery collections and other collections including the national archives;

(b)   medieval castles, archaeological sites, burial mounds, ruins, monuments and statues.

287 It may also be difficult or costly to attribute a cost or valuation to heritage assets which are donated where such assets are rarely sold on the open market. Where assets are purchased by a party who then shortly afterwards donates the asset to the charity, the purchase price should be considered as reliable cost information and could be used as a reference point for the fair value of donations of similar assets. Where an asset is partly purchased by the charity and partly donated, a reasonable estimate of the cost or value to the charity should be able to be made. Gifts on death or lifetime transfers of significant value may also carry valuations for inheritance tax purposes that may provide sufficient reliability.

288 Heritage assets should be included in a separate row in the balance sheet and can be further analysed, in the notes to the accounts, into classes appropriate to each charity e g collections, artefacts, and historic houses. An appropriate depreciation policy should be applied in accordance with paragraphs 258 to 261. As explained in paragraph 259 certain heritage assets may have an indefinite useful life and a high residual value resulting in any depreciation charge being immaterial.

289 Where assets of historical, scientific or artistic importance are held by a charity but not for preservation or conservation purposes, they cannot be regarded as heritage assets. Examples of assets that do not fall within the heritage assets category include situations where a charity:

(a)   holds and occupies an historic building as its administrative offices or as part of a property investment portfolio unrelated to any preservation or educational purpose;

(b)   has in its possession works of art, or a collection of historic importance, or antique furnishings within its boardroom, as a store of wealth, the retention of which is unrelated to any objectives of preservation or education;

(c)   occupies a functional property that is used to house or display a collection of heritage assets (unless the property itself is held for preservation or conservation purposes).

290   Charities may be required by trust law to retain an asset indefinitely for its own use/benefit and are effectively prohibited from its disposal without external consent. Such assets are termed inalienable. Inalienability, of itself, does not preclude capitalisation of an asset.

291   Inalienable assets that do not fall within the definition of heritage assets, should be capitalised and disclosed in the relevant categories of balance sheet and in related notes. For example:

(a)   An investment property will be included as an investment within fixed assets, valued at open market value and disclosed as part of investment properties within the investment notes.

(b)   Functional properties used by a charity in undertaking its activities are included within tangible fixed assets and are included at cost or valued on an existing use basis unless of a specialised nature when a depreciated replacement cost (see Glossary GL 18) valuation is adopted.

(c)   Tangible fixed assets other than properties are included at cost or valued at open market value.

292   Inalienable assets, by their nature, will belong to a charity's restricted funds, often being permanent endowment.

293   Abbeys, Monasteries, Cathedrals, historic Churches and ancient centres of learning may not meet the heritage asset definition as the preservation of the buildings they occupy is unlikely to be the primary objective of the charity. Such assets might nevertheless be considered integral to the activities of the charity and this may give rise to difficulties in ascertaining an estimate of the current cost of construction of an asset that has the same service potential as the existing one. For example, a new structure could recreate the floor area and seating capacity of a medieval Cathedral but such a structure would not recreate the uniqueness of the original in terms of the religious and historical significance. In such cases a valuation of previously non-capitalised assets may be impractical and the notes should contain a statement to that effect explaining why conventional valuation techniques cannot be applied. Similar issues may arise in the context of artefacts contained within and associated with such structures e g religious artefacts contained within a cathedral or historic church.

Disclosure

294   Information on heritage assets (whether or not they have been capitalised) should be given in the notes to the accounts. The notes should contain:

(a)   an analysis or narrative that enables the user to appreciate the age, scale and nature of the heritage assets held and the use made of them;

(b)   either:
(i)   details of the cost (or value) of additions and disposals of heritage assets during the year; or
(ii)   where details of cost or value are not available (non-capitalisation in previous periods), a brief description of the nature of the assets acquired or disposed of, together with the sales proceeds of any disposals;

(c)   accounting policy notes explaining the charity's capitalisation policy in relation to heritage assets and the measurement bases adopted for their inclusion in the accounts.

A4: Investment Assets

295   Investment assets (including investments and investment properties (Glossary GL 39) and cash held for investment purposes) should be classified as a separate category within fixed assets except where the intention is to realise the asset without reinvestment of the sale proceeds. In such a case, it should be reclassified as a current asset. The reason for this is that investment assets are generally held with the overall intention of retaining them long-term (ie as fixed assets) for the continuing benefit of the charity in the form of income and capital appreciation.

Valuation of Investment Assets

296   All investment assets other than programme related investments (see paragraph 308), should be shown in the balance sheet at market value or at the trustees' best estimate of market value as described below. Market value best represents a true and fair view of the value of these assets to the charity, given the duty of the trustees to administer the portfolio of investment assets so as to obtain the best investment performance without undue risk. Investment assets should not be depreciated. All changes in value in the year, whether or not realised, should be reported in the "gains and losses on investment assets" section of the Statement of Financial Activities (see paragraph 219).

297   Most freely tradable investments will have a readily available market price eg shares on a recognised stock exchange. For investment assets for which there is no readily identifiable market price the trustees should adopt a reasonable approach. For example:

(a)   Shares in unlisted companies may be valued by reference to their underlying net assets or earnings or the dividend record, as appropriate.

(b)   Where the cost of obtaining a valuation by one of the methods in (a) above outweighs the benefit to the users of the accounts, or lacks reliability, the investment may be included at cost.

298   For investment assets other than shares or securities (eg property), the trustees may use any reasonable approach to market valuations which must be done at least every five years, subject only to obtaining advice as to the possibility of any material movements between individual valuations. If there is a material movement the assets must be revalued. Where a charity has a number of such assets it will be acceptable for valuations to be carried out on a rolling basis over a five-year period.

Disclosure

299   The investment asset note to the accounts should disclose separately:

(a)   investments held primarily to provide an investment return for the charity; and

(b)   programme related investments (Glossary GL 47) that the charity makes primarily as part of its charitable activities.

300   Where values are determined other than by reference to readily available market prices (Glossary GL 41), the notes to the accounts should disclose who has made the valuation, giving:

(a)   the name and qualification (if any) of the valuer and whether they are a member of staff or a trustee or external to the charity; and

(b)   the basis or bases of valuation.

301   In the rare case where the size or nature of a holding of securities is such that the market is thought by the trustees not to be capable of absorbing the sale of the shareholding without a material effect on the quoted price, the trustees should summarise the position in the notes to the accounts. If they are able to do so, the trustees should give an opinion in the notes to the accounts on how much the market price should be adjusted to take this fact into consideration.

302   The notes to the accounts should show all changes in values of investment assets and reconcile the opening and closing book values. This information may be provided in a table format as set out in Table 9.

Table 9.   Analysis of Movement of Investments

	£
Carrying value (market value) at beginning of year	
Add: Additions to investments at cost	
Less: Disposals at carrying value	
Add/deduct Net gain/(loss) on revaluation	
Carrying value (market value) at end of year	

303   The notes should also show the total value of investment assets at the end of the financial year divided between distinct classes of investment. This would normally include:

(a)   investment properties;

(b)   investments listed on a recognised stock exchange or ones valued by reference to such investments, such as common investment funds, open ended investment companies, and unit trusts;

(c)   investments in subsidiary or associated undertakings or in companies which are connected persons (Glossary GL 50);

(d)   other unlisted securities;

(e)   cash and settlements pending, held as part of the investment portfolio;

(f)   any other investments.

304 Items in categories (a) to (f) of paragraph 303 above should be further analysed between:

(i)   investment assets in the UK (see paragraph 305 below);

(ii)   investment assets outside the UK.

305 The total value of shares or investment schemes (including common investment funds, open ended investment companies and unit trusts) relating to companies listed on a UK stock exchange or incorporated in the UK are treated as investment assets in the UK and no further analysis is required of whether such entities invest their funds in the UK or outside the UK.

306 Further details should be given in the notes to the accounts of any particular investment that is considered material in the context of the investment portfolio.

307 The notes to the accounts should indicate the value of investments held in each category of fund. This may be included in the overall analysis of assets held in the different category of funds (see paragraph 75(a)).

A4b: Programme Related Investments

308 Programme related investments are defined in the Glossary (GL 47) and should be disclosed separately within the investment asset category from those investments intended primarily to generate a financial return for the charity.

309 Programme related investments should generally be included in the balance sheet at the amount invested less any impairments (in the case of equity or loans) and any amounts repaid (in the case of loans). Impairments should be charged to resources expended on charitable activities. Similarly a loan subsequently converted to a grant would be charged to charitable activities.

310 Where a gain is made on the disposal of a programme related investment, then the gain should either be set off against any prior impairment loss or included as a gain on disposal of fixed assets for the charity's own use and recorded under "other incoming resources" (see paragraph 147).

Disclosure

311 Where the use of programme related investments forms a material part of the work of the charity, or the amounts form a material part of the investment assets of the charity, the notes to the accounts should show all changes in carrying values of programme related investments, including any impairment losses, and reconcile the opening and closing carrying values of such investments.

312 The notes should also analyse programme related investments held between equity, loan and other investments and indicate the charitable objectives, programmes or projects the investment supports.

B: Current Assets

313 Current assets other than current asset investments (see paragraph 296) should normally be recognised at the lower of their cost and net realisable value.

Disclosure

314 Where there are debtors which do not fit into any of the following categories, the headings may be added to or adapted as appropriate to the type of debtor or creditor and nature of the charity. Debtors should be analysed in the notes to the accounts between short term and long term (after more than one year) giving amounts for the following:

(a)   trade debtors;

(b)   amounts due from subsidiary and associated undertakings;

(c)   other debtors;

(d)   prepayments and accrued income.

315 Where long term debtors are material in the context of the total net current assets, they should be separately shown in the balance sheet (see paragraph 249).

316 Where investments are held as current assets the same disclosure is required as for fixed asset investments (see paragraphs 299 to 307).

C: Current Liabilities and Long-term Creditors

317 Liabilities should normally be recognised at their settlement value. In the case of provisions, this will be the amount that an entity would rationally pay to settle the obligation at the balance sheet date or to transfer it to a third party at that time and may therefore involve discounting (see paragraph 323).

Disclosure

318 Where there are creditors which do not fit into any of the following categories, the headings may be added to or adapted as appropriate to the type of creditor and nature of the charity. The totals for both short-term and long-term creditors should each be separately analysed in the notes giving amounts for the following:

(a)   loans and overdrafts;

(b)   trade creditors;

(c)   amounts due to subsidiary and associated undertakings;

(d)   other creditors;

(e)   accruals and deferred income.

319   Where a charity is acting as an intermediary agent (as opposed to a custodian trustee) for another organisation, as described in paragraph 112, then any assets held and the associated liabilities should be separately identified in the notes to the accounts but not included in the balance sheet. The notes to the accounts should provide sufficient detail so that the reader of the accounts understands the relationship and nature of the transactions between the charity, the funding organisation and the recipient of the funds.

320   The details in paragraph 319 should also be provided when the charity is acting as an intermediary but is the principal as described in paragraph 113. However, in this case the assets and liabilities will be included in the balance sheet.

C3: Provisions for Liabilities and Charges

321   Expenditure resulting from provisions that arise due to a legal or constructive obligation (as per FRS 12) should be accounted for in the Statement of Financial Activities in accordance with paragraphs 148 to 163. Such provisions should be appropriately analysed in the balance sheet between liabilities due within one year and those falling due after one year.

322   The amount recognised as a liability should be the best estimate of the expenditure required to settle the present obligation at the balance sheet date or to transfer it to a third party at that time. When calculating this amount consideration should be given to:

(a)   the timing of the cash flows;

(b)   future events and uncertainties which may affect the amount required to settle the obligation.

323   Where provisions are accrued in the current financial year but are to be paid over several years then future payments may have a reduced value in today's terms (current value). Where the effect is material, the outflow of resources required to settle the obligation at the balance sheet date should be discounted to their present value. The discount rate used should reflect the current assessments of the time value of money and the risks specific to the provision. The interest rate either for the cost of borrowing or investment could be an appropriate discount rate.

324 The best estimate of the liability should be reviewed at the balance sheet date and adjusted appropriately. If a transfer of resources is no longer needed to settle the obligation then the amount of the liability no longer representing an obligation should be deducted from the resources expended category to which it was originally charged in the Statement of Financial Activities.

325 Where a charity has earmarked part of its unrestricted funds for a particular future purpose, this intention to expend funds in the future is not recognised as a provision for a liability in the accounts. Such earmarked amounts may be recorded by setting up a designated fund (see paragraph 68).

Disclosure

326 Particulars of all material provisions for liabilities and charges accrued in the balance sheet as liabilities should be disclosed in the notes. Similarly, particulars of all material commitments in respect of specific charitable projects should be disclosed if they have not been charged in the accounts.

327 These particulars should include the amounts involved, when the commitments are likely to be met and the movements on commitments previously reported. Particulars of all other material binding commitments should also be disclosed (eg operating leases).

328 The notes should distinguish between those commitments included in the balance sheet as liabilities and those that are intentions to spend and are not included, but in both cases should detail:

(a)   the reason for the commitments, giving separate disclosure for material projects;

(b)   the total amount of the commitments, including amounts already charged in the accounts;

(c)   the amount of commitments outstanding at the start of the year;

(d)   any amounts charged in the Statement of Financial Activities for the year;

(e)   any amounts released during the year due to a change in the value in the commitments;

(f)   the amount of commitments outstanding at the end of the year and an indication as to how much is payable within one year and over one year.

329 Any designated funds relating to intentions to spend not included as liabilities should be separately disclosed as part of the unrestricted funds of the charity and appropriately described in the notes. The purpose of the disclosure is to identify that portion of the unrestricted funds that has been set aside to meet the commitments. Activities that are to be wholly financed from future income would not form part of such designation.

D: Defined Benefit Pension Scheme Asset/Liability

330 Any asset or liability derived from a surplus or deficit in a defined benefit pension scheme (calculated in accordance with FRS 17: Retirement Benefits) should be included within this category and disclosed on the face of the balance sheet.

331 A surplus or deficit in a defined benefit scheme will normally give rise to an asset or liability within the unrestricted funds of the reporting charity. The circumstances in which the pension asset or liability may accrue to a restricted fund are set out in paragraphs 433 to 442.

332 Recommendations on the application of FRS 17 to charities and the required accounting methods and disclosures are set out in a separate section on accounting for retirement benefits in paragraphs 430 to 448.

E3a: Share Capital

333 A number of charities, eg Industrial and Provident Societies, are constituted with a share capital. A small number of charities incorporated as companies under the Companies Act may also have share capital. Usually this is a nominal amount (such as £10) and although this is legally "owners equity", the prohibition on owners benefiting from this share ownership effectively means that money contributed for share capital forms part of the unrestricted funds of the charity. Nevertheless, company law requires share capital to be shown separately in the balance sheet.

E3c: Revaluation Reserve

334 Charities that are companies are required to report, in respect of their unrestricted funds, the difference between the historic cost of fixed assets (including investment assets) and their revalued amount as a revaluation reserve.

E3d: Pension Reserve

335 When there is a surplus or a deficit on a defined benefit pension scheme that results in an asset or a liability being recognised by the charity, the recognition of the pension asset or liability will result in the creation of a pension reserve. This reserve will be negative in the case of a liability. If the pension asset or liability relates only to unrestricted funds then this reserve will be part of unrestricted funds. If, however, the criteria set out in paragraphs 438 to 442, are met and the pension asset/liability is allocated to a restricted fund, then the pension reserve will be part of that restricted fund.

Other Balance Sheet Matters to be Covered in the Notes to the Accounts

Guarantees

336 All material guarantees given by the charity, and the conditions under which liabilities might arise as a result of such guarantees, should be disclosed in a note to the accounts.

Financial Derivative Disclosure

337 There are occasions where charities make use of financial derivative products to ameliorate the risk associated with normal operations (eg currency forward contracts), holding investments or borrowing (eg interest rate hedging). Such derivatives as are used will be in response to a charity's risk management and an explanation of the reasons for their use should be provided as part of the discussion of risk in the Trustees' Annual Report.

338 It is not normally appropriate for charities to hold derivatives for any other reason than to ameliorate risk as this would involve establishing a non-charitable trade. As a result, it would not normally be necessary to value the derivative products separately from the underlying investment or debt.

Disclosure

339 The notes to the accounts should indicate what derivative products are in use by the charity and indicate their impact on the risks of the underlying asset or liability to which they relate. The description of the products held should be in sufficient detail so that the reader of the accounts can understand what the charity's position would have been with, and without the derivatives, and should give an indication of the costs and benefits of the derivative products.

Contingent Assets and Liabilities

340 A charity may have contingent assets and liabilities as defined in FRS 12 (Glossary GL 11 and GL 12 and Appendix 2: FRS 12).

341 A charity should not recognise incoming or outgoing resources or gains and losses arising respectively from contingent assets or contingent liabilities in the Statement of Financial Activities or the balance sheet.

342 Contingent assets are not recognised because it could result in the recognition of incoming resources that may never be realised. However, when the realisation of the incoming resources is virtually certain, then the asset is not a contingent asset and the resource/gain arising should be included in the Statement of Financial Activities as an incoming resource and in the balance sheet as a debtor.

343 Where it becomes probable that there will be a future outflow of resources to settle an item previously regarded as a contingent liability, it should cease to be contingent and should be accrued in the accounts. The amount of the liability should (except in extremely rare circumstances where no reliable estimate can be made) be capable of being estimated with reasonable accuracy at the date on which the accounts are approved.

344 The probability of a contingent asset or liability resulting in a future transfer of resources (to or from the charity) should be continually assessed and the recognition of the asset or liability should be reviewed as appropriate.

Disclosure

345 Material contingent assets and liabilities should be disclosed in the notes to the accounts unless the probability of a future transfer of resources (to or from the charity) is extremely remote – in which case no disclosure is necessary.

346 The accounts should disclose the nature of each contingency, the uncertainties that are expected to affect the outcome, and a prudent estimate of the financial effect where an amount has not been accrued. If such an estimate cannot be made, the accounts should explain why it is not practicable to make such an estimate.

347 Where there is more than one contingent asset or liability, they may be sufficiently similar in nature for them to be grouped together as one class and be disclosed in a single statement.

348 Where a liability has been accrued but there is still a contingent liability arising from the same set of circumstances then the notes to the accounts should link the provision and the contingent liability.

Loan Liabilities

349 If any specific assets (whether land or other property) of the charity are subject to a mortgage or charge given as security for a loan or other liability, a note to the accounts should disclose:

(a)   particulars of the assets which are subject to the mortgage or charge;

(b)   the amount of the loan or liability and its proportion to the value of the assets mortgaged or charged.

350 The amounts and interest and repayment terms of all inter-fund loans (including any loans from permanent endowment and summarised, if necessary) should be disclosed in the notes to the accounts. Loans made to trading subsidiaries, the security provided, the interest payable and the repayment terms should be disclosed as a separate item in the notes to the accounts.

CASH FLOW STATEMENT

Application

351 The preparation of a cash flow statement is a requirement of FRS 1 for all charities above the small companies thresholds (see Appendix 2: FRS 1) in England, Wales and Scotland. The object of the cash flow statement is to show the cash received and used by the charity in the accounting period.

352 Wherever a cash flow statement is prepared it should comply with the requirements of FRS 1 subject to the following paragraphs.

353 The analysis of the cash movements should accord with the charity's operations as reported in its Statement of Financial Activities, and be given in appropriate detail. The starting point will normally be "net incoming/outgoing resources before other recognised gains and losses" in Table 3.

354 Movements in endowments should not be included in cash flows from "operating activities" but should be treated as increases or decreases in the financing section. This is achieved as follows:

(a) cash donations to endowment should be treated as additions to endowment in the "financing" section;

(b) the receipts and payments from the acquisition and disposal of investments should be shown gross in the "capital expenditure and financial investment" section of the cash flow statement. A single row should then be included in this section showing the net movement in cash flows attributable to endowment investments. A corresponding row should be included in the "financing" section for the same amount. The row in the "financing" section should reflect the cash into/(cash out of) the endowment fund whereas it will be the opposite direction in the "capital expenditure and financial investment" section;

(c) on the rare occasion when payments are made out of permanent endowment this should be shown as a decrease in the "financing" section;

(d) transactions which do not result in cash flows should not be reported in the cash flow statement (eg depreciation, revaluations, accruals,) but may need to be disclosed (see paragraph 355).

Disclosure

355 The disclosure requirements of FRS 1 will depend upon the exact basis of preparation and content of the cash flow statement for each charity but the following are some of the more common disclosures:

(a) major transactions not resulting in cash movements should be disclosed in the notes if necessary for an understanding of the underlying transactions. For instance the release of expendable endowment;

(b) cash (and any financing) movements should be reconciled to the appropriate opening and closing balance sheet amounts; and

(c) a reconciliation of cash flows from "operating activities" within the cash flow statement to the net incoming resources/expenditure row of the Statement of Financial Activities.

DISCLOSURE OF ACCOUNTING POLICIES

The Basis of the Preparation of Accounts

356 Charity accounts should include notes on the accounting policies chosen. These should be the most appropriate in the particular circumstances of each charity for the purpose of giving a true and fair view. The policies should be consistent with this SORP, Accounting Standards and relevant legislation. FRS 18: Accounting Policies explains how accounting policies should be determined.

357 Accounting policies are the principles, bases, conventions and rules by which transactions are recognised, measured and presented in the accounts. They are supplemented by estimation techniques where judgement is required in recording the value of incoming and outgoing resources and of assets and liabilities. It is essential that the accounts are accompanied by an explanation of the basis and estimation techniques on which they have been prepared. Accounts are normally prepared on the basis that the charity is a going concern and must include relevant, reliable, comparable and understandable information.

358 The notes regarding the basis of preparation of the accounts should state that the accounts have been prepared in accordance with:

(a) this SORP and accounting standards or with this SORP and the FRSSE (see Appendix 5 paragraphs 5.2.1 to 5.2.2);

(b) the Charities Act or the Companies Act or other legislative requirement; and

(c) the historic cost basis of accounting except for investments (and if applicable, fixed assets) which have been included at revalued amounts.

359 If the accounts depart from accounting standards in any material respect, this should be stated in the accounting policies giving the reason and justification for the departure and the financial impact. Similarly the following details should be given for any material departure from this SORP:

(a) a brief description of how the treatment adopted departs from this SORP;

(b) the reasons why the trustees judge that the treatment adopted is more appropriate to the charity's particular circumstances; and

(c) an estimate of the financial effect on the accounts where this is needed for the accounts to give a true and fair view.

360 If any branches (Glossary GL 4) have been omitted from the accounts, the reason for omission should be given although the individual branches do not need to be named. Reference should also be made to any related organisations (such as supporters associations or subsidiaries not consolidated) explaining the accounting treatment adopted.

Specific Policies

361 Trustees should explain in the notes to the accounts the accounting policies they have adopted to deal with material items. Explanations need only be brief but they should be clear, fair and accurate. Changes to any of the policies that result in a material adjustment to prior periods should be disclosed in detail. The following are some examples of matters for which the accounting policies should be explained where the amounts involved are material. Trustees should only include those notes which are relevant to their charity.

Incoming Resources Policy Notes

362 The policy for including each type of material incoming resource should be given. This will normally be on a receivable basis but may need further details in some cases, for instance:

(a) a description of when a legacy is regarded as receivable;

(b) the basis of recognition of gifts in kind and donated services and facilities, specifically covering when such items are not included in the Statement of Financial Activities and the methods of valuation;

(c) the basis of recognition of all grants receivable, including those for fixed assets, and how the grants are analysed between the different types of incoming resources;

(d) whether any incoming resources are deferred and the basis for any deferrals;

(e) the basis for including subscriptions for life membership;

(f) whether the incoming resources from endowment funds are unrestricted or restricted;

(g) whether any incoming resources have been included in the Statement of Financial Activities net of expenditure and the reason for this.

Resources Expended Policy Notes

363 These policy notes may include:

(a) The policy for the recognition of liabilities including constructive obligations should be given. Where the liabilities are included as provisions, the point at which the provision is considered to become binding and the basis of any discount factors used in current value calculations for long term commitments should be given. This is particularly applicable to grants, the policy for which should be separately identified.

(b) The policy for including items within the relevant activity categories of resources expended should be given. In particular the policy for including items within:
(i) costs of generating funds;
(ii) charitable activities;

(iii)   governance costs.

(c)   The methods and principles for the allocation and apportionment of all costs between the different activity categories of resources expended in. (b). This disclosure should include the underlying principle ie whether based on staff time, staff salaries, space occupied or other. Where the costs apportioned are material, then further clarification on the method of apportionment used is necessary, including the proportions used to undertake the calculations.

Assets Policy Notes

364   The policy for capitalisation of fixed assets for charity use should be stated including:

(a)   whether each class of asset is included at cost, valuation or revaluation and the method of valuation where applicable;

(b)   the value below which fixed assets are not capitalised;

(c)   whether or not heritage assets are capitalised and if not, the reason why (eg lack of reliable information, cost/benefit reason etc: see paragraph 283 to 287), specifying the acquisition and disposal policies for such assets;

(d)   the rates of depreciation applying to each class of fixed asset; and

(e)   the policy with respect to impairment reviews of fixed assets.

365   The policy for including investments in the accounts should be given. This should be at market value but may need to be modified for the valuation of:

(a)   investments not listed on a recognised stock exchange;

(b)   investment properties; and

(c)   investments in subsidiary undertakings.

366   The basis of inclusion in the Statement of Financial Activities of unrealised and realised gains and losses on investments should be stated.

367   The basis for inclusion of stocks and work in progress (where relevant the amount of unsold or unused goods and materials should be given).

Funds Structure Policy Notes

368   A brief description should be given of the different types of fund held by the charity, including the policy for any transfers between funds and allocations to or from designated funds. Transfers may arise, for example, where there is a release of restricted or endowed funds to unrestricted funds or charges are made from the unrestricted to other funds.

369   The policy for determining each designated fund should be stated.

Other Policy Notes

370 These could include policies for the recognition of the following:

(a) pension costs and any pension asset or liability;

(b) foreign exchange gains and losses;

(c) treatment of exceptional items;

(d) treatment of finance and operating leases;

(e) treatment of irrecoverable VAT.

SUMMARY FINANCIAL INFORMATION AND STATEMENTS

General Principles

371 Some charities publish financial information or summaries in a format different from the statutory accounts. Such information or summaries are often included in a non-statutory annual review or in fundraising literature. There are two basic types of such summaries:

(a) Summarised financial statements which should be based on the full financial statements and communicate key financial information without providing the greater detail required in the full accounts (for example, as contained in the notes to the accounts).

(b) Summary financial information which presents information on a particular aspect of a charity's finances for example, an analysis of incoming resources or expenditure on particular activities of a charity. Such information does not purport to summarise the full statutory accounts.

372 The distinction between summarised financial statements and summary information is set out in Table 10 below:

Table 10.   Contrasting Characteristics of Summarised Financial Statements and Information

Characteristics of: Summarised financial statements	Summary financial information
Includes a summary of the Statement of Financial Activities and/or Balance Sheet.	Draws information from only parts of the accounts.
The summary is derived from statutory accounts.	May be based on interim accounts or other financial information as well as statutory accounts.
A financial statement that purports to be a Statement of Activities or Balance Sheet or summary thereof.	Makes no reference to either of these primary statements.

Characteristics of: Summarised financial statements	Summary financial information
Represents the entire finances of a charity or a charity group.	Represents analysis eg. of a particular activity or region.

373 As charitable companies are not listed companies, the provisions of section 428 of the Companies Act 2006 concerning statutory summarised financial statements do not apply. However the provisions of section 427 of the Companies Act 2006 relating to the publication of non-statutory financial statements do apply. The recommendations set out below in relation to summarised financial statements are consistent with these statutory provisions applying to companies. There are no legal provisions for other charities.

374 As the form in which such information or summaries will be produced will vary considerably, depending on the purpose for which they have been prepared, it is not practicable to give detailed recommendations on the content of summary financial information or summarised financial statements. The general principles which should be followed are set out below.

375 Regardless of the intended circulation of any summary financial information or summarised financial statements, the full Annual Report and accounts must always be produced. Any summarised financial statements:

(a)   should contain information on both the Statement of Financial Activities and the balance sheet;

(b)   should be consistent with the statutory accounts; and

(c)   should not be misleading by either omission or inappropriate amalgamation of information.

376 Summary financial information will not necessarily contain information on both the Statement of Financial Activities and balance sheet but should nevertheless present information consistent with the statutory accounts and not be misleading by either omission or inappropriate amalgamation of information.

Summarised Financial Statements

377 Summarised financial statements should be accompanied by a statement, signed on behalf of the trustees, indicating:

(a)   that they are not the statutory accounts but a summary of information relating to both the Statement of Financial Activities and the balance sheet;

(b)   whether or not the full accounts from which the summarised financial statements are derived have as yet been externally scrutinised (whether audit or independent examination, or (for years prior to 1 April 2008) reporting accountant's report); and

(c)   where they have been externally scrutinised, whether the report contained any concerns such as a qualified opinion, limitation of scope, etc;

(d)   where the report contains any concerns, eg is qualified, contains an explanatory paragraph or emphasis of matter, sufficient details should be provided in the summarised financial statements to enable the reader to appreciate the significance of the report;

(e)   where accounts are produced only for a branch of the charity (see paragraph 77), it must be clearly stated that the summarised financial statements are for the branch only and have been extracted from the full accounts of the reporting charity (giving its name);

(f)   details of how the full annual accounts, the external scrutiny report (as applicable) and the Trustees' Annual Report can be obtained;

(g)   the date on which the annual accounts were approved;

(h)   for charities registered in England and Wales, say whether or not the Trustees' Annual Report and accounts have been submitted to the Charity Commission, and for charities registered in Scotland, say whether or not the Trustees' Annual Report and accounts have been submitted to the Office of the Scottish Charity Regulator; and

(i)   where the charity is a company incorporated under the Companies Acts:
    (i)   whether the summary financial statement contains additional information from the directors' report and, if so, that it does not contain the full text of that report; and
    (ii)   whether the auditor's statement under section 496 of the Companies Act 2006 was qualified or unqualified, and if qualified disclose the qualification statement and additional relevant information; and
    (iii)   whether the audit report was qualified in respect of the Companies Act 2006 sections 498(2)(a) or (b) and section 498(3), and if so disclose the auditor's statement in full.

378   If the full accounts have been externally scrutinised, a statement from the external scrutineer, giving an opinion as to whether or not the summarised financial statements are consistent with the full annual accounts, should be attached.

Summary Financial Information

379   Any other summary financial information, in whatever form, should be accompanied by a statement on behalf of the trustees as to:

(a)   the purpose of the information;

(b)   whether or not it is from the full annual accounts;

(c)   whether or not these accounts have been audited, independently examined or subject to a reporting accountant's report;

(d)   details of how the full annual accounts, trustees' report and external scrutiny report (as appropriate) can be obtained.

SPECIAL SECTIONS

380   The main text of the SORP deals with the recommended accounting practice for those charities producing full accruals accounts. Some charities will have to meet additional requirements and the following sections have therefore been provided to explain the additional recommendations applicable to particular arrangements or structures that charities may adopt.

(a)   Consolidation of Subsidiary Undertakings – paragraphs 381 to 406.

(b)   Accounting for Associates, Joint Ventures and Joint Arrangements – paragraphs 407 to 418.

(c)   Charitable Companies – paragraphs 419 to 429.

(d)   Accounting for Retirement Benefits – paragraphs 430 to 448.

(e)   Accounting for Common Investment Funds and Investment Pooling Schemes – paragraphs 449 to 451.

Consolidation of Subsidiary Undertakings

Purpose and Scope

381   The purpose of consolidated accounts is to present a true and fair view of the state of financial affairs of all the group interests of the reporting charity including its subsidiary undertakings. The principles and methods of consolidation are covered by FRS 2. These principles should be applied irrespective of whether the parent charity and its subsidiaries are companies or otherwise constituted.

382   Consolidated accounts are a set of accounts prepared in addition to those prepared for the parent itself and to those prepared for each of the subsidiary undertakings in its own right.

383   A parent charity (Glossary GL 44) must prepare consolidated accounts including all its subsidiary undertakings (Glossary GL 44) where their preparation is either a requirement of company law or where the gross income of the group, the parent charity and its subsidiary undertakings together (Glossary GL 44), exceeds the threshold set by the Regulations made under the Charities Act 1993 or the Charities and Trustee Investment (Scotland) Act 2005 (see appendix 4), except where:

(a)   FRS2 provides for exclusion of certain subsidiary undertakings from consolidation (see paragraph 384); or

(b)   The gross income, after consolidation adjustments, (Glossary GL 31) of the group in the accounting period is below the group accounts preparation threshold (see Appendix 4); or

(c)   There is no statutory requirement to prepare group accounts and the results of the subsidiary undertaking(s) are not material to the group; or

(d)   The subsidiary is not a company and, by virtue of being a special trust or a charity subject to a uniting direction under s96 (5) or (6) of the Charities Act 1993, has had its accounts aggregated with that of the reporting charity.

384   FRS 2 allows subsidiaries to be excluded from consolidation in certain limited circumstances (severe long-term restrictions which substantially hinder the exercise of the parent undertaking's rights over the subsidiary undertaking's assets or management or subsidiary held only for sale). It is unlikely that these exclusions will generally apply to a charitable group.

385   Charities utilise subsidiary undertakings for a variety of purposes including undertaking non-charitable trading, for investment purposes and carrying out charitable activities. The difference between profit and not-for-profit undertakings is not sufficient of itself to justify non-consolidation. However, where a subsidiary undertaking is a registered company which is insolvent and is being wound up then the subsidiary undertaking can be excluded from consolidation.

Charitable Subsidiaries

386   Most non-company charitable subsidiaries will be included in the aggregated accounts of the controlling charity, as they will either be restricted funds or endowment funds of the charity (see Paragraph 383(d)). However, on occasions, a charity may control another charitable entity that does not meet the definition of a special trust, for example, because the objects of the subsidiary are wider than those of the parent charity. Where the tests for control (the parent's ability to direct and benefit) are met, the charitable subsidiary should be consolidated. Benefit to a parent charity may arise where the services and benefits provided by the charitable subsidiary to its own beneficiaries also contribute to the objectives of the parent charity or in terms of cash flow to the parent charity. Where (unusually) a subsidiary charity's objects are substantially different from the parent charity, the benefit test of control will not be met and so no consolidation should take place.

387   A subsidiary that is a charity with objects narrower than its parent will need to be accounted for by the use of one or more restricted fund columns in the consolidated accounts.

Determining whether a Subsidiary undertaking meets the Control test

388   Subsidiary undertakings can be identified by the measure of control (Glossary GL44) exercised by the parent charity. FRS2 outlines how such control can be determined in the context of:

(a)   voting rights (mainly stemming from share ownership); and/ or

(b)   dominant influence over the Board or activities of the subsidiary.

This embodies the requirements of the Companies Act 2006 which should be followed by those undertakings registered under this Act.

389   A similar relationship to that of a parent and subsidiary undertaking may arise where the parent charity transacts with another undertaking in such a way that all the risks and rewards of the transactions remain with the parent undertaking. An example is when the ownership of the assets is transferred to another entity whilst retaining exclusive use of those assets and meeting the costs of maintaining them. Such undertakings are regarded as quasi-subsidiaries and should be accounted for in accordance with FRS 5.

390   A charity, however constituted, should be regarded as a subsidiary undertaking where the parent charity has the power to exercise, or actually exercises, dominant influence or control over the subsidiary or the parent and subsidiary are managed on a unified basis. Control can arise in any of the following situations:

(a)   the charity trustees and/or members and or employees of the parent charity are, or have the right to appoint or remove, a majority of the charity trustees of the subsidiary charity; or

(b)   the governing document of the subsidiary charity reserves to the parent charity's trustees and/or members the right to direct, or to give consent to, the exercise of significant discretion by the trustees of the subsidiary charity.

391   The basis for treating a non-company charity as a subsidiary is that the connection between it and some other charity is such that the operating and financial policies of the former are likely to be set in accordance with the wishes of the latter. This is likely to be the case where one of the relationships described in the previous paragraph exists, but trustees may, in a particular case, be able to produce evidence to the contrary.

392   Where the objects of a charity are substantially or exclusively confined to the benefit of another charity, the issue of control requires particular consideration. For example, friends' groups, on occasions, form separate charities to give support to an established charity whilst retaining legal discretion as to the nature and timing of its support. In such cases the formal powers identified in paragraph 390 may not exist but dominant influence may arise less formally. For example, the benefiting charity may set out in outline the nature or timing of the support it wants to achieve. Alternatively the parent charity may intervene on a critical matter. Where evidence exists of such dominant influence being exercised the criteria for consolidation should be regarded as being met.

Method of Consolidation

393   The normal rules will apply regarding the method of consolidation, which should be carried out on a line-by-line basis as set out in FRS 2.

394   All items of incoming resources and resources expended should be shown gross after the removal of intra-group transactions. Clearly it is desirable that similar items are treated in the same way. For instance, incoming resources from activities to generate funds in the charity should be combined with similar activities in the subsidiary, and charitable activities within the charity should be combined with similar activities in the subsidiary. Similarly, costs of generating funds and/or governance costs in the subsidiary should be aggregated with those of the charity.

395   Each charity should choose appropriate category headings within the permissible format of the Statement of Financial Activities and suitable amalgamations of activities. The headings used should reflect the underlying activities of the group. If it is not possible to exactly match items between the subsidiary undertaking and the parent charity, segmental information should be provided so that the results of the parent charity and each subsidiary undertaking are transparent (see paragraph 405).

Filing of Accounts

396 For financial years beginning on or after 1 April 2008 where consolidated accounts are required to be prepared under the Charities Act 1993 these must be prepared in accordance with the Charities (Accounts and Reports) Regulations 2008 and filed with the Charity Commission and should include the individual accounts of the parent charity. In Scotland consolidated and individual accounts must be prepared and filed in accordance with the Regulations. Charitable companies prepare group accounts in accordance with section 399 of the Companies Act 2006 where the preparation of group accounts is required by company not charity law. To ensure information is available about the parent charity alone where the group and parent charity's accounts are included in the same set of consolidated accounts, as well as two balance sheets there should be two Statements of Financial Activities (one for the group and one for the parent).

397 However, consolidated accounts are often filed with the Commission omitting the Statement of Financial Activities for the parent charity. The Commission is prepared to accept these accounts as long as gross income/turnover and results of the parent charity are clearly disclosed in the notes. The group accounts must still contain the entity balance sheet of the parent charity. The Commission retains the power to require the production and filing of any individual charity Statement of Financial Activities and similarly members of the public have a legal right to request this statement.

Disclosure

398 There should be a separate comment in the Trustees' Annual Report concerning the activities and performance of each of the charity's material subsidiary undertakings (see paragraph 53).

399 Where consolidated accounts are prepared, the policy notes should state the method of consolidation and which subsidiaries or associated entities are included and excluded from the consolidation.

400 The notes to the consolidated accounts should give the position of the group as well as the parent undertaking.

401 The notes to the accounts should state the aggregate amount of the total investment of the charity in its subsidiary undertakings and, unless the subsidiary is not material, in relation to each one:

(a)   its name;

(b)   particulars of the parent charity's shareholding or other means of control;

(c)   how its activities relate to those of the charity;

(d)   the aggregate amount of its assets, liabilities and funds;

(e)   a summary of its turnover and expenditure and its profit or loss for the year (or equivalent categories for charitable subsidiary undertakings).

402 If there are any minority interests external to the group, similar details to those in the above paragraph should be provided relating to the minority interest held in the subsidiary undertakings including any restrictions that may be placed on the group's activities.

403 If a charity has a large number of subsidiary undertakings such that the disclosure in paragraph 401 would result in information of excessive length being given, the information need only be given in respect of those undertakings whose results or financial position materially affected the figures shown in the charity's annual accounts. The full disclosure should be made available (in the same way as the accounts) to any member of the public upon request.

404 In addition, if, following paragraphs 383 to 384, subsidiary undertakings are excluded or consolidated accounts are not prepared then the trustees should explain the reasons in a note to the charity's accounts with reference to each excluded subsidiary undertaking.

405 As stated in paragraph 395 segmental information may need to be provided where the aggregation and adjustments required to consolidate financial information may obscure information about the different undertakings and the activities included in the consolidated accounts. It is important that the presentation adopted and disclosure in the notes is sufficiently detailed to distinguish the key results of the charity from those of its subsidiary undertakings. Examples of those items that should be separately disclosed include the costs of generating funds, the costs of charitable activities and governance costs.

406 In consolidated accounts, funds or reserves retained by subsidiary undertakings other than funds available to be used in carrying out the charity's objects should be included under an appropriate separate fund heading in the balance sheet (eg funds retained within a non-charitable subsidiary).

Associates, Joint Ventures and Joint Arrangements

Introduction

407 This section explains the additional accounting requirements in consolidated accounts where a charity has associates, joint ventures or joint arrangements.

Identification

408 FRS 9 covers the accounting for associates, joint ventures and joint arrangements and provides detailed guidance on how to determine the relationship between the entities involved. Where these exist, consolidated accounts should be prepared subject to the exemptions in paragraph 383.

409 Where a charity has a long term participating interest in another undertaking and exercises significant influence over its operating and financial policy then this is likely to be an associate undertaking. Where a charity beneficially holds 20% or more of the voting rights in any undertaking, it will be presumed to have a participating interest and significant influence over its operating and financial policy, unless the contrary is shown.

410 Charities providing grants or making programme related investments may on occasions combine funding with the provision of advice or expertise and on occasions may be invited by the recipient charity to provide or nominate a charity trustee with particular skills or expertise. Where the recipient charity operates with a small trustee body, this might be construed as creating an associate. An associate will be created if the nomination or appointment is used in conjunction with a formal or informal agreement to exercise significant influence through direct involvement in setting the recipient charity's operating and financial polices. Where the charity trustee appointment is simply used to provide advice or expertise to the recipient charity whilst allowing the charity to adopt its own policies and strategies then an associate relationship is unlikely to be created.

411 In a joint venture situation, a separate entity is jointly controlled by two or more undertakings, all of which have a say in the operations of the joint venture, so that no single investing undertaking controls the joint venture but all together can do so. It is possible for a charity to beneficially hold 20% or more of the voting rights in an undertaking but for the management arrangements to be such that control is clearly shared with the other partners and hence the undertaking is a joint venture as opposed to an associate.

412 Often charities also undertake joint arrangements where they may carry out activities in partnership with other bodies but without establishing a separate legal entity.

Methods of Accounting for Associates, Joint Ventures and Joint Arrangements

413 Associates should be included in the accounts based on the net equity method. The consolidated Statement of Financial Activities should show the net interest in the results for the year in the associates as a separate row after the "net incoming resources/(resources expended) before transfers" row. In the balance sheet, the net interest in associates should be shown as a separate row within fixed asset investments. Where the charity's rights to the associate's assets are severely limited (eg because the majority prohibit any dividend distribution) then this should be reflected in the valuation.

414 Joint ventures should be accounted for on a gross equity method. This method requires the reporting entity to present its share of the gross incoming resources of joint ventures on the face of the consolidated profit and loss account (Statement of Financial Activities in charities). However, this does not form part of the group incoming resources and must be clearly distinguished. For charities this can be achieved by including gross incoming resources from joint ventures in the Statement of Financial Activities on a line-by-line basis with an additional row showing the total share of gross incoming resources from joint ventures as a reduction in total incoming resources. In addition a row showing the net interest in the results for the year in the joint ventures as a separate row after the "net incoming resources/(resources expended)" row must be included (this may be combined with that of the associates). In the balance sheet the share of the gross assets and the gross liabilities should be shown in a linked presentation within fixed assets investments.

415   Where there are gains and losses on investments and unrealised gains on other fixed assets, the net share relating to associates should be shown on a separate row, with the gross share relating to joint ventures being shown either on a separate row or combined with the appropriate lines on the Statement of Financial Activities.

416   Where there is a joint arrangement, the charity's gross share of the incoming resources and resources expended and the assets and liabilities should be included in the accounts in the same way as for a branch per paragraphs 77 to 81. If under the arrangement the charity is jointly and severally liable for an obligation, it should accrue the part of the obligation for which it is responsible and treat the part of the obligation which is expected to be met by the other parties as a contingent liability.

Disclosure

417   The following disclosure should be given in respect of each associate and joint venture and this will normally be compliant with FRS 9:

(a)   its name;

(b)   the charity's shareholding and other interests in it;

(c)   the nature of the activities of the associate or joint venture;

(d)   the charity's interest in the results showing separately its share in:
    (i)   gross incoming resources by type;
    (ii)   costs of generating funds;
    (iii)   expenditure on charitable activities;
    (iv)   expenditure on governance;
    (these first four items may need to be adapted in the case of associates or joint ventures that are not charities)
    (v)   the net results (where tax is payable, the share of the results pre and post tax and the share in the tax should be shown);
    (vi)   gains or losses on investments and the share in unrealised gains on other fixed assets;
    (vii)   fixed assets;
    (viii)   current assets;
    (ix)   liabilities under one year;
    (x)   liabilities over one year;
    (xi)   the different funds of the charity;
    (xii)   contingent liabilities and other commitments;

(e)   particulars of any qualifications contained in any audit or other statutory report on its accounts, and any note or reservation in those accounts to call attention to a matter which, apart from the note or reservation, would properly have been referred to in such a qualification.

418   For joint arrangements, the notes to the accounts should provide appropriate details of the charity's commitments in the arrangement.

The SORP in relation to Charitable Companies in the UK

Introduction

419 This section explains the position of this SORP with respect to charitable companies. In following this SORP, charitable companies will normally meet most of the reporting requirements under the Companies Act. However, the SORP does not reproduce these requirements in full and a charity should have regard to its own circumstances when considering the application of the Companies Act. In addition to following the main section of this SORP and the other special sections as applicable, there are certain further requirements which must be met by charitable companies. Ways of meeting the most common of these requirements are suggested below, but these too should be considered in the light of the company's individual circumstances.

Accounts and Reports

420 Charitable companies must comply with the Companies Act 2006 with respect to the form and content of their accounts. This Act also stipulates the contents of the annual (directors') report. In England and Wales, strictly, the directors of charitable companies have to prepare both that report, and the Trustees' Annual Report under Part VI of the Charities Act 1993, but the Charity Commission is prepared to accept the directors' report for filing under Part VI if it also contains the information required under Part VI. In Scotland charitable companies should comply with both the Companies Act 2006 and the trustee reporting requirements of SORP. Charitable companies (unlike non company charities) do not have an exemption to leave out the names of the directors from the Annual Report.

421 The Companies Act 2006 requires a company to prepare annual financial statements which give a true and fair view of its state of affairs at the end of the year and of its profit and loss for that year. In addition, Paragraph 3(3) of Part 1, section A of Schedule 4 to the Companies Act 1985, which remains in force until superseded by Regulations made under the Companies Act 2006, requires the directors to adapt the headings and subheadings of the balance sheet and profit and loss account in any case where the special nature of the company's business requires such adaptation.

422 The requirement to show a true and fair view and to adapt the accounts for the special nature of charity means that there is a strong presumption that charitable companies will, in all but exceptional circumstances, have to comply with this SORP in order to meet the requirements of company law. Particulars of any material departures from this SORP are required to be disclosed in accordance with paragraph 359.

The Statement of Financial Activities and the Summary Income and Expenditure Account

423 All charitable companies registered under the Companies Acts must include an income and expenditure account in their financial statements. The Statement of Financial Activities is designed to include all the gains and losses of a charity which would be found in both the income and expenditure account and the statement of total recognised gains and losses as required by FRS 3. A separate income and expenditure account is therefore not necessarily required. Circumstances where it will probably be required may arise where the income and expenditure account cannot be separately identified within the Statement of Financial Activities and there are items which may be open to challenge if they are included in an income and expenditure account, such as:

(a)   movement on endowment (capital) funds during the year; and

(b)   unrealised gains and losses arising during the year.

Whilst unrealised gains and losses are not allowed in the income and expenditure account, most of these are included in the Statement of Financial Activities below the point at which a conventional income and expenditure account would end as explained in paragraph 424. Furthermore – where charities adopt a policy of continuous revaluation of investments (as explained in paragraph 219) there may be no realised gains to report and all the revaluation movements will be classified as unrealised gains.

424   Where the Statement of Financial Activities of a charitable company does not include any of the items in paragraph 423, it may not need to produce a separate summary income and expenditure account but the headings in the Statement of Financial Activities should be changed so that:

(a)   the title clearly indicates that it includes an income and expenditure account and statement of total recognised gains and losses (if required); and

(b)   there is a prominent sub total entitled "net income/(expenditure) for the year" which replaces or is in addition to the heading of "net incoming/(outgoing) resources for the year".

Care should also be taken to ensure that all realised gains and losses are included in the Statement of Financial Activities in such a way that they fall within the bounds of the headings for (a) and (b) within the income and expenditure account. Particular attention may need to be given to impairment losses and reversals which, in accordance with the guidance in FRS 11, are realised in some circumstances and unrealised in others.

425   Where a summary income and expenditure account is required, it should be derived from and cross-referenced to the corresponding figures in the Statement of Financial Activities. It need not distinguish between unrestricted and restricted income funds but the accounting basis on which items are included must be the same as in the Statement of Financial Activities. It should show separately in respect of continuing operations, acquisitions and discontinued operations:

(a)   gross income from all sources;

(b)   net gains/losses from disposals of all fixed assets belonging to the charity's income funds;

(c)   transfers from endowment funds of amounts previously received as capital resources and now converted into income funds for expending;

(d)   total income (this will be the total of all incoming resources – other than revaluation gains – of all the income funds but not for any endowment funds);

(e)   total expenditure out of the charity's income funds;

(f)   net income or expenditure for the year. In practice, the format may need to be modified to comply with specific statutory requirements or those of the charity's own governing document.

426   Charitable companies which require a summary income and expenditure account and which prepare consolidated accounts should prepare a summary income and expenditure account for the group.

Revaluation Reserve

427   Where fixed assets are revalued upwards, a revaluation reserve will arise being the difference between the original depreciated cost or valuation of the asset and the revalued amount. Separate reporting of the reserve is not significant for charities as they do not distribute profits, but a revaluation reserve will, nevertheless, arise. This will form part of the funds in which the revalued assets are held. In certain circumstances (as described in FRSs 11 and 15), impairment losses or other downward revaluations can be offset against the revaluation reserve.

428   To comply with the Companies Act 2006, charitable companies must separately disclose the revaluation reserve in respect of their unrestricted funds within the relevant funds section on the face of the balance sheet but may change the heading as appropriate. This may be best effected by use of a prominent inset.

Summary Financial Information

429   Charitable companies should follow the recommendations in paragraphs 371 to 379 but their summary financial information should also include a statement indicating whether or not the statutory accounts for the relevant year(s) have been delivered to the Registrar of Companies and contain such additional information as required by section 427 of the Companies Act 2006 and Regulations made thereunder.

Accounting for Retirement Benefits

Introduction

430   There are two main types of retirement benefit schemes: defined contribution schemes and defined benefit schemes. Definitions for both appear in the glossary (GL 16 & GL 17). Details of how to account for each are included in this section.

431   A charity participating in a multi-employer defined benefit scheme, where the contributions are set in relation to the current service period only, or where the charity is unable to identify its share of the underlying assets and liabilities on a consistent or reasonable basis, should account for its contributions to the scheme as if it were a defined contribution scheme. Where a charity is unable to identify its share of the underlying assets and liabilities of the scheme, the disclosures set out in paragraph 446 should be provided.

432   The cost of a defined contribution scheme recognised in the accounts is equal to the contributions payable to the scheme in the accounting period. These pension costs should be allocated across the relevant resources expended categories of the Statement of Financial Activities set out in paragraph 177. The note disclosures in relation to such schemes are set out in paragraph 445.

Defined Benefit Schemes

433 FRS 17: Retirement Benefits substantially affects charities that operate defined benefit schemes (see Appendix 2: FRS 17). The surplus/deficit in a defined benefit scheme is the excess/shortfall of the value of the assets in the scheme over/ below the present value of the scheme liabilities. In accordance with FRS 17 principles:

(a)   An asset should be recognised to the extent that the employer charity is able to recover a surplus either through reduced contributions in the future or through refunds from the scheme.

(b)   A liability should be recognised to the extent that it reflects its legal or constructive obligation of the employer charity.

Similar principles should also be adopted in relation to the provision of death-in-service and incapacity benefits, that are not wholly insured, and provided through a defined benefit pension scheme.

434 Full actuarial valuations of a defined benefit scheme should be undertaken by an independent, qualified actuary at intervals not exceeding three years and updated annually at the charity's balance sheet date to reflect current conditions.

435 A surplus or deficit in a defined benefit scheme normally gives rise to an asset or liability within unrestricted funds of the reporting charity. The reporting charity will normally be the employer and have control as to the future use of a surplus recovered either in the form of reduced contributions or a refund from the scheme. Similarly, where a liability arises through a legal or constructive obligation to make good a deficit, this liability will normally rest with the main charity's unrestricted funds.

Allocation of Retirement Benefit Costs and Gains

436 The change in the defined benefit asset or liability (other than that arising from contributions payable to the scheme which affect the surplus or deficit in the scheme) should be analysed into the components identified in FRS 17. However these will only be recognised through the Statement of Financial Activities on full implementation of FRS 17. (See Appendix 2 for FRS 17 implementation date and transitional arrangements.)

437 Pension costs may be allocated between the resources expended categories of the Statement of Financial Activities on the basis of the charity's own computations. The basis of the allocation should be reasonable and consistent. Allocations of pension costs based on the staff costs of employees within the scheme is one approach, although other approaches (e g allocation based on pension contributions payable) may also produce an equitable allocation. Allocation of the components should be based on the following:

(a)   The changes relating to current or past service costs and gains, and losses on settlements and curtailments should be allocated to the appropriate resources expended categories set out in paragraph 432.

(b)   Pension finance costs arising from changes in the net of the interest costs and expected return on assets should be allocated to the appropriate resources expended categories set out in paragraph 432. Income arising from these changes should be recognised as an incoming resource and separately disclosed where material.

(c) Where past service costs, or gains or losses on settlements or curtailment, are material in the context of the particular expenditure (or income) category in which they are recognised, the amounts should be disclosed as exceptional in accordance with FRS 3 – Reporting Financial Performance (see Appendix 2).

(d) Actuarial gains and losses arising should be recognised within the "gains and losses" categories of the Statement of Financial Activities under the heading "actuarial gains and losses on defined benefit pension scheme".

Restricted Funds

438 A pension asset should be recognised as accruing to a restricted fund only where it can be demonstrated that the economic benefit of the asset will accrue to a particular fund through reduced contributions or refunds. Similarly, a pension liability should be allocated to a particular fund only where it is demonstrable that a constructive liability arises to fund the deficit and could properly be met from the particular fund. Such a situation may arise where staff are specifically engaged on a long-term project funded from restricted income. This allocation may be undertaken on the basis of the charity's own computations. Liaison with the provider of a particular restricted fund may be necessary in order to establish the basis on which any pension asset or liability is allocated to that fund and therefore the pension costs that may be properly charged through it.

439 Any allocation of a pension asset or liability to a restricted fund should be reviewed on an annual basis. Where staff changes or cessation of a particular project indicate that the economic benefits or obligations will no longer accrue to that particular fund then the asset or liability should be allocated to the unrestricted funds by means of a transfer of funds through the Statement of Financial Activities.

440 Where the criteria for the recognition of a pension asset or liability within restricted funds are met, the related pension costs should be recognised within the restricted funds column of the Statement of Financial Activities. The components of the pension cost should be recognised within the same Statement of Financial Activities categories and on the same basis as set out in the preceding paragraphs.

441 A restricted fund may, however, incur staff costs without the criteria for the recognition of a pension asset or liability within the restricted fund's balance sheet being met. For example, a restricted fund may be of a short-term nature or staff may be frequently transferred between activities creating uncertainty as to the fund which will ultimately recover any surplus or meet future contributions resulting from any deficit. In such circumstances, the restricted funds column of the Statement of Financial Activities may still be recharged with an appropriate portion of the current service cost component of the pension cost relating to the staff engaged in activities within restricted funds. Such a recharge within the Statement of Financial Activities would, as with any recharge, also necessitate a balance sheet adjustment between fund balances. The balance sheet of the unrestricted funds should, however, continue to recognise the overall pension asset or liability.

442 When past service costs and gains and losses on curtailments and settlements arise, such costs may be recharged to restricted funds only when a charity can demonstrate the costs relate to present staff engaged in the activities of the restricted funds.

Disclosures

443 The disclosure requirements for pension scheme contributions are given in FRS 17. This section summarises the key points.

444 Where a defined contribution scheme is operated by a charity, the notes to the accounts should disclose:

(a)   the nature of the scheme;

(b)   the costs for the accounting period; and

(c)   the amount of any outstanding or prepaid contributions at the year end.

445 FRS 17 disclosure requirements for defined benefit pension schemes are detailed and charities should refer to the text of the standard in completing their disclosure notes. The notes to the accounts should include the following information:

(a)   the nature of the scheme;

(b)   the date of the most recent full actuarial valuation;

(c)   the contributions made in the accounting period and any agreed contribution rates for future years;

(d)   the main financial assumptions used at the beginning of the period and at the balance sheet date;

(e)   the fair value of scheme assets analysed between equities, bonds and other assets and their expected rates of returns;

(f)   the present value of the scheme liabilities and the resulting surplus or deficit compared with the fair value of the scheme assets;

(g)   an analysis of the amounts for each of the component parts of the defined benefit costs charged or credited through the Statement of Financial Activities.

446 Where a charity operating a defined benefit scheme has established that the employer's share of underlying assets and liabilities cannot be identified on a consistent and reasonable basis (eg by confirmation from the scheme administrators or actuaries) this fact should be disclosed. Any available information about the existence of the surplus or deficit in the scheme and the implications of that surplus or deficit for the employing charity should be disclosed together with a brief explanation of the general circumstances giving rise to this position.

447 When a charity operating a defined benefit scheme discloses a material pension liability, the notes to the accounts (or Trustees' Annual Report in the explanation of the policy on reserves) should explain the impact, if any, on resources available for general application. If a pension liability exceeds the balance on unrestricted funds, the note should also explain any limitations placed on any restricted fund of the charity to contribute to any resource requirements arising from the disclosed liability.

448 If a material pension asset is disclosed, the notes to the accounts (or Trustees' Annual Report) should explain the nature of the economic benefit derived from the asset and give an indication of the period over which any benefit in terms of reduced contributions will accrue to the charity.

Common Investment Funds and Investment Pooling Schemes

449 The trustees of Common Investment Funds (CIFs) in England and Wales, other than pooling scheme funds (see paragraph 450), should prepare their accounts and Trustees' Annual Report in accordance with the relevant accounts and reports regulations for CIFs made under part VI of the Charities Act 1993 (regulations made in 2008 ensured these requirements are consistent with the SORP for Authorised Funds issued by the Investment Management Association in December 2005) and any subsequent regulations which may be made. The trustees of Common Deposit Funds (CDFs) should also meet the relevant requirements that regulations place on such funds.

450 Some charities may operate a pooling scheme (Glossary GL 46) for the investments under the control of a single body of trustees common to the investing charities. Sometimes such arrangements are governed by a formal Charity Commission scheme but the pooling of investments may also be an informal arrangement under the Trustee Act 2000. This SORP does not provide details on how to operate or manage pooling schemes where underlying investments funds are apportioned between the investing charities or their funds on a similar basis to that adopted by unit trusts.

451 Where a pooling scheme holds investments for the separate funds of a single reporting charity, the scheme will form a restricted fund of the reporting charity. The assets of the pooled fund are the investments held and its liabilities are the share of these investments due to the funds of the reporting charity which have invested through the pooling arrangements. Its income and costs will accrue to the funds investing in the pool. Therefore, when accounts are prepared for the reporting charity, the assets, investment income and related costs of the pooling scheme fund will appear in the funds investing in the pool. The notes to the accounts simply disclose the pooling of investments with the underlying investments, income and costs being disclosed as part of the investment disclosures of the reporting charity. Thus to the reader of the accounts the pool will not be visible as a separate fund.

APPENDIX 1: GLOSSARY

GL 1   Activity Classification of costs

1.1   An "activity classification of costs" is the aggregation of costs incurred in pursuit of a defined activity (eg provision of services to elderly people or counselling), and is achieved by adding together all the costs (salaries, rents, depreciation etc) relating to that specific activity.

1.2   The three main 'high level' activities that charities preparing accruals accounts will report on are generating funds, charitable activity and governance costs of the charity.

GL 2   Actuarial Gains and Losses

2.1   Changes in the actuarial deficits or surpluses that arise because the actuarial assumptions, in relation to pension or other retirement benefit schemes, have changed or events have not coincided with the actuarial assumptions made for the last valuation.

GL 3   Audit Threshold

3.1   This is the threshold (which may include income, expenditure and asset limits) above which a charity will be required to have a statutory audit.

GL 4   Branches

4.1   "Branches" (which may also be known as supporters' groups, friends' groups, members' groups, communities or parishes which are part of a common trust etc.) are entities or administrative bodies set up, for example, to conduct a particular aspect of the activities of the reporting charity, or to conduct the activities of the reporting charity in a particular geographical area. They may or may not be legal entities which are separate from the reporting charity.

4.2   For the purpose of this SORP a "branch" is either:

(a)   simply part of the administrative machinery of the reporting charity; or

(b)   a fund shown in the accounts as a restricted or endowment fund. Two types of entity are covered by this category, each of which should be treated as linked to the reporting charity for accounting purposes:

(i)   a separate legal entity which is administered by, or on behalf of, the reporting charity and whose funds are held for specific purposes which are within the general purposes of the reporting charity. "Legal entity" means a trust or unincorporated association or other body formed for a charitable purpose. The words "on behalf of" should be taken to mean that, under the constitution of the separate entity, a substantial degree of influence can be exerted by the reporting charity over the administration of its affairs; or,

(ii)   in England and Wales, a separate legal entity not falling within (i) which the Charity Commission has united by a direction under section 96(5) or 96(6) of the Charities Act 1993 should be treated as linked to the reporting charity for accounting purposes.

4.3 This definition has been adopted to reflect the provisions of the Charities Act 1993 allocating responsibility for accounting in the case of multicellular charities. FRS 2 expressly disapplies its requirements where they are not consistent with a particular statutory accounting framework. Consequently, charitable bodies which are controlled by other charitable bodies will not normally be subject to the requirements of that standard where they are treated as "special trusts" under the Charities Act 1993 or are the subject of a direction as mentioned above in paragraph 4.2(b)(ii). Also see the definition of "parent undertaking and subsidiary undertaking" (see GL 44 below).

4.4 Some of the characteristics of a branch are:

(a) it uses the name of the reporting charity within its title;

(b) it exclusively raises funds for the reporting charity and/or for its own local activities;

(c) it uses the reporting charity's registration number to receive tax relief on its activities;

(d) it is perceived by the public to be the reporting charity's local representative or its representative for a particular purpose;

(e) it receives support from the reporting charity through advice, publicity materials, etc.

4.5 If the branch exists to carry out the primary objects of the charity, typically it will receive funds from the reporting charity for its work and may be staffed by employees of the reporting charity.

4.6 If the branch is not a separate legal entity, all funds held by a branch will be the legal property of the reporting charity, whether or not the branch has a separate bank account.

Organisations which are not Branches

4.7 Some charities may be known as "branches" within a particular organisational or network structure, but if their level of administrative autonomy from the reporting charity – as determined by their constitutions – is such that legislation requires them to be treated as separate accounting entities, then they should not be regarded as "branches" for accounting purposes but should prepare separate accounts for submission to the appropriate regulatory authority. Such "branches" may also be subsidiaries.

4.8 Other examples of organisations which are not "branches" for the purpose of these recommendations include:

(a) groups of people who occasionally gather together to raise funds for one or a number of different charities; and

(b) special interest groups who are affiliated to a particular charity, but do not themselves undertake charitable activities (including fundraising for the charity).

GL 5   Capital

5.1 In the context of charity law "capital" means resources which become available to a charity and which the trustees are legally required to invest or retain and use for its purposes. "Capital" may be permanent endowment, where the trustees have no power to convert it into income and apply it as such, or expendable endowment, where they do have this power (see Appendix 3).

5.2 Capital is also used in its various accounting meanings, such as the capital elements of fixed assets, working capital or share capital.

GL 6   Charity

6.1 A "charity" is any institution established for purposes which are exclusively charitable. Where the institution is involved in more than one activity, operates more than one fund, or is not centralised into one unit of operation, the term is used in this statement to include all those activities, units and funds which fall within the scope of either a single governing instrument (or instruments supplemental to the main instrument) or for which the trustees are otherwise legally liable to account (eg branches, as defined in paragraph GL 4 above).

GL 7   Charity Trustees

7.1 "Charity trustees" has the same meaning as in s97(1) of the Charities Act 1993 and section 106 of the Charities and Trustee Investment (Scotland) Act 2005, that is the persons having the general control and management of the administration of a charity regardless of what they are called. Custodian trustees and nominees are not within this definition (see GL59).

7.2 For instance, in the case of an unincorporated association the executive or management committee are its charity trustees, and in the case of a charitable company it is the directors who are the charity trustees.

7.3 Those concerned in any way with the administration of charities should note that the status of a charity trustee is defined in terms of the function to be performed, and not by reference to the title given to any office, or membership of any committee or committees.

GL 8   Common Investment Funds

8.1 Common Investment Funds (CIFs) are collective investment schemes that are similar to authorised unit trusts and are for charity investors only. They are investment vehicles providing diversification of investment to reduce risk, and are tax efficient, administratively simple and cost efficient. They are deemed by law to be charities themselves and enjoy the same tax status as other charities.

8.2 CIFs set up by schemes made by the Charity Commission under section 22 of the Charities Act 1960 or section 24 of the Charities Act 1993 are open to charities in England and Wales, Scotland and Northern Ireland.

GL 9 Connected Charities

9.1 "Connected charities" are those which have common, parallel or related objects and activities; and either:

(a) common control; or

(b) unity of administration (e g shared management).

9.2 Within this category may be charities which come together under one umbrella organisation or are part of a federal structure. Also see related parties (GL 50).

GL 10 Constructive Obligation

10.1 An obligation that derives from an entity's actions where:

(a) by an established pattern of past practice, published policies or a sufficiently specific current statement, the entity has indicated to other parties that it will accept certain responsibilities; and

(b) as a result, the entity has created a valid expectation on the part of those other parties that it will discharge those responsibilities.

GL 11 Contingent Asset

11.1 A possible asset that arises from past events and whose existence will be confirmed only by the occurrence of one or more uncertain future events not wholly within the entity's control.

GL 12 Contingent Liability

12.1 This is either:

(a) A possible obligation that arises from past events and whose existence will be confirmed only by the occurrence of one or more uncertain future events not wholly within the entity's control; or

(b) a present obligation that arises from past events but is not recognised in the primary statements because:
  (i) it is not probable that a transfer of economic benefits will be required to settle the obligation; or
  (ii) the amount of the obligation cannot be measured with sufficient reliability.

GL 13 Costs of Generating Voluntary Income

13.1 Costs of generating voluntary income comprise the costs actually incurred by a charity, or by an agent, in inducing others to make gifts to it that are voluntary income (see GL 61).

(a)   Such costs will include the costs of producing fundraising advertising, marketing and direct mail materials, as well as any remuneration payable to an agent. It will normally include publicity costs but not those used in an educational manner in furtherance of the charity's objects.

(b)   Such costs will exclude fundraising trading costs (see GL 26).

GL 14   Custodian Trustee

14.1   "Custodian Trustee" includes for present purposes any other non-executive trustee in whose name property belonging to the charity is held. (See also "trustee for a charity" GL 59).

GL 15   Deferred Income

15.1   Deferred income consists of resources (normally cash) received by a charity that do not meet the criteria for recognition as incoming resources in the Statement of Financial Activities as entitlement to the incoming resource does not exist at the balance sheet date. This will arise for example, in the case of resources received but not yet earned (in the case of a contract) which is deferred to match with performance under the contract or where the conditions attaching to a grant prevents its immediate recognition.

15.2   Deferred income is not recognised in the Statement of Financial Activities until the charity is entitled to the incoming resource and instead is disclosed as a liability in the balance sheet (see paragraph 318).

GL 16   Defined Benefit Pension Scheme

16.1   A pension or other retirement benefit scheme other than a defined contribution scheme (see GL 17). Usually, the scheme rules define the benefits independently of the contributions payable, and the benefits are not directly related to the investments of the scheme.

GL 17   Defined Contribution Pension Scheme

17.1   A pension or other retirement benefit scheme into which an employer pays regular contributions fixed as an amount or as a percentage of pay and will have no legal or constructive obligations to pay further contributions if the scheme does not have sufficient assets to pay all employee benefits relating to employee service in the current and prior periods. An individual member's benefits are determined by reference to contributions paid into the scheme in respect of that member, usually increased by an amount based on the investment return on those contributions.

GL 18   Depreciated Replacement Cost

18.1   Depreciated Replacement Cost is defined in FRS 15.

18.2   The objective of depreciated replacement cost is to make a realistic estimate of the current cost of constructing an asset that has the same service potential as the existing asset.

GL 19 Designated Fund

19.1 See Appendix 3 (App 3.1).

GL 20 Donated Services and Facilities

20.1 Donated services and facilities could include gifts of facilities, beneficial loan arrangements, or services from volunteers. Used to be known as intangible income (see GL 37)

GL 21 Endowment Fund

21.1 See Appendix 3 (App 3.3).

GL 22 Ex gratia Payment

22.1 Ex gratia payments are payments made at the discretion of trustees and not as a result of a contract or other legal obligation.

22.2 Ex gratia payments are of two distinct types:

(a) Those made by a charity in relation to its charitable activities (e g extra payments to retiring employees). These will not normally need to be disclosed.

(b) Those where a charity believes it is expedient to make in relation to an obligation which is not within its charitable objects and powers. This may be, for example, to settle a claim in respect of a legacy that would otherwise consume charitable resources in legal expenses. (see paragraph 240)

GL 23 Fair Value

23.1 Fair value is the amount for which an asset could be exchanged or a liability settled between knowledgeable, willing parties in an arm's length transaction.

23.2 The object of fair value measurement is to estimate an exchange price for the asset or liability being measured in the absence of an actual transaction for that asset or liability.

GL 24 Financial Derivative

24.1 A financial derivative is a security, such as an option or futures contract, whose value depends on the performance of an underlying security. In their simplest form derivatives can be used to reduce the cost and/or risk associated with holding or acquiring assets.

GL 25 Functional Fixed Assets

25.1 "Functional fixed assets" are those assets which are used for charitable purposes (i e to undertake the activities that are within the charity's objectives).

GL 26   Fundraising Costs

26.1   Fundraising costs consist of two categories:

(a)   Costs of generating voluntary income – see GL 13 above and

(b)   Fundraising trading costs which comprise the costs of trading to raise funds including the cost of goods sold and any other costs associated with a trading operation.

GL 27   Funds

27.1   A "fund" is a pool of resources, held and maintained separately from other pools because of the circumstances in which the resources were originally received or the way in which they have subsequently been treated. At the broadest level a fund will be one of two kinds: a restricted fund or an unrestricted fund (see Appendix 3 for the legal position as regards the various funds of a charity.)

GL 28   Governance Costs

28.1   These are the costs associated with the governance arrangements of the charity which relate to the general running of the charity as opposed to those costs associated with fundraising or charitable activity. The costs will normally include internal and external audit, legal advice for trustees and costs associated with constitutional and statutory requirements e g the cost of trustee meetings and preparing statutory accounts. Included within this category are any costs associated with the strategic as opposed to day to day management of the charity's activities.

GL 29   Grant

29.1   A grant is any voluntary payment (or other transfer of property) in favour of a person or institution. Grant payments, when made by a charity, are any such voluntary payments made in furtherance of its objects. The payment or transfer may be for the general purposes of the recipient, or for some specific purpose such as the supply of a particular service. It may be unconditional, or be subject to conditions which, if not satisfied by the recipient, may lead to the grant, or property acquired with the aid of the grant, or part of it, being reclaimed.

GL 30   Grants and/or Contract Income

30.1   A payment made to a charity for the purpose of providing goods or services may be by way of grant or contract. The main distinction is that grant payments are voluntary whereas contracts are normally legally binding between the payer and the charity: the payment is not then voluntary and is not a grant. The distinction is important because:

(a)   a contractual payment will normally be unrestricted income of the charity, but a grant for the supply of specific services will normally be restricted income;

(b)   the nature of the payment may be relevant to its VAT treatment.

30.2   It is not always easy in practice to decide whether a particular arrangement is or is not intended by the parties to be a legally binding contract for the supply of services. If, under the arrangement, the payer, rather than the recipient charity, has taken the lead in identifying the services to be provided, or if the arrangement provides for damages to be paid in the case of a breach of its terms, rather than, say, for total or partial refund of the payment, it is more probable that there is a contract for the supply of services. If there is no such contract, the rights and obligations of the parties will depend primarily on the law of trusts and conditional gifts, rather than on the law of contract.

30.3   Certain grant arrangements may not be contractual in law but nevertheless have the characteristics of a contract, in that the conditions attaching to the grant only give entitlement to the recipient of the funding (and a liability to the grant provider) as the goods or services specified in the grant terms are provided. Such arrangements are termed performance related grants (see GL 45 Performance-related Grants).

GL 31   Gross Income

31.1   Gross income is a term used within the Charities Act 1993 to determine the thresholds made by the Regulations under that Act (and the Companies Act in relation to charitable companies). The thresholds govern the requirements (in England and Wales) for account's scrutiny, the preparation of accruals accounts by non-company charities, submission of reports, accounts and an annual return to the Charity Commission. Gross income does not include the gains from investments, nor asset revaluation gains nor any resources received in endowment funds. It will however include funds released from endowments.

31.2   Gross income is separately defined for the statutory thresholds that apply in Scotland. The same principles apply in Scotland and the detailed definition of gross income is contained in the Charities Accounts (Scotland) Regulations 2006 (SSI 2006: No 218).

31.3   In relation to consolidated accounts, gross income will relate to aggregate gross income of the group after any adjustments arising from consolidation (eg inter-group sales).

GL 32   Heritage Assets

32.1   Heritage assets are assets of historical, artistic or scientific importance that are held to advance preservation, conservation and educational objectives of charities and through public access contribute to the nation's culture and education either at a national or local level. Such assets are central to the achievement of the purposes of such charities and include the land, buildings, structures, collections, exhibits or artefacts that are preserved or conserved and are central to the educational objectives of such charities.

32.2   Examples of these assets are:

(a)   Charities with preservation objectives may hold specified or historic buildings or a complex of historic or architectural importance or a site where a building has been or where its remains can be seen.

(b)   Conservation charities may hold land relating to the habitat needs of species, or the environment generally, including areas of natural beauty or scientific interest.

(c)   Museums and art galleries hold collections and artefacts to educate the public and to promote the arts and sciences.

GL 33   Historic Asset

33.1   See GL 32 above: Heritage Assets.

GL 34   Inalienable Asset

34.1   An asset which a charity is required by law to retain indefinitely for its own use/benefit and therefore cannot dispose of without external consent, whether prohibited by its governing document, the donor's wishes or in some other way. Normally the asset will belong to the charity's "permanent endowment", where it is held on trusts which contemplate its retention and continuing use but not its disposal. However, in the case of a gift-in-kind of a "wasting asset", such as a building, a long lease or a nondurable artefact, the terms of trust may not have provided for its maintenance in perpetuity or its replacement. In that case the endowment will be expended to the extent of the aggregate amount of its depreciation or amortisation properly provided for in the annual accounts (ie based on its currently anticipated useful life).

GL 35   Income

35.1   In the context of charity law, income refers to resources received that must be expended within a reasonable time of their being received. This contrasts with capital funds (see definition GL 5 above).

35.2   The term income is also used in its more general accounting sense.

GL 36   Incoming Resources

36.1   Incoming resources means all resources which become available to a charity including contributions to endowment (capital) funds but excluding gains and losses on investment assets. Gross incoming resources includes all trading and investment income, legacies, donations, grants and gains from disposals of fixed assets for use by the charity. Incoming resources should be recognised in the Statement of Financial Activities when the effect of a transaction or other event results in an increase in the charity's assets.

36.2   This term is to be distinguished from the statutory term gross income (see GL 31).

GL 37   Intangible Income

37.1   Intangible income is the term used by previous Charity SORPs to refer to what is now known as Donated Services and Facilities (see GL 20).

GL 38   Investment Management Costs

38.1   Investment management costs include the costs of:

(a)   portfolio management;

(b)   obtaining investment advice;

(c)   administration of the investments;

(d)   rent collection, property repairs and maintenance charges.

38.2   Valuation fees incurred for accounting purposes would normally be charged to the governance cost category of the relevant funds that hold the properties being valued.

38.3   Costs associated with acquiring and disposing of investments would normally form part of the acquisition cost of the investment or reduce the return on disposals. These costs are therefore not part of investment management costs.

GL 39   Investment Property

39.1   Subject to the exceptions in paragraph 39.2 below, an investment property is an interest in land and/or buildings:

(a)   in respect of which construction work and development have been completed; and

(b)   which is held for its investment potential, any rental income being negotiated at arm's length.

39.2   The following are exceptions from the definition:

(a)   A property which is owned and occupied by a company for its own purposes is not an investment property.

(b)   A property let to and occupied by another group company is not an investment property for the purposes of its own accounts or the group accounts.

GL 40   Liability

40.1   A liability is an obligation of an entity to transfer economic benefits which:

(a)   is expected to be settled by the entity parting with assets or in some way losing an economic benefit; and

(b)   results from past transactions or events; and

(c)   embodies a present duty or responsibility to one or more other entities that entails settlement at a specified or determinable future date, on the occurrence of a specified event, or on demand; and

(d)   results from a duty or responsibility which obligates the entity either legally, or practically (a constructive obligation), because it would be financially or otherwise operationally damaging to the entity not to discharge the duty or responsibility.

A moral obligation – such as results from the making of a non-contractual promise – does not create a liability unless it meets the definition above.

GL 41   Market Value

41.1   "Market Value" is the price at which an asset could be, or could be expected to be, sold or acquired in a public market between a willing buyer and willing seller. For traded securities in which there is an established market, the market value basis that is to be used in the valuation for the balance sheet is defined as the midpoint of the quotation in the Stock Exchange Daily Official List or at a similar recognised market value. For other assets it is the trustees' or valuers' best estimate of such a value.

GL 42   Material

42.1   Materiality is the final test of what information should be given in a particular set of accounts. An item of information is material to the accounts if its misstatement or omission might reasonably be expected to influence the economic decisions of users of those accounts, including their assessments of stewardship. Immaterial information will need to be excluded to avoid clutter which impairs the understandability of other information provided.

42.2   Whether information is material will depend on the size and nature of the item in question judged in the particular circumstances of the case. Materiality is not capable of general mathematical definition as it has both qualitative and quantitative aspects. The principal factors to be taken into account are set out below. It will usually be a combination of these factors, rather than any one in particular, that will determine materiality.

(a)   The item's size is judged in the context both of the accounts as a whole and of the other information available to users that would affect their evaluation of the accounts. This includes, for example, considering how the item affects the evaluation of trends and similar considerations.

(b)   Consideration is given to the item's nature in relation to:
(i)   the transactions or other events giving rise to it;
(ii)   the legality, sensitivity, normality and potential consequences of the event or transaction;
(iii) the identity of the parties involved; and
(iv)   the particular headings and disclosures that are affected.

42.3   If there are two or more similar items, the materiality of the items in aggregate as well as of the items individually needs to be considered.

42.4   Trustees are responsible for deciding whether an item is or is not material. In cases of doubt an item should be treated as material.

42.5   This process may result in different materiality considerations being applied depending on the aspect of the accounts being considered. For example, the expected degree of accuracy expected in the case of certain statutory disclosures e g trustees' remuneration, may make normal materiality considerations irrelevant.

GL 43   Operating and Financial Review

43.1   An operating and financial review (OFR) is a form of reporting currently adopted by many quoted companies and is designed to provide a balanced and comprehensive analysis of:

(a)   the development and performance of the business of the entity during the financial year;

(b)   the position of the entity at the end of the year;

(c)   the main trends and factors underlying the development, performance and position of the business of the entity during the financial year; and

(d)   the main trends and factors which are likely to affect their future development, performance and position, prepared so as to assist investors to assess the strategies adopted by the entity and the potential for those strategies to succeed.

43.2   The Accounting Standards Board withdrew Reporting Standard 1: Operating and Financial Review and reissued the contents as a statement of best practice Reporting Statement: Operating and Financial Review (OFR). There is currently no requirement for charities to prepare an operating and financial review although a number of this SORP's reporting recommendations for the content of the Trustees' Annual Report are consistent with OFR reporting.

GL 44   Parent Undertaking and Subsidiary Undertaking

44.1   In relation to a charity, an undertaking is the parent undertaking of another undertaking, called a subsidiary undertaking, where the charity controls the subsidiary. Control requires that the parent can both direct and derive benefit from the subsidiary.

(a)   Direction is achieved if the charity or its trustees:
(i)   hold or control the majority of the voting rights, or
(ii)   have the right to appoint or remove a majority of the board of directors or trustees of the subsidiary undertaking, or
(iii)   have the power to exercise, or actually exercise, a dominant influence over the subsidiary undertaking or
(iv)   manage the charity and the subsidiary on a unified basis.
For a fuller definition, reference should be made to sections 1161 and 1162 Companies Act 2006.

(b)   Benefit derived can either be economic benefit that results in a net cash inflow to the charity or can arise through the provision of goods or services to the benefit of the charity or its beneficiaries.

44.2   Paragraphs 381 to 406 explain how to account for subsidiary undertakings within the consolidated accounts of a parent undertaking. This includes the exemptions from consolidation and the particular circumstances in which a charity can be considered to be a subsidiary undertaking of another charity.

GL 45   Performance Related Grant

45.1 The term performance-related grant is used to describe a grant that has the characteristics of a contract in that:

(a)   the terms of the grant require the performance of a specified service that furthers the objectives of the grant maker; and

(b)   where payment of the grant receivable is conditional on a specified output being provided by the grant recipient.

GL 46   Pooling Scheme (see also GL 8)

46.1 A Pooling Scheme is a class of Common Investment Fund that provides for the pooling of investments belonging to two or more charities (which may be special trusts) which are administered by the same trustee body as the body managing the Pooling Scheme. Such schemes are referred to as Pool Charities and may be established with or without a formal scheme of the Charity Commission or the Courts.

GL 47   Programme Related Investments

47.1 Programme related investments (also known as social investments) are made directly in pursuit of the organisation's charitable purposes. Although they can generate some financial return (funding may or may not be provided on commercial terms), the primary motivation for making them is not financial but to further the objects of the funding charity. Such investments could include loans to individual beneficiaries (e g for housing deposits) or to other charities (for example, in relation to regeneration projects).

GL 48   Provision

48.1 A provision (as defined in FRS 12) is a liability of uncertain timing or amount. It is recognised when a charity has a present obligation (a legal or constructive obligation exists at the balance sheet date) as a result of a past event, it is probable that a transfer of economic benefits will be required to settle the obligation and the amount can be reliably estimated.

GL 49   Public Benefit Entity

49.1 The Accounting Standards Board's Interpretation for Public Benefit Entities of the Statement of Principles for Financial Reporting defines such entities as follows:

'Public benefit entities are reporting entities whose primary objective is to provide goods or services for the general public or social benefit and where any equity has been provided with a view to supporting that primary objective rather than with a view to providing a financial return to shareholders.'

GL 50 Related Parties

50.1 Related parties include all of the following:

(a) Any charity trustee and custodian trustee of the charity;

(b) Any person or body with:
   (i) either the power to appoint or remove a significant proportion of the charity trustees of the charity. All or a majority of the trustees should always be treated as a "significant proportion". Fewer than 50% of the trustees may be a "significant proportion" if they collectively have a dominant influence on the operation of the charity, as, for example, is likely to be the case if one body has the power to appoint/remove 7 of a body of 15 trustees, and 8 other different bodies had the right to appoint/remove 1 each,
   (ii) or whose consent is required to the exercise of any of the discretions of those trustees,
   (iii) or who is entitled to give directions to those trustees as to the exercise of any of those discretions.

(c) Any institution connected with the charity, and any director of such an institution. An institution is connected with a charity if either:
   (i) it is controlled by (in Scotland managed or controlled by) the charity. "Controlled" means that the charity is able to secure that the affairs of the institution are conducted in accordance with its wishes. A charity will control another if it is trustee of that charity or has power to appoint or remove a significant proportion of its trustees; or
   (ii) a participating interest in it is beneficially owned by the charity. "Participating interest" means that the charity:
      (a) is interested in shares comprised in the equity share capital of the body of a nominal value of more than one fifth of that share capital; or
      (b) is entitled to exercise or control the exercise of more than one-fifth of the voting power at any general meeting of that body.

(d) Any other charity with which it is commonly controlled. Common control exists if:
   (i) the same person, or persons have the right to appoint a majority of the charity trustees of both or all the charities; or
   (ii) the same person, or persons, hold a majority of the voting rights in the administration of both or all of the charities.

Persons who are related with each other through family or business relationships should be treated as the same person for the present purposes.

A charity is not necessarily related to another charity simply because a particular person happens to be a trustee of both. It will only be related if one charity subordinates its interests to the other charity in any transaction because of this relationship.

(e) Any pension fund for the benefit of:
   (i) the employees of the charity; and/or
   (ii) of any other person who is a related party of the charity.

(f)   Any officer, agent or employee of the charity having authority or responsibility for directing or controlling the major activities or resources of the charity; and

(g)   Any person connected to a person who is related to the charity including:
  (i)   members of the same family or household of the charity trustee or related person who may be expected to influence, or be influenced by, that person in their dealings with the charity;
  (ii)   the trustees of any trust, not being a charity, the beneficiaries or potential beneficiaries of which include a charity trustee or related person or a person referred to in (i) as being connected with a charity trustee or to a related person, as the case may be;
  (iii) any business partner of a charity trustee or related person, or of any person referred to in (i) or (ii) as being connected with a charity trustee or to a related person, as the case may be;
  (iv)   any body corporate, not being a company which is controlled entirely by one or more charitable institutions, in which:
    (a)   the charity trustee has, or the charity trustee and any other charity trustee or trustees or person or persons referred to in (i), (ii) or (iii) above as being connected with a charity trustee, taken together, have a participating interest; or
    (b)   the related person has, or the related person and any other related parties of the charity, taken together, have a participating interest.
  (v)   Any person or body who makes available to the charity the services of any person or body as a charity trustee is connected with a charity trustee.

GL 51   *Reserves*

51.1   The term "reserves" has a variety of technical and ordinary meanings, depending on the context in which it is used. In this SORP the term "reserves" (unless otherwise indicated) describes that part of a charity's income funds that is freely available.

51.2   This definition of reserves therefore normally excludes:

(a)   permanent endowment funds;

(b)   expendable endowment funds;

(c)   restricted funds;

and any part of unrestricted funds not readily available for spending, specifically:

(d)   income funds which could only be realised by disposing of fixed assets held for charity use and performance related investments.

51.3   Individual charities may have more or less reserves available to them than this simple calculation suggests for example:

(a)   expendable endowments may be readily available for spending; or

(b)   unrestricted funds may be earmarked or designated for essential future spending and reduce the amount readily available.

51.4 For further information, see the Charity Commission's publication CC19 on Charities' Reserves.

GL 52 Resources Expended

52.1 Resources expended means all costs incurred in the course of expending or utilising the charity's funds.

This includes all claims against the charity upon being recognised as liabilities by the trustees, as well as all accruals and payments made by the trustees of a charity, and all losses on the disposal of fixed assets (other than investments), together with all provisions for impairment of tangible fixed assets or programme related investments.

52.2 This is to be distinguished from total expenditure (see GL 55 below).

GL 53 Restricted Fund

53.1 See Appendix 3 (App 3.2).

GL 54 Support Costs

54.1 Support costs are those costs that, whilst necessary to deliver an activity, do not themselves produce or constitute the output of the charitable activity. Similarly, costs will be incurred in supporting income generation activities such as fundraising, and in supporting the governance of the charity. Support costs include the central or regional office functions such as general management, payroll administration, budgeting and accounting, information technology, human resources, and financing.

GL 55 Total Expenditure

55.1 Total expenditure was a term used within the Charities Act 1993 to determine the thresholds that govern the requirements (in England and Wales) for accounts scrutiny, submission of reports, accounts and an annual return to the Charity Commission. For accounting periods beginning on or after 27 February 2007, the criterion of total expenditure is no longer used.

GL 56 Total Return Approach to Investment

56.1 The total return approach to investment management allows trustees to manage investments without the need to take account of whether the return is income (dividends, interest, etc.) or capital gains and losses. Normally a total return approach cannot be adopted in relation to permanent endowment funds, though the Charity Commission can enable this for charities in England and Wales. Further details are given in Appendix 3 (paragraph 3(g)).

GL 57 Trading

57.1 In a strict legal sense, trading activities are those carried out under contract, whether at the point of sale or otherwise, where goods and services are provided in return for consideration for those goods or services. Normally, trading activities are carried out on a regular basis with a view to making profits, though it is possible that some one-off activities could be regarded as trading.

57.2 However, in an economic sense, trading can be regarded as the provision of goods and services in return for a payment whether or not this payment is in fact under contract. Therefore, certain incoming grants which are, in a legal sense, donations, but which have specific terms attached to them such that a charity becomes entitled to the payment on the provision of specified goods or services, are in the context of this SORP recognised on the same basis as trading income (see Performance Related Grant: GL 45). This is because the charity has an obligation to provide the specific services or goods in the same way that it would have to provide them under contract. If it fails to provide the goods or services then, if the funds are by way of grant, this will be a breach of trust, but if they are by way of contract, this will be by way of breach of contract. The legal remedies of the funding body are different depending upon the circumstances.

57.3 Similarly, the sale of donated goods is in a legal sense regarded as the realisation of a donation. However, in the context of this SORP it is regarded as trading, and recognised as an activity for generating funds (See paragraph 137), because it is so similar to the sale of bought in goods as to be indistinguishable in the actual processes involved except for the legal distinction.

57.4 For income, corporation and value added tax purposes trading must be interpreted within the meaning of the legislation governing those taxes.

GL 58   Trustees

58.1 Has the same meaning as charity trustees.

GL 59   Trustee for a Charity

59.1 "Trustee for a charity" means any person (other than the charity itself, or a charity trustee of the charity) who holds the title to property belonging to the charity, and so includes a custodian trustee and a nominee.

GL 60   Unrestricted Fund

60.1 See Appendix 3 (App 3.1).

GL 61   Voluntary Income

61.1 Voluntary income comprises gifts that will not normally provide any return to the donor other than the knowledge that someone will benefit from the donation. They will thus exclude any gifts that are quasi-contractual (in that a certain service to a certain level must be provided) but they would include gifts that must be spent on some particular area of work (ie restricted funds) or given to be held as endowment. Voluntary income will normally include gifts in kind and donated services, for example gifts in kind as part of an international aid programme.

Glossary of terms relating to Pension Scheme Accounting under FRS 17

The following definitions are specifically needed to understand pension scheme accounting. Where definitions are more generally applicable they are included in the main glossary above.

GL 62   (Pensions) Actuarial gains and losses

62.1   See definition GL 2 in the main glossary.

GL 63   (Pensions) Current service costs

63.1   The increase in the present value of scheme liabilities expected to arise from employee service in the current period.

GL 64   (Pensions) Curtailment

64.1   An event reducing the expected years of future service of present employees or reducing for a number of employees the accrual of defined benefits for future years service, e g early termination of employees' services or termination or amendment of scheme terms affecting benefits accrued by future service.

GL 65   (Pensions) Defined benefit pension scheme

65.1   See definition GL 16 in the main glossary.

GL 66   (Pensions) Defined contribution pension scheme

66.1   See definition GL 17 in the main glossary.

GL 67   (Pensions) Expected rate of return on assets

67.1   Average rate of return, including income and changes in fair value but net of expenses, expected over the remaining life of the related obligation on the assets held by the scheme.

GL 68   (Pensions) Interest cost

68.1   The expected increase during the period in the present value of the scheme liabilities because the benefits are one period closer to settlement.

GL 69   (Pensions) Multi-employer pension scheme

69.1   This is a defined contribution pension scheme or a defined benefit pension scheme where more than one employer participates.

GL 70   (Pensions) Past service cost

70.1   The increase in the present value of scheme liabilities relating to employee service in prior periods arising in the current period as a result of the introduction of, or improvements to, retirement benefits.

GL 71   *(Pensions) Projected unit method*

71.1   An accrued benefits valuation method in which the scheme liabilities make allowance for projected earnings. An accrued benefits valuation method is a valuation method in which the scheme liabilities at the valuation date relate to:

(a)   the benefits for pensioners and deferred pensioners (ie individuals who have ceased to be active members but are entitled to benefits payable at a later date) and their dependants, allowing where appropriate for future increases, and

(b)   the accrued benefits for members in service on the valuation date.

The accrued benefits are the benefits for service up to a given point in time, whether vested rights or not.

GL 72   *(Pensions) Retirement benefit*

72.1   All forms of consideration given by an employer in exchange for services rendered by employees that are payable after the completion of employment.

GL 73   *(Pensions) Scheme liabilities*

73.1   The liabilities of a defined benefit scheme for outgoings due after the valuation date.

GL 74   *(Pensions) Settlement*

74.1   An irrevocable action that relieves the employer (or the defined benefit scheme) of the primary responsibility for a pension obligation and eliminates significant risks relating to the obligation and the assets used to effect the settlement. For example, the payment of a lump sum in exchange for surrender of rights, the purchase of an annuity to cover benefits, or the transfer of scheme assets and liabilities relating to employees leaving the scheme.

APPENDIX 2: APPLICATION OF ACCOUNTING STANDARDS

App 2.1   Accounting standards are developed in the UK by the Accounting Standards Board and are referred to as Financial Reporting Standards (FRSs). Accounting standards developed by its predecessor body the Accounting Standards Committee and adopted by the ASB continue to be known as Statements of Standard Accounting Practice or SSAPs. Accounting standards are authoritative statements of how particular types of transaction and other events should be reflected in accounts and accordingly compliance with accounting standards will normally be necessary for accounts to give a true and fair view. Accounting standards need not be applied to immaterial items. In applying accounting standards it is important to be guided by the spirit and reasoning behind them.

App 2.2   The main role of the Urgent Issues Task Force (UITF) is to assist the ASB with important or significant accounting issues where unsatisfactory or conflicting interpretations of standards have developed. UITF Abstracts apply where accounts are intended to give a true and fair view. They should be regarded as part of the body of practices forming the basis for determining what constitutes a true and fair view and should be read in conjunction with accounting standards. UITF Abstracts need not be applied to immaterial items. As with accounting standards it is important when applying UITF Abstracts to be guided by the spirit and reasoning behind them.

App 2.3 Subsequent to the consultation on this SORP, in December 2004 the Accounting Standards Board issued five new accounting standards (FRS 22 to FRS 26) as part of its strategy for convergence with International Financial Reporting Standards. In addition FRS 2: Accounting for Subsidiary Undertakings has been amended to reflect changes to the Companies Act 1985 (now section 1162 of the Companies Act 2006) and a new standard, FRS 27: Life Assurance, applying to life insurance businesses, was issued.

App 2.4 The following table includes a brief summary of these new standards. Four of these standards will become fully mandatory for charities who adopt fair value measurement rules (unless the FRSSE is applied) for accounting periods beginning on or after 1 January 2006. Where allowed by the relevant standard, charities may adopt them early, and where charities so do, reference should be made directly to the relevant standard. The presentational requirements of FRS 25 Financial Instruments: Disclosure and Presentation apply to charities for accounting periods beginning on or after 1 January 2005. Although charities are unlikely to issue equity, this standard will also be relevant in determining the classification of liabilities based on the substance of the arrangement.

App 2.5 The following table provides a summary of the accounting standards and Urgent Issues Task Force abstracts extant at the date of issue of this SORP and their applicability to charities. The standards should only be applied in so far as they are relevant to activities being carried out by an individual charity. Where this is the case the summaries below should not be relied upon as a substitute for reading the full text of the standard.

Statements of Standard Accounting Practice (SSAPs)

SSAP 4 Accounting Treatment of Government Grants	SSAP 4 deals with the accounting treatment and disclosure of government grants and other forms of government assistance, including grants, equity finance, subsidised loans and advisory assistance. It is also indicative of best practice for accounting for grants and assistance from other sources.	A gift of a tangible fixed asset (or grant to purchase) is recognised in full with the recipient charity's entitlement to the asset. Any restriction on the asset's future use is recognised by allocating the asset to a restricted fund rather than deferring the recognition of the asset. Any residual liability to the donor arising from, for example, the asset's future sale, is disclosed as a contingent liability unless the event that would trigger repayment of the grant becomes probable in which case a liability for repayment is recognised.
		This SORP provides the most appropriate interpretation of SSAP 4 for charities. In particular, grants for fixed assets should not be deferred though normally they will have to be accounted for in a separate fund (see paragraph 111).

SSAP 5 Accounting For Value Added Tax (VAT)	SSAP 5 follows the general principle that the treatment of VAT in the accounts should reflect an entity's role as a collector of the tax and VAT should not be included in income or in expenditure whether of a capital or revenue nature. However, where the VAT is irrecoverable, it should be included in the cost of the items reported in the financial statements.	Many if not all charities will suffer irrecoverable VAT either because they are not registered or have a mixture of activities which are zero and standard rated, exempt and outside the scope of VAT. The irrecoverable tax should be included in the relevant cost headings on the face of the Statement of Financial Activities and not shown as a separate item though separate disclosure of the amount may be made in the notes to the accounts.
SSAP 9 Stocks and Long-term Contracts	SSAP 9 gives guidance on the values to be included in the balance sheet of stocks and long-term contracts and the criteria for recognition of income and expenditure on such items within the profit and loss account (Statement of Financial Activities for charities).	Equally applicable to charities as to other entities.
SSAP 13 Accounting for Research and Development	SSAP 13 provides guidance on three broad categories of activity, namely pure research, applied research and development. The standard defines these categories and specifies the accounting policies that may be followed for each.	Equally applicable to charities as to other entities.
SSAP 17 Accounting for Post Balance Sheet Events	SSAP 17 defines the period for post balance sheet events and describes the accounting treatment for adjusting and non-adjusting events. Adjusting events are those which provide additional evidence of conditions existing at the balance sheet date. Non-adjusting events are those which concern conditions that did not exist at the balance sheet date. SSAP 17 has been replaced by FRS 21 for accounting periods beginning on or after 1 January 2005	Equally applicable to charities as to other entities.
SSAP 19 Accounting for Investment Properties	SSAP 19 requires investment properties to be included in the balance sheet at their open market value, but without charging depreciation.	Equally applicable to charities as to other entities.
SSAP 20 Foreign Currency Translation	SSAP 20 generally requires, in individual financial statements, that each transaction should be translated into the entity's local currency using the exchange rate in operation at the date of the transaction. In consolidated accounts the standard allows two alternative methods of translation of a foreign entity's financial statements, depending on whether the enterprise is a separate quasi-independent entity, or a direct extension of the trade of the investing entity. See also FRS 23 and FRS 24.	Generally applicable to charities entering directly into transactions overseas or with branches or subsidiaries overseas. Gains should be recorded as other income in the Statement of Financial Activities and losses as a support cost of the relevant activity category. Where the standard permits gains and losses to be taken to reserves, these should be shown as a separate row in the Statement of Financial Activities after "net incoming/outgoing resources."

Statements of Standard Accounting Practice (SSAPs)

SSAP 21 Accounting for Leases and Hire Purchase Contracts	SSAP 21 describes how to identify and account for finance leases, operating leases and hire purchase contracts both for the lessee and the lessor.	Equally applicable to charities as to other entities.
SSAP 25 Segmental Reporting	SSAP 25 requires the disclosure by class of business and by geographical segment of turnover, segment result and segment net assets. The turnover disclosure is required by all companies otherwise the disclosure is mandatory only for PLCs, banking and insurance companies and those over ten times the threshold for medium sized companies.	This will only be applicable to the largest charities. The disclosure requirements in the SORP for details of activities by function meets the spirit of SSAP 25 for turnover by class of activity. The disclosure by geographical region and segment net assets would be additional.

Financial Reporting Standards (FRSs)

FRS 1 Cash Flow Statements (Revised 1996)	FRS 1 (Revised 1996) requires reporting entities within its scope (from 6 April 2008 where two of £6.5m gross turnover; £3.26m gross assets; 50 employees) to prepare a cash flow statement in the manner set out in the FRS.	Paragraphs 351 to 355 explain the applicability of FRS 1 to charities.
FRS 2 Accounting for Subsidiary Undertakings	FRS 2 sets out the conditions under which an entity qualifies as a parent undertaking which should prepare consolidated financial statements for its group, the parent and its subsidiaries. It also sets out the manner in which consolidated financial statements are to be prepared.	Paragraphs 381 to 397 explain consolidation and the applicability of FRS 2 to charities.
FRS 3 Reporting Financial Performance	FRS 3 requires a layered format for the profit and loss (income and expenditure) account split between continuing, newly acquired and discontinued operations. It has effectively outlawed extraordinary items. The standard also requires a statement of total recognised gains and losses to be shown as a primary statement. A note of historical profits, which is a memorandum item, is also required as is the disclosure of earnings per share.	The Statement of Financial Activities combines both the income and expenditure account and the statement of total recognised gains and losses and meets charity law. Exceptional items should be disclosed on a separate row within the activity to which they relate. The additional requirements for charitable companies are explained in paragraphs 423 to 426. Earnings per share is not relevant to charities.
FRS 4 Capital Instruments	FRS 4 requires capital instruments to be presented in financial statements in a way that reflects the obligations of the issuer and the impact on shareholders equity. Most parts of this standard are superseded by FRS 25.	Not generally applicable to charities following this SORP

Financial Reporting Standards (FRSs)

FRS 5 Reporting the Substance of Transactions	FRS 5 requires that the substance of an entity's transactions is reported in its financial statements. This requires that the commercial effect of a transaction and any resulting assets, liabilities, gains and losses are shown and that the accounts do not merely report the legal form of a transaction.	Equally applicable to charities as to other entities.
FRS 6 Accounting For Acquisitions and Mergers	FRS 6 sets out the circumstances in which the two methods of accounting for a business combination (acquisition accounting and merger accounting) are to be used. The FRS sets out five criteria that must be met for merger accounting to be used. If they are not met then acquisition accounting should be used.	The principles of merger accounting are applicable to charities where two or more charities merge. However where funds are merely transferred from one charity to another this may constitute a gift or in the case of a restricted fund simply the administrative transfer of the restricted fund from one set of trustees to another. Two of the five criteria apply to shareholders funds and so will not be applicable to charities. Charities cannot merge with non-charitable companies and so acquisition accounting will have to be used where such companies are acquired.
FRS 7 Fair Values in Acquisition Accounting	FRS 7 sets out the principles of accounting for a business combination under the acquisition method of accounting. It explains what "identifiable assets and liabilities" means and how to determine their fair values. The difference between the sum of these fair values and the cost of acquisition is recognised as goodwill or negative goodwill.	Equally applicable to charities as to other entities where acquisition accounting is used.
FRS 8 Related Party Disclosures	FRS 8 determines who and what are "related parties" and the disclosures necessary to draw attention to the possibility that the reported financial position and results may have been affected by the existence of related parties and by material transactions with them.	Paragraphs 221 to 233 explain the application of FRS 8 with respect to charities.
FRS 9 Associates and Joint Ventures	FRS 9 sets out the definitions and accounting treatments for associates and joint ventures, two types of interests that a reporting entity may have in other entities. The FRS also deals with joint arrangements that are not entities.	Paragraphs 407 to 418 explain the applicability of FRS 9 to charities.
FRS 10 Goodwill and Intangible Assets.	FRS 10 requires purchased goodwill and intangible fixed assets (where marketable) to be capitalised on the balance sheet and amortised over their life, normally regarded as 20 years, subject to impairment reviews.	FRS 10 covers common occurrences of goodwill and intangible assets. Where a charity has an intangible asset which does not meet the criteria under the standard it should not be included in the primary statements but details of the asset and its financial effect should be disclosed in the notes to the accounts.

Financial Reporting Standards (FRSs)

FRS 11 Impairment of Fixed Assets and Goodwill	FRS 11 sets out the principles and methodology for accounting for impairments of fixed assets and goodwill. The carrying amount of an asset is compared with its recoverable amount and, if the carrying amount is higher, the asset is written down. Recoverable amount is defined as the higher of the amount that could be obtained by selling the asset (net realisable value) and the amount that could be obtained through using the asset (value in use). Impairment tests are only required when there has been some indication that an impairment has occurred.	Paragraphs 267 to 272 explain the applicability of FRS 11 to charities.
FRS 12 Provisions, Contingent Liabilities and Contingent Assets.	FRS 12 describes the circumstances in which a provision (a liability that is of uncertain timing or amount) may arise and how it should be measured and recognised in the financial statements. It also describes how to account for contingent assets and liabilities.	FRS 12 is generally applicable to charities. Paragraphs 148 to 163 and 321 to 329 describe some particular application points to charities.
FRS 13 Derivatives and other Financial Instruments	The Financial Reporting Standard on derivatives (FRS 13) must be followed by a reporting entity that has any of its capital instruments listed or publicly traded on a stock exchange or market. A capital instrument is an instrument issued by a reporting entity as a means of raising finance and includes shares, debentures, loans and debt instruments. The FRS is therefore neither applicable to nor designed for charities.	Although FRS 13 is not applicable to charities, much of what would need to be disclosed is required in the SORP. In particular: <ul><li>Amongst the requirements of the FRS are those to disclose details of financial assets and liabilities, which can include most current assets and current liabilities, investments and derivatives. Disclosure of all these items is required by the SORP.</li><li>FRS 13 requires disclosure of the financial risk profile of the entity. Disclosure of risks, including financial risk, is required in the Trustees' Annual Report as part of the general disclosure on risk.</li><li>The FRS also requires an explanation of derivatives in particular and this is also required in the SORP.</li><li>The SORP also indicates that the notes to the accounts should disclose what derivative products are in use by the charity and the role that financial instruments play in creating or changing the risks that the entity faces in its activities. (see paragraphs 337 to 339).</li></ul>
FRS 14 Earnings Per Share	This is superseded by FRS 21 for accounting periods beginning on or after 1/1/2005	Not applicable to charities.

Financial Reporting Standards (FRSs)

FRS 15 Tangible Fixed Assets	FRS 15 sets out the principles of accounting for tangible fixed assets, with the exception of investment properties. In principle all fixed assets should be capitalised at cost or at revalued amount. However, where an enterprise chooses to adopt a policy of revaluing some assets, all assets of the same class must be revalued and the valuations kept up to date.	The principles of FRS 15 are generally applicable to charities and are embodied in the balance sheet section of this SORP. However, there are relaxed criteria for the valuations of charity assets and certain heritage assets need not be capitalised in certain circumstances as explained in paragraphs 279 to 294. As noted in paragraph 265 and 266 where a charity adopts a policy of revaluation of tangible fixed assets, the SORP allows in the case of land and buildings such valuations to be undertaken by a suitably qualified trustee or employee.
FRS 16 Current Tax		FRS 16 is generally not applicable to charities. However, the government have paid compensation payments to charities for 5 years from April 1999 for the removal of ACT credits on the payment of UK dividends. These payments should be included as part of a charity's investment income.

FRS 17 Retirement Benefits	FRS 17 sets out the accounting treatment for retirement benefits such as pensions and medical care during retirement. On the full implementation of the standard the main requirements are:
	
	(a) pension assets are measured using fair values,
	
	(b) pension scheme liabilities are measured using the projected unit method and discounted using the current rate of return on a high quality corporate bond of equivalent term and currency to the liabilities,
	
	(c) the pension scheme surplus (to the extent it can be recovered) or deficit is recognised on the balance sheet,
	
	(d) the movement in the scheme surplus/deficit is analysed into:
	
	  • the current service cost and any past service cost, recognized in operating profit,
	
	  • the interest cost and expected return on assets, recognised as other finance costs, and
	
	  • actuarial gains and losses recognised in the statement of total recognised gains and losses.
	
	FRS 17 (As amended in November 2002) includes the following transitional arrangements:
		Equally applicable to charities. Specific guidance on the application of the standard is given in the special section beginning at paragraph 430

Financial Reporting Standards (FRSs)

(a) For accounting periods ending on or after 22 June 2001, closing balance sheet information (no comparatives required) is to be given in the notes only.

(b) For accounting periods ending on or after 22 June 2002, opening and closing balance sheet information and performance statement information for the period (no comparatives required) is to be given in the notes only.

(c) For accounting periods beginning on or after 1 January 2005, the standard is fully effective.

FRS 18 Accounting Policies

FRS 18 sets out the principles to be followed in selecting accounting policies and the disclosures needed to help users to understand the accounting policies adopted and how they have been applied. Its objective is to ensure that:

- an entity adopts the accounting policies most appropriate to its particular circumstances for the purposes of giving a true and fair view;

- the accounting policies adopted are reviewed regularly to ensure that they remain appropriate, and are changed when a new policy becomes more appropriate to the entity's particular circumstances; and

- sufficient information is disclosed in the financial statements to enable users to understand the accounting policies adopted and how they have been implemented.

It requires disclosure of the extent to which financial statements comply with any relevant SORP. Where an entity's financial statements fall within the scope of a SORP, the entity should state the title of the SORP and whether its financial statements have been prepared in accordance with the SORP's provisions currently in effect. In the event of a departure, the entity should give a brief description of the departure from recommended practice, the reasons why the treatment adopted is judged more appropriate, details of any disclosures recommended by the SORP that have not been provided and the reasons why they have not been provided.

Equally applicable to charities as other entities. The disclosure of compliance with any relevant SORP has particular relevance in the context of the charity sector where adherence to this SORP is expected.

The implementation of this SORP may involve the analysis and presentation of incoming resources and resources expended across different SoFA categories and the allocation of support costs to activity categories within the SoFA. The SoFA for the preceding period should be restated to ensure consistent presentation.

Although this SORP does not change the basis of asset and liability recognition, it does provide more detailed guidance on the recognition of performance related grants which may result in some charities amending their accounting policies and where the effect of such a policy change is material, a restatement of comparative amounts will be necessary.

The appropriateness of accounting policies adopted are judged against the objectives of:

(a)   relevance,

(b)   reliability,

(c)   comparability, and

(d)   understandability.

FRS 19 Deferred Tax	FRS 19 requires full provision to be made for deferred tax assets and liabilities arising from timing differences between the recognition of gains and losses in the financial statements and their recognition in a tax computation. The general principle underlying the requirements is that deferred tax should be recognised as a liability or asset if the transactions or events that give the entity an obligation to pay more tax in the future or the right to pay less tax in the future have occurred at the balance sheet date.	Not generally applicable to charities due to tax exemptions available. However the standard will be of relevance in consolidated accounts that include non-charitable subsidiaries particularly those that adopt a policy of full or partial profits retention rather than full distribution of taxable profits through gift aid provisions. Where it is a subsidiary's practice to make a gift aid payment of all of its taxable profits to its parent charity, subsequent to its reporting year end, which qualifies for tax relief in that earlier period a provision for deferred tax is unlikely to be necessary.
FRS 20 Share-based Payments		Not applicable to charities
FRS 21 (IAS 10) Post Balance sheet event's	FRS 21 sets out the recognition and measurement requirements for two types of event after the balance sheet date: • Those that provide evidence of conditions that existed at the balance sheet date for which the entity shall adjust the amounts recognised in its financial statements or recognise items that were not previously recognised (adjusting events). For example, the settlement of a court case that confirms the entity had a present obligation at the balance sheet date. • Those that are indicative of conditions that arose after the balance sheet date for which the entity does not adjust the amounts recognised in its financial statements (non-adjusting events). For example, a decline in market value of investments between the balance sheet date and the date when the financial statements are authorised for issue. FRS 21 applies for accounting periods beginning on or after 1 January 2005	Equally applicable to charities as other entities. The determination after the balance sheet date of the amount of a gift aid payment to a parent charity by a subsidiary undertaking is an adjusting event, if the subsidiary had a present legal (eg. a deed) or a constructive obligation at the balance sheet date. Where a present obligation is demonstrable at the year end, an adjustment is made where post balance sheet calculations provide greater accuracy in the measurement of the existing liability e g to equate the gift aid liability more closely to taxable profits. Designations reflect intentions as to the future application of funds held at a particular balance sheet date and do not reflect an external transaction or present obligation to a third party. As such they fall outside the scope of FRS 21. However, the spirit and reasoning behind the standard would suggest that charities would designate for future projects or plans envisaged at the balance sheet date and adjust such estimates to accord with any more accurate information that became available after the year end.
FRS 22 (IAS 33) Earnings per share	This standard only applies to entities whose ordinary shares are traded or in the process of issuing such shares.	Not Applicable to Charities

Financial Reporting Standards (FRSs)

	This standard supersedes FRS 14 for accounting periods beginning on or after 1 January 2005.	
FRS 23 (IAS 21) The Effects of Changes of Foreign Exchange Rates	An entity may carry on foreign activities in two ways. It may have transactions in foreign currencies or it may have foreign operations. In addition, an entity may present its financial statements in a foreign currency. This standard prescribes how entities should include foreign currency transactions and foreign operations in their financial statements and how they should translate financial statements into a presentation currency.	Applicable to charities that are applying FRS 26.
	The standard applies to entities applying FRS 26, In effect this means listed entities are required to apply the standard for accounting periods beginning on or after 1 January 2005 and unlisted entities preparing their accounts in accordance with the fair value accounting rules set out in the Companies Act 1985 will be required to adopt it for accounting periods beginning on or after 1 January 2006.	
	This standard replaces the requirements set out in SSAP 20 from when the new standard is applied.	
FRS 24 (IAS 29) Financial Reporting in Hyperinflationary economies	FRS 24 prescribes how an entity whose functional currency is the currency of a hyperinflationary economy should report its operating results and financial position. It also provides guidance on determining whether an economy is a hyperinflationary economy.	Will not apply to charities unless the functional currency in which they report is subject to hyperinflation and FRS 26 has been adopted.
	The standard applies to entities applying FRS 26. In effect, this means listed entities are required to apply the standard for accounting periods beginning on or after 1 January 2005 and unlisted entities preparing their accounts in accordance with the fair value accounting rules set out in the Companies Act 1985 will be required to adopt it for accounting periods beginning on or after 1 January 2006.	
	Where this standard is applied it replaces UITF 9.	
FRS 25 (IAS 32) Financial Instruments: Disclosure and Presentation	The objective of FRS 25 is to enhance the understanding of users of accounts of the significance of financial instruments to an entity's financial position, performance and cash flow.	Presentational requirements apply to charities for accounting periods beginning on or after 1 January 2005.

	The presentation requirements of this standard deal with the classification of capital instruments issued between debt and equity and the implications of that classification for dividends and interest expense. The presentational disclosures required by the standard apply to accounting periods beginning on or after 1 January 2005 with earlier adoption not being permitted. The disclosure requirements apply to entities applying FRS 26 only. In effect this means listed entities are required to apply the standard for accounting periods beginning on or after 1 January 2005 and unlisted entities preparing their accounts in accordance with the fair value accounting rules set out in the Companies Act 1985 will be required to adopt it for accounting periods beginning on or after 1 January 2006.	Disclosure requirements apply to charities that are applying FRS 26.
FRS 26 (IAS 39) Financial Instruments: Measurement	This standard introduces for the first time requirements for the measurement of financial instruments. It implements in full the measurement and hedge accounting provisions of IAS 39 as published by the International Accounting Standards Board. This standard applies to listed entities for accounting periods beginning on or after 1 January 2005. Unlisted entities preparing accounts in accordance with fair value accounting rules set out in the Companies Act 1985 are required to apply the standard for accounting periods beginning on or after 1 January 2006 and may voluntarily apply it for accounting periods beginning on or after 1 January 2005.	Applicable to charities that are companies and adopt an accounting policy that measures financial instruments at fair value for accounting periods beginning on or after 1 January 2006.
FRS 27 Life Assurance	FRS 27 applies to all entities with a life assurance business (including a life reinsurance business), and is effective for accounting periods ending on or after 23 December 2005, except that some smaller friendly societies are exempt until 2006 or 2007.	Will only apply to charities in the even of them undertaking life insurance business.

Financial Reporting Standards (FRSs)

FRSSE Financial Reporting Standard for Smaller Entities	The FRSSE brings together the relevant accounting requirements and disclosures from the other accounting standards and UITF abstracts, simplified and modified as appropriate for smaller entities. The FRSSE is an optional standard but entities adopting it are exempt from applying all the other accounting standards and UITF abstracts. Financial reporting is continually evolving and therefore the FRSSE needs to be updated, roughly on an annual basis, to reflect new or revised accounting standards and UITF abstracts.	Paragraphs 5.2.1 to 5.2.2 in Appendix 5 explain the applicability of the FRSSE to smaller charities. Whilst it can be followed there are certain principles and notes within this SORP which apply to all charities and should be included in the accounts.

Urgent Issues Task Force (UITF) Abstracts

UITF Abstract 4 Presentation of long-term debtors in current assets	Such items should be separately disclosed on the face of the balance sheet or in the notes to the accounts.	Equally applicable to charities as to other entities.
UITF Abstract 5 Transfers from current assets to fixed assets		Applicable in principle to charities but unlikely to arise in practice.
UITF Abstract 9 Accounting for operations in hyper-inflationary economies	See also FRS 24.	Only applicable to charities which operate in countries where such conditions exist.
UITF Abstract 11 Capital instruments: issue call options	See also FRS 25 and FRS 26	Not generally applicable to charities.
UITF Abstract 15 Disclosure of substantial acquisitions		Not applicable to charities.
UITF Abstract 17 Employee share schemes		Not applicable to charities.
UITF Abstract 18 Pensions costs following the 1997 tax changes in respect of dividend income (to be replaced by FRED 20)	The probable reduction in actuarial value as a result of pension schemes no longer being able to claim tax credits on dividends should be spread over the remaining service lives of current employees in line with SSAP 24.	Equally applicable to charities as to other entities.
UITF Abstract 19 Tax on gains and losses on foreign currency borrowings that hedge an investment in a foreign enterprise		Not generally applicable to charities.
UITF Abstract 21 Accounting issues arising from the proposed introduction of the Euro		Generally applicable to charities though it will have limited impact unless the UK adopts the Euro.

Urgent Issues Task Force (UITF) Abstracts		
UITF Abstract 22 The acquisition of a Lloyd's business		Not applicable to charities.
UITF Abstract 23 Application of the transitional rules in FRS 15	Provides transitional rules on the use of prior period adjustments where tangible fixed assets which were previously treated as a single asset are identified as having two or more major components with substantially different useful economic lives.	Equally applicable to charities as to other entities.
UITF Abstract 24 Accounting for Start-up Costs	Addresses whether start-up costs that cannot be included within the cost of a fixed asset may nevertheless be carried forward. Start-up costs that do not meet the recognition criteria under relevant accounting standards should not be carried forward, but recognised as an expense when incurred.	Equally applicable to charities as to other entities.
UITF Abstract 25 National Insurance contributions on share option gains		Not applicable to charities.
UITF Abstract 26 Barter transaction for advertising	An entity involved in publishing or broadcasting may agree to provide advertising in exchange for advertising services provided by its customers, rather than for cash consideration. Income from advertising undertaken on such a barter basis is only recognised where persuasive evidence exists that the advertising opportunity could have been sold for an equivalent sum of cash.	Equally applicable to charities as to other entities.
UITF Abstract 27 Revisions to estimates of useful economic lives of goodwill and intangible assets	This abstract states that a change from non-amortisation of goodwill or intangible assets, on the grounds that the life of the asset is indefinite, to amortisation over a period of 20 years or less, should not be reported as a change in accounting policy. In such a circumstance, the carrying amount of the goodwill or intangible asset should be amortised over the revised remaining useful life.	Goodwill rarely arises in the context of charity accounts; the treatment of intangible assets applies equally to charities as to other entities.
UITF Abstract 28 Operating lease incentives	A lessor may provide an incentive for the lessee to enter into a new or renewed operating lease. It requires that the relevant income or expense be recognised over the life of the asset, or until a market rent will be payable, on a straight-line basis unless another systematic basis is more representative of benefit flows.	Equally applicable to charities as other entities.

**Urgent Issues Task Force
(UITF) Abstracts**

UITF Abstract 29 Website development costs	Websites are used for a variety of activities, including promotion of services and goods, taking orders and provision of information. Many entities incur significant costs in developing such websites. Certain website development costs may be capitalised only where they lead to the creation of an enduring asset delivering benefits at least as great as the amount capitalised.	Generally applicable to charities. Charities' websites may however also provide economic benefit without being related to cash flow, for example, the provision of educational information to beneficiaries of the charity. To the extent that the relationship to such benefits is sufficiently certain such costs may be capitalised.
UITF Abstract 30 Date of award to employees of shares or rights to shares		Not applicable to charities.
UITF Abstract 31 Exchanges of businesses or other non-monetary assets for an interest in a subsidiary, joint venture or associate.	Entities may transfer businesses or other non-monetary assets in exchange for equity in a subsidiary, joint venture or associate. This abstract deals with accounting for such transactions in consolidated accounts, in particular issues surrounding reporting the transaction at fair values or book values.	Equally applicable to charities as other entities.
UITF Abstract 32 Employee benefit trusts and other intermediate payment arrangements	This abstract applies when an entity sets up and transfers funds to an employee benefit trust (or other intermediary) and the trust's accumulated assets are used to remunerate the entity's employees (or other service providers). The abstract clarifies how the principles for FRS 5 – Reporting the Substance of Transactions should be applied.	Not generally applicable to charities.
UITF Abstract 33 Obligations in capital instruments	This abstract deals with the classification of capital instruments. A capital instrument, other than a share, which involves an obligation to transfer economic benefits will be treated as a liability in the single entity financial statements of the issuer unless that obligation would not be considered in accordance with the going concern concept. See also FRS 25 and FRS 26.	Equally applicable to charities as other entities.
UITF Abstract 34 Pre-contract costs	This abstract is intended to bring consistency to the treatment of costs incurred in bidding for and securing contracts to supply products or services. It requires costs incurred before it is virtually certain that a contract will be obtained to be charged immediately as expenses. Directly attributable costs incurred after that point should be recognised as an asset and charged as expenses during the period of the contract.	Equally applicable to charities as other entities.

Urgent Issues Task Force (UITF) Abstracts

UITF Abstract 35 **Death-in-service and** **incapacity benefits**	This Abstract clarifies the accounting required by FRS 17 'Retirement Benefits' for the cost of death-in-service and incapacity benefits, where such benefits are provided through a defined benefit pension scheme. The Abstract requires that, where the benefits are not wholly insured, the uninsured scheme liability and the cost for the accounting period should be measured, in line with other retirement benefits, using the projected unit method. The effect is that the valuation of uninsured benefits reflects the current period's portion of the full benefits ultimately payable in respect of current members of the scheme; the cost of insured benefits is determined by the relevant insurance premiums.	Equally applicable to charities as other entities.
UITF Abstract 36 **Contracts for sales of** **capacity**	Entities in some industries (such as telecommunications and electricity) sell rights to use capacity on their networks, sometimes entering into exchange or reciprocal transactions ('capacity swaps'). This Abstract sets out the limited circumstances under which transactions in capacity should be reported as sales, and the proceeds reported as turnover.	Not generally applicable to charities.
UITF Abstract 37 **Purchase and sale of own** **shares**	See also FRS 25 and FRS 26.	Not applicable to charities.
UITF Abstract 38 **Accounting for ESOP** **Trusts**		Not applicable to charities.

APPENDIX 3: THE FUNDS OF A CHARITY

The purpose of this appendix is to explain the legal position as regards the various funds of a charity and the implications this has for the way in which the funds are accounted for.

App 3.1 Unrestricted Funds (including designated funds)

1(a) Unrestricted funds are expendable at the discretion of the trustees in furtherance of the charity's objects. If part of an unrestricted fund is earmarked for a particular project it may be designated as a separate fund, but the designation has an administrative purpose only, and does not legally restrict the trustees' discretion to apply the fund. Some trustees have power to declare specific trusts over unrestricted funds. If such a power is available and is exercised, the assets affected will form a restricted fund, and the trustees' discretion to apply the fund will be legally restricted.

1(b) Whether or not trustees have the power to create restricted funds by declaring a trust, unrestricted funds can be spent on the same purposes as restricted funds, for example by spending more on a project for which a restricted grant has provided funding. In practice therefore unrestricted funds may be transferred to meet any overspending on a restricted fund.

1(c) A power of accumulation will allow trustees to create or augment endowment funds (restricted capital funds) from income funds (restricted or unrestricted). Without this power trustees may not create endowment from income funds. Trustees need to be aware that if they use income funds to erect, extend or improve a building on land which is an endowment asset, then those income funds will normally become permanent endowment.

App 3.2   Restricted Funds

2(a) Restricted funds are funds subject to specific trusts, which may be declared by the donor(s) or with their authority (e g in a public appeal) or created through legal process, but still within the wider objects of the charity. Restricted funds may be restricted income funds, which are expendable at the discretion of the trustees in furtherance of some particular aspect(s) of the objects of the charity. Or they may be capital (ie. endowment) funds, where the assets are required to be invested, or retained for actual use, rather than expended.

2(b) Where incoming resources are for goods or services and, upon full performance of the service, any surplus funds can be retained and used for general purposes, the incoming resources and related expenditure will most likely be unrestricted. However, if upon full performance any surplus is retrievable by the donor then the resources are most likely to be restricted.

2(c) Where funds are provided for fixed assets, the treatment of the fixed assets acquired with those funds will depend on the basis on which they are held. The terms on which the funds were received may require that the fixed asset which is provided should be held by the charity on trust for a specific purpose. Alternatively, if the charity's governing instrument allows them to do so, the trustees may choose to settle the fixed asset on trust for a specific purpose implied by the appeal (this will be legally binding as opposed to an administrative decision taken by the trustees to include assets in a designated fund). In either case the asset will form part of restricted funds, as will a fixed asset which has itself been given to the charity on trust for a specific purpose. There is, however, no general rule and the treatment will depend upon the circumstances of each individual case.

App 3.3   Endowment funds

Introduction

3(a) An endowment fund where there is no power to convert the capital into income is known as a permanent endowment fund, which must generally be held indefinitely. This concept of "permanence" does not however necessarily mean that the assets held in the endowment fund cannot be exchanged (though in some cases the trusts will require the retention of a specific asset for actual use e g a historic building), nor does it mean that they are incapable of depreciation or loss. What it does mean is that the permanent endowment fund cannot be used as if it were income (ie to make payments or grants to others), however certain payments must be made out of the endowment, such as the payment of investment management fees where these relate to investments held within the endowment. Where assets held in a permanent endowment fund are exchanged, their place in the fund must be taken by the assets received in exchange. "Exchange" here may simply mean a change of investment, but it may also mean, for example, the application of the proceeds of sale of freehold land and buildings in the purchase or improvement of freehold property.

3(b) Trustees may have the power to convert endowment funds into expendable income; such funds are known as expendable endowments. Expendable endowment is distinguishable from "income" in that there is no actual requirement to spend the capital unless, or until, the charity trustees decide to. The fund must be invested to produce income which should be spent for the purposes of the charity within a reasonable time of receipt. If such a power to expend the capital of the expendable endowment is exercised, the relevant funds become restricted or unrestricted income, depending upon whether the trusts permit expenditure for any of the purposes of the charity, or only for specific purposes.

Expenses Related to Endowment Investments

3(c) Any expenses incurred in the administration, or protection of endowment investments should be charged to capital. For example, the fees of someone who manages endowment investments, or the cost of improvements to land held as an endowment investment. Only where the trusts of the charity provide to the contrary, or there are insufficient funds in the endowment to meet such costs, can they be charged against the other funds held by the charity.

3(d) However where charities have land held as endowment investments, then rent collection, property repairs and maintenance charges would normally be charged against the relevant income fund as would the cost of rent reviews. Valuation fees and other expenses incurred in connection with the sale of such land would normally be charged to capital, ie. against the gain (or added to the loss) realised on the disposal.

3(e) Valuation fees incurred for accounting purposes would normally, in the case of endowment investments, be charged to capital and recorded in governance category of resources expended.

3(f) All incoming resources derived from assets held as endowment investments should be included in the Statement of Financial Activities. Normally the income forms part of the unrestricted funds but if the application of the income is restricted to a particular purpose the income and corresponding expenditure should be appropriately identified in the restricted funds. Any income not spent at the year end should be carried forward in the appropriate unrestricted or restricted fund.

Total Return on Investment for Permanent Endowment

3(g) In England and Wales, the Charity Commission may give the power to adopt a total return approach to investment (for definition see Glossary: GL 56) to charities with permanent endowment. This power may be taken by new charities and will normally be given to existing charities by Order under section 26 of the Charities

Act 1993 which specifies required accounting and reporting disclosures. New charities with such a power are expected by the Charity Commission to mirror these disclosures. The key elements of this approach are:

(i) The charity concerned must hold a permanently endowed fund, the assets of which are required to be invested to produce an investment return.

(ii) Because the return received from investment will not be "labelled" as either income or capital (as it would be under the standard rules), trustees can allocate the return between the present and future beneficiaries in the way they consider best gives effect to their duty to be fair to all beneficiaries.

(iii) In any one year, total return is the whole of the investment return received by a charity, regardless of how it has arisen.

(iv) The accumulated total return, less any part of the return which the trustees have previously applied for the purposes of the charity, or have previously allocated to income funds, is referred to as the unapplied total return.

(v) The accounting treatment, where the total return approach to investment is adopted, is specified in the order granting the power and is summarised below.

Accounting Treatment for Total Return

3(h) Where a charity with the necessary authority adopts a total return approach to investment (See Glossary GL 56), the entire investment return initially accrues to an unapplied total return fund. Any income earned on the endowment investments and any capital gains or losses will be shown in the relevant row of the Statement of Financial Activities in the endowment column.

3(i) The total return, less any part of the return which has previously been applied for the purposes of the charity, or has previously been allocated to income funds remains in the unapplied total return fund. This fund remains part of the permanent endowment until such time as a transfer is made to income funds.

3(j) Any transfer from the unapplied total return fund to either unrestricted or restricted income funds will be shown on the transfer row of the Statement of Financial Activities as appropriate.

3(k) Paragraph 75(e) of the SORP sets out necessary note disclosures in relation to transfers between funds and movements in the unapplied total return.

App 3.4   General Points

Asset Gains and Losses

4(a) If a gain is made on the disposal of an asset, the gain will form part of the fund in which the asset was held. An unrealised gain on an asset will also form part of the fund in which the asset is held. Similarly, unrealised losses and provisions for depreciation and impairment of an asset will reduce the fund in which the asset is (or, in the case of a realised loss, was) held. In order to ensure that gains, losses and provisions are added to or deducted from the correct fund, it is therefore essential to know which assets and liabilities are held in which fund.

Restricted Income and Expenditure

4(b) The trustees of a charity will be in breach of trust if they expend restricted income otherwise than in furtherance of that aspect or those aspects of the objects of the charity to which expenditure is restricted. It is therefore essential that due care is taken to spend out of a particular restricted income fund only where the trusts so permit. Expenditure may be charged to a restricted fund which is not at the time in credit, or not in sufficient credit, where there is a genuine anticipation of receipts which can properly be credited to the fund in order to meet the expenditure (eg where a decision has been taken to invite donations for that fund). The fund which is actually drawn upon to finance the expenditure should be held upon trusts which are wide enough to permit the expenditure (in case the expected receipts do not materialise). But if expenditure has been charged to an unrestricted fund, it should not subsequently be recharged to restricted fund receipts simply in order to increase the fund of unrestricted income.

App 3.5   Fund Assets and Liabilities

5(a) It is also important for the trustees to ensure that the assets and liabilities held in a fund are consistent with the fund type; if a fund which, because of donor restrictions, must be applied in the short term is represented by assets which cannot reasonably be expected to be realised in the short term, there is a real possibility that the charity will not be able to apply the funds as directed.

App 3.6   Income Application

6(a) Where restricted income has been invested prior to application for a suitable charitable purpose, any income/gains derived from the investment will be added to, and form part of, the restricted income fund in question. Income derived from the investment of capital (endowment) funds may be applied for the general purposes of the charity (unrestricted income), unless a specific purpose has been declared by the donor for the application of the income from the capital fund in question. Such income will be applicable for that purpose and will be restricted income. Gains from the realisation of investments in a capital (endowment) fund form part of the fund itself.

APPENDIX 4: THRESHOLDS

App 4.1   Thresholds for Small Companies

1.1 The current thresholds in the Companies Act 2006 section 382(3) for qualification as a small company. The thresholds effective from 6 April 2008, are as follows:

Any 2 of the following 3 conditions:

(i)   Annual turnover (gross income for charities) not exceeding – £6,500,000

(ii)   Balance sheet total not exceeding – £3,260,000

(iii)   Average number of employees not exceeding – 50

For accounting periods which are shorter or longer than 12 months the thresholds should be adjusted in proportion to the accounting period.

The size parameters are subject to periodic amendment. The latest change was made in April 2008 under The Companies Act 2006 (Amendment) (Accounts and Reports) Regulations 2008 and applies to accounting periods beginning on or after 6 April 2008.

App 4.2   Thresholds for FRSSE

2.1   Any charity which comes under the above thresholds, whether or not it is a company, may be able to apply the Financial Reporting Standard For Smaller Entities (FRSSE) as described in Appendix 5 paragraphs 5.2.1 to 5.2.2.

App 4.3   Charities Act 1993 (England and Wales) Threshold for the preparation of accruals accounts

3.1   As at 28 February 2005: Gross income above £100,000 (set by SI 1995: No 2696 The Charities Act 1993 (Substitution of Sums) Order 1995) (unless and until this is revised).

App 4.4   Charities Act 1993 (England and Wales) Threshold for audit

4.1   For accounting periods beginning on or after 27 February 2007: Gross income above £500,000 or gross assets exceeding £2.8m and gross income exceeding £100,000 (set by the Charities Act 1993 as amended by the Charities Act 2006, first commencement Order) (unless and until this is revised).

App 4.5   Charities and Trustee Investment (Scotland) Act 2005 Threshold for the preparation of accruals accounts

5.1   Charities with a gross income of £100,000 or more (set by SSI 2006: No. 218, The Charities Accounts (Scotland) Regulations 2006).

App 4.6   Charities and Trustee Investment (Scotland) Act 2005 Threshold for audit

6.1   Gross income of £500,000 or more, or gross assets exceeding £2.8m (set by SSI 2006: No. 218. The Charities Accounts (Scotland) Regulations 2006).

App 4.7   Charities Act 1993 (England and Wales) Threshold for the preparation of group accounts

7.1   Following the Charities Act 2006 (Charitable Companies Audit and Group Accounts Provisions) Order 2008, and the Charities (Accounts and Reports) Regulations 2008, for financial years beginning from 1 April 2008 any parent charity where the aggregate gross income of the group, the parent charity and its subsidiaries, exceeds £500,000 after consolidation adjustments, must prepare group accounts. The form and content of group accounts is set out in the Charities (Accounts and Reports) Regulations 2008. However where a charitable company is required by section 399 of the Companies Act 2006 to prepare group accounts, its group accounts are prepared under the Companies Act 2006.

App 4.8   Charities and Trustee Investment (Scotland) Act 2005 Threshold for the preparation of group accounts

8.1   Any parent charity where the gross income of the group, the parent charity and its subsidiaries, is £500,000 or more after consolidation adjustments, must prepare group accounts under the Charities and Trustee Investment (Scotland Act 2005 and associated Charities Accounts (Scotland)) Regulations 2006. However where a charitable company is required by section 399 of the Companies Act 2006 to prepare group accounts, those group accounts are prepared under the Companies Act 2006, as well as the above Act and Regulations.

APPENDIX 5: ACCOUNTING FOR SMALLER CHARITIES

Particular accounting disclosures and the activity basis for the analysis of income and costs within the Statement of Financial Activities may not be relevant information for the users of accounts prepared by smaller charities. Similarly, the level of detail provided in the Trustees' Annual Report is likely to be dependent on the structure, size and complexity of the charity and be proportionate to the needs of the users of the report. This appendix lists the concessions at the date of publication of this SORP.

App 5.1   Cash-Based Receipts and Payments Accounts

5.1.1   There are many relatively small charities with very simple structures and no control of other organisations. The vast majority of them will have cash and deposit accounts but few other assets. Apart from charitable companies (see 5.1.4) these charities will often find that cashbased receipts and payments accounts meet both their needs and those of others who read their accounts. This form of accounts contains a summary of money received and money spent during the year and a list of assets at the end of the year.

5.1.2   In England and Wales, charities whose accounts 'form and content' are governed by the Charities Act 1993, may choose between preparing accruals accounts and receipts and payments accounts provided their gross income is not over £100,000.

5.1.3   Scottish charities for which accounts are prepared under the Charities and Trustee Investment (Scotland) Act 2005 and associated Regulations, are eligible to prepare receipts and payments accounts provided their gross income is under £100,000.

5.1.4   Small charitable companies must always prepare accruals accounts and are not covered by these concessions.

5.1.5   As this SORP is applicable to accruals accounts, no specific recommendations on cash based receipts and payments accounts are provided within this SORP although as explained in paragraph 6 such charities are encouraged to analyse their receipts and payments based on the activities undertaken. Charities registered in Scotland and preparing receipts and payments accounts must ensure they meet the requirements of the Charities Accounts (Scotland) Regulations 2006. Both the Charity Commission and OSCR produce detailed guidance on the preparation of receipts and payments based accounts.

App 5.2   The Financial Reporting Standard for Smaller Entities (FRSSE)

5.2.1   Any charity (whether or not it is a company) which is under the thresholds for small companies, as described in the Companies Acts (see Appendix 4), can follow the Financial Reporting Standard for Smaller Entities (FRSSE) in preparing its financial accounts except where it conflicts with this Charities SORP, in which case this SORP should be followed. Charities which follow another SORP or have to prepare additional accounts in a format required by other bodies, such as HM Treasury, may find that they cannot follow the FRSSE for these purposes. The FRSSE is not relevant to charities preparing cash-based (receipts and payments) accounts.

5.2.2   In following the FRSSE, the accounts will meet most of the requirements of the SORP for smaller entities. However:

(a)   The accounts should include a Statement of Financial Activities in place of a profit and loss account and statement of total recognised gains and losses.

(b)   The principles of fund accounting should be adopted throughout the accounts. This will include appropriate descriptions of the funds and notes showing the composition of the funds and the differentiation of funds on the balance sheet.

(c)   All investments, including investment properties, must be shown at market value.

(d)   Those foreign exchange gains and losses which may be allowed to be taken to reserves (as prescribed in the FRSSE) must be shown in the gains and losses section of the Statement of Financial Activities.

(e)   Those exceptional items which are required to be shown after operating profit must be shown in an appropriate place on the Statement of Financial Activities.

(f)   If a charity applying the FRSSE prepares consolidated accounts, it should apply the relevant accounting practices and disclosures required by accounting standards and the SORP in relation to consolidated accounts.

App 5.3   Accounting statements of Smaller Charities

5.3.1   The SORP provides a number of concessions for smaller charities that are not subject to a statutory audit (see Appendix 4 Audit thresholds). The concessions cover the Statement of Financial Activities and notes to the accounts:

(a)   In relation to the Statement of Financial Activities, smaller charities do not need to analyse either resources expended or incoming resources by activity categories within the Statement of Financial Activities. They may instead choose resource classifications to suit their circumstances.

(b)   Where a small charity adopts an alternative approach to analysis within the Statement of Financial Activities certain note disclosures may no longer be necessary, for example, where these disclosures relate to the constituent costs of an activity category or where relevant information is provided on the face of the Statement of Financial Activities. The disclosure paragraphs affected by this are set out below:

Details	Paragraph References
Analysis of activities that have generated funds	122
Analysis of incoming resources from charitable activities	146
Support Costs analysis	166–167
Apportionment of Costs	175–176
Breakdown of costs of generating voluntary income	183–184
Analysis of fundraising trading costs	186
Analysis of charitable activity costs	191–194
Analysis of grantmaking or associated support costs by activity	202, 203(b)
Analysis of governance costs	212

(c)   Smaller charities are not required to give details of staff emoluments in bands (paragraph 236).

5.3.2   These concessions are intended to reduce the detail of reporting requirements placed on smaller charities, though any such charity wishing to follow the full recommendations of the SORP is encouraged to do so.

App 5.4   Trustees' Annual Reports of Smaller Charities in England and Wales

5.4.1   In England and Wales, all registered charities are required to produce a Trustees' Annual Report.

Regulations made under the Charities Act 1993 provide for charities that are not subject to a statutory audit (see Appendix 4 Audit thresholds) to produce an abbreviated Trustees' Annual Report. This concession applies to all charities required to produce the report, and includes charitable companies.

5.4.2   The minimum content of the abbreviated Trustees' Annual Report is summarised in Table 11.

Table 11. Contents of the Trustees' Annual Report for a smaller charity (England and Wales – not subject to a statutory audit)

		SORP Paragraph
Reference and administrative information	The name of the charity	41(a)
	Any other name by which a charity makes itself known	41(a)
	The charity registration number (or Scottish Charity Number) (if any)	41(b)
	The company registration number (if applicable)	41(b)
	The address of the principal office of the charity;	41(c)
	The names of the charity's trustees or trustee(s) for the charity on the date the report was approved. (where any charity trustee is a body corporate, the names of the directors of that body corporate should also be provided)	41(d)
	The names of any other person who served as a charity trustee in the financial year	41(e)
Structure Governance and Management	The nature of the governing document and how the charity is (or its trustees are) constituted	44(a)
	The methods adopted for the recruitment and appointment of new trustees,	44(b)
Objectives and Activities	A summary of the objects of the charity as set out in its governing document.	47(a)
	Summary of the main activities undertaken in relation to those objects.	47(e)
Achievements and Performance	A summary of the main achievements of the charity during the year	(54)
Financial Review	Policy on reserves	55(a)
	Details of any fund materially in deficit and the circumstances giving rise to the deficit and steps being taken to eliminate the deficit.	55(b)
Funds held as Custodian Trustee	A description of the assets which they hold in this capacity.	59
	The name and objects of the charity (or charities) on whose behalf the assets are held and how this activity falls within their own objects.	
	Details of the arrangements for safe custody and segregation of such assets from the charity's own assets.	

APPENDIX 6: THE CHARITY ACCOUNTING REVIEW COMMITTEE (2003/5)

Membership

Chairman

David Taylor

Members

Denis Cathcart

Andrew Dobson

James Dutton

Pesh Framjee

Keith Hickey

Richard Hellewell

Gareth Jones

Raymond Jones

Roger Morris

Paul Palmer

Adrian Randall

Kate Sayer

Ian Smith

Committee Secretary

John Kerry

Technical Secretary

Ken Ashford

Appendix 1(A1)

SORP INFORMATION SHEET 1 – TECHNICAL APPLICATION ISSUES

1. ANNUAL REVIEW PROCESS

1.1. The Charity Commission and the Office of the Scottish Charity Regulator are the joint SORP making body and as such are required by the Accounting Standards Board's (ASB) code of practice to undertake annual reviews of the SORP. These reviews are undertaken in conjunction with the SORP Committee and in particular considered:

- any implications for the SORP of new or proposed accounting standards;

- any evidence of widespread failure to follow any part of the guidance; and

- any developments within the sector that suggests further guidance on accounting matters is desirable.

1.2. The current SORP was issued in March 2005, and although its early implementation was encouraged, the effective date of implementation is for accounting periods beginning on or after 1 April 2005. The purpose of this Information Sheet, which provides informal guidance on the application of the SORP, is to assist practitioners in their preparation of financial statements. This Information Sheet does not form part of the SORP, nor has it been reviewed by the ASB, rather it attempts to explain and illustrate what is already recommended by the SORP, but does not carry the authority of the SORP.

2. INDEX OF TOPICS:

Accounting treatment for grants (section 3)

The Charities Act 2006 and disclosures for grant-making charities (section 4)

Investment management costs (section 5)

Bank interest and other finance costs (section 6)

The business review and company charities (section 7)

The operating financial review and reporting by charities (section 8)

3. ACCOUNTING TREATMENT FOR GRANTS

3.1. Grant income received is analysed, in the Statement of Financial Activities (SoFA), as either voluntary income (paragraph 121) or incoming resources from charitable activities (paragraph 145) depending upon the character of the grant. Preparers of accounts have sought clarification as to how grant income should be analysed between the income categories of the SoFA and, in particular, whether the receipt of a restricted grant is equivalent to a performance related grant which should be categorised as incoming resources from charitable activities.

3.2. Contractual income derived from the provision of goods and services to beneficiaries will always be analysed as incoming resources from charitable activities. The SORP also recognises that some grants contain conditions that require the performance of a specified service where payment is conditional on a specified output being achieved (See SORP Glossary GL 45). Such grants are termed performance related grants and have conditions which make them similar in economic terms to trading income (See SORP Para.143) and are also analysed as incoming resources from charitable activities within the SoFA.

3.3. Simply because a grant is restricted to a particular purpose of the recipient charity does not mean it should be recognised as a performance related grant (See SORP Para 100). Restricted grants, that do not create a service requirement, are normally analysed as restricted voluntary income (see SORP Glossary GL 61). However, even where the conditions attaching to grants do not create specific performance related conditions, the funding may often be provided on terms that clearly require the funds to be utilised to support particular service providing activities of the charity. Where the nature of the conditions attaching to a restricted fund are such that they create a service requirement that must be met by the charity then the grant funding should also be analysed as incoming resources from charitable activities.

3.4. Voluntary income comprises gifts that will not normally provide any return to the donor other than the knowledge that someone will benefit from the donation. Voluntary income will normally include gifts in kind and donated services (See SORP Glossary GL 61). Grants received for the general purposes of the charity or do not have particular service requirements are analysed as voluntary income (See SORP Para 144 and Para 121 (b)).

4. THE CHARITIES ACT 2006 AND DISCLOSURES FOR GRANT-MAKING CHARITIES

4.1. Schedule 8 to the Charities Act 2006, clause 133, on implementation in England and Wales, will provide that "there shall be no provision in the Regulations made under section 42 of the Charities Act 1993 that requires the charity trustees of a charity that is a charitable trust created by any person (the settlor), to disclose in the statement of the accounts, either the identities of recipients of grants made out of the funds of the charity, or the amounts of any individual grants so made, if the disclosure would fall to be made at a time when the settlor or their spouse or civil partner was still alive."

4.2.   For charitable trusts in England and Wales where this provision applies, the Charities Act 2006 will allow further grant disclosure exemptions in addition to those already set out in SORP paragraph 200.

4.3.   The SORP does not, in any case, require details of grants made to individuals to be disclosed. In the case of institutional grants, the SORP requires disclosure of the name of the institution supported and the total value of grants made to it. Disclosure is limited to grants that are material in the context of grantmaking and requires the disclosure of a sufficient number of institutional grants to provide a reasonable understanding of the range of institutions supported.

4.4.   Following the implementation of the Charities Act 2006 in England and Wales, the disclosures of the names of institutions supported by grants and the amount of funding they received will be discretionary in law during the lifetime of the settlor (or their spouse or civil partner) of a charitable trust that has funded the grant.   This discretion does not extend to charities registered or operating in Scotland.

4.5.   For other grantmakers where clause 133 of schedule 8 to the Charities Act 2006 does not apply, the only grounds for non-disclosure of this information remain those set out in SORP paragraph 200 and paragraphs 208 and 209.

4.6.   The objectives of the SORP include improving the quality of financial reporting and therefore the grant information disclosures recommended by the SORP remains recommended practice for all grantmaking charities in the UK.

5.   INVESTMENT MANAGEMENT COSTS

5.1.   A principle of the SORP is that all incoming resources should be reported gross. Paragraph 187 of the SORP recommends that where investment management fees have been deducted from investment income by investment managers that the charity should show investment income gross before the deduction of such fees and report the costs of managing investments separately within the SoFA.

5.2.   With collective investment schemes, such as unit trusts, or common investment funds, investment management costs may be included within the bid-offer spread or recovered by transaction and portfolio charges rather than by a fee charged directly to the charity.

5.3.   Where it is not practicable to ascertain the actual or a notional apportionment of costs charged to the individual participants of such schemes with reasonable accuracy then the investment income received should be reported without adjustment.

6.   BANK INTEREST AND OTHER FINANCE COSTS

6.1.   Interest and other finance costs may arise from short term borrowing to fund working capital or from longer term borrowing to fund the operating assets of a charity. Preparers of accounts have questioned whether such interest costs should be allocated to activities funded by the loan or whether such costs should be regarded as a cost of generating funds.

6.2.   The SoFA provides an activity classification of costs. Where interest has arisen in order to finance a particular activity then it would generally be allocated to that activity. Interest costs that cannot be directly allocated to a particular activity will generally be apportioned on a reasonable basis as with other support costs.

7.   THE BUSINESS REVIEW AND COMPANY CHARITIES

7.1.   Section 417 of the Companies Act 2006 requires the Director's Report to include a 'business review'. These provisions are brought forwards from section 234(1) (b) and section 234ZZB of the Companies Act 1985 which applied to accounting periods beginning on or after 1 April 2005. Small companies are relieved from this reporting requirement by section 417(1). Medium sized companies need not disclose the performance information so far as they relate to non-financial information (section 417(7)).

7.2.   Charitable companies applying the SORP's recommendations for the Trustees' Annual Report are likely to meet the general requirements for a business review if an expanded narrative is provided on the risks and uncertainties faced by the charity.

7.3.   The content of a business review and the SORP paragraphs that are likely to meet these requirements are summarised in the table below:

Contents of statutory business review Sections 417 Companies Act 2006	SORP 2005 paragraph reference
A fair review of the business.	Paragraph 36
Description of principal risks and uncertainties.	Paragraph 45 & 53(d)
Review the development and performance in the financial year, and the position of the business at the end of the year. The review should be balanced and comprehensive and consistent with the size and complexity of the business	Paragraphs 53(a) 53(d) and Paragraph 55
The review must, to the extent necessary for an understanding of the development, performance or position include: a) analysis using key performance indicators, b) where appropriate, analysis using other key indicators, including environmental and employee matters (applicable only to large companies).	Paragraph 53
Key performance indicators means factors by reference to which the development, performance or position of the company (or group) can be measured effectively.	Paragraph 36 & 53(a)
Where a group, the report shall address the performance of both parent and subsidiary.	Paragraph 53

7.4.   In practice charities subject to statutory audit, through their compliance with the SORP's recommendations, are likely to be compliant with the requirements of the business review provided they include an explanation of the risks and uncertainties facing the charity.

8. THE OPERATING FINANCIAL REVIEW (OFR) AND REPORTING BY CHARITIES

8.1. In 2005, the requirement to prepare an OFR was repealed by Statutory Instrument 3442/2005. The OFR was considered too prescriptive and the business review (see above) was considered to cover much of the ground covered by the OFR in a more proportionate way. The ASB withdrew 'Reporting Standard 1: Operating and Financial Review' following the repeal of the regulations and reissued the contents as a statement of best practice 'Reporting Statement: Operating and Financial Review' (the Reporting Statement) in January 2006.

8.2. The SORP does not create any requirement for charities to prepare an OFR. However, the SORP's recommendations for a Trustees' Annual Report already cover a number of the key disclosures recommended by the Reporting Statement.

8.3. The Reporting Statement was written with quoted companies in mind, but is also applicable to other entities, including charities, that choose to prepare an OFR. The Reporting Statement was developed as best practice and is not mandatory even for quoted companies.

8.4. Where the trustees, particularly of larger charities, choose to expand their reporting to encompass a full OFR, they are encouraged to make reference to the Reporting Standard. Indeed, the principles put forward by the statement may also be helpful to trustees more generally in the preparation of their annual report.

8.5. The table below, which provides a synopsis of the OFR, may be helpful to charities considering expanding their annual report into a full OFR. Particular areas which the SORP Committee considers are not currently addressed by the SORP are highlighted in **bold**.

Contents of best practice OFR	SORP 2005
A balanced and comprehensive analysis consistent with the size and complexity of the business of: a) development and performance in the financial year b) position at the end of the year c) main trends and factors underlying the development, performance and position during the year d) the main trends and factors which are likely to affect future development, performance and position so as to assist 'members' to assess the strategies adopted and potential for success	Paragraphs 36, 47, 53, 57
In supplementing the accounts, provide additional explanations of amounts and explain the conditions and events that shaped the information in the financial statements	Paragraphs 10, 21,35 & 36
Key elements of disclosure: a) nature of the business including a description of the market, competitive and regulatory environment and entity's objectives and strategies b)development and performance both in the financial year and in the future c) resources, principal risks and uncertainties and relationships that may affect long-term value d) position of the business including **liquidity** performance both in the financial year and in the future	Paragraphs 47, 53, 57 & 55

Details of particular matters, where appropriate, to provide a balanced and comprehensive analysis: a) **environmental matters** and related policies b) **employees** and related policies c) **social and community issues** and related policies d) persons with whom entity has contractual or other arrangements essential to the business e) other matters	Paragraphs 44 & 51
Director's strategies for achieving the objectives of the business	Paragraph 47
Include key performance indicators both financial, and where appropriate, non financial used by directors to assess progress against their stated objectives	Paragraph 53
For each KPI disclosed, disclose key matters including definition and calculation	–

Appendix 1(A2)

SORP INFORMATION SHEET 2 – CHARITIES SORP INFORMATION

STATEMENT OF PRINCIPLES FOR FINANCIAL REPORTING INTERPRETATION FOR PUBLIC BENEFIT ENTITIES

1. BACKGROUND

1.1 The Charity Commission and the Office of the Scottish Charity Regulator are the joint SORP-making body and as such are required by the Accounting Standards Board's (ASB) code of practice to keep the SORP under review.

1.2 As part of its work, the SORP Committee may issue "Information Sheets" which seek to clarify the application of the SORP or particular recommendations contained with the SORP. Information Sheets do not amend the SORP and are advisory in nature and are released to assist preparers and auditors of accounts in applying the SORP's recommendations.

1.3 In June 2007 the ASB published its 'Interpretation for Public Benefit Entities of the Statement of Principles for Financial Reporting' (the Interpretation). The Interpretation sets out the principles that the ASB believe should underlie the preparation and presentation of general purpose financial statements of public benefit entities including charities.

1.4 The primary purpose of the Interpretation is to provide a coherent frame of reference to be used in the development of SORPs or other specific guidance for public benefit entities and to assist preparers and auditors faced with new or emerging issues.

1.5 Whilst the Interpretation does not override the requirements of existing accounting standards and SORPs, as part of its work, the SORP Committee considered the Interpretation, at its October 2007 meeting, to ensure the Interpretation's key principles are consistent with the recommendations contained in SORP 2005. As noted in paragraph 61(d) of SORP 2005, the Interpretation was at a discussion document stage when SORP 2005 was published.

1.6 The SORP Committee concluded that there are no fundamental issues which require addressing by a revision to the current SORP at this stage. However, it was felt that the results of the SORP Committee's consideration, set out as an Information Sheet below, would be helpful to preparers of accounts and auditors.

1.7 It should be noted that Information Sheets do not form part of the SORP, nor are they reviewed by the ASB and therefore do not carry the authority of the SORP.

2. INDEX OF TOPICS:

- Objective of financial statement and defining class of user

- Multi-period liabilities

- Residual interests and designations

- Donated services

- Grants for financing capital projects

- Accounting for business combinations

3. OBJECTIVE OF FINANCIAL STATEMENTS (INTERPRETATION PARAGRAPHS 1.1 TO 1.10) AND DEFINING CLASS OF USER (INTERPRETATION 1.11 TO 1.16)

3.1 SORP 2005 (paragraph 10) recognises the accountability and stewardship role of financial reporting but does not mention specifically its role in economic decision making. SORP 2005 recognises a variety of users of financial information including donors, beneficiaries and the general public, however, unlike the Interpretation does not identify a defining class of user.

3.2 The Interpretation provides a detailed analysis of the objective of financial statements noting that many people may have an interest in the financial information of an entity. The Statement of Principles, on which the Interpretation is based, puts forward, in relation to profit-orientated entities, the rebuttable assumption that financial statements focus on the interests that investors have in the reporting entity's financial performance and financial position and in so doing focuses on the common interest that all users have in these matters.

3.3 Public benefit entities, including charities, have no such investors and therefore the Interpretation puts forward funders and financial supports as being similar to investors in profit-orientated entities in terms of their information requirements.

3.4 SORP 2005 deals with the question of the objective of financial statements in less detail than the Interpretation and offers no conclusion as to a defining class of users. The Interpretation deals with an issue not fully addressed by the SORP and therefore assists preparers and auditors deal with an emerging issue that will require consideration by the SORP Committee in developing any new SORP.

4. MULTI-PERIOD LIABILITIES (INTERPRETATION – PARAGRAPHS 4.29 TO 4.34)

4.1 SORP 2005 noted that certain grants may contain specific conditions that closely specify a particular service to be performed where the conditions for payment are linked to the performance of a particular level of service or units of output delivered. Often the grant maker will have negotiated the services to be provided to it or its beneficiaries. The SORP refers to such grants as performance-related grants and they are recognised as resources expended to the extent to which the specified services have been provided.

4.2 Under SORP 2005 grant liabilities may also arise as a result of a constructive obligation. Where a multi-year funding agreement has been entered into and a specific funding commitment made to a grant recipient then a liability results and the conditions attaching to the grant will determine whether a liability is recognised for the full funding commitment.

4.3 In developing the Interpretation the ASB's Committee on Accounting for Public-benefit Entities (CAPE) gave considerable thought to this issue. The SORP's approach is consistent with that of the Interpretation.

4.4 The Interpretation confirms that a general or policy statement of an intention to provide goods and services to beneficiaries in accordance with objectives will not necessarily give rise to a liability. The accounting treatment of specific commitments depends on whether:

• The obligation is such that the entity cannot realistically withdraw from it;

• The commitment has been communicated to the other party; and

• The commitment is performance related.

The Interpretation states that where the commitment, giving rise to the obligation, is not performance related a liability arises at the time the commitment is made.

5.   RESIDUAL INTERESTS AND DESIGNATIONS (INTERPRETATION – PARAGRAPHS 4.41 TO 4.44)

5.1   Residual interests are disclosed as "funds" in charity accounting and are arrived at by deducting all of an entity's liabilities from its assets. The Interpretation recognises there may be different classes of residual interest that require disclosure, in particular, where resources are held for a particular purpose (a restricted fund) this creates a separate class of residual interest in the balance sheet.

5.2   The nature of the residual interest should be clear from the disclosure in the accounts. The Interpretation, however, goes a stage further than the existing SORP by stating that where, in the event of a winding-up, the ultimate interest would be required to be distributed in a particular way then that fact should be disclosed. Charity law would require a distribution on winding-up to reflect the nature of the restriction represented by a restriction or special trust. Whilst uncommon, some dissolution clauses in governing documents of charities may be more prescriptive than the charity law requirement and in such cases, to be consistent with the Interpretation, an additional disclosure would be required by a minority of charities.

5.3   The Interpretation, however, does not regard designations as creating a separate class of residual interest. This is consistent with the SORP where designations are defined as being part of unrestricted funds earmarked for a particular project. The designation has an administrative purpose only and does not legally restrict the trustees' discretion to apply the fund.

5.4   Paragraph 325 of the SORP reminds trustees that where part of the unrestricted fund is earmarked then this intention to expend funds in the future is not recognised as a provision but may be recorded by setting up a designated fund. The SORP does not create a requirement to set-up designations and is silent on how designations are disclosed apart from reminding trustees that designations remain part of the charity's unrestricted funds.

5.5   Designations were first introduced into the SORP to help explain that funds disclosed within the balance sheet should not be equated with funds immediately available for expenditure as they may have been "earmarked" for a particular purpose. Designations should, under the SORP, also be quantified and explained within a charity reserves policy (paragraph 55) – this was an attempt by SORP to help ensure designations were not used purely as a window dressing technique.

5.6   The Interpretation concludes that designations reflect no more than management intention and correctly points out, as does SORP, that a separate class of residual interest (a fund) is not created. The Interpretation is however more specific and states designations should not lead to the recognition of a transaction in the financial statements (paragraph 4.44). Such information could be disclosed in the notes to the accounts but would more normally be disclosed in the accompanying information (i.e. Trustees Annual Report in the case of a charity).

5.7   The SORP does not create a requirement for designations to be recognised within the primary statements and the SORP is clear that designation has an administrative purpose only, and does not legally restrict the trustees' discretion to apply the resources represented by the designation. The explanation of designations required within reserve policies takes us a long way towards the approach provided within the Interpretation.

5.8   The SORP Committee had considered these issues in the context of the development of the 2005 SORP. The Committee has taken the view that designation provided useful information helping users understand the funding position of a charity. It has also been pointed out that there is no legal prohibition on providing additional information within the separate categories of funds identified by the balance sheet and [the Committee] is not convinced, at this stage, that the identification of a designation within a particular fund would be construed by users of accounts as either resulting from a transaction or as creating a separate class of residual interest.

6. DONATED SERVICES (INTERPRETATION – PARAGRAPHS 4.47 TO 4.51)

6.1   The issues surrounding the recognition of the contribution of volunteers in charity accounts has been the subject of sector debate for a number of years. The Interpretation confirms that where volunteering, has an economic impact on an entity that impact should be reflected in the accounts but highlights that in practice it may not be possible to measure some services with sufficient reliability and consequently such services should not be recognised.

6.2 If reliability of measurement issues can be overcome then recognition would take place provided the charity would otherwise have purchased the service (evidence of economic contribution). Under this approach a charity would need to demonstrate that the services provided to the charity would be purchased if volunteers were not available.

6.3 The SORP also recognises that donated services should be recognised where the benefit (economic contribution) is reasonably quantifiable and measurable. The SORP concludes that these tests are likely to be met where the service is provided by an individual (volunteer) as part of a trade or profession but excludes "general" volunteers on the basis that their contribution cannot be reasonably valued in financial terms. Whilst the Interpretation does not over-ride a SORP, and the underlying principle is similar, the Interpretation places emphasis on whether the service would be purchased in the absence of volunteers whilst the SORP looks at whether the service is provided in the course of a trade of profession and excludes the valuation of "general" volunteers.

6.4 In relation to other services or facilities donated to a charity (for example, free advertising, office accommodation etc) the SORP would again require recognition if the benefit to the charity is reasonably quantifiable and measurable. Again, this approach is not considered inconsistent with the principles of the Interpretation.

7. GRANTS FOR FINANCING CAPITAL PROJECTS (INTERPRETATION – PARAGRAPHS 5.32 TO 5.37)

7.1 The Interpretation states that grants and donations should be recognised as gains unless there are conditions to be met. Where conditions are substantially or virtually certain to be met the gain should be recognised.

7.2 The Interpretation points out that a repayment condition applying to a capital grant, in the event of a future sale of the asset, would not prevent recognition where the decision to sell was within the reporting entity's control.

7.3 Whilst the Interpretation recognises that a capital grant (a grant to finance a capital project, for example, the acquisition or construction of a tangible fixed asset) can represent a subsidy there is no mention of a deferral of its recognition although if the gift establishes an interest (presumably for the donor) in the residual interests then the transaction should be treated as a capital contribution.

7.4 The approach put forward by the Interpretation is seen as consistent with SORP 2005.

7.5 It is important to note that where the Interpretation deals with "capital contributions" (see paragraphs 4.52 to 4.55 of the Interpretation) that this term includes only transactions that establish a financial interest (a right to participate) in the residual interest (funds) of an entity.

Charities are unlikely to receive capital contributions of this [commercial] type as transactions with donors and other funders, including the receipt of capital grants (see 7.3 above) or gifts of endowment, generally create a gain for the charity that is recognised within the Statement of Financial Activities. The SORP does not provide recommendations on accounting for "capital contributions" received as they are unlikely to arise in the context of charities.

8.   ACCOUNTING FOR BUSINESS COMBINATIONS (INTERPRETATION – PARAS 8.10-14)

8.1   Despite the direction taken by International Financial Reporting Standards, the Interpretation continues to recognise that an amalgamation of two or more reporting entities can take a number of different forms. The Interpretation points out that the fact that a business combination involves public benefit entities does not in itself influence whether the business combination is accounted for as an acquisition or a merger. This is again consistent with the accounting options allowed by the SORP.

8.2   Helpfully the Interpretation also explains that under acquisition accounting where the acquisition is carried out at nil or nominal consideration the excess of fair value of the assets acquired over the fair value of the liabilities assumed should be treated as a gain and recognised as income (or a loss where net liabilities are acquired). The SORP is currently silent on this matter. This approach is consistent with the accounting advice currently provided by the Commission with the exception that **restricted funds that constitute a special trust would normally be dealt with by a transfer of trusteeship and the accounting would reflect the legal nature of such transactions.**

8.3   The Interpretation clarifies that the excess of the fair value of assets over liabilities acquired represents a gift of the value of one 'business' to another that should be recognised as income. In charity accounting the effect is likely to be that any 'negative goodwill' arising under FRS 10: 'Goodwill and intangible assets' in context of an acquisition by gift (or nil consideration transfer) would be recognised as income and not deferred.

INDEX

References are to paragraph numbers.